The Chesapeake House

The Chesapeake House

Architectural Investigation by Colonial Williamsburg

EDITED BY CARY CARSON & CARL R. LOUNSBURY

Published in association with

The Colonial Williamsburg Foundation by

The University of North Carolina Press,

Chapel Hill

The paper in this book meets the guidelines for permanence and durability of the Committee on Production Guidelines for Book Longevity of the Council on Library Resources. The University of North Carolina Press has been a member of the Green Press Initiative since 2003.

Library of Congress Cataloging-in-Publication Data
The Chesapeake house : architectural investigation by Colonial Williamsburg / edited by Cary Carson and Carl R. Lounsbury.
pages cm
Includes index.
ISBN 978-0-8078-3577-7 (cloth: alk. paper)
1. Architecture, Domestic—Chesapeake Bay Region (Md. and Va.)
2. Architecture, Colonial—Chesapeake Bay Region (Md. and Va.)
3. Vernacular architecture—Chesapeake Bay Region (Md. and Va.)
I. Carson, Cary, editor of compilation. II. Lounsbury, Carl, editor of compilation. III. Colonial Williamsburg Foundation, sponsoring body.
NA7235.M32C485 2013
728.09755'18—dc23   2012028590

ILLUSTRATIONS WITHOUT CAPTIONS p. ii: detail of Wales (photo by Willie Graham); pp. 10–11: clapboard wall in the cellar of Bowling Green (photo by Willie Graham); pp. 62–63: River Edge (photo by Jeff Klee); pp. 204–5: Springfield (photo by Willie Graham); pp. 284–85: Tulip Hill (photo by Willie Graham); p. 393: 315 High Street, Petersburg, Virginia (photo by Willie Graham).

Chapter 1 frontispiece: Aerial view of Jamestown Island, © Cameron Davidson. Chapter 17 frontispiece: Lumberyard at a rail siding, courtesy of Norfolk and Western Historical Photograph Collection, Norfolk Southern Archives, Norfolk, Virginia.

17 16 15 14 13   5 4 3 2

Contents

Acknowledgments

The origins of this book go back more than a quarter of a century. Talk of writing the "office book" surfaced in the Architectural Research Department at the Colonial Williamsburg Foundation sometime in the early 1980s, not long after many of the authors of this volume first began extensive fieldwork in the Chesapeake region. Although we did not know precisely the structure or content of the book, we were certain of two things. The information and insights gained from our extensive examination of hundreds of early buildings in Maryland and Virginia would shape what we wrote. In addition to returning to many of the large gentry houses, which many earlier scholars had studied, we believed that our fieldwork would reveal a richer and more complex history if armed with a new set of questions to ask of these familiar mansions. More important, we also intended to look at nearby slave houses, outbuildings, and many other building types that had previously been ignored but were no less part of this historical landscape.

We also knew that this book would be a collective endeavor, the product of many hands. Academic scholarship is usually a solitary affair, the result of a single individual being engaged in archival research. By contrast, architectural research carried out by historians in museums such as Colonial Williamsburg invariably requires a group effort. Recording a building works best when two or more people are involved. It is more efficient to have a pair of hands holding one end of a tape and another recording the measurements at the other. More details can be seen, more information recorded, and more theories posited when fieldwork is conducted by a team. The sheer amount of work involved in simply recording a building, let alone developing a plausible scenario accounting for its age and subsequent development, is time consuming and far harder when done alone.

The field of architectural research encourages fellowship, and we have been amply rewarded over the years by working with many people who have been dedicated to understanding, protecting, and restoring the early buildings of our region. Although this volume has nine authors, the number of people who have contributed to it in some fashion is much greater by far. We are forever grateful to the thousands of home owners, public officials, churchwardens, curators, custodians, and others who have opened their buildings for our investigations. Only rarely have we been denied permission to examine a building, even when we have knocked unbidden on a door of an intriguing house deep in the backwoods. We acknowledge and appreciate the help of those countless numbers who in no small way contributed to this book by their hospitality.

A project as large as this could not have been accomplished without the resources of many institutions, foundations, and friends of Colonial Williamsburg. We are deeply appreciative of the early and enthusiastic support of Lilla and Christopher Ohrstrom of The Plains, Virginia. The Catesby Foundation and the Ohrstrom Foundation funded the early research, paint analysis, and drawings for this project. Thanks to the late William O. Harrison Jr., Michael A. Harrison, and Kathryn Nell Harrison of Texas, a family with deep Virginia roots that stretch back to Benjamin Harrison I. Their gift helped to underwrite fieldwork, digital imaging, and paint analysis. The generosity of Scott and Debra Duncan of Edmond, Oklahoma, made it possible to do dendrochronological testing on important structures and helped us finish the manuscript and assisted in its publication. Grants from the Richard Gwathmey and Caroline T. Gwathmey Memorial Trust and the Roller-Bottimore Foundation of Richmond supported research and the production of images.

Since the early 1980s, the Architectural Research Department at Colonial Williamsburg has employed a number of individuals who came with formidable research and field recording skills. Some of these have moved on to positions elsewhere, but we have benefited from our association with Travis McDonald, Vanessa Patrick, Peter Sandbeck, Michael Bourne, Myron Stachiw, Mary Keeling, John Bernard, Mark Shara, Doug Taylor, William Macintire, Charles Bergengren, Harry Bradley, Jeff Bostetter, and Camille Wells. Jeff Klee replaced Mark R. Wenger in 2004 as our newest colleague. His investigative skills, prowess with electronic drafting, sharp intellect, and good humor has made him an inestimable member of our department ever since. We would like to acknowledge Jeff as the tenth author of this book, since his contributions to its publication have been numerous and timely.

We are also grateful to Janet Murray-King and Wendy Sumerlin for their administrative support over the years. Jonathan Owen has done yeoman work in finding, scanning, and cataloging the images that appear in this book. He has helped our office keep track of the thousands of drawings, photographs, and documents generated from numerous projects. We are indebted to past and present members of the Colonial Williamsburg library and photography lab for supplying research material and illustrations for this project. These include Susan Berg, Mary Keeling, Liz Ackert, Del Moore, Juleigh Clark, John Ingram, Gail Greve, George Yetter, Doug Mayo, Marianne Martin, Cathy Grosfils, Rebecca Scheetz, Barbara Lombardi, Tom Green, Dave Doody, Tom Austin, Kathy Rose, and Lael White, who tracked down obscure volumes, answered our inquiries, scanned images, arranged and photographed new ones, and digitized and improved old photographs from our collections.

Other colleagues at Colonial Williamsburg who have helped us in many ways in this and other projects include Laura Barry, Linda Baumgarten, Edwin Boscana, Colin Campbell, Andrew Edwards, Lisa Fischer, Patricia Gibbs, Graham Hood, Jim Horn, Ron Hurst, Dani Jaworski, Kevin Kelly, Kelly Ladd Kostro, Mark Kostro, Angelika Kuettner, Erin Kuykendall, Nicholas Pappas, Meredith Poole, Julie Richter, Peter Ross, Linda Rowe, Ken Schwarz, Thomas Taylor, Lucy Vinciguerra, Matt Webster, Garland Wood, and Susan Zarecky.

We have worked with scores of colleagues, especially members of the Vernacular Architecture Forum, an organization that was established in 1980 to encourage fieldwork among a new generation of architectural historians. During these more than thirty years, we have welcomed many newcomers into the field, and we have learned and been encouraged by the work that they do in this region as well as in other parts of the country. Our work has also drawn upon the knowledge of specialists from many different fields, including curators, paint analysts, dendrochronologists, archaeologists, architects, conservationists, contractors, and craftsmen. Among the many friends, colleagues, and professionals outside our home institution, we have benefited from the assistance of Nat Alcock, Janet Appel, Jeff Baker, Heather Barrett, Bill Beiswanger, David Bergstone, Catherine Bishir, Susan Borchardt, Bennie Brown, David Brown, Richard Candee, Ray Cannetti, Lois Green Carr, Barbara Carson, Charles Carter, Randolph Carter, Tom Carter, Allen Chambers, Bill Cole, Sarah Cooleen, Abbott Lowell Cummings, Eric Deetz, Claire Dempsey, Mary Louise de Sarran, Garrett Fesler, Ritchie Garrison, Billie Graham, Bryan Green, Gardiner Hallock, Gina Haney, Thane Har-

pole, David Hazzard, Elizabeth Gallow Heavrin, Herman J. Heikkenen, Bernard Herman, Charles T. Hodges, Warren Hofstra, Quattro Hubbard, Carter C. Hudgins, Carter L. Hudgins, Silas Hurry, Kate Hutchins, Rhys Isaac, John Jeanes, Carolyn Keen, Bill Kelso, Susan Kern, Glenn Keyes, Julie King, Peter Kurtze, Mark Kutney, Matthew Laird, Gabrielle Lanier, John Larson, Neil Larson, Catherine Lavoie, Ann Carter Lee, Betty Leviner, Ruth Little, Natasha Loeblich, Calder Loth, Nick Luccketti, Al Luckenbach, Gerard Lynch, Louis Malon, Richard Marks, Ann Martin, Catherine Matsen, Jamie May, Martha McCartney, Turk McCleskey, Lawrence McLaughlin, Martha McNamara, Jim and Marilyn Melchor, John Mesick, Dan Miles, Henry Miller, Hugh Miller, Marcia Miller, Barbara Mooney, Brown Morton III, Fraser Neiman, Louis Nelson, John O'Rourke, Alain and Merry Outlaw, John Pearce, Phil Pendleton, Dennis Pogue, Jonathan Poston, Gigi Price, Matt Reeves, Karen Rehm, Tom Reinhart, Rick Revoire, Selden Richardson, Daves Rossell, Jean E. Russo, Robert St. George, Doug Sanford, Bob Self, Diane Shaw, Karen Shriver, Pam Simpson, Michael Southern, Gary Stanton, Garry Wheeler Stone, Beverly Straube, Jane Sundburg, Polly Tayloe, Robert Teagle, Reid Thomas, Sarah Thomas, Evan Thompson, Paul Touart, Kirsten Travers, E. Paul Treanor, Dell Upton, Marc Wagner, Donna Ware, Priscilla Wellford, Frank Welsh, Mitch Wilds, Richard Guy Wilson, and Michael Worthington.

In addition to these individuals, we thank the many archivists and librarians who have made our work over the years much easier, especially those staff members at North Carolina Division of Archives and History, Southern Historical Collection at the University of North Carolina, Duke University Library, Virginia State Library, Virginia Historical Society, Virginia Department of Historic Resources, Alderman Library at the University of Virginia, Historic American Buildings Survey, Library of Congress, Maryland State Archives, Maryland Historical Society, Winterthur Museum and Library, South Carolina Historical Society, Historic Charleston Foundation, Massachusetts Historical Society, Peabody Essex Museum, and Museum of Early Southern Decorative Arts.

Thanks also to all the professionals and volunteers at the many historic house museums across the region who have invited us to crawl through their attics, peel away modern plaster, and dig through their archives, especially the directors, curators, and research staff at the Adam Thoroughgood House, Belair, the Charles Carroll House, the Chase-Lloyd House, the Hammond-Harwood House, Hampton, Historic St. Mary's City, Homewood, London Town, the Paca House, Pemberton Hall, Riversdale, and the Teackle Mansion in Maryland; Octagon and Tudor Place in Washington, D.C.; and Bacon's Castle, the Ball-Sellers House, Berkeley, the Carlyle House, Christ Church, Lancaster, Ferry Farm, the Francis Land House, Gadsby's Tavern, Gunston Hall, Jamestown Rediscovery, Kenmore, the Lynnhaven House, Magnolia Grange, Menokin, Monticello, Montpelier, Mount Vernon, the Patteson-Schutte House, Poplar Forest, Prestwould, Rosewell, Scotchtown, Shirley, Stratford, the Thomas Nelson House, Westover, the Wickham House, and Wilton in Virginia.

The steady hand of English Heritage illustrator Allan Adams produced many of the cutaway illustrations. Trey Tyler, Terry Ammons, Gibson Worsham, Richard Worsham, Forrest French, Malcolm Ammons, Bay Koulabdara, Dolly Holmes, Roger Guernsey, Billie Graham, Peter Inker, and Jeff Klee were responsible for the digital drawings and three-dimensional models. Tricia Miller made the technical drawings. We appreciate the ability of all of these to translate our field notes into finely wrought images.

For his enthusiasm and encouragement for this project, we thank David Perry, editor-in-chief of the University of North Carolina Press. When deadlines loomed and were missed, he never got discouraged but gently prodded us to keep focused. Thanks also to other members of the staff of the press, including Paul Betz, Caitlin Bell-Butterfield, Kim Bryant, Heidi Perov, and Susan Garrett for guiding this book through to publication.

Finally, we would like to acknowledge the sufferance and support of our spouses, family members, and friends, who have heard us talk about this book for too long. To finally hold it in their hands may be some recompense for their patience.

Architectural Spatial Abbreviations Used in Floor Plans

B	Buttery	GC	Great Chamber	OH	Old Hall
Bh	Brewhouse	GR	Great Room	P	Parlor
BkP	Back Parlor	H	Hall	Pch	Porch
Bn	Barn	HBR	Hall Back Room	Ps	Passage
BP	Best Parlor	IR	Inner Room	Pv	Privy
BR	Back Room	K	Kitchen	Py	Pantry
C	Chamber	L	Library	Q	Quarter
Cl	Closet	Lo	Lobby	S	Study
Cr	Cellar	LoR	Lodging Room	Sd	Shed
D	Dining Room	LP	Little Parlor	SDr	Small Dining Room
DP	Dining Parlor	LR	Little Room	SH	Smoke House
DR	Drawing Room	MH	Meat House	Sn	Saloon
Dy	Dairy	NH	New Hall	Sr	Service
E	Entry	NR	New Room	W	Withdrawing Room
F	Fireplace	O	Office		
G	Granary	OD	Old Dining Room		

KEY TO DRAFTING CONVENTIONS USED TO DISTINGUISH PHASES OF CONSTRUCTION AND SUBSEQUENT ALTERATIONS

Period I
Period II
Period III
Period IV
Period V
Period VI
Modern or Unknown

Period I Framing
Period II or Unknown Framing
Period III Framing

The Chesapeake House

1 *Introduction*

CARY CARSON

Colonial Williamsburg has earned many reputations since its founder, John D. Rockefeller Jr., began restoring the capital of eighteenth-century Virginia in 1927. Yet no part of its fame is so firmly fixed in popular imagination as its association with early American architecture. Millions of visitors to Williamsburg and millions more who have seen "Rockefeller's restoration" only in magazine illustrations find it hard to forget the handsome public buildings where so much American history took place, the period taverns famous for their peanut soup and game pie, and most of all the attractive shops and houses that line the city streets. The houses especially feature in shelter magazines and home-decorating handbooks, season after season. Homebuilders have copied them far and wide (and inappropriately) from New England to Minnesota to California. Hardly a week goes by when Colonial Williamsburg's staff of architectural historians doesn't get calls, letters, or e-mails from people seeking advice about the right way to fix up their own old houses. Occasionally, in the aftermath of a Hurricane Hugo or a Katrina, the Colonial Williamsburg Foundation's architectural specialists are flown to disaster areas to do for devastated buildings what the National Guard and the Red Cross do for the people whom the storms leave homeless. By now, the name "Colonial Williamsburg" is synonymous with architectural expertise.

The authors of this book are those selfsame experts. Most of us are or have been employees of the Colonial Williamsburg Foundation for many years; a few of us are independent researchers with whom the rest of us frequently collaborate. We all gladly share what we know about early buildings, but, until now, usually with one person or one group at a time. By writing this book, we hope to reach a much-wider audience of students, teachers, preservationists, and architectural experts in other parts of the country, old house buffs, and history lovers generally. Here at last, assembled between two covers, is the knowledge we inherited from our predecessors, plus everything else our generation has brought to the task

of renewing Colonial Williamsburg's worldwide reputation in this field.

The fact that our interdisciplinary team of historians, archaeologists, curators, and conservators works for a history museum is not without consequence for the study of domestic architecture. In an age when all buildings were designed locally and built mostly with materials prepared on site, architecture varied significantly from region to region. Colonial Williamsburg takes regional history to heart. It has to. Every outdoor history museum occupies a given time and place in the past. It therefore stands to reason that field research undertaken by the foundation has always been narrow and deep. The narrow part focuses on those tablelands across Virginia and Maryland that water the Chesapeake Bay (Fig. 1.1). The Bay and its tributaries were the locus of a seventeenth- and eighteenth-century agricultural economy organized principally around the production of tobacco for export overseas and eventually food crops for sale to hungry cities nearer by. As historian Lorena Walsh explains in her scene-setting chapter, the tobacco economy forced planter-settlers who migrated to these shores to make different choices than those made by colonists elsewhere. The one choice that impressed its mark on architecture almost immediately was the advantage to be gained by cultivating the crop with a labor force of indentured English servants and enslaved Africans. The tobacco economy and the slave society it fostered effectively drew boundaries around the watershed that the authors of this book call the Chesapeake region. Likewise, tobacco and slave labor gave the Chesapeake house a special function and appearance that distinguished it from farmhouses and town houses beyond the region, to the north in Pennsylvania and southward along the Albemarle Sound into the Carolinas, and even in the western counties of Maryland and Virginia, where the Piedmont economy and the farm labor it employed made different demands that required different kinds of buildings. This book then is the product of a museum research program that has explored one region, its buildings and its records, relentlessly, for almost ninety years. Chesapeake architecture is now the most exhaustively studied seventeenth- and eighteenth-century building tradition in North America. Not even New England has been so thoroughly pored over and analyzed.

Working for a history museum has influenced the scholarship presented in these pages in another respect. Whatever renown it enjoys for its architectural collection and the antique furnishings on view in its exhibition buildings, Colonial Williamsburg remains a history museum first and foremost. That means that the restored buildings and decorative arts have been assembled ultimately to set the stage for a telling of the American story that gives starring roles to the participants, not to the settings or the props. The men and women who lived in Williamsburg or came to town on business or pleasure occupy center stage in the museum's educational mission. It therefore behooves us, the foundation's curators and architectural historians, to learn how buildings and furnishings actually worked for the people who acquired and used them.

That intrinsic connection between dwellings and dwellers guides our research and now provides the underlying rationale for this book. The buildings we study belonged to an age before factory-made materials and mechanized transportation had begun chipping away at the localness of

bespoke architecture. Surviving indigenous buildings retain their value as prime sources of historical evidence about people who lived long before the modern world homogenized everyday life. Those people are our ultimate quarry in this study—men and women of European and African descent, rich and poor, free and enslaved, native born and newcomers—in short, all who resided in the two neighboring colonies (and eventually the independent states) of Virginia and Maryland. Their story—how the houses they built gave architectural shape to their relations with everybody who shared their domestic space—is that part of our book that answers to the title, *The Chesapeake House*.

The most conspicuous figures in this landscape were the great planters, who, though relatively few in number, dominated the scene that travelers to the region remarked on at the time (Fig. 1.2). They figure disproportionately in this and all other studies of Chesapeake architecture because their buildings enjoyed a better chance of survival. But, could you yourself be a time-traveler back 200 years ago, you would encounter other landscapes less familiar now but well known then to a cast of characters that will appear frequently throughout this book. In the neighborhoods around every great estate, you would, for instance, find a countryside that swarmed with ordinary people who seldom or never set foot on a gentleman's property and only occasionally crossed paths with the local grandees at church, the courthouse, the muster field, or by chance along the highway (Fig. 1.3). The commonplace world of small freeholders, tenant farmers, indentured servants, and most slaves assumed a much-reduced scale—smaller farms, modest wooden farmhouses, fewer specialized farm buildings, and here and there a solitary quarter that lodged the two, three, four, or five bondsmen that were all the chattel laborers that most slave owners could afford. Not surprisingly, few of these smaller farmhouses remain standing today, and eighteenth-century slave cabins and agricultural buildings are fewer still. What we know about such ephemeral structures comes instead from archaeological excavations, written records, and, occasionally, drawings.

Were you to take an even-wider-angle view across the Chesapeake landscape, you would glimpse yet another Tidewater setting in the far distance—the region's urban settlements, such as they were. An increasingly complex Chesapeake economy gave rise to a few genuine towns and cities by the middle of the eighteenth century—for example, Norfolk, Williamsburg, Yorktown, and Petersburg in Virginia and Annapolis, Oxford, and Chestertown in Maryland (Figs. 1.4, 1.5). The time-traveler's eye would also pick up a sprinkling of lesser gathering places—wharves and warehouses with adjacent stores and taverns located at landings along some of

Fig. 1.1. The Chesapeake region.

Fig. 1.2. "Horsdumonde, the house of Colonel Skipwith, Cumberland County, Virginia," 1796.
Drawing by Benjamin Henry Latrobe. (Courtesy of the Maryland Historical Society, 1960.108.1.2.4)

the larger creeks and rivers (Fig. 1.6). Inland, yet more stores and taverns clustered around courthouses and jails at county seats (Fig. 1.7). Such settlements notwithstanding, the Chesapeake region remained overwhelmingly rural before the Revolution and only marginally less so afterward.

These three typical landscapes set the scenes that play out in the following pages. They are animated landscapes everywhere you look. The scenery is crowded with actors. Some are the "undertakers," craftsmen, tradespeople, and laborers who planned, built, finished, and furnished the Chesapeake house. Storekeepers, merchants, ship captains, and London agents managed the supply lines that equipped the builders with the tools and materials that could not be manufactured economically in the colonies. Still other players are the householders themselves, whose lifestyles further shaped and reshaped their dwellings from the inside, out according to the uses they made of their homes and the ways they altered those uses over time. In effect, the cover of this book works like the front door to any one of the hundreds of houses described herein. Open it and discover not empty rooms, but furnished, functioning, living interiors. Chapter 2, "Architecture as Social History," is a primer to the research strategy that led to the choice of buildings we have studied

and the methods we have employed to understand what dwellings can tell us about people's house habits, which back then were so different from our own.

Explaining those methods and sharing our findings are the principal purposes of this volume. They are the promise implied by the book's subtitle, a pledge to readers to describe the practice of architectural investigation by Colonial Williamsburg. A chapter on modern field-working techniques explains the tools and methods architectural historians use today to measure, photograph, and otherwise record structures in the field. Some were pioneered by our predecessors and have remained useful ever since; others our own generation has invented or improved upon. All demonstrate that field-recording methods depend first, foremost, and fundamentally on the questions that researchers believe are the most important ones to ask about houses and their inhabitants. Questions lead to hypotheses, hypotheses to tests, tests to a search for pertinent evidence, and the discovery of evidence to methods of recording and storing information that can be shared reliably with other people in books like this one. Most readers will never have an opportunity to visit the buildings in question and evaluate the evidence themselves. Field-recording techniques therefore quarry the

Fig. 1.3. Countryside around Williamsburg, Virginia, 1781. Detail of map by Nicholas Desandrouin.
(Rochambeau Collection, Library of Congress)

(top) Fig. 1.4. "Sketch of York town, from the beach, looking to the West," 1798. Drawing by Benjamin Henry Latrobe. (Courtesy of the Maryland Historical Society, 1960.108.1.4.9)

(bottom) Fig. 1.5. "Old Annapolis, Francis Street," 1876. Painting by Francis Mayer. (The Metropolitan Museum of Art, Rogers Fund, 1916 [16.112], Image © The Metropolitan Museum of Art)

Fig. 1.6. "View down James river from Mr. Nicolson's house above Rocketts [Landing]," 1796.
Drawing by Benjamin Henry Latrobe. (Courtesy of the Maryland Historical Society, 1960.108.1.39)

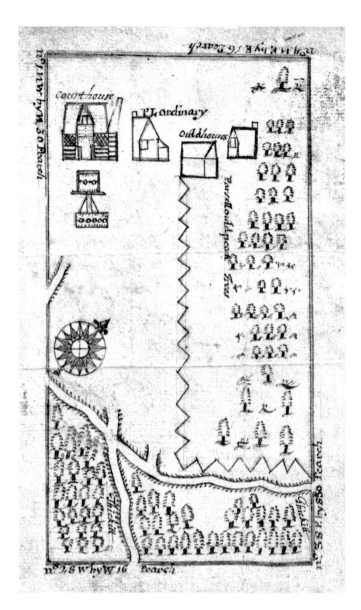

Fig. 1.7. Plat of Charles County, Maryland, courthouse grounds, 1697. (Maryland State Archives)

tial settlements at Jamestown (Virginia) and St. Mary's City (Maryland) through the 1830s. Two additional chapters describe housing for servants and enslaved Africans and their typical plantation workplaces, including farm buildings. These essays engage ongoing historical debates about the region's agricultural diversification and a labor system increasingly based on slavery. They raise questions about the transfer of ideas and expectations from the Old World and the conditions that immigrants encountered in the colonies that encouraged innovation and rewarded risk-taking. Some essays explore the impact of class and race on the design of buildings and their layout on the landscape. Others tell of contests between polite and popular culture and the diffusion of store-bought consumer goods and the spread of etiquette-book manners, even to remote rural backwaters. Still other essays chart the growth of modern pleasure towns and the gradual adoption of urban lifestyles by country folk. All are familiar topics to American historians. Here they acquire the three-dimensional settings that ground these issues in real-world built environments. A conversion takes place in the process. Subjects well understood by economic, social, cultural, and urban historians are reformulated to contribute to a newer-fangled history of American material life, a 400-year-old story that takes account of people's increasingly complex dependence on man-made objects to communicate their relationships with one another and to steer their daily progress through the social worlds they inhabited.

A book about architecture should also be a "brass tacks" book about the building process. Ours is that too, starting with Carl Lounsbury's chapter, "The Design Process." He and later authors find that building practices took shape in the colonies in response to pressures and conditions that challenged people's conventional notions about what a house should be. How Virginians and Marylanders then organized themselves to meet their new needs also reflected circumstances that often were peculiar to the region. The strategies they employed were themselves remembered-from-home, on one hand, and on another were a response to the new realities of life in Virginia and Maryland. How, for example, did clients and builders from different regions in the British Isles reach a meeting of minds on an acceptable design for structures to accommodate their start-over lives in North America? How were building trades in the colonies organized to accomplish construction work? In the case of plantation housing for slaves, what domestic arrangements were white masters content to leave to the very different cultural

building blocks needed for our own scholarship and for its future reinterpretation by those who follow us.

The architectural evidence we and other field-working historians have collected since 1980 rivals the treasure trove assembled by the restoration architects who worked for Rockefeller three-quarters of a century ago. Their work and ours, added together, form the substance of the book. The following sixteen chapters are organized into four parts, starting with the opening essays on our goals and methods followed by a concise economic and social history of the region. Part 2 treats the design and use of buildings front and center. It gives architectural dimension to historical problems that figure prominently in broader academic and professional literatures. Here, though, our prime audience is expected to be those general readers who often share the authors' specialized interests but usually lack their formal training. Three chapters trace the development of regional house forms and shifts in domestic lifestyles, from the ini-

preferences of their African bondsmen? Both the chapter on building design and Edward Chappell's on slave quarters and workplaces raise these questions about the production of material culture by introducing readers to the men and women who formally planned and built Chesapeake dwellings and others who informally adjusted those accommodations to meet their own preferences and everyday needs.

Skilled and semiskilled craftsmen in the building trades show up for work in Parts 3 and 4. Carpenters, bricklayers, blacksmiths, glaziers, painters, plasterers, paperhangers, and more left behind the physical evidence that Williamsburg's field-working historians have systematically collected, photographed, and recorded in abundance. These chapters bring together almost everything that the Williamsburg team has learned and considers worth remembering about the development of timber framing in the region, the brickmason's arts, the variety and specialized use of hardware, and the many ways that rooms were trimmed, plastered, painted, and papered to help define their functions and, in the case of rooms that were open to outsiders, fine-tune their capacity to communicate clear social messages. They provide a richly illustrated guide to the regional forms, variations, and chronologies of building elements, ranging from molding profiles and framing methods to nail types and bonding patterns.

The value of this information is further enhanced because the authors have based their work, wherever possible, on firmly dated buildings rather than those whose age can only be guessed at. Nearly 100 structures featured in this study have been accurately dated by dendrochronological (tree-ring) analysis. For years, Colonial Williamsburg partnered with Dendrochronology, Inc., and more recently with the Oxford Dendrochronological Laboratory in England. These collaborations became the largest such research programs in the country. Dendrochronology takes the guesswork out of dating old buildings. Firm dates make possible trustworthy chronologies of everything from floor plans and architectural moldings to imported nails, hardware, and the ingredients in paint. To the degree that British-made ironmongery, pigments, wallpapers, and the molding planes used to fashion architectural trim were imported into other American colonies, information anchored on datable buildings in Maryland and Virginia should make these chapters about materials and finishes useful benchmarks for readers who study early houses anywhere along the eastern seaboard.

A concluding chapter explains how factory production and mass transportation gradually transformed the building trades in Maryland and Virginia in the years before the Civil War, thus bringing the centuries-old story of strictly handmade buildings to a close.

Readers will find these pages replete with fully developed examples of fieldwork and archival research that demonstrate the value of objects treated as important primary evidence for the study of the past. As such, there is much source material here for classroom teachers, who sometimes express disappointment at the dearth of publications they can recommend to students. Newcomers to the study of material culture, they insist, need model studies that show, step-by-step, how archaeologists and field-working historians find meaning in objects that appear at first glance to be less articulate and less forthcoming than the written records so familiar to most historians. Here students can examine up close a research methodology that starts with the collection and careful recording of physical evidence, proceeds to date it and discover its historical associations with owners and users, then sorts information compiled from multiple buildings and sites into suggestive patterns, and finally draws broad historical inferences from those patterned correlations. Gradually, a bigger picture comes into view, one that helps explain the complicated role that furnished dwellings and fashioned landscapes came to play in the evermore materialistic world that our forebears have bestowed on us. The approach and the investigative procedures tested and refined at Colonial Williamsburg can be applied far beyond the boundaries of the region studied here.

No book, not even this one, can match the revelation that comes from visiting an architectural mecca like Williamsburg or Annapolis. If you have not done so already, you should. If you have but have not returned, treat yourself again. Experiencing architecture in three dimensions engages more faculties than just your mind or your eyes alone. Reading this book beforehand will enhance your appreciation for standing structures in several ways. You will see more. It will open your eyes and focus your attention on things that escaped your notice before. It will deepen your awareness of the scholarship that lies behind ancient buildings restored to their long-lost appearances. Best of all, it will have taught you skills that prepare you to become a knowledgeable architectural investigator in your own right.

Ends & Means

2 Architecture as Social History

Every scholarship has a moral center. Research and writing are meaningful as long as the center holds. Eventually, compelling new truths tarnish the old verities, and scholars move off in directions that realign their work with their changing values.[1] The essays in this volume represent the mature scholarship of men and women who discovered more than thirty years ago that conventional wisdom about architecture was more acceptable to their teachers than it was to them. As graduate students, we, the authors of this book, began learning our trade when buildings were still strictly regarded as works of art. Architectural history was an activity that sorted buildings into styles, traced those styles back to Old World precedents, and judged the worth of individual structures by rules more appropriate to beauty contests. Aesthetic perfection marked the moral center of the scholarship we learned at school.

Once out on our own, our generation lost no time professing its atheism to the elders' faith in the primacy of truth and beauty. The aesthetic character of buildings no longer answered the most important questions—the moral questions—that students of architecture were and still are eager to investigate. Instead of style (how buildings look), we now study function (how buildings work). In place of landmarks (enduring monuments), we see landscapes (animated social settings). The moral center of our scholarship rests squarely on the conviction that architecture, intentionally or not, gives physical form to the way people treat other people who share their space. It follows that the historical study of architecture reveals how planners and builders have created human environments intended to enforce the social rules that they themselves preferred, while those whom the plans and buildings were thrust upon have often ingeniously subverted this received architecture to their own purposes. In other words, the authors of this book see architecture as an instrument of social politics, politics with a small "p"—buildings, towns, and landscapes enlisted in the ceaseless, self-serving tug-of-war that fuels the central dynamic in a democratic society.[2]

Many influences account for this approach to the study of architecture, influences that left their mark on other branches of scholarship as well. One seems peculiar to architectural history. A surprising number of men and women in our field work for historical societies, preservation agencies, and outdoor history museums rather than colleges and universities. There is a connection between our employment by these nonacademic institutions and the social meaning we attach to the buildings we study. The work we do every day—surveying buildings in the field, recording their complicated histories in photographs and measured drawings, and sometimes using that information to design museum reconstructions—all are activities that involve the kind of investigative fieldwork that lays bare the social uses of architecture.

Readers will find both in the pages of this book—a description and demonstration of the field-working methods employed by architectural historians at Colonial Williamsburg and a full setting out of the results that that work has produced. The authors are either staff historians in the Research Division at the foundation or frequent collaborators with the division. For all, field recording is indivisible from the interpretation of architecture as social history.

Museums have been havens for field-working historians for a long time. Colonial Williamsburg, for instance, has employed them in every generation going all the way back to the truth-and-beauty days. This continuous tradition needs to be noted here because the differences among past, current, and future approaches to the study of historical architecture are not differences between those who do and those who do not do field research. Instead, it is the use every generation makes of the information so collected to answer the questions they consider important enough to ask in the first place.

In the next chapter, on field-working methods, Edward Chappell tells how the architects who were engaged in the early restoration of Williamsburg scoured the countryside in search of eighteenth-century buildings to serve as design models for the houses, shops, and public buildings they were restoring and reconstructing in the colonial capital.[3] So do we today. The similarity between them and us ends there. Architects in the 1950s, 1960s, and early 1970s filled their sketchbooks with very different kinds of drawings than those we make today, and back in the drafting room, they used them for very different purposes. Eighty-five years after its founding, restored Williamsburg has become a museum of their several different perspectives and approaches, in effect, a museum within a museum. Its re-created streetscapes not only evoke the semblance of the eighteenth-century Tidewater town that tourists see, but, to knowing eyes, they are also a retrospective exhibition of the foundation's successive attempts to make the three-dimensional buildings that line the streets teach the lessons that their designers intended to communicate to the visiting public.

A quick look at three Williamsburg buildings will show how field-working methods have developed over the years into the coherent research strategy successfully employed by the contributors to this book. The Capitol, the Governor's Palace, and the Courthouse have been chosen on purpose. All three are exhibition buildings open to the public and are therefore accessible to readers who may want to test for themselves the social history approach to architecture described in these pages.

The two most prominent public buildings in eighteenth-century Williamsburg, the Capitol and the Governor's Palace, had burned down long before John D. Rockefeller Jr. purchased the sites and announced his intention to reconstruct the buildings on their original foundations. Remains of the old walls were duly excavated and recorded. This rudimentary exercise in archaeological fieldwork was then used to interpret a contemporary copperplate engraving of both structures and a Thomas Jefferson sketch of the Palace floor plan (Fig. 2.1). The excavated evidence from the Capitol confounded the École des Beaux-Arts–trained architects responsible for designing its reconstruction. They dismissed as "inconceivable" clear evidence that the original builder located the entrance "off center." One of them explained that "architects in 1700 or before were as little likely to do that as architects would be today." Trusting that their own aesthetic sensibilities were more closely attuned to those of the original builder, Henry Cary, they concluded that the perplexing evidence produced by the archaeologists should be respectfully set aside and a symmetrical front reconstructed instead.[4]

They made better use of field research at the Governor's Palace (Fig. 2.2), where excavators unearthed a double-pile plan that Rockefeller's architects quickly identified as "Anglo-Dutch" in style and traced back to English design books and specific country houses in Britain.[5] These prototypes were then exhaustively mined for the treasure trove of "authentic" architectural details that is always needed to complete a full set of working drawings for a reconstructed building.

As completed in 1934, the Capitol and the Palace are now quite literally museum pieces to the scholarship that raised them from the grave. Bricks and mortar set in stone their creators' blindness no less than their erudition (Fig. 2.3). The original scholar-designers, trained as architects, had eyes only for those things that architects back then saw in the work of their respected predecessors—elegantly resolved plans, classicism by the book, honest materials, and handwork exquisitely executed by master craftsmen. They seldom pictured period rooms inhabited by the full cast of characters that made up households and staffed workplaces in the eighteenth century. Occasionally, a fashionable gentleman-owner's presence was implied, or an upwardly mobile artisan's, in one of the tidy frame houses built along the Duke of Gloucester Street. Otherwise, there was nary a sign of the enslaved servants, the wage-earning staff, the workmen, housekeepers, kitchen help, gardeners, stable hands, venders, tutors, and calling tradesmen, or, for that matter, even a householder's wife and children, all of whom once upon a

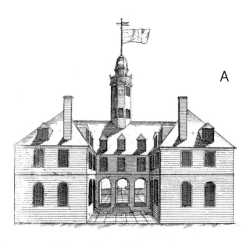

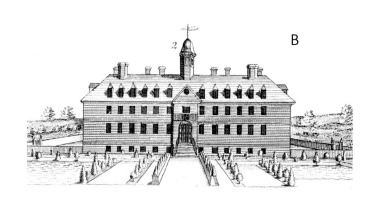

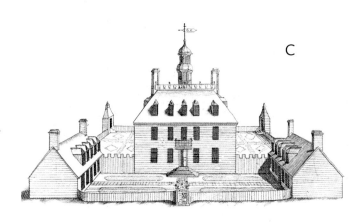

Fig. 2.1. A: Capitol; B: College of William and Mary; C: Governor's Palace. Images from the (Bodleian plate (detail), engraver unknown, c. 1737; D: Measured sketch of the ground floor of the Palace drawn by Thomas Jefferson, early 1770s. (Courtesy of the Massachusetts Historical Society)

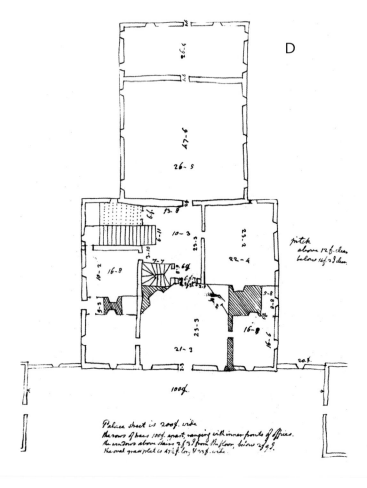

time had been busy about the house from sunup to sundown everyday. The architects who made "Rockefeller's restoration" famous to readers of the magazines *House Beautiful* and *House and Garden* simply were not curious to know how the buildings they restored had functioned as anything more than showrooms. They did not interrogate the evidence for answers that would have told them otherwise (Fig. 2.4).

Fifty years later, the restorers of the Courthouse on Market Square—another exhibition building now open to the public—approached that project altogether differently. They began by asking how legal proceedings in the municipal and county courts that shared the building had required the unusual layout of rooms and special fittings that the Courthouse provided when newly built in 1771. Fieldwork and research in written records went forward hand in hand. There was nothing novel about that by 1982. Ever since Paul Buchanan and James Waite restored Henry Wetherburn's Tavern down the street from the Courthouse in the late 1960s, reading the physical evidence that alterations to old buildings leaves behind and interpreting it in light of related documents such as probate inventories had become standard operating procedure at Colonial Williamsburg (Fig. 2.5).[6]

The team of researchers at the Courthouse pushed the evidence even harder. They wanted to know how the building had been staffed by officers of the court, where they worked, how and when they admitted petitioners, where lawyers, jurors, clerks, constables, prisoners, and defendants were accommodated, how the courtroom was fitted out and furnished to assist the court proceedings, and what spaces were reserved for the throng of spectators who attended court days in eighteenth-century Virginia. The objective was not, as it had been several decades earlier at the Capitol, to cre-

Fig. 2.2.
Excavated site
of Governor's
Palace and
gardens,
early 1930s,
Williamsburg.

Fig. 2.3.
Supper room,
Governor's
Palace, as
furnished in
1934.

(clockwise from upper left)

Fig. 2.4. Bedchamber, Governor's Palace, mid-1930s, published in House & Garden magazine, November 1937. Bruehl / House & Garden / Condé Nast Archive. Copyright © Condé Nast.

Fig. 2.5. Restoration of Wetherburn's Tavern, Williamsburg, 1968.

Fig. 2.6. Courtroom drama at the Williamsburg/James City County Courthouse, 1771, as restored in 1991.

ate a dignified court chamber befitting proud patriots intent on asserting their rights to self-government. The goal at the Courthouse was to reproduce realistically a fully functioning eighteenth-century courtroom interior where modern-day visitors could see with their own eyes how ordinary towns-people back then had learned the art of self-government by suing their neighbors for every penny they could get. Field-work was informed by a thorough study of the county court system, the officers who ran it, and the people who passed through it.[7] The research results laid the groundwork for the restoration of Williamsburg's first exhibition building to be interpreted exclusively by actors, who now use the furnished interior exactly as it had been used 240 years ago by the men and women they portray (Fig. 2.6). Reconstructing action as well as the architectural setting in which it took place has become the ultimate road test for field researchers, a perfor-mance standard they demonstrate in the chapters to come that deal with floor plans and room uses.

FOREGROUND: HABITATS

By now, field researchers have accumulated a significant body of test results. They have learned that embedded in the fab-ric of most buildings is evidence to answer three questions that are key to understanding how a structure functioned as a regulator of people's social behavior, that is, how its architec-tural form choreographed the movements of the inhabitants and their encounters with one another.

The sequence of questions begins by asking where were the entrances into a building and, from there, into each room, and how did passages, staircases, and closed and locked doors control the flow of traffic through the interior. Second, social historians inquire as to what activities oc-curred in each and every space within a building, recognizing that room functions often changed according to the time of day, the season of the year, and the calendar of events. Finally, once they understand the evidence of room use, investigators look for signs that tell them how adjoining rooms and spaces worked in combination. Public and private buildings alike were usually planned to perform a variety of simultaneous or sequential tasks that were anticipated by an arrangement of rooms that gave access from one to another. Field-working architectural historians have discovered that frequently there was a pecking order in these suites of rooms. One or more rooms was superior to the others, and one or more suites was superior to lesser groups of rooms in large buildings. They have learned to look for architectural features that signaled this relative importance, visual signals to which users in the eighteenth century were keenly attuned.

Taken together, access, function, and coordination added up to every user's practical experience with the buildings where they lived and worked. All three usually left traces in the architectural record. Much of this book describes how skilled field-workers recognize and interpret this three-dimensional evidence. The exercise is usually far from straightforward. Most historical buildings have been altered many times to meet the changing needs of later users. Walls get moved, fireplaces are blocked, and doors and windows are retrimmed. Architectural historians must sort out these alterations and put them into chronological order before they can ask of each historical period, *who entered where, what did they do where, and how were a building's many func-tions organized spatially and temporally under one roof.*[8] In practice, structural evidence and social information are lay-ered on top of each other in a stratigraphy that is often as complicated as any archaeological site. Here on paper, we can explore them, one by one, to see how each sheds light on the lived-in experience of architecture.

ACCESS AND CIRCULATION

Few buildings are open to everybody, at least not everybody equally. Because four walls often enclose what is private or personal or exclusive or precious or sacred or secret or pres-tigious, access is restricted to those who belong and to those who wait upon those who belong. Architecture sorts them out, starting usually at the door. Inside, the restrictions al-most always become increasingly selective and directed.

Access into and around the Williamsburg Courthouse perfectly illustrates the principle at work in an eighteenth-century civic building. Only one entrance, one double front door, opened into this hall of popular justice (although re-cords tell us that clamorous spectators sometimes climbed through open windows to get a better view!). Immediately inside, a large courtroom presented all comers with a maze of barriers, gates, closed doors into side rooms, raised plat-forms, and reserved seating (Fig. 2.7). On court days, an un-dersheriff directed traffic from an elevated box built against the wall. Justices, jurors, officers of the court, and lawyers were allowed to pass the bar through two gates guarded by the undersheriff on his side of the room and a constable on the other. Only the justices were free to mount the platform at the far end of the room and take seats on the dais. Jurors sat on a floor-level bench with their backs against the plat-form. The lawyers were corralled into a cramped enclosure barely two steps inside the gates. Everybody else was left standing in an undifferentiated space reserved for spectators behind the bar. Doors to two jury rooms remained closed

tic functions. A formal front entrance into a reception hall delineated a processional axis running through a ballroom in the center of the house to a formal exit from the supper room into the park and promenade behind the Palace.

A third, narrower doorway on the west side of the house led to a service yard ringed with kitchens, pantries, sculleries, and other work buildings mostly involved in food preparation. This clearly was a service entrance. It connected through a small lobby to the butler's pantry on one side and on the other to a room used as a staging area for meals served in the dining room across the passage. The governor's guests saw nothing of slaves' and servants' activities unless the butler stepped out of his office or until footmen emerged from the warming room to wait on table. Partitioning the house into these social zones controlled circulation on each floor. Two separate flights of stairs ensured that masters and servants would not meet unexpectedly between floors. A service stair twisted its way from cellar to attic inside the walls just beyond the door to the warming room. Ladies and gentlemen, of course, had no business in the cellars or attics, so the grand staircase intended for their use ascended only one flight from the parade rooms on the ground floor to the superior bedchambers above.

Such a fully developed social plan might be expected in a governor's official residence, even though the one in Williamsburg was a fairly modest gentry house by English standards. In fact, architectural historians find evidence of social partitioning in houses of all ranks in Virginia and Maryland. The divisions not only separated masters from servants and gentlefolk from rustics; sometimes they carved out private space for multiple or extended families living under one roof. For instance, while many enslaved Africans were quartered in individual one-room cabins, others occupied duplexes, two houses combined into one building. The surviving slave quarters at Prestwould Plantation in Mecklenburg County, Virginia, is one such double house where care was taken to keep the two apartments completely separate and noncommunicating, even in the attic (Fig. 2.8). Three households of enslaved farmworkers on the early nineteenth-century Bacon's Castle plantation in Surry County, Virginia, shared a single building with separate, side-by-side, front doors that opened directly into each of two small ground-floor rooms and another door in the middle that led upstairs to a third apartment in the attics. Where slaves lived in lofts above kitchens and stables, masters sometimes were careful to build an outside staircase that bypassed the work room

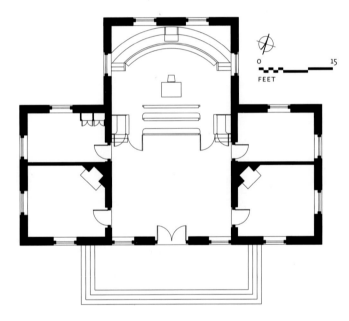

until jurors retired into the rooms to consider their verdicts. The courtroom's architectural fittings admitted or excluded all who entered this (and every other) eighteenth-century courthouse according to their social rank and their role in the legal proceedings.

Domestic architecture sorted and circulated inmates by different rules, but no less effectively. The plan of the Governor's Palace in Williamsburg that Thomas Jefferson drew before moving in as chief executive shows what can be learned about life above and below stairs by paying attention to the placement of entrances, interior doorways, staircases, and corridors (Fig. 2.1D). There were three doors to and from the Governor's Palace, a dwelling with both civic and domes-

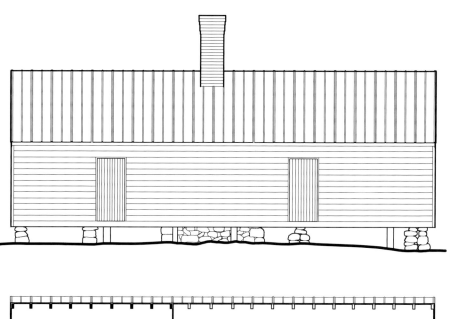

Fig. 2.8. Plan and elevation, slave duplex, 1780s, enlarged c. 1840, Prestwould Plantation, Mecklenburg County, Virginia.

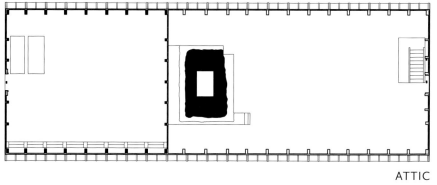

ATTIC

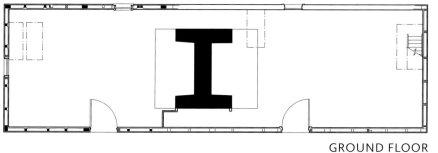

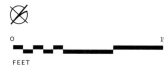

GROUND FLOOR

below, which was full of food that might be pilfered or tools that could be stolen or vandalized (Fig. 2.9).

Men and women at all levels of society felt a strong need to create for themselves some measure of personal space, however small. Archaeologists excavating slave houses in the Chesapeake have come to expect that earthen floors inside slave dwellings will be perforated with subterranean pits. Those located nearest the hearth were often communal root cellars. Others—Landon Carter referred to them as slaves' "holes and boxes"—appear to have been personal safety deposit boxes belonging to individuals.[9] Fraser Neiman has made the insightful observation that these smaller subfloor pits occur most frequently in dormitory-style quar-

ters where unrelated workers bunked together, perhaps each inmate rolling out his bedding on the loose boards that covered his personal hideaway.[10] Others have wondered if the pits were not a response by slaves to a new provisioning system whereby scrimping masters replaced daily rations of fresh food with a weekly allotment of corn and salted pork that required storage.[11] The frequency of these private lockers diminishes on early nineteenth-century sites at just the time when more slave owners were coming to appreciate the advantage of housing their laborers in family groups. Everywhere, even in the meanest hovel, architectural historians find dwellings and workplaces carved up to accommodate the users' social needs.

Fig. 2.9. Plan and elevation, Dixon's Purchase, 1858, St. Mary's County, Maryland. An outside staircase led to slave quarters in the attic above the log kitchen.

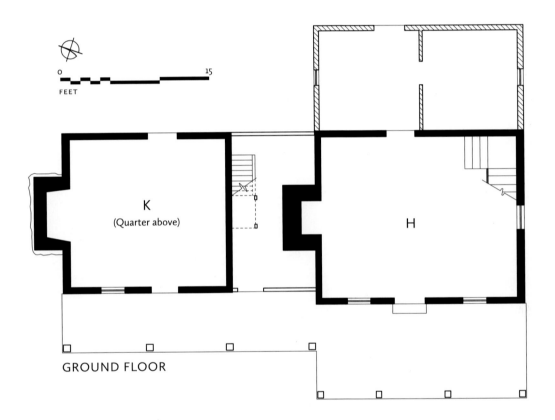

ELEVATION (with porch removed)

0   15
FEET

K
(Quarter above)

H

GROUND FLOOR

There can be no social history without accounting first for the makeup of society. Who belonged? Who did not? The same stricture applies by extension to every community of inmates who inhabit a building, be it mansion or cabin. Architecture and man-made landscapes have always been prime instruments for enforcing the rules of inclusion and exclusion.[12] Different rules apply in different places, and they undergo amendment as people's social ideals shift and are redefined.[13] To study the social uses of architecture, researchers must therefore first identify who was present in the buildings they investigate and where they were and were not welcome to go. Only then are historians ready to ask what activities occurred there.

ROOM USE

Broadly speaking, the function of all buildings is specialized to some degree. That is not to deny that structures often changed uses in times past. An eighteenth-century building built as a storehouse, for instance, might be called a dwelling or a tavern the next time it appeared in the records. Likewise, it is no contradiction to observe that many buildings served multiple purposes simultaneously. The keeper of the store in this example might typically have devoted his large front room to sales, a back room to bookkeeping, the cellar to storage, and the attic chambers to his own lodgings. The variations seem endless.

But they are not. One more generalization can be drawn from the multiplicity of architectural alternatives that researchers observe in the field and encounter in written records, namely that the solutions that buildings offer to the needs they are built to meet are never infinite. A builder's repertory of choices is restricted in practice to a relatively small number of alternatives familiar to him and his clients, to variations on those designs that he can imagine and they will accept, or to innovations that they propose and he can build. These limits are established by culture and custom. If they were not, if they were entirely random and idiosyncratic, only biographers would be interested in knowing how life was lived in a particular person's house or workplace. Every building would be a unique creation. Fortunately for social historians, buildings and the activities that take place inside them almost always follow widely accepted conventions and conform to broadly shared cultural patterns. That is what makes social behavior social. Patterned behavior holds the secret to understanding how groups of like-minded people have treated other groups in times and places like seventeenth- and eighteenth-century Virginia and Maryland. This chapter opened with the statement that parsing out the everyday dynamics of human society is ultimately the work that today's social and architectural historians set out to do. Often, they pursue their quarry into architectural spaces. There, inevitably, they focus attention on the individual rooms where social interactions took place because rooms are the containers for the activities that the room users believe are most appropriately performed there rather than someplace else. A building's function is the sum of its room uses added together.

Once more, but now from this different perspective, the Williamsburg Courthouse provides an instructive example (see Fig. 2.7). The building contained five rooms in all: one jury room for each of the two courts that met there, an office apiece for their clerks, and a large, open courtroom in the middle. The four smaller rooms were mostly reserved for meetings, desk work, and the storage of court books. The courtroom served more complicated uses. It was subdivided by the various gates and fences already described, not just to usher the participants to their appointed places but also to create distinct activity zones where they performed their assigned roles in the court proceedings. Those formalities scripted a sequence of "court day" activities that can be re-created on paper from the clerk's record books and re-created physically from the layout of spaces and the special fittings that literally moved the participants through the docket. Other times, when the clerk received petitions

and prepared documents on "rules day," he used the room altogether differently.

Legal procedures drew the blueprints that laid out three-dimensional spaces inside courthouses. Likewise, liturgy and ritual set out the plans of churches, and manufacturing processes determined the layout of workshops and factories. Daily living followed routines that shaped domestic interiors in similar fashion. Being less formal or mechanistic, house habits encouraged the wider variations in behavior that put a field-worker's powers of observation to the test when investigating historic dwellings. Sometimes special equipment or built-in furniture such as ovens, buffets (for storing tablewares), or valance hooks (for suspending bed curtains) indicates clearly how a particular room was fitted out and, therefore by implication, what activities took place there. Those clues are rare. More often, completely empty architectural spaces give no indication of their original function. Most rooms had to be furnished before they could perform their intended tasks. Consequently, curators have become architectural historians' invaluable partners in identifying room uses. Curators study how furniture and furnishings were arranged and used. They can call on this specialized knowledge to make social history sense out of a helpful class of documents known as probate inventories. These court-ordered lists record the contents of thousands of early houses, often room by room, sometimes giving the rooms their common names. Inventory studies thus can be combined with architectural fieldwork to create a kind of playbook in which knowledgeable curators and social historians can follow the activities that took place in the interior spaces they study.

The role that furnishings played in defining—and redefining—room use can be vividly seen in houses where multiple inventories, made at different times, reveal how the same physical spaces, differently furnished, served different uses for different occupants. Bacon's Castle, in Surry County, Virginia, is not only the oldest surviving building in the Chesapeake region; it also is unusually well documented by three room-by-room inventories (Fig. 2.10).[14] The first records the contents of the house in 1711, furnished as it had been since shortly after it was built in 1665 and, by and large, as it continued to be through 1728 when the second list was made. The instructive comparison comes with a 1755 inventory. By then, the great-grandson of the builder, Arthur Allen, had modernized the old house, moved the most antiquated pieces of furniture to lesser rooms, and acquired a few newer things better suited to the genteel lifestyle expected of a prominent planter by the middle of the eighteenth century. A quick look inside reveals how furniture and fittings modi-

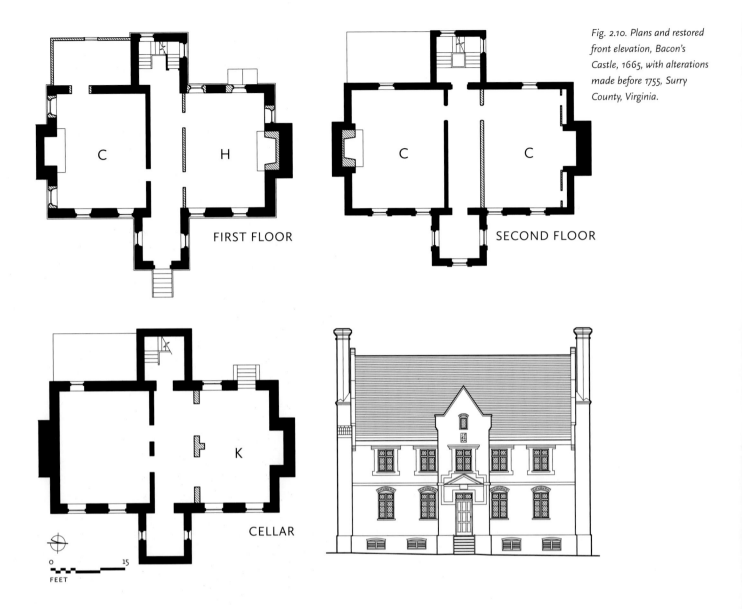

FIRST FLOOR

SECOND FLOOR

CELLAR

0   15
FEET

Fig. 2.10. Plans and restored front elevation, Bacon's Castle, 1665, with alterations made before 1755, Surry County, Virginia.

fied room functions, even though the names by which they were called—"hall" and "chamber"—remained the same for ninety years.

Seventeenth-century visitors to Bacon's Castle entered the house through a central porch tower directly into the hall, the larger of the two downstairs rooms. It was furnished with a great many chairs—eighteen to be exact—plus two tables for taking meals, an open cupboard to store and display plate and tablewares, a daybed for the idle rich, a desk and bookcase for the business of getting rich, and two chests to lock up valuable table linens and bulk yard goods. In short, the hall was the all-purpose daytime living room and the nerve center of the plantation.

The smaller room next door, though called a "chamber" and furnished with two not-so-special beds, was mainly a storeroom for valuables. There Allen kept the family's stock of fine sheets, pillowcases, napkins, and tablecloths, a mortar and pestle for powdering spices, two sugar boxes, and a dis-

tillery. This strong room for precious table linens was separate from, yet convenient to, the adjacent dining area, and the expensive sweeteners and seasonings were safely locked away from the cooks in the cellar kitchen, to whom Mistress Allen must have doled them out as needed.

The principal bedrooms, furnished with the most expensive beds hung with curtains and valences, were located upstairs in two more rooms called "chambers" but in effect a great chamber and an anteroom or dressing chamber. These were not just sleeping chambers. They, too, like the hall downstairs, were equipped for entertaining guests. Fashionable, high-backed cane chairs offered seating for twelve in Allen's bedchamber and another six in the dressing room.

Two generations later, by the middle of the eighteenth century, Bacon's Castle looked positively superannuated on the outside, but inside, the hall and ground-floor chamber had been transformed into modern if unexceptional living spaces. Remodeling helped; newfangled furniture helped

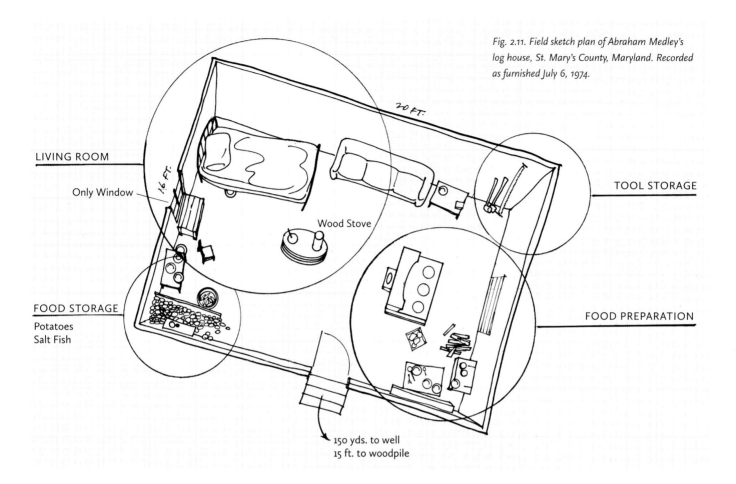

LIVING ROOM

Only Window

Wood Stove

FOOD STORAGE
Potatoes
Salt Fish

TOOL STORAGE

FOOD PREPARATION

20 FT.

16 FT.

150 yds. to well
15 ft. to woodpile

Fig. 2.11. Field sketch plan of Abraham Medley's log house, St. Mary's County, Maryland. Recorded as furnished July 6, 1974.

even more. A partition had been inserted into the hall, creating a passage between it and the chamber, and, although the size of the hall was thereby reduced, the formal entryway added a foyer where visitors could be kept waiting before— and if—they were invited into the hall. That room was now a more restricted space, in keeping with gentry protocol. The hall itself had been refenestrated, and the old lime-washed walls had been dressed up with raised panels, chair boards, and a garnished mantelpiece. Members of the younger generation held on to some of their grandparents' antique furniture—the "old" desk and bookcase, the "old" cane couch, and sixteen oak-framed backstools still upholstered in Russian leather. But the dining tables covered with turkey carpets had been replaced with large, oval walnut tables, and, in the same vein, a fashionable "beaufet"—a proper china closet— had banished the hoary old court cupboard to a back room. Where forty years earlier the hall had been an everything-except-sleeping kind of room, by 1755 it had become primarily a formal room for dining, taking tea, and showing off a galaxy of silver, glass, and fancy earthenware in the buffet.

The uses of the other rooms remained much the same, improved here and there by the addition of modern furnishings. Although the downstairs chamber no longer functioned as a storeroom, it still was only a secondary bedroom.

The best bedchambers upstairs continued to double as the family's private apartments and entertaining rooms for special guests, equipped with looking glasses and tea tables since sometime after 1728.

The furniture and other domestic goods that became ever-more-plentiful in the eighteenth century enabled affluent householders to partition the gentry house into specialized activity areas—public entertaining rooms designed for company, private apartments for family and intimates or special friends, and workrooms for the help. Increasingly, as the century drew to a close, even poor people acquired similar but cheaper household furnishings in unprecedented numbers.[15] For them, the placement of furniture was as important as the function it served. Its arrangement organized the way they lived in their one- and two-room houses by subdividing the little space at their disposal into zones of activity marked off by furnishings in place of solid walls. Probate inventories seldom describe very small houses, and, when they do, they reveal even less about the placement of their contents. Once in a great while, folklorists record ethnographic evidence that shows that there is rhyme and reason even to one-room living. Abraham Medley, for example, fitted out his nineteenth-century log cabin in St. Mary's County, Maryland, with furniture and appliances he acquired in the 1920s and 1930s, but he arranged them as earlier residents must also have arranged their things to create several invisible "rooms" within the one-room cabin (Fig. 2.11).[16] Interviews with Mr. Medley and a carefully recorded furnishing plan of the 16- by 20-foot dwelling revealed a hierarchy of spaces delineated entirely by Medley's possessions placed where they best assisted the way he used his single room dwelling day and night.

COORDINATED ROOM USE

In the absence of such living informants, students who study more distant pasts must collect visual clues to discover the relative importance that people assigned to rooms or parts of rooms in private houses and public buildings. For everyone, for rich and poor alike, daily living always entailed a sequence of events from the moment of rising in the morning to retiring at night. Some of those events, usually the ones that involved social interactions, were considered more significant than others. When performed indoors in the eighteenth century, the settings where activities such as dining, tea taking, and entertaining company took place were often signified by architectural embellishments or specialized furnishings. People with genteel sensibilities had a keen eye for such place-markers.

Today the movable furniture is gone, but the architectural telltales remain for field-working social historians to recognize and record. To untrained modern eyes, these social calibrations seem preposterously arcane. Sitting magistrates in Virginia courthouses, for instance, occupied elevated benches that measured half an inch wider than the jurors' benches; jurors' benches, in turn, were a full inch wider than the narrow perches reserved for those "mercenary pleaders," the lowly lawyers (see Fig. 2.7).[17] House carpenters deliberately selected wrought nails to spike down floorboards in ordinary rooms, T-headed flooring nails in the better rooms, and concealed edge-nails in the best—frequently all in the same building. Their published price books calculated the cost of these refinements down to the penny. Builders took great pains to trim doors and door cases according to the relative status of the rooms on each side. They calibrated these embellishments so exactly that users then and historians now can literally follow a trail of moldings in a fashionable gentry house from its formal front entrance up the stairs and down the passages to all the other socially significant rooms in the building. Whatever the carpenters left unsignified, painters and paperhangers often completed. Prussian blue and "stone" gray colors and printed papers were widely accepted as superior wall treatments for parlors and passages by the third quarter of the eighteenth century; a coat of red-brown

paint was good enough for secondary spaces. Color coding even reinforced slave codes at some Anglican churches in Virginia, where the pews that were restricted to African worshippers, "who are not allowed to mix with whites," were painted jet black.[18]

Several chapters at the heart of this book—chapters on hardware, paint, wallpaper, and architectural decoration—describe at length this remarkable system of differentiating architectural elements. The authors were among the first to recognize the system and understand its operation because our generation was the first to ask how buildings gave physical form and visual direction to the routine business of daily living.[19]

Those questions, and the search for answers they set in motion, direct scholars' attention to a fourth dimension that ought to figure in social architectural studies—the time dimension. Everyone's daily round of activities is always and only a string of sequential events from morning until night. The significance accorded to some more than to others sets the pace and regulates the timing that make a shopgirl's routine so different from the life of a woman of leisure, or a slave's labors so different from the shopgirl's. While such rhythms varied from person to person according to age, gender, race, class, wealth, days of the week, seasons of the year, and, of course, personal preference, they also exhibited broad similarities—recognizable patterns—within cohesive cultures, or, perhaps more accurately, within closely knit communities. That is only another way of saying that the organization of people's daily calendars—that deliberate if habitual sequencing of necessary and recurring activities for which we moderns now use personal Blackberries and iPhones—has always been subject to the same influences that give speech, dress, foodways, folk art, folk music, and vernacular buildings their distinctive twang, flavor, sound, and look.

How surprising then that virtually no historian has studied this most basic temporal organization of human behavior or tried to account for the conspicuous differences between one people's set of routines and another's.[20] Patricia Gibbs, a former colleague at Colonial Williamsburg, is one of only a few who even bothered to assemble the elementary information from which such studies might proceed. Consulting diaries and other time-specific historical sources, she reconstructed daily schedules for a "typical" slave woman cook in a Virginia gentry household, a "typical" teenage girl in such a family, and, last of all, the mother of the teenage girl, a "typical" urban housewife—all from the second half of the eighteenth century and all from the hour of rising in the morning to retiring at night.[21] By locating each woman's round of activities on a "typical" gentry townstead in Williamsburg, say, for example, Peyton and Betty Randolph's house and property, and by imagining the rooms furnished according to inventories of the period, the inquiring social historian can picture how three lives in motion intersected, overlapped, and sometimes went their separate ways in the course of an average day (see Fig. 15.9). Time-use studies of London and the north of England reveal that class and gender had an effect on the time of day that people got up in the morning, began working, stopped working, and went to bed, that plus the nature of the activities in which they were engaged.[22] Furthermore, these habitual patterns changed over the course of the eighty years covered in the studies, from 1750 to 1830. People on different schedules can disturb or inconvenience others in the same household depending on their proximity. Did such considerations figure consciously or unconsciously in the choices that builders of new houses made among alternative room layouts or in others' decisions to reassign room uses in older dwellings? Unquestionably, the daily rhythms of people's lives shaped and were shaped by the buildings and landscapes they shared with their housemates.

By now it should be obvious that an approach suited to the investigation of single buildings can be enlarged to explore the use of nearby related structures and the outdoor spaces in between that make up their workaday setting. We use words like "homestead," "farmstead," and "factory site" to acknowledge that most people live and work in extended landscapes that reach beyond the four walls of a solitary house, barn, or workshop. The activities they pursue in these larger settings and their interactions with others they encounter there invite the same three questions that inform the study of single structures, albeit on a larger scale and with greater attention to coordination among the many parts.[23]

BACKSTORY: CHESAPEAKE BUILDINGS IN PERSPECTIVE

Access, activities, and adjacency, transformed by the alchemy of time, animate the social history of both architecture and landscape. For some years now, scholars have been patiently assembling that history, piece by piece, the pieces usually delineated by regional or national boundaries, time periods, cultures, or classes. Our work at Colonial Williamsburg is no different. As broadly conceived as we intend this book to be, it deals mainly with dwellings and farm buildings in Maryland and Virginia that men and women of mostly English descent built for themselves and their tenants, servants, and African slaves over a period of approximately 230 years. Readers may be surprised to discover that much happened in those two centuries to transform living conditions for all

residents of the Chesapeake region. Be that as it may, our story amounts to only one chapter, or maybe just a few pages, in the much-larger account of architecture as social history that historians and archaeologists have begun to write by putting flesh-and-blood people back into the domestic settings where once upon a time they lived and worked.

A glimpse of the bigger picture adds greater perspective to developments that we pick up in this book only when Englishmen and Africans began settling in the southern colonies. From as long ago as the early Middle Ages in Western Europe and the sixteenth century in West Africa (the dawn of our current knowledge of domestic architecture in that region), dwelling houses have sheltered two categories of human occupants: those whom custom regarded as the primary inhabitants and all others to whom those inhabitants opened their doors.[24] Like churches, shrines, workplaces, and a multiplicity of leisure-time retreats, dwellings have always been meeting places—residences first and foremost, yes, but never totally private hideaways such as a recluse or a hermit inhabits. That said, unlike most other structures that communities build to serve their social needs, dwellings have usually enforced a distinction between insiders and outsiders and have convened both under one roof in social interactions where the former, the inhabitants, invariably initiated whatever invitation brought the latter into the dwelling, be it as boarders, free and unfree laborers, guests, wards, or kinfolk. The primary occupants were usually family, in the many forms that that basic social unit has assumed the world over. These were the men, women, and children who regarded their dwelling place as their home, whether they owned it or not.

This much applies broadly to social histories of architecture in Europe, Africa, the American colonies, and, for that matter, far and wide across the globe. The narrative continues with greater precision in Britain and Northern Europe than the current state of scholarship allows elsewhere. In those parts of the Old World that planted colonies in North America, two developments appear to have been driving forces behind changing architectural traditions in the 500 years between, say, 1400 and 1900. One regulated the admission of outsiders into the vernacular house; the other affected the creature comforts of the primary inhabitants. Strands from both storylines weave through the pages of this book. Therefore, a Cliffs Notes synopsis may help readers follow the action.

Impossible as it is to generalize about the economic and cultural circumstances that determined whom householders welcomed into their company, a trend is discernible. Over the course of several centuries, subordinates of all kinds—vassals, servants, farmhands, hired help, and, of course,

Fig. 2.12. The comforts of home for a gentleman and slaveholder in Williamsburg, third quarter of the eighteenth century.

Fig. 2.13. The discomforts of everyday life for enslaved black families in Williamsburg, third quarter of the eighteenth century.

people enslaved—were gradually excluded from their masters' dwellings, especially as full-time boarders. The rooms where they had formerly worked, eaten, and slept also disappeared, or were put to different uses. Simultaneously, changing notions of hospitality brought larger numbers of visitors, guests, and companions into householders' homes. These were men and women whom the principal inhabitants regarded as social equals. Little by little, rooms for their entertainment supplanted spaces that had been occupied previously by domestics. Thus, houses became more formal. Partitions and furnishings drew harder lines between public entertaining rooms and private family apartments and between those various superior spaces and the netherworld of cellars, backrooms, and outbuildings inhabited by an increasingly invisible servant underclass. These developments were reaching full pitch by 1700, and readers will encounter them frequently throughout this book.

They will also find ample evidence of the second long-range trend in domestic living that modernized the Western European house: people's rising expectations concerning their comfort and privacy. That too had a history that preceded the settlement of North America. Nor had it been

resolved by the seventeenth century when house builders in the Chesapeake colonies were still trying to decide whether to heat their parlors, to dine separately from their farmhands, and to retire at night to private bedchambers. A hundred and fifty years later, most householders had finally made those choices. But, as readers will find in chapters that deal with the design and furnishing of gentry houses toward the end of the eighteenth century, similar concerns had by then raised expectations and standards to new levels. Houses after 1800 increasingly made provisions for individual bedrooms and special-purpose workrooms, and they introduced improved technologies for heating, cooking, and lighting. By increments, domestic architecture already was tending in the direction of the individualistic, self-indulgent, woman-centered home place that middle-class Victorian house builders eventually perfected and that we moderns have only mass-produced and supersized.

Other subplots enliven the social history of houses, but these two themes dominate the literature because they squarely address the questions that our generation finds most compelling. The many ways that buildings were deliberately designed to admit and accommodate some people

Fig. 2.14. Williamsburg's restored and reconstructed buildings have given street credibility to dramatizations of "Revolutionary City" since 2006.

and not others—literally the ins and the outs—selected the commonwealth of inmates who become our historical informants. The many ways that buildings were planned, equipped, and furnished to the greater advantage of some more than others—the haves and the have-nots—show us exactly how the comforts of home have been unevenly bestowed. It bears remembering that the dynamic mainspring that has driven social change ever since Europeans colonized North America is ultimately to be found in the personal and homely pleasures of everyday life—or in the keen disappointment of their denial (Figs. 2.12, 2.13).

SEQUEL: THEATERS OF EVERYDAY LIFE

The brevity of the foregoing synopsis necessarily compresses a long and complicated history into a one-page executive summary. It leaves no place to hide the moral justification that validates this scholarship. Our generation of historians takes pains to repopulate the buildings we study because only that kind of research supports certain fundamental convic-

tions we share. They start with the belief that, whatever else can be said about them, landscapes, cities, and buildings are created to give useful form to the things that people do to, for, and with everybody else who cohabits those places. We also believe that, by studying everybody's buildings, we historians make our own special contribution to every American citizen's obligation to be curious about other Americans—to heed one another's hopes and needs and to discover and chronicle the struggles that have led to their fulfillment or, alternatively, to their frustration when they go unfulfilled. Finally, many who see value in this approach to studying architecture share the ultimate conviction that such scholarship, however modestly, provides a historical understanding that educates the conscientious citizen's commitment to social justice and to keeping alive this country's everlasting promise that the future can improve on the past.

So there it is. Decades ago, as recent graduates, we rallied around the "new social history" banner, believing that we had learned the secret to writing a fuller and fairer account of the building arts in America. We supposed that

that would be our contribution to a much larger narrative of social change. Our study of the past would open other people's eyes to the fact that today, too, built environments still weigh heavily in favor of the wealthy and powerful. The success of our ambition to redefine architectural scholarship can be read—and judged—in the pages of this book. Our even greater aspirations to be public historians can be experienced by all who visit the buildings we have chosen to reconstruct at Colonial Williamsburg with the knowledge so gained—an asylum, a plantation slave quarter, a blacksmith's workshop retooled as a Revolutionary War armory, a "people's court," the in-town quarters and work buildings where enslaved Africans labored in service to Peyton and Betty Randolph, a hypothetical (but thoroughly researched) small planter's farmstead on the edge of town, and most recently a

dissenter's haven, Richard Charlton's Coffeehouse. By making such ordinary structures our highest priority, the Colonial Williamsburg Foundation's architectural historians have literally set the stage for daily theatrical performances that have again recast Rockefeller's restoration in yet another guise. Today Williamsburg is a "Revolutionary City." It features a live-action drama called "Becoming Americans" (Fig. 2.14). The story the street actors tell, the story of Americans' unfinished "struggle to be both free and equal," plays against an architectural background that scholarship has made into something much more than mere scenery. The places and spaces that stage our telling of history today were the very crucibles where the events themselves were originally fired and fused before they were cast in the form of a brand-new nation.[25]

3 *Fieldwork*

EDWARD A. CHAPPELL

Readers might assume that the authors of this book invented most of the methods used herein. We did not. While we have refined the techniques to suit work for a museum that portrays life in the past through buildings, we have borrowed freely from earlier generations of researchers, each with its own preoccupations. For all of us, fieldwork forms the core of our research. Our predecessors and colleagues in other institutions have taught us much.

The first people to give careful attention to early houses in the Chesapeake region were hagiographers intent on placing great men in grand houses, most prominently Mount Vernon. Eventually, that quest shifted to houses notable for their revered design qualities rather than their tenants. Architects in search of a formal but homegrown American style found rich material in the field, in historic structures they measured and recorded in ways that we still employ. Draftsmen and photographers sought the most classically inspired enrichments in the biggest houses and captured them in beautifully delineated drawings and large-format photos.

Begun in 1927, the restoration of eighteenth-century Williamsburg widened the search beyond the obvious models for modern suburban mansions. Tasked with restoring and reconstructing hundreds of buildings in the colonial city, everything from privies to the Governor's Palace, the project architects, Perry, Shaw, and Hepburn of Boston, set out to learn the full grammar of early Chesapeake building. Their draftsmen scoured eastern Virginia and Maryland for early details to record, learn, and use in the colonial capital (Fig. 3.1). The designers brought a new level of obsessiveness to the enterprise. The first resident architect, Walter M. Macomber, fondly recalling the attention he and his colleagues paid to the shapes of simple architectural moldings, later regretted that he never found time to write a definitive history of the cyma.[1]

Two people involved in the early restoration created broader roles for Chesapeake houses in the nation's written architectural history. In 1922, Fiske Kimball, the first archi-

tectural scholar to study the area professionally, combined what he believed were seventeenth-century houses with later mansions to create a broader East Coast study that charted changes in both building form and ornament. Thomas Waterman followed Kimball's lead in an effort to explain stylistic evolution of the grandest eighteenth-century Virginia houses. Waterman drew heavily on fieldwork, which he illustrated with his own measured plans.[2] Like us, he and Kimball used houses they studied in the field to develop a narrative about architectural change in the region.

During the Great Depression, a federal program went far in raising standards for architectural recording and ex-

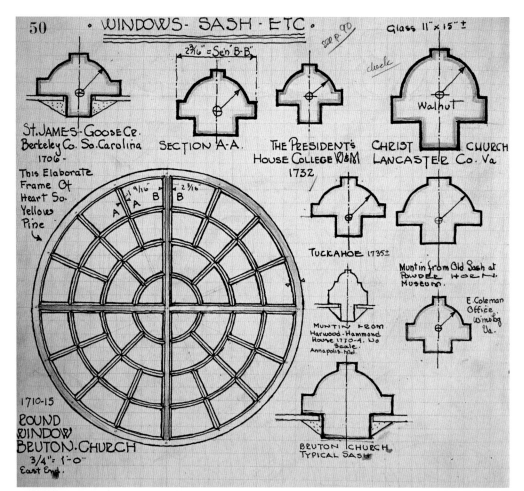

Figures within the sketch:

50 · WINDOWS · SASH · ETC ·

Glass 11" × 15" ±

St. JAMES-GOOSE Cr.
Berkeley Co. So. Carolina
1706 -
This Elaborate
Frame Of
Heart So.
Yellow
Pine

2³⁄₁₆" = Sec'n B-B'

SECTION A-A.

THE PRESIDENT'S
HOUSE COLLEGE W&M
1732

Walnut

CHRIST CHURCH
LANCASTER Co. Va

TUCKAHOE 1735±

Muntin from Old Sash at
POWDER HORN.
MUSEUM.

E. Coleman
Office
Window
Va.

MUNTIN FROM
Harwood-Hammond
House 1770-4. No
Scale.
Annapolis. Md.

1710-15
ROUND
WINDOW
BRUTON · CHURCH
3/4" = 1'-0"
East End.

BRUTON CHURCH
TYPICAL SASH

Fig. 3.1. Measured window details in the 1936–52 sketchbook of Colonial Williamsburg architect Singleton P. Moorehead. (Special Collections, Colonial Williamsburg Foundation)

panding the scope of architectural field research. Begun in 1933, the Historic American Buildings Survey (HABS) was influential in establishing guidelines for how to record early structures more comprehensively in measured drawings and photographs, which became available in the public domain. Draftsmen and photographers working for this Works Progress Administration program made Virginia one of the most extensively studied states. Their surveys included buildings without the aesthetic qualities that Kimball and Waterman admired (Fig. 3.2).

Thirty years later, an international preservation movement, responding to the accelerating destruction of historic structures worldwide, promoted a more liberal definition of buildings and landscapes worth saving. In this country, state governments used funding provided by the 1966 National Historic Preservation Act to carry out city, county, and regional surveys that offered employment for many young field-workers to record a large and varied architectural legacy that remained unstudied.

Folklorist Henry Glassie provided intellectual direction and inspiration to this generation of surveyors. In a remarkable manifesto, *Folk Housing in Middle Virginia*, he wove together threads of French structuralism and linguistic analysis to identify unconscious rules governing the variable form of Chesapeake houses.[3] Drawing plans and construction details in a careful but seemingly simple manner, Glassie persuasively made interpretation of deep-seated regional culture more important than identifying the first or the finest designs.

Dell Upton brought comparable theoretical constructs to State Historic Preservation Office fieldwork when he came to the Virginia Historic Landmarks Commission in 1974. Using probate inventories and measuring house plans, Upton sought to explain how patterns in the arrangement of functions generated houses of superficially different form. Influenced by Edmund Morgan's *American Slavery, American Freedom*, Upton saw a fractured past, one defined by oppositions of fine and unrefined, leisure and work. Slavery shaped the Chesapeake house as profoundly as any architectural design book. Upton and historian Cary Carson included new archaeological findings with their fieldwork to discover a history of rudimentary construction practices in the region. They argued that the expensive workmanship Williamsburg restoration scholars and even Glassie understood as an architectural heritage of the early Chesapeake was only half the story.[4]

Fig. 3.2. Long Lane Farm, St. Mary's County, Maryland. (HABS, 1937)

The field had come a long way since the first Chesapeake field-workers drooled over exotic balusters and fanciful chimneypieces. Carson made archaeological evidence for less-durable seventeenth-century houses comprehensible by showing the evolution of surviving Maryland houses in annotated HABS drawings. These Maryland records are another precedent for our own fieldwork, which draws most directly on modern archaeological methods, with their related graphics and interest in interpreting changing patterns of past life rather than solely in design.

Our approach to fieldwork is indebted to these predecessors. If it is different, it is in how various research modes are combined and intensified and in the general objectives of the inquiry. Intensity, in our case, grows from both the demands of literal restoration and the need to harvest newly exposed information during interventions like mundane repairs. We pay much attention to finish, but only in a contextual perspective rather than as worshipers at the altars of venerable design and skillful craftsmanship. We are as interested in representative examples of poor work as in admirable expressions of skillful craftsmanship. As evidence, they offer equal value.

We assembled a small team of architectural historians

at Colonial Williamsburg in the early 1980s, one that substantially remained together and has engaged in fieldwork for the past three decades. We quickly encountered detailed questions looming about the character and use of rooms in the long-lost Governor's Palace, the region's first insane asylum, and buildings at the town's wartime ironworking site. We were also asked, by the way, how a late colonial store was arranged, including its office and residential space. We soon began to ask our own questions about a greater spectrum of eighteenth-century housing as well as the traditional dates ascribed to surviving houses. The nature of work buildings and housing for enslaved residents of the Chesapeake became an essential inquiry. The physical investigation of buildings, supported by archival research, has continued to provide the best available answers to these and countless other questions. More broadly, it has allowed us to explore how, at least architecturally, the town appears somewhat at odds with developing historical perceptions of the countryside where most people lived. We have been relatively liberal in investigating sites that directly address no projects of the moment but that seem too valuable to lose without analysis. We collect data for what they contribute to understanding of life in the early Chesapeake, not simply because they answer a narrow research question like the proper shade of blue for the governor's ballroom.

Our fieldwork involves three overlapping efforts: recognizing changes, sorting out dates, and discovering variability that reveals human choice and ideology. All three focus on historic use and meaning. The objective is to read the physical evidence as a means of understanding past intentions and patterns of behavior. This approach is sometimes called building archaeology because it involves uncovering and recording layers of evidence. Like good archaeology of any stripe, the method builds interpretation on foundations of scrupulously analyzed data.

Few preindustrial buildings survive intact, if intactness is defined as original condition upon completion. Even the humblest of old buildings reflect changing uses and standards of accommodation. Some change is immediately recognizable—a doorway that has been blocked or a staircase that has been removed. Producing measured drawings helps the observer assemble that evidence in a methodical manner. A small wooden building behind a house at New Kent Courthouse offers an illustrative example. Outwardly, it appears to be a conventional kitchen of about 1850, with sawn weatherboards and a brick chimney. A look inside, however, reveals that it had been cheaply built with walls of round logs and had been served by a wooden smoke hood that preceded the present exterior chimney. Smoke hoods were a crude and early method of collecting smoke and heat in one bay of a building without constructing a chimney extending from floor to rooftop. Recording a simple plan and sections of the one-room building helped us recognize framing remnants of the hood, which had included angled studs lapped to an overhead joist and carried up to create a rectangular funnel that directed smoke through the attic to a hole in the ridge of the roof, possibly topped by a low wooden stack (Fig. 3.3). Parts of the feature were demolished long ago, but four of the studs survived (Fig. 3.4). These show that the inside of the hood was lathed and plastered while the outside was sheathed with boards. The record drawings include the brick chimney added when the kitchen was made more habitable several decades later. Likewise, the drawings capture clues for the form of small unglazed windows closed with an out-swinging shutter, as well as later nineteenth-century improvements and mid-twentieth-century extensions. In this case, the earliest details are arguably most important simply because remains of smoke hoods and unglazed windows, once common in the region, now survive in only a handful of buildings. Mid-nineteenth-century changes to the kitchen are also important when understood as part of late

antebellum efforts to improve workers' accommodations in response to abolitionism. The drawings, photographs, and written summary are essential for recording the significant elements of both phases as well as more recent additions.

A second modest kitchen-quarter offers a more complex example of field recording in which all periods clearly are significant and where only a few photos would miss most of the story. As a boy in the 1870s, prominent African American educator Robert Russa Moton lived with his parents in a two-room-plan tenant house standing near planter Samuel Veneble's own house in Prince Edward County, Virginia (Fig. 3.5). Like many black families in the postwar South, the Motons occupied what had previously been a divided work building and lodging for slaves, with two separate doors to similar-size ground-floor rooms. Measuring the plan of the house helped us understand the spaces and circulation, including a change from two stairs leading to separate sleeping rooms in the dimly lit attic to a single stair used by the Moton family to reach their two upstairs bedrooms, with one located beyond the other (Figs. 3.6A, 3.6B). The drawings document the existing stair and the framing for the earlier one, which was removed after 1865, as well as the addition of a doorway between the lower rooms.

These alterations fit the general pattern found in the transformation of former slave houses into tenant houses in the postwar period. On the other hand, a peculiarity of this building is that it was more expensively finished than most kitchen quarters from the period between 1820 and 1840. Recording older mortises in the wall frame with relative dates of posts and studs helped us recognize that the early nineteenth-century arrangement was itself a substantial alteration of an earlier landowner's hall-chamber house. The earlier house had a different plan and circulation pattern, consisting of a direct entry into a larger hall with an internal door opening into a smaller chamber (Fig. 3.6C). Both rooms had fireplaces in gable-end chimneys. Typical of such Chesapeake houses, it had a single stair placed against the partition in order to reach both upper bedchambers independently, now evident only in joints and spacing of the upper joists. The attic rooms were as unfinished for the earlier landowning white family as they were for subsequent poor black ones.

Here the framing demanded close study and the field drawings needed to be systematically annotated to sort out the evolution of the house. A plan recording each piece of wood without identifying its relative date or noting evidence for missing members would have captured only the building's final era, in severe decline. Based on more detailed recording, three sequential plans summarize a much more

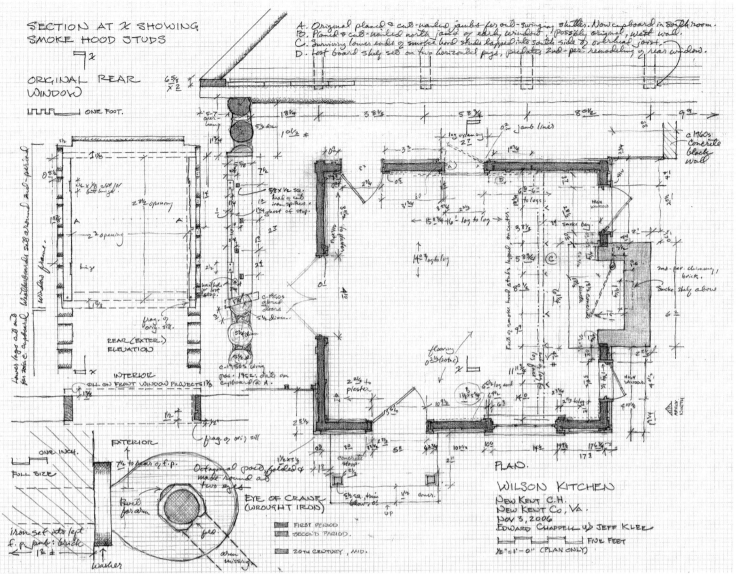

SECTION AT X SHOWING
SMOKE HOOD STUDS

ORIGINAL REAR
WINDOW

A. Original planed & cut-nailed jambs for out-swinging shutters. Now cupboard in south room.
B. Planed & cut-nailed with jambs of early window, possibly original, west wall.
C. Surviving lower ends of smoke hood studs lapped into south side of overhead joist.
D. Lost board shelf set on two horizontal pegs, predates 2nd-per. remodeling of rear window.

REAR (EXTER.)
ELEVATION

INTERIOR

EXTERIOR

EYE OF CRANE
(WROUGHT IRON)

■ FIRST PERIOD
■ SECOND PERIOD.
■ 20TH CENTURY, MID.

PLAN.

WILSON KITCHEN
NEW KENT C.H.
NEW KENT CO, VA.
NOV 3, 2006
EDWARD CHAPPELL w/ JEFF KLEE

½"=1'-0" (PLAN ONLY)

(top) Fig. 3.3. Annotated field drawing of the Wilson Kitchen, New Kent County, Virginia.

(bottom) Fig. 3.4. Attic of the Wilson Kitchen with angled studs and plaster lath remaining from its frame smoke hood.

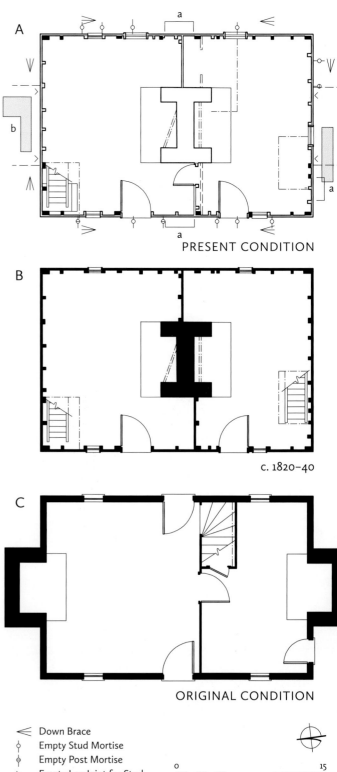

(left) Fig. 3.5. R. R. Moton House, Prince Edward County, Virginia.

(right) Fig. 3.6. R. R. Moton House plan. A: Present condition with evidence of alterations; B: Condition c. 1820–40; C: Original condition.

PRESENT CONDITION

c. 1820–40

ORIGINAL CONDITION

⋘	Down Brace
⌀	Empty Stud Mortise
⌀	Empty Post Mortise
>	Empty Lap Joint for Stud
a	Original Door Locations
b	Archaeological Excavations
■	Original Framing
□	Later Framing

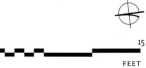

complex history that ranged from it being home to a white planter family, then to two enslaved black families, and later to a newly freed black family who raised an exceptional son.

Modern technologies are increasingly applied to answer questions raised by field observation. Tree-ring dating, for example, played an important role in the Moton House. The builder's use of distinctive triangular false plates in framing the roof, as well as planed and beaded joists ornamenting the lower rooms, suggested a relatively early date for the house. According to the dendrochronologists who studied original parts of the frame, the house was built of timber from southern yellow pine trees cut in the winter of 1745–46, which is surprisingly early for a part of the Piedmont with few colonial settlers before 1732.[5] As a result, a fully developed Anglo-Chesapeake house rather than any of a number of rude log cabins became the earliest building known to survive in this and surrounding counties.

The Moton House illustrates how subtle and sometimes obscure evidence can best be collected and interpreted through careful field drawings. Fieldwork involves more than the neutral representation of a building or the recording of its most elegant or archaic details. Drawing plans and photographing details are easy technical exercises that can be achieved by laser-guided automata. Digital scanning now offers an especially efficient means of capturing complex shapes and textures. What demands rigor is the analysis of the evidence, a process that involves a continual interplay between recording and interpretation. We always seek to represent the physical history of a particular site accurately, but

Fig. 3.7. Westover, 1750–51, Charles City County, Virginia.

the ultimate goal is to wring meaning from the built form. Meaning is derived from context: first, an artifact's spatial context—its position within a structure or site—and second, its chronological context. Another principal quarry then is date.

William Byrd II famously describes having sex with his wife on a billiard table in a secret diary filled with similarly intimate glimpses into the private life of a rakish and educated Virginia planter. Yet the diary reveals so little about the settings of these events that generations of historians have wrongly assumed they happened in the house his son built six years after the old man's death. Neither Byrd nor the pool table ever saw the present Westover (Fig. 3.7).[6] Even the most literate or famous often left no written record of the construction and alteration of their houses. Two of the seminal works based on model fieldwork for their time are flawed by muddled chronologies. Both Waterman in *Mansions of Virginia* and Glassie in *Folk Housing in Middle Virginia* based confident stories of cultural change on misreadings of the physical evidence.

As the following chapters will demonstrate, buildings are filled with clues that can be used to date their construction

and alterations. How bricks were laid, wood was cut, house frames were assembled, exteriors were finished, and doors were hung changed in the more than two centuries addressed in this book. Recognizing timing for the arrival of bookish classical woodwork or the shift from hand-wrought nails to machine-cut ones could have saved Waterman and Glassie some confusion in their analysis of building patterns in the region. These and other details, however, need to be read in the context of where they were used. In which room of the house, in what building on a property, on what owner's property in the community, and where within the region did these features appear? Context matters.

Carefully mortised and tenoned frames characterized superior construction in the eighteenth century, but fieldwork shows that braces and vertical timbers were still lapped and pegged or spiked together in poorer work, like on an early nineteenth-century kitchen at Bayside Farm in St. Mary's County, Maryland. Water-driven sawmills were established in the Tidewater by 1689, but slave labor made pit-sawing by hand the common practice in Maryland and Virginia until the Civil War.[7] Hand-wrought HL hinges went out of common use with the widespread availability of cast-iron butt

(top) Fig. 3.8. Thomas Everard House, Williamsburg, before restoration.

(bottom) Fig. 3.9. Plan, Thomas Everard House, from Marcus Whiffen, The Eighteenth-Century Houses of Williamsburg (1960).

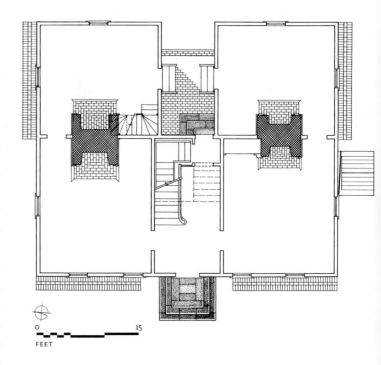

hinges after 1800, but the old-fashioned hinges still found use in cellars and slave quarters as late as the 1840s.

More critical reading of the physical evidence and dendrochronology have demonstrated that most Chesapeake buildings once thought to be seventeenth century actually date from the first half of the eighteenth century. Exposed and molded framing, closed string stairs with chunky balusters, and decorated hinges were long believed to indicate a seventeenth-century date for houses like Belle Farm and Resurrection Manor. We now know these to be solidly eighteenth century. Their heavy details appear archaic only when compared to the more refined finishes of the mid-eighteenth century and later. However, the evolutionary lines of form and finish follow varied routes within the region as well as in the household. Central passages and hidden wall frames appeared earlier in Williamsburg, for example, but the most refined masonry and elaborate woodwork both appeared in houses of the Tidewater countryside well before it did in their counterparts in either colonial capital.

Dating the phases of even seemingly simple houses is sometimes a protracted affair, requiring substantive investigation. The tale of discovery at the Moton House includes an architectural historian moving in with flashlights, tape

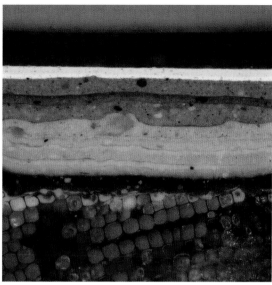

Fig. 3.10. Photomicrographs of paint strata on chair boards (left) and wainscot (right) in Thomas Everard's parlor. Samples taken under visible light at 100x magnification. The earliest layers of paint on the chair boards are absent on the wainscot.

measures, and small mirrors on sticks for a few days. The same architectural historian's job in Williamsburg often involves repeated efforts to sort out the dates of changing forms and finishes in a single building. Our understanding of the Thomas Everard House is still evolving after sixty years of careful looking. A public armorer and protégé of Governor Alexander Spotswood named John Brush built himself a center passage house prominently situated on Palace Green next to the residence of his patron (Fig. 3.8). He acquired the lot in 1717, and historians have rightly assumed he built the house within the two years required by the trustees of the city. We investigated this with dendrochronology and found that twelve tulip poplar rafters in the main roof were from trees felled in 1718. Rafters in a surviving rear wing were from trees cut two years later, indicating that Brush added the wing in 1720, fulfilling an original intent expressed in his rear placement of chimneys in 1718.[8]

Colonial Williamsburg architect John Henderson and his colleagues studied the house carefully for several years in preparation for a full restoration in 1949. Henderson struggled to decipher how the house had evolved after Brush's work. He recognized that woodwork was of several eras, but he lacked the microscopic data we could bring to the study, so he had trouble with the sequence. Writing in 1960, Marcus Whiffen felt there was evidence for Brush having built a more modest hall-parlor house with direct entry into the principal room, and with plain plastered walls from floor to ceiling. He plausibly imagined that builder Henry Cary Jr. and his wife, Elizabeth Russell, added most of the refined woodwork in the second quarter of the century, and that Williamsburg mayor Thomas Everard built the wings (Fig. 3.9). Whiffen was clearly wrong about the addition of the passage and the late date of the wings, but his argument for Cary producing

some of the woodwork was logical. Cary built the President's House and chapel at William and Mary. One might easily see his hand in the stair, a remarkably showy piece for a relatively small house. Its carved brackets, in fact, resemble those at Rosewell (1726–37), Tuckahoe (1733), and Carter's Grove (1751–55), and they equal in richness the carving on the altarpiece at Bruton Parish Church (1752). Any argument for this as Brush's stair seemed credulous.

We had an opportunity to look behind twentieth-century plaster and siding in 1994, finding that plaster in the side rooms had originally extended between exposed wall plates and bases, without chair boards or wainscot. Paint analysis showed that existing chair boards were added to the rooms, were painted, and then accumulated grime before wainscoting was inserted below (Fig. 3.10). A number of pieces seemed to fall into place. The elaborate stair substantially blocked a rear doorway that was part of the original frame, causing the door to be moved. Paint analysis suggested that the wainscot and doorways in the passage were contemporary with the stair—that virtually all the passage finish was of a single date.[9] Most surprising, though, was the fact that there was absolutely no evidence for an earlier stair or any wall finish predating the passage wainscot. Could it mean, then, that rough framing was exposed in the entrance and that no stair better than a ladder existed for thirty years? Unlikely as it seemed, we were forced to accept this as the strongest interpretation for more than a decade. Then, in 2006, we asked the Oxford Dendrochronological Laboratory to study the existing stair structure and treads. Much to our surprise, they found that four datable pieces—one tread, two step ledgers, and a trimmer—all were made from trees cut in 1719. None of the pieces was recycled.[10]

Remarkably, then, armorer John Brush built the house

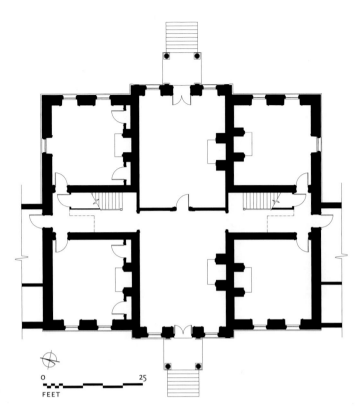

with an up-to-date stair passage that was surprisingly well finished for a tradesman in 1718–20, even for an associate of Spotswood. The carved stair brackets were based on a relatively familiar and probably unpublished British model for first-rate brackets, more roughly carved here than by later craftsmen working for fancier plantation clients. The passage doorframes were also a funky version of ornamental work, with awkward crossettes above and below. If taken as an example of its era, then, Brush's house illustrates that well-connected urban tradesmen could build a somewhat larger and more fashionable house several decades before many landowners and modest officeholders in the Chesapeake countryside did. But the tradesman's house was unevenly finished, with riven clapboards on the roof above a classical modillion cornice and plain plastered rooms beyond the fancy entry. And it took two more generations to create a very genteel house, concluding with two phases of work by the mayor of Williamsburg.

Our understanding of the story continues to evolve. Recent examination of the stair reveals that two different joiners produced elements of its finish, the second of whom more carefully turned his classical balusters. He did this to replace lost pieces, leaving relic mortises and other evidence of change, as though the stair had been vandalized and substantially repaired around the era of the Civil War. Remnants of the earliest paint on the replacement parts confused us by resembling an original primer, until we

recognized the sequence of layers on the later woodwork began only halfway through paint stratigraphy on the older members. Out of the confusion of paint layers appeared a previously unknown nineteenth-century phase of history-conscious house repair.

Confusing or straightforward, such empirical research provides a correction to book-bound architectural history, which holds the real subject beyond scholars' confident reach. Without careful fieldwork, historians are reduced to commenting superficially on subjects such as the manner in which some wealthy builders fished their house designs from published sources. Robert Beverley's Blandfield (1769–72) is a good example of plans and elevations developed from James Gibbs's *Book of Architecture* (1728) (Fig. 3.11). By not looking closely at the building, historians fail to see meaningful details, such as how Beverley chose to omit most of the interior doorways in Gibbs's plans, making circulation through his own house more controlled than in the English prototypes. Gibbs's designs portray all rooms opening directly into adjoining rooms, making movement easy and the plan more porous (Fig. 3.12). But Beverley's guests, family, and servants reached the four corner rooms on the main floor only by traversing a pair of stair passages flanking an entrance hall and connecting with covered routes to the wings. Only when his grandson altered the house in the 1840s did the circulation pattern more closely follow that proposed by Gibbs. Armchair scholars likewise miss Robert Beverley's physical signals that the hall, central drawing room, and southeast (right) side rooms were the superior parts of the house, not all those on either the front or river-side rear. Or that the form of both wings was derived from Chesapeake kitchen-slave quarters resembling the Moton House and intended to accommodate domestic workers and service before his son recast one for a more familiar pattern of extended family use. Even at a relatively well-documented house such as Bland-field, physical evidence expands upon information gleaned from family records.

Sorting out changes and dates are the first steps toward the more useful job of recognizing variation and its social functions. Whether inside a single building, or among associated buildings, or between regions, variation is meaningful. Varied quality of construction and finish makes buildings and their spaces legible, especially those from the eighteenth and early nineteenth centuries. Careful study of the details described throughout this book rises above dilettantism only when the details are recognized as choices made

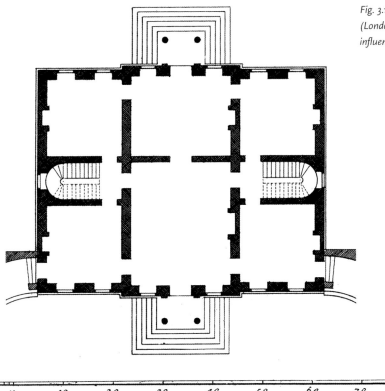

Fig. 3.12. *Plate 63, after James Gibbs,* A Book of Architecture *(London, 1728), detail. This is one of several plates in the book that influenced the design of Robert Beverley's Blandfield.*

that reflect economic conditions, social attitudes, and strategies for living.

One factor affecting variation in the preindustrial Chesapeake was the high cost of workmanship. Research by Upton, Carson, and others since the 1970s has demonstrated that careful joinery and refined finish were not as predictable as once thought, based on what was seen in Annapolis, Williamsburg, and most surviving rural houses. Carpentry in the eighteenth-century Chesapeake was not simply an age-old way of working that was carried on uncritically. Indeed, carefully crafted work represents a substantial investment by people with sufficient wealth to pay for and reason to desire labor-intensive building construction, as well as sufficient confidence in their future to invest in nonessential fabric.[11] For superior framing and wooden finish, production meant cutting down trees, squaring the logs, sawing them into pieces, and trimming the joints or planing them into shape—all by hand. Window glass, oil paint, and wallpaper were comparably laborious to produce and expensive to purchase, especially when all were imported.

Both the cost of preindustrial production and the complex social requirements of building clients made almost all surviving pre-Revolutionary Chesapeake houses visually hierarchical. Various buildings within a community differed in quality far beyond the obvious point that rich people usually built better than the rest. Buildings within a group owned by a single individual varied; and spaces within a single building did so as well. When a few wealthy planters expended additional funds on certain ancillary buildings to create formal settings for their houses, other buildings on the same property could be visible but beneath notice. Stables, corn houses, and tobacco houses were often cheaply built, and poor housing for field hands saw little improvement until affected by a new consciousness among owners after the Revolution.

The study of housing over the century or so spanning the American Revolution, therefore, is particularly suited to careful investigation of finish. By the mid-eighteenth century, British and Chesapeake builders had developed a grammar of construction finishes, which were distilled from their interpretation of Roman moldings and extended to elements like window muntins and shaped handrails not known by the ancients. They combined these elements freely with exterior finishes like round butt shingles and riven clapboards, which had evolved from everyday construction practices with no connection to classicism. One job of the field-worker is to translate this complex language.

Finish animates forms and suggests intent. Variation in finish was for two principal purposes: to communicate relative status and to direct movement. At the most simple level, doors had a superior side, and that face was turned toward the guest or resident moving from one space to the next: from passage to reception room and then to secondary reception room and beyond. Doorways at Rural Plains in Hanover County, Virginia, for example, have architraves, raised

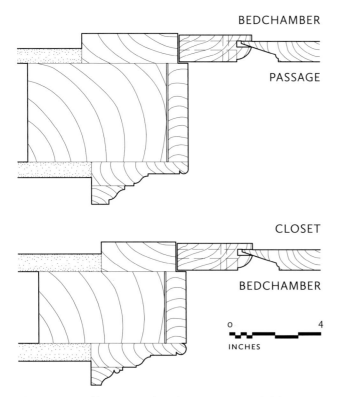

BEDCHAMBER

PASSAGE

CLOSET

BEDCHAMBER

0   4
INCHES

Fig. 3.13. Door architraves. Marmion, King George County, Virginia.

panels, and molded stiles and rails on the passage side, contrasting with plain frames, flat panels, and unmolded stiles and rails on the room side. Such simple systems extend into private space. The Rural Plains pattern is used upstairs at Marmion, for example, where bedchamber doors face the passage and closet doors face the chambers (Fig. 3.13). Routes marked by such signals can be predictable or unpredictable, indicating habits or perspectives otherwise unexpected. At Blandfield, broad, leafless doorways signaled the only route from the entrance hall to the pair of stair passages giving access to four corner rooms. At the Judge John Brice House in Annapolis (1739), superior moldings were applied to the inside of a stair enclosure no larger than a closet on the upper floor, suggesting that the elder Brices were intended to reach their superior second-floor bedchamber by way of the narrow private stair rather than up the main stair and through a second-floor passage (see Fig. 14.18).

Most commonly, variation in detail expresses the intended social meaning of spaces within eighteenth-century houses. Hierarchical distinctions are almost always made between floors and among rooms on each floor. In general, the level of expense decreases as one moves from the most to the least public spaces, often with the exception of the circulation space. Thus, the first floors of hall-chamber and single-room rural houses often have plastered walls and visible beaded or chamfered joists, while sleeping rooms in the attic remain entirely unfinished. On the first floor, halls (the principal re-

ception room) are usually treated as superior to chambers, and passages are sometimes superior to halls. A simple illustration can be found at the John Orrell House in Williamsburg. From the passage and the hall to the back room, the trim changes from a 7½-inch chair board to a 6-inch chair board. Chair boards are entirely omitted on the second floor. In 1762, silversmith James Geddy installed double architraves in his dining room, contrasting with single architraves in his passage, parlor, first-floor chamber, and all spaces upstairs. A subsequent owner added wainscot, cornice, and double architraves to the parlor. Successful tradesmen in the towns and middling planters shared certain strategies for applying the grammar with their wealthy neighbors, though it provided a vehicle for the rich to overshadow them in degrees of refinement as well as size of construction.

Because of their scale and multiplicity of social signals, the largest Chesapeake houses display particularly elaborate internal decorative hierarchies. When Charles Carter remodeled Shirley in 1772, he confined pilasters to the superior, first-floor bedchamber and used complex paneling with Ionic entablatures and baroque door pediments in the two connecting reception rooms, more richly finished with carving in the larger room. There are fourteen spaces on the three main floors at Shirley, each space with some different handling of the finish to clarify its intended status. In short, the degree of attention Walter Macomber and his colleagues brought to the subtleties of eighteenth-century Chesapeake woodwork remains useful for contemporary social historians as long as they read the variations within their settings.

Increasingly, stratigraphic analysis of paint reveals that color could play a major supporting role in the social system of gentry house construction. Virtually all woodwork on the main floors at Blandfield was painted off-white, with the doors dark brown, around 1772. Simple woodwork in the upper passage was left unpainted. However, Robert Beverley's orders for wallpaper and fabrics reveal wide variation in the colors of different spaces, with some rooms clearly enjoying a bold and unified palette. At Shirley in the 1770s, all woodwork was also painted off-white, except in the best room, where there was a carved, oak-leaf mantel frieze brightly glazed with green.[12]

The remodeled Shirley and the newly built Kenmore (1772–76) in Fredericksburg share fundamental spatial similarities and demonstrate how richly varied media were used to define the intended quality of spaces and direct movement through them (Fig. 3.14). Both have a pair of reception rooms treated en suite, which occupy the full river side of the first floor, with the larger room opening directly onto a scenic garden or yard with a river view (Fig. 3.15). Both also

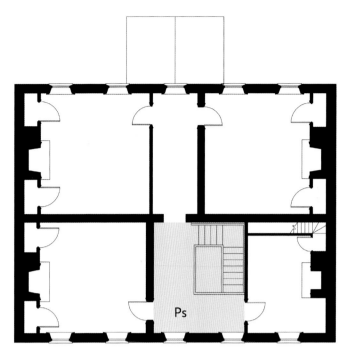

SECOND FLOOR

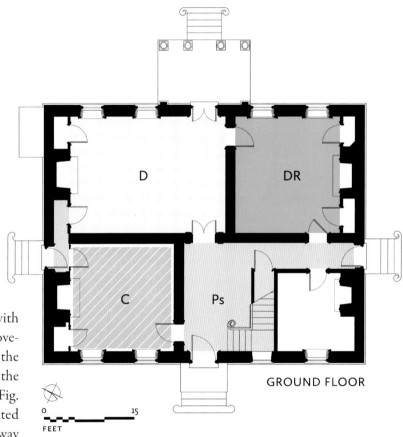

GROUND FLOOR

(left) Fig. 3.14. Kenmore, 1772–76, Fredericksburg. A subsequent owner added the rear porch to overlook grounds descending toward the Rappahannock River.

(right) Fig. 3.15. Plans, Kenmore, Fredericksburg, showing disposition of plain blue wallpaper in the dining room, flocked green paper in the drawing room, and plain yellow paper in circulation spaces, extending to an axial passage upstairs. Plaster in the ground-floor chamber was painted blue-green and all other plaster was whitewashed.

have a sizable stair hall on the land side, communicating with the larger reception room on axis. At Shirley, formal movement was directed by mounting polished brass hinges on the two doors into and out of the best room and elaborating the internal link with geometrically worked transoms (see Fig. 12.18A). At Kenmore, Fielding Lewis's builders added fluted pilasters during construction to a round-transomed doorway in the same position, heightening attention on the portal to parties and beckoning guests past a plain doorway into the best bedchamber.

Kenmore illustrates that sustained investigation can reveal a depth of variation not initially apparent, even within a house that has survived with much first-period fabric still in place. Kenmore's builders used a classical dado, mantels carved with rococo and neoclassical friezes, elaborate plaster overmantels, and fine decorative plaster ceilings in the large

dining room and smaller parlor, called "Drawing Room" in Lewis's 1782 probate inventory.[13] Together, they make up one of the richest ensembles of interior finish in the late colonial Chesapeake. During the most recent work, restoration director Matthew Webster found that a 1770s plasterer also installed bolection (raised) moldings to form large panels between wainscot and cornice in the dining room. The first-floor chamber was finished in a different manner,

Fig. 3.16. Drawing room, Kenmore.

with old-fashioned raised-panel wainscot and a paneled wall (Waterman called it countrified), another carved mantel, and original decorative plaster confined to a small head of Apollo radiating rays of sunlight overhead.

Paint analysis shows that the woodwork was blue-green throughout the main floors over a pink primer, with brown room doors and bases. In spite of most early plaster having been stripped, careful exploration around the windows and doors revealed blue wallpaper in the dining room and green flocked wallpaper in the drawing room. Ghosts near edges of plaster in the drawing room showed that the flocked paper was outlined with decorative borders. Plaster walls in the first-floor chamber were painted the same blue-green in oil, contrasting with white plaster in the smallest first-floor room and all upper chambers. Circulation space was finished with plain yellow paper, carried up to an arched doorway into an inner second-floor passage. Remarkably, we found that a tight, closetlike, end passage through which slaves brought food from a detached kitchen to the dining room was also

papered in yellow, because it could be glimpsed by diners when servants opened its door.[14]

How does one add up the pieces? Lewis's joiners installed relatively literal classical details like wainscot resembling temple plinths in the two reception rooms. A craftsman recorded only as "the stucco man" strengthened the link between the two public rooms, using virtuoso plaster work on the ceilings and overmantels, as did hangers of colored paper (see Fig. 14.15).[15] The 1782 inventory reveals that the larger room easily entered from the passage was used for formal dining, leaving the flocked drawing room as an inner room into which guests withdrew, perhaps separating women from men after dinner. The talented stucco man created a sprawling landscape with Aesop's Fables characters for picturesque and pedagogical effect over the dining room mantel and a more simply conceived floral overmantel for the drawing room (Fig. 3.16). Plasterers were further called upon to clarify that the larger room was the best space by applying raised moldings to the dining room walls, making big white-edged rectangles on the blue paper. The first-floor bedchamber opens only into circulation space, not directly into reception rooms. Its functions have a foot in both realms, public and private. The inventory makes clear that it contained mahogany furniture, and it was a visually celebrated space, with a richly carved mantel planted on the paneled chimney wall, but with no plaster overmantel (Fig. 3.17). Stationed hierarchically midway between reception rooms and upper bedchambers, its plastered walls were painted in oil to match the woodwork—cheaper than wallpaper but superior to the whitewash applied to plaster in the chambers upstairs. It was both the finest private room and the cheapest public space.

Everything seems in order with new evidence for richer finish, the better to inspire designs for bankers' boardrooms and bolster arguments for the superiority of Homo Chesopeakus. But one should not be so easily beguiled. Lewis's probate inventory refines and complicates observations in the field, recording a rough parity in the quality of furnishings in the reception rooms and a lower status for those in the first-floor chamber. As Upton observed, the fourth first-floor room in a Chesapeake Georgian house is the wild card in the deck, with undefined or idiosyncratic use. At Kenmore, it is a miniature room with a handsomely carved little mantel. Located across the side passage from the drawing room, was it a scene for more intimate use such as tea and toilet or a private study? Two pieces of evidence indicate otherwise, at least by 1782. Lewis's inventory lists a cheap tulip poplar bed valued at only ten shillings in the "Small Room," along with quantities of fine dining and bed textiles, suggesting the combination of sleeping space for a domestic servant and storage of valuable accoutrements of hospitality and rest. The mantel, surprisingly, has the variety of small burn marks that one finds in low-status rooms such as the unfinished cellar, the marks of cheap iron crusie lamps used by workers to light their spaces more economically than candles. Both the document and the physical evidence suggest that, by a relatively early date, the small room beside the service door was servant occupied. They offer a reminder that genteel settings were often not used as their builders intended. House owners' changing priorities and fortunes, resistance from workers, and wishes of new occupants all could challenge the template the builder so carefully crafted. In short, the evidence allows one to put what archaeologists would call a post-processual spin on the notion that gentry society evolved and dominated by means of increasingly orchestrating their houses and public spaces. Fieldwork often reveals intention more reliably than use, and the field-worker should be mindful that understanding use may require more than a straightforward decoding of construction details.

Fig. 3.17. First-floor chamber, Kenmore.

A deeper level of inquiry seeks reasons for such obsessive marshaling of details in a house. Precisely why owners and builders employed various materials to establish the intended quality of spaces and routes to them is an essential question. At its most obvious, superior domestic architecture is a means of public presentation and, as Mark Girouard suggests for the English country house, political advancement. The most costly pre-Revolutionary Virginia houses were built by those already involved in or aspiring to leadership of the colonial government.[16] Successful Williamsburg tradespeople built or rented smaller refined houses in the 1760s and 1770s as equally clear markers of their commercial success and social aspiration. Some such male masters of hand trades took up a lower tier of officeholding. Certain women in trade as well as the men populated a rank of Williamsburg society much more clearly defined architecturally by the 1760s than in John Brush's generation.

However, the field-worker can see that the extent of the carefully planned variation suggests a desire for self-

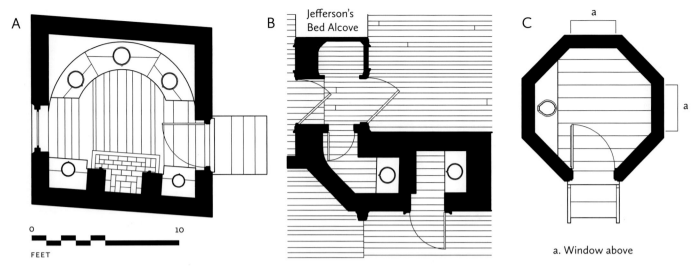

A

0   10
FEET

B
Jefferson's
Bed Alcove

C
a

a

a. Window above

Fig. 3.18. Plans of privies. A: Westover, Charles City County, Virginia; B: Monticello, Albemarle County, Virginia; C: Poplar Forest, Bedford County, Virginia. Interior privies at Monticello were illuminated by skylights and exterior ones at Poplar Forest by windows located high on their walls.

fashioning that extends past, or below, front-stage presentation. Probate inventories make clear that beds with elaborate fittings were among the most costly furnishings in elite houses, and they were spread well beyond the semiprivate first-floor chambers in ornate gentry houses like Kenmore. The bedchambers of lowest status in grand houses, like those on the third floor at Shirley and Westover, are nonetheless nicely trimmed and plastered. The same is emphatically not true for most domestic servants' work and living spaces in attics and cellars, which were usually left unfinished. In the era when Newtonian concepts of natural order in the universe reached the ordinary literate wealthy, elite people's spaces were cast as orderly settings for respectable life, public and private. A large house such as Kenmore permitted an owner like Lewis to provide each guest, family member, and chosen members of the extended household with domestic space refined according to his or her station. Variations allowed him to arrange them in the order of his choosing.

The attention of art and architectural historians commonly falls on ancillary buildings only when they become part of the composition as subordinates for the central structure in a formal ensemble. Even then, remarkable evidence for the lives and outlooks of residents is usually ignored. The most costly of privies offer a startling example. At their grandest, late eighteenth-century gentry privies were small public spaces with multiple holes in seats set against paneled wainscot. At Drayton Hall in South Carolina, Dr. Charles Drayton equipped the best holes with elegantly curved arm rests, like superior chairs at a dining table. At Westover, William Byrd III arranged the adult holes in an apsidal seat in front of a raised masonry shelf as a miniature version of the elevated seat that distinguished the superior position of justices like himself in Virginia courtrooms of the same era. Byrd added a domestic degree of comfort by including a fireplace, facing the central hole and flanked by children's seats (Fig. 3.18A).

For Byrd and Drayton, privies were arenas only partially more restricted than reception spaces in their houses, places for display and hospitality, offering refined space and comfort, if not food and drink. Eighteenth-century paintings and prints of diners and drinkers reveal that the custom of males relieving themselves in the company of other males was common practice. Gentry privies simply moved the activity into a more specialized space, in which the property owner offered a genteel setting with himself at the center or sharing the stage with his peers. Such stage setting reflected the old regime's intensified effort at cementing social and political leadership, increasingly challenged from below.[17] In the Chesapeake, designs so overtly and eccentrically supporting absolute hierarchy largely disappeared with the Revolution and increased concern for domestic privacy.

Jefferson at Monticello and Poplar Forest provides a clear contrast to Byrd. His own exterior privies are also prominent features on the landscape. At Monticello, they are highly visible stone pavilions with stepped roofs and finials, terminating the front service wings. At Poplar Forest, they are octagonal, dome-roofed follies located beside earth mounds, again flanking the house while buffered by the artificial hills. But these and interior toilets in both houses are all private, solitary spaces, without glazed windows at eye level (Figs.

3.18B, 3.18C). For his own Monticello toilet, located beside his bedchamber and library, Jefferson elaborately conceived a light shaft passing through upper floors and an equally complex sewer system below, all employed to avoid use of a conventional window and chamber pot. It is literally his most intimate space, the opposite of the socially expansive facilities conceived by Byrd and Drayton. Jefferson is merely an early and prominent actor in the privatization of post-Revolutionary houses, rather than the sole eliminatory hermit of his class.

Looking at buildings that are as complex as an ostentatious gentry house or as seemingly mundane as an outbuilding, the inquisitive field-worker is likely to find useful evidence for builders' intentions and users' experiences and how their use evolved. It is by looking further afield that the observer recognizes how those experiences fit with or deviate from patterns of class, time, and region. Phenomena achieve significance in context, and context for eighteenth-century buildings cannot be fully recovered in the library.[18]

An example of what field surveys reveal that inventories and deed records cannot is that throughout the Chesapeake the extent of refined building leaped after the Revolution and the nature of finish was gradually transformed. Weighed against trifling numbers of pre-Revolutionary buildings surviving in the Chesapeake, great numbers from the following decades make it broadly evident that a larger segment of the rural population began to build well, however small the structures. In a region with declining crop yields and land values, farmers with middling holdings of 200 to 500 acres increasingly built permanent houses of four or more well-finished rooms. Growth in substantial housing was even more dramatic in the towns and in cities like Baltimore and Richmond. Increasing consistency within gradations of urban housing indicates new commercial class formation dramatically contrasting with the society and its patchwork accommodation along the streets of Annapolis and Williamsburg. Changing ideas about how houses should be rendered inside makes recording the full range of finishes all the more useful. The Georgian emphasis on hierarchy and on rendering the social order in material form was displaced by a preference for better and more-lasting finish throughout the house. Expansive fieldwork reveals that, more and more, builders carried plaster or planed sheathing into minor spaces like habitable attics and cellars rather than confining it to the core of the dwelling.

Ornament as well as extent of simple finish expressed the shift toward architectural assertion by middling people. Industrial production and neoclassical taste accompanied widespread consumption of amenities in the Chesapeake as well as in Britain. Neoclassicism could be bought by the yard in architectural materials as well as in textiles. At the most refined level, tradesmen like Robert Wellford in Philadelphia produced scenes of triumphal gods and graceful goddesses in plasterlike composition that their workmen or local carpenters could apply to mantels and doorways. Comparable figural ornament had been rare before the Revolution, confined to a handful of examples imported or commissioned by governors such as Virginia's Lord Dunmore, regional leaders like Lewis, and the richest Annapolitans, as recently as the 1770s. New attitudes of appropriateness and factory production led planters and merchants such as Accomack County's John Wharton, who would have never considered using figural ornament before the Revolution, to extend it from parlors and dining rooms to fourth- and fifth-best rooms (Fig. 3.19). Only through fieldwork does the scholar perceive the expanded use of such decoration, from a royal governor or two to hundreds of relatively successful postwar merchants. Joiners and turners in every corner of the region offered equal degrees of adornment in more eccentric compositions of geometry set spinning, for the front rooms of countless farmers and attorneys. Raised and carved elliptical ornaments were multiplied exponentially and painted in harlequin patterns and colors in the hinterlands of Maryland, North Carolina, and Virginia (Fig. 3.20).

The character of finish changed dramatically again in the second quarter of the nineteenth century, substantially affecting how it can be studied. If the design imperative in the new republic was imagination, packing the maximum amount of ornament into woodwork, that of the antebellum era was starkness—the opposite, reducing walls and elements to the essential shapes. Mantels became pairs of piers supporting thick lintels, with minimal molded relief; surbases (molded chair boards) and cornices disappeared. Houses like Blandfield and Rosewell were stripped of most or all of their costly old finish and re-skinned with plain, heavy woodwork and a sea of perfectly flat plaster. It looked as though a new species had taken up residence. Most important, the change marked a sharper decline of the hierarchical house. Consistency trumped variation. Moldings used around doors and windows dropped to a single or several shapes within a house. James Coles Bruce, one of the region's richest planters, built Berry Hill in 1842–44, an oversized and pretentious temple-form house. Behind the eight-columned portico, his builder, Josiah Dabbs, used only three kinds of interior trim: Greek aedicules in public spaces, double architraves in private rooms, and single ones in service areas. The move

(top) Fig. 3.19. Mantel, second-floor bedchamber, Wharton Place, Accomack County, Virginia. Painstakingly removing paint layer by layer on the mantels at Wharton Place, conservator Stephen Marder found that around 1808 Philadelphia tradesmen wrote the titles of neoclassical ornaments on the wooden elements as well as incorporating the name of the manufacturer, Robert Wellford.

(bottom) Fig. 3.20. Mantel from Hunt House, Pittsylvania County, Virginia. Conservator Amelia Bagnall Jenson removed portions of late nineteenth-century paint (darker areas) to reveal eight colors and numerous patterns of paint applied around 1820 to some fifty paterae and rosettes, eight levels of bead and cable moldings, a fireplace surround resembling shark's teeth, and other turned and carved ornaments. Original paint is visible on the upper left quarter, left side of the central panel, and around the left plinth.

represents more than a change in fashion. A deeper shift was the rise of popular faith in the house as "home," more important throughout as the scene for family nurturance than as a stage for personal presentation. Quickly, toward midcentury, the relative significance and thus architectural character of public space and private space approached equality.

Architectural recording needs to respond to the nature of the evidence as well as the scholar's research agenda. Mid-Georgian houses are perfectly suited to careful recording of circulation patterns and gradations of finish. Complex variations in kaleidoscopic post-Revolutionary woodwork demand extensive crisp photography, paint investigation, and perhaps even some drawings in the early twentieth-century manner. The Greek house is an easier game, allowing the researcher to focus on space and its developing use without the aid of subtle evidence from finish. In either case, the potential for a new generation of study is evident, one that captures the full spectrum of construction and offers it accessibly to scholars and generalists who bring their own special interests to the study of people's houses.

Examples from the New Kent kitchen and R. R. Moton's boyhood house to Bruce's Berry Hill illustrate that much architectural history best relies on a balance between careful field recording and broader study of patterns. Sorting out dates, variation, and alteration within individual buildings and landscapes provides a solid basis for expansive interpretation. Like good dirt archaeologists, architectural historians in the Chesapeake do best when their ideas drive them back into the field, and the resulting data enriches evolving interpretations.

4 Migration, Society, Economy, & Settlement
1607–1830

LORENA S. WALSH

The dwelling and work buildings built by or for the people who migrated to the Chesapeake colonies reflected a combination of Old World models and New World conditions. Voluntary migrants came from many different regions of England, Scotland, and Ireland, with a scattering from continental Europe. Each group brought its own local building traditions. Forced African migrants, who began arriving soon after the first European settlers, retained knowledge of varied West and Central African building practices. Once settled, both groups encountered yet other solutions for shelters that Native Americans had devised. Thus the houses and other structures that early migrants were called upon to build could draw on a multiplicity of imported traditions. Harsh conditions and the continued need for all Old World migrants to adapt to a different climate and disease environment forced surviving migrants to improvise on traditional practices. The need arose for new sorts of farm buildings and for novel solutions to the problems of housing domestic and agricultural workers where almost everyone's livelihood depended on the production of a single staple export crop, tobacco, raised primarily by indentured servants and, later, enslaved workers. A hundred years later, by the middle of the eighteenth century, the Chesapeake economy had become more mature and more diversified and the population in older areas was now primarily native born. Economic change required different kinds of agricultural buildings, and the accompanying economic prosperity enabled wealthy planters and merchants to construct large, handsome houses and middling residents to build more finished ones. Geographic expansion into the Piedmont and the arrival of new groups of European immigrants on the western frontier introduced new influences on housing. Finally, independence from Britain brought changes in the character of new in-migrants, significant out-migration, alterations in the crops that residents produced and in the means for getting them to market, and increased urbanization. These economic and social devel-

opments further affected the choices Chesapeake residents made about housing after the American Revolution.

MIGRATION AND SOCIETY

European migrants, like Northern European colonizers throughout the Americas, encountered an abundance of land and other natural resources in the seventeenth-century Chesapeake but were handicapped by a chronic shortage of labor and the capital needed to take advantage of New World resources. Establishing settlements, building forts for shelter from Native Americans and European rivals, clearing land

48

Fig. 4.1. Jamestown street scene around 1660. A small port where Old World settlers and goods arrived and New World products were shipped.
Painting by Keith Rocco based on research by the Colonial Williamsburg Foundation. (Courtesy of National Park Service/Keith Rocco)

for farming, learning how to raise crops suitable for food in unfamiliar environments, erecting houses and more work buildings, and building up herds of Old World livestock all required massive amounts of labor. Moreover, in order to procure essential supplies from their homelands, settlers had either to produce products in demand in Europe or to earn income to buy them through trade with other regions. Producing cash crops in addition to food crops required even more labor but was critical to maintaining a viable enterprise, since stay-at-home investors willing to risk capital in colonial ventures demanded quick returns. Settlers could eventually compensate for the scarcity of imported capital by generat-

ing much of it themselves through pioneering farming. But in order to remedy the shortage of workers, colonists who hoped to prosper quickly turned to novel solutions that involved varying degrees of unfree labor (Fig. 4.1).

The southern mainland colonies were the second most important destination for British migrants to the Americas in the seventeenth century, after the West Indies. Between 100,000 and 150,000, or roughly one-third of those who left Britain, moved to the Tobacco Coast. The initial stream came primarily from England and Wales, in larger numbers vis-à-vis the total population than those involved in better-known transatlantic migrations of the early nineteenth cen-

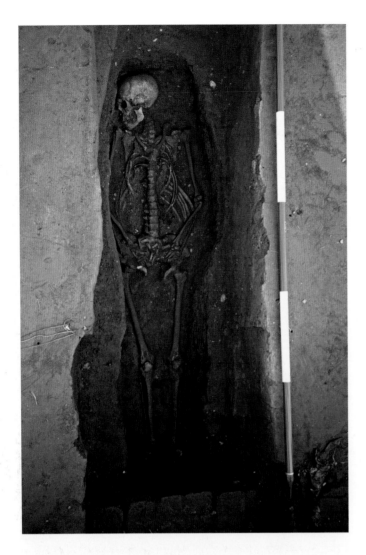

amounts of nonhuman capital and began almost immediately to contribute to the economic development of the colonies, both as farm builders and as consumers.[2]

Migrants who could not afford their own fares could most readily obtain passage to southerly staple-producing colonies where planters were willing to pay their transportation costs in return for bound service for specified periods of time. The disparity between the price of labor in the Old and the New Worlds led merchants to take an active interest in recruiting and transporting servants to places where they were much in demand. Across the seventeenth century, servants made up at least 60 percent of the emigrant total. The peak migration decades of the 1630s through the 1660s have been characterized as a "poverty-driven with high overseas demand" movement. English migrants were pushed out primarily by deteriorating economic conditions at home, although some Puritans, Catholics, and Quakers also had religious motivations for emigrating. Most potential migrants were enticed by the hope of earning good wages in the colonies and eventually of acquiring land of their own.[3]

Old World immigrants experienced a period of sickness during their first years in the Chesapeake; as many as a fifth may have died within twelve months. Consequently, the transportation of substantial numbers of workers resulted in only modest increases in the total population. Malaria occasionally reached pandemic proportions, and if it was not always deadly, it frequently left survivors in poor health, unable to withstand other diseases (Fig. 4.2). In addition to newcomers, children and pregnant women were particularly susceptible. Since male servants outnumbered female servants by three to one across much of the century, even those who survived the "seasoning" ordeal had limited marital opportunities to contribute to population growth. The combination of high mortality and unbalanced sex ratios, compounded by restraints on marriage and reproduction among bound European workers and low reproductive rates among enslaved Africans, delayed the onset of natural population increase. Virginia and Maryland remained immigrant societies for much of the first century, subject to rapid turnovers of population, stunted family life, and social and political instability.[4]

The earliest Chesapeake migrants were usually either gentlemen or bound servants, thereby reinforcing the founders' initial expectation that they would re-create the hierar-

tury. The majority of Chesapeake settlers came from the south and west of England, primarily from the cities of London and Bristol and the counties surrounding them. Many came from urban backgrounds, and others who had been born in more distant places had moved first to one of these cities. Later-arriving migrants were drawn from more diverse areas: Ireland, Scotland, and the environs of Liverpool, for example, whose merchants entered the tobacco trade and began recruiting servants for plantation work in northwestern England and northern Wales.[1]

European immigrants fell into one of two categories, broadly speaking: a smaller one composed of free families with sufficient resources to finance the move themselves and a larger one composed primarily of young, single men who could not afford an ocean passage without help. The free minority (about one out of five Chesapeake migrants in the seventeenth century) exerted a disproportionate influence on the economic, social, political, and cultural development of the places to which they moved. Furthermore, they contributed more to natural population increase than did single bound laborers. They brought with them substantial

chical, stratified communities of landlords and tenants they remembered from home. But few of the gentlemen survived the rigors of the lethal environment or were willing to commit themselves permanently to the raw new land. Moreover, the ready availability of land weighed against tenancy as a viable option, although for a decade or so after most early settlers arrived, those who came without capital remained in dependent, subordinate positions. Because the Europeans were unable to transform the resident Native Americans into a willing or even an unwilling workforce, indentured servitude quickly became the means by which planters recruited desperately needed laborers. England was perceived to be overpopulated, so it appeared to make sense for colonists to turn first to fellow countrymen to fill the labor gap.[5]

Migration from England to the Chesapeake accelerated from the 1630s through the early 1660s, fueled by favorable tobacco prices. Servants accounted for the majority of newcomers, but many later arrivals were free migrants of modest means who came in family groups. These new immigrants helped to transform Chesapeake society into a community of households headed mostly by small or middling planters. Prosperous times enabled even ordinary planters to purchase servants to develop their plantations and also helped many former indentured laborers who served out their terms to move into the ranks of landowners and become respected members of local communities in their own right.

By the mid-1660s, the best land in the most densely settled areas had been taken up. Furthermore, the price of tobacco began falling. Consequently, fewer free migrants were willing to move to the Chesapeake. This was also the case for indentured servants, whose numbers remained stable in the 1660s and 1670s before falling off in the 1680s and 1690s as economic conditions in England improved and population growth slowed. Periodic deportation of orphans, vagrants, convicts, and war prisoners from the British Isles did little to alleviate labor shortages in the colonies. European wars between 1689 and 1697 and again from 1702 to 1713 also served to dampen emigration. The flow of new arrivals increased again in the early eighteenth century, but the numbers were smaller than previously and the migrants themselves were "betterment-driven with selective demand." Young and unskilled English and Irish flocked to Maryland and Virginia during the brief years of peace at the turn of the century; thereafter, the emigrant servant population became increasingly male, literate, and skilled. Voluntary migrants became choosier about their destinations, and colonial employers became discriminating about the sorts of indentured servants they would buy.[6]

Scholars have yet to establish firm estimates of the num-

bers of European immigrants who entered the Chesapeake region between 1700 and about 1780. Most agree that the total did not surpass the volume of newcomers in the seventeenth century and likely did not equal it. Eighteenth-century migrants are known to have included more people from other parts of the British Empire and from continental Europe and fewer English men and women. Early in the century, Irish indentured servants, French Huguenot refugees, and a sprinkling of Dutch, Swedes, and Swiss, along with Jacobite prisoners transported after the rebellions of 1715 and 1745 in Scotland, added diversity to older areas, as did Acadians from Canada displaced by the French and Indian War. German and Scotch-Irish migrants, traveling overland from Pennsylvania, established settlements in the Shenandoah Valley in the 1730s. Most free migrants settled either in Tidewater towns or in the Piedmont or the Valley as the century progressed, since open land was no longer available in older rural counties. Germans came primarily in family groups and tended to settle in sparsely populated frontier areas more successfully than other groups. They managed to establish and reproduce a separate distinctive European culture. Some 40,000 British and Irish convict servants, mostly young unskilled males, were transported into the region between 1718 and 1775. Indeed, convicts constituted nearly 10 percent of Maryland's white population in 1755. A French traveler to Virginia commented ten years later on the effects of the "new" immigration there: "The number of Convicts and Indented servants imported to virginia [is] amazing, besides the numbers of Dutch and Germans which is also Considerable." The percentage of foreign-born residents rose across the eighteenth century in newer settled areas. In contrast, whites living in the old Tidewater counties after 1700 had less direct personal knowledge of their parents' European home and felt bound together by increasingly dense kinship networks and local concerns. Newcomers from abroad found it difficult to become fully accepted there.[7]

The arrival in 1619 of twenty-some Africans captured in a raid on Iberian shipping began an experiment by wealthy Chesapeake planters and officials with enslaved African labor. At first it was a novel solution to New World labor shortages, but one that they would look on as a potentially profitable alternative to white indentured servants by the 1640s. Barbadian settlers enthusiastically embraced African slavery in that decade; island planters had sufficient assets to acquire large numbers of these increasingly expensive workers. Just before midcentury, slaves already outnumbered servants on West Indian plantations by approximately two to one. The introduction of the more lucrative sugar crop in the 1650s sped up a process already under way. The ensuing sugar boom led Northern Europeans to concentrate their efforts on supplying slaves to Caribbean markets, where rising demand drove up their prices. Planters along the Tobacco Coast offered too small a market to attract most English traders, and the English government's campaign against Dutch commercial supremacy in the 1650s and 1660s cut off the settlers' main supply of black workers. A succession of monopolies granted by Charles II restricted entry into England's African trade and reduced the supply of slaves, especially to minor markets. Nonetheless, by the 1650s, most members of Virginia's provincial elite had managed to acquire some Africans through international connections, and, seeking more in the 1660s, they turned to West Indian suppliers. Blacks amounted to 5 percent of Virginia's population by 1671. By the late 1670s, the leading Chesapeake planters and provincial officeholders were already thoroughly committed to slave labor; county level officers followed their example as fast as their more limited resources permitted.[8]

Regular, direct shipments of slaves from Africa began in the mid-1670s, probably rose markedly in the 1680s, and increased sharply when the slave trade was formally opened to all merchants in the British Empire in 1698. Once the price of laborers fell—from around £30 sterling for a prime hand in the mid-1650s to about £15 in the 1680s—slavery expanded rapidly. That said, slaveholding remained confined almost entirely to colonial officeholders prior to 1700; in Virginia, only about 10 percent of inventories of nonofficeholding decedents included slaves, and a similar situation prevailed in Maryland. By the late 1690s, wealthy planters throughout the region had chosen slavery irrevocably. Aside from an occasional indentured artisan with special skills, they had come to rely entirely on enslaved workers for agricultural labor. Roughly 5,000 new Africans were brought into the region from 1680 to 1697. No less than 4,500 more arrived between 1698 and 1703. The numbers increased still further to over 13,000 between 1704 and 1718, followed by another 17,000 between 1719 and 1730. Bristol merchants began aggressively contesting London's dominant role in the African trade, as did those from Liverpool a few years later, with the result that Chesapeake planters benefited from the increasing competition, as well as from another decline in the price they paid for slaves owing to a depression in West Indian sugar prices.[9]

The transition to slave labor was swift and dramatic throughout the region. Between 1680 and 1720 the enslaved population of the region increased at almost twice the rate of the white population. In the decade between the mid-1680s and the mid-1690s the aggregate unfree labor force changed from primarily indentured servants to primarily slaves. Although blacks were only about 13 percent of the total population in 1700, they were already a third of all workers. Working conditions that Africans endured deteriorated in proportion to their increase in numbers. So long as Africans were a minority in the bound workforce, Europeans and Africans usually shared both work routines and dwelling spaces more or less equally. They are known to have socialized, had sexual relations, and run away in mixed groups. But once planters acquired appreciably more slaves, masters systematically intensified work requirements for Africans, denying them any claim to English workers' customary rights to food of reasonable quantity and quality or to adequate clothing, shelter, and leisure, as well as stripping them of any significant freedom for themselves or their children. By the early eighteenth century, European bondsmen increasingly refused to live and work with slaves. Those who came under contract demanded and received separate quarters and work assignments and better food and clothing. Meanwhile, as discussed in chapters 6 and 8, houses and landscapes were increasingly rearranged to impose a rigid physical separation of masters from bondspeople.[10]

As lifelong service and hereditary slavery for blacks became firmly established in both practice and law, and as the chances for surviving a term of service marginally increased, the interests of term and heredity-bound servants inevitably diverged. Shirking work and running away continued to be strategies to which all bound laborers might resort, sometimes individually and sometimes in groups. But even though opportunities for eventual economic advantage were severely diminished, the assurance of eventually moving out of a debased servile status, coupled with the promise of some minimal freedom dues at the end of their terms, still afforded European servants incentives for completing their contractual obligations. Laborers relegated to involuntary lifelong bondage had no such motivation. Plantation discipline became more severe and more systematic as the proportion of blacks in the total population rose. "Foul means must do, what fair will not," in William Byrd II's words. Force was increasingly required and tolerated by whites, both to extract unwilling labor and to prevent violent insurrections (Fig. 4.3).[11]

The diminished supply of servants and higher prices for their purchase drove many small planters out of the labor market and concentrated unfree workers on large estates. Disparities in wealth between rich, middling, and poor increased, marked by rigid disparities in social status. Consequently, the proportion of ordinary planters fell in older Chesapeake communities in the last quarter of the seventeenth century. The decline was accompanied by a large in-

Fig. 4.3. Slave punishment, painting by unidentified artist, c. 1825. (Colonial Williamsburg Foundation)

crease in the size of the bound labor force and the numbers of former servants who were unable to join the ranks of tenant farmers or landowners. Population turnover remained high in older areas. Almost all free immigrants moved on, as did many former servants who failed either to secure land or to find marriage partners.[12]

When significant in-migration ended, adult sex ratios became more evenly balanced, making marriage and family formation possible for a greater proportion of men. The proportion of children rose dramatically as creole women married at relatively young ages and so had more children than their immigrant mothers. Mortality rates improved somewhat without the high seasoning losses associated with new immigrants and with the slightly stronger immunities to local diseases that creoles possessed. Nearly all native-born men were eventually able to find wives; because natives married earlier and lived longer, their marriages lasted twice as long as marriages among immigrants.

These improvements stabilized society. Other trends did not. Opportunities for getting rich quickly diminished as established planters exhausted the high rates of return that had once been earned by farm building and as the local population shifted from an artificially high proportion of productive adult immigrants toward a normal demographic balance in which approximately half of the residents were dependent children who were too young to contribute much to family income. The early ambition to make and spend a fortune

quickly was gradually replaced by more prosaic concerns about making an ordinary living. Continued shortages of bound labor among all but the already well-to-do prevented most householders from significantly improving their economic positions. It was not until around 1730, when a similar demographic transition occurred in the enslaved black population, that the proportion of bound laborers in the Chesapeake began to approach levels last seen in the 1660s.[13]

From 1730 to 1760, the number of black inhabitants expanded more than threefold, partly by natural increase, but also partly from the forced migration of at least 51,000 additional Africans. The "Golden Years" for Chesapeake planters were to a large extent made possible by the exploitation of thousands of unwilling forced African migrants and their enslaved offspring at a time when service in the colonies held fewer attractions for Europeans. By midcentury, most new African captives were purchased by residents of the Piedmont—the rest were purchased by Tidewater planters of lesser means. As the black population grew ever larger, slaveholding spread wider and deeper. Middling planters became as dependent on and committed to slave labor as their wealthier neighbors were. Increasingly, planters inherited or hired slaves in addition to buying them outright. On the eve of the Revolution, as many as three-quarters of all householders in some Tidewater areas owned or hired at least one slave.[14]

Although historians have argued that unbalanced sex ratios among forced African migrants seriously thwarted family formation and interrupted cultural continuities, the imbalance was in fact significantly less than that among European migrants. African cargoes brought to this peripheral region fell below the overall Atlantic average of 170 men to 100 women; instead, they ranged from 1.25 to 1.5 men for each woman. All else being equal, African migrants to the Chesapeake region should have stood better chances for marrying, procreating, and reproducing Old World cultures than did Europeans. But for these migrants nothing was equal. The slave regime severely constrained both biological and cultural reproduction.[15]

New evidence on the Chesapeake slave trade reveals greater homogeneity in the geographic origins, languages, and customs of transported Africans than was once believed. The proportion of seasoned slaves transshipped to Virginia and Maryland from the West Indies has been exaggerated. It is now known that there was much less initial random mixing of African groups than had been supposed (Fig. 4.4).

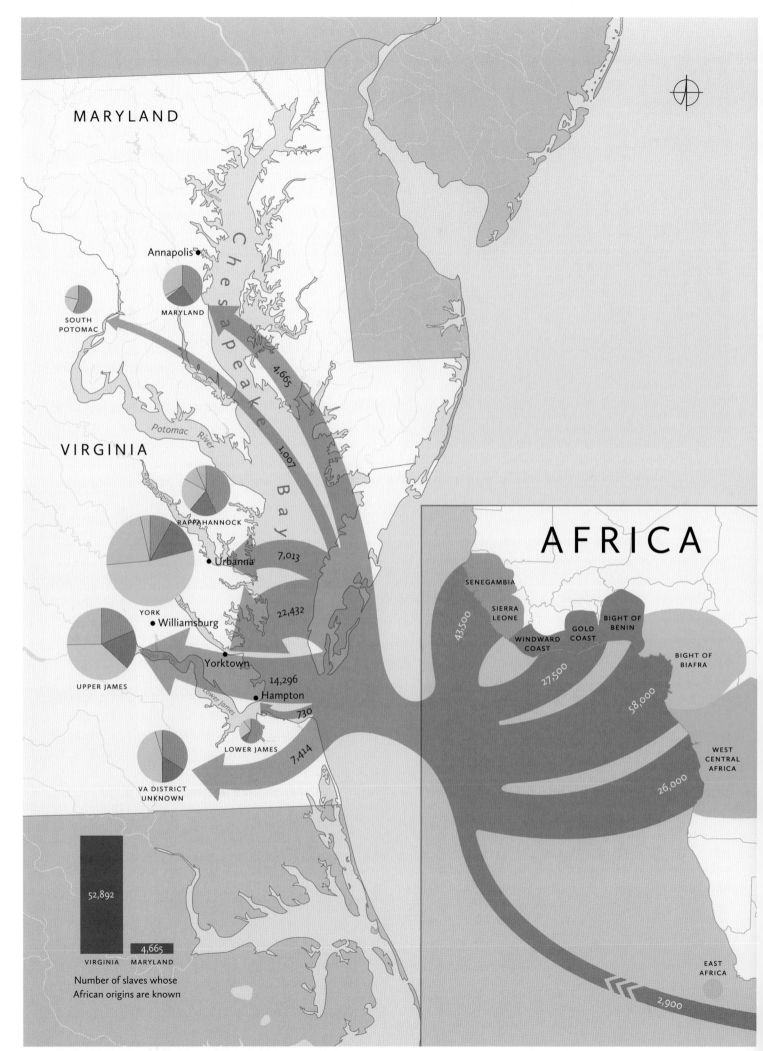

Fig. 4.4. Map of West Africa origins and American destinations of slaves imported to Virginia and Maryland.

More than half the number of Africans brought to the Upper Chesapeake (the Virginia Potomac basin and Maryland) in the eighteenth century came from the upper parts of the West African coast, from Senegambia on the north, to a second region extending from the Cassamance River to Cape Mount (the region that today includes Sierra Leone in the center), then easterly along the Windward Coast (which encompasses Ivory Coast and Liberia), and ending on the Gold Coast (present-day Ghana). In contrast, about three-quarters of the Africans delivered to the Lower Chesapeake (the York and Upper James basins) came from more southerly parts of Africa, from the Bight of Biafra (now eastern Nigeria) or West Central Africa (the Congo and Angola).[16]

Whether these differing forced migration streams had any effect on local slave cultures in the region is a strenuously debated topic. A considered assessment, supported by recent archaeological discoveries, suggests major differences between the Upper and Lower Chesapeake in the potential for cultural continuities with West Africa. Large numbers of Ibo and West Central Africans brought to lower Virginia possessed greater linguistic and cultural homogeneity than did the more diverse groups taken to the Upper Chesapeake. Thus it is possible that evidence for greater cultural continuities may be discovered in lower Tidewater Virginia and perhaps in parts of the Piedmont where newcomers from these same African regions were most concentrated.[17]

Nearly 17,000 additional new captives arrived in the Chesapeake after 1760. Even so, African-born individuals made up an ever-decreasing proportion of the black population. It has been estimated that early in the century half the blacks in the region had been born in Africa, but by 1750 their numbers had fallen to about one-quarter, and by 1770 their numbers were under 10 percent. Syncretic adaptations became increasingly likely as settled Africans adopted more elements of European culture and as the proportion of creoles with no direct knowledge of Africa and greater familiarity with Anglo-European culture steadily rose. Support networks rooted in biological kin ties replaced earlier ones based on co-resident strangers, quasi kin, and countrymen and countrywomen. English increasingly became the lingua franca instead of African languages or pidgins. That said, consistent evidence for widespread cultural change appears only in the last quarter of the century when a critical proportion of first- and second-generation Chesapeake-born children survived to become decision-making adults.[18]

Immigration of all kinds ceased early in 1775 when war broke out between Britain and the thirteen colonies. When immigration resumed in the 1780s, its nature was permanently changed. Post-Revolutionary immigration differed markedly from population movements in the colonial period. Almost all newcomers involved were free, voluntary migrants, rather than primarily unfree and often involuntary movers. The trade in British convicts was not resumed after the war, and even voluntary indentured servitude disappeared by the early 1800s. Virginians and Marylanders, unlike their Lower South counterparts, decided not to resume the transatlantic slave trade after the war. Many now condemned the international commerce in human chattels, although fewer rejected slavery itself. Most free migrants chose to move to areas that offered more economic opportunities than did the slave societies of the Upper and Lower South. Those seeking wage labor fared better in states that had abolished or were in the process of ending slavery, while those drawn by the lure of land moved to newer settlements in the West.

Indeed, there was substantial out-migration of free whites from the Tidewater areas after the end of the American Revolution. This was accompanied by substantial forced migration of blacks to the Ohio country and especially to Kentucky and Tennessee. White and black populations in older areas stagnated, except for those in rapidly growing towns and cities. Urban areas did attract some of the new waves of European immigrants, who left England, Ireland, Scotland, Germany, and France to try their fortunes in America. They were joined in the 1790s by French-speaking refugees fleeing the Haitian Revolution.[19]

The changed nature of in- and out-migration after the Revolution reflected the fact that the problem of labor shortages in the Chesapeake had been resolved through the natural reproduction of the enslaved population. By then, larger slaveholders owned as many and sometimes more workers than they needed, and by the 1810s they were moving or selling slaves west and south, where labor-short frontier planters bid up their price. With declining economic opportunity and diminished labor needs in the older rural areas, a region that was once a land of immigrants became an inbred stagnating backwater, sending out a mix of voluntary and involuntary migrants to exploit the richer natural resources to be found in the ever-expanding West.

ECONOMY AND SETTLEMENT

Initially, seventeenth-century planters set out to exploit farmland, which was abundant and cheap, and make the most of labor, which was scarce and dear. The colonists developed a new system of husbandry. In the process of learning how to survive in an unfamiliar and often hostile environment and in finding staple export products that they could exchange for imports, they soon abandoned most

European agricultural practices. In their place they adopted girdling and slash-and-burn clearing, long fallows, and hoe culture from Native Americans, all to the purpose of growing maize and tobacco. Their own principal contributions to the Indians' agricultural economy were the introduction of domestic livestock and the use of metal tools. At first they concentrated on maximum production of tobacco from freshly cultivated lands. The annual work cycle was almost wholly shaped by the seasonal demands of tobacco. Production of food crops—primarily maize—was usually limited to the requirements of self-sufficiency. Almost all essential manufactures were imported. This simplified early Chesapeake agriculture system required only limited numbers and kinds of farm buildings.[20]

Although contemporaries maintained that "tobacco is our meat, drinke, cloathing and monies," in reality the staple accounted for only approximately two-thirds of an average planter's annual market income, not the 90 percent one would infer from export statistics alone. Local markets were an important source of income and in many years meant the difference between profit and loss. Subsistence production outside the market—the provision of food, shelter, fuel, washing, and other services consumed in the home—was worth as much as export earnings. Over time, householders increased their wealth not from adding to their local or export earnings or from increasing subsistence production but from making farm improvements, adding value to undeveloped land through clearing, fencing, building houses and barns, and planting orchards.[21]

Since there were few alternative sources of market revenue, tobacco production and the exchange of export earnings for imported goods and services continued to drive the seventeenth- and early eighteenth-century Chesapeake economy. It was, however, the lure of earning income well above subsistence, rather than a shortage of options for securing subsistence itself, that sustained generations of "sotweed" planters. Because tobacco demanded little capital to start production—a cleared patch of land and a few simple tools were all that was needed—and because it earned few returns to scale, freed servants and tenant farmers seized the opportunities that tobacco culture held out as eagerly as did wealthier landowners. Small farmers, who often owned just a few indentured servants, were the major producers in the region until the last quarter of the century.

By then, an early undifferentiated tobacco-centered agricultural economy had evolved into three distinct subregional economies. For the first half century or so, Chesapeake tobacco growers weathered falling prices by increasing the number of plants a worker could tend and by making improvements in curing and packing the crop. From 1640 to 1675, annual gross revenues per laborer amounted to roughly £15 sterling constant value. However, by the mid-1670s, prices fell to a point at which most planters in the Lower James basin and the lower Delmarva peninsula, where soils suitable for tobacco were rare, curtailed the staple or dropped it entirely and turned instead to the production of naval stores, timber, cider, small grains, corn, and livestock. By 1700, residents of these marginal areas made up about 20 percent of the total Chesapeake population, but they produced less than 10 percent of the tobacco in the region. Earnings per capita from the staple fell to well under £1 in the peripheral areas, and most market income was earned by trading with other mainland colonies and the West Indies, not the mother country.

Although economic conditions in the rest of the Tidewater remained more closely tied to the fortunes of the export market, two other tobacco-producing subregions developed in the 1650s. Planters in the York basin and part of the Rappahannock started to produce a unique sweet-scented strain that sold well in the British domestic market. This tobacco usually commanded higher prices than did oronoco, the more common sort produced everywhere else in the region. Planters fortunate enough to own the limited acres on which the sweet-scented strain flourished prospered disproportionately in the second half of the seventeenth century. Their profits enabled them to buy up a larger share of the African slaves transported to the area, acquisitions and wealth that propelled them to the top of the political establishment in Virginia. Sweet-scented tobacco lands supported over 40 percent of the population by 1700. It also was home to a higher proportion of bound labor than the other two economic subregions. However, this subregion produced only about 40 percent of total tobacco exports, owing to the fact that sweet-scented growers developed different techniques for cultivating, processing, and packing their crops that improved the quality and raised the value of their tobacco but did not expand volume. Sweet-scented producers usually shipped their tobacco to England on consignment, the growers assuming the risk of shipment in the hope of gaining the highest possible prices in Europe.

The third subregion, the oronoco-producing areas of Maryland's lower Western and upper Eastern Shore, the Virginia side of the Potomac, and parts of the Rappahannock watershed, was where a third of the total population lived in 1700, but it produced about half of all tobacco exports. Oronoco growers offset the lower prices their more ordinary product commanded by making larger crops rather than by trying to improve the leaf itself. They usually sold their crops locally to British merchants or Scottish storekeepers, accepting lower prices in return for cash in hand. The merchants shipped the oronoco product to Britain, or, after the turn of the eighteenth century, re-exported it to new continental European consumers. Laborers earned about £5 a year from tobacco up to 1700, while annual per capita market income averaged around £2 in both sweet-scented and oronoco areas.[22]

Returns from the two strains tended to diverge during the first half of the eighteenth century: good times for growers of one sort were paralleled by poor returns for producers of the other. Annual tobacco income per worker fluctuated between £2 and £6, but income per capita dropped to between £.75 and £2. Prices—and returns—converged again only after Maryland adopted a tobacco inspection system in 1747 similar to that initiated by Virginia in 1733. Then, finally, in the third quarter of the century, Chesapeake residents as a whole enjoyed higher tobacco prices coupled with more favorable terms of trade with Britain and expanded commerce with other colonies. This general prosperity enabled them to purchase increasing quantities of consumer goods, which improved standards of living for all economic groups.

Domestic markets also expanded alongside the staple trade as the makeup of the population changed and the economy diversified. Tobacco growers everywhere had already by the 1690s wrung as much efficiency as they could from their field hands. Thereafter, output per worker fell in older areas. Furthermore, per capita incomes fell more steeply than did income per laborer as the white population shifted from a predominantly immigrant workforce to one that was largely native born. This change produced a permanent increase in the proportion of young dependents to productive adult workers. Planters needed a strategy to meet new local demands created by the changing demographic structure. Wealthy or not, they devoted more time and energy to producing goods and services for a growing resident population. They also began replacing imports with local manufactures and raising a greater mix of crops and livestock. Richer families were able to diversify more than poorer ones, and so enjoyed more hedges against external market fluctuations by meeting their own needs for leather, shoes, yarn, cloth, beverages, furnishings, and tools.[23]

The estuarine geography of the region and the dispersed settlement patterns encouraged by tobacco culture forestalled the growth of significant urban communities in the Chesapeake region. Landings and warehouses were the entire infrastructure required to carry on trade. It was only during the 1690s that town development began in earnest, aside from the original, small, poorly sited capitals at Jamestown and St. Mary's City. Attempts to create additional towns had been one of the standard remedies that colonial legislatures resorted to, to counter depressed tobacco prices, centralize trade, encourage economic diversification, and promote crafts, mostly for naught. Around the turn of the century, some of the paper towns the legislatures laid out, such as Yorktown and Norfolk, Virginia, and Oxford, Maryland, began to attract a few pioneering merchants, artisans, and inevitably tavern keepers. Two new formally planned capital towns—Annapolis and Williamsburg—were founded as administrative centers but became cultural watering holes as well. They provided a clientele for the only significant concentrations of artisans producing luxury goods. Gradually, genteel housing, designed to meet the social needs of fashion-conscious town dwellers, made an appearance in these arenas of conspicuous consumption and public display. By 1750, both capitals had about 1,000 residents living in roughly 100 households. Their populations doubled by 1775. Elsewhere hamlets and villages of 100 to 500 residents also grew up around tobacco warehouses and country stores, and small towns numbering as many as 1,000 inhabitants emerged at fall line transshipment points. Nevertheless, townspeople remained a tiny minority throughout the colonial era (Fig. 4.5).[24]

Over time, the fortunes of the oronoco tobacco strain increasingly dominated economic conditions along the Tobacco Coast, it being the only variant that could be successfully cultivated in newer Piedmont areas west of the fall line, where tobacco culture and slavery spread rapidly after the 1720s. There, virgin soils and liberal land-granting policies encouraged expansion from the old and comparatively crowded Tidewater counties. From the 1730s, settlers from Pennsylvania entered the Shenandoah Valley and created another culturally and economically divergent subregion. The Germans and Scotch-Irish who moved into the Shenandoah Valley developed a separate economy based on grains grown on family farms; planters and slaves who moved in from the east remained a minority in far western settlements. Tidewater rulers increasingly had to take into account the political and economic concerns of an expanding upland population by midcentury. While 90 percent of the population still lived in the lowlands, 40 percent had moved beyond the fall line twenty-five years later.[25]

Once planters could find no further means for increasing the amount of tobacco a field hand could raise, their efforts to replace diminishing returns from the sale of tobacco dominate the story of eighteenth-century agriculture. These initiatives not only included expanded import replacement strategies, but also the addition of maize and wheat as major

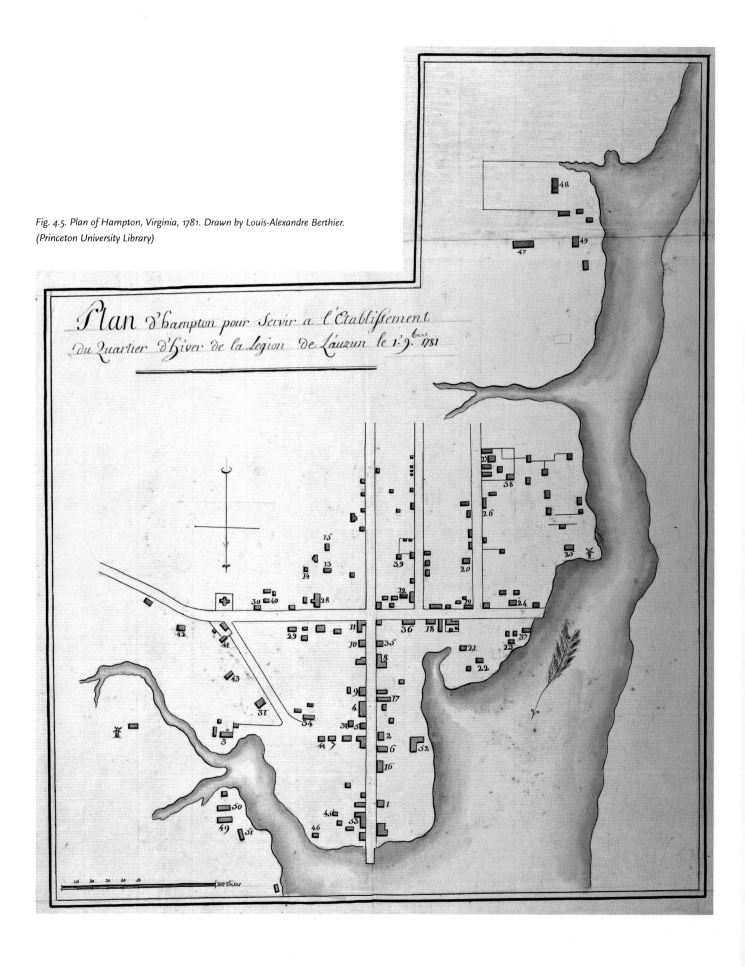

Fig. 4.5. *Plan of Hampton, Virginia, 1781. Drawn by Louis-Alexandre Berthier.*
(Princeton University Library)

Plan d'hampton pour Servir a l'Etablissement du Quartier d'Hiver de la Legion de Lauzun le 1.9.bre 1781

Fig. 4.6. The scene that Lewis Miller sketched in 1870 resembled many western Virginia farmsteads a generation or two earlier in the persistence of log outbuildings and split rail fences. (Colonial Williamsburg Foundation, Gift of Dr. and Mrs. Richard Kain)

revenue crops and livestock to produce manure for fields and to boost yields. These changes in crop mix entailed a gradual shift from hoe to plow culture, more division of labor by gender among bound workers, and fuller use of the entire labor force year round. Slaves bore the brunt of expanded and intensified work regimes, once planters discovered that by carefully coordinating crop cycles they could grow more grain with little or no reduction in tobacco production. Tobacco and grains produced approximately equal revenues on large plantations from about the middle of the eighteenth century, and most export earnings came from a combination of tobacco and wheat. Planters seldom made a choice between one export crop and the other. Instead, they continued to grow both crops—and corn as well. On Piedmont farms, too, grains grown for sale supplemented tobacco. Soils better suited to wheat and forage crops produced larger yields, which offset the disadvantage of higher transportation costs from the interior (Fig. 4.6). As will be seen in chapter 9, this more diversified agriculture required a wider array of supporting farm buildings. Small planters through-

out the region realized few benefits from these changes, since they usually lacked sufficient land, labor, and draft animals to produce much surplus grain. A combination of improved tobacco markets and increased revenues from grains enabled planters who owned slaves to increase annual gross farm revenues per worker from around £10 earned in the decades between 1680 and 1740 to £15 in the third quarter of the eighteenth century. As discussed in chapter 7, with increased agricultural incomes, elite planters could more readily afford to build new brick Georgian houses.[26]

The outbreak of the American Revolution led to severe economic depression. British naval blockades cut Chesapeake farmers off from international and intercolonial markets. Most planters responded by curtailing the production of all market crops. No longer able to buy imported manufactures, they devoted their energies to producing fibers, making cloth, boiling salt, brewing alcohol, and finding ways to pay their taxes. Most Chesapeake residents found themselves in severely reduced straits by 1781, for many reasons, including absenteeism due to government or military service, loss of income from market crops, destructive British raids, slave desertions, loss of rents from tenants who could not or would not pay, depletion of livestock herds and timber reserves, high taxes, scarce specie, and the deterioration of buildings, fences, and other infrastructure. Once hostilities ended, Chesapeake residents made concerted efforts to make up for years of lost revenues. But few planters were able to resume full crop production before 1785, and a postwar economic bust, falling land prices due to out-migration, scarce money and credit, unpaid prewar debts, and continued high taxes all contributed to a prolonged economic malaise. Entrepreneurially minded residents became more optimistic after the Constitution was adopted and a national government was organized, in 1789, and economic conditions improved.[27]

Most planters at first returned to their traditional staple and revived the trading arrangements they had had with British merchants before the war. Tobacco remained the dominant element in the 1780s economy, import-replacement strategies were curtailed, and heavy imports of British manufactures and British credit resumed. However, the old colonial economy was finally brought to an end by the abolition of the national tobacco monopoly at the outset of the French Revolution in 1791 and by the closing of French and other continental markets with the outbreak of war in Europe. For the first time ever, many planters decided to drop tobacco entirely in favor of grains, hay, dairy products, and livestock. Per capita earnings from tobacco declined everywhere except in the Virginia Piedmont and Southside counties, where tobacco production continued to expand and outputs per laborer were sometimes higher than those achieved before the war. As will be discussed in chapter 9, corn houses and granaries largely replaced tobacco houses by 1798 in those areas that shifted almost entirely out of tobacco, while barns and specialized livestock shelters became more common.[28]

The size and functions of Chesapeake towns and cities also changed with the shift from a colonial to a national economy. After 1791, American merchants, who had largely controlled the wheat and West Indian trades prior to the Revolution, took over the tobacco export and European merchandise supply lines as well. Baltimore, with over 13,000 residents and extensive connections both to the West and to foreign and domestic ports, was already the nation's fifth-largest city in 1790; by 1830, it had grown to be the second-largest, with a population of over 80,000, surpassed only by New York City. Norfolk and Richmond were also among the twenty most populous cities in the young republic. Alexandria, Georgetown, Petersburg, and Washington, D.C., ranked in the top thirty. Even interior trading centers like Frederick and Hagerstown, Maryland, and Lynchburg,

Virginia, supported larger populations than once lived in Williamsburg and Annapolis. These expanding commercial centers became centers of political and cultural life as well. Notwithstanding, merchants and bankers in the region proved no match for the entrepreneurs of New York City and Philadelphia. Little by little, these northern cities replaced London, Glasgow, Liverpool, and Bristol as the main sources of credit and the distribution centers from whence Virginians and Marylanders obtained both imported and American-made manufactured goods.

The shift into grain farming that commenced in the early 1790s, much praised by agricultural reformers at the time and by many twentieth-century scholars since, brought temporary prosperity, largely to a privileged few. Grains created more serious environmental problems than the application of "scientific" farming solved. Unlike tobacco, raising wheat involved economies of scale. Middling to large planters were better positioned than were small growers to benefit from the high grain prices inflated by the Napoleonic Wars. Generally speaking, the outlook for Chesapeake farmers was favorable, despite the Embargo of 1808 and renewed war with Britain between 1812 and 1815, at least until 1818 or 1819. Besides high overseas demand for grain, rapidly growing urban populations expanded markets for hay, dairy products, meat, seafood, firewood, and perishable produce.

Revenues earned by large producers again pulled far ahead of those of smaller farmers in the early years of the nineteenth century, just as they had in the difficult years between 1680 and 1730. Big planters who shifted their crop mix to match volatile markets and tailored their slave labor forces to fit that mix were rewarded with significant returns from major field crops as well as growing revenues from livestock sales. Not all abandoned tobacco entirely, and planters who grew grain every year and tended tobacco when prices were favorable did better than most farmers who dropped it altogether. Gross revenues per laborer among large slave owners rose to about £25 sterling constant value between 1790 and 1807 and averaged over £35 between 1810 and 1818, almost certainly the highest returns seen in the region prior to the Civil War. Newly available nonagricultural investments—urban real estate, bank stock, and shares in internal improvement companies—also contributed to big planter prosperity. In contrast, planters who owned few or no slaves realized gross revenues of only about £15 per worker, no better than their earnings before the Revolution.[29]

The fortunes of middling planters varied in the immediate post-Revolutionary era. Many moderately prosperous families in parts of the Tidewater such as Virginia's Northern Neck and Elizabeth City County on the Lower Peninsula, pulled up stakes to move west or into cities. Those who remained may have experienced downward economic mobility. Economic inequality increased as the farms they left behind were often divided into smaller parcels or worked by slaves owned by absentee buyers. In other mainland Tidewater and Piedmont counties, middling planters had more success in raising some combination of tobacco and grains and were much more likely than their poorer neighbors to stay put. The changing crop mix encouraged new investment in agricultural buildings and other farm improvements. In still other areas where diversified farming was well established before the Revolution, including the upper and lower Eastern Shore and the environs of Norfolk and Baltimore, new overseas markets and more regular opportunities to sell grain, timber, livestock, and naval stores to urban populations raised revenues for middling as well as large farmers. In these places, the temporary spate of postwar prosperity encouraged families to replace prewar impermanent housing with small but more durable and better-finished houses.

Farmers could choose between three general courses of action from the 1780s to 1820 or so. They could relocate to newly opened western settlements where they might continue farming in the old ways with better results. Many chose this course. By 1790, more people lived beyond the fall line— 43 percent in the Virginia Piedmont and Southside and 20 percent in the Shenandoah Valley and trans-Appalachian west—than remained in the old Tidewater counties, including the Eastern Shore. Chesapeake out-migrants also supplied many settlers to the new states of Kentucky and Tennessee and to parts of southern Ohio, Indiana, Illinois, and Missouri. Many stay-at-homes followed the second course: they followed farming practices that involved a land-consuming crop progression of tobacco, corn, wheat, and finally fallow, accompanied by extensive plowing, which led to massive soil erosion in much of the region. Even zealous advocates of improvement recognized that when farmers required "speedy supplies" just to make ends meet, they had no choice but to grow crops that sold for the most money. At best, that meant extracting the greatest product possible from the soil "without entirely destroying future prospects of crops from their lands." Indeed, since land prices in most areas east of the Blue Ridge did not rise between 1775 and 1830, soil mining was not an irrational choice, especially among farmers who might eventually move farther west.[30]

The third course, abandoning traditional, land-mining, labor-saving Chesapeake husbandry for European-style high farming, was primarily an option for those wealthy enough to forego immediate profits long enough to divert labor to the arduous business of keeping fields under perpetual cultivation and of improving the appearance of holdings that agricultural reformers now perceived of as "slovenly." The marked changes in crop mix and cultivation techniques accompanying the shift into grain farming permanently altered ratios of land to labor, sometimes leaving planters with more workers—especially women and children—than they needed. Masters opposed to breaking up slave families often had to settle for lesser revenues than those who were willing to dispose of "surplus" hands through some combination of selective sales, forced westward migration, selective manumissions, apprenticeships, and increased slave hiring.[31]

Out-migration and the transfer of resources westward, coupled with falling agricultural productivity in regions left behind, led to a drop in per capita exports throughout the South. By the early 1790s, they were only half what they had been in the 1770s. Exports from more northerly areas meanwhile equaled or surpassed prewar levels. The proportion of national private wealth held by New Englanders and Middle Atlantic residents consequently increased, while that of the Chesapeake residents fell. By the time the worldwide economic depression following the Napoleonic Wars hit the Chesapeake in 1819, the region was already reeling from competition for markets from settlers in Kentucky and Tennessee, who farmed fresher, better lands. Neither Chesapeake tobacco planters nor wheat farmers could successfully compete with the new western states after 1820. Little by little, wealth, social status, and national political power slipped away from old planter families in Maryland and Virginia. They looked back nostalgically to a mythical colonial golden age while engaging in an increasingly insular and retrogressive defense of chattel slavery and a slave society.[32]

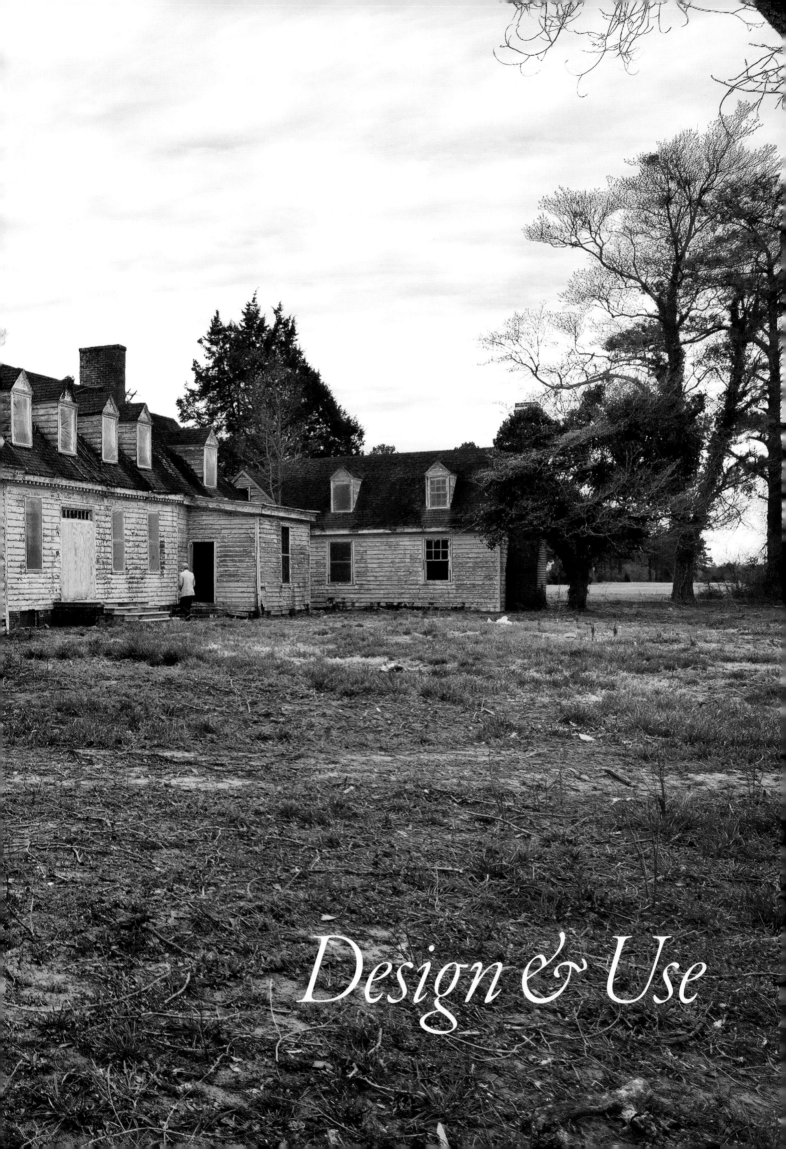

Design & Use

5 *The Design Process*

CARL R. LOUNSBURY

The design process in the early Chesapeake was a collective endeavor that involved numerous individuals who had the ability to shape the form of a structure at various stages during the construction of a building, from initial discussions to the final coat of paint. Rather than a static method whose source emanated from an architect's drawings and set of written specifications, the conceptualization and execution of a building's design from its plan to its ornamentation was far more fluid, as clients, contractors, and craftsmen played important and often variable roles in the process.

Clearly delineated responsibilities characteristic of modern design had not developed, as the émigré English architect Benjamin Henry Latrobe discovered to his detriment in one of his earliest commissions in America. Latrobe set out to launch his architectural career in this country in 1796 but discovered that neoclassical design had scarcely made an impact in Virginia, and his choice of Norfolk to make his debut was less than propitious. The town had flourished in the late colonial period as a tobacco port, but in the decades following its destruction during the Revolutionary War, it had barely recovered from the disruptions of the transatlantic trade. Latrobe encountered "an illbuilt and unhealthy town," where the "ruins of old houses" were "almost as numerous as the inhabited houses." Of those that had survived, he observed, "the stile of houses of private Gentlemen is plain and decent, but of the fashion of 30 Years ago. They are kept very clean and independent of papering, which is not universal, fitted up much in the English style."[1] Norfolk seemed impervious to contemporary English fashion, a throwback to another era when dwellings contained massive exterior chimneys, floor-to-ceiling raised-panel wainscoting trimmed with heavy moldings, and stout sash muntins.

Latrobe realized that down-at-the-heels Norfolk held little promise for his talents and soon moved on to more thriving locations. However, before he left, he designed for merchant William Pennock a neoclassical house filled with details that were novel for Norfolk and most of the Chesa-

peake. The three-story town house with its hipped roof and one-story pedimented Greek Doric porch featured polygonally shaped entertaining rooms on the back side and a sweeping oval staircase ascending in a two-story entrance hall, characteristic of the neoclassical penchant for elliptical spaces and forms. Equally novel in the Pennock design was the detailing (Fig. 5.1). Rather than traditional heavy molded railings and turned balusters, Latrobe introduced an oval-shaped spiraling handrail with square balusters. The apertures had symmetrical architraves and corner blocks, features that were repeated in the ceiling design (Fig. 5.2). He recessed the window sash in the jambs, and all the moldings were based on Greek forms rather than traditional Roman ones.

As with so many other projects that he would undertake in America, the execution of the design fell into the hands of craftsmen who understood little of the new style. Latrobe

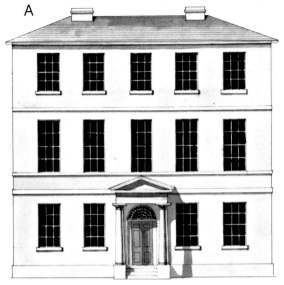

A

Elevation on the Mainstreet.

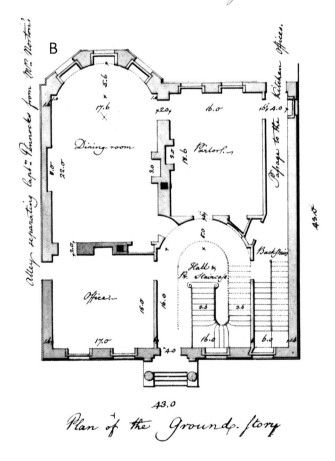

B

Plan of the Grounds story

(left) Fig. 5.1. Benjamin Henry Latrobe, design drawings of the Pennock House, 1796, Norfolk, Virginia. A: Elevation; B: Plan. (Library of Congress)

(right) Fig. 5.2. Benjamin Henry Latrobe, view of the entrance hall, Pennock House. (Library of Congress)

found that "Mr. Gracie an ingenious Scotch joiner," who had fabricated the woodwork of the house, was "wedded to the heavy wooden taste of the last century" and that "no part of the plan had been accurately set out. The front was totally altered: all the sash frames, instead of being in reveals, were solid, and placed on the outside, and no two sides of the bow window were equal, or set out from the same center. The chimneys occupied double the space requisite for them. . . . The cornices which I designed, were deemed too plain and Mr. Ferguson was employed to furnish such as were *tastier* and *finer*." To expedite completion of the project, Latrobe found it "necessary to accommodate the original plan to the blunders committed by the workmen, to combat their prejudices and obstinacy, and to inform their ignorance."[2] The builders simply ignored many of the innovative features of the design and instead had reverted to more familiar regional forms—a gabled roof, window frames set flush with the face of the wall, large chimney stacks, and a heavy modillion cornice. Even if the craftsmen had been more competent or were trained to follow faithfully the sketches of the architect, it

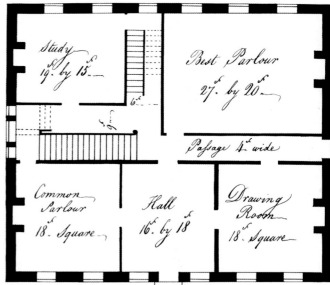

(left) Fig. 5.3. Secretary Thomas Nelson House, Yorktown, c. 1765, showing the damage suffered during the 1781 siege of the town. Drawing by Benjamin Henry Latrobe, 1796. (The Library of Virginia)

(right) Fig. 5.4. Plan, Secretary Thomas Nelson House, Yorktown. Drawing by Thomas Hunt, 1765. (Royal Institute of British Architects Library Drawings Collection)

is difficult to see how Latrobe's design would have survived unaltered. There were just too many novelties for tradition-bound workmen to absorb—from the recessed sash to the Greek moldings. For one thing, few joiners in Norfolk at the time had a plane with a blade that could form the elliptical shape of Latrobe's moldings.[3]

As the town house commission illustrates, the design process in the early Chesapeake can be interpreted from a hierarchical model of cultural development that has long been a staple of architectural history.[4] This perspective starts with the premise that there are academic or metropolitan forms that constitute the core ideals of a given period, which gradually spread to the cultural periphery. In the case of early American architecture, it has often focused on tracing the introduction of design precedents through architectural innovators such as Latrobe or through the medium of prints and books and assessing their eventual reception in provincial cities and remote corners of British America, generally observing a case of diminishing fidelity to the original forms by lesser skilled craftsmen in the backwaters.[5] Yet this is a one-sided, ahistorical view that seldom takes into account the perspective of the locals. Did most residents of Norfolk really want all the novelty that Latrobe had packed into his design?

From Jamestown's beginnings to Latrobe's frustrating experience in Norfolk two centuries later, the design and construction of buildings bore the imprint of many different hands. Latrobe's designs are well known, but less has been

said about the impact of craftsmen such as Gracie and Ferguson in determining the form and finish of early buildings. This chapter explores the design process, specifically the changing ways in which buildings were devised. In a letter to an English business acquaintance in 1765, Thomas Nelson, longtime secretary of the colony of Virginia, described in great detail the two-story brick house that he "designed by himself" in Yorktown (Figs. 5.3, 5.4).[6] Nelson may not have relied upon the services of a gentleman such as Latrobe for the plan of his dwelling, but the attribution of the house solely to the wits of its owner tells only part of the story.

The source of design did not originate solely from architectural drawings or from decisions made by an architect or even a client. In fact, drawings did not command a preeminent position in the transmission of architectural ideals in early America but only supplemented or clarified other ways of communicating intentions, including the reliance upon the expertise of craftsmen. Often what was not expressed in drawings or written specifications remained in the domain of the builder to resolve during construction. In laying out the specifications for an Anglican church in Maryland, the vestrymen called for "sufficient" pilasters or buttresses to support the brick walls as the "workman shall think fitt," leaving the design to his discretion.[7] Although the history of design in the early Chesapeake centers upon the introduction and adaptation of metropolitan ideas, the course of that transformation was charted on the construction site and at the workbench. The authority of the drawing board had not trumped

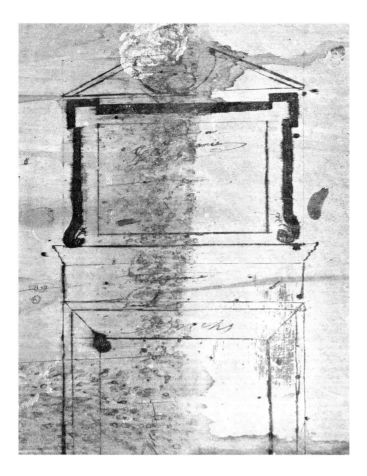

practical experience on the building site. Unfortunately, most of that process occurred in conversations between clients and workmen or in schematic sketches executed on a piece of paper or material at hand, ephemeral communication that left little record (Fig. 5.5). Nothing survives to describe the means by which Secretary Nelson transformed his ideas into a physical reality, but he must have been deeply engaged with the numerous craftsmen who oversaw the task of integrating individual preferences with regional practices. To ignore the instrumental role played by workmen in the design process, no matter how difficult to document, is to misunderstand the nature of architectural change.

THE FORMATION OF A REGIONAL TRADITION: DESIGN IN THE SEVENTEENTH CENTURY

Distinctive regional building practices emerged in the Chesapeake region within a few decades of first settlement. By the second quarter of the seventeenth century, colonists had become acutely aware that their most common manner of building had diverged from standard English patterns—so much so that they referred to the new forms as "Virginia houses," a term that was used throughout Virginia and Maryland. From the rich variety of English building practices, they carefully selected and adapted construction

methods and plan types that best suited their own particular needs and technological capabilities. The exigencies of the frontier disrupted many Old World patterns. An unhealthy climate with an appalling mortality rate disrupted the formation of familiar patterns of domestic life. In the allocation of scarce resources in an uncertain world, the construction of fine houses with masonry chimneys and well-crafted interior finishes in the manner that had transformed English housing standards in the late sixteenth century stood beyond the capabilities of most settlers. They made do with inferior buildings with simplified construction techniques built for the moment rather than for the future.[8]

The first generation or two of immigrant craftsmen adapted their skills to the conditions of settlement, distinguishing between well-framed "English houses," with stout posts, beams, and braces fastened with mortise and tenon and dovetail joints, and the far more prevalent form of mass mud wall construction—later supplanted by riven clapboard carpentry—that they were called on to construct on most sites. Earthfast construction, which eschewed the use of masonry foundations, appeared from the earliest days of Jamestown's settlement and must have been familiar to English craftsmen as an alternative method to the more labor-intensive braced framing. However, as the archaeological record suggests, until the last decades of the seventeenth century Chesapeake builders experimented with a variety of plan types and different methods for erecting frame structures.

With few commonly accepted ways of building, new projects needed explicit explanations. While most matters were worked out on the building site, documents describe a society striving to find those forms that worked best. In 1635, members of an Anglican vestry on the Eastern Shore felt compelled to describe the plan of a new parsonage. The house was to be "forty foot long and eyghteene foot wyde and nine foot to the wall plates and that ther shalbe a chimney at each end of the house, and upon each side of the chimneys a rome, the one for study, the other for a buttery alsoe a pertition neere the midest of the house wth an entry and two doures the one to goe into the kitching the other into the chamber."[9] Little was taken for granted. Room functions and the number and placement of chimneys, partitions, and doorways needed articulation. Their instructions omitted mention of framing systems or finishes, issues that were probably resolved in discussions between the carpenter and members of the building committee. They may have provided some additional details—the number of windows or the type of hardware that would be installed—but the execution of the work was left in the hands of the craftsman, whose training and experience made him the arbiter of construction methods.

Despite variations in plan and earthfast construction methods, some building practices coalesced to form recognizable regional patterns fairly early. The occasional use of thatch and lime rendering gave way to riven clapboards as the principal covering material for roofs and walls. A cheap material easily worked to four- or five-foot lengths, clapboards provided structural rigidity to underbraced wall and roof frames. They were sometimes used as an alternative to plaster for interior sheathing and as flooring in secondary spaces such as lofts. Although clapboard lengths did not dictate the type of earthfast construction that appeared, the logic of arranging bay systems with major posts located at regular intervals of 8 or 10 feet and studs and rafters on 2- or 2½-foot centers became apparent to carpenters across the region (see Fig. 10.4).

By the middle of the seventeenth century, the system became rooted in the way colonists thought about buildings. Building specifications describe structures in so many "lengths of boards" or "feet of housing." For example, in 1651 a carpenter contracted "to build a house of six lengths of boards." The house was to be 20 feet wide, which suggests that the building was erected with 10-foot bay systems using 5-foot-long clapboards as covering. The overall length of the house would have been 30 feet.[10] A few years later, James Hugate agreed to build for Thomas Swann "one small quartering house of twenty-five or thirty foot long and so much other out houses as will make up the sum of ninety foot of housing. The Bredth of them not to be under fifteen nor above twenty foot. . . . Swann is to allow Hugate 125 lbs. Tob. [tobacco] &c. for every length of boards so built allowing five foot to each length of boards."[11] As long as there was little distinction between the framing and finish of a dwelling, service structure, or agricultural building, Chesapeake builders estimated carpentry costs by the linear foot, a practice that would survive through the eighteenth century, especially when riven clapboard structures with unfinished interiors such as barns or tobacco houses were contemplated.

The cryptic description of the buildings that Hugate was to erect for Swann illustrates the manner in which buildings were designed. The written agreement described the general characteristics of the building—the size and the type of materials to be used. It also stipulated the responsibilities of each party. Swann, the client, agreed to lend the carpenter "a couple of hands to assist him with the woods to saw timber to bring it in place as also to help him rear, one to hand

boards to him for covering, and find all manner of Nayles and other things as shall be necessary and useful about the same." For his part, Hugate, the carpenter, agreed to remain on the job once engaged and not go off to work on other projects. To ensure that Hugate completed his obligation, Swann agreed to allow him the use of a house on the property as well as land to plant corn for sustenance. In terms of building, those things left unsaid in writing were to be "done as the said Swann shall contrive and give directions" on the building site.[12] In face-to-face conversations, the client and his builder resolved issues concerning the quality of the framing, the placement of chimneys, partitions, stairs, doors, and windows, the type of flooring, the wall and ceiling finishes, and ornamental details. Swann and his builder probably used standing structures as references to the form and quality of these features. The discussions may have been very detailed, but for the most part craftsmen were left on their own to resolve framing issues and devise finish details based on their expertise and recognized standards.

The agreement between Swann and Hugate presumed a set of commonly accepted conventions about the building and its workmanship, conceptual models shared by the client and builder that emanated from a combination of traditional English practices and local experience. These rules for building were shaped and could be transformed by changes in patterns of domesticity, social attitudes, and technological capabilities. For example, after more than four decades in the New World, colonists understood the peculiar qualities of regional building materials. Certain woods withstood rot or warping better than others. As earthfast construction became the most common method for building, colonists prized the durability of oaks, locusts, and heart cypress and pine and appreciated the ease with which oak could be riven into long lengths. By midcentury, most contracts had little need to mention the types of woods to be used in building, only emphasizing the use of heartwood over sapwood. Builders and presumably most clients understood standard practices and therefore felt no obligation to state the obvious, which was covered by a phrase often inserted in contracts that specified that craftsmanship was to be executed in a "workmanlike manner." It denoted what was commonplace and could be taken for granted from what was novel and had to be spelled out.

TRADITIONAL DESIGN SOURCES

Regional design became rooted when colonists reached a consensus on what constituted the shape and appropriate finish of a house or the hallmarks of workmanlike craftsmanship. Precedent set the tone for new work, and by the late seventeenth century regional building practices had coalesced into recognizable patterns. In most cases, clients had no desire to deviate from past forms but sought to replicate buildings that were known to them. They were not averse to novelty, but most had little reason to seek it out for workaday structures. Building specifications sometimes used shorthand references that recognized this commonality and acknowledged mutual understandings and expectations among contracting parties. In 1747, the vestrymen in a Virginia parish agreed to build a new 26- by 50-foot wooden church that was to be finished "in the usuall manner of building chappells."[13] In his 1762 will, Charles Carter of Cleve made provision to build, for his daughter-in-law, "two 40 foot Tobo. [tobacco] Houses, according to the common methods of building in Virginia."[14] Both the churchwardens who would have contracted with a builder for the chapel and the executors of Carter's will would have known their client's intentions. By midcentury, a secondary chapel in a small parish would have stood on masonry foundations, been sheathed with beaded weatherboards, and been covered with shingles. The tobacco houses would have been constructed with earthfast frames of posts set at regular intervals with the walls and roof covered with clapboards (see Fig. 10.1).

Building contracts sometimes singled out specific features to copy without describing them, fully confident that all parties would understand the standard form or manner of execution. The 1785 specifications for the fittings of a Virginia courthouse called for "the usual lawyers bar and justices bench."[15] Since the beginning of the eighteenth century, nearly all courtrooms were built with a raised magistrates' platform containing a curved bench for the justices, which was enclosed by a balustraded railing. Lawyers' bars stood some feet opposite the justices' bench and consisted of one or two narrow benches enclosed by a similar railing, a feature that had gained currency in courtrooms in the second quarter of the eighteenth century. Thus the justices were relying upon conventional forms that had changed little in more than half a century.[16]

A standing structure sometimes served as an exemplar of a well-ordered plan or of a well-constructed frame or exhibited clever brickwork worthy of emulation. Neighboring buildings also provided a gauge for estimating costs and materials or judging new workmanship and warned potential builders of the shortcomings of certain forms or construction methods. Sometimes, an entire building might be singled out for replication. At other times, the inventory of features on the original model might be altered slightly, such as substituting batten doors for panel doors or a wooden floor for a stone

one. Occasionally, only a particular feature might be picked out, such as a fine modillion cornice on a neighbor's dwelling. In 1665, the vestry of Christ Church Parish in Middlesex County, Virginia, decided to build a new structure "according to ye Modall of ye Middle-plantacon Church in all respects."[17] The chancel and west doorways at the newly rebuilt church in Jamestown caught the eye of vestrymen in the neighboring parish of Bruton in 1679 when they were planning to build a new brick church at Middle Plantation. Rather than copying the Jamestown doorways directly, the building committee wanted theirs to be a foot higher and half a foot wider, presumably finding some fault in the size of the originals.[18]

References to specific buildings as models helped define expectations of clients and served as gauges to judge the work of builders. In 1685, Middlesex County magistrates ordered the construction of a new courthouse and stipulated that it should "be at least of equall goodness and Dimentions with ye Brick Court house lately built in Gloucester County." To make sure that Robert Beverley, the gentleman who agreed to undertake the project, did not misunderstand the intentions of the magistrates, they reiterated that the building should be finished in all respects "as well as Gloucester Court house."[19] The Middlesex magistrates looked to a neighboring county for the source of their design, a practice that was extremely common throughout Virginia and Maryland in the seventeenth and eighteenth centuries. Northampton County officials cited their northern neighbor on the Eastern Shore of Virginia in building a new prison in 1690 "of the same dimension as the logg'd prison by Accomack County Courthouse."[20] The similarity of many churches, courthouses, and prisons is due to this blatant copying of nearby buildings and was seldom the product of a craftsman or master builder peddling a plan or his services from place to place.[21] The formation of new counties or parishes or the growth and maturation of older ones often precipitated the construction of new buildings, which, for the most part, looked back to the parent jurisdiction for architectural direction. In 1743, the magistrates in newly established Louisa County ordered built "a courthouse, prison, stocks such as the old ones were in Hanover County," where many of them had sat in session before the county was subdivided.[22] They knew exactly the kind of buildings that they would be getting, including a rather elegantly proportioned arcaded courthouse, which had been constructed only a few years earlier at Hanover.

Occasionally, buildings further afield might serve as models. Provincial buildings or the dwellings of important planters inspired some designs. Legislative and general court sessions attracted a steady stream of visitors to the capitals

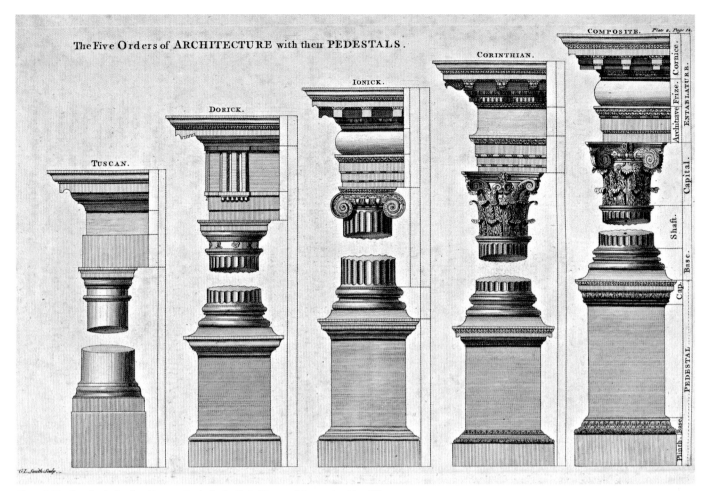

The Five Orders of ARCHITECTURE with their PEDESTALS.

TUSCAN.

DORICK.

IONICK.

CORINTHIAN.

COMPOSITE. *Plate 9. Page 14.*

Fig. 5.6. *The five classical orders: Tuscan, Doric, Ionic, Corinthian, and Composite. Isaac Ware,*
A Complete Body of Architecture *(London, 1756).*

of the two colonies, which provided an opportunity for planters and merchants to study in some detail the latest architectural fashions that arose on the streets of eighteenth-century Annapolis and Williamsburg. The completion of the double-pile Governor's Palace in Williamsburg at the beginning of the 1720s may have set the pattern for the spate of similar two-story gentry houses built in the following decades, though no documentary references give attribution to that specific source for a design. The influence may have been more general in terms of proportions, scale, and finishes. The impact of the capitol on courthouse design in Virginia can be traced more directly in terms of details and overall forms. In planning their new courthouse in 1726, justices in Norfolk County patterned the apsidal end of the building after the curved ends of the capitol and specified that the "seats for ye justices end & barrs in the same manner as in the General Court house."[23] A few years earlier, the vestry of St. Peter's Parish in New Kent County wanted its new church wall "to be in all Respects as well Done as the Capitol wall in Williamsburgh."[24] Alexander Spotswood's 1711 plan for a cruciform church to replace the earlier Bruton Parish Church in

the capital probably inspired the construction of cruciform churches in Tidewater Virginia over the next few decades, especially the church in Hampton, which was completed around 1728 by Williamsburg builder Henry Cary, and the one erected in Norfolk in 1739.[25]

THE INTEGRATION OF CLASSICAL DESIGN PRINCIPLES IN CHESAPEAKE BUILDING

Beginning in the last decades of the seventeenth century and continuing through the end of the eighteenth century, a new design aesthetic eclipsed many of the older patterns that had characterized the Chesapeake. Craftsmen and their clients began to subscribe to an aesthetic promulgated by British builders, which in turn was based on Renaissance ideas derived from the authoritative precedent of the five ancient orders of classical architecture (Fig. 5.6). The plainest and shortest order was the Tuscan, and the most elaborate and elongated was the Composite. The elements that made up the constituent parts of each order—the pedestal, column, and entablature—were precisely proportioned according to the rules codified by Renaissance architects such as Sebastiano Serlio, Ottavio Scamozzi, and Andrea Palladio, who had based their observations on ancient Roman buildings. Classical design offered an inherent relational logic, which could be manipulated like a Bach fugue to create multiple variations within the parameters of a given form. British theorists and popularizers duly followed the prescriptive rules devised by the Italians, offering detailed plates of the orders and their individual components and describing their appropriate use.

In truth, design was rarely as meticulous as classical theory. Few builders adhered to the degree of specificity laid out in the treatises. Instead, craftsmen developed shorthand rules that violated many of the canonical standards but nonetheless followed the spirit of classical proportioning and detailing. Except for the self-taught pedant Thomas Jefferson, most clients in the Chesapeake accepted the more relaxed approach to classical design practiced by their workmen. George Washington, who professed his "ignorance of Architectural principles," gave expression to this prevailing attitude when he observed that "Rules of Architecture are calculated . . . to give symmetry, and just proportion to all the Orders, & parts of buildings, in order to please the eye. Small departures from strict rules are discoverable only by skilful Architects, or by the eye of criticism; while ninety nine in a hundred—deficient of their knowledge—might be pleased with things not quite orthodox."[26]

Contracts and accounts describe a new language of building that reflected the increasing importance of massing, scale, and symmetry. Drawings came into regular use in the design of major buildings as a medium to discuss the arrangement of spaces and explore the proportional relationship of different elements to one another. Clients and craftsmen self-consciously used fashionable words such as "modillion" and "surbase" to indicate a new desire to disguise the structural frame beneath applied decorative elements whose forms derived from English interpretations of Renaissance classicism.[27] Exposed framing members carefully finished with chamfers gradually disappeared in the eighteenth century, replaced by smooth planar surfaces, wainscoting, and cased work. Craftsmen retired their hollow and round chisels and purchased molding planes with blades shaped to run Roman moldings. Architraves with classical moldings, raised panel wainscoting, and chimneypieces appeared along with classically proportioned apertures containing sash windows with wide muntins and crown glass imported from London and Bristol. Because Chesapeake craftsmen had integrated many elements of earthfast construction into their building habits, including the paring back in size of many of the major framing members, it was easier for them to hide these elements beneath wainscoting or plastered surfaces than for their compatriots in the New England colonies, where builders continued to erect frames with massive corner posts and summer beams that had to be boxed and jutted out beyond the wall and ceiling planes.

PROPORTION

Ideas associated with classical architecture make their first appearance in building documents in the last quarter of the seventeenth century. For the first time, contractual agreements stressed the relationship of parts to the whole—described in the use of the term "proportionable." Batty Langley, a promoter of classical design, proclaimed "true proportions [to be] the fundamentals and very life of architecture."[28] Most buildings erected in Britain and her American colonies from the late seventeenth century onward were astylar, that is, erected without an applied order. In lieu of columns and pediments, there was an implied order that governed the design of most buildings. These informal rules divided a facade into three sections—the foundations, the principal stories, and the eaves. These corresponded to the division of a classical order into its three principal components—plinth or base, column, and entablature. Horizontal elements in the facade—the water table, stringcourse, and cornice—sometimes expressed these implied divisions. Doors, windows, and cornices were to be "in proportion" to the height of the walls, the principal element for determining the general aesthetic appearance of a building. The dentilated cornice of a church in Truro Parish in Fairfax County was to be "in Proportion to the hight of the Walls (which are to be twenty two feet and an half)."[29] Apertures were also proportioned within themselves. Most windows were twice as tall as they were wide, one of the proportions recommended by Renaissance theorists such as Palladio (Fig. 5.7). Although laymen and builders alike recognized that classical rules dictated the precise size of these elements, few took the trouble to design them to such rigorous standards, an attitude that would provoke the ire of those such as Thomas Jefferson and Benjamin Latrobe who took a more scholarly approach to design.[30]

Classical ideals dictated that internal functions should be expressed on the exteriors in abstract ways. The stories that contained the most important rooms—public reception spaces—often had the largest windows, and corresponding stories that contained service spaces or private chambers had smaller openings. This rule was by no means formulaic but depended as much upon the social custom of a country or region. For example, the principal entertaining rooms in Italian

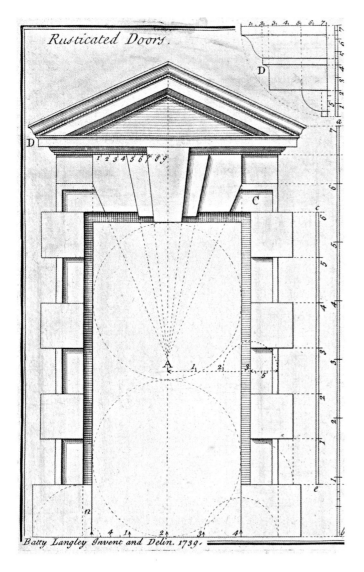

Fig. 5.7. *"Rusticated Doors," Plate XXIX, Batty Langley*, The City and Country Builder's and Workman's Treasury of Designs *(London, 1740). The image shows the proportioning of the door opening as being twice as tall as it is wide, a standard ratio found in the Chesapeake region in the late colonial period.*

Renaissance palaces were on the second floor, or *piano nobile*, and architects designed facades that recognized this arrangement. British dwellings in the seventeenth and early eighteenth centuries did not follow the Italian model—many entertaining rooms remained on the ground floor, as they had been for many generations, or were divided between the first and second stories. English town house design in the late seventeenth and early eighteenth centuries rarely distinguished between the size of ground-floor and second-story windows. However, by the time that neo-Palladian taste became established in the 1720s, more and more buildings began to be built in a manner that reflected the social hierarchy of floor levels.[31] The largest openings were on the second story, lighting the principal public spaces, while the apertures for the bedchamber and service floors above graduated proportionally in size to reflect their private and subservient roles.

Classical proportioning permeated the Chesapeake but was shaped in ways that reflected local conditions. Most colonists lived in one-story dwellings, so the hierarchy of aperture openings had little application. Those few planters and merchants who chose to build two-story dwellings varied from the metropolitan standard by choosing to maintain the ground floor as the principal story. With the kitchen, laundry, pantry, and other domestic functions relegated to detached structures, there was no need to raise the entertaining rooms above a full-height service floor. Bacon's Castle, Stratford, and the second-period wing at Green Spring were rare exceptions (see Fig. 6.18). Two-story dwellings erected by the second quarter of the eighteenth century almost invariably have larger apertures on the ground floor with smaller openings lighting the bedchamber story above.[32]

In a much more subtle way, the facades of Chesapeake houses exhibited regional preferences. The percentage of openings to wall mass was much lower in the Chesapeake than in London and in other American colonies (Fig. 5.8). Two dozen gentry houses erected in Maryland and Virginia in the half century before the American Revolution had door and window openings that composed between 12 and 30 percent of the front facade between the water table and the cornice. On average, 19 percent of the facade was pierced by apertures. By comparison, the percentage represented by the openings in the front facade of houses of the same period and size in Massachusetts ranged from 24 to 33 percent, with a mean average of 28 percent. Houses in or near Philadelphia had a slightly higher percentage, ranging from 22 to 38 percent, with the average being 32 percent.[33] In contrast, town houses and individual houses in London during the same period were built with apertures that composed between 25 and 40 percent of the entire facade. Although there may be a slight chronological trend toward a smaller ratio of void to solid in the metropolis in the latter part of the century, no such variation appears in the Chesapeake sample.[34] Climatic differences may have had some influence. English buildings may have been calibrated to accommodate more light in rooms for a variety of reasons. In some cases, town houses were more difficult to light because of shared party walls, so those windows on the street and rear facades had to suffice. A colder climate with more diffuse sunlight probably argued for larger windows as well. However, larger windows meant a greater loss of heat during winter months. Concomitantly, the hot climate of Virginia argued against a superabundance of apertures that would fill rooms with additional heat. Economic and aesthetic factors also affected differences between

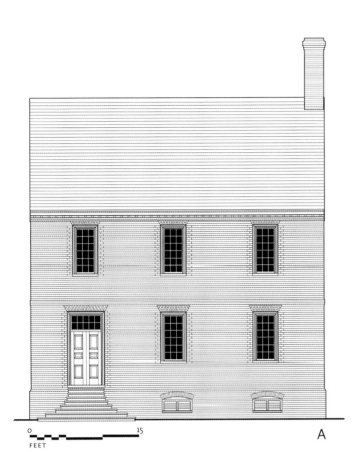

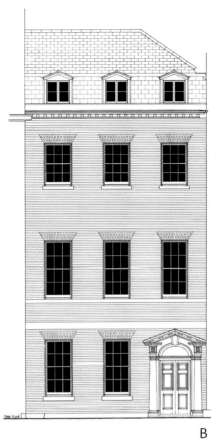

Fig. 5.8. In general, the front facades of most Virginia houses had a much smaller ratio of door and window openings to wall mass than facades in London. A: Palmer House, Williamsburg, c. 1755; B: 43 Parliament Street, London, 1753, after Cruickshank and Wyld, London: The Art of Georgian Building (1975). (Courtesy of Dan Cruickshank)

0 ... 15
FEET

A

B

English and Chesapeake standards. Glass, lead, and paint were costly imports to the colonies. The expense of labor to fabricate brick arches, rubbed openings, sash, and glazing, usually calculated by the square foot or square yard, also had an impact in the long run on the way colonists thought about the design of their houses. Local social customs in this case overshadowed metropolitan design trends.

Public architecture, too, saw the adaptation of English Palladian design to match the Chesapeake experience. Anglican vestrymen in eastern Virginia and parts of southern Maryland used the British tradition of large-scale apertures to light parish churches. Following the Great Fire in London in 1666, Christopher Wren updated church design in a classical style, making compass-headed, segmental, circular, oval, and Venetian windows standard forms in his many designs. By the late seventeenth century, compass-headed windows became part of ambitious church designs, as can still be seen in the west towers of the Newport Parish and Jamestown churches.[35] In order to accentuate their public nature, church openings were scaled in proportion to the pitch of the walls.[36] Rather than constructing a double tier of domestic-size windows, as was common in churches and meetinghouses throughout the mid-Atlantic and New England, Virginia vestrymen choose to build a single set of large openings. For example, the walls of Williamsburg's Bruton

Church stand 19 feet high between the water table and the cornice and are punctuated by a single band of compass-headed windows that measure 5 feet in width and 12 feet in height.

SYMMETRY

Along with proportion, symmetry was an integral part of classical design. It was considered by theorists to be the balance and harmony of constituent elements with each other and as a whole. The term "symmetry" derived from the Greek and was used in the colonial period in much the same manner as "proportion" to describe the comparative relationship of various parts in terms of magnitude, position, and quantity. The notion of symmetry governed the placement of one building in relation to another, but also regulated the pattern of ornament in a decorative element. It imbued a design with a consciously structured effect that, when done well, evoked a sense of naturalness or repose, an attribute much prized in eighteenth-century America.

Out of these general connotations, the term could be more narrowly applied to describe what English architect Isaac Ware called "respective symmetry," now referred to as "bilateral symmetry," wherein elements reflect a mirror image on either side of an imaginary center line. The con-

Fig. 5.9. Small house at Walnut Valley showing the placement of the door and window openings on the front facade, 1815, Surry County, Virginia.

scious application of this kind of symmetry was pervasive in the layout of cities, the plan of formal gardens, the appearance of facades, and the arrangement of rooms and elements within them. It helped define the hierarchical relationship of buildings and elements by defining an axis or central focus around which elements were arranged. Contemporary fashion encouraged the creation of a forecourt at the Governor's Palace in Williamsburg, but it was bilateral symmetry that gave pattern to the space with a pair of matching offices flanking a central walk (see Fig. 2.1C). Even if only one office was functionally necessary, symmetry required a second one, and their subordinate position and smaller size served to accentuate the significance of the main house.

Although its impact was ubiquitous, it was seldom rigidly applied, as some aspects of building and the use of spaces refused to lend themselves to its implied rules. For example, variations appear in the manner in which apertures were laid out in building facades. Not all windows and doors were evenly spaced on a facade, and bilateral symmetry was given short shrift in some buildings. A subtle manipulation of symmetry occurred in some Virginia parish churches, where the long wall windows did not line up opposite one another but were staggered slightly in some places to accommodate the placement of the pulpit against one wall or the chancel door in the other. A number of structures followed older rules of locating doors and windows in places where they best suited the function of the room or building, with any concern for a symmetrical arrangement being entirely secondary.

This more traditional design logic is evident in many one-room dwelling houses, especially those that were timber-framed, where angled wall braces and major posts often dictated the location of apertures. In the Chesapeake, wood dwellings that were between 16 and 22 feet in length often contained a door and a single window on the front facade. Carpenters generally did not place the door opening in the center of the facade but located it slightly off center. One of the doorjambs often marked the centerline of the wall. This is where a doorpost, often the only large intermediary post between the two corner posts, was located. The door was hung off the post. If there was a window in this facade, it was located one or two studs distant from that center doorpost in the other half of the facade that was not pierced by the door opening. This pattern is evident in the small house at Walnut Valley on the south side of the James River, where the front and rear facades are identical, with a door and window lighting the one-room ground floor (Fig. 5.9).[37]

(above) Fig. 5.10. *George Reid House, late eighteenth century, Williamsburg.*

(below) Fig. 5.11. *Plans. A: George Reid House; B: George Wythe House.*

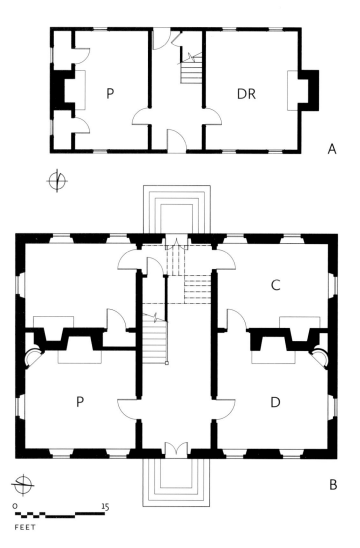

Even in larger houses, the arrangement of openings was sometimes dictated by internal considerations of the plan, which mitigated or violated rules of bilateral symmetry on the outside. The George Reid House in Williamsburg is a late eighteenth-century, one-story, center-passage frame dwelling with an asymmetrical front facade (Figs. 5.10, 5.11A). Although the center of the doorway splits the length of the house evenly, the front wall has only three windows. One is located on one side of the door and two are on the other, an arrangement that also appears on the rear facade. The symmetry is disturbed even further by the fact that one gable-end chimney is internal and the other is external. While two dormers line up with a window and center door, the third falls between a pair of windows.

Inside the Reid House, the placement of the windows is prescribed by the plan. Although the two ground-floor rooms are of equal size, the one with the internal chimney has a pair of closets in line with the front of the fireplace opening, making the room smaller in size than the one on the other side of the passage. The single window lighting this smaller room is centered between the gable-end wall and the passage wall. With the closets, it appears slightly off center in the room. In the larger room, the pairs of windows on the

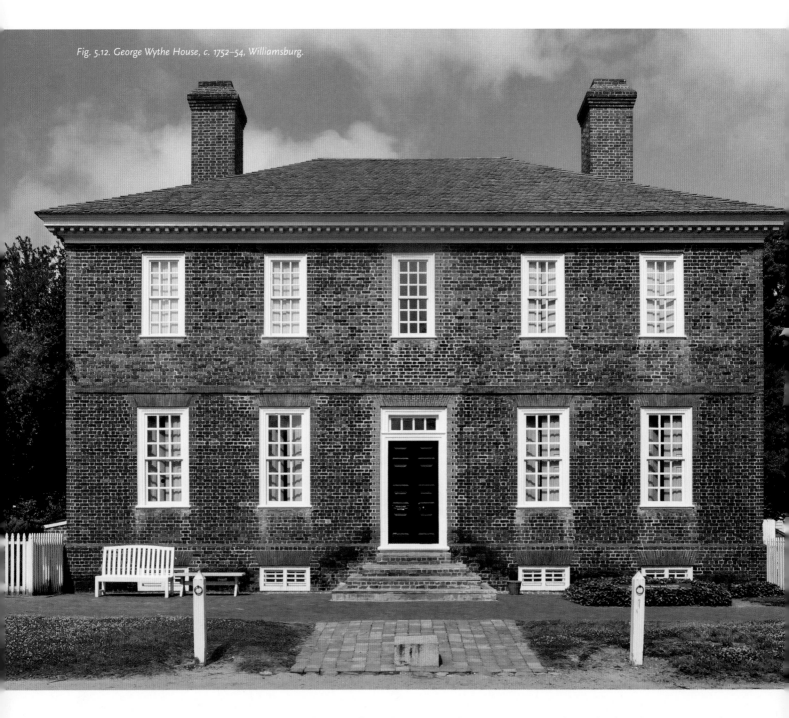

Fig. 5.12. *George Wythe House, c. 1752–54, Williamsburg.*

front and rear facades are spaced the same distance from the gable-end wall and the partition wall. From the contiguous wall to the leading edge of the window jamb, the space is 2½ feet, which also matches the width of the openings themselves. The spacing between the two windows in this room is 5 feet, or twice the window width or the same distance as the window combined with the corner spacing. The logic of this internal symmetry, however, is not to be seen on the exterior, which reads as an irregular facade.

Window placement was often a negotiation between the needs of the plan and the desire for exterior balance. The arrangement of windows in dwellings with center passages and flanking rooms of unequal size proved challenging.

Windows were commonly pushed as close to internal partition walls as possible for the sake of the rhythmic harmony of the exterior. The one-story Powell House in Williamsburg appears to have a symmetrical facade on its front elevation with two windows on either side of the front door. In fact, the doorway was built slightly off center to allow one of the inner windows to be placed within the center passage. Even by moving the window closer to the doorway, the rest of the windows are not evenly spaced. An offset center passage at Westover also incorporates a window within the passage so that one of the major entertaining rooms is lit by three windows and the smaller one opposite it contains two, but the openings are regularly aligned (see Figs. 3.7, 7.19B).

In buildings where exterior symmetry was paramount, craftsmen strove to hide visual irregularities near the center or at the corners, compensating by devising wider widths of wall panel in the end bays or on either side of the central doorway. Sometimes the pattern was carefully worked out so that all the solids between the apertures were the same width, as was the case at two Williamsburg houses—the Everard House, a five-bay frame dwelling (1718–20), and the more pretentious two-story Wythe House (see Figs. 3.8, 3.9) (Figs. 5.11B, 5.12). The front facade determined their placement. On the side elevations, plan dictated their location. At the Wythe House, a single window lights the side wall in each of the two front rooms. The window is centered on the inside in the straight length of the side wall between the front corner and the beginning of the framing of a corner buffet that sits at an angle between the side wall and the internal fireplace wall. In the smaller back rooms, the side window is centered between the rear facade and the partition wall separating the front and rear rooms. Such was the resolution of this design, that from the outside, the two windows on the side elevations are located exactly the same distance from the corners as the end windows on the front and rear elevations.

HIERARCHY OF ORNAMENTATION

As in the past, the response to this new style of design coalesced into a regional pattern that distinguished and limited the decorative treatment of a building into a few predictable forms. Fundamental to the development of design schemes was the correlation between the quality of a space and its social importance. For those who devised plans for a dwelling, tobacco house, or church, the layout and interrelationship of spaces created an intrinsic logic of emphasis of detailing. Those buildings or rooms that Chesapeake colonists considered symbolically or socially important were given the most elaborate decorative treatment, with fancier woodwork and finishes than secondary structures or spaces. In a dwelling, public entertaining rooms such as a parlor or dining room were inherently more important than a bedchamber or dressing room. It was the place where the status of the family was on display. The superior status of the room dictated that it receive a far richer treatment of details compared to the relative simplicity of the subsidiary rooms. Similarly, a kitchen played a much more important role in the life of a family than did the woodshed or a workroom.

The hierarchy of space also worked vertically, as the best spaces appeared generally on the ground floor, with subsidiary work and storage spaces located below the main floor

and secondary bedchambers placed above. Only in Annapolis did some late colonial merchant houses eschew this trend, containing second-story *piano nobiles*. Otherwise, in the most imposing structures, this hierarchy was expressed through the use of different materials or in the scale of apertures. When first constructed, the basement of Stratford was devoted to dry and wet storage, and the brickwork at this level differs dramatically from that of the main floor above. Laid with larger bricks and wider mortar joints than the story above, the basement appears as a solid, rusticated foundation that supports the main living space. As in many other buildings, the segmental arches of the basement apertures contrast with the more refined gauged-and-rubbed, flat jack arches of the windows above, yet another visual clue as to the relative significance of the two stories.

DRAWINGS

With the growing specialization of room functions and building types and the increasing elaboration of finishes, the language of building required more explicit instructions. In the late colonial period, contracts became far more detailed in order to cover the myriad choices made by clients. On more ambitious structures, written explanations and basic drawings were essential in order to avoid misunderstandings among the contracting parties. It is no coincidence that architectural drawings first appear in the region in the late seventeenth century, when new ideas about plan, form, and finishes forced clients, committees, and craftsmen to think about design beyond traditional ways.

Because architectural drawings have formed the basic means of communicating design ideas for so long, it may be hard to imagine their novelty in colonial America. Many individuals simply did not understand drafting conventions or the abstract ideas they communicated about scale, circulation, and lighting. George Washington, for example, confessed his "unaccustomedness to drawings" in a letter to a craftsman who had sent him a plan of proposed decorative work for Mount Vernon.[38] Few drawings have survived from the colonial period since they were considered as little more than ephemeral aids in the design process that were tossed aside after construction began or the project reached a successful conclusion. Nearly all drawings that may have once accompanied contracts for the construction of private dwellings have disappeared. A handful exist for civic projects—courthouses and prisons—which, because of their public nature, were preserved in official court records. Some were drawn to scale with a considerable degree of accuracy, while others were more hastily penned with the aid of no drafting

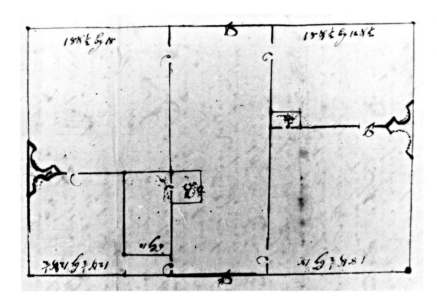

Fig. 5.13. Richard King, drawing for a house, 1719, Yorktown. (Pole Papers, Clerk's Office, Northampton County, Virginia)

equipment or straightedge, with the dimensions scrawled across the paper (see Fig. 2.1D).

Sometimes public building committees, formed to oversee the design, construction, or repair of a courthouse or church, called on craftsmen or contractors to supply drawings for new work. The Reverend Patrick Henry and members of the vestry of St. Peter's Parish in New Kent County agreed with builder William Walker in 1740 to erect a steeple and vestry room according to a plan "drawn by the said Walker."[39] The vestry of St. Andrew's Parish in St. Mary's County paid Richard Boulton £5 "for drawing a plan" of a new brick church in 1767.[40] Both Walker and Boulton contracted with the respective parishes to build their designs, but on a few occasions building committees commissioned drawings from individuals who did not undertake the work. On the whole, these individuals were well-known craftsmen and undertakers who lived nearby.

By the end of the eighteenth century, a few individuals began to advertise their design services. Besides contracting work, the firm of James Hogan, George M'Cutchan and Company, "Architects and Builders," formerly of Dublin but operating in the growing town of Baltimore in 1784, provided "plans, elevations and estimates, for any building."[41] The following year, Joseph Clark of Annapolis claimed a similar range of skills, boasting especially of his competence in composing designs and drawing "plans, elevations and sections of buildings of all kinds in civil architecture."[42] While these and other men emphasized their facility with drafting equipment, none lived entirely by their design work but depended upon their skills as artisans and contractors. Benjamin Latrobe was the first person in the region to make a self-conscious break with this tradition and establish a career based solely on his design skills.

Throughout the colonial period, most drawings used in the design process were floor plans, or "plats," as they were sometimes known in the late seventeenth and early eighteenth centuries (Fig. 5.13). They provided a means for all those involved in devising the design of a building to settle upon the placement of doors, windows, chimneys, and partitions. In the case of churches and courthouses, plans also located the shape and position of built-in fittings, such as pews, pulpits, altar rails, magistrates' benches, sheriff's boxes, and lawyers' bars. Elevations appear to have been less common. They provided an overall appearance of a building, showing the height of the walls and roof and the size of apertures, and may have been a handy means for estimating construction costs. Even rarer were sections that illuminated the vertical relationship of elements within the building, such as a roof frame, ceiling, and floor level. Craftsmen devised them for particularly unusual circumstances—detailing the construction of a novel roof truss or locating the arch of a compass roof. Such a drawing clarified the intentions of the magistrates in a Virginia county whose 1765 specifications for a prison called for walls of triple thickness, to be capped by a solid brick vaulted roof covered with clapboards.[43]

Drawings and agreements paid careful attention to those matters where there was a range of forms, details, materials, and workmanship to consider. New elements that might eventually capture the imagination of a client had to be described in some detail at first. If accepted, over time they too would become part of the standard repertoire, requiring less comment in contractual agreements. The tripartite Venetian window with a large central arched section flanked by narrower square-headed openings was unknown in Chesapeake architecture before the second quarter of the eighteenth century. Because of its complexity, the window became a showpiece used to adorn the east windows of English parish churches, public buildings such as town halls, and stair windows in dwellings of some pretense. One of the first appearances of the form in the Chesapeake was in an Anglican church in Maryland. The 1733 specifications for St. Paul's, Baden, called for a small three-part window in the west gable end at gallery level. In the east end of the church above the communion table, there was to be "a Large Window in three Lights the middle Light Eight feet high and three feet wide in the Clear the two side Lights seven feet four Inches high and two feet wide in the Clear."[44] These two windows were illustrated in a number of drawings associated with the design, which have since been lost, making it difficult to determine their precise shape. It is not clear from the specifications whether the central element of these three-part windows was to be compass-headed or whether the entire window was encased in a single frame beneath a large relieving arch. Since the west gable has been rebuilt and the east window heavily reworked, it is impossible to tell from existing evidence. The vestry reused the same specifications for the design of St. Thomas, Croom, in 1742.[45] Unfortunately, this church too has lost evidence for the Venetian windows in the east and west walls due to later alterations. The Venetian window was no longer a novelty in the Chesapeake by midcentury. When the vestry in Maryland's Trinity Parish agreed with builder John Ariss to construct a new church in 1752, the specifications simply called for "a Window at the Altar piece after ye Venetian Fashion" and made no reference to any drawings of the form, since it had become a staple in Anglican church design in Maryland.[46]

AGENTS OF CHANGE: CRAFTSMEN

There were three conduits through which architectural forms and design ideas filtered into the Chesapeake. First and foremost, there were the skilled craftsmen—carpenters, joiners, cabinetmakers, brickmakers, masons, and stone-carvers, who were trained in Britain and immigrated to the Chesapeake. From earliest settlement in the first decade of the seventeenth century through the years leading up to the American Revolution, and even afterward, there was a steady stream of craftsmen who decided to take their chances in the New World. Each generation brought with them the latest architectural fashions, along with their knowledge of the "art and mystery" of their craft. They carried their English tools and their understanding of how they were to be used to give form to the new classical design vocabulary. A few had training and experience far beyond what could be obtained in the colonies. London-trained carver James Wilson not only

Fig. 5.14. William Buckland, 1734–74. Portrait by Charles Willson Peale. (Yale University Art Gallery, Mabel Brady Garvan Collection)

brought his skills as a wood-carver to Williamsburg in the mid-1770s, but he also fabricated "all Kinds of Ornaments in stucco, human Figures and flowers, &c. Stucco Cornishes in Plaster, carved or plain, after the best Manner" of metropolitan fashion.[47] Although only twenty-eight years old when he left Glasgow, Scottish joiner Robert Robinson had already labored several years in Edinburgh and Kelso and had supervised the construction of a church in Inverness.[48] Others were young men just at the beginnings of their careers, who, no doubt, looked to the labor-starved Chesapeake as a place where they could exercise their trades without the restrictions of an entrenched guild system or too much competition. Perhaps spotting an opportunity for quick advancement, twenty-one-year-old William Buckland, a native of Oxford who had just finished several years of apprenticeship as a joiner in London, took up an offer in 1755 to supervise the interior finishes at Gunston Hall for George Mason (Fig. 5.14).[49]

A number of craftsmen had no choice about emigrating but were transported to Maryland and Virginia after being convicted of crimes at home. Vessels unloaded their human cargo of convict servants at ports across the region. Carpenters, blacksmiths, bricklayers, painters, plasterers, and stonemasons found themselves placed on the auction block, where their services for the next three or four years were sold to the highest bidder. Houses such as Stratford, Shirley, and Mount Vernon were built and finished in part by the skills of convict craftsmen.[50] William Buckland supplemented the versatility of his contracting business in the 1760s and early 1770s by purchasing the indentures of joiners, plasterers, and carvers from this stream of skilled labor, as well as indentured servants who had not run afoul of the law. Though he ran the risk of supervising a shop of recalcitrant workmen, many of whom took the opportunity to flee his service, Buckland must have prized their sometimes highly developed skills and knowledge of the latest London styles.[51] In a 1771 letter in which he tried to entice his wealthy neighbor Robert Carter III into transforming Nomini Hall into a stylish summer residence, Buckland claimed to have "Some of the Best Workmen in Virginia among whom is a London Carver a masterly Hand."[52]

While Carter did not rise to Buckland's bait, other members of the gentry on the Northern Neck of Virginia and merchants in Annapolis were more than willing to turn this ambitious builder loose on their houses, giving him a wide latitude to explore English Palladian design motifs at places like Gunston Hall, Mount Airy (original interiors now lost), the Hammond-Harwood House, and the Chase-Lloyd House (see Figs. 7.20, 7.24). Buckland and his shop of craftsmen ornamented these dwellings with enriched moldings, carved mantels and stairs, and decorative details rare to most Potomac River plantations. He supervised the construction of a few compact houses that explored the use of polygonal bays in the manner reminiscent of the Thames River villas of Robert Taylor. In a series of design vignettes discovered on the back of a window architrave at Gunston Hall, Buckland pushed his penchant for polygonal forms in a plan for the Prince William County Courthouse, partly succeeding in moving the traditional rectangular Virginia courthouse plan in a new direction.[53]

For all his novelty, Buckland chose, perhaps on the insistence of his clients, to integrate his work with regional practices, especially in terms of plan. Through the influence of local bricklayers, he also incorporated a number of distinctive Maryland features in his Annapolis designs, including the use of pilastered facades (see Fig. 7.25). His English-trained craftsmen might introduce a new detail for a turned baluster, but in general they produced raised panel wainscoting, ogee-shaped bench brackets, and double architraves that were indistinguishable from their British or New England counter-

parts. This architectural DNA of classical design permeated all corners of the British Empire. The manner in which these elements were used and combined, however, was determined by local circumstances, which gave rise to the formation of distinctive regional patterns.

AGENTS OF CHANGE: BRITISH PRECEDENTS

A second conduit for the spread of metropolitan ideas was through ordinary colonists, crown officials, and Anglican ministers, who may have had an acute sense of design or a heightened consciousness of the dwellings, public buildings, commercial structures, and furnishings of their genteel acquaintances, kinsfolk, and business associates. A few elite, native-born colonists traveled to England to receive an education, conduct business, or even visit relatives. Although most never set out to deliberately study aristocratic houses, castles, gardens, and churches for design details, their travels shaped or reinforced more general ideas about architectural aesthetics. In 1750, William Beverley and a coterie of fellow Virginians combined sightseeing with business that took them from Yorkshire to London. Along the way, they visited York Minster and Beverley Minster and "viewed Chatsworth a noble house." In London, Beverley and John Carlyle of Alexandria "dined at Majr F[airfa]x's house which is beautiful & had a kind entertainment & he carried us to ye play house [at] Covent Garden," an evening that allowed them to muse on the different settings and modes of genteel levity.[54]

Whether Chesapeake natives or British born, Anglican clerics traveled to Lambeth Palace in the capital to be ordained by the Bishop of London, whose diocese encompassed the American colonies. The Reverend Jacob Henderson of St. Barnabas in Maryland claimed a familiarity with the ecclesiastical structures of the metropolis and reckoned his own church to be "as decent as any in London that I have seen & I have been in most great churches."[55] If visitors and immigrants did not possess the technical knowledge of tradesmen or were not even keen students of design, they certainly understood from what they saw the symbolic significance of an arcade, cupola, or compass-headed window and the appropriate architectural settings for public and private display. Embedded in their memories were conceptual models of dwellings, civic structures, churches, and gardens.

Even if they had never traveled to Britain, literate residents of the Chesapeake read the latest novels and newspaper accounts, exchanged letters, and generally kept abreast of social currents in the mother country. Augmenting this descriptive view of the British landscape were visual images—prints and other graphic sources, which ranged from topographical subjects to satires on social mores. They illustrated street scenes and drawing rooms, real places and imaginative settings, many of which recorded contemporary architectural fashions.[56] Prints from Hogarth and less well-known artists were sold across the Chesapeake region by booksellers and storekeepers.[57] Whether tacked to the walls of taverns or hung in frames in gentry houses, images of the metropolis and Britain permeated the far reaches of the empire.[58]

AGENTS OF CHANGE: ARCHITECTURAL BOOKS

Architectural books provided a third source for the transfer of design ideas to the Chesapeake. Beginning in the late seventeenth century, English publishers produced scores of books—large portfolios of design drawings by noted architects, scholarly treatises on the classical orders, topographical guides to the ruins of ancient Rome, pocketbook manuals for measuring materials.[59] From the early eighteenth century, but especially after about 1740, the number and variety of publications devoted to building increased in Maryland and Virginia as well as in the rest of the American colonies.[60] A few were expensive folios that primarily contained plans and elevations of aristocratic houses on a scale far beyond any Chesapeake grandee's dreams. Because of their cost and their content, most of these volumes appeared in the libraries of planters and merchants, not in those of contractors or craftsmen, and provided little in the way of practical advice about building methods or useful information about building design. Rarely did owners mine these treatises as guides for building. Except for a few notable exceptions—Thomas Jefferson being one—the architectural education gained from costly English, French, and Italian books on design, topography, and aesthetics more closely resembled antiquarian scholarship. It was simply one part of the curriculum of a gentleman's classical education.

Smaller builder's books reached a broader audience. They generally described methods of proportioning and the laying out of difficult elements such as stairs, arches, and roof frames and contained a number of plates illustrating display elements such as frontispieces, chimneypieces, and staircases. Planters and merchants bought these books, often to ascertain if their craftsmen were overcharging them compared to standard London rates.[61] On occasion, individuals purchased or borrowed these books specifically to inform their building projects. They may have consulted the catalog of illustrations to convey to their joiner or carver an image of what they had in mind for a staircase or a stair bracket. In 1747, lawyer and planter John Mercer bought four architectural books as he began the construction of Marlborough on Potomac Creek. He promptly loaned the books to Fairfax County joiner William Bromley, who was hired in 1748 to finish the interior woodwork of the house. Bromley spent two years in Mercer's employment fitting out the interior woodwork, perhaps taking his cue from the many illustrations in these publications.[62]

Although few studied these books as carefully as Thomas Jefferson, Chesapeake gentlemen occasionally assimilated the instructive comments about the appropriate forms and use of the classical orders that invariably prefaced the illustrations. Batty Langley offered his *Workman's Treasury of Designs* "for the common Good of all *Men of Reason*, whose Business require the Knowledge of this Art," which included not only craftsmen but also clients such as the building committees that supervised the design and construction of public buildings.[63] In 1771, members of the vestry of Truro Parish in Fairfax County must have read Langley, for they noticed that the dimensions of the altarpiece erected in Pohick Church were "not according to the proportions of Architecture" and that Daniel French, the undertaker, was "authorized and desired to make the same according to the true proportions of the Ionic order."[64]

Building books circulated more widely among tradesmen. Major contractors and specialist craftsmen such as plasterers, carvers, and joiners purchased or borrowed these books to inform their own design vocabulary or to lure prospective clients to invest in a novel feature.[65] Some craftsmen received their only formal education in the classical orders by studying these inexpensive builder's manuals. Most books illustrated the five ancient orders, explicated the grammar of classical design, and provided useful information on mensuration. A few instructed craftsmen on the manner of laying out multicentered arches or framing steeples, tasks that they encountered rarely in their building careers. At the very least, craftsmen received the rudiments of English Palladian philosophy concerning the hierarchical arrangement and massing of buildings, the appropriate use of ornament, and the rules governing the proportioning of individual elements.

William Buckland owned at least fourteen books, including titles by Batty Langley, William Salmon, Robert Morris, Abraham Swan, and Isaac Ware, who were among the most popular authors of this genre.[66] Buckland's collection was extraordinarily large by Chesapeake standards, as such books were by no means commonplace. Most craftsmen probably never owned any at all, and those who did generally had only one or two in their possession. However, some books may have circulated among craftsmen, as John Mercer's loan to William Bromley suggests.

Both the authors and the consumers of these books had no illusions that the illustrations of chimneypieces, staircases, pulpits, doorways, and house plans should be copied with absolute fidelity. Rather they saw them as inspirations for improvisation. In *A Book of Architecture* (1728), James Gibbs published a collection of designs that he thought might "be of use to such Gentlemen as might be concerned in Building, especially in the remote parts of the Country, where little or no assistance for Designs can be procured. Such may be here furnished with Draughts of useful and convenient Buildings and proper Ornaments; which may be executed by any Workman who understands Lines, either as here Design'd, or with some alteration, which may be easily made by a person of Judgment."[67] As Gibbs presciently understood, those architectural books that would have the greatest impact on actual design in the Chesapeake and the American colonies were the ones that were most easily adaptable to local requirements, aspirations, and skills.

Many such books contained little more than fanciful concoctions devised by men such as Abraham Swan and William

Pain, whose lack of experience, Benjamin Latrobe observed, had "given them leisure to speculate, and to build *castles in the Air*."[68] In *British Architect* (1745), Swan offered "a great variety of new and curious chimney-pieces, in the most elegant and modern taste," to suit every client's aesthetic preference. Most of the designs, with their swirling foliage and enriched moldings, however, found little favor among the few tobacco planters and merchants who could afford to lavish money on vigorously carved chimneypieces. An ingenious carver such as William Bernard Sears, who had worked with William Buckland at Gunston Hall in the late 1750s, reworked one of Swan's fanciful designs for George Washington at Mount Vernon in the mid-1770s.[69] For the small dining room chimneypiece, Sears eliminated the scrolled pediment that crowned the original design and flattened the proportions of the overmantel and firebox so that it would fit the height of the room (Fig. 5.15). Although he followed the pattern of ornamentation in Swan's design, he removed the foliage that projected across the side backbands of the overmantel frame, added a dentilated course below the shelf, and

liberally altered the foliage details but yet remained faith-
ful to the overall form of the foliage. In 1773, the vestry in
Washington's parish of Truro specified that mason William
Copein was "to make a stone font for the Church according
to a Draught in the 150th plate of Langleys Designs being the
uppermost on the left hand."[70] Such an explicit reference is
extremely rare in the records of the early Chesapeake. Most
documents are quite silent on issues of design precedents.
Even with such clear instructions, Copein modified the font
design, adding an extra ring of moldings around the lower
part of the bowl.

Much of the architectural history that has been written
about early America has asserted the primacy of architectural
books in communicating ideas among builders and their clients. In the first scholarly overview of colonial architecture,
published in 1922, Fiske Kimball argued that "the adoption
of the new style came about in America in the same way in
which it did . . . in England: through the making of its form
universally accessible to intelligent workmen, or even, laymen, by means of books."[71] Historians since Kimball have
exhausted these books hunting down precedents for various
Chesapeake buildings and their details—to little avail.[72]

Thomas Waterman claimed a design in Gibbs's *A Book of
Architecture* as the prototype for the south facade of Mount

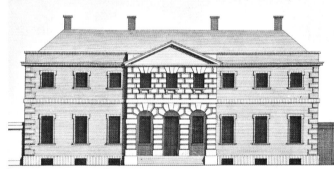

(top) Fig. 5.16. *South facade, Mount Airy, 1760–64, Richmond County, Virginia.*

(bottom) Fig. 5.17. *"A Design for a Gentleman in Dorsetshire," Plate 58, James
Gibbs,* A Book of Architecture *(London, 1728).*

Airy, John Tayloe's residence on the Rappahannock River,
built in the early 1760s.[73] He asserted that the rusticated
and arcaded central three bays corresponded closely to plate
58, "A Design for a Gentleman in Dorsetshire," except that
the height of the second story had been enlarged in the Virginia design (Figs. 5.16, 5.17). From *Vitruvius Scoticus*, he
discerned an elevation for Haddo House, a seven-bay dwelling with a projecting central pedimented block connected
to flanking offices by curved covered ways, as the inspiration
for Mount Airy's north front. Unfortunately, the latter had
not been published when Tayloe was contemplating his new

house, thus making the Haddo design purely coincidental and indicative of the universality of many elements in the Anglo-American design vocabulary in the mid-eighteenth century.[74]

The Gibbs design seems a much more plausible attribution, but Waterman did not pursue the question of why Tayloe chose this unusual form for his dwelling. How did he come across a copy of Gibbs's design in the first place? Did he own a copy of the book or was he shown one by a neighbor or a builder? Did he discuss the design with neighbors or friends?[75] What was it about this thirty-year-old design that appealed to the Richmond County tobacco planter, businessman, and avid horseman? Tayloe's selection of a design with an arcade was novel for domestic architecture in the region where such a form had a long association with public building. What motivated Tayloe to look beyond standard practices? Perhaps the rhythmic quality of the nearby double-arcaded Richmond County Courthouse, erected in 1750 by Tayloe's neighbor Landon Carter of Sabine Hall, inspired him to use Plate 58 with its arcaded piazza. Waterman was equally silent in explaining why so few others chose to follow Tayloe's route and crib their house designs from imported books.

Once conditioned to think about architectural precedent in this bookish fashion, it is easy to overlook the complexity of the design process in early America, where plans and elevations seldom moved from illustration to construction site with such ease. Local influences almost always intervened to transform these designs. As Tayloe's friend and mentor Edmund Jennings II had observed from London when told about his design, "Every Scituation & plan must be adapted to ye Country & Climate."[76] Mantels, fonts, and other features may have leapt off the page into Chesapeake buildings, but entire house designs never did. What need did tobacco planters such as Tayloe have for houses of aristocratic proportions or plans that did not match their domestic and public lives? Mount Airy was a house of its place and time, not an abstraction drawn without reference to local conditions. The builder grafted a fragment from an English design book onto a plan that reflected the personal needs and social aspirations of a wealthy tobacco planter on the fringe of the British Empire. The system of ornamentation and the level of elaboration derived from regional building practices that were tempered by the taste and pocketbook of the client. Tayloe built on a massive scale with locally quarried ashlar masonry, an undertaking that was prohibitively expensive to practically everyone else. The copying of an English design precedent with features that had little currency in Chesapeake domestic architecture further emphasized the social gulf that separated Tayloe from his neighbors.

Yet there is more to bookish quotations than social prestige. From a design perspective, many of the academic ideas promoted in these books became integrated into local practices. As in genetic recombination, craftsmen in the Chesapeake reworked the standard Georgian elements to form new models—from a framing system to the hierarchical treatment of room finishes. The combination of plan, patterns of ornamentation, and construction methods invariably reveals a regional tradition. Although the interior of Mount Airy was gutted by fire in the 1840s, surviving fragments of the woodwork suggest that William Buckland, who was employed by Tayloe to finish the interior, must have supervised the fabrication of elaborate ornamentation that stood outside standard models. It is tempting to suggest that many of the showpieces derived from architectural books in Buckland's possession. However, it is just as plausible to ascribe such features to the imagination of his workmen, many of whom were well versed in contemporary forms.

Architectural books may have been a source for new ideas among some builders and clients, but generally most publications that circulated in the Chesapeake in the eighteenth century were often little more than ciphers of contemporary design or exotic improbabilities. The creative capacity of the carver and joiner had not been superseded entirely by images from the printed page. It is simply much more difficult to document the ephemeral act of design at the workbench than it is to trace a form in published sources. If the case for the significance of architectural books in the Chesapeake in the eighteenth century has been overstated in the past, they were still by no means marginal in the spread of architectural knowledge. They made a modest contribution to the diffusion of contemporary ideas about proportioning and the proper use and detailing of the architectural orders. Finally, they did provide the source for fanciful display elements such as carved chimneypieces and frontispieces that found their way into the dwellings of a few planters such as John Tayloe and the merchants who provided William Buckland with his livelihood in Annapolis in the early 1770s.

❖ The design process in the early Chesapeake was very different from the one that has been portrayed by earlier scholars. It involved a far more complex interaction between metropolitan examples and inspirations and regional practices than previously acknowledged. The transatlantic connection was imperfect. The American colonies were simply too far away and too different culturally from English society to be merely an unreflective extension of British architectural taste. As early as the second quarter of the seventeenth century, the economic and social exigencies of the emerging Chesapeake tobacco-growing economy spurred the establishment of distinctive building practices based on the simplified carpentry of earthfast construction. The plantation culture that evolved pared down the English inheritance by reducing plan forms to a few types that worked best and that exploited the plentiful supply of timber and the concomitant shortage of hardware and high cost of masonry to build in wood in ways that diverged from English methods. Those practices became the norm over the next century, and new design ideas, forms, and details, as Benjamin Latrobe discovered in Norfolk, had to overcome or fit into the "prejudices and obstinacy" of those traditional ways of envisaging and constructing buildings.

The impact and spread of novelty on traditional ways of thinking about building design and finishes depended upon a variety of circumstances and the intermingling of complex social, economic, environmental, and technological factors. Some new ideas were readily accepted; a few were quickly rejected; still others were altered to accommodate local practices. Changes in the layout of basic house forms signaled fundamental shifts in the way people worked, cooked, dined, entertained, and slept in their dwellings. Aesthetics, too, played an important role in shaping architectural form, especially when individuals began to perceive of their buildings as prestigious commodities, hallmarks of their social aspirations. By the late seventeenth century, the English in-terpretation of Renaissance classicism served as the model for new design. Skilled contractors, carpenters, joiners, carvers, and bricklayers grasped its fundamental rules and details and translated this knowledge into building practices that matched their clients' needs and ambitions. Construction methods and patterns of ornamentation changed significantly over time and developed regional manifestations in the course of those transformations. The interior finish of the first houses built in the new city of Norfolk in the 1690s, with their exposed framing elements, large chamfered manteltrees, and leaded casement windows, contrasted with the wainscoted rooms, decorative chimneypieces, and large sash windows that Latrobe encountered there a century later.

Despite his awkward beginnings with the Norfolk town house, Latrobe eventually became instrumental in reshaping the practice of architecture in his newly adopted country. By the time of his death in 1820, craftsmen were better versed in reading architectural plans and had long experience in running Greek moldings. Workmen grudgingly had come to respect the expertise of the architect in the building process. Yet this watershed in architectural design in the early national era did not entirely eliminate many of the regional building practices that had developed in the colonial period. Latrobe's neoclassicism was but the latest transatlantic wave of academic design to make a splash on the shores of America. Its reception was typical of earlier fashions—a mixed welcome followed by a thorough domestication. Chesapeake builders integrated new forms into their designs and at their workbenches in ways that continually moved regional practices in new directions.

6 *Plantation Housing*

SEVENTEENTH CENTURY

CARY CARSON

Moving house is always disruptive. Moving house across the Atlantic Ocean in the seventeenth century had to be arduous and disorienting, even for willing emigrants; for indentured servants, enslaved Africans, and transported felons, whose destiny lay in other people's hands, the prospects were downright terrifying. Whatever reasons took migrants to the Chesapeake colonies, every new arrival expected that he or she would have to make a new home at the end of the journey, or make do with a home that somebody else would thrust upon him or her. Even that expectation was an illusion to those whose ideas of home were the ones they brought with them. Getting truly settled—in effect, coming to terms with a world full of surprises—took the rest of the seventeenth century in the southern colonies. It required adjustments that no migrants accurately foresaw and that none therefore anticipated. So much was utterly unfamiliar—a staple economy enthralled to tobacco, a punishing agricultural calendar, a coercive labor system, a deadly disease environment, and, as the century drew to a close, a set of new social rules to sort out the haves from the have-nots. The resolution of these challenges to immigrants' traditional Old World customs and practices set the stage for later developments in the architectural culture of the region, the substance of the chapters to follow. The preamble to that story, told here, must come first.

English colonists were traditional peoples no less than were the West African bondsmen who arrived at the same landings by different ships. All were bearers of deeply ingrained, intensely local, folk cultures. Back home, both in England and in Africa, local builders had developed dwellings and farm buildings that housed the distinctive customs by which members of those cultures organized society, maintained family and social relations, and made their living. The structures they had grown up in were the only ones that felt right. No Africans and few Englishmen had ever seen an architectural design book in the seventeenth century, and, while long-distance travelers observed unfamiliar vernacular

buildings in the regions through which they journeyed, these were people whose only experience of architecture was a living experience, a personal experience. English immigrants arrived in the New World expecting sooner or later to replicate the buildings they had left behind and the way of life those buildings had accommodated. They knew nothing else. Still, such hopes often turned out to be "Castles in the Air," in the words of one seasoned observer, who knew from experience that reality was likely to confound the unwary newcomer's most cherished dreams.[1]

Understanding those realities is the first step to understanding how the experience of settling the Chesapeake colonies created new vernacular traditions—the new ways of building buildings and the new ways of living in buildings that are the subjects of this book.

O STRANGE NEW WORLD

Homesteaders on the Chesapeake frontier encountered checks to their expectations everywhere they turned. Even basic building materials were a surprise to many. Virginia and Maryland were prodigiously supplied with timber for those familiar with timber-frame construction in England's wooded regions, but there was next to no stone for the many other immigrants who came from areas where masonry, rubble, and various earthen materials substituted for a severe shortage of buildable timber. Even those for whom an "English fram'd house" was a familiar memory were shocked to discover that professional carpenters were so scarce in the colonies, and so sought after, that they regularly charged three times what carpenters received for the same work in England. Greenhorn settlers soon learned to adjust their expectations downward. "Labor is so intolerably dear," one sadder but wiser homebuilder wrote back to England, "that the building of a good house, to you there will seem insupportable ... notwithstanding we have timber for nothing but the felling & getting in place." Instead, almost everyone made do with houses in which "not one tittle of workmanship" was better than "Tobacco house work."[2] For that matter, newly arrived immigrants were further surprised to observe that established planters had made the cheaply framed "Virginia house" a positive virtue by turning it to their economic advantage. They had to. Transplanted colonists could not look forward to inheriting hand-me-down farmsteads from their fathers and grandfathers. Newcomers had to start from scratch. The savvy ones soon learned to invest their limited resources in the land and labor that promised a quick return. A fully framed dwelling wasted precious capital; a "Virginia house" could help a planter squeak by until he got his feet firmly on the ground. Homesteaders were advised over and over again that "an ordinary House and a good Stock is the Planter's Wisdom."[3]

Unfamiliar building materials, sky-high labor costs, and the economies of homesteading were three realities that altered the hopes of unsuspecting immigrants who fancied that someday they would build a house like those that they and their former neighbors had been accustomed to at home. These were the practical circumstances that influenced the choice of materials and methods of construction that are discussed at length in later chapters. There were other conditions of everyday life in the Chesapeake colonies that challenged settlers' cultural assumptions even more profoundly. They too took a toll on the immigrant's idealized notion of what a house should be and further altered the lives of those who made new homes on the earliest Maryland and Virginia frontiers.

Every immigrant brought along a set of mental house plans, in which the rooms were arranged and furnished to suit the only domestic habits that she or he had ever known. Neighbors in the British Isles had shared many unspoken assumptions about the rightness of those arrangements, despite all the variations that custom and individual circumstances allowed. By contrast, Chesapeake neighbors were likely to be perfect strangers at first, people from some other region in England where vernacular buildings and household customs were notably different. Rival traditions were put to the test in the colonies, not deliberately, of course, and probably not often consciously. The winnowing process was evolutionary. The fittest imported traditions prevailed against less suitable alternatives or, more accurately, adapted most successfully to the unfamiliar circumstances with which every "Virginy-planter" had to cope.[4]

The novelties began with his cash crop—tobacco—which almost no one had grown in England. "King tobacco" was an absolute monarch. It demanded obeisance from a planter's family and field hands every daylight hour during the spring and summer growing seasons to the exclusion of almost all other activities except cultivating food crops. Seasoned planters reckoned that "Sowing, plantinge, weedinge, wormminge, gatheringe, Cureinge, and making up" a planter's annual tobacco crop "consumes tenn monthes at least, if not eleven."[5] Various by-employments and home industries had been activities that English farmhouses and farmsteads had often accommodated, indoors or in specialized service buildings. Because there was little time for such sidelines on the Chesapeake frontier, room was seldom set aside for them on early Chesapeake plantations.

If the tyranny and drudgery of growing tobacco were not reminders enough of the strange new world where planters had come to seek their fortunes, they only had to look across the hominy pot at the inmates with whom they shared their bed and board. Chesapeake households little resembled the family-centered social groupings of blood relations and seasonal help that lived together on most English farmsteads or, for that matter, the extended, women-centered families typical of households in West Africa. The colonies attracted a disproportionate number of young, unmarried males—indentured "four year slaves" from Britain in the first decades and, then increasingly after the 1640s, young African men enslaved for life.[6] Many field hands never found a mate or fathered families. The lucky ones who did, often came to an unlucky end before their time. Exceptionally high mortality rates broke up many young families prematurely, left orphans in the care of guardians, and led to remarriages and broods of half-siblings, either beginning the homesteading cycle all over again or prolonging it into the next generation. Family life, as newcomers remembered it from home, was difficult to replicate for freedmen and unattainable for bondsmen. Just as the absence of various domestic industries subtracted rooms from Virginia and Maryland houses, the presence of so many strangers separated, segregated, and otherwise rearranged people's living quarters on typical Tidewater plantations.

House plans—the arrangement of rooms and the connections between them—usually adjust gradually to people's lives, much as a new shoe slowly conforms to the foot that wears it. A chronology of house planning over several generations can therefore be read as a record of the particular circumstances that reshaped domestic life in the Chesapeake colonies in the seventeenth century. Builders quickly learned to substitute readily available building materials for scarce ones, and they could build bigger and better dwellings as soon as their fortunes improved. But few could escape the cultural amalgam and the hard facts of life and death that quickly began to rearrange familiar English regional house plans into numerous experimental configurations. Little by little, these innovations hardened into a new and different Chesapeake tradition of vernacular architecture before the end of the century.

NEW ARRIVALS

Sea-weary travelers desired a dry roof over their heads more than they wanted comfortable accommodations on making landfall in America. Chronicle writers such as John Winthrop Jr., Captain John Smith, Edmund Plowden, and others describe caves, canvas awnings, and mat-covered wigwams where colonists just off the boat found temporary shelter. But they say not one word about housekeeping in these makeshift hostelries.[7] Several early pit houses excavated at sites along the James River—notably at Flowerdew Hundred and Jamestown—reveal nothing about the arrangement or use of space in these hastily roofed warrens in the ground (Fig. 6.1).[8] Nor does the discovery of two wattle-and-daub cottages built inside the Jamestown Fort of 1607 reveal whether they were partitioned into two or more small rooms; in fact, it is only presumed that they served as barracks-like dwellings (Fig. 6.2).[9] Bodies and baggage were probably squeezed

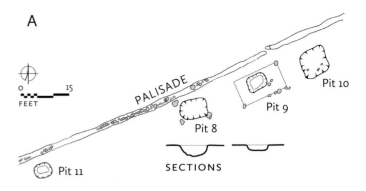

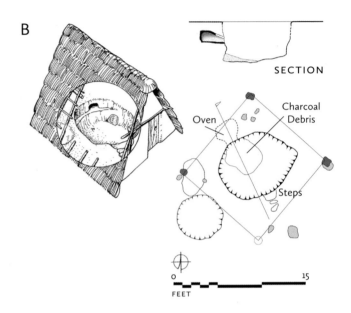

Fig. 6.1. Early pit houses and storage cellars in Virginia. A: "Holes within the ground" used as shelters and maybe storehouses by the builders of James Fort (c. 1607), Jamestown Island, Virginia, after Jamie May and David Givens (Courtesy Jamestown Rediscovery, Preservation Virginia); B: Pit house with clay oven, may have been later used exclusively as a bakehouse, Site 44PG82, feature 3 (c. 1619), Flowerdew Hundred, Prince George's County. (Courtesy of Harrison Institute Archives, University of Virginia Library)

into berths even less commodious than the bunk beds that fitted out so-called guesthouses where later new arrivals to Virginia were said to be housed by 1620—pallets "foure foot broad, six foot long, and two foot height from the ground [stacked one on top of another] in equall distance, and with partitions of Boords between them."[10] The Virginia Company records give us a glimpse of those early bonanza years when company officials could barely keep up with the flood of fortune seekers and indentured servants who needed temporary lodgings. One agent reported to his superiors that he had assigned six servants to one such guesthouse, but, finding it overcrowded, "I have doubled the number of houses and put but three to one hous, and for the new men which

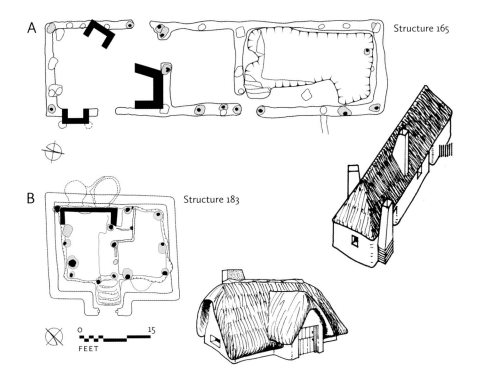

A

Structure 165

B

Structure 183

0 — 15
FEET

Fig. 6.2. Wattle-and-daub barracks and workshops, Jamestown Fort, Structures 165 and 183 phase III, (1607–8), Jamestown Island, Virginia. (Courtesy Jamestown Rediscovery, Preservation Virginia)

are to come, I have already built a guest hous of forty foote long and twentie foot wide to receive them at there first landing."[11] While these company accommodations were probably among the best, they are a reminder that most newcomers roomed temporarily in makeshift shelters until they settled out on landholdings of their own or were quartered by employers.

For enslaved Virginians, and probably for many unmarried servants too, living in barracks continued to be commonplace well into the eighteenth century. A home quarter at Carter's Grove built c. 1750–75 included a structure that was considerably larger than a single family dwelling and may have been a bunkhouse for single men (and maybe women), whose only personal space was the storage lockers they dug into the earthen floor and covered with loose boards (Fig. 6.3A).[12] A generation earlier, Lewis Burwell's neighbor, James Bray III, had converted an old tobacco house or hay barn into a dormitory for a new gang of field hands, whom he probably bought directly from a slaver, judging from their African names (Fig. 6.3B).[13] Hardly better than stabling for animals, the communal quarters intended for enslaved laborers cannot have been much different in the seventeenth century.

Freeholders often fared little better than servants and slaves, but, being their own masters, they had choices. Once out on their own, many greenhorns made a strictly pragmatic decision to start small—to build only a hall, "that Rome

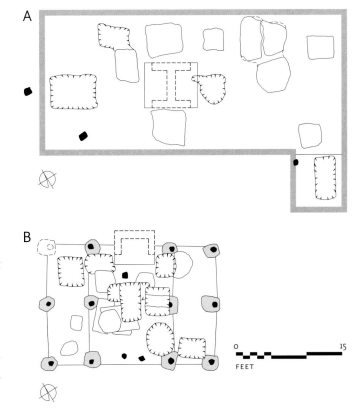

A

B

0 — 15
FEET

Fig. 6.3. Bunkhouse lodgings for slaves or servants. A: Structure 1, c. 1750–75, home quarter, Carter's Grove Plantation, James City County, Virginia. Ground-laid log or frame walls left no archaeological remains. B: Barn converted into dormitory for enslaved field hands, Structure 50, 1730–50, Utopia Quarter, Bray Plantation, James City County, Virginia, showing numerous repairs and additions to the subfloor pits. Hachure marks indicate deeper pits, 12 to 34 inches below earth floor.

which is their Kitchen, their Chamber, their all," as one eye-witness described such cots.[14] It was a choice that landlords and smallholders made over and over again through the end of the eighteenth century, when the first federal tax rolls record thousands of log and frame houses with wooden chimneys, many no larger than 12 by 14 feet.

First-generation immigrants who could afford more than one room usually set about building houses that organized interior space into the same familiar configuration of rooms that had given order to their domestic arrangements back home, wherever those had been. "Homelike" was the word they used to describe those recollections. Predictably therefore, archaeological excavations on dwelling sites occupied in the first half century of settlement in the Chesapeake colonies reveal a wide variety of regional house plans from Britain. The archaeological evidence presents a complex picture, not only because conditions in the Chesapeake forced newcomers to adjust to their new surroundings almost as soon as they arrived, but also because British vernacular building traditions had themselves been yielding to significant social pressures since the sixteenth century. In other words, the idealized models that colonists remembered from home were often already works in progress before they crossed the ocean.

SEGREGATION IN BRITISH FARMHOUSES

Broadly speaking, two cultural developments eroded traditional ideas about farmhouse accommodations in Britain over the course of the seventeenth century. One was a growing preference on the part of profit-seeking farmers to treat field hands and domestic menials as wage earners, not servants to whom they owed bed and board. The other was an inclination to treat themselves as a class apart, as ladies and gentlemen better bred, more refined, and ultimately superior to and therefore deserving to be separate from, the men and maids whom they employed in the barn and the kitchen. This capitalistic outlook on labor and the accompanying spread of gentility among prosperous landowners reordered domestic relations and reorganized household space. These influences were felt sooner in some regions and overseas colonies than in others and differently from place to place, depending on the strength of local customs. The resulting variations account for the several different plan types that newcomers to the Chesapeake colonies built in the first decades of settlement, before the inevitable process of trial and error narrowed the smart choice down to a one-story, two-room, frame house with a detached kitchen.

In England, three long-term trends had combined to drive

servants in husbandry out of their employers' households, where these young, unmarried men and women had traditionally resided for a year at a time, usually from harvest to harvest.[15] The country's steadily growing population, beginning late in the sixteenth century and lasting into the 1650s, created a labor surplus that gave employers opportunities to reduce their operating costs by employing day laborers instead of servants hired on annual contracts. A second trend, a rising cost of living, up sharply until approximately 1650 before it leveled off, reinforced the wisdom of hiring laborers as needed instead of boarding them expensively for twelve months at a time. Finally, wheat prices rose faster than prices for animal products, again until the mid-1650s, thereby rewarding farmers who specialized in growing field crops that required only seasonal labor compared to the graziers and dairy farmers who needed drovers and herders year round.[16] By the end of the century, every careful farmer in Britain understood his choices: "Whether it be better for a Housekeeper to have his Work Manag'd by Day-Labourers, or by [live-in] Domesticks, is a Point likewise of some Consideration in the Oeconomy of a Family." It all came down to pounds and pence: "Domesticks may be a greater Charge, because we are obliged to pay and provide for them, even when they do no Service. . . . Day-Labourers ly more easily upon us, as being paid no longer than they work." Increasingly, until midcentury at least, employers looked to the bottom line and concluded that "'tis better to have Work wanting for our Servants than Servants for our Work."[17]

Laborers hired by the day went home to their own cottages at night. Gradually, the little community of household inmates—farmer, family, and boarding servants—ceased to live side by side from one year to the next. Medieval house plans that had accommodated this domestic menagerie began yielding in the late sixteenth century to a changing social scene that reflected these new economic realities. The hall, a portmanteau space in vernacular houses where all manner of daytime and nighttime activities traditionally took place, was left with less to do when the master of the house no longer presided over a table set for boarders as well as for kinfolk, when wage laborers slept at home, and when various indoor activities withdrew from the hall to specialized rooms or service buildings that were added for those purposes. The old hall was rehabilitated strictly as a kitchen in some parts of the country; in others it became the family's sitting room or parlor. Almost everywhere, these changes were under way by the time English farmers set sail for the colonies.

Frequently, the earliest fault lines appeared along the cross passage. This ubiquitous corridor had been the through-

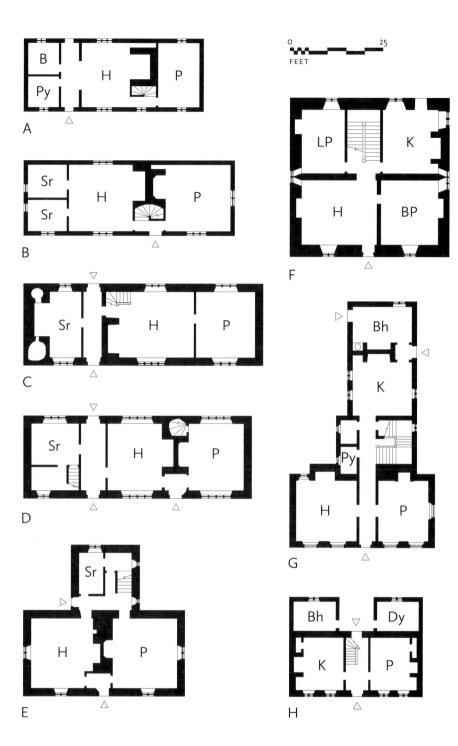

Fig. 6.4. Seventeenth-century English farmhouse plans familiar to immigrants to the American colonies. Based on specific recorded structures from A: Norfolk, 1580–1600; B: Suffolk, early seventeenth century; C: Somerset, 1627; D: Somerset, 1661; E: Derbyshire, 1670; F: Lincolnshire, 1658; G: Oxfordshire, 1685; H: Cambridgeshire, 1725.

fare that brought all traffic into a yeoman's medieval house, visitors through the front door at one end and the farmer, farmhands, and kitchen help through a back door from the barnyard and the farmstead beyond (Fig. 6.4A). Later builders, intent on not giving casual laborers the same run of the house that contractual servants had once enjoyed, sometimes forwent a cross passage altogether, the front door opening instead into a small lobby built against a chimney stack (Fig. 6.4B).

Elsewhere, cross passages were retained in regions that responded less quickly to changes in the agricultural economy. Many farmers in the West Country, parts of southern En-gland, Wales, and the northern highlands continued to treat the hall as the hub of the house, for cooking and eating meals, craftwork, and socializing. Across the passage, the newest innovation was a "downhouse" kitchen, for dairying, baking, brewing, salting, and curing (Fig. 6.4C). The parlor, located at the upper end of the hall and still usually unheated, was not yet a place of retreat for the householder and his friends so much as his and his wife's bedchamber—cold, small, but removed from the hubbub of the central hall.[18] The emigration of tens of thousands of yeomen and husbandmen from the West Country and south Wales to Virginia and Maryland in the middle decades of the seventeenth century caught this older cross-passage house plan at a critical moment in its development. Retention of the passage and the creation of a second, heavy-duty, downhouse kitchen turned out to have unforeseen applications for Chesapeake planters eager to place physical barriers between themselves and their workforces of indentured servants and enslaved Africans.

Those developments get ahead of the story. The population and price trends in England that had given employers an upper hand for half a century flattened out or reversed in the decade of the 1650s. A shortage of available labor and lower maintenance costs revived the practice of hiring servants on annual contracts and brought lodgers back into employers' dwellings during the second half of the seventeenth century. But frequently the old relationships based on mutual obligations and mutual dependency were not restored. Something else had come along in the meantime to change forever the old-fashioned recognition that servants in husbandry were simply the sons and daughters of one's neighbors passing through an adolescent stage in life before young people married and became householders in their own right. The new element was an emerging perception that the squirearchy and its numerous village imitators were imbued with cultural attributes that set them permanently apart from the laboring classes below them. Called "gentility" at first, it was the forerunner of eighteenth-century politeness.[19]

Self-important gentlemen were therefore inclined, when building or renovating, to divert servant traffic from those parts of the house that they reserved for themselves and their social peers. Newly class-conscious farmers often took the first step toward segregating domestic accommodations by remodeling their parlors into sitting rooms. There those who no longer sat down at meals with the men and the maids were free to dine with family and friends behind closed doors. Parlor manners did not always go hand in hand with the new employer-worker relationship, not in Britain and not among Britons overseas. Some farmers in England and planters in the colonies experimented with house plans that retained the old-fashioned cross passage and the common hall while also providing a modern parlor with its own separate outside doorway and sometimes a secondary staircase leading to private chambers overhead (Fig. 6.4D). These were people caught in the middle, rural folk who still toiled alongside their servants and yet were not immune to peer pressures from family and neighbors to keep a better sort of company on special occasions. Such improvisations occurred over the course of the seventeenth century and, thus depending on where they came from, were known to many immigrants to America.

Hybrid house plans reveal the confusion and ambiguity that attends complex social and cultural transformations. They are also signposts that point toward the next general resolution in vernacular traditions. By 1700, innovations that had begun a hundred years earlier in regions where market farming was first introduced had spread to farmhouses all over England. Cross passages disappeared. Dining tables and seating furniture pushed bedsteads out of parlors. Sleeping chambers colonized the territory above stairs with bedrooms that no longer led from one to another but were entered separately from connecting corridors.

Little by little, over the course of the seventeenth century, class consciousness and its genteel accoutrements refashioned country dwellings into the image of their city cousins. Two-room hall-and-parlor farmhouses, houses without a separate service room, came readymade for the face-lift that gave vernacular buildings a symmetrical appearance so much admired by growing numbers of fashion-conscious village aesthetes (Fig. 6.4E). Larger houses struggled to conform. Service rooms that once stood alongside halls and parlors or occupied cross wings now moved around behind the house into lean-to sheds or full-sized back rooms. So eventually did kitchens, thereby leaving the hall free to become a dining room or formal entertaining room, beginning in the second half of the seventeenth century. The segregation of masters and servants and the removal of sleeping chambers from downstairs parlors pushed traditional houses further in the direction of formality by dividing them, both front to back and upstairs and downstairs, between public spaces— rooms for show—and those back-of-the-house workrooms and private chambers that visitors never saw. The demise of the cross passage made way for a more or less symmetrically placed front door—sometimes reached through a porch tower, sometimes through an ornamental frontispiece— that then opened directly into the larger of the two front rooms (Fig. 6.4F). Shortly before and after the end of the century, the entry space itself began to be partitioned into a newfangled center passage (Figs. 6.4G, 6.4H). Superficially it resembled the cross passage of old, but it served an altogether different purpose in the gentleman's formal house. No longer was it the thoroughfare along which all domestic traffic flowed. On the contrary, center passages were waiting rooms. They assisted in the important business of dividing a gentrified residence into separate social zones. They provided a no-man's-land where unfamiliar callers could be stopped and screened before they were admitted into the public rooms on either side, or, as passages increasingly held a formal staircase, to superior entertaining rooms on the floor above. Unworthy callers were sent around to the servants' entrance behind the house.

Socially and culturally, the English vernacular farmhouse made a longer journey over the course of the seventeenth century than the ocean crossing that meanwhile had brought it to America.

TRIAL AND ERROR

There these transitional ideas incubated while settlers in Maryland and Virginia staked their claims and began grubbing out a livelihood. Initially, they endured huts and hovels, then cobbled together clapboard-covered starter houses. Characteristically though, as Thomas Nairne wrote from a later frontier farther south in the Carolinas, transplanted Britons never let go of the idea of eventually building a proper farmhouse. The intermediate house—Nairne characterized it as a homesteader's "small house"—usually served, he said, "for a kitchen afterwards when they are in better Circumstances."[20] Archaeological excavations in the Chesapeake region have shown that sometimes newcomers' circumstances were good enough, soon enough, to build full-sized farmhouses, even when they were still cutting corners on materials and construction costs. "Very meane and Little" was the way one Maryland observer described ordinary dwellings in that colony, but he also conceded that "generally" they were built "after the manner of . . . farme houses in England."[21] He must have meant houses that contained more than one or two rooms to warrant that analogy. Not every homesteader squeezed into a one-room cottage. Prospective settlers bound for the town of Henrico in Virginia were promised that each would "finde a hansome howse of some foure roomes or more if he haue a family."[22] Promotional pamphlets notoriously exaggerated the truth, but, true or not, this one is useful because it puts a number—four rooms minimum—on what were people's optimistic expectations. Occasionally, they were not disappointed. A few of the earliest earthfast or post-in-the-ground buildings that archaeologists have discovered in Virginia and Maryland approached the standard promised by promoters. They make an instructive group of buildings because they catch various English vernacular house plan ideas before they lost their regional personalities. Together, these buildings establish a baseline from which to measure the subsequent development of a homegrown vernacular tradition in the South.

Three early houses that show little deviation from English models were built by colonists sent to Virginia in 1618 by the Martin's Hundred Society, one of several privately financed colonizing ventures licensed by the Virginia Company (Figs. 6.5A, 6.5B, 6.5C).[23] These were the most fully developed dwellings built by the Martin's Hundred settlers, one located

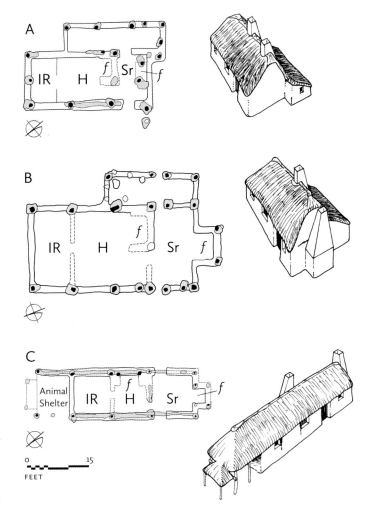

Fig. 6.5. Early wattle-and-daub farmhouses with cross-passage plans. A: John Boyse House, Site H, Structure A, c. 1620–22; B: Governor William Harwood Plantation, Site A, Structure C, c. 1625; C: Company compound, Wolstenholme Town, Site C, Structure D, c. 1620–22. All from Martin's Hundred, James City County, Virginia.

inside their fortified base camp, Wolstenholme Town, and two others on nearby farmsteads. They also built numerous one- and two-bay structures at these and other settlements in the neighborhood that must have served as cottages, quarters, work buildings, and barns.

The three farmhouses were all laid out on the same plan, presumably on purpose. The principal entrance into each opened into a cross passage that gave direct access to a heated workroom on one side—a "downhouse" domestic processing area—and, farther along the passage, into a hall on the other. As usual in similar English houses, an unheated inner chamber lay on the other side of the hall opposite the cooking hearth. The dwelling located inside the company compound at Wolstenholme Town incorporated an open-sided animal shelter on the end of the building beyond the inner room, but there is no evidence that this byre was entered from the house (see Fig. 6.5C).

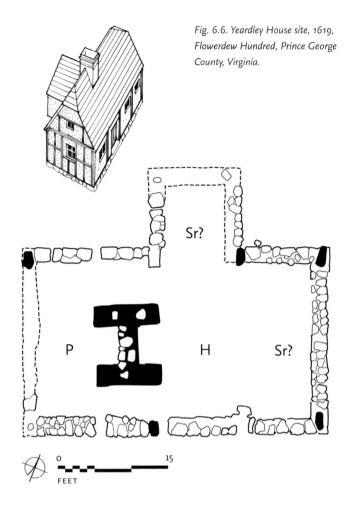

Fig. 6.6. Yeardley House site, 1619, Flowerdew Hundred, Prince George County, Virginia.

These three cross-passage houses at Martin's Hundred show that some immigrants to Virginia were well acquainted with vernacular building traditions that accommodated households in which masters and servants still worked and lodged together under one roof. The passage was still everybody's entrance. The hall was probably still a multipurpose common room. Specialized service rooms were still integral parts of the whole house and were still reached from the passage. The heavy-duty downhouse kitchen in particular was well suited to the relatively large number of men—approximately 25 percent of the workforce at Richard Claiborne's Kent Island colony—who were "imployed in the Ketchin to beate corne [into cornmeal] and dresse Victualls" in the course of preparing meals for the gangs of indentured servants who staffed these early joint stock company plantations.[24] It is easy to understand why colonists from those parts of Britain that had not wholly adopted the wage labor system before 1620—William Harwood, for example, hailed from Barnstaple, Devonshire—might suppose that a cross-passage house plan, to them so familiar, would be ideally suited to their plantations in Virginia. Indentured servants, after all, were contract laborers too, entitled to bed and board, as were servants in husbandry, but for a period of several years in-

stead of one. Enslaved Africans, who only just began arriving in the colony the same year that Martin's Hundred was settled, would not become a significant alternative source of labor—or a threatening alien presence on Chesapeake plantations—for another generation. So, at first, the cross-passage dwelling appeared to some colonists to be a perfect halfway house for masters and servants alike, each helping the other get a successful start in their New World home.

Reality turned out otherwise, one more unwelcome surprise that forced settlers to improvise in the Chesapeake colonies. The earliest adventurers guessed wrong about their fellow countrymen whose transportation costs they paid in return for their labor. Indentured servants often proved to be unruly as well as expensive. Usually they were strangers, not near neighbors or young people from villages in the region, as many servants in husbandry had been. Mostly, too, they were young men—adolescent males, 3,000 miles from home, restless, boisterous, on the loose and on the make. Masters finally concluded that such misfits made poor housemates and expensive lodgers. To adjust, they took elements from the same kind of cross-passage houses that were built at Martin's Hundred and radically reshuffled them to create a new form of segregated housing that was at once more economical and better suited to living with rascals and ruffians on remote wilderness plantations.

Those lessons took two or three decades to become common knowledge. Meanwhile, colonists from other parts of England were building houses that already separated householders' private quarters from servants' workrooms and lodgings. Archaeologists have excavated several three- and four-unit structures where a lobby entrance and an internal chimney stack physically separated a parlor on one side from a hall/kitchen and one or more service rooms on the other. Thirty miles upriver from Martin's Hundred, Sir George Yeardley founded another fortified settlement, at Flowerdew Hundred, in the same year, 1619. The principal dwelling there was an earthfast structure four bays long (Fig. 6.6).[25] Its archaeological footprint can be read as one of two possible variations on the familiar three-room lobby entrance plan. An H-shaped chimney warmed a small parlor on one side and a two-bay hall on the other, which may also have doubled as the settlement's official courtroom and assembly hall. Alternatively the hall/kitchen may have been partitioned at the far end to provide the usual buttery or pantry services. If not there, those functions were probably accommodated in a 10- by 10-foot room built off the back of the hall. Either way, the house at Flowerdew Hundred is recognizable as a parlor/lobby/hall/service room farmhouse in which the householder could withdraw into his private room to escape

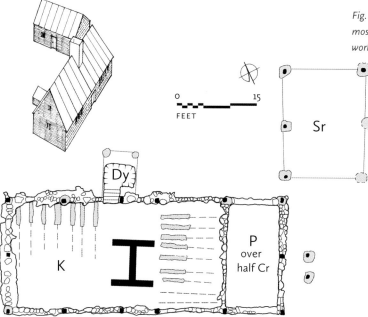

the cooking and other domestic activities—and possibly sometimes even public meetings—that took place in the hall/kitchen.

Archaeologists have investigated a lobby entrance dwelling in Maryland built by someone else who sought the advantages of a house divisible. John Lewger, secretary to the colony founded by Lord Baltimore, built a large house called St. John's on the outskirts of the capital, St. Mary's City, four years after it was settled in 1634 (Fig. 6.7).[26] He deliberately planned a private residence in which he could also host sessions of the general court and meetings of the assembly, which brought together as many as forty lawmakers. These gatherings were held in a very generous parlor at the east end of the house. Lewger's hall/kitchen occupied the other end, its cooking hearth sharing a brick and timber chimney stack with the fireplace in the parlor. Entry to a third room, a service room, a subterranean dairy built off the back of the house, was gained down a short flight of steps from inside the hall/kitchen.[27]

Other colony officials besides Lewger and Yeardley built houses with halls and parlors separated by a central chimney and lobby entry. Three more have come to light in Virginia, all among the earliest substantial houses in the region. One belonged to Samuel Mathews I, a self-made tobacco baron, councilor, Indian fighter, and political maverick. Mathews Manor was timber-framed, but it earned a compliment as "a fine house and all things answerable to it" (Fig. 6.8A).[28] Mathews seems to have built it sometime in the late 1630s. About the same time, Richard Kemp, another member of the Governor's Council and the colony's secretary, built the first of two similar hall-and-parlor houses, this one his

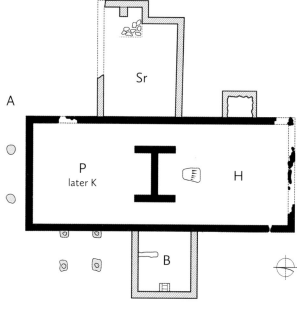

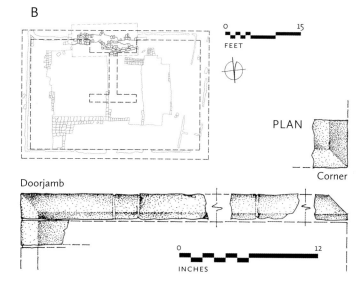

Fig. 6.8. Early hall-and-parlor houses in Virginia. A: Mathews Manor site, c. late 1630, Newport News, Warwick County. Mathews may later have renovated his dwelling to accommodate meetings of the court in the hall by moving the kitchen into the former parlor and adding a buttery/dairy and possibly a brewhouse. B: Richard Kemp's town house site, Structure 44, 1638–39, Jamestown, showing sketch plan of 1935 excavation (gray lines), selected features from the 1994–95 excavation, and chamfered water table bricks.

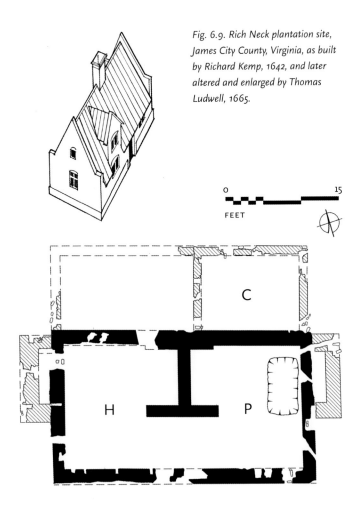

Fig. 6.9. Rich Neck plantation site, James City County, Virginia, as built by Richard Kemp, 1642, and later altered and enlarged by Thomas Ludwell, 1665.

0   15

FEET

residence at Jamestown (Fig. 6.8B). Governor John Harvey pronounced it "the fairest that ever was knowen in this countrye for substance and uniformity."[29] The substance was brick; the plan may have contributed to its uniformity. Kemp repeated both when he built Rich Neck in 1642, his country seat near Middle Plantation (Fig. 6.9).[30] The coincidence of five known hall/lobby/parlor houses built by high government officials is striking. The explanation is perhaps to be found in Governor Harvey's complaint to his superiors in England that his own private Jamestown residence (possibly another lobby-entry house) was frequently called into service as the colony's statehouse and official guesthouse as well.[31] There and elsewhere, lobby entrances may have sorted and separated callers on official business as efficiently as they divided common rooms from family apartments.

Not all large lobby-entrance houses relegated the service rooms to ells, wings, or sheds behind the house. Excavations on the John Hallowes site, Westmoreland County, Virginia, recovered the foundations of a five-bay structure in which three rooms—parlor, hall/kitchen, and services—formed a single range, the parlor and hall separated by a shared H-shaped chimney and the end bay given over to a cold service room convenient to work performed in the hall (Fig. 6.10).[32]

This house on the Northern Neck, built sometime in the 1660s, was probably one of the last that admitted both masters and servants through the same front door while directing them, once inside, to those spaces where they separately belonged. Increasingly, from midcentury onward, householders felt less and less comfortable about encountering servants, not to mention Africans, anywhere within doors, even in the no-man's-land of an entrance lobby. As the century wore on, hard-pressed tobacco lords felt more and more pressure to economize, as their English brethren had done, by putting farmworkers out of the house and into subsistence quarters of their own.

A house fraught with these tensions and ambiguities—and another English prototype tested for its fitness to conditions on the Chesapeake frontier—was a so-called manner house, constructed about 1670 by a substantial tenant farmer on property owned by Thomas Pope, a merchant-planter also of Westmoreland County (Fig. 6.11).[33] The principal dwelling on the Clifts Plantation replicated a hybrid cross-passage plan that provided a second, additional porch and lobby entrance, presumably for users of the adjacent parlor (compare Fig. 6.4D). A passage located at the working end of the house admitted servants and slaves directly into a dairy and a shed beyond, but it also gave them access through another doorway into the hall, which was kitchen and mess for family and farmhands alike. The small parlor at the far end of the house, though provided with a hearth, was probably only a sleeping chamber originally, not the family's dining room, which it may have become later when it was doubled in size. Distribution analyses of ceramic shards and tobacco pipestem fragments show that during the day the tenant and his farmhands labored shoulder to shoulder in a nearby workhouse in which they processed farm produce for bulk storage. We are left to guess what the occasions might have been when the householder stepped into the porch and entered his house through the doorway that was off-limits to the passage passengers. The answer may have been ambiguous even at the time, for thirty years later Thomas Pope's own son closed the residence to farmhands and reserved the entire dwelling for his own use.

House plans that provided both private and service entrances reinforced the age-old division of many English farmhouses into lodging rooms at one end and food preparation activities at the other. Leonard Calvert, Maryland's first governor, built a "large fram'd house" at St. Mary's City shortly after 1634 in which the layout of rooms closely resembled the Clifts ground plan (Fig. 6.12).[34] A room-by-room inventory compiled some thirty years later almost certainly echoes the functions of rooms in Calvert's dwelling, despite

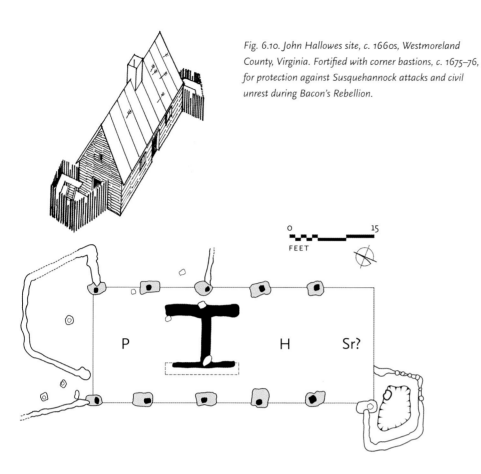

Fig. 6.10. John Hallowes site, c. 1660s, Westmoreland County, Virginia. Fortified with corner bastions, c. 1675–76, for protection against Susquehannock attacks and civil unrest during Bacon's Rebellion.

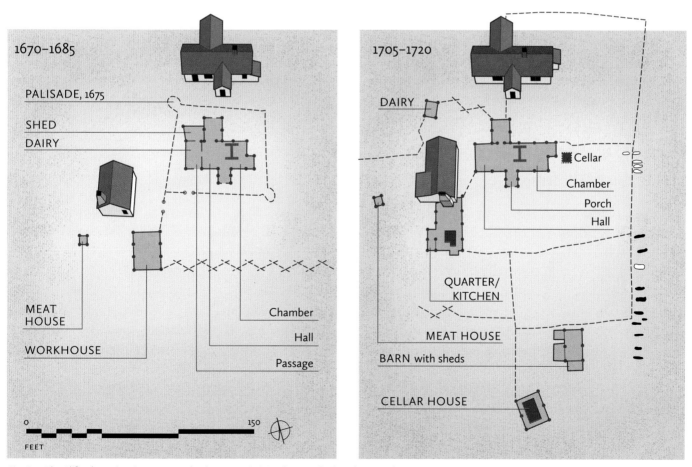

1670–1685

PALISADE, 1675

SHED
DAIRY

MEAT
HOUSE

WORKHOUSE

Chamber

Hall

Passage

1705–1720

DAIRY

Cellar

Chamber

Porch

Hall

QUARTER/
KITCHEN

MEAT HOUSE

BARN with sheds

CELLAR HOUSE

Fig. 6.11. The Clifts plantation site, Westmoreland County, Virginia, shown as built and tenanted, c. 1670–85, left, and later altered for owner occupancy, c. 1705–20, right.

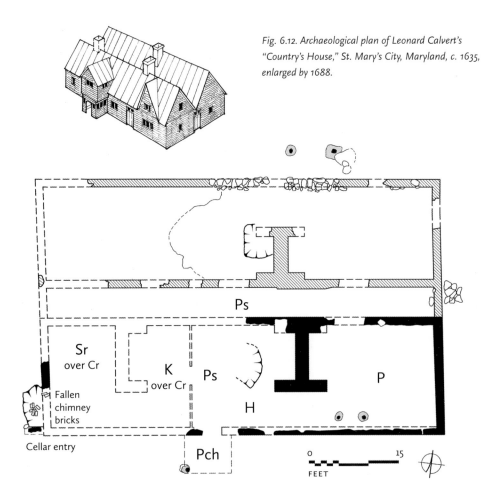

Fig. 6.12. *Archaeological plan of Leonard Calvert's "Country's House," St. Mary's City, Maryland, c. 1635, enlarged by 1688.*

later alterations.[35] A "Hall" occupied its traditional location on the working side of an H-shaped chimney and was probably the room in which the governor's kitchen staff cooked daily meals. A room called "Kitchen," adjoining the passage and provided with a separate chimney and a root cellar, was likely used for food processing, explaining the presence of "one copper in the Kitchen." Those functions were assisted by the later addition of an adjacent storeroom and cellars for meat and wine. Refuse recovered from the yard outside the west end yielded concentrations of coarseware milk pans and butter pots. In contrast, a scatter of refined tablewares located a "Parlor," "Lodging Chamber," and "Bed chamber" at the other end of the house. This 18- by 20-foot space on the other side of the central chimney may have been built as a single, average-to-large-size room that combined all three functions—dining, socializing, and sleeping. Its partition into separate small rooms for each activity probably came later, after the structure was acquired for the colony's first official statehouse and leased to an innkeeper when the General Assembly and the courts were not in session. If so, the publican's renovations to the "Country's House" (it is his 1668 inventory that lists the rooms by name) conformed to the customary allocation of space that his patrons expected in dwellings of this size.

These several early houses had not yet lost a family resemblance to their English forebears. They fall into place in a larger pattern of archaeological evidence that Fraser Neiman was the first to recognize. He collected statistically comparable information from a sample of sixty-five dated structures—a few still standing and the others known from excavation.[36] From this sample, he drew two observations that help explain the development of the region's vernacular building tradition away from its Old World origins toward the full-blown manifestation that it became by the end of the seventeenth century. First, he noted that the number of houses providing three or more main rooms steadily declined and finally disappeared around 1680. Second, his analysis further demonstrated that houses in which a lobby and chimney occupied the same middle bay also dropped out of use at approximately the same time, about 1680, when planters began showing a marked preference for two-unit houses containing only a ground-floor hall and a parlor. Usually both were heated by chimneys built into the gable ends. The front door in such houses opened directly into the larger room, the hall, there being as yet no formal passageway separating the two downstairs rooms. A staircase, or sometimes two, rose to attic chambers in closets alongside one or both chimneys or up one side of the partition that divided the hall from the inner room or parlor. As a practical matter, planters were shedding unwanted baggage from home and jerry-rigging the rest into farmhouses that were better suited to the colonies.

PLANTATION APARTHEID

What life lessons had Marylanders and Virginians learned by the third quarter of the century that encouraged them to abandon various traditional three- and four-part house plans in favor of dwellings with only two rooms downstairs, whether built expensively of brick or cheaply with earthfast posts and riven (split) clapboards? One certainly was their discovery that tobacco agriculture left little time for baking, brewing, bolting, cheese making, weaving, and other country by-employments common in Britain. Consequently, tobacco growers had scant need for the separate rooms where such chores were often performed in English farmhouses. Even the room names "buttery" and "milk house" (or its synonym "dairy") seldom appear together in Virginia and Maryland probate inventories, suggesting that their traditionally different functions—storage for drink and foodstuffs and storage for milk, butter, and cheese—soon merged into a single storeroom on Chesapeake plantations or were absorbed into the kitchen. By the end of the century, the term "buttery" had all but disappeared, and by then most dairies had moved outside to become stand-alone service buildings as well. Robert Beverley described what had become a typical Chesapeake scene by 1705 when he noted that "all their Drudgeries of Cooking, Washing, Daries, etc. are performed in Offices detacht from the Dwelling Houses, which by this means are kept more cool and sweet."[37]

The removal of domestic chores from the farmhouse proper is an important clue to the main reason that the number of rooms declined in plantation houses after the middle of the seventeenth century. It was not just the activities themselves that departed from the typical dwelling house. Increasingly, the servants and slaves who performed these tasks were put out as well. Bondsmen were not day laborers, of course. They could not be hired only when needed and left to fend for themselves when not, the expedient favored by economizing farmers in Britain. But planters could reduce their operating costs by feeding and housing laborers in separate quarters. Falling tobacco prices on the world market beginning in the 1620s gave them a powerful incentive to cut corners where they could. Although the staple economy experienced cycles of boom and bust, farm prices trended steeply downward for most of the century. A pound of Virginia tobacco that sold for two or three shillings in 1620 brought a

penny a pound by the late 1670s. Granted, the prices that planters paid for many essential goods and services declined too—prices for grain and meat as food supplies became more dependable, prices for clothing and tools as competition increased among a growing number of merchants, and the cost of credit as the settled colonies lowered the risks for lenders. It also helped that the cost of contracting with indentured servants remained stable for thirty years, through the 1660s, and then dropped still lower in the early 1670s.[38]

Even so, tobacco prices tumbled furthest and fastest of all. Beginning in the 1620s, planters began searching for ways to boost productivity while at the same time reducing production costs. Selective breeding produced higher-yielding strains of tobacco. Improved cultivation techniques increased the number of plants a worker could tend—tenfold by 1670.[39] As farmers in England had been learning as well, there were also gains to be made by shaving pennies off the cost of maintaining the workforce. Feeding servants and slaves a constant diet of cornmeal hominy was one shortcut. Jasper Danckaerts, traveling across the Eastern Shore of Maryland in 1679, observed the connection between tobacco growing and diet: "The servants and negroes after they have worn themselves down the whole day, and come home to rest, have yet to grind and pound the grain, which is generally maize, for their masters and all their families as well as themselves, and all the negroes to eat."[40] While hardscrabble planters were likely to take their dinner from the hominy pot too, as the Dutchman observed, archaeologists have discovered that generally masters enjoyed a more varied—and therefore a somewhat more costly—diet than the gruel they fed their field hands.[41]

Different fare for different folks was easiest to enforce when the grinders and pounders of corn prepared and took their meals separately in detached kitchens and when their quarters were removed from the planter's house and table. The employment of indentured servants encouraged such social segregation. The reason was not that most contract laborers were incorrigible rogues, whores, and vagabonds, as was alleged at the time and has been since. They were overwhelmingly unattached, adolescent males, eighteen to twenty-two years old, too far from home and kin to invoke the reciprocal obligations that both masters and servants in husbandry honored in English parishes, where everyone had a reputation to protect. Colonies collected strangers. Indentured servants came without relations or reputations. Consequently, planters incurred no social cost when they made a strictly pounds-and-pence decision to move servants' workplaces, messes, and quarters into separate buildings in the farmyard. Just as the ship captains who transported servants to the colonies valued "whome they carry at no other rate then theire passage-mony," so the planters who assumed those costs had no reason to value laborers for anything more than the work they performed and the profit they could earn during their term of service.[42] Treating servants as investments made two kinds of sense—financially, because planters could feed and house workers less expensively in separate quarters, and socially, because quartering servants separately removed from the family circle persons who were in every sense strangers, young people without family connections in the immediate community or even in the wider region.

Nor were bound servants the only outsiders whom planters had to find room for. While many Chesapeake plantations grew most of the food and fodder consumed on the farm, they depended heavily on itinerant craftsmen to supply the specialized skills needed to build buildings, cooper casks and barrels, repair tools, tan leather, cobble and patch shoes, and tailor clothing. In England, those services were often supplied locally. In the thinly settled southern colonies, only craftsmen who traveled from farm to farm could make a living by their trade, and, anyway, whatever time field hands did not spend tending the labor-intensive tobacco crop showed up on the bottom line. So periodically throughout the year, planters hosted and boarded various carpenters, coopers, blacksmiths, and other wage earners, many of them recent immigrants, or by the 1660s and 1670s ex-servants. Their numbers swelled the mongrel population that attached to Chesapeake plantations—skilled workers staying for days or weeks at a time and indentured servants for a period of years.

Eventually, a workforce of enslaved Africans added to the mix a people so alien to Englishmen's experience and so repugnant to their sensibilities that the influx of slaves into the region turned the segregation of plantation labor into something approaching apartheid. Slaves began replacing English-speaking servants on large plantations operated by provincial officeholders as early as the 1630s and 1640s, then increasingly on smaller farms after 1680.[43] As their numbers grew, the distance between masters and bondsmen widened into a chasm. In the eyes of Britons raised in the English countryside, black-skinned men and women from Africa and the West Indies appeared indescribably "outlandish" and their behavior "beast like."[44] To their ears, the babble of "harsh jargons" was not only an ever-present reminder of Africans' exoticness, but a practical barrier to the basic communication that overseers needed to manage laborers, short of brute force.[45] That slaves "understand not our Language nor me their's" became a constant refrain in planters' letters back to England.[46] Otherness led to loathing. As a rare (and anonymous) African voice complained to the Bishop of London,

"To be plain they doo Look no more up on us than if wee ware dogs."[47] On the other hand, for the wealthy planters who were the first to acquire gangs of Africans, chattel slavery was the logical next step in their relentless search to grow tobacco as economically as was humanly—or, if necessary, inhumanly—possible. It was well known that "the Low Price of Tobaccoe requires It should be made as cheape as possible, And . . . Blacks can make it cheaper than whites."[48] The reasons were simple. Africans could be put to the hoe without regard to gender; they could be forced to live in "wretchedly constructed" shelters no better than housing for farm animals; and they could be kept alive on a subsistence diet sufficient only for the work they performed.[49]

The switch to slave labor accelerated and completed a transformation in the vernacular landscape that the presence of indentured servants and numerous itinerant craftsmen had begun. A traveler through the region in 1687 described the scene that met his eyes everywhere he went: "Whatever their rank, & I know not why, they [planters] build only two rooms [for themselves] with some closets on the ground floor, & two rooms in the attic above; but they build several like this, according to their means. They build also a separate kitchen, a separate house for the Christian slaves [and] one for the negro slaves."[50] This entry in Durand de Dauphiné's travel journal gives us the clearest picture we have of the former, three-part, cross-passage, English farmhouse now deconstructed by the realities of life on the Chesapeake frontier. The workaday "downhouse" kitchen had been removed altogether from the house proper to become a nearby ancillary building; servants' nighttime lodgings in attics and lofts and their places at the communal table were relegated to a second stand-alone structure, a quartering house; accommodations for Africans required still another cheaply built quarters on farms where Negroes had not yet replaced the "Christian slaves" completely. Durand might have added one last detail, that Virginia's largest planters were already taking measures to separate the races even farther by housing more of their English servants on home plantations and more blacks at remote outlying quarters managed by an overseer.[51] What was left—indeed, all that remained of the transplanted English prototype—was the planter's hall, his parlor or sleeping chamber, and some rooms in the attic. Best of all, such gentleman planters had their houses all to themselves and their families. As the new governor Lord Effingham promised his wife, who was preparing to join him in Virginia in 1684, we "shall have the great house entirely to ourselves, which will be suffitiently large enough, having a pantrey, washhouse, and Laindry without doors."[52] A homegrown vernacular building tradition in the South had emerged fully developed by 1680.

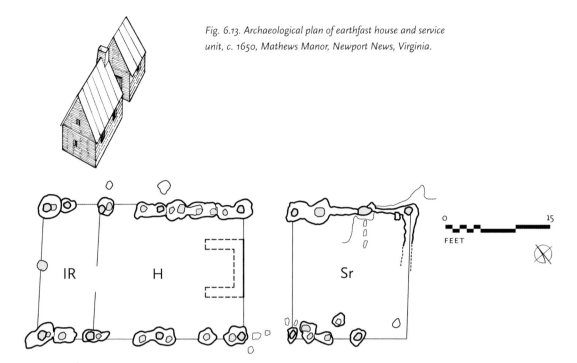

Fig. 6.13. Archaeological plan of earthfast house and service unit, c. 1650, Mathews Manor, Newport News, Virginia.

IR   H   Sr

0 ___ 15
FEET

This architecture of apartheid would last as long as slavery itself and would spread throughout the Cotton South with westward-trekking slaves and masters from Virginia and Maryland.

Durand's journal records the end of the process in the Chesapeake colonies. Archaeological excavations reveal its beginning and subsequent development. Planters began building detached kitchens as early as the 1620s. In cross-passage houses, the uncoupling took place along the corridor, thereby making a new freestanding cookhouse out of the old "downhouse" kitchen/workroom, a servants' realm anyway. The separation left behind the hall and inner chamber for the more exclusive use of planters and their families. The first experiments in this direction may have involved nothing more than leaving the passage unroofed. That is one plausible interpretation of the excavated ground plan of an earthfast house on the Mathews Manor estate from about 1650 (Fig. 6.13). A space 8 feet wide separated the service from the hall and parlor/chamber. Was this just an unusually wide interior corridor, or was it an open passageway alongside a workroom that the builder had set adrift from the house proper?

Elsewhere, the archaeological record is unequivocal. St. John's, the well-made house that John Lewger built at St. Mary's City in 1638, was sold to Simon Overzee, a merchant, in 1653 (see Fig. 6.7). Overzee, a notoriously sadistic slave owner, immediately removed the kitchen (and the African cooks) into a nearby workhouse, retrofitted with a new chimney, and the old dairy from its shed attached to the house into a separate milk house. The former hall/kitchen become

a domestic space serving a function that was compatible with a "Nursery" built off the backside by Charles Calvert ten years later. Calvert too owned slaves as well as English servants. "For a Quarter," he built "a little House near to the Gate," probably to accommodate whichever group of laborers was not already sleeping in the renovated kitchen.

Colonel Thomas Pettus built a strikingly similar timber-framed, hall-and-parlor house in James City County, Virginia, about 1641 (Fig. 6.14A).[53] At first, the (presumed) kitchen was a freestanding structure located immediately behind the house, but later Pettus added another bay, combined it with a milk house and cistern, and attached the whole to the backside of his dwelling, possibly in the same rearrangement of quarters and work spaces that required several more structures in the nearby farmyard. One seems to have been an unheated workhouse and another a two-room building with a large hearth and a cellar underneath. Either one may have bunked Pettus's farmhands.

If assigning particular inmates to specific domestic spaces remains a matter of guesswork at some sites, the distribution of artifacts excavated at the Clifts Plantation in Westmoreland County documents very precisely the physical alterations that planters were then making to buffer themselves and other whites from the presence of enslaved laborers imported from Africa. The son of the absentee landlord, Thomas Pope, moved himself to the Clifts about 1705 and altered the former tenant house to restrict entry by farmworkers (Fig. 6.11). The passage was closed and workrooms were pulled down or moved to outbuildings. Pope enlarged the old, three-bay workhouse to become the plantation

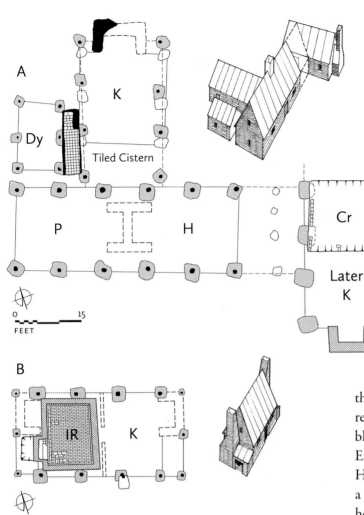

Fig. 6.14. A: Colonel Thomas Pettus plantation site, c. 1641–50, James City County, Virginia; B: Tenant house site, c. 1675–91, Utopia Quarter, Pettus plantation, James City County, Virginia. The house later became a quarter for servants or slaves when Pettus installed a brick-lined cellar for dry storage of plantation supplies or produce.

kitchen and a quarter. The distribution pattern of ceramic and pipestem evidence, very different from the pattern laid down thirty years earlier, indicates that whites and blacks were cooking, eating, socializing, and sleeping separately by the turn of the century. The hall in Pope's dwelling, now entered exclusively through the front door, served as a dining room for the planter's own family and friends, while his bedchamber, enlarged twice before 1730, turned into a sitting parlor. Even in death, the races went their separate ways, whites to a graveyard adjoining the orchard and garden; blacks to a plot along a fence line beyond the barn.

Savvy planters quickly learned from their successful neighbors how to fine-tune their farmsteads to eke out a living on the tobacco frontier. Along the way, they reaped some unintended benefits by banishing kitchens, cooks, and common diners from their hearth and hall. "By this means," Robert Beverley noted in 1705 in respect to absent kitchens, they keep their houses "more cool and sweet." Twenty years later, another writer, describing the segregated plantations he encountered everywhere in the region, believed that "the smell of hot victuals, offensive in hot weather," was, in fact,

the principal reason that kitchens and workrooms had been removed from slaveholders' dwelling houses. By then, 1724, black Africans were so rapidly and thoroughly replacing English and Irish servants on Chesapeake plantations that Hugh Jones could no longer remember, or even imagine, a time when the "common planters," whose "pretty timber houses" he described in *The Present State of Virginia*, had lived under the same roof with the hired help.[54] His amnesia certainly owed something to English Virginians' repugnance for African Virginians. It also reflected newfangled cultural aspirations that bring us back to the hall-and-parlor house to consider its further development in the closing decades of the seventeenth century.

COMPANIONABLE SPACES

Kitchen odors are as good a place to start as any. Far away from Virginia's sultry summers, British architects had been campaigning to remove smelly kitchens from gentlemen's living quarters since the 1660s. Sir Roger Pratt favored a basement location. There, "no dirty servant may be seen passing to and fro by those that are above, nor noises heard, nor ill scents smelt."[55] Dear, dear!—what had become of England's great seigniorial lords that they were lately so offended by a grubby scullion, coarse talk, or the smell of frying fat?

The answer—a growing tendency to value class over rank—we have already observed among prosperous British farmers in the second half of the seventeenth century, men much less substantial than Roger Pratt's clients, who, notwithstanding, were no less eager to acquire the attributes of cultivated gentlemen. The man of culture displayed his learning, manners, and sensibilities to his social equals rather than parading his largesse indiscriminately before his assembled household or to all his neighbors without distinction. "Those that are above" were learning to prefer peer group acceptance before community approbation.

Those same anxieties and ambitions, when present in the colonies, make it harder for historians to determine the function of rooms in the Virginia house. Not all halls were equal, it stands to reason. Not all hall-and-parlor houses were used the same way. Durand de Dauphiné's observation that everyone lived in houses with two ground-floor rooms came with a qualifier—"regardless of rank." When rank is taken into account, distinctions are discernible. Leaving aside a universe of smaller cottages, those "containing one Ground Room and a Garret above" that many "a poor Man" leased for 40 shillings tobacco, there were a great many small farmers for whom a house with two ground-floor rooms, a hall and a chamber, essentially a kitchen and a sleeping room, was all the house they ever had or thought they needed. For example, the tenants who occupied Thomas Pettus II's Utopia Quarter had no choice but to cook and eat in the hall, there being no other kitchen anywhere on the property (Fig. 6.14B).[56] After their evening meal, they could withdraw to a bedchamber warmed by a separate hearth, which may indicate that the chamber served as a sitting room as well. More frequently, the sleeping chamber, the "inner room," had no source of heat, as at Bennett Farm and River Creek, two neighboring small plantations in York County, Virginia.[57] These and other similar two-unit dwellings were still thoroughly traditional farmhouses, used exactly as comparable cottages were in Britain, especially if the indentured servants who are known to have worked at both Bennett Farm and River Creek rolled out their blankets on the hall floor at night after the common mess was cleared, the cooking pots were put away, and the master and mistress had retired for the night into the adjoining inner room. This basic hall-chamber cottage had housed the traditional farmer's household for centuries.

Planters of higher rank also built houses that contained only two downstairs rooms, as Durand reported, houses that left an archaeological footprint that is often indistinguishable from a traditional cottage of the same plan. For that matter, some well-to-do freeholders were content with a single, large, ground-floor room and one or more sleeping chambers in the loft, for example, the builder of the Woodward-Jones House in Suffolk, Virginia (Fig. 6.15). We now understand the reason. Halls in houses belonging to

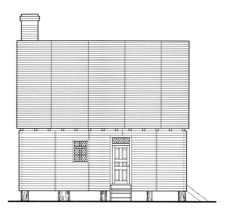

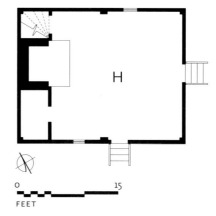

Fig. 6.15. *Plan and reconstructed elevation, Woodward-Jones House, 1716, Suffolk, Virginia.*

these larger planters were no longer called on to do double duty as kitchens, common rooms, and servants' lodgings, and, where parlors adjoined, those rooms were fast becoming comfortable bedsitters, just as they were in many English farmhouses. The relocation of services to separate outbuildings on Chesapeake plantations started the gentleman farmer's hall-and-parlor house, or even hall-only house, developing in a direction quite different from the superficially similar one- and two-unit houses inhabited by tenants and ordinary freeholders.

To what purpose? The answer is best guessed at by solving Fraser Neiman's riddle about the disappearance of lobby entrances and internal chimneys. Why, he asks, did houses that had been entered through a vestibule located in a central chimney bay all but vanish after 1680, to be replaced by those in which the front door opened directly into the hall, and from there an internal doorway giving access to a smaller inner chamber or parlor?[58] He conjectures that householders preferred a layout of interior space where masters or mistresses in one room could easily keep watch on untrustworthy domestics working in the other. Surveillance may have been one consideration. But, given the fact that servants and slaves now usually worked, ate, socialized, and slept mostly outside the planter's house, there has to be a more compelling reason to explain not just why planters built new houses with direct communication between hall and parlor but also why many others went to considerable trouble and expense to convert older, lobby-entry houses to the new model plan invariably in the closing decades of the seventeenth century.

Such conversions involved expensive renovations. Taking the trouble to tear down and rebuild chimneys, reframe floors and ceilings, plaster walls anew, and patch roofs seems excessive just to reduce pilfering and vandalism by servants and slaves. Might there be another explanation? Could the "persons of quality" whom Durand was surprised to find living in such small houses have had another motive altogether?

Looking ahead at later developments in regional house plans puts the disappearing lobby into a longer perspective and also suggests a rhyme and reason for the design decision that turned halls and parlors into a suite of communicating rooms intended for company in the houses of gentleman-planters, beginning as early as the 1660s. Dell Upton has worked out the end of the story.[59] He has demonstrated that the three functions that had gradually collected in the parlor—sleeping (the oldest use), private dining, and socializing or "setting" with social equals—were each reassigned to a separate adjoining room by the second quarter of the eighteenth century. Beds were sometimes simply moved upstairs, although often the best bedchamber remained on the ground floor, where it occupied a new room built in a wing or ell off the back of the house. From inside, it was entered directly through the parlor space from which it had just taken leave. These bedchamber ells first appeared about 1730.

Meanwhile, the convivial, company-keeping activities that had gravitated to parlors in the seventeenth century migrated back to the old hall, once it was closed to the swarm of servants who had formerly congregated there. No longer a kitchen, a mess, or a bunkhouse, the hall was left with little to do; hence, the space was ready and waiting to assume a new role in genteel households as a reception hall and quasi-public entertaining room. At first, before central passages became commonplace, the newfangled hall was invariably the room into which the front door opened directly, although sometimes through a porch. An appropriate new name for the room was slow to catch up with its evolving new use. As late as 1737, vestrymen in Truro Parish, Virginia, building a new glebe house, had to use both the old term and a new one—"hall or entertaining room"—to describe the intended function of the principal downstairs room.[60] Eventually, such social spaces came to be known as "drawing rooms" in ambitious planters' houses.

These first two defections from the parlor freed that room to specialize in the one function that they left behind, intimate dining for family and peers. The dining parlor, suitably equipped with tables and chairs, gradually turned into

a formal "dyninge room," set apart and so designated as early as 1651 in Virginia and 1688 in Maryland.[61] Its popularity spread rapidly in the eighteenth century, thus completing the trio of domestic living spaces that was said to be all that a Virginia gentleman ever wanted in a house—"a bed, a dining room, and a drawing room for company."[62]

The suite of complementary hall-cum-entertaining room and dining room became the modern reincarnation of the old hall and parlor. The two rooms functioned together, as two formal settings for the performance of synchronized activities that needed to flow back and forth between the larger entertaining room and the adjacent dining room. Awkward, old-fashioned, internal chimneys got in the way. Tearing them down and rebuilding them into the gables was therefore a small price to pay for creating a unified social space where planters with genteel sensibilities could comport themselves and entertain their friends in a style to which increasingly they were pleased to be accustomed.

The transformation took place surprisingly quickly in circumstances where householders discovered that antiquated dwellings no longer suited their lifestyle. For instance, Thomas Ludwell immediately renovated an otherwise handsome brick house outside Middle Plantation, which he bought secondhand in 1665, not long after he showed up in Virginia with a commission from Charles II appointing him secretary of the colony (Fig. 6.9). Similarly, Ludwell's younger brother, Philip, later reconfigured two dwellings he acquired in a Jamestown row house in the 1690s, as had George Lee, a London merchant, slave trader, and part owner of another Jamestown row, ten years earlier (Fig. 6.16).[63] Class-conscious social climbers thrived in urban places, even in such start-up towns as Williamsburg, the capital city of Virginia, newly founded in 1699. One of its earliest lot owners, William Robertson, bought a conventional, one-story, timber-frame "fixer-upper," built in 1695, and pulled it around into alignment with the gridded street pattern in the new capital (Fig. 6.17).[64] By 1718, he had thoroughly remodeled the hall-and-parlor house by carving up the hall to make room for a central passage (one of the earliest in the colony), a dining room, and a small, narrow chamber into which he managed to wedge a corner fireplace. It was cramped, but it gave him the complement of ground-floor rooms that an urban and urbane gentleman required.

Thus, gentry houses in the Chesapeake colonies began reserving public rooms for company and private apartments for family in much the same way and at exactly the same time that fashionably self-conscious British farmhouses first assumed the trappings of gentility. The innovators in Virginia and Maryland came from a rising generation of well-to-do

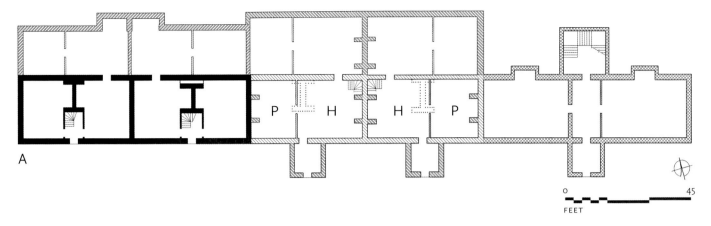

A

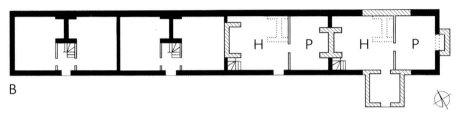

B

Fig. 6.16. A: Site of row house, Structure 144, Jamestown Island, Virginia, built, enlarged, two center units renovated by Philip Ludwell, and statehouse added to east end, 1663–c. 1694; B: Site of row house, Structure 115, Jamestown Island, Virginia, built 1663, two east-end dwellings reconditioned c. 1681 by George Lee.

planters, many newly arrived in the colonies during the Commonwealth years and immediately following the restoration of Charles II. They were enterprising men with Royalist sympathies and connections to prosperous mercantile firms in London and Bristol or with relations among English landowners. Newcomers often married into older gentry families in the colonies, and many quickly became provincial and county officeholders. They had wealth to spend. They put it to work assembling a labor force of African slaves, investing in Governor William Berkeley's Indian trade cartel and speculating in large tracts of land on the Northern Neck and the Southside frontier below the James River. Their spectacular ascendancy superseded the generation of self-made grandees who had come to power after the dissolution of the Virginia Company in 1624; their boundless greed touched off a civil war with hard pressed smallholders in 1676; and their near overthrow in Bacon's Rebellion hardened their determination afterward to use their wealth and power to reinforce their dominant position in society as much by cultural prowess as by the offices they controlled and the influence they wielded. These were men with an Atlantic worldview, metropolitans and cosmopolitans who regarded the colonies as a lucrative enterprise but a cultural backwater. "Society that is good & ingenious," one of them, William Fitzhugh, opined, "is very scarce, & seldom to be come at except in books."[65] Fitzhugh and others like him set out to civilize Virginia and Maryland society, partly by building the first houses in the region that actually resembled illustrations to be found in books.

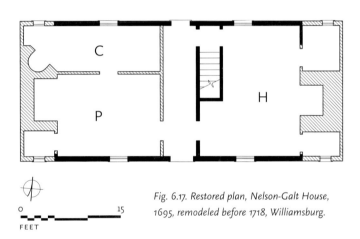

Fig. 6.17. Restored plan, Nelson-Galt House, 1695, remodeled before 1718, Williamsburg.

Not that colonists really did consult architectural pattern books in this period. They did not have to. Bookish novelties were much in the air by the 1640s and 1650s and much on the minds of sophisticated gentlefolk, who preferred the good and ingenious society of peers to the respectful homage of their retainers and lesser neighbors. Such a man was Sir William Berkeley, younger son of a pedigreed West Country family, a gentleman of the privy chamber in the court of Charles I, and twice governor of Virginia, the first time beginning in 1642.[66] By his own admission, he too was "fond of, and in need of society," once he settled into his new life 3,000 miles distant from the royal court.[67] His solution was to amass an estate that eventually totaled more than 7,000 acres and to build a mansion house where he could live comfortably and entertain in style.[68]

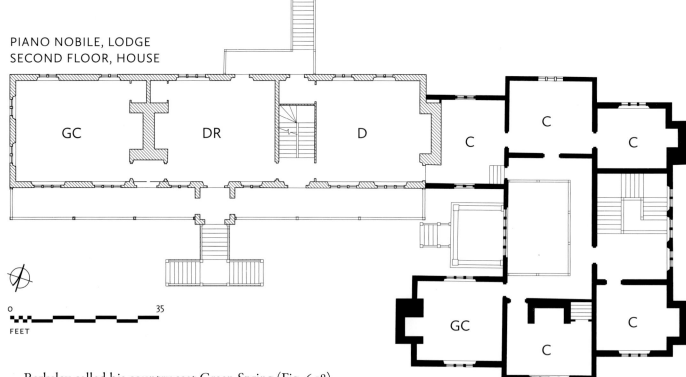

PIANO NOBILE, LODGE
SECOND FLOOR, HOUSE

GC   DR   D

C
C   C

GC   C
C

0   35
FEET

Berkeley called his country seat Green Spring (Fig. 6.18). It was an easy ride four miles from Jamestown. He patented the tract in 1643 and began building immediately. The gabled brick house, two stories high with garrets, was said to be "in hand" by early 1645.[69] Noteworthy is how it both resembled and departed from the diagrammatic plan of a generic English country house published in 1613 and reissued in 1635, not because Gervase Markham's *The English Husbandman* was Berkeley's inspiration, but as a reminder of the architectural tastes that the governor-general brought to Virginia. They fell somewhere between conservative and progressive. Markham's "model of a plaine country mans house" was altogether typical of gentry building in Britain since the sixteenth century (Fig. 6.19).[70] A "Great Hall" at the center of the building that he illustrates connected a projecting service wing on one side to a range of superior entertaining and lodging rooms on the other. Together they formed a large H-shaped or U-shaped plan. So did the central hall and wings at Green Spring. A service range at its north end held the kitchen, buttery, and another small room. A matching wing on the other side, entered from the south end of the hall, contained three more ground-floor rooms, all with fireplaces: one or more parlors (Markham's "Dining Parlor for entertainment of strangers" is probably an apt description of one), a traditional English withdrawing room in all likelihood, and perhaps a bedchamber.

A closer comparison between the excavated foundations of Green Spring and the illustration in Markham shows that Berkeley's thinking, conventional in the overall layout of his house, had advanced with the times in two or three notable

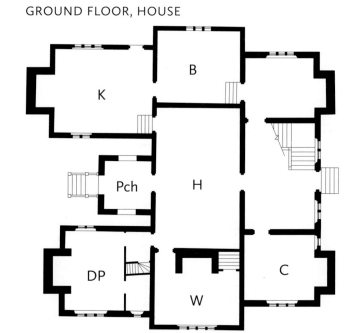

GROUND FLOOR, HOUSE

B
K
Pch   H
DP   C
W

Fig. 6.18. Reconstructed ground plan, William Berkeley's country house (1643–45), and second-floor plans, house and banqueting lodge (by 1674) at Green Spring, James City County, Virginia. Plans developed from excavated footings, drawings and notes by Benjamin Henry Latrobe (1796–97), and comparable British buildings.

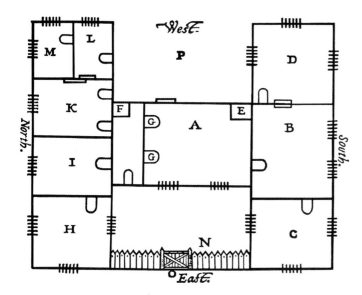

respects. Before the middle decades of the seventeenth century, halls in great men's houses were traditionally arranged to reflect the social hierarchy of the family members, servants, and villagers who frequently gathered there to accept the manor lord's hospitality. Everyone entered the house through an off-center passage that opened into the "lower" or inferior end of the hall through a partitionlike screen or solid wall. At mealtimes, servants carried food and drink from the kitchens and butteries across the passage, through the screen, and down the length of the hall to the master's high table at the superior "upper" end, or alternatively into his private dining parlor immediately beyond. When Markham wrote *The English Husbandman*, those age-old customs were still living traditions almost everywhere in the British Isles and, for that matter, in Britain's American colonies as well. As we have seen, several early (and much smaller) three-unit dwellings in Virginia perpetuated the high-end/low-end distinction as long as the hall remained a common meeting place for people from different social ranks (see Fig. 6.5).

But not at Berkeley's house, not by 1645. Hierarchy was absent in the great hall at Green Spring. A brick porch on the west front brought the governor's guests into the room at its center, not into a narrow passage at one end, thereby erasing all low- and high-end distinctions in the hall itself. The result was the creation of a socially ambiguous space that made equal demands on all who entered. Berkeley entertained countless officials, foreign visitors, and other dignitaries at Green Spring during his long residence in the colony. Doubtless, he received them formally in his spacious open hall, a room more than 30 feet long, 20 feet wide, two full stories tall, atrium-like, and lit from above by a row of high, front-facing windows. On occasion, he probably entertained in this entrance hall as well, although in what manner is im-

possible to say without an inventory to tell historians how the room was furnished. The absence of a chimney adds to the impression that a room redolent with ancient symbolism had here assumed a much more modern function. It had become a formal reception hall.

In that capacity, it served another new use, also typical of the most forward-looking, upper-gentry houses in Britain. The reception hall was a vestibule from which Berkeley invited his intimate friends and honored guests deeper into the house. Green Spring introduced provincial Virginians to a second architectural innovation no less portentous than the reception hall. Berkeley's was the first double-pile house built in the colony, a structure with two adjoining ranges of full-sized rooms lying back to back. A second large space, directly behind the front hall, was part stair hall and part passage. It held a grand, open-well staircase that ascended around the walls to a second-floor landing and from there probably continued to the garrets at the top of the house. Berkeley's own great chamber and those used by his family filled out a superior suite of upstairs apartments in the south wing; lesser chambers occupied the second floor above kitchen and service rooms.

Years later, Berkeley's widow reminisced that her husband's country estate in Virginia had been "I thinke . . . the finest seat in America & the only tollerable place for a Governour."[71] Her tribute aptly described the fifteen- or sixteen-room mansion that Berkeley built to satisfy his "need of society" in faraway Virginia. From the start, Green Spring was unrivaled anywhere in British North America. It was the country's first fully developed English country house set in an expansive parklike landscape that its builder intended as the fullest expression of a cultivated gentility that he was determined not to find only in books.

The governor's ambition to make Green Spring an even more splendid backdrop for court life in Virginia set off a second round of building soon after he was restored to his post following Charles II's restoration in 1660. The new work, finished by 1674, introduced Virginia grandees to a whole new world of civilized living, London-style (Fig. 6.20). Berkeley's scheme was not to replace the house he had built only fifteen years earlier but to erect an additional range of

Fig. 6.20. Reconstructed view of Green Spring house and lodge by 1674, James City County, Virginia, looking north from the garden. Inset: Thumbnail sketch of Green Spring in 1683 from John Soane survey of "Governor's Land." (Reproduced by kind permission of the Trustees of the William Salt Library, Stafford, England). (Perspective drawing courtesy of Roger Guernsey)

rooms extending westward from the old service wing across the entire north end of his walled garden, a distance of 97 feet. The garden was integral to his plans, for he intended the new structure to serve much like a park lodge, banqueting house, or bellaria—a place of informal retirement overlooking the baroque garden he had already developed within a walled enclosure that formed the forecourt to the house itself. Such park and garden structures were usually separate retreats on English estates, removed from the house itself. Berkeley chose to attach the new suite of rooms to the older house for reasons unknown. Possibly he regarded Green Spring itself as a retreat from his in-town residence at nearby Jamestown.

A ground-story loggia, arcaded below and no doubt balustraded above, ran the full length of the new structure. At its center, a divided flight of stairs rose from the garden to the platform that formed the flat roof of the loggia. From the top of the stairs the entrance led through an open-sided brick porch built in the artisan mannerist style that was high fashion among London builders during the reign of Charles I and remained popular in the provinces through the 1660s. Visually a frontispiece, the pedimented porch, centered on the garden-facing facade, signaled an unconventional and completely unhierarchical arrangement of rooms within, as suited a building intended exclusively for entertaining the governor's social peers. Loggias often provided viewing plat-

forms attached to the fronts of hunting lodges and garden banqueting houses on seventeenth-century English estates.[72] Berkeley's loggia served the same purpose. It overlooked his garden.[73] When he and his guests tired of strolling along the paths, they climbed the staircase and stepped out onto the gallerylike loggia to take in fine perspective views of the parterres below and probably the governor's famous deer park in the distance.

Garden gazing and convivial socializing were a perfect aperitif to the main course of activities that awaited Berkeley's guests in three, large, upper-story entertainment rooms behind (see Fig. 6.18). Almost equal in size and all heated, the trio of rooms strongly resembled the classic sequence of special entertaining rooms found in English country houses, by 1660 usually termed dining chamber, drawing room, and bedchamber.[74] The rooms functioned en suite. They were party rooms. Berkeley's guests gathered in the first to dine and banquet (a word referring to elaborate desserts). They withdrew into the middle room between courses or to give servants time to reset the table or prepare adjacent spaces for other uses. Alternatively, the antechamber might serve as a dayroom and a dressing chamber for the distinguished guest or guests who lodged in the third room, the bedchamber. The point to be observed is that these self-contained apartments were reserved for special people and special occasions. They did not replace the family's everyday use of the dining parlor off the hall or disturb their customary sleeping arrangements in the south wing.

Green Spring, house and lodge together, provided the most lavish and elaborated entertainment space in any known public or private structure in seventeenth-century British North America. Berkeley set a standard that became the new measure of refinement in Virginia. Others took notice. The same Colonel William Fitzhugh who shared the governor's yearning for good society described his own house on the Northern Neck, Eagle's Nest, as "furnished with all accommodations for a comfortable & gentile living." Like Green Spring, it was a very large house, thirteen rooms, the best four hung with tapestries or painted cloths and nine "plentifully furnished with all things necessary & convenient."[75]

The desire to create domestic settings reserved for the entertainment of gentlefolk pushed the development of building traditions in the Chesapeake colonies still further away from their ancient vernacular origins. Eventually, gentry houses in the South came to resemble formal dwellings everywhere in the English-speaking world, for gentility was inherently peripatetic and cosmopolitan. Its value as a mode of visual communications depended on the observance of formal rules of behavior that could only be performed in standardized architectural settings wherever knowledgeable ladies and gentlemen assembled.[76] That said, each region in Britain and in Britain's overseas colonies arrived at this more or less common architectural form along different paths. In Virginia and Maryland, the formal gentry house did not reach full development until the eighteenth century, a story that remains to be told in the next chapter. But decades earlier, some of the region's greatest planters and merchants had already begun shuffling spaces in what was still an evolving regional house plan as they tried to find room for the companionable activities in which true gentlefolk engaged.

Green Spring serves as a benchmark. The reception hall, ground-floor dining parlor, and upstairs great chamber in the house itself, plus the suite of three entertaining rooms in the 1660s extension, were all as pedigreed English as were the U-shaped plan and the lodge-like addition. Not so another two-story brick house built across the James River in Surry County in 1665, "Arthur Allen's brick house," as his neighbors called it in his lifetime—and since then known as Bacon's Castle (see Fig. 2.10).[77] Unlike the governor, Allen favored a design that borrowed from the flux of local practice, despite his choice of a pattern-book facade, shaped gables, and artisan mannerist decoration. In plan, Bacon's Castle

appears to conform to the preference among Chesapeake planters for two ground-floor rooms, a larger hall (entered here through a two-story porch tower), and a smaller, more intimate private chamber. Already, menial slaves and servants had been made to disappear (except when bidden), although not to a separate kitchen in the usual way, but underground, to a cookroom and pantry in the cellar, a netherworld entered from outside the house down a bulkhead staircase. How much this arrangement owed to Allen's knowledge of fashionable English practice and how much to emerging local custom is impossible to say. Either way, the effect was the same: the two principal ground-floor rooms were left free for day-use family living and polite entertainment, but in this case with an important exception to common practice elsewhere in Virginia. Allen and his son, Arthur Allen II, chose to entertain their guests somewhat differently than was typical among most other planters.[78] Their so-called hall was actually a dining parlor. Two tables, eighteen chairs, a cupboard, a desk, a daybed, and enough knives and forks to set a dinner table for ten furnished it for every activity except sleeping. The adjoining smaller room, though heated, was pointedly not a parlor but rather a secondary bedchamber and storage room termed simply "the chamber."

The Allens' most expensive "high bedsteads," hung with curtains and valences, were set up upstairs in the rooms over the hall and the chamber, rooms also furnished with looking glasses, chests of drawers, and twelve and six cane chairs, respectively. Though these second-floor rooms were not named as such, their furnishings indicate that the smaller room functioned as a great chamber and that the larger one (into which the staircase opened) was its antechamber and dressing room, although it too held a fine, but less valuable, curtained bed. A dozen imported cane chairs were more than enough for members of the Allen family; therefore, they must have been intended for guests who were invited upstairs during the day. Master Allen may have received them dressed in his "morning Gound [gown]," perhaps while taking his ease on the "Cain Couch" that matched the chairs. The dressing room was certainly where he put on his "Waring Clothes" and the "bob wig" that the inventory takers recorded in this anteroom "over the Hall." At night, "Two Negro men," manservants Boatswain and Salisbury, slept nearby in hammocks, one in each room. From outside, the greater importance accorded to these upstairs rooms was plainly signaled by heavy brick window frames picked out with white plaster, very much in the mannerist tradition.[79] At Bacon's Castle, the Arthur Allens experimented with one solution to a gentleman's desire for companionable spaces. Downstairs, they fitted out the hall as a dining

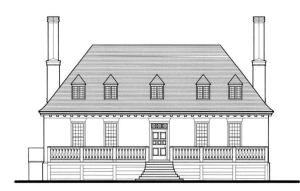

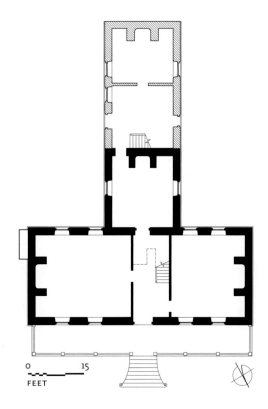

```
0        15
  FEET
```

Fig. 6.21. Plan and reconstructed elevation, Fairfield, Gloucester County, Virginia. The lodge was built in 1694 and enlarged with the addition of a residential wing about 1710. The size and shape of the original window openings suggests that Lewis Burwell II was one of the gentlemen whom Robert Beverley mentioned in 1705 as having built improved houses, with "their Windows large, and sasht with Cristal Glass."

Gentlemen living on remote plantations occasionally went to extreme lengths to create private watering holes to attract and entertain the kind of polite society that was beginning to frequent spa towns in England and in port cities in the northern colonies and the islands but that had no urban venues in the Chesapeake region until later. A man's well-appointed parlor, dining room, or great bedchamber were not always equal to the task. Four neighbors in Westmoreland County, Virginia, came to that conclusion in 1670. Together they subscribed to the building of a "Banquetting House." No doubt smaller in scale, it functioned like Berkeley's party house at Green Spring, but in their case it was "for the continuance of [a] good Neighborhood."[80] Every May, each man in rotation (and, after him, his heirs) was obliged to make "an Honorable treatment fit to entertain the [other] undertakers thereof, their wives, mistress[es], & friends yearly and every year" thereafter. Their banquet hall was in effect a clubhouse. A few very wealthy planters had the inclination and the resources to build clubhouses all their own. Lewis Burwell II, of Gloucester County, Virginia, for instance, constructed a highly sophisticated and ornate structure in 1694 immediately adjacent to his older dwelling house at Fairfield plantation (Fig. 6.21).[81] Here, too, three exceptionally large and lofty entertaining rooms occupied the entire *piano nobile* elevated on a high English basement. As at Green Spring, the host and his guests could take in views of the gardens and surrounding landscape from an open veranda that ran the full length of the front facade. This impressive structure was not enlarged and converted to a residence until Nathaniel Burwell took over the property after 1705. Nor would the elder Burwell be the last great country squire to build a freestanding banqueting lodge alongside his seventeenth-century dwelling house. That distinction belongs to Robert "King" Carter, who began hosting lavish balls and "dancing assemblies" as late as 1727 at his then-brand-new monumental party house at Corotoman.[82] The story of sociable architecture continues in a subsequent chapter where it moves to the public and private ballrooms

parlor, while furnishing two superior chambers upstairs as rooms for leisurely entertainment and perhaps sometimes private soirees in the best bedchamber. Upper-floor living may have been second nature to Arthur Allen I, raised in the West Midlands, where best bedrooms were traditionally located above stairs. Or he may have acquired such cosmopolitan tastes during his years as a merchant of Bristol before he shifted operations to Virginia.

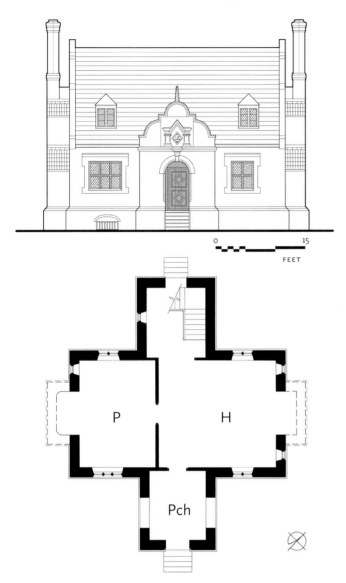

Fig. 6.22. Plan and reconstructed elevation, John Page House, 1662, Middle Plantation (Williamsburg), Virginia. Page, a planter, merchant, land speculator, and high-ranking official, operated a large brickyard and tile works on the site. The many molded bricks that have been discovered suggest ornamental brickwork, perhaps in the artisan mannerist style.

Fig. 6.23. Cartouche, Page House, Middle Plantation.

and commercial assembly rooms that finally lured country gentlemen into the region's growing towns and cities.

In their different ways, Green Spring, Bacon's Castle, and Fairfield put innovative room arrangements and room uses to early tests, some of which eventually coalesced into the mature gentry house found throughout the Chesapeake colonies in the eighteenth century. The experiments included the double-pile plan, the hall as reception room, the staircase (or stair tower) aligned directly behind a centered front entrance, suites of superior entertaining rooms above stairs, and the combination of ball and banquet rooms with smaller withdrawing rooms for card-playing, polite conversation, and the exchange of other social pleasantries. Progressive though these elements were, each trial was flawed in

ways that became unacceptable to later generations: Green Spring because its old-fashioned, U-shaped plan lacked (in the words of a contemporary architectural critic) the desired "connexion, and unity, without crossing to and fro" from one wing to another;[83] Bacon's Castle because polite visitors increasingly disliked passing through a lived-in hall to reach the principal entertaining rooms upstairs;[84] and Fairfield and other specially built banquet houses because they were only annexes and not fully integrated into the regular flow of mansion living.

Needless to say, such defects little concerned the vast majority of seventeenth-century freeholders in Maryland and Virginia. Even most of those lesser gentlemen who put out tentative feelers toward polite society in this period might refurnish their old halls and parlors, but usually nothing more. A few, like planter and entrepreneur John Page of Middle Plantation (later Williamsburg), went so far as to clear the hall for social entertaining by pushing the staircase into a tower appendage behind the house and the entrance and reception functions into a large front porch (Figs. 6.22, 6.23).[85] All the same, Page's stylish brick house of 1662, though replete with mannerist ornament, was only one story high. Inside, it provided his family and guests with no more than the usual ground-floor hall and parlor (or chamber) and two or three attic bedchambers above.

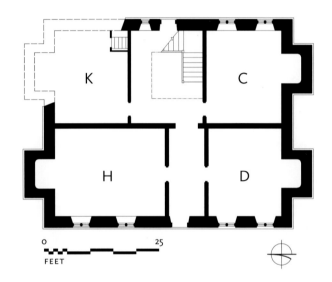

Fig. 6.24. Arlington, Northampton County, Virginia, reconstructed ground plan and elevation.

Architecturally, it was a startling advance on any building seen to date in this or any colony in North America.[86]

The builder of Arlington, Berkeley loyalist John Custis II (c. 1628–96), was born of English parents but raised in the cosmopolitan milieu of mercantile Rotterdam before he emigrated to Virginia in 1651.[87] Over the next twenty years, he amassed a fortune by planting, trading, and moneylending from his domain in Accomack (later Northampton) County. Finally, in 1674, at the zenith of his career, he hired an English bricklayer named Ralph Deane, trebled his workforce of servants and slaves, and set about building the "Great house" he called Arlington (Fig. 6.24). It was enormous by the standards of the day: 54 feet across the front, 43 feet deep, and (according to a contemporary observer) "three stories high besides garrets."[88] The prominent garrets were lit by cross gables, not dormers.

Rows of gables were of a piece with the handling of the masonry walls. They rivaled the most exuberant artisan work in England and the Netherlands. Portions of the curtain walls, all laid in English bond, were left exposed, the joints between courses tinted with red iron oxide and red ocher pigments and scored to simulate vining. Elsewhere, the walls were covered with roughcast plaster ornaments in the shape of hearts and spirals, all studded with quartz pebbles and then whitewashed (Fig. 6.25A). The overall composition of the ornamental design is lost, but its astonishing effect on passersby is not hard to imagine.

Whatever sophistication Arlington lacked in its outward appearance was compensated twice over in its compact and unified plan. Even more than its gaudy red-white-and-glitz exterior, Custis's house impressed by its awesome size and austere lines. Arlington was a towering block of a building, a double-pile mass almost as deep as it was wide. No porches, no stair towers, no forward-thrusting wings interrupted its severely rectangular outline. Only pairs of matching chimney stacks broke the sheer sweep of wall across each gable. Rising off the tablelands that spread over the Eastern Shore, Arlington loomed on the landscape as only a few other great plantation houses were to do again half a century later. To Custis's neighbors in 1675, this masonry behemoth must have looked like something come from outer space.

Custis or his builder—whoever devised the plan—was able to consolidate the structure's silhouette in this manner by finding solutions to the design problems that cluttered other seventeenth-century house plans. In his will, Custis mentioned a "hall" and a "dineinge Roome" by name.[89] Al-

Eventually, the design problems that arose from these early attempts to adapt regional house plans to the novelties of genteel living were resolved by incorporating projecting wings, porches, and towers into the block of a compact rectangular structure and by disposing rooms and passages more coherently within a double-depth plan. In the southern colonies, such developments took place well after 1700, indeed mostly after 1720. We should therefore reserve discussion of compact plans to the following chapter, as indeed we would were it not for one extraordinary and prescient exception, another Virginia house as prophetic of architectural developments yet to come as Green Spring had been a generation earlier. Ironically, Berkeley himself fled to Arlington in the darkest days of Bacon's Rebellion after the sack of Jamestown in September 1676. Even as the rebels barricaded themselves inside his beloved Green Spring, the beleaguered governor and his fugitive court got an unexpected introduction to John Custis's brand-new prodigy house on the Eastern Shore.

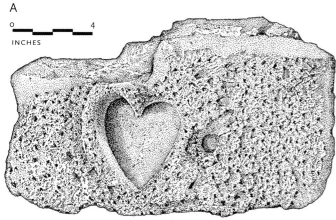

A

0   4
INCHES

ATTIC WINDOW JAMB

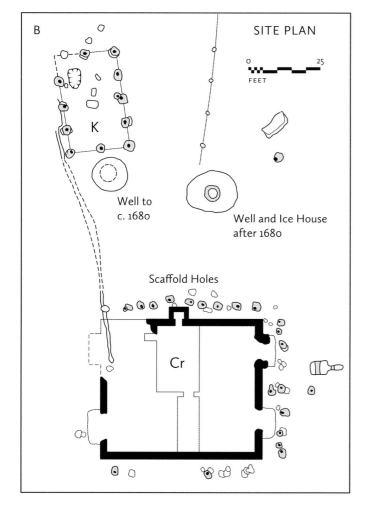

B   SITE PLAN

0   25
FEET

K

Well to
c. 1680

Well and Ice House
after 1680

Scaffold Holes

Cr

Fig. 6.25. A: Roughcast ornament from front gables, Arlington;
B: Archaeological site plan. Architectural features include an older
earthfast structure reused as an outside kitchen by 1693.

then when Custis threw open his new house to William Berkeley in 1676, the fugitive governor and his travel-weary companions must have been quite surprised to find themselves invited into a corridor the likes of which was still largely unfamiliar even to those with recent knowledge of high society in Britain. Such a passage presented the newcomers with two choices. Their host may have directed them through the doorway that led into the hall, the premier ground-floor entertaining room and additionally, at mealtimes, an anteroom to the dining room across the passage on the other side. The latter was another important public room whose furnishings included a "great Dutch Presse and [a] Gilded lookeinge Glass." Or new arrivals at Arlington may have been offered a second choice: they may have been shown down the length of the passage to a grand staircase that ascended to the floor above. There almost certainly Custis was prepared to receive guests in his "great Parlour," a superior room where he kept an expensive "presse made of Cedar and black walnut." This parlor may also have served as an anteroom to his own well-appointed bedchamber, in which he is known to have entertained neighbors and guests on various occasions. The two rooms together may have formed the same sort of superior suite of second-floor rooms that Arthur Allen maintained at Bacon's Castle.

Arlington could accommodate a large staircase and as many as four public and quasi-public entertaining rooms entirely within the four walls of the house proper because it redistributed the services and family apartments vertically rather than horizontally. The arrangement was a radical departure from age-old house-planning traditions. With no low- or high-end distinctions to respect, a good-sized kitchen could be tucked into one corner of the four-square plan. (Cooks and scullions may have used a short cellar stairs inside the kitchen to reach storage rooms for food and drink in the basement.) Similarly the bedchambers. Custis's own room was paired with the great parlor on the second floor or, alternatively, occupied the other rear corner room below. Either way, family and guests could avail themselves of three additional full-size chambers on the two main floors and an unknown number of finished attic chambers in the garrets. All were accessible from the stairwell centered between the corner rooms in the rear range. Traffic that once shuttled back and forth across traditional halls to reach upstairs parlors and chambers in separate wings now passed up and down a staircase that was only a step or two away from every

most certainly, these were two, side-by-side, front rooms on the ground floor, clear proof that here all traditional notions of architectural hierarchy had been banished without a trace. Entry space for the formal reception of guests, the usual business of a porch, was pulled directly into the hall at Arlington and very possibly into a central passage between the two front rooms, if a pair of foundation walls in the vaulted cellar underneath supported corresponding partitions on the floor above (Fig 6.25B). If so, if Arlington was one of the earliest dwellings in the colony to feature a formal center passage,

room in the house. This efficient arrangement had been prefigured at Berkeley's Green Spring mansion. The idea took thirty more years to reach maturity at Arlington. A few comparable structures were built about the same time in other colonies. Drax Hall on Barbados (c. 1650) and Province House in Boston (1676–79) were two. But no equally ambitious, equally sophisticated, equally modern gentry house was attempted again in Virginia for another generation, not until Henry Cary began drawing up plans for an official residence for Governor Alexander Spotswood in the new capital city of Williamsburg. That story most definitely belongs to the next chapter.

Arlington, Green Spring, Bacon's Castle, Fairfield, William Fitzhugh's Eagle's Nest perhaps, and maybe Philip Calvert's great brick mansion at St. Mary's City, Maryland—all were buildings that raised domestic standards to a higher level in the Chesapeake colonies. Some followed English practice more faithfully than not; others absorbed innovations from local vernacular tradition more readily than not. All numbered among the "large Brick Houses of many Rooms on a Floor, and several Stories high" that Robert Beverley reported had "of late very much improved" gentry housing in the region.[90] Together they tell us just how far architectural design had advanced before the end of the century. But these prodigy houses were anomalies too, dead ends in a sense. None gave rise to a design tradition that continued unbroken into the next century. In truth, construction of most of them stretched their builders' resources to the breaking point, even in the prosperous 1660s and 1670s. Then, beginning in 1680, the tobacco market slumped again, and thereafter prices remained low almost everywhere until 1700, improving only here and there until prosperity returned to the region as a whole after 1730. While rich planters fared better than their smaller neighbors, their advantage—they had the wherewithal to replace English servants with African slaves—drew off capital resources that otherwise they might have spent on ambitious building projects. Not by chance did the next boom in gentry house building coincide with the return of higher prices in the 1730s.

"King Tobacco" has been the dominant presence throughout the story this chapter set out to tell. No greater tyrant so ruthlessly disabused English settlers of their cherished notions of "home." No taskmaster begrudged them so little time from their labors in the fields or gave them so little encouragement to pursue the supplementary by-employments that had always helped country people in England make ends meet. No paymaster cut homesteaders so little slack in the allocation of their limited resources. No slave driver filled their tiny, clapboard-covered cottages with so many strangers. Tobacco was the absolute monarch of the Chesapeake. No one escaped its despotic rule completely. Even John Custis—who was given to styling himself "King Custis" in the presence of his lesser neighbors—even he had bowed before the colony's supreme sovereign for the twenty-some years that he pinched pennies in a small, secondhand, post-in-the-ground dwelling while amassing the fortune he needed to build Arlington. And later he submitted to another iron rule of tobacco's economy, its insistence on efficiency. As black Africans rapidly replaced English servants on his workforce after 1677, he too succumbed to the harsh logic of removing them and removing their kitchen workplace from under his own roof and relegating both to separate outbuildings.[91]

Everyone, great and small alike, came to terms with His Majesty Tobacco. When eventually a pretender appeared in the guise of an etiquette-enforcing Master of Ceremonies, only the region's wealthiest tobacco barons could afford a house and furnishings that met his demands. Notwithstanding, even they were obliged to compromise with realities that already by the third quarter of the seventeenth century had produced a brand-new vernacular building tradition in the slaveholding South. Fashion and gentility would make modest appearances in many more Chesapeake households in the decades to come, but only gradually. Until then, the vast majority of planters in Virginia and Maryland made do with clapboard cottages hardly larger or better than the cabins in which they quartered their slaves, albeit separately.

Furnished Lives

No one lives in an empty house. The buildings featured in this book were, of course, furnished (however sparsely) before they could be used in the ways the authors describe. Furnishing the Chesapeake house is another book-length subject all by itself, too large and complicated to do justice to in these pages. Still and all, the question must be asked. How did furnishings—every householder's tools for living—pattern the lives of the men and women who once occupied these houses and were the cast of characters in the social history narrative that this book ultimately sets out to tell?

The accompanying illustrations provide a shorthand answer. Each equips and furnishes an almost identical small house at fifty-year intervals—from 1650 to 1700 to 1750 and finally to 1800. The architectural renderings are based on information from documents and archaeological evidence, and, in the case of the last two drawings, from a surviving structure in Westmoreland County, Virginia, the Rochester House. The furnishings are drawn from real life as well, from specific documents, usually probate inventories, representing the same four time periods—1654, 1702, 1755, and 1795.[1] The last two record household furnishings inventoried at the Rochester House itself, a generation apart. Taken together, the four illustrations pack into a one-size-fits-all container an encapsulated history of household furnishings used throughout the region for 150 years. In larger houses, the same tables, chairs, bedsteads, cooking equipment, and other familiar objects were distributed to separate rooms with specialized functions and even to outbuildings. Houses with multiple rooms figure disproportionately in books like this one because more of them survived into modern times. Be that as it may, many freeholders in Maryland and Virginia occupied farmhouses no larger than those pictured here—a downstairs hall and an attic chamber overhead. Nor were such householders the poorest planters in the region. Far from it. Modern readers may be surprised to learn that the decedents whose probated estates were used to furnish the three eighteenth-century houses illustrated here were all slave owners, and the man who hired a carpenter to build him a house in 1654 called himself a "Gentleman." In other words, small as they were, these four unexceptional dwellings concentrate in the space of one hall and one chamber a distillation of furnished lifestyles that were known to many property holders throughout the Chesapeake region from the seventeenth century well into the nineteenth.

Described in the building agreement as "a fifteen foot house Square with a welsh [wooden] Chimney," this cottage, "well beseeming and fitting a Gentleman," was floored above and below with pine planks, and the walls were lined with riven clapboards. The contract further required the carpenter to build "a handsome Joined Bedstead," a joined table, six stools, and three wainscot chairs. Those, plus a cooking pot, tablewares, assorted buckets and baskets, and chests and boxes for linen storage, rounded out a fairly standard kit of furnishings and utensils for most reasonably affluent planters in the 1650s. The bedstead, hung with curtains for warmth more than privacy, was the most intensively used real estate inside this tiny 225-square-foot hall. Here the master and mistress slept, had sex, gave birth, horsed around with their young kids, nursed the sick and elderly, and sooner or later passed away. In addition, the downstairs room was the center of food preparation and food consumption. A bulky chest for storing textiles and a closet under the stairs for tools that had to be kept safe and dry took up still more precious floor space. Overhead, an unlit and unheated attic chamber combined dry storage for farm produce with nighttime quarters for children, servants, house slaves, and now and then temporary boarders. All other house life accommodated itself to the principal indoor activities that took place in the hall—namely, cooking, eating, and sleeping.

Fifty years later, middling planters still lived much as their parents and grandparents had, but now they enjoyed a few additional comforts, which began with improvements to the dwelling itself. Timber-frame chimneys gave way to brick stacks, plastered walls replaced clapboards, and larger casement windows admitted more sunlight. Bedsteads hung with curtains were still a well-to-do planter's most valuable piece of furniture. Also much desired by 1700 was an assortment of frying pans, roasting spits, and other kitchen utensils needed to prepare more varied meals than could be stewed in a hominy pot. Householders who could afford only one or two small improvements preferred a well-equipped hearth even to bedsteads, tables, and chairs. The additional kitchenwares not only cluttered the fireplace and nearby work tables, but the more elaborate meals they were used to prepare meant that cooks and kitchen activities occupied that half of the hall for longer hours every day. That one all-purpose room was getting crowded and busier. By 1700, housemates in some parts of the region had to make still more room for flax and spinning wheels and shoemaking tools for the production of goods at home that they once had imported from abroad. Family members or itinerant craftsmen who were engaged in spinning, tailoring, and shoemaking might sometimes find extra workspace in attics and outbuildings, which now were usually better lit.

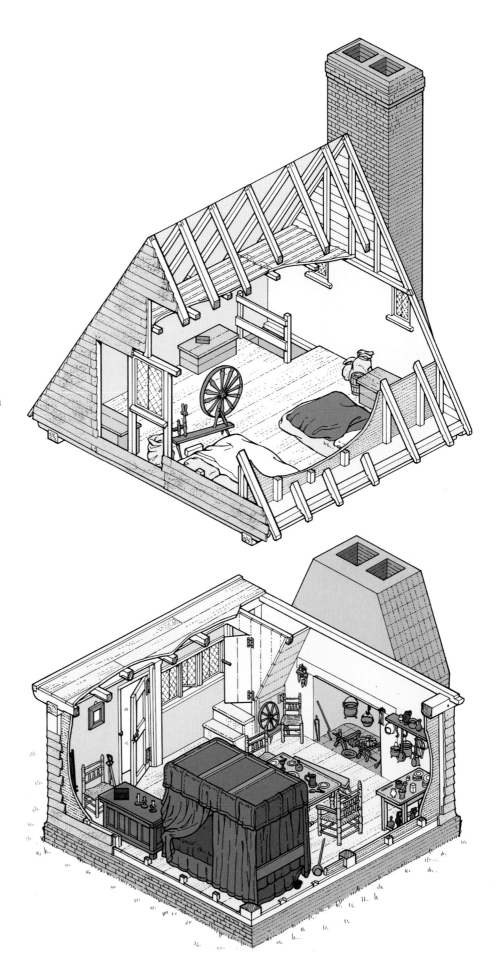

The next half century placed greater strains on almost all Chesapeake houses. Accordingly, even some of the smallest added square footage and spilled into cellars. The relentless spread of fashionable living was the culprit. Witness the house in Westmoreland County that appraisers inventoried after John Rochester's death in 1754. The 285-square-foot hall had served his family, as it had his father and mother, as both bedroom and kitchen, the latter further accessorized with a bulky food safe. Now, though, the center of the room was dominated by a stylish oval dining table. Another one and nine matching rush-bottom chairs were pushed up against the walls ready and waiting for a company of Rochester's friends and social peers. As equals, each could be offered an identical seat at his convivial table and served from sets of matching plates and stemmed wineglasses. The presence of a secretary desk implies other connections with the outside world. So doing, it brought yet another activity into the same one room where Rochester's wife and probably one or more of his female Negroes were often busy cooking and washing while keeping watchful eyes on their small children sometimes underfoot. The Rochesters' older children still slept in the attic, but at midcentury they were more comfortable in beds raised on frames in a ceiled chamber heated from a small fireplace. Farmhouse life continued much as before, except that now more prominence was given to furniture, cooking utensils, and tablewares that occasionally did double duty when the family entertained polite company.

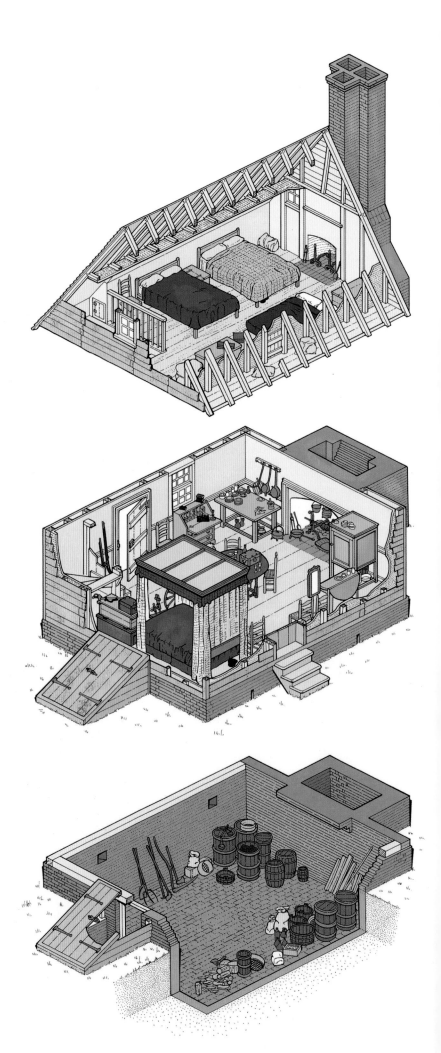

By 1800, the march of fashion and the reign of etiquette were bursting houses at the seams. Entertaining rooms multiplied exponentially in larger houses as family apartments and workrooms withdrew farther and farther behind the scenes and upstairs. Fashionable living in houses as small as the Rochester House now often pushed cooking activities (and with them the cooks) out of the house altogether into a separate kitchen. The former kitchen fireplace became a seasonal heating source and a warmer for food and beverages brought in at mealtimes from the outside cook house. The best bed, a chest or two, and sometimes a housewife's spinning wheel remained behind in the hall only because there was no good alternative. Otherwise, that room was given over almost wholly to the leisure pursuits that had turned countryman John Rochester II into a gentleman farmer. He and his family had developed a taste for tea and coffee and acquired the pots, cups and saucers, tea table, and coffee grinder needed to prepare and serve these newfangled beverages to themselves and visitors. Stools and benches were things long gone. Appraisers inventoried twenty-nine chairs in Rochester's house, small as it was. Some were hand-me-downs, but his leather chairs came in sets of eight and a dozen, in other words, identical seating for genteel men and women of equal social standing. Little by little, middling farmers were becoming as well furnished as only grandees had been 150 years earlier.

Is that simply another way of saying that the more things changed, the more they stayed the same? Not when historians look beyond the objects themselves or their numbers and ask what tasks they performed and whom those activities brought into these rooms. The 1650s farmhouse was primarily a place of rest, shelter, and nourishment for planters, wives and children, and farmhands, both enslaved and free, who went to and fro many times in the course of their daily chores. By 1700, such dwellings had also become workplaces, not just for those on kitchen detail, but for women and children and periodically for itinerant craftsmen engaged in home industries. Small houses were all that and, by 1750, plantation offices and increasingly social centers as well. Seldom again would such a menagerie of inmates be thrown together in a single room—family members, black and white farmworkers and kitchen help, business associates, and now and then neighbors and strangers expecting the polite company of other ladies and gentlemen. For by 1800 people's genteel aspirations had grown so powerful that they purged entertaining rooms everywhere of all but those who had pretensions to respect-

ability and, of course, the minions who served them but who worked and slept someplace else. Dwellings themselves often remained little changed for decades. In the meantime, new furnishings extended their usefulness by accommodating the continually evolving lifestyles of their inhabitants.

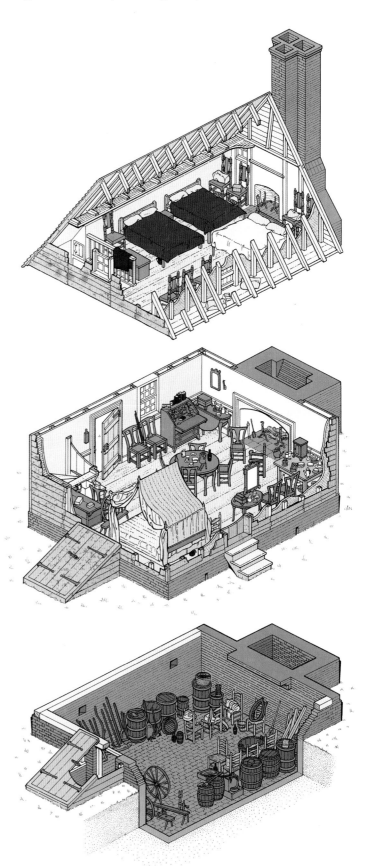

7 Town House & Country House

EIGHTEENTH AND EARLY NINETEENTH CENTURIES

MARK R. WENGER

Every old house in this book has served to categorize, divide, and facilitate daily activities for the succession of families. Each of those families came with expectations as to how it wished to live and how their dwelling should assist. To meet those expectations, it was often necessary to alter the house in some way. Bound into every old dwelling, then, is the story of how people made their lives, how they changed the business of living, and how those changes reflected the interplay of larger social and economic forces.

Beginning in the 1970s, historians and archaeologists launched a new exploration of early building in the Chesapeake Bay region, focusing on the architectural consequences of social change in the colonies of Maryland and Virginia. In the decades since, these scholars have created a new understanding of the "great house" and the social roles it filled. That story begins during the last decades of the seventeenth century, when a small cadre of families rose to social and political dominance—an event that coincided with the first efforts of these people to present the facts of their ancestry with illuminated pedigrees and correctly rendered coats of arms, and to celebrate themselves with painted portraits and silver vessels adorned with armorial engraving.[1] Material things figured ever more prominently in the effort to establish and maintain a place at the apex of Chesapeake society. Increasingly, architecture gave shape and substance to the dynastic aspirations of these leading families. As early as 1705, Robert Beverley noted that the dwellings of certain Virginians were "of late very much improved; several Gentlemen there, having built themselves large Brick Houses of many Rooms on a Floor, and several Stories high. . . . Of late they have made their Stories much higher than formerly, and their Windows large, and sasht with Cristal Glass: and within they adorn their Apartments with rich Furniture."[2]

Most persons, rich and poor, had once lived in ways that were qualitatively similar one to the other, but now the wealthy planter's house and possessions became conspicuous emblems of social rank and political attainment.[3] This

change utterly transformed the better sort of dwelling, which was now built more substantially and with more attention to finish than before. But this "genteel house" was not merely the old house with more embellishment or better materials. To meet new social demands, it had to be reorganized and enlarged. This elaboration of the Chesapeake dwelling was not a linear development in which each new plan form succeeded and then vanquished the one before. It proceeded instead like the branching of a tree and so produced an ever-growing repertoire of concurrent planning options.

Any attempt to understand this process faces an important limitation. Virtually all Chesapeake houses surviving from the seventeenth and eighteenth centuries are unrepresentative, in the sense that their original occupants stood much closer to the top of the social pyramid than to the bottom.[4] Nonetheless, these are the houses that are physically present today and available for study. Because surviving houses (with their infinite variation and subtlety) are the most informative, and because complex houses best illustrate the ways in which architecture responded to social need, this essay will emphasize standing houses and the people who first lived in them. This essay, then, is largely about gentry houses and gentry ways. It will consider the houses and lives of those who, through the ownership of land, by professional practice, or through commerce, garnered wealth sufficient to partake of the emerging consumer culture described elsewhere in this book.

Having said that, it is important to note that the architectural universe of genteel folk included houses that seem quite modest by current standards—some having just one ground-floor room. These simplest dwellings offer a useful vantage point from which to consider the development of early house-planning traditions in Maryland and Virginia.

At the heart of virtually every house, regardless of plan, was a multipurpose room called the "hall." Rich or poor, every Chesapeake resident's idea of "house" began with this all-important space. It was the conceptual center, the "irreducible core" of every dwelling. For many colonists, including some persons of fairly substantial means, this hall was literally "all the house there was."[5]

John Rochester's single-room dwelling, built in Westmoreland County, Virginia, in 1745, exemplifies the type (see Portfolio I). The original character of the interior remains uncertain, but externally, the massive brick chimney and the drawn wooden shingles that once covered the front slope of the roof would have given the place a suitably genteel aspect. In 1782, tax records placed Rochester among the top 19 percent of Westmoreland landowners; evidently, one-room dwellings were not limited to the lower orders of society.[6] Prior to completion of the main house at Monticello, Thomas Jefferson set up housekeeping in a single room at the southern end of his mountaintop compound. To a friend he declared that "I have here, like the cobbler, but one room, which serves me as kitchen and chamber, I might add as parlor and study as well."[7]

True to Jefferson's characterization, single-room dwellings brought together a promiscuous mix of people, activities, and things, but it would be misleading to suggest that this aggregation was necessarily disordered or undifferentiated. In Maryland and North Carolina, twentieth-century inhabitants of such houses spoke of discrete areas apportioned to specific individuals or activities, despite the absence of physical divisions (see Fig. 2.11).[8] This seems to have been true of eighteenth-century householders as well. The following news account of a lightning strike at the house of James Smith, a tailor in Prince Edward County, Virginia, allows us to visualize how families actually occupied such spaces. "In the room below . . . Mary Smith, wife of the above mentioned James Smith, stood ironing some clothes at a table near the end which was struck, with her back towards the chimney, and a box iron in her hand. She was knocked down." James Smith himself, who was "sitting on the working board, was struck across his thighs, but no mark appeared." A third person, "a young man who was lolling on a feather bed, near the wall where the lightning struck, with his legs resting on the work board, got a pretty large mark above one of the knees." There was yet another resident in the tiny house, a twelve-year old boy, who was "standing near the table above mentioned, sifting meal." He too was knocked down by the lightning bolt.[9]

Like Beatrix Potter's "Tailor of Gloucester," Smith sat cross-legged upon the work board that was emblematic of his trade, probably at the window, where the light was sufficient to work his needle. Mistress Smith stood before the fireplace, immersed in domestic chores, while a male youth—a son or perhaps an apprentice—lay on the floor, his feet propped on the board. At the table, where all would later eat, another young male stood preparing food. Sewing, ironing, cooking, dining, and sleeping—each had its particular, customary place in this domestic tableau; each was tethered to some landmark in the room. In the colonies of Maryland and Virginia, the history of house planning is largely the story of extracting one or more of these functions from the hall and placing them somewhere else—in another room, or in another building altogether.

TWO ROOMS

Strange as it seems, this one-room house is not the beginning of that story. A comprehensive review of the archaeological literature for early Chesapeake sites led Willie Graham to conclude that one-room houses were rare before the early decades of the eighteenth century.[10] In a previous chapter, we saw that the bulk of the typical Chesapeake dwelling diminished significantly at the end of the seventeenth century, as servants and service spaces were spun off into separate accommodations. The remaining core incorporated two ground-floor rooms of unequal size, and it was this two-room house that became the foundation for future developments. How did such dwellings function?

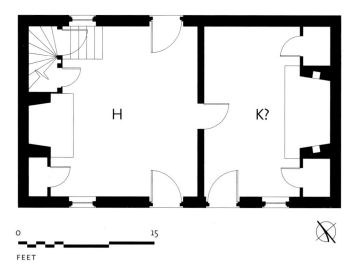

0
15
FEET

Fig. 7.1. Plan. Sturgis House, Northampton County, Virginia. In houses with no central circulation space, separate doors could provide independent access to the ground-floor rooms. The smaller room was normally used for sleeping or socializing. In this case, the size of the fireplace suggests that the smaller room may have served for cooking.

THE HALL

By the second quarter of the eighteenth century, a two-room house with chimneys at each end had become the reflexive choice of Virginians and Marylanders alike (Fig. 7.1). Throughout the previous century, the larger room, the hall, had functioned as an informal, all-purpose living space. By its very nature, the hall was a public room—typically it served as the primary point of entry and for that reason was sometimes called the "Outer Room." In such cases, merely crossing the planter's threshold placed visiting strangers in the midst of his domestic world. The hall was open to many sorts of people, engaged in varied activities, surrounded always by a wide range of commodities and domestic objects.

The second quarter of the eighteenth century witnessed profound changes in the social concept and physical character of this space, changes that involved the growing importance of genteel entertainment among elite families.[11] This new interest in public "hospitality" found expression in the growing array of formal equipage genteel folk acquired during the first two decades of the eighteenth century, though the process of accumulation had begun decades earlier. In 1686, William Fitzhugh wrote to an associate in Bristol, England, about his Virginia property, which included "my own Dwelling house, furnished with all accommodations for a comfortable & genteel living, as a very good dwelling house, with 13 Rooms in it, four of the best of them hung, nine of them furnished with all things necessary & convenient & all houses for use well furnished with brick Chimneys."[12]

Fitzhugh's letter reminds us that gentility embraced house and contents equally and that public rooms mattered most. In Fitzhugh's case, these spaces were furnished to be "comfortable & genteel," while others merely reflected the dictates

of necessity and convenience. His order for an elegant silver table setting reflected a new concern for the appearance of the meal and of the room in which it took place.[13] "I esteem it as well politic as reputable, to furnish my self with an handsom Cupboard of plate which gives my self the present use & Credit, is a sure friend at a dead lift, without much loss, or is a certain portion for a Child after my decease."[14]

Since there were few dedicated "dining rooms" at the time, this impressive collection of silver was almost certainly intended for Fitzhugh's hall. Just two years later, William Byrd I of Charles City County, Virginia, ordered what soon became the standard kit of hall furniture for his best room: "1 dozen best Rushia lether chairs, 1 small, 1 middlcing & 1 large ovall table." In contrast with items of "best" quality for this hall, the furniture for Byrd's inner room was to be "neat, but cheap."[15] Like William Fitzhugh, Byrd was determined to meet the needs of every dinner guest individually. At Fitzhugh's house, each had his own plate and flatware; at Byrd's, each was to have his own chair—no seating of the company on benches, no serving of the guests from a communal vessel.

These furnishings imply that Virginians came to identify hospitality with the hall, and the room's architectural appointments soon reflected that fact. Once a repository for virtually any movable object or commodity the planter owned, the hall came to be a place of formal reception, where all the owner's best possessions were assembled and displayed.[16] The formal character of this new hall—one observer called it the "entertaining room"—was defined by what the planter put there, but also by what he removed.[17] After 1700, beds began to disappear from the hall, as the master either retreated to the chamber or to the room above it. After 1720, it was rare to find anyone sleeping in the best room. By 1750, the practice had ceased entirely among the gentry set. Gone, too, were the workaday implements and bulk commodities enumerated in earlier inventories. Growing quantities of refined consumer goods now took their place, but it was no longer acceptable for even these things to lie about in plain view.

This is no time to flail at the thicket of folklore surrounding closets. For now, it is enough to say that closets were rare in these parts until the last quarter of the seventeenth century, and even then, the term often referred to a small room where the master or his mistress could be alone. Nonetheless, as a snowballing interest in refined living began to fill the house with consumer goods, closets-as-storage began to emerge in response.

THE CHAMBER

The smaller component of the two-room house, often called the "parlor," took its name from English room-naming traditions and, ultimately, from French, in which "parler" means "to speak." This name derived from the room's original function as a place for conversation and related social activity. In these parts, however, the space went by several other names, including "inward room," "little room," or "chamber," all describing either its function, its size, or its relationship to the other space. Among these, "chamber" (essentially a bedroom) became the most common.

From the beginning, this chamber was closely associated with female endeavor.[18] If any room in the house could be regarded as belonging to the mistress, it was this one. Here the planter's wife kept her bed, while the master himself often slept in the hall or in the second-floor room above, as Arthur Allen seemingly did at Bacon's Castle (see Fig. 2.10).[19] Consequently, the chamber became a kind of administrative center from which the mistress managed the day-to-day operation of her household. Here were kept the "precious stores for the table"—tea, coffee, sugar, physic (medicine), candles, linens, and such—all under lock and key, all in her care.[20] Most often these objects resided in a freestanding cupboard, though built-in cupboards for this purpose occasionally survive. An example at Smith's Fort, in Surry County, Virginia, is particularly revealing. The time and expense lavished on this installation, with its circular head and raised panels, leaves no doubt of its symbolic importance. Like the intricately adorned leather baskets in which matriarchs later carried their keys, the cupboard symbolized the mistress's position as manager of the household. To facilitate that role, her room was often situated between the hall and the out-of-door activities that served it. In some houses, a doorway led from her room directly into the service or kitchen yard (Fig. 7.2).

Access to this inner room was more selective than for the hall, but that limitation did not equate with complete privacy. In addition to its function as a sleeping space and housekeeper's office, the chamber served as a quasi-public sitting room where it was common to see four or even six chairs. Amazingly, appraisers counted seventeen chairs in the first-floor chamber of Robert "King" Carter's house at Corotoman—not a place for solitary ruminations![21]

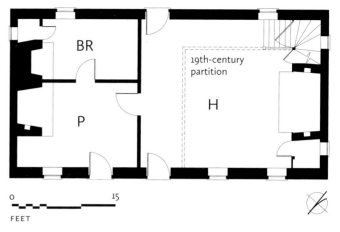

Fig. 7.2. Restored plan. Williams Green, after 1731, Somerset County, Maryland.

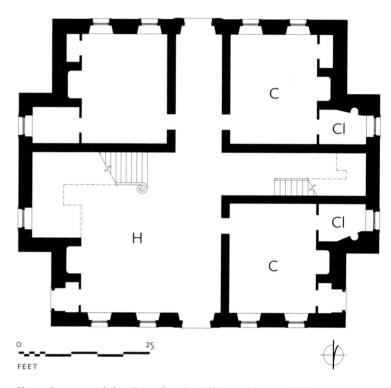

Fig. 7.3. Reconstructed plan. Rosewell, 1726–37, Gloucester County, Virginia.

Inventories suggest that most early chambers shared this public dimension. As late as the 1750s, probate records listed tea tables and tea equipage in sleeping rooms above and below stairs. Tea drinking, of course, was typically a public ritual.[22] The equipment of these rooms for tea reflected an expectation that persons outside the immediate circle of family and friends would be present on some occasions.[23] Significantly, the term "closet," used in the sense of a private study, appears most frequently in late seventeenth- and early eighteenth-century records—suggesting that early chambers afforded little real privacy, hence the need for some genuine place of retreat (Fig. 7.3).

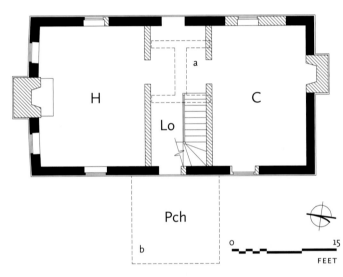

a. Center-chimney lobby-entry plan altered to its current center-passage arrangement in the 1820s.

b. Extent of original porch tower that was removed as part of the 1820s renovation.

Fig. 7.4. Plan and reconstructed elevation. Carvill Hall, c. 1695–1709, Kent County, Maryland. It appears that the house originally had a porch and an internal lobby in front of the chimney.

LOBBIES AND PORCHES

For the packaging of these two ground-floor rooms—hall and chamber—we generally imagine a house with chimneys at either end, but this was not always the case. In chapter 6, Cary Carson explained that the ground-floor rooms of certain houses were heated by a shared chimney positioned near the middle of the building. Judging from the rarity of early survivors, this type of house rapidly diminished in favor after 1700. Carvill Hall in Kent County, Maryland (1695–1709), and the Sands House, in Annapolis (c. 1739), may be the ear-

Fig. 7.5. Benches in the porch at Malvern Hill, c. 1700–25, Henrico County, Virginia. These were intended for the use of persons not admitted to the best room, or, in warmer weather, for members of the family. The large arches suggest that this porch was conceptualized not as a part of the dwelling's interior space, but as an exterior appendage. The small room above was often denominated as the "porch chamber." (Cook Collection, Valentine Richmond History Center)

liest Maryland examples now standing, though Carvill Hall has lost its chimney (Fig. 7.4). In each case, a lobby and stair stood against the front flank of the chimney, affording controlled access to the ground-floor rooms and to the upstairs. At Carvill Hall, moreover, a porch tower (also lost) originally sheltered the entry. Something of the actual character and function of such porches is captured in a nineteenth-century photograph of Malvern Hill in Henrico County, Virginia, where built-in benches still lined the walls (Fig. 7.5). It was here that black servants and whites of low estate waited, the former for a summons from the master, the latter for an opportunity to communicate with the master on some matter of business.[24]

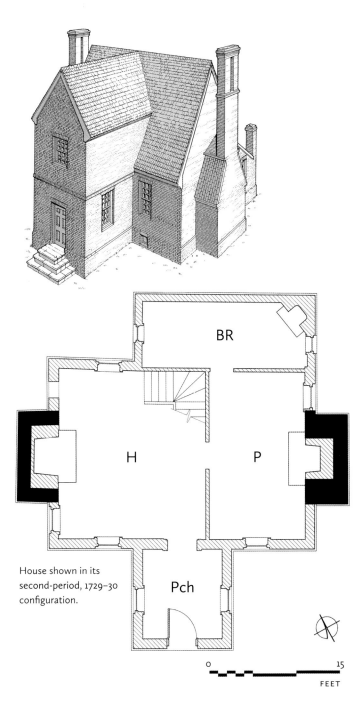

House shown in its
second-period, 1729–30
configuration.

*Fig. 7.6. Plan and elevation. Matthew Jones House, c. 1720, remodeled and
encased in brick in 1729, Newport News, Virginia. The enclosure of this porch
leaves little doubt that the builder regarded it as a part of the house interior.*

Conceived as a kind of waiting room, porches like the
ones at Carvill Hall and Malvern Hill signaled the new importance of the hall as a formal entertaining room and, thus,
the need to exclude certain kinds of people from that space.
In Virginia, the trend is best represented by the Matthew
Jones House, an earthfast frame house encased in brick with
a porch in 1729 to provide a more genteel experience in the
hall (Fig. 7.6). The emergence of the lobby and porch as a
means of formalizing and managing interactions with others
portended still other changes to the planter's dwelling.

TWO NEW ROOMS

The second quarter of the eighteenth century witnessed two
important additions to the hall-chamber house described
above—the passage and the dining room. Like the formal-
ization of the old hall, the introduction of these spaces was
closely allied to the growing importance of public entertainment among the gentry. Having achieved an elevated place
in the new social order, well-to-do Marylanders and wealthy
Virginians displayed that attainment through the liberal
entertainment of visiting guests, a convivial practice called
"hospitality." To say that hospitality was partly calculated for
show in no way discounts the planter's genuine desire for fellowship. Prompted by the weary solitude of life in a "silent
country," planters opened their houses to friend and stranger
alike.[25] Genteel travelers presenting themselves at the front
door of most any planter could expect to find fellowship, a
meal, and a bed. Indeed, gentlemanly status was defined in
part by the capacity to engage in acts of liberality.[26]

THE PASSAGE

The concept of hospitality implied sociability, of course, but
it also set limits on sociable conduct. Not all visitors were invited to enter the planter's hall or sit at his table. As we have
seen, the task of deciding whom to admit was facilitated at
first by the "porch," a partially enclosed appendage that sheltered the front door and provided seating for those who were
not allowed to cross the threshold. Dell Upton has argued
that this function was later assumed by a central hallway or
"passage" that extended the full depth of the house. Con-
ceptually, he suggests that the old porches were "drawn into
the house" to create these passages (Fig. 7.7) (see Fig. 2.10).
Probate records mentioned porches well into the eighteenth
century, but beginning in the 1730s and 1740s the passages
surpassed them in number and significance. Now it was the
passage where visitors paused, awaiting an invitation to enter
the formal room beyond.[27]

Three recorded incidents reveal how the sorting process
worked. During a 1785 visit to Virginia, Robert Hunter
nervously presented himself at the house of a Gloucester
County grandee, whereupon "entering the house we were
received by Mr. [Warner] Lewis himself, a polite, elegant
gentleman. We . . . made an apology for our situation, as
we certainly had intended to have proceeded immediately
to York, if the weather would have permitted us. We told
him our names, when he politely desired us to walk into the
parlor, where there were several gentlemen."[28] Everyone present understood the significance of this encounter in Lewis's

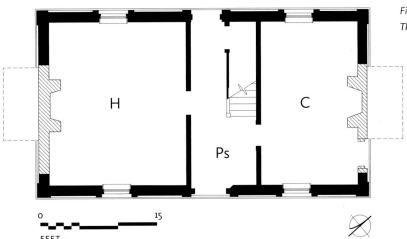

H

C

Ps

0   15
FEET

passage. After a brief period of evaluation, Hunter and his companion were invited to enter the best room, a verdict of acceptance that the diarist acknowledged with evident relief.

Not all comers fared so well. When Alexander Macaulay visited Williamsburg in 1783, he was obliged to wait in a passage populated with black servants before seeing Mrs. Campbell. Peevishly, he wrote that "as I did not approve of waiting for her in the passage, I . . . led Bettsy into the cold parlour." By entering without invitation, Macaulay committed a spectacular breach of etiquette, contesting the servants' assessment of his social identity.[29]

Tutor Philip Fithian's account of life at Nomini Hall describes a different sort of encounter, one between Robert Carter III and a slave. According to Fithian, Carter's slave entered the passage with deferential awe: "About ten an old Negro Man came with a complaint to Mr Carter of the Overseer. . . . The humble posture in which the old Fellow placed himself before he began moved me. We were sitting in the passage."[30] Like Macaulay, Carter's slave was allowed no further than the passage. Again, the entry acted as a barrier, restricting access not to Carter's person, but to the inner sanctum of his domestic establishment.

Virginians identified this best room with formal entertainment and sought, increasingly, to hold it aloof from the comings and goings of the household. The introduction of a central passage met this need by providing independent access not only to the various ground-floor rooms but to the chambers "above stairs" as well.

In this way, the passage became the crossroads of the house. Chesapeake families also came to appreciate the practical advantages of this new space as a refuge from the heat of summer. As early as 1724, Hugh Jones remarked that some Williamsburg houses were provided with "a passage generally through the middle of the house for an air-draft in summer." In 1732, William Hugh Grove similarly commented

that "the Manner of Building is much alike. They have a broad Stayrcase with a passage thro the house in the middle which is the Summer hall and Draws the air."[31] Grove's term, "summer hall," is significant, for it points to the growing importance of the passage as a living space and emphasizes the seasonality of its use.[32]

In mid-July of 1735 William Fairfax amplified these observations, writing that Virginians frequently "have a large Porch before the Door & generally another behind the House, in one of which or [in the] Hall & passage they always sit & frequently dine & sup but the musquitos there are very troublesome."[33] This remark is useful in adding porches to the repertoire of sitting and dining spaces used by Virginians in warm weather. It seems that Fairfax used the term "porch" in the older sense, connoting the open, ground-floor space of a projecting tower, usually with an enclosed room above. If we take his remarks literally, the porch and passage were as suitable for dinner—the main meal of the day—as for supper, the later, lighter meal at day's end.

Unlike the porch, the passage seems to have been an urban innovation. In Virginia, most of the earliest examples were associated with the region around Williamsburg and Yorktown. In 1717, John Custis of Williamsburg wrote to London for "good Comicall diverting prints to hang in the passage of my house."[34] The following year, Williamsburg gunsmith John Brush and impresario William Levingston built houses on adjoining lots. Both of these dwellings originally had passages and both exhibit unconventional methods of framing to accommodate the stair opening; evidently, the stair passage was still new enough at this time that carpenters were still trying to solve the problems presented by a large stair aperture at the rear wall.

In 1719 appraisers mentioned a passage in the Williamsburg inventory of Rowland Jones. About the same time, Richard King prepared a simple floor plan for what became

Fig. 7.8. "Mum S. at work in the minor hall— Dynes Hall—Brisk near her dozing." Watercolor by Diana Sperling. (Courtesy of Mrs. Nony Ollerenshaw)

Swan Tavern, to be built in Yorktown, just down the road from Williamsburg (see Fig. 5.13). Moreover, John Blair of Williamsburg built a new house in 1722, which, despite its covering of riven clapboards, boasted a central passage (see Fig. 7.10A). At this early date, Williamsburg and Yorktown, with their many new houses and ideas, appear to have driven the development of house planning in Virginia.[35]

Social considerations were certainly important in the emergence of the passage, but seasonality was also central to the concept of this space. During the summer of 1781, Sarah Nourse of Berkeley County, (West) Virginia, complained often of her discomfort from heat and humidity. If breezes allowed, she occasionally remained "upstairs"— in the ground-floor passage—dressed only in a "shift" or undergarment, sometimes taking her meals there. When the breezes failed, she found it necessary to seek relief in the cellar, where she reported working, dining, and, occasionally, having tea.[36]

Landon Carter of Sabine Hall, in Richmond County, Virginia, seems to have used his passage as a similar place of resort. In 1775, William Lee wrote to Carter, promising him "a line to repose on in a hot afternoon in ye cool passage." Sometime later, Carter remarked in his diary on the "Gale's Pattent bedsteads on a new plan," adding, "I want one for my Passage in summer." Likewise, when, in July of 1774, tutor Philip Fithian visited George Turberville in Westmoreland County, Virginia, he found the captain seated with his company "in a cool passage." Clearly, Virginians made seasonal adjustments in their use of domestic space, and the passage played an important role in that process.[37]

The importance of this "summer hall" during the warmest months can be seen in the 1760 inventory of Virginia planter Gawen Corbin. Among the articles assembled in Corbin's passage, Westmoreland County appraisers found a couch, twelve chairs, three tables, a corner cupboard, a candle stand, and a harpsichord.[38] Clearly, someone was living here, where doors at either end could be thrown open to "draw the air." The illustration above, an English watercolor, offers an idea of what life in the passage may have looked like on such occasions (Fig. 7.8). A woman sits at an open door, where there is air and sufficient light to carry on with her needlework. This woman was the prime administrator of her household (note the key basket that stands on the table). Her proximity to the doorway may explain the folding screen listed in the 1772 inventory of York County resident Thomas Hornsby, undoubtedly intended to exclude the curious stares of persons in the street.[39]

THE DINING ROOM

The growing refinement of life among the Chesapeake gentry made new demands on the planter's house. Genteel life centered on the institution of hospitality, and the ritual enactment of hospitality centered on the meal. In time, this tended to elaborate the meal and thus the planter's table. The first quarter of the eighteenth century witnessed the proliferation of specialized wares and of forms intended solely for display—dish rings to elevate serving pieces, jelly glasses to display vividly colored desserts, and ornamental figures of sugar, laid over with gold leaf, merely to look at. All the while, matching sets of chairs, dishes, and utensils invested the table with opulence and formality.[40]

The new significance of the meal led some householders to create a separate venue for that all-important event. At first, they accomplished this by transforming their chambers (or parlors) into dining rooms. Probate records reflected this trend by the end of the 1720s, when small oval dining tables and related equipage began to appear in the inner room, even when the planter or his wife continued sleeping there.

John O'Sheal, of Norfolk County, Virginia, maintained one of these transitional dining spaces at the time of his death in 1749. Besides a bed, his "Parler" furniture included fourteen chairs, two square mahogany dining tables, a mahogany tea table and tea board, tea china, several punch bowls, and a desk containing a set of money scales. At the time of the inventory, the square dining tables would have been quite fashionable, allowing O'Sheal the option of entertaining four persons or six, as the occasion required. Eventually these square tables would eclipse the older, oval form in popularity. In later decades, too, the desk and money scales would come to be a common fixture in Virginia dining rooms, assisting in the conduct of business after women left the table. Whatever O'Sheal's appraisers chose to call it, this was a formal dining space, and the quality of its furnishings reflected that purpose. Though the hall was equipped with similar furnishings, comparable articles in the parlor were consistently assigned higher values.[41]

In Richmond County, Virginia, the 1750 inventory of

Leroy Griffin provides a revealing case of resistance to the new terminology. Griffin's appraisers enumerated the contents of a space called the "Chamber" but identified the room directly above as being "over the Dining Room."[42] Nonetheless, probate inventories from the second quarter of the century show a noticeable trend toward spaces called "dining room." Admittedly, the designation had appeared in Chesapeake records long before this—in some cases as early as the 1660s—but it was not until the late 1720s and the early 1730s that it was applied consistently to dedicated dining spaces.[43]

Like the introduction of the central passage, the emergence of these dining rooms may have found inspiration in Williamsburg, where in 1722 the Governor's Council called for painting the "Great Dining Room" of the governor's house (see Fig. 2.1D).[44] Though the Governor's Palace remained unfinished at the time, Lieutenant-Governor Alexander Spotswood had set up housekeeping there in 1714, and it was probably under his roof that many well-to-do people first experienced hospitality in a large, lavishly appointed space dedicated solely to the meal. After 1730, the incidence of the term "Dining Room" in probate records begins to grow. If we add in the chambers and parlors with dining equipment and no beds, the trend accelerates impressively in the 1740s, 1750s, and 1760s.

THREE ROOMS AND (SOMETIMES) A PASSAGE

Once the smaller room adjoining the passage was given over to dining, some other room often became the primary sleeping space. Occasionally it stood against the rear of the old parlor or chamber, taking on the name "back room." Just as parlors and chambers without beds grew in importance during the 1740s, so too did the incidence of these "back room" spaces.[45]

In houses where the chamber continued to function as the primary sleeping space, the adjoining "back room" sometimes served as a kind of study and repository for male gear—books, edged weapons, guns, razors, fishing gear, and the like. In regard to privacy, such spaces may have functioned like the "closets" at Rosewell, providing a place in which to enjoy true solitude.[46]

Of these two arrangements, it was the former—a chamber attached to the rear of the dining room—that prevailed. The identity of the dining room as a space given wholly to meals was firmly established by 1750—after that date inventories rarely mentioned dining rooms with beds. The term "chamber," referring to the principal sleeping space, survived this transition, but the use of "parlor" to identify the princi-

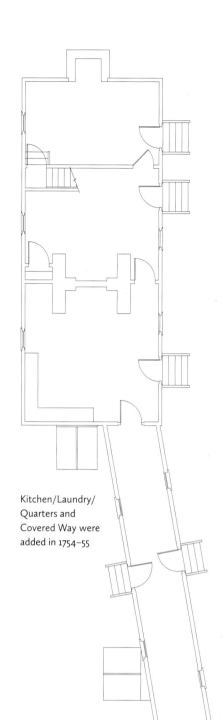

Kitchen/Laundry/
Quarters and
Covered Way were
added in 1754–55

pal sleeping space rapidly waned. Confusingly, the term later became synonymous with "hall."

In the decades leading up to midcentury, a new constellation of three rooms—hall, dining room, and chamber, sometimes with a passage—had emerged as the standard complement of spaces in substantial houses. This expanded repertoire of domestic spaces soon broke open the axial, two-room box that had long been the planter's house, leading to a reformulation of the dwelling's external form. By the 1750s, the resulting "three-room" house became a staple of house planning among the Chesapeake gentry.

Among these three-room dwellings, the earliest survivor is probably the Williamsburg house of William Robertson, built over a period of three years, 1715–18 (Fig. 7.9). Now subsumed within the later dwelling of Peyton Randolph, it was a cubic structure, with three ground-floor living spaces plus an entry, all distributed around a central chimney. This plan made but little of the entry. At this early date, the room was simply a means of independent circulation, another of Upton's porches, drawn into the house. Nonetheless, its physical connection to both the hall and the dining room underscored the public character of those spaces, while highlighting the privacy of the chamber, which stood completely apart from the entry.

Three-room dwellings were often the product of alteration. In houses already built, one could obtain a new dining space by adding a new hall. Sometimes this was a matter of simple extension. The Williamsburg house of John Blair is perhaps the earliest example. As mentioned earlier, Blair first built his house, a central passage, hall-and-chamber dwelling, in 1723. In 1737 he added a new hall at one end and then appropriated the old hall for dining (Fig. 7.10A). To serve

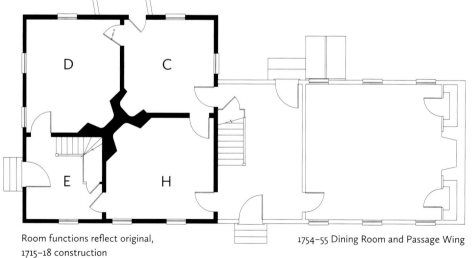

Room functions reflect original,
1715–18 construction

0   15
FEET

1754–55 Dining Room and Passage Wing

Fig. 7.9. Plan. Robertson Tenement, 1715–18, enlarged 1754–55 by Peyton Randolph with a service wing to the north and a passage and dining room to the east, Williamsburg.

A

0   15

FEET

Fig. 7.10. Plans. A: John Blair House, 1723, enlarged 1737, Williamsburg; B: Sotterley, 1704, enlarged 1715, 1732, 1762–63, 1768–70, St. Mary's County, Maryland; C: Kingston Manor, 1760s–80s, St. Mary's County, Maryland.

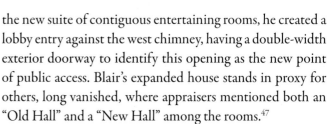

B

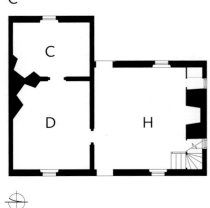

C

the new suite of contiguous entertaining rooms, he created a lobby entry against the west chimney, having a double-width exterior doorway to identify this opening as the new point of public access. Blair's expanded house stands in proxy for others, long vanished, where appraisers mentioned both an "Old Hall" and a "New Hall" among the rooms.[47]

The new dining space could also assume the form of a rear ell, as at Sotterley, in St. Mary's County, Maryland, where the rear dining room—clearly an addition—was added by 1715 (Fig. 7.10B).[48] Hall, dining room, and chamber—Marylanders had settled on the same constellation of living spaces as Virginians, but that is not to say that the results were always congruent. At Sotterley, a narrow passage in the rear wing led from the hall, in the front range, back to a stair by the dining room chimney. This little corridor removed traffic from the dining room—but not from the hall. While Virginians often chose to mediate between all three living spaces with some

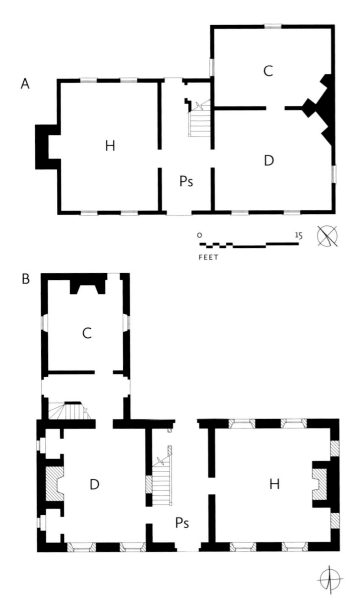

Fig. 7.11. Plans. A: Harwood House, c. 1750–70, Williamsburg; B: Hewick, c. 1750, Middlesex County, Virginia.

ity of the three-room idea. At Providence Plantation, Kent County, Maryland, the hall was the largest room, entered directly from the exterior. As at Kingston Manor, the main stair ascended beside the hall chimney. The chamber is identified by its exterior doorway and by the back stair ascending to the upper floor. As usual, this chamber joined to the back of the dining room and protruded from the rear of the main range. The one-story kitchen connected to what was probably the dining room. Attaching a kitchen directly to the house was more common on the Eastern Shore of Maryland than elsewhere in the Chesapeake. Here, the wing appears to be an early structure, showing that the practice was not confined to the post–Civil War period as was typically the case in Virginia. A single chimney served the principal room, while the dining room and chamber shared a chimney with corner fireplaces, a common arrangement in Maryland and Virginia alike.

The Williamsburg house of bricklayer Humphrey Harwood exhibited a similar plan, but with a passage, an arrangement more common in Virginia (Fig. 7.11A). As at Kingston Hall, the chamber protruded only a short way beyond the rear of the main range and so was covered by an extension of the main roof. Again, a shared, gable-end chimney with corner fireplaces served the dining room and chamber.

At Hewick, in Middlesex County, Virginia, a small passage separated the chamber from the main range of the house (Fig. 7.11B). This circulation space afforded independent access to the dining room and chamber from the service compound, allowing the mistress to move unobserved between chamber and kitchen while servants passed between kitchen and dining room. At the same time, it placed the chamber one remove farther from the dwelling's public core. Logistically, this passage was an enlarged version of the shared vestibule that occasionally joined the chamber and dining room to the service yard. Carter's Grove, in James City County, illustrates the latter sort of scheme.

As the ground floor of the Chesapeake House manifested these changes, the upper floor was also evolving. The Williamsburg dwelling of carpenter Seymour Powell, a hall-and-chamber house with a side passage, presented a novel exterior mass, having a gambrel roof as the crowning element (Fig. 7.12) (see Fig. 10.28). While it made an obvious contribution to the building's external appearance, this roof was most important for what it did inside—augmenting avail-

sort of entry or corridor, the same three rooms often stood together without distinct circulation in Maryland houses.

Williams's Green, in Somerset County, Maryland, is an early three-room dwelling with no passage or porch (see Fig. 7.2).[49] It illustrates how the old axial house form could be retained by compressing the dining room and chamber in a front-to-back pairing, opposite the hall. Even with no passage, one could still have independent access to the hall and dining room by creating separate front doorways to each, as was originally done here.

At Kingston Manor, a pre-Revolutionary house in St. Mary's County, Maryland, the chamber protruded from the rear of the main range, creating an L-shaped footprint that was more characteristic of three-room houses in both colonies (Fig. 7.10C). Like Williams's Green, this house had no passage, so the stair ascended beside the hall fireplace.

A related plan, dating to 1781, illustrates the durabil-

Fig. 7.12. Powell-Hallam House, c. 1753, Williamsburg.

able space "above stairs." This gambrel or "Dutch" form, first seen in the Chesapeake during the 1740s, reflected the growing importance residents ascribed to the upper floor in the decades leading up to the Revolution and the consequent elaboration of those spaces.[50] The result was an imposing new form that communicated something of the owner's ascendant position as a successful tradesman.

FOUR ROOMS AND A PASSAGE

Planning developments did not end with the emergence and elaboration of the three-room house. Occasionally, the addition of a small, fourth room completed a perfectly rectangular plan and thus unified the dwelling's outward form. The Moore House in Yorktown is perhaps the best example (Fig. 7.13A). In North Carolina, Edenton's Cupola House, built for Francis Corbin 1757–58, is another. In both cases, hall, dining room, and chamber assume the familiar, L-shaped configuration, but with a small, unheated closet positioned behind the hall.

Sometimes the fourth room became a heated living space, but one without a strongly defined social function. While appraisers referred consistently to the "hall," "dining room," and "chamber," the fourth room went by a host of different names—"Nursery," "Study," "Mrs. Wormley's Room," "the Yellow Room," or "Little Parlour." The best that appraisers could do for a consistent name was the functionally neutral term "Back Room." The Yorktown house of Thomas Nelson illustrates this arrangement (Fig. 7.13B). As at the Moore House, the hall, dining room, and chamber form an L-shaped apartment of interconnected spaces. However, the fourth space, referred to as the "Back Room" in a 1789 inventory, is accessible from the passage only.[51]

The "problematic" identity of this fourth room helps us make sense of Thomas Jefferson's sketch plan for a house prepared sometime after 1765 (Fig. 7.14). Customarily, we think of Jefferson as a "citizen of the world," though it is clear that he regarded himself as a Virginian first and foremost. If there were any doubts as to where his center of gravity lay, this crudely rendered plan lays them all to rest. In the best Virginia tradition, he envisioned a hall or "parlour," a "dining room," and a "chamber." Like his neighbors, though, Jefferson was unsure what to call the fourth room—and so left it blank. Whatever Jefferson borrowed from the canons of classical architecture, it was always grafted onto a locally derived understanding of what constituted an acceptable house.

The mention of Jefferson calls to mind the Williamsburg house of George Wythe, where Jefferson read law as a young man. In its original state, this house codified the four-room, central-passage formula—hall and dining room in the front, chamber behind (and communicating with) the dining room, and a fourth room behind the hall, accessible only from the rear of the passage (see Fig. 5.11B). In Wythe's

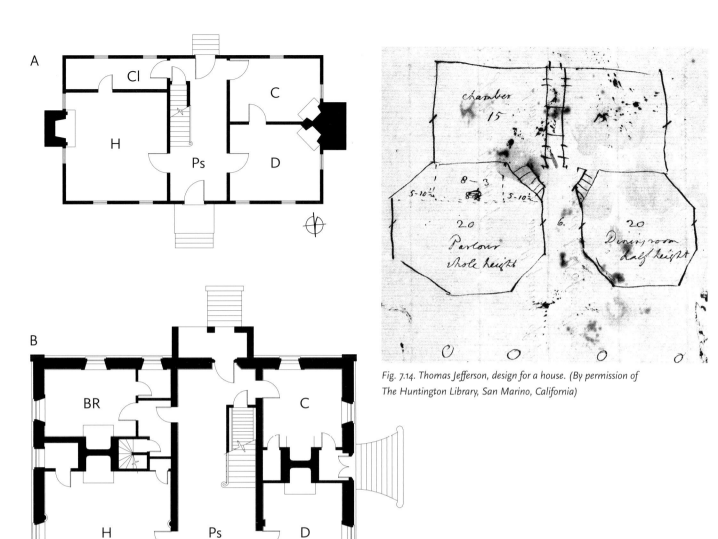

A

CI
H
Ps
C
D

B

BR
C
H
Ps
D

0   15
FEET

Fig. 7.13. Plans. A: Moore House, c. 1750, Yorktown, Virginia; B: Nelson House, 1729, Yorktown, Virginia. The Nelson plan represents probable room designations in the construction period. By 1789 the dining room had come to occupy the largest room.

Fig. 7.14. Thomas Jefferson, design for a house. (By permission of The Huntington Library, San Marino, California)

time, the latter space appears to have functioned as a study. Nowadays this house is everyone's idea of "Georgian symmetry," but there was nothing inevitable about its carefully considered design — this dwelling was the product of a tortuous evolutionary process. Even if the plan was bilaterally symmetrical, the logistical scheme of the ground floor was not.

Four Mile Tree, in Surry County, Virginia, better illustrates the hierarchical nature of this so-called Georgian-plan house; every ground-floor room is a different size, expressing its relative importance in the overall scheme of the interior

(Fig. 7.15A).[52] Taking the traditional triad of hall, dining room, and chamber as the organizing principle for this plan, the hall was surely the largest and the best room, having cupboards for display of the owner's finest possessions. In that case, the dining room was probably the smaller space to the east. Normally, that would place the chamber in the room behind, but here that space was originally unheated. Clearly, the principal bedchamber was the heated room behind the hall.

Owing to its location, this space was sometimes called the "Hall Back Room." Augustine Washington had such a room in 1743, and the internal divisions of his house probably resembled the ones at Ferry Farm, near Fredericksburg (Fig. 7.15B). Judging from the appraised value of Washington's "hall back room" furnishings, it too served as the best sleeping space.[53] The *smaller* of Washington's rear spaces was called the "back room," and that was likely the situation at Four Mile Tree. In other cases, when the room opposite the chamber was the largest, it could function like the "Little Parlor" at another Washington house, Mount Vernon, where

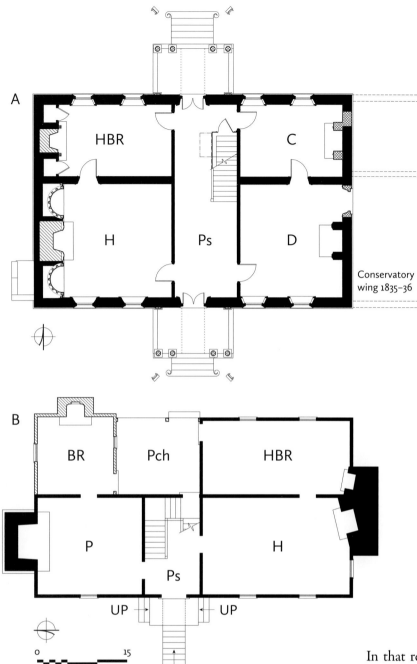

the family could congregate on the rare occasions when there was no company (see Fig. 7.32B).[54]

Unlike many houses of the period, Four Mile Tree turned its back to the river, despite the dwelling's dramatic situation overlooking the James. The stair faced the land side of the house, where the best rooms stood ready to receive guests arriving from that direction. But while the internal organization of the house favored those who arrived by the county road, the exterior was formulated to present suitably impressive faces to the road and the river alike, ascribing equal importance to each.

In that regard, it resembled the Wythe House, though the two dwellings are very different externally. At the Wythe House, the upper rooms are two full stories in height, while at Four Mile Tree they are encompassed within a "hip-on-gambrel" roof (see Figs. 5.12, 15.16). In both instances, the importance of these spaces was acknowledged in the ample provisions made for light and heat. The unitary mass of such houses appeals to modern tastes, but this was not the most common choice for early Virginians and Marylanders.

ADDITIONAL OPTIONS — REAR SHEDS

The four-room, central-passage plan could be packaged in a number of ways, depending on the importance ascribed to the upper rooms. More often, the main range was one full story in height, with corresponding rooms on the upper

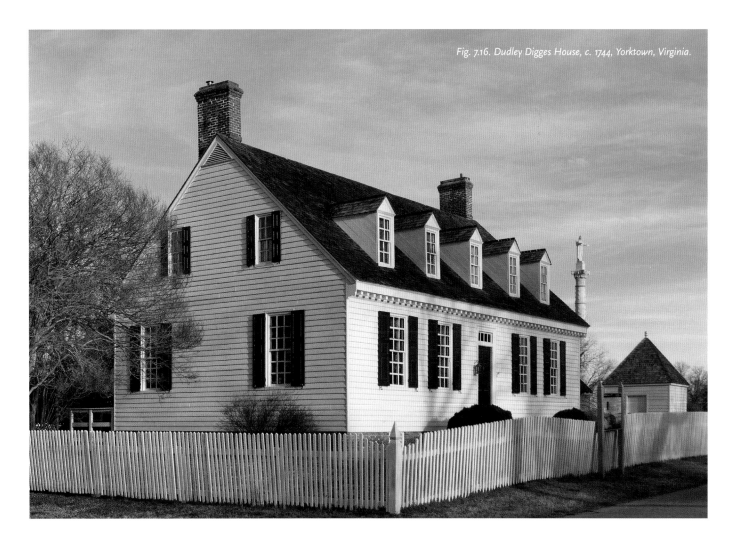

Fig. 7.16. Dudley Digges House, c. 1744, Yorktown, Virginia.

floor housed under the roof. The back rooms stood within a rear shed, its roof framed against the rear slope of the main range. Alternatively, the main roof could simply extend over the rear shed, leaving the back wall and floor of the shed lower than in the front.

THE UPPER FLOOR

Occasionally, the rear file of ground-floor rooms was taken into the main body of the house and the roof symmetrically framed over the full depth of the structure, which still stood just one full story in height. The Dudley Digges House in Yorktown, Virginia, was formulated in this manner (Fig. 7.16). These houses tend to date from midcentury or later, by which time the Chesapeake house frame had evolved to accommodate double-pile plans.

If an imposing facade and spacious upper rooms were sufficiently important considerations, the front range of the house could rise to two full stories with a one-story rear shed framed against the back wall, as at the Ludwell House in Williamsburg. More interesting and visually arresting is The Reward in Kent County, Maryland, a compromise among

the options previously noted. Like a dog on hind legs, this house rears up to present a two-story front to approaching strangers, while appearing as a low shed in the rear.

Houses of two full stories were not as common as their prevalence today would suggest; indeed, documents suggest that they were exceptional.[55] Certainly they were unusual in their emphasis of the upper floor and the activities centered there. A survey of early Virginia inventories revealed that fireplace equipment was uncommon in upper rooms until the end of the eighteenth century. Significantly it is during this period that we first see evidence of families withdrawing to the upper floors of their houses, resulting in houses with no ground-floor chambers. Some of these had two-story porticos accessible from the upper floor. The great porticos at Shirley, added in a 1770s refit of the house, are among the earliest such features to survive in the region (Fig. 7.17). For practical reasons, the porches and porticos that brought the outdoors upstairs were typically associated with houses having full-height second stories, but examples of two-story porticos attached to gambrel-roof houses like Sandy Point or Tedington, in Charles City County, Virginia, or Exeter, in Loudoun County, dem-

Fig. 7.17. Shirley, 1738, porticos 1770s, Charles City County, Virginia.

Fig. 7.18. Monticello, 1770–85, enlarged 1796–1809, Albemarle County, Virginia.

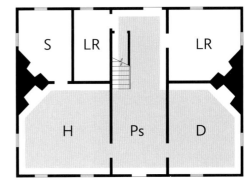

Plan reconstructed from documents

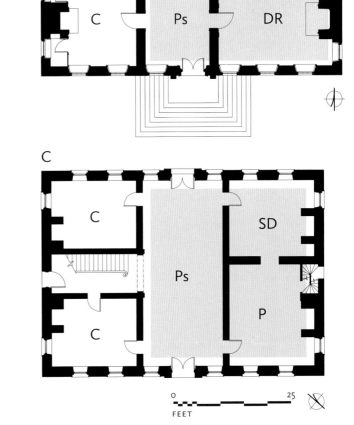

Fig. 7.19. Plans. A: St. Mark's glebe house, reconstructed plan, 1772, Culpeper County, Virginia. The public space of the dwelling, delineated in red, bisects the private space; B: Westover, 1750–51, Charles City County, Virginia; C: Sabine Hall, 1738, Richmond County, Virginia. The stair at Westover faced the river, not the land-side approach. This orientation occurred most often in the best houses such as Tuckahoe, Carter's Grove, and Mount Vernon.

onstrate the determination with which some owners pursued this amenity, even when existing conditions made it frightfully awkward.

As never before, these porticos connected Chesapeake houses to the landscapes around them. Even interior spaces were drawn into this "dialogue." Jefferson's Monticello, adorned with a polygonal bay in the parlor and a grass-green floor in the entry, is the most celebrated instance (Fig. 7.18). Each of these examples represented a new conception of the dwelling's relation to its setting, an ideal expressed in the ever-expanding variety of topographically inspired names current during the late colonial and early republican eras— Rose Hill, Belle Plain, Bon Aire, Bellevue, Grove Mount, and, yes, Monticello.[56]

PUBLIC/PRIVATE, INSIDE/OUTSIDE

Adequate as all of these houses appear to us, householders and builders continued to manipulate existing formulas in hopes of achieving a more satisfactory division between public and private realms. A building specification drawn on the eve of the Revolution nicely illuminates the problem they saw. In 1772, the vestry of St. Mark's Parish, Culpeper County, Virginia, authorized construction of a glebe house having four rooms and a central passage on the ground floor (Fig. 7.19A). The public spaces—hall, dining room, and passage—were to have surbase-height wainscoting, while the private spaces—chamber and study—were to have chair boards and bases only. Through this allocation of interior trim, the vestrymen sought to distinguish the dwelling's public and private domains. Yet when the plan is laid out according to their directions, the public passage bisects the dwelling's private domain.[57]

An obvious solution was to position the hall and dining room on the same side of the passage. This arrangement drew a clear line of separation between the public and private zones of the house, making a coherent entity of the hall, passage, and dining room. To further distinguish public and private zones, some Virginians moved the passage off of the dwelling's central axis, enlarging the public spaces at the expense of the private ones. Westover, in Charles City County (1750–51), embodies this solution (Fig. 7.19B). During a visit there in 1783, Thomas Lee Shippen identified the two larger ground-floor rooms as "Dining Room" and "Drawing Room" but did not mention the smaller spaces on the opposite side of the passage; evidently, these functioned as chambers and thus were inaccessible to visitors.[58]

As an alternative to the Westover arrangement, a lateral, auxiliary passage was sometimes carved out of the two rooms composing the private end of the house. Sabine Hall, in Richmond County, Virginia, illustrates this option (Fig 7.19C). According to Landon Carter's 1779 inventory, the two smaller rooms by the stair served as bedchambers, while the larger spaces opposite the stair functioned as the "Parlor" and the "Small Dining Room." The plan was an ideal one, since it effected a rational division of the house into public and private areas and left the passage wholly uncluttered. Modern accounts frequently refer to dancing in such passages—a reasonable idea, one would think, yet no early documents substantiating the claim have come to light.[59]

With dancing or without, the Sabine Hall plan was highly suitable for another reason—its ambiguous orientation. Without a stair, the passage offered no clear directional cues, so that in some sense, the house faced both ways. Whichever door one entered, the experience was essentially the same. As at Four Mile Tree, the equivalence ascribed to land and river fronts found expression on the exterior of the house, where identical facades greeted all comers—whether arriving by land or returning from the terraced garden before the river.

Gunston Hall, built for George Mason between 1755 and 1759, represents a related solution to the problems of orientation and privacy (Fig. 7.20). As at Sabine Hall, three public rooms—hall, dining room, and passage—formed a compact, public entity, while smaller, private rooms stood across the passage, flanking a longitudinal service corridor (Fig. 7.21B). Unlike at Sabine Hall, however, the main stair at Gunston Hall rises from the main passage. Outdoors, a long, axial drive served to highlight the importance of the dwelling's land front. Persons who traversed that approach and en-

tered by that doorway were greeted by the sight of Mason's magnificent stair, situated at the far end of the passage and framed by a pair of lavishly adorned arches. Immediately to the right of the land-front doorway was the principal room of reception—the hall (perhaps called the "parlor" or "drawing room" in this case). Adorned with carved chinoiserie ornaments, it was one of the most floridly decorated spaces in all of Virginia. After dinner, women probably withdrew to this space—perhaps the exotic appointments were intended to express the room's female association.[60]

Doorways to the privileged realms of dining room and garden stood beyond the archway. For eighteenth-century Virginians, an invitation to dine at the host's table was a special demonstration of acceptance. Those who enjoyed this favor at Gunston Hall moved deeper into the house to dine in the richest space of all—a river-front room with Doric appointments well calculated to express the male associations of that space (see Fig. 16.12).[61] Situated on the far side of the house, Mason's dining room looked out over a carefully conceived, ornamental landscape. It was more for this prospect than for any approach from the garden or river that Mason situated his best room on the far side of the house.

The garden, of course, was more than an object for viewing from the house. Judging from William Byrd's diary, admittance to the planter's garden was, like an invitation to dine, a notable dispensation.[62] Mason organized his garden around a central allee, adorned with low box hedges, flanked by planting beds, and terminating at an overlook from which one could enjoy a view of the river. This landscape was best appreciated from the elevated deck of a polygonal, river-front porch. There, Mason and his company could seat themselves and enjoy the view, or simply pause before descending to the garden. As one gazed back toward the house, Mason's porch became the focal point of the dwelling's river-front facade. It was a place from which to see the garden—and an ornament to be seen from it. Its demi-octagonal form purposefully evoked the imagery of garden structures—a summer house attached to the great house.[63]

By addressing land- and river-front landscapes, George Mason, like Landon Carter, managed to face his house both ways. Mason's plan also made the most of the dwelling's private spaces. One of these served the family as a dining room on occasions when there was no company, and when Mason wished to be alone he appropriated the space as a study. Significantly, Mason's son later described this room in purely logistical terms. Situated behind the stair, it "looked by two south windows immediately on the garden, which adjoined the house on its south front and into which it opened by an outer door and porch . . . [via] a door and short passage

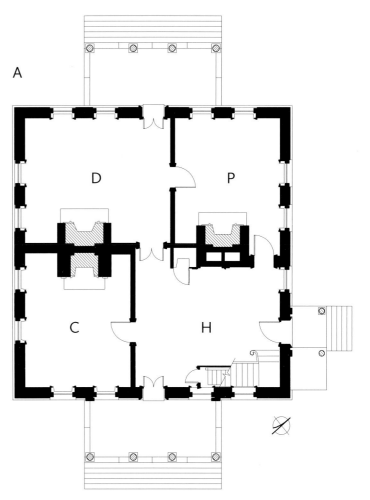

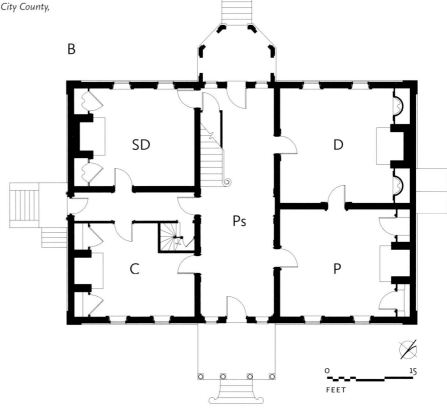

(left) Fig. 7.20. Passage with a pair of arches framing the stair, Gunston Hall, 1755–59, Fairfax County, Virginia.

(right) Fig. 7.21. Plans. A: Shirley, 1738, remodeled 1772, Charles City County, Virginia; B: Gunston Hall, 1755–59, Fairfax County, Virginia.

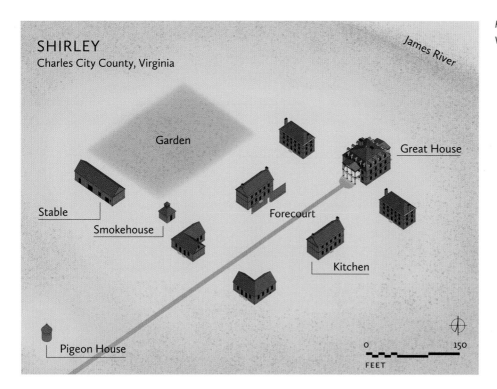

SHIRLEY
Charles City County, Virginia

James River

Garden

Great House

Stable

Smokehouse

Forecourt

Kitchen

Pigeon House

0   150
FEET

Fig. 7.22. Site Plan. Shirley, Charles City County, Virginia, house and service buildings.

from that room. . . . It was in a measure detached from the rest of the house, having a direct and . . . private way into the garden."[64]

The little passage ran laterally between the study and Mrs. Mason's chamber, bisecting the private end of the house. There, it allowed family and servants to move without fanfare between the private rooms, the garden, the service yard, and, by a private stair at one end, to the second floor. George Mason's well-considered plan effected a clear division of the house while accommodating the river-front/land-front dichotomy.

Shirley, in Charles City County (1738), is an early and ambitious example of this dual orientation (see Fig. 7.17).[65] Inside the land-front door, visitors found an imposing entry, one of the two largest rooms in the house (Fig. 7.21A). This was surely the intended entry, for it shared two important attributes with the central passages of other houses—it was unheated and it provided independent access to the second floor.[66]

The present stair dates to a remodeling carried out by Charles Carter shortly after 1770, and it is Charles's magnificent interior that visitors to Shirley now see. Beyond the land-front entry stands the largest and best room, probably the dining room, judging from a nineteenth-century pair of brass cocks on the far side of the chimney. Situated on the river-front side of the house, this sumptuous room afforded prospects up, down, and across the James. A broad exterior doorway led family and guests out of this dining room into the ground story of the portico, down to the lawn, and, beyond that, to the river. Like George Mason's polygonal porch, this appendage was a feature to be seen from the adjoining landscape and, in this case, from the James River. Just as the west portico at Monticello was of sufficient scale to read from afar, so too, Charles Carter ensured that Shirley's two-story portico was large enough to provide a suitable focal point for this, the river-front facade.

Equally important, though, was the function of Shirley's portico as a space for living. Virginians in this period generally spoke of sitting "in the porch." At Shirley and at certain other sites, this spatial conception of porch was expressed in the interior appointments that adorned it—cornices, surbases, and even plaster give the appearance of an outdoor room.

Like the river-front portico, that on the land-front side was sufficiently grand to read from afar, in this case as visitors moved toward the compound along the long axial approach road. To emphasize the importance of this procession and celebrate the climactic moment of arrival, four massive outbuildings, each as large and substantial as a well-built gentry house, defined a monumental forecourt—to reach the house, it was necessary to move through this space (Fig. 7.22). In addition to these forecourt buildings, two more brick structures, now destroyed, flanked the main house, aligned on its longitudinal axis. No doubt they housed necessary functions, but they also served to extend the frontage of the compound when viewed from the river. Together with the river-front portico, they extended the visual impact and "reach" of the entire composition.

All major elements in the compound at Shirley—the approach road, the outbuildings, the porticos, the entry, and the dining room—were distributed in such a way as to elevate the arriving visitor's experience while affording impressive views from the house toward the river and from the river toward the house. As if to emphasize the equivalence of land- and river-front landscapes, the porticos on both fronts were identical. Like George Mason and Landon Carter, cousin Charles succeeded in having it both ways.

THE URBAN SETTING

Shirley's interior arrangement anticipated a number of related houses in Annapolis, houses in which the best ground-floor room was situated on the "back" of the house. This general scheme, realized in several variations, has been christened the "Annapolis Plan," based on its prevalence in that city. As at Shirley, the desire for a dual orientation was the underlying idea. First among these was the Judge John Brice House, built about 1739 (see Fig. 14.18). The "Passage" (so named in a 1768 inventory) contained the main stair and faced the street, while the largest and most opulent room— the "Parlour"—faced the garden. To the left of the front door was the dining room, from which a private stair descended to the kitchen below. Situated between the parlor and the dining room was the "Red Chamber." This space had all the earmarks of that room customarily occupied by the mistress of the household—no communication with the passage, a separate exterior doorway, and a private stair to the upper floor.[67]

To the right of the front door, partly hidden below the main stair, was a small space referred to in the inventory as the "Lockd Room." Despite its confined situation, this room had heat, light, and even a small closet in the space below the stair. This is believed to have been an office, a feature that would soon typify the grander sort of Annapolis houses, typically occupied by merchants.[68] Here, just within the front door, Brice received those who wished to speak with him on some matter of business.

The John Ridout House is a more developed and sophisticated example of the type (Fig. 7.23). As at the Judge John Brice House, the entry faces the street, and from this space the main stair makes its way to the second-floor rooms. The large room on the right-hand retains an original buffet, including the slide on which footmen mixed punch or other beverages at the end of the meal—clearly, this was the din-

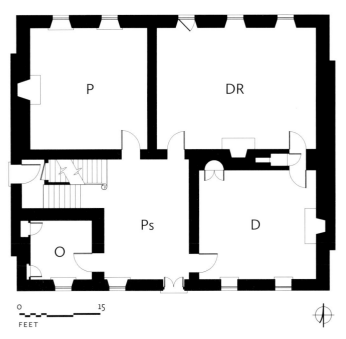

Fig. 7.23. Plan. John Ridout House, 1764–65, Annapolis.

ing room. It follows that the larger space on the garden front was the withdrawing or "drawing" room (a new synonym for the term "hall"), the place where company gathered after meals. The adjoining ground-floor space communicates directly with the entry and has none of the provisions for private movement as in the "Red Chamber" of the Judge Brice House. Together with its fine appointments, the logistics of this room suggest that it functioned as a public space, probably a parlor, where visitors were first received or perhaps where the family convened on informal occasions. A tiny room by the front door seems to have functioned as an office from which to conduct business, as in the Judge Brice House. The stuccoed ceiling, a rarity in Chesapeake houses, gives the space an uncommon touch of opulence, indicative of the importance Ridout attached to these activities.

Both of the best public rooms looked out over the garden, and each had its own door to the exterior. To clear the back of his property for a garden, Ridout gathered all service functions in under the house. To shield this garden from the street, he erected a brick wall across the front of the property. Practically speaking, these arrangements all worked well enough, but the importance of the garden-front rooms found no satisfactory expression on the exterior of the house with its two-door porch.[69]

The Hammond-Harwood House addressed this problem more successfully (Fig. 7.24). First, services and ancillary spaces were distributed along the front of the lot, screening the garden from public view. The street-front facade of the main house was elegant but restrained in its appointments.

Fig. 7.24. Street facade,
Hammond-Harwood House,
1774, Annapolis.

Fig. 7.25. Garden facade, Hammond-Harwood House.

Fig. 7.26. Dining room, Hammond-Harwood House, Annapolis.

Wonderful as it is, this was the lesser of the dwelling's two main facades. On the garden front, William Buckland created a projecting pavilion, heavily articulated with pilasters and a full-height entablature, all expressing the social importance of the landscape it addressed (Fig. 7.25).

Inside, the dining space—the biggest and best ground-floor room—occupied the place of honor, looking out to the garden behind the house (Fig. 7.26). The drawing room was situated on the upper floor, a rare thing in Chesapeake houses. After meals, this separation transformed the ladies' withdrawal into a suspenseful procession toward what ultimately became a beautifully decorated room. At the same time, this up/down arrangement allowed both of the best rooms to front on the garden in a way that ascribed something like equal importance to both. To emphasize that equivalence, the appointments of the ground-floor circulation space left no doubt of the public path leading upstairs.

What suited this plan type to the urban setting of Annapolis was its capacity to present an adequate face to street and garden alike. Similar considerations account for the deployment of Kenmore, now within the city limits of Fredericksburg, Virginia, constructed from 1772 to 1776 for Fielding

and Betty Lewis (see Fig. 3.14). Originally, the house stood on the outskirts of the town, in the manner of a villa, fronting toward the road, with the Rappahannock River at its back. A 1781 inventory fails to enumerate the rooms, though it appears that the parlor was the larger, river-front room, having the most chairs, the best looking glass, the finest fireplace equipment, a large collection of books, but no dining equipment (see Fig. 3.15). The smaller river-front room was surely the dining room, with the second-best fireplace equipment, all of the dining equipage, several tables, and ten mahogany chairs. Also on the ground floor were two chambers, the better one being on the left as one entered by the stair, to judge from the fireplace equipment and the quality of the bedstead. Behind the stair, and accessible from the side passage only, was the smaller chamber. This was furnished with a press full of linens and a poplar bedstead, in addition to the least expensive fireplace tools. Perhaps this little room was conceived initially as an office, similar to that of Judge John Brice. In the end, it may have served Mrs. Lewis instead as a place from which to manage the household, like "Mrs. Randolph's closet" at the Peyton Randolph House in Williamsburg. Alternatively, it may have served as a housekeeper's room, similar to the pantry at the Governor's Palace, where Lord Botetourt's butler occasionally reclined on a day bed.

As in Annapolis, the plan worked well on a site where both orientations were important—the best rooms looking out to the river, while the entry and the chambers faced the Fredericksburg road. As in some other houses of the period, a vestibule adjoining the better chamber led out to the kitchen yard—but also to the principal public room. By this little passage, Mrs. Lewis could reach the kitchen and the parlor without crossing the passage.[70]

SOCIAL AND ARCHITECTURAL CHANGE

Exquisitely divided houses of the sort discussed here were mostly products of the quarter century leading up to the American Revolution. The middle decades of the eighteenth century had been a time of social and material efflorescence in the Chesapeake colonies. Landowners, merchants, professionals, and tradesmen all rode high on a wave of prosperity, driven by expanding markets for agricultural goods and by the easy terms on which credit was available from British merchants willing to bet on tobacco's future. Many of the largest and most elaborate mansions in Maryland and Virginia were completed—or at least begun—during this period. Looking across the landscape, the ascendancy of the Chesapeake gentry was everywhere apparent.

But just as planter oligarchs approached the height of their wealth and power, historians tell us that the social edifice on which they stood supreme began to shift. Religious and social upheavals associated with the Great Awakening created enormous tensions among the various elements of society. The success of dissenting preachers in attracting new followers presented a serious challenge to the established church and the social order it upheld. The American Revolution intensified these problems, eroding conventions of deference that had once characterized relations between the gentry and those who stood below them in the social hierarchy. The existing order of things appeared to be unraveling.[71]

The planter's sense of impending chaos was heightened by the economic difficulty of the post-Revolutionary period—when the Chesapeake colonies entered a period of decline, and thus of lowered expectation, with many families struggling merely to maintain the level of existence established by the previous generation. Easy credit had allowed that generation to indulge in luxury and competitive display, but now many were reduced to a humiliating state of indebtedness and dependency. In a society that regarded personal independence as the very core of genteel identity, this was anathema. Increasingly, Marylanders and Virginians came to view the vanity and excess of public life with misgivings, even revulsion. According to historians, these circumstances began to undermine the public orientation of gentry society.[72]

In response, gentry families began to withdraw from public affairs and from the conviviality that had once characterized life at the apex of society. Now gentlemen frequently declined to serve on vestries or to sit on county courts. Travelers who had once taken for granted the planter's openhanded hospitality now found it necessary to carry letters of introduction.[73] By all accounts, gentry houses eventually reflected these circumstances. Various scholars have identified the architectural manifestations. Henry Glassie sees an alteration in the attitude of houses revealed in their plans and their relationship to the road: outwardly oriented dwellings—"extensive" in Glassie's parlance—became "intensive," that is, inwardly oriented. In a similar vein, Dell Upton comments on the growing tendency to suppress the stair and otherwise close off visitors' access to the private areas of post-Revolutionary houses. Rhys Isaac also sees the existence of the central passage as facilitating a withdrawal from public life, while Camille Wells explains how, in the post-Revolutionary period, servants were often banished to the kitchen, where they could be summoned by mechanical call bells. The house, she suggests, became more effective in separating the public and private spheres of domestic life. In the popularity of symmetrical, articulated houses, Marlene Heck finds a desire to delineate the public and private areas of the house more clearly, and thus enhance the dwelling's suitability as a refuge from society.[74]

All of this is perfectly true, but we tend to think of the phenomenon described here as a retrograde movement, a retreat. It is important to remember, however, that in effecting these changes, the Chesapeake gentry made an affirmative step toward something. As external pressures on gentry society continued to build, other forces were beginning to transform that society from within. Social historians suggest that the period between 1750 and 1800 witnessed deeply important changes in the structure and ideology of the family. The extended household of earlier times gave way to a more tightly drawn unit, usually limited to the circle of one's immediate kin. Where the old model of family had featured patriarchy as the basis of social harmony, the relationships and interactions within the nuclear family of the post-Revolutionary period were more companionate, influenced by the sentimentalism associated with evangelical religion. A corollary to this development was a growing sense of individual autonomy and a new emphasis on the creation and expression of emotional bonds within the group. Increasingly, children

A

B

0   25

FEET

became the focus of the family's energies and attention. Indeed, the very notion of childhood as a separate phase of life
was a product of this period. These changes soon found expression in portraiture, which became decidedly less formal
and assumed a new, emotional dimension.[75]

After 1750, probate records began to mention spaces denominated according to their association with children—
the "Nursery," "Humberston's Room," "the Boy's Room,"
"the Girls' Room," and so on. In the decades on either side of
the Revolution, we see an emergent infrastructure of childhood, accompanied by a growing emphasis on children in
the daily routine of the family. Increasingly withdrawn from
society, this "sentimental" family, as some have called it,
turned inward, seeking to expand the private sphere of domestic existence.[76]

By the end of the eighteenth century, the changing character of family life was transforming gentry houses. Prominent in this reformation was that ground-floor sleeping
space called "the Chamber." Virginians and Marylanders
had long associated the mistress of the household with this
room, where appraisers typically found the assorted and valued commodities entrusted to her care. We have seen that
this room functioned in a quasi-public way and that as late
as the 1750s one could expect to find a tea table and equipage there. By 1760, however, the tea ceremony—and all it

implied about the presence of strangers—had disappeared
from sleeping spaces completely.

Nonetheless, appraisers continued to list as many as six
chairs in some of these rooms. Evidently, the chamber continued to function in a social way, but it was now off-limits to
those outside the circle of kin, serving a much narrower slice
of society. In 1786, Robert Hunter described how families
used such rooms. Lodging with relatives in what is now Tappahannock, Virginia, Hunter occasionally read aloud in the
upstairs chamber of his cousin, Catherine McCall. On one
such occasion, at least four people were present—three family members, including Hunter, and also Catherine's suitor.[77]

During the second half of the eighteenth century, Virginians came to regard the ground-floor chamber as an inner
sanctum of family life. John Mason's boyhood memories of
Gunston Hall centered almost entirely on his mother's chamber. Dismissing the public house in a few brief sentences,
Mason went on to describe the chamber and his experiences
there at great length, enumerating the contents of one closet
and then the other. But he did not stop there. One by one, he
inventoried and discussed every drawer in his mother's chest
of drawers as well. Clearly, young Mason and his mother
spent much, even most, of their time in this one room. The
chamber was, in every sense, the center of their world.[78]

Among Virginians, the expansion of private life was soon

reflected in a tendency to enlarge the ground-floor chamber substantially, so that it became a kind of sitting room, in some cases the biggest room in the house. The entire east wing of St. George Tucker's Williamsburg house was taken up by a new chamber and two smaller rooms adjoining (Fig. 7.27A). Because the chamber-as-sitting-room offered little real privacy, we see a resurgence during this period in the use of the closets mentioned earlier—one for each spouse in this case—a measure of the new autonomy that husband and wife now enjoyed.

Chamber suites of this kind came to be identified with houses of the better sort during the last quarter of the eighteenth century, and people devised various ways of relating the components of these suites. Eppington, in Chesterfield County, was begun by Francis Eppes in the late 1760s and enlarged by adding the one-story wings about 1790 (Fig. 7.27B). At the western end of this expanded house was Eppes's chamber suite, which, like Tucker's, included a room for sleeping, plus two smaller unheated spaces adjoining. In this case, however, a contiguous room, probably a "little parlor" or some such space, continued to function as the room in which the family sat when company did not demand their presence in the public rooms.[79]

The informal character of this new kind of chamber and its importance in daily routine are captured in Margaret Bayard Smith's account of an 1828 visit to James and Dolley Madison at Montpelier. The visitor described how "after the first salutations were passed, Mrs. M invited us in to a chamber, where we might make ourselves comfortable, she said. She led the way to an elegant little chamber, on the same floor and adjoining her own, furnished with crimson damask and looking out on the beautiful lawn. She sent a maid to attend us and said she would return by the time we had exchanged our damp clothes. This she soon did and she then carried us in to her own chamber. It was very large and commodious and furnished with every convenience and much elegance." She continued: "Before a large sopha lay her work. Couches, easy-chairs &c. invited us to ease and comfortable indulgence. I told her I had no notion of playing lady visitor all day and sitting prim in the drawing room with our hands before us, and if she would resume her work, we would sit with her and work too. It was so agreed. She drew Anna on the sopha beside her and gave her a half dozen pretty books to look over, while, drawing a French arm chair . . . close by her I reclined at my ease, while we talked—and oh, how we did talk."[80]

Evidently, Mrs. Madison's chamber was more than a place to lay her head, and it is clear that Mrs. Smith regarded her admission to this space as a special favor. The couches, easy

chairs, and needlework were obvious cues for Mrs. Smith's offer to dispense with formalities and spend the time fruitfully engaged.

Her account leaves no doubt that the chamber had become an important focus of daily life among the well-to-do. It remained such well into the nineteenth century. In 1839, Mrs. Robert Tyler, a daughter-in-law of President John Tyler, offered this revealing description of her mother-in-law's chamber: "The room in the main dwelling furthest removed and most retired is the chamber, as the bedroom of the mistress of the house is always called in Virginia. This . . . is a most quiet and comfortable retreat, with an air of repose and sanctity about it; at least I feel it so, and often seek refuge here from the company, and beaux and laughing and talking of the other parts of the house."[81] Like Smith's Montpelier account, this description portrays the chamber as a female space, a refuge that stood aloof from the rest of the house. Already, the phenomenon of domesticity is apparent here, fully developed. In future decades, Americans would extend this idea of a "refuge" to include the entire house.

At the same time that Chesapeake grandees expanded the chamber and narrowed the compass of its society, they also drew the space deeper into their houses. This development had consequences for the dwelling's internal organization and outward form. By the end of the eighteenth century, the ground-floor chamber had moved to the upper floor or to a wing, which afforded more space at greater distance from the public rooms than had been possible in conventional houses. Articulated dwellings were particularly suited to this development, a matter worth exploring in greater detail.[82]

Benjamin Harrison completed his Prince George County seat, Brandon, shortly after 1795 (Fig. 7.28). Others have noted that the house was based on plate III of Robert Morris's *Select Architecture*, first published in 1752 (Fig. 7.29). As a domestic environment, however, Brandon functioned in ways that had little to do with Morris's plan; indeed, its organization corresponded precisely to changes that were overtaking gentry life and gentry houses in the years following the Revolution.

At the center of Harrison's dwelling stood a large articulated block, composed of an entry or saloon, and above it, a single sleeping space, reserved, perhaps, for the use of important visitors—a kind of state bedchamber. To either side were single-story wings that accommodated spaces for entertainment—a dining room and drawing room. Together with the second-floor chamber, this triad of ground-floor public spaces formed a visually distinct, ceremonial core—the physical plant of Harrison's public existence. The fam-

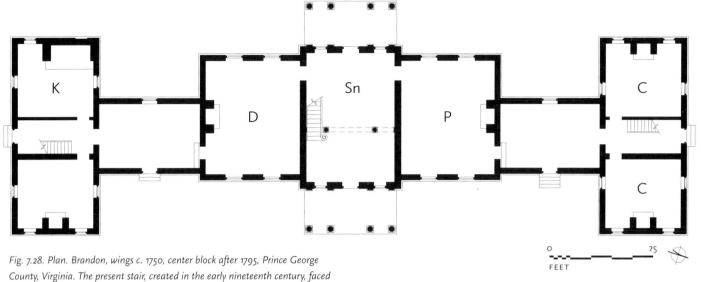

Fig. 7.28. Plan. Brandon, wings c. 1750, center block after 1795, Prince George
County, Virginia. The present stair, created in the early nineteenth century, faced
the river, but the land front of the house has always been the main approach.

Fig. 7.29. Top: Brandon, Prince
George County, Virginia.
Bottom: Plate 3, Robert Morris,
Select Architecture (London,
1752).

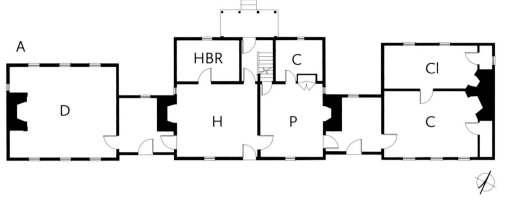

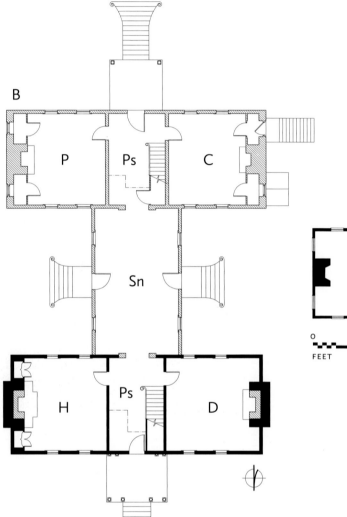

ily's quarters were detached from this core, standing at one extremity of the complex. Physically and psychologically, the resulting arrangement dramatically increased the distance between Harrison's front door and the center of his private world. Gathered into a two-story domestic wing, these chambers answered an identical mass at the other end of the complex housing kitchen and servants. Like the Harrison family, these servants were drawn out of the house and collected at the end of a taut umbilicus.

The conventional cubic house was broken down and redistributed along a single axis, driving public and private

zones as far apart as the connective tissue of the house would allow. The result was an imposing, symmetrical composition, modulated to express the importance of each part relative to all the others. Changing patterns of domestic life had impelled Virginians to build a new kind of house, one that separated public and backstage areas of the domestic establishment more effectively. Among these symmetrical, articulated houses, Brandon was unusual in collecting public functions at the center of the dwelling. A more common solution was to distribute all spaces along a continuum, moving from the most public at one end to the most private at the other. This was the case at Eppington, where the new chamber wing, at one extremity, answered a large dining room at the other (see Fig. 7.27B).

The symmetry of these expansions challenges Jan Lewis and Rhys Isaac's characterization of the post-Revolutionary era as a time of retrenchment. The immensity of Eppes's dining room contravenes the idea of a gentry class under siege and in retreat. The private zone of the house was greatly en-

Fig. 7.31. Tuckahoe, Goochland County, Virginia.

larged here, but so too was the family's capacity to engage in public life. At the same time that Francis Eppes added a chamber suite at one end of the house, he added a large, elegant dining space at the opposite end, the biggest and best of all the rooms at Eppington.

Wales, in Dinwiddie County, Virginia, was another of these symmetrical expansions, probably dating to the 1780s (Fig. 7.30A). As at Eppington, the additions seem to have included a chamber suite on one hand and a large, elaborate room for entertainment on the other. At the time of its completion, the public room at Wales ranked among the most impressive domestic spaces in the region. Far from effecting a retreat, Wales and other houses like it served to accom-

modate an expanding world of private life while maintaining—or even enlarging—the family's role in public life. In so doing, they reflected the prevailing desire to reconcile the conflicting demands of public and private existence.

Tuckahoe, the boyhood home of Thomas Jefferson, was one of the earliest and most radical efforts to make these opposing realms cohabit more happily (Fig. 7.30B). The original, land-front range of the house was completed shortly after 1733; the saloon and the wing beyond it were under construction in the 1750s (Fig. 7.31).[83] During a visit here in 1783, Thomas Anburey explained the logic of the dwelling's arrangement: "[The] house seems to be built solely to answer the purposes of hospitality. . . . It is in the form of an

H, and has the appearance of two houses, joined by a large saloon. . . . In one the family reside, and the other is reserved solely for visitors."[84] Colonel Randolph's house was really two houses, deployed in such a way as to effect a total separation between the public world of conviviality in the front and the private world of family and servants in the rear.

Wigwam, expanded for Governor Giles in 1815, bears no resemblance to Tuckahoe externally, though it seems to have functioned in a similar way (Fig. 7.30C). Apparently, the front pile embraced a suite of public rooms for reception and entertainment of guests, while the back wing probably accommodated the family. In this case, the better of the front rooms may have served as a parlor or drawing room and the lesser room as a bedchamber for favored guests. At the far end of the passage was the dining room—in some respects the most elaborate of the three main spaces.

To the rear of this dining room is the other house, essentially a hall/chamber dwelling with a vestibule and stair separating the two rooms. The first space beyond the dining room probably served as a kind of sitting room where members of the household engaged one another informally. The back room is likely to have been the chamber. An added tower at the rear of the private wing afforded enclosed circulation between these rooms and additional chambers above. Only when guests were present would Giles and his family have emerged from the simpler routine of life in this back dwelling. At the time of their construction, Tuckahoe and Wigwam were among the most elaborate domestic buildings in their respective localities. Colonel Randolph and Governor Giles expected to entertain often, but both men wished to hold that undertaking "at arm's length." To achieve this, each man built what were, in effect, two distinct houses.

This public/private dichotomy allows us to make sense of Thomas Jefferson's 1779 design for remodeling the Governor's Palace in Williamsburg. Owing to his kindred ties with the Randolphs of Tuckahoe, Jefferson was familiar with the convention of paired dwellings, and he later proposed to remake the Governor's Palace according to this formula. By collapsing the old ballroom into the body of the existing structure, he would have expelled all services from the existing pile, relocating these, along with the family's quarters, in a rear wing (see Fig. 2.1D).[85]

In other cases, Jefferson was more subtle in his effort to segregate public and private zones of the house. Like other dwellings examined here, Monticello was the product of a late eighteenth-century expansion. In this campaign of construction, Jefferson created a haven of solitary endeavor centered on the chamber, while providing, at the opposite end of the house, new spaces for waiting visitors and overnight guests (Fig. 7.32A). In his attempt to mediate the tug-of-war between social and solitary endeavors, Jefferson built a house that was actually quite conventional in its segregation of these realms—the Eppses, the Tuckers, and others had already done the same.

George Washington's reconstruction of Mount Vernon, in 1774–76, reflected similar aims and produced comparable results (Fig. 7.32B). As completed, the house embraced a large and sumptuously appointed banqueting room at one end and a private suite for General and Mrs. Washington at the other. These quarters occupied two floors, but, like Jefferson's lair, they created a self-contained world of domestic activity. Above stairs was a large chamber, which apparently functioned as Mrs. Washington's sitting room as well. On the ground floor was a closet for those precious objects that tradition would have entrusted to her care, but these were now the purview of Washington's butler, Frank. Adjoining this space was Washington's library, which served the general as sitting room and study. Like the library at Monticello, this space was the master's alone, and others entered only with his permission. As at Monticello, this suite was adjacent to, yet emphatically segregated from, the public side of the house. Like Jefferson, the Washingtons were able to enter or leave their apartment without passing through the public rooms. It is tempting to see in this arrangement the special circumstance of Washington's celebrity, but the evidence on this point is quite clear: he conceived and began execution of this scheme prior to becoming the father of his country. At this juncture, Washington was just one of many affluent Virginians rebuilding a house to achieve new levels of refinement in private as well as public living.

Similarly, the enlargement and remodeling of Montpelier, initiated by James Madison in 1797 and revived in 1809, had less to do with Madison's notoriety as constitutional architect than with his desire to accommodate two households—his own and that of his parents—while undertaking a wider range of public and private activity (Fig. 7.33). In this case, however, his creation of private suites at both ends of the house—one for his mother and one for his library—pushed the grand public space into the middle of the house, as at Brandon. There it functioned as the principal room of reception and as a kind of museum to edify visitors and thus to provide a basis for conversing intelligently with them.[86]

Based on the houses examined here, it appears that we must rethink our notion of the Virginia gentry's withdrawal from society. Throughout the period under consideration, Virginians were surely remaking their houses to achieve greater privacy, but many of these people were also enlarging the public side of their lives. Greater autonomy and per-

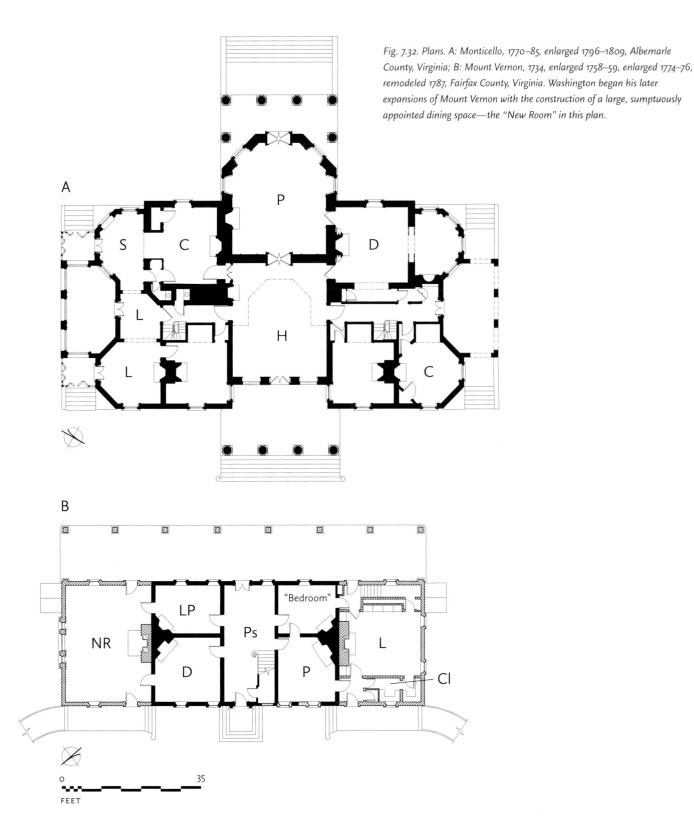

Fig. 7.32. Plans. A: Monticello, 1770–85, enlarged 1796–1809, Albemarle County, Virginia; B: Mount Vernon, 1734, enlarged 1758–59, enlarged 1774–76, remodeled 1787, Fairfax County, Virginia. Washington began his later expansions of Mount Vernon with the construction of a large, sumptuously appointed dining space—the "New Room" in this plan.

sonal privacy did not necessarily equate with the atrophy of public existence. Instead, the period witnessed an expansion and enrichment of both spheres. This event owed less to the transformation of Virginia society, real though it was, than to the changing nature of the family, to new ideas of individual autonomy, and to the continuing progress of genteel refinements. Gentility was not limited to public aspects of life. It refined and elaborated public and private aspects of living equally and so demanded greater provision at both ends of the house.

This public/private mode of expanding houses became an enduring legacy in the region's domestic architecture, continuing well into the nineteenth century. Marlene Heck has identified a number of Piedmont examples, but these symmetrical houses are greatly outnumbered by later, asymmetrical versions, especially in the Tidewater regions of Maryland

Fig. 7.33. Sequential development of Montpelier, Orange County, Virginia. The first expansion created two houses under one roof. Nelly and James Madison Sr. occupied the old house on the right, James Jr. and his new wife lived in the addition. A second remodeling created commodious private wings for both families and a large drawing room in which to receive company.

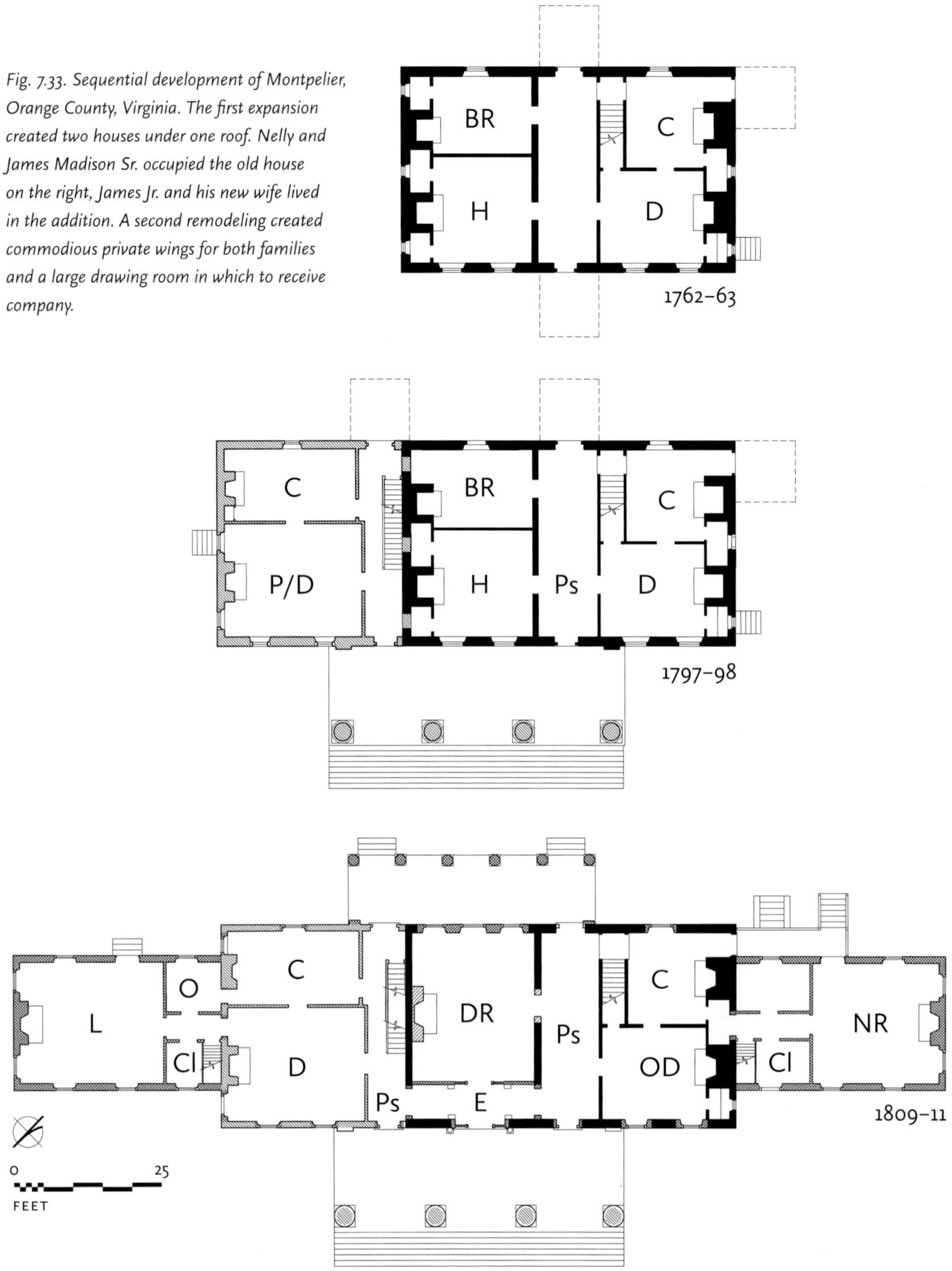

and Virginia. After 1800, new public and private components were often collapsed into a single two-story wing, erected against one end of an earlier single-story house. This addition usually provided a new best room on the ground floor and a large new bedchamber above. In most cases, the addition included a new passage as well. The Jordan House, in Isle of Wight County, now destroyed by neglect, was an early example in which the new building passed across the end of the existing structure and so became the front of an expanded and reoriented dwelling.

Most often though, the addition was deployed on-axis with the earlier house, as at the Coke-Garrett House in

Williamsburg, a relatively late example of the type, completed in 1837 (Fig. 7.34). This dwelling is unusual in that the existing house did not communicate directly with the new passage. Occasionally, the entry remained in the older part of the house. Marlborough, in King and Queen County, began life around 1805 as a side-passage house, so it was necessary to add only the public rooms and the chambers above when the house was enlarged. In this instance, however, the addition was raised on a high basement to accommodate service spaces below, resulting in a "split level" arrangement, with stairs leading from the passage up to the parlor and down to the cellar.

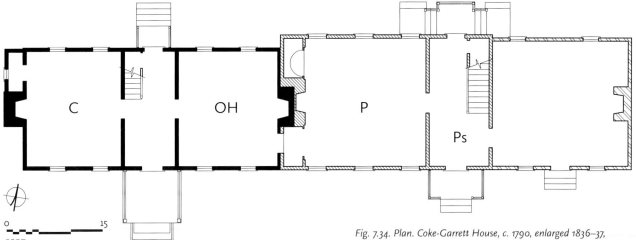

Fig. 7.34. Plan. Coke-Garrett House, c. 1790, enlarged 1836–37, Williamsburg. The house was expanded by adding a parlor wing, which contained an entertaining room below stairs and a large bedchamber above.

In Cecil County, Maryland, Rose Hill was first built as a conventional hall-and-chamber, central-passage house, one full story in height, with upper rooms accommodated within a gambrel roof. In 1837, General Thomas Marsh Foreman completed a two-story brick addition that included "an entry, rather narrow, and two parlors" below and commodious bedchambers above, another example of the house type discussed above. But Sidney George Fisher saw it differently, deeming it "exactly a third-rate city house," a reference to the system of rating urban properties for tax and insurance purposes.[87] In Fisher's eyes, Rose Hill, with its narrow brick addition, looked more like an urban house with its attached back building than a proper country house—a measure of the influence Philadelphia exerted in this region of Maryland. As in the grander projects at Monticello and Mount Vernon, the enlargement of these smaller houses responded to new social habits demanding larger, more opulent public rooms in which to entertain visitors and larger, more remote spaces in which to grow the family. Yet even these houses failed to solve the public/private dilemma entirely.

SERVANTS AND STRANGERS

Amid a growing polarization of the Chesapeake planter's house between public and private activity, the varied functions required of the passage—entry point for visitors, waiting room for servants, and summer sitting room for the family and guests—became increasingly fraught with problems. Some sort of separation was necessary if these now-incompatible uses of the space were to be sorted out satisfactorily.

One house in particular illuminates the effort to segregate the activities that had once filled the passage. At Prestwould, in Mecklenburg County, Virginia, Sir Peyton Skipwith

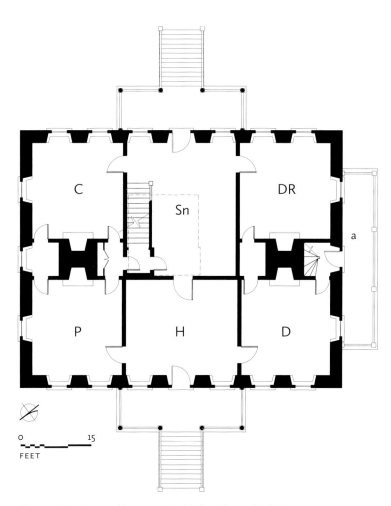

Fig. 7.35. Plan. Prestwould, 1794–95, Mecklenburg County, Virginia. The bell that summoned servants from the kitchen was mounted at "a" under the roof of the porch.

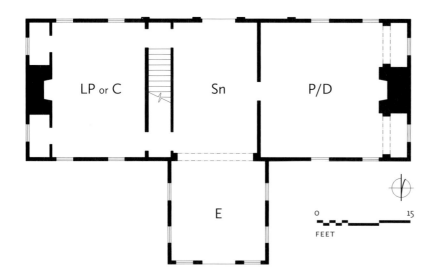

LP or C	Sn	P/D

E

0   15
FEET

Fig. 7.36. Plan. Nanzatico, 1801, King George County, Virginia. The extension of the passage was built on the land-side approach. On the opposite side, a two-story classical frontispiece faced the river and possibly a garden. Removing the stair from Nanzatico's entry produced a large, unimpeded passage or saloon. As at Menokin in Richmond County, the main room may have served as both parlor and dining room. Perhaps the smaller room, secluded behind the stair, functioned as a chamber or as a sitting room for family members.

divided the middle third of the ground floor into two rooms (Fig. 7.35). At the land-front door was a "Hall" in which to receive and seat strangers. Beyond this space, at the river-front entry, was the "Saloon," a much larger room where the family sat in warmer weather. Significantly, the stair rose from this unheated river-front room—beyond the view of those seated in the hall. In this way, it was possible to divide the family from strangers who sat in the hall, probably on the Windsor settee that stood there. At the same time, Skipwith's plan placed the upper floor one additional remove from the front door. Having removed strangers from the family's summer sitting room, Skipwith banished waiting servants from the house altogether. As part of the original construction, he installed a system of house bells, mounted on the exterior of the house above the plastered ceilings of the porches (see Fig. 12.23). In this way, servants stationed in the separate kitchen, on one of the porches, or in some remote service space, could hear any summons. From the kitchen-side porch, a back stair allowed servants to reach the upstairs chambers without passing through the rest of the house. To an unusual degree, this merger of architecture and technology allowed the Skipwiths to control their contact with other elements of society.[88]

Even in dwellings less ambitious than Prestwould, bell systems provided a way to remove servants from the house. These had been around since the middle of the eighteenth century, but remained quite rare until after the Revolution. To be sure, this trend owed something to the proliferation of illustrated catalogs from ironmongers and brass founders in Britain, but it was a growing desire among the Chesapeake gentry to remove servants from the dwelling's public realm that contributed most to the popularity of these systems at the end of the eighteenth century.

Where there were no bell systems to summon servants from remote locations, the open piazza—an increasingly popular form in the post-Revolutionary period—provided a place for servants to sit during idle moments. Occasionally, these porches were equipped with built-in benches for the purpose. Like Windsor chairs in the planter's passage, they provided serviceable accommodation for servants and for those waiting to see the master. Fixing these benches in place against the house or porch railings ensured a measure of decorum in the way people positioned and carried themselves.

Like the passage, though, piazzas and their seating were occasionally used by family members. It is this latter function of the porch that illuminates the meaning of small rooms attached to certain houses in the Rappahannock Valley. Extruded from one end of the passage, these rooms were essentially enclosed porches. The example at Nanzatico (1801), in King George County, Virginia, is visible from the land-side approach (Fig. 7.36). Here it could have accommodated servants and strangers, but the extensive glazing and the embellishment typically afforded such spaces suggests that they were intended for the family's use as well. In that context, it is useful to note that the interior separation of this appendage from the passage is equivocal, more symbolic than actual. Just across the Rappahannock River, in the quasi-urban confines of Port Royal, Virginia, two such rooms stand on the side of the house opposite the street, where they probably afforded a view of the garden in one instance (Brockenbrough House) or of the Rappahannock River in the other (Townfield). In this respect, they functioned like George Mason's polygonal porch at Gunston Hall, being a sort of ground-level lantern or garden house from which to view the landscape.[89]

❖ We have seen how at the beginning of the eighteenth century the Chesapeake planter's concept of "house" began with that all-important room called "the hall." From this solitary room, containing most of the planter's possessions and domestic activities, we have traced the conceptual elaboration of the dwelling as it responded to social trends, ones that placed new emphasis on public hospitality and display but also on social segregation. Initially, these developments were a matter of extracting certain kinds of people, activities, and things from the hall—servants, cooking, beds, and so on—and putting them somewhere else.

A growing repertoire of domestic spaces—hall, dining room, passage, chamber, and more—was the result. The introduction of these new spaces forced open the axial box that had been the two-room house, clearing the way to innovation in the dwelling's external form. Physically, logistically, and visually, houses became more complex, conforming with ever-greater precision to a growing list of social requirements. As hospitality and especially dining came to be the main event in gentry life, many Chesapeake householders dedicated a separate room to the meal and to the glittering equipage that accompanied it. Chesapeake families became increasingly conscious of the social place they occupied and thus chose to exclude certain categories of people from the circle of their society. Porches, lobbies, and, eventually, passages served to remove black servants and some whites from the scenes of conviviality.

As consumer goods became an important measure of social standing, owners came to regard their dwellings as settings for the display of these things. The buffet or cupboard, originally a freestanding piece of furniture, was now incorporated into the house. Inevitably, this and other architectural elements became a part of the display. The chimney, previously hidden within the body of the house, was now divided and moved to the gables, where it became more sculptural and was more easily displayed to advantage. Meanwhile, the stair abandoned its place by the chimney of the great room, moving to the new passage, where it girded the far end of the room in a riot of molded, turned, and jigsawn ornament.

The new intensity of formal public life led planters to create a "back room" or "little parlor" where the family could simply "be" when no performance was required. Indeed, the emergence of boxlike "Georgian-plan" houses during the second quarter of the eighteenth century was associated in some degree with this new fourth room, which implied a rectilinear ground-floor plan and thus a unitary mass. The appearance of these "backstage" rooms also reflected a new concept of family that looked inward, focusing on the immediate circle of kin and on the lives of children. This idea, with its greater emphasis on individual autonomy, served to enlarge the private sphere of domestic life.

However, the desire for privacy that led planters to create family sitting rooms soon impelled them to more drastic experiments. At first, this meant simply stirring the contents of "the box" to achieve a more satisfactory division between private and public space. Eventually, some householders chose to dispense with that container altogether, distributing the contents in a single rank of modulated parts, each of a size and form suitable to its social importance. This sort of house celebrated the continuing importance of hospitality, but it also placed the widest possible separation between the public and private spheres of the house. Even this was not enough for some, who chose to build instead what amounted to two distinct houses under one roof.

In the aftermath of the American Revolution, the rhetoric of liberty and equality highlighted the moral embarrassments of slavery and contributed to a breakdown of deference and social hierarchy among whites. Increasingly, householders sought to shield their families more effectively from arriving strangers and to make slavery less visible in the experience of those who occupied the great house. Initially, these efforts to "close" the house did not discount the importance of hospitality. However, they did prepare the way for a new conception of the house—current by the middle of the nineteenth century—as a place of refuge from an immoral world. This idea, central to the so-called cult of domesticity, was promoted by northern reformers, yet its practical implications concerning privacy and access were congruent with the changing needs of a people among whom the central fact of social existence up to that time—the institution of slavery—was increasingly under attack. All of this set the stage for continuing change in the way Chesapeake residents lived and built.

8 *Housing Slavery*

EDWARD A. CHAPPELL

Every building in this book was raised with profits from the labor of enslaved Africans or African Americans.[1] Slavery built the Chesapeake economy and shaped its landscape. Income from slaveholding enabled some planters to erect extraordinarily ambitious houses and others more comfortable dwellings. Slaves also labored in the construction of these buildings, from hauling materials to fashioning finish joinery. The circumstances in which they lived in towns and in the countryside ranged far beyond the rural cabin and fireside hearth of popular image, an impression popularized in *Uncle Tom's Cabin* and nurtured by proslavery advocates in the early 1850s.[2] Accommodations for most slaves in the eighteenth century consisted of rudimentary shelters and makeshift spaces, often no more than a cheap bed in an unheated cellar or a pallet on a kitchen floor. By the 1780s, roughly half of the residents of Williamsburg were enslaved, as were about a third of the residents in Annapolis. Yet no purpose-built slave housing survives in either capital from before the Revolution, and few such buildings from any period have been identified archaeologically in over eighty years of excavation.[3] Separate structures to house slaves were more common in the countryside, at least where plantations with large numbers of field hands required more accommodations than could be found among leftover spaces in houses and outbuildings. For the Chesapeake region as a whole, only a few enslaved domestics and field-workers had decent accommodations by eighteenth-century white standards; the vast majority dwelled in wretched circumstances. In a region where housing conditions were extremely modest for most inhabitants, enslaved Africans and African Americans made do with small, poorly lit, cold, unventilated spaces that provided the lowest degree of privacy and comfort.[4] Any personal space they claimed was usually of their own making.

The efforts of slave owners to wrest profit and domestic support from enslaved laborers while separating themselves

from the people and processes determined the nature of this housing. Factors that affected housing decisions included the wealth of an owner, the number of people in his service and their family composition, the nature of their work, and the perception that the enslaved shared an inherent racial inferiority. Influenced by political, economic, and religious attitudes, planters' views about accommodating their bondspeople shifted over time. The formation of African American families and the changing nature of agricultural labor contributed to slaves' developing a degree of agency in their material welfare, which ultimately changed the form and quality of housing just as owners' taste for propriety grew and their sense of appropriate management evolved. So the character of workers' housing was dynamic even as it was generally poor.

Enslaved workers occupied a spectrum of low-status environments in the century and a half before the Civil War. This diversity was less the function of the relative beneficence or cruelty of different masters than it was of their different strategies employed in balancing three imperatives: durability, discipline, and economy. The enslavement of domestic laborers and field-workers allowed owners to see them as investments from which maximum value could be derived by limiting the cost of housing and of work buildings, as well as that of food and clothing. But how much was just enough? The answer to that question varied significantly from place to place and between the colonial and antebellum periods. That it was asked, and the way in which it was answered, reveals much about white inhabitants' conception of slavery and the social function of architecture.

QUARTERS

Before the Revolution, owners of fewer than eight or nine slaves often relegated them to kitchens, work buildings, and parts of the principal house. Those owning larger numbers of people were more likely to construct separate buildings or additional spaces, both often called "quarters." Use of the term is illustrated by the vestry of Christ Church Parish in 1672 when it approved payment for finishing a house for its minister and for building "a Quarter for his servants."[5] In 1775, widow Dinah Archer of Norfolk was awarded use of certain rooms in her deceased husband's house as well as the "north room of the kitchen, commonly called the quarter."[6] This was not the only name used. "Negro house," cabin, hut, and dwelling house referred also to workers' housing. The Dorchester County, Maryland, Orphans' Court directed a guardian in 1770 to build a new kitchen and repair the old one "to make it fit for a quarter or negro house."[7]

The term "quarter" was likewise applied to the area or plot of land where slaves lived. A visitor to Virginia in 1736 noted that "A Negro Quarter is a Number of Huts or Hovels, built at some Distance from the Mansion-House; where the Negroes reside with their Wives and Families."[8] "Quarter" was also the term used for secondary, outlying farms on which a slave or white overseer managed field-workers. In the richest tobacco-growing regions, the population in these dispersed settlements ranged from ten to thirty people, often residing in two to four rooms. By contrast, outlying quarters in non-tobacco areas like the lower Eastern Shore contained far fewer people. In 1686, Stafford County planter William Fitzhugh noted that his thousand-acre property included

"three Quarters well furnished, with all necessary houses, ground & fencing, together with a choice crew of negroes at each plantation . . . with stocks of cattle and hogs at each quarter."[9] Williamsburg resident John Custis reported to his friend Peter Collinson in 1742 that "I dayly ride to my near Qrs wch are 3 or 4 miles out of Town."[10]

FIELD LABORERS

Colonial planters confronted the question of how to extract maximum work with the minimum investment most directly with field-workers. A principal motivation for separating slaves from owners' houses was as a means for enforcing leaner diets for laborers.[11] Poor housing was a corollary. On home plantations and more distant quarters, housing for field-workers was cheaply built, even compared to the "Virginia houses" in which early owners lived.[12] Philip Morgan observes that ephemeral construction reflected the peripatetic nature of tobacco cultivation, as planters regularly moved workers and cultivation from exhausted fields to fresh ones.[13] In the 1750s, blacks on David Curle's plantation in Elizabeth City County lived in "a pen made of Poles and covered with Pine-Brush, and in bad weather [they] retire to the Neighbors for shelter." Around 1788, Robert Carter valued eleven "Negro cabins" on his Coles Point plantation at just £3, while assessing a barn, granary, and storehouse together at £87.[14]

Low valuations could reflect modest scale as well as meanness of construction. Dimensions of slave quarters give hints to the relative size of intended resident populations throughout the eighteenth century. Larger buildings offered their own economy as a means of crowding more residents together. By 1745, Robert Bolling reported that he employed fifteen slaves over the age of sixteen on property where he himself did not reside in Amelia County. The team of men and women may have all occupied a "Quarter 16 by 20 Shedded & Lofted with outside chimney," worth £7.10, at a tobacco tract called Sampsons.[15] Advertisements in the *Virginia Gazette* before 1781 listed buildings on rural quarters that ranged from 40 by 20 feet down to 12 by 8 feet. The average-size house contained about 345 square feet, which would be comparable to a structure measuring 20 by 17 feet.[16] Buildings specifically listed as quarters in Dorchester County, Maryland, Orphans' Court valuations between 1745 and 1770 ranged from 150 to 540 square feet, with an average of 303 square feet, none of them suggesting rows of near-identical cabins.[17]

The various sizes affected how occupants arranged their lives. Buildings of shallow spans reduced cost by limiting the weight of joists and length of rafters. A common depth for houses of late colonial landowners was 16 to 18 feet, which provided space for bedchambers upstairs.[18] When the depth of workers' houses was reduced to less than 14 feet, headroom in the loft was substantially lowered, making the upstairs little more than an uncomfortable space into which people could crawl and sleep. More often it meant there was simply no loft. Before the nineteenth century, quarters greater than 14 or 15 feet deep were usually intended to house a larger population than a single kinship group. It is worth asking why planters like Bolling made such varied choices, building some quarters larger in order to crowd more residents together and others too small to shelter many, often on the same plantation. Family formation is part of the answer.

The development of black families and the decline in the importation of Africans into the Chesapeake had profound effects on the nature of the region's enslaved population, and historians have argued that there were parallel changes in their housing. Allan Kulikoff observes that most very young children remained with their enslaved mothers but were likely to be separated at an early age. He contends that people held in smaller numbers by small planters were less likely to reside with their partners and children.[19] Lorena Walsh recounts that by the early 1730s Virginia's preeminent slaveholder, Robert Carter, provided separate housing for married slaves and that there was general movement toward providing individual cabins for families.[20] Russell Menard sees gender balance from creole population growth ending what he calls "barracks-like existence" for enslaved males in the lower Western Shore of Maryland by the 1750s. Philip Morgan, too, sees nonkinship crowding as substantially declining through the century.[21]

Yet the emerging pattern for the first three-quarters of the eighteenth century is that wealthy tobacco planters commonly crowded field laborers together in groups with limited respect for kinship. It should not be inferred from listing slaves in family groups such as those in Carter's probate inventory that each kinship group was housed separately. Categories in an inventory do not necessarily equate with units of housing. Indeed, the African American population of the Chesapeake achieved natural reproduction by the mid-eighteenth century—earlier in some subregions—in spite of crowded conditions and the common pattern of one parent living distant from the other.[22]

Archaeology offers a useful perspective on the question of accommodation for workers in the region and its variability over the eighteenth century. Even though the sample remains small and weighted toward the largest planters, primarily in eastern Virginia, it has provided new data with which to weigh assumptions about widespread change in housing. Soil-stain ensembles confirm the meager size of some houses and give evidence of larger households crowded together. They also suggest the pervasive manner in which residents responded to crowding by modifying their buildings with the construction of subfloor pits. The most concentrated sample of sites appears at three James City County plantations. Among the earliest are three successive quarters located at Utopia, an outlying plantation held by James Bray II (d. 1725), his son, James Bray III (d. 1744), and Lewis Burwell IV (d. 1784), who married the younger Bray's widow. From the beginning of the eighteenth century until about 1730, enslaved residents at Utopia occupied two rooms of a 28- by 12-foot earthfast frame house. Near the hearth of the single wooden chimney, archaeologists discovered a cluster of several sizable pits. Such multiple pits, many of which have been found dug into the dirt floors of eighteenth-century Chesapeake slave house sites, seem to indicate the presence of non-family groups. Fraser Neiman has argued that the pits were a means for unrelated individuals forced to share a single living space to separate and defend their food supplies and other possessions.[23] Although the presence of the pits alone cannot reveal the precise composition of a dwelling's inhabitants, larger numbers of pits within specific dwellings suggest that a significant degree of crowding was present, in contrast to houses with few or no pits, which are generally smaller. Multiple pits fell from use in later quarters composed of family households, most clearly evident on sites dated after 1790–1800, although single cellar pits continued to be useful for storage into the mid-nineteenth century.

The first earthfast house at Utopia was followed by another with two 16-foot square rooms, one with a fireplace around which pits were concentrated. Residents dug an additional eight pits in the unheated room, suggesting both rooms were occupied by unrelated people (Fig. 8.1). By the end of the 1720s, another 28- by 12-foot house was built, containing two or three rooms but with just one fireplace with a single pit nearby.[24] Residents of this building may have been kinship-based with less reason to separate their possessions into separate storage spaces. The three buildings coexisted for a while, built around an uneven courtyard with a cooking pit near the center. Such sizable quarters, which Neiman has called "satellite farms," often included a small food storehouse controlled by an overseer, who may also have been enslaved.[25]

The Bray family had this ensemble demolished and rebuilt nearby around 1730–50 in a more compact layout. On the new site, numerous people appear to have crowded into a 12- by 16-foot room served by a fireplace and flanked by two

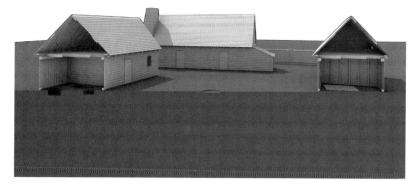

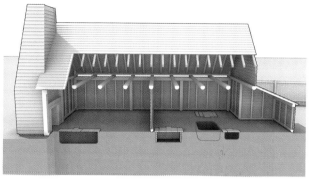

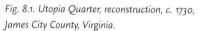

Fig. 8.1. Utopia Quarter, reconstruction, c. 1730, James City County, Virginia.

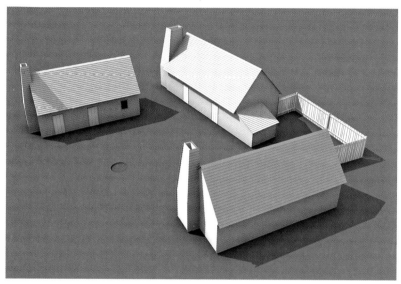

6- by 16-foot sheds. Residents dug twelve pits in the floor of the central room, three or more in each of four phases. Other residents occupied an adjoining 16- by 12-foot house, with a total of three pits.[26] In spite of the evident crowding, residents worked at making the quarters livable by constantly cleaning waste away from a broad yard between the houses.[27] In 1750–75, this building was replaced by a two-room, roughly 32- by 22-foot house of more regular form with a chimney at both ends. Again, numerous people crowded into the two heated rooms, digging four to six pits in each of four phases. Two separate pits nearby suggest that by 1775 single-unit houses were built within 50 feet, arguably for two families.[28] This new arrangement probably combined mass housing with separate accommodation for certain workers, who were possibly related. The yard space shared by the houses continued to be kept clean, despite also being used for outside cooking.

Two nearby James City County sites illustrate similar patterns at field quarters associated with their owners' grand Georgian houses. By midcentury, some wealthy planters began to arrange two sizable rooms for workers around a central brick chimney. It was a kind of building that was more durable than ones with wooden chimneys and smoke hoods, but it saved money by limiting the amount of masonry to a single chimney. It also distinguished the quarters from the end-chimney houses of white Virginians and Marylanders. Lewis Burwell IV built such a house around 1750 to accommodate field-workers at his home plantation, Kingsmill, roughly half a mile from his mansion. This consisted of two 20- by 18-foot rooms flanking a central chimney set against the rear wall, apparently without providing a third fireplace for a 16-foot-deep shed. Although the form was widely used later as two-family quarters, the Kingsmill building appears to have been crowded with a number of residents, including unrelated individuals, who dug eight pits in the rooms. About a decade later, residents filled in these pits and dug a dozen new ones before abandonment around the end of the Revolution. Nearby, a 24- by 20-foot house sheltered additional people who divvied up their possessions into six separate pits.[29]

The shift to mixed agriculture would ultimately change the practice of both slavery and house building in the Chesapeake. Although it was not necessarily accompanied by pro-

Fig. 8.2. Carter's Grove Quarter, c. 1750–75, as reconstructed 1987–90, James City County, Virginia.

visions for separate housing or a reduction in crowding, even at the large holdings, selective change was under way. When planter Nathaniel Burwell reached his majority in 1771, he inherited Carter's Grove, including the grand James River house built by his father, Carter Burwell, in 1751–55 (see Fig. 11.16). The son diversified crop production and built a new house for some of his slaves a few hundred feet from the mansion. Following the pattern established on tobacco-growing plantations, Burwell planned for perhaps twenty people to occupy two rooms, each roughly 21 feet by 20 feet and heated by a central chimney (Fig. 8.2).

The structure is known only from the arrangement of its eleven storage pits in two or three rooms. These contrast with a pair of larger, 9- by 6-foot pits that indicated the presence of a different variety of two-room house 30 feet away. The latter appears to be the remnant of a smaller, two-family house, probably built after the larger building. Two smaller pits nearby may represent single-family houses, which likewise postdate the larger structure. One of these houses was conceivably occupied by an overseer. All the excavated pits were filled when the buildings were demolished and Burwell moved the laborers to Frederick County, in 1796–97.[30]

Response to African American family formation can be read in developments at Utopia in the 1720s through Carter's Grove in the 1770s. Separate single pits suggest housing that accommodated family groups without the need for multiple pits. Variations in the size and configurations of buildings at all three sites indicate the range of spaces assigned to slaves, permitting a fuller interpretation of what might otherwise be read as changeless poverty. A broader counting of measurable Tidewater Virginia quarters and their pits finds declining size and fewer pits, suggesting an increase in kin-based households in the later eighteenth century.[31] Yet it is clear that all the phases at Utopia, Kingsmill, and Carter's Grove continued to crowd numerous people—possibly the majority at the respective plantations—into houses not divided by kinship.[32] Why would exceptions be made? What would cause a planter to provide smaller, more private quarters for some workers alongside crowded, ephemeral housing for others? Was family status or change in crop production the primary cause of variation?

The midcentury correspondence of Joseph Ball, a wealthy, absentee slave owner with plantations on the Northern Neck of Virginia, lays out the decision making that informed the provision of housing for favored slaves as well as for people he considered solely as field hands. Ball, like the richest pre-Revolutionary planters, drew a distinction between agricultural laborers subject to generalized and arm's-length treatment and a handful of domestic workers with whom he was intimately acquainted. That acquaintance provided some opportunity for negotiation between the enslaved and their owner. For the slave owner to receive the labor he sought, there could be some reciprocal benefit reflecting the worker's prior experience.[33] Ball's detailed letters from England between 1744 and 1758 to his nephew and plantation manager Joseph Chinn at Morattico include directions for construction and repair of housing for his workers that was clearly calculated to maximize the return on his investment. For most of his field hands, dry and secure accommodations as well as sufficient food and clothing were his chief intents.

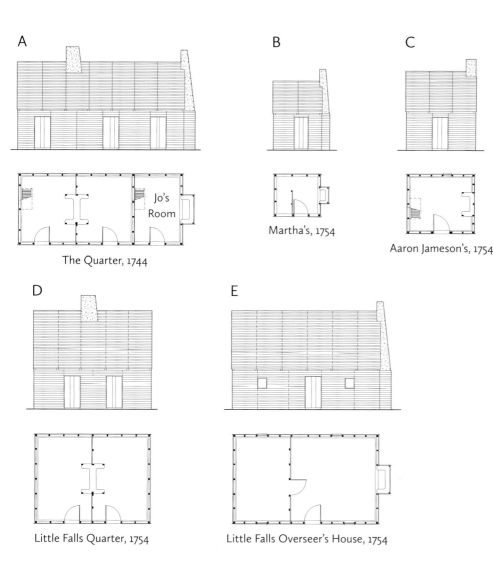

A

Jo's
Room

The Quarter, 1744

B

Martha's, 1754

C

Aaron Jameson's, 1754

D

Little Falls Quarter, 1754

E

Little Falls Overseer's House, 1754

This contrasts with the considerable concern he showed for the privacy and general condition of a few individuals he knew best.

In 1744, Ball wrote to Chinn about the construction of a three-unit house he called "the Quarter," intended to shelter a man named Jo, with whom he had close acquaintance, and other, unspecified people. It was to be frame and the walls were to be filled with poor-quality brick and mortar as insulation. There were to be two plastered wooden chimneys, one serving Jo's room and another between the two rooms occupied by "the other Negroes" (Fig. 8.3A). Brickwork was to be used in the shared wall to separate Jo from his fellow residents. The loft was to be laid with reused plank to make it available for sleeping. Ball omitted reference to the size of the building or any windows, but he desired secure doors and a dry floor. "And there must be Good plank Doors, and well hung with Iron hinges . . . and there must be Locks to the Doors; which I shall send. And the floors must be rais'd higher than the Ground without."[34]

A second letter, also sent in 1744, addressed rebuilding old houses at a quarter called the Forest, in Lancaster

County. Ball directed Chinn to rework the deteriorated houses in a manner that made them secure from cold, moisture, and intrusion. Like Robert Carter, who had called for lathing and nogging the frame walls of all his slave quarters in 1727, Ball also sought to make the walls solid with brick filling. In addition, he instructed Chinn to "let them be well Coverd, weatherboarded, and latt'd & fill'd, and the floors rais'd higher than without, and a Good plank Door, with Iron hinges, & a Good Lock & key: and let there be good Substantial Cills, of white oak, or Chestnut laid a little way in the Ground, and Jamy's Quarter must have the Shade [shed] pull'd away; and the End Cill at the Chimney must be set a Good hight above Ground; and be made up with dirt."[35] Nothing in these detailed instructions, however, demonstrates a concern to expand the overall living space or to provide privacy for family groups.

Ten years later, in February 1754, Ball wrote about a young enslaved woman named Martha, who had traveled to England with him as a child and whom he was now sending back to Virginia. Martha was to have a small new house at a farm quarter, where she would be introduced gradually to field labor. He asked his nephew to "take care of her, and let her have a Cabbin built up in one of the Quarters, with a Bed place in it and a Door to the Cabbin (which must be larger than the Bed place) with a Lock and Key to it: she must be used Tenderly the first Year at least; for she has been used to live well here."[36] Though he was consigning Martha to field-work, Ball sought a house for her with private, lockable accommodation and a separate sleeping space, however minute. Especially favored slaves were sometimes provided with a separate room or loft for sleeping. Landon Carter gave his gardener Johnny a small inner room, though he was angered to discover that the slave had used it to hide runaways.[37]

Within two weeks, Ball wrote again about Martha's treatment and specified that she should "live with her Mother: and a Cabbin built up for her Seven foot Long, and Eight foot wide, and Lathed and filled so as to be thorough dry before cold weather (Fig. 8.3B). I would have her put in but for half a share this first year: or she should prove sickly for nothing, but to keep her a little out of Idleness; and the next year for a whole share."[38] Martha's dwelling represents the extent of the accommodation given to a favored slave—only 56 square feet, tight to the weather but no masonry chimney, a lockable door but no glazed windows.

Still mean, but considerably better, were the accommodations Ball specified in 1754 for Aaron Jameson (whose surname suggests he may have been of mixed race). Born in Virginia, Jameson was carried to England as a boy and, like Martha, was now returning to be put to field labor. In spite of his new fate, Jameson was to have a superior house of his own built at Morattico, one in which he could secure all his possessions. Ball enumerated an uncommonly long list of goods belonging to Jameson and stipulated that they were to be "in his own custody in his own Little House." These included specialized cooking equipment, a violin, twelve shirts, pairs of stockings, shoes, boots, and much bedding, which contrasts with the two blankets and two or three shirts allotted to Ball's other workers. Ball stated:

His Beding is Quite New & Clean and I would have it kept so; and to that End would have him to ly in the Kitchin Loft when he is at Morattico; and in some Clean Place when he is in the Forrest. I would forthwith after his arrival have one of the worst of my old Bed steads cut short & fit for his Mattress. . . . And as soon as can be I would have a framed House Twelve foot long, and ten foot wide built for him . . . [and a plastered wood chimney well built] and the whole House must be Lathed and filled, and the Lock I have sent with him put upon the Door; and the Door must be made wide enough to take

his Great Harness barrel; and all this must be done as soon as possible that it may be soon dry in hot weather (Fig. 8.3C).[39]

Ball called for the house to have masonry foundations or durable bottom sills set in the ground and a raised floor. The ceiling height was to be no more than about 7 feet below an attic floored with salvaged boards. He also sent a note directing that Jameson "must ly in the Kitchin Loft till he is otherwise provided for: and must put his Great Cask Either in the Kitchen or in the old Milk house."[40] His house was to contain 120 square feet, more than twice the 56 square feet specified for Martha. Jameson's is the only case in which Ball expressed concern for cleanliness or raising his bed above the floor. That floor was still to be clay, however, and Ball did not call for windows in this superior accommodation.

Shortly after these specifications for Jameson's "Little House," Ball included directions for slave housing and an overseer's house at Little Falls, a distant quarter in King George County, when sending clothes for the workers, with the best reserved for Jameson and another favored male slave. He wrote:

I have sent you by Capt. Payne Nails Enough as I think to build what House you want for which here is bill of Lading and Invoice. I would have them all built upon the Top of the Hill: and the Dwelling houses first; and Lathed & filled that they may be Dry to live in as soon as may be. And let there be good fires kept to dry them; they must ly in the Tobacco house in the mean time. Let the quarter be twenty foot long, and 15 foot wide and fireplace in the Midle. And let the Overseers House be Twenty five foot long & fifteen foot wide, with a part partitioned off at one End [Figs. 8.3D, 8.3E].[41]

Ball's field-workers were to occupy several modest structures. Two were new two-room houses with wood and clay chimneys. Another was a rebuilt duplex with two rooms of 150 square feet each. A slightly larger hall-chamber house was planned for an overseer, which was three times the size of Jameson's house. He expressed no interest in housing together any family groups that may have existed among his field hands, but he gave special attention to three slaves with whom he was intimately acquainted. Each was to have a separate room or house, with 56 square feet for the woman and 120 for one of the men. And yet, just as he bunked his field hands in a tobacco barn while their quarters were under construction, he felt the kitchen attic to be suitably private and hygienic for Aaron Jameson as a temporary dwelling.

Ball made economic calculations when planning accommodations intended for Jameson and other slaves—whether or not they were to have separate housing, raised floors, much headroom, lockable doors, and such. Within a narrow range of options, he was very specific about the comparative quality of the buildings. All were to be relatively cheap, with earth floors rather than wooden ones, but they were to have frames lifted off the ground rather than secured with earth-fast posts. He intended them, then, to be more permanent than most tobacco houses and more secure against the cold. Yet, like owners of the James City County plantation quarters, he was selective in which people were to be offered privacy. At least in his midcentury case, that selection had more to do with the planter's own personal relationships than kinship groups within the workforce.

Ball's perceptions of appropriateness are cast in sharper relief by comparing the housing for enslaved field-workers with that he considered reasonable for white overseers, whom he characterized as "a parcel of Slubbering Sons of bitches." The slubbering Little Falls overseer received a hall-chamber house with 325 square feet on the main floor. For another overseer, Henry Pullen, Ball told Chinn to underpin an old house that he had bought and to relay boards on sleepers to provide a cheap wooden floor. He suggested that Pullen could reside there on the condition that he "make Good any Damages that may be done, by breaking the windows, or Greasing [soiling] the house, or the Like, else not; for I see no reason, why I should keep a Fine House with sash windows for an overseer." That settled, the old overseer's house was to be repaired and used for stripping tobacco.[42]

The Ball letters offer an unusually detailed account of how one Chesapeake planter conceived of housing for enslaved field-workers, who remained unnamed and uncounted in the correspondence, and for the three unmarried slaves who received special attention. Like his neighbors, Ball felt that he looked after his slaves, and he echoed the arguments advanced by many proslavery planters in the decades before emancipation when he favorably compared the condition of slaves "that have a Good Master" within his own region to that of French peasants.[43] His concern for their welfare may well have led him to devote unusual attention to some of his workers' accommodations, but the sparseness of his housing specifications for his field laborers is fully consonant with the evidence found by archaeologists. If Ball saw himself as "a Good Master," it was in the guise of a careful manager who protected his inherited Virginia estate and motivated his workers with incentives and force. Better accommodation, the promise of handed-down clothing, and the use of a horse for limited travel were all favors Ball extended to

Jameson as inducements for submissive behavior. The use of these "soothing arts," of course, was always in the context of harsh discipline. Preferential treatment for some, no matter the motivation, did not change the brutish reality for all. Ball wrote that if Jameson were to become unruly, Chinn should have him bound, severely whipped, and pickled, followed, if needed, by iron restraints on his neck and, failing that, his legs, "for as he is my Slave he must and Shall be obedient."[44]

Like the diary of Landon Carter, another Northern Neck planter, Ball's letters reveal that owners' evolving personal relationships with workers and the degrees to which their demands were met affected their conferred status and their treatment, including their housing, in the late colonial period.

DOMESTIC WORKERS AND WORKPLACES

Unlike field hands, whose rough work and distance from the main house made it easier for masters to treat them indifferently, eighteenth-century enslaved domestics labored and lived with their masters in close proximity. Whether in town or on the plantation, they rarely had separate residences. In households staffed by fewer than ten or a dozen servants, most slept in ancillary spaces in and around their master's dwelling. Even at Robert Carter III's elaborate Nomini Hall, tutor Philip Fithian described a kitchen and workhouse but no separate quarters near the mansion house.[45] The poor quality of freestanding quarters erected before the Revolution is reflected in their rarity—virtually none survive. Only quarters closely associated with elite houses remain. Clearly, there were more Negro houses nearby than the standing record indicates. Executors for Peter Randolph offered his Williamsburg property for sale in 1767, reporting that it had "a good kitchen, a servant's house of the same dimensions, two new stables . . . [and] a coach house." The same year, William Carter advertised for a runaway woman named Venus, whom he suspected "was harboured by other slaves in Kitchens and quarters in and about the town." A Fredericksburg property was offered in 1780 with "a coach house, stables, and houses for servants."[46] But advertisements for urban properties in Virginia and Maryland rarely included such references before 1800.

The majority of domestic slaves bedded down not in separate, purpose-built housing, but in outbuildings, principally in kitchens. Despite the central role that dining played in genteel hospitality, preparation of food by black cooks was such a low-status activity that most slave-owning Virginians and Marylanders separated cooking and meal preparation from their halls and dining rooms. As early as 1665, Arthur

Allen removed cooking to a cellar room at Bacon's Castle. More commonly, planters built separate kitchens, as did John Page and Thomas Ludwell at Middle Plantation. This choice had the additional advantage of removing the smells, sounds, and occasional dangers of cooking from the owner's house. Exterior kitchens became the favored choice by the end of the seventeenth century and remained so through the middle of the nineteenth century. In Williamsburg, some seventy-five detached kitchens are known from the eighteenth century, compared to little more than a half dozen cellar ones in residences and public houses.[47] In Annapolis, the ratio of detached to cellar kitchens is similar. Owners' concerns for separating themselves from the unappealing activities and by-products associated with cooking is vividly evident in President James Madison's decision when he expanded Montpelier in 1811–13 to insulate only the ceilings of cellar kitchens, buffering the refined rooms above from the sounds and smells of cooking.

Their removal from the house, their work function, and the provision of heat made kitchens the default choice for housing servants cheaply. It could be their sole accommodation on urban sites and on all but the largest plantations. Even on elite plantations, the kitchen might be the principal shelter for the domestic workers, who were housed separately from field hands. Richard Henry Lee made such a distinction when he recorded that he "gave Quarter & Kitchen people each half a bushel of salt."[48]

Like quarters, kitchens in the Chesapeake were lowly regarded, reflected in the inferiority of their construction and maintenance. The Dorchester County Orphans' Court records indicate that by the third quarter of the eighteenth century all but the poorest white households in the county had detached kitchens, and they were among the more poorly finished and cheaply valued structures on any site. The principal dwelling houses were the superior structures on these plantations, followed by milk houses and dairies. Kitchens were consistently of poorer quality, and quarters, smokehouses, cornhouses, and stables were the lowest. Weatherboarded frame walls were usually associated with dwellings and milk houses, while other buildings were commonly log, reflecting housewives' closer association with dairy processing than the dirtier labor involved in meat preparation and cooking. Building hierarchy within these farms was evident in the materials and finishes. When the Dorchester County kitchens were frame, their siding was riven clapboards more often than weatherboards. When the dwelling house walls were built of hewn log, those of the kitchen, quarters, and lesser buildings were unhewn logs. The 1774 inventory of Hannah Hayward's property is representative. Her house

TABLE 8.1. Wall Materials Identified in Dorchester County, Maryland, Orphans Court Appraisals, 1760–1775

	BRICK	FRAME	LOG
Dwelling houses	3	52	36
Kitchens		14	29
Milk houses		12	1
Smokehouses		1	23
Quarters			11
Stables			9
Corn houses			45

Note: Superior materials characterized white-occupied dwelling houses and milk houses. Materials for kitchens were better than those for smokehouses, slave quarters, stables, and corn houses.

TABLE 8.2. Roof Materials Identified in Dorchester County, Maryland, Orphans Court Appraisals, 1760–1775.

	SHINGLES	FEATHEREDGE SHINGLES	CLAPBOARDS
Dwelling houses	21	12	16
Kitchens	3	2	12
Smokehouses	2		8
Quarters	1		3
Corn houses		10	14

Note: Superior materials characterized white-occupied dwelling houses. Materials for kitchens were better than those for smokehouses, slave quarters, and corn houses.

and milk house were both frame, her kitchen was made of logs hewn square, a smokehouse was also log, while the quarter was built with cheaper round logs. The Orphans' Court records make it clear that in the hierarchy of structures on domestic sites, quarters consistently fell at the bottom, with kitchens slightly higher (Tables 8.1, 8.2).

One extensive entry in the Dorchester County records illustrates the pattern across a range of constructional quality. In 1774, well-off orphan Mary Nevitt and her family occupied a substantial frame house in Cambridge, Maryland, and owned five farms rented to white tenants. The poorest lacked a separate kitchen while all the others had kitchens inferior to the dwellings in construction and condition. The family's large house was in good repair with sawn weatherboard siding, a round-butt shingle roof, and plank floors. It contrasted with the "old framed clapboard kitchen with a bad brick chimney the whole scarcely worth noticing" that stood in the yard. Their most comfortable tenants, Henry and James Trego, occupied a two-story, 20- by 16-foot frame house finished with sawn weatherboards and round-butt

Fig. 8.4. Kitchen Quarter, c. 1760, Gould Hill, Hanover County, Virginia.

shingles. It was served by a large wooden kitchen finished with riven clapboard siding and featheredge shingles, an inferior variety. The four log buildings—a quarter, henhouse, stable, and corn house—were all in very bad order. A poorer tenant, James Layton, occupied a 20- by 16-foot dwelling with a shed, built of hewn logs, with a brick chimney and wooden floors. His kitchen was built of unhewn logs with a wood chimney and apparently an earth floor. Two smokehouses, two corn houses, and a quarter were all built of round logs as well.[49]

At the other end of the spectrum, the best cookrooms on the largest plantations and urban lots were better than James Layton's log dwelling house, especially when they were designed to be part of a pleasing view from the mansion house or to serve as a frame for the principal edifice. At Kingsmill and the Hammond-Harwood House, large sash windows in the kitchen were part of the formal composition that made the cookroom well lighted. Such design favored the aesthetic delight of the owner and his guests over comfort and ease for workers within, and with a little ingenuity the additional expense of glazed openings could be avoided. A fine pair of c. 1760 freestanding flankers to a now-lost but

once lavish house called Gould Hill in Hanover County contained a cookroom and laundry below lodging rooms in the full upper story. The brick walls are finely executed, with rubbed-and-gauged work on central Venetian windows and rectangular outer windows ornamenting the long walls. But the outer windows were blind openings and provided no light for servants toiling at large fireplaces (Fig. 8.4). Contrasting with the exceptional exteriors, the interiors were completely unfinished.

Whatever their quality, kitchens, like quarters, were crowded with black bodies. In most cases, people were packed into rooms of less than 300 square feet. Eighteenth-century owners showed little concern about having many people congregating day and night in the space in which cooking took place. Just how many was revealed when a fire swept through the kitchen at Rosewell one night in 1741, killing eleven slaves who were asleep in the building.[50] The shared understanding that kitchens, like quarters, were black zones, not black and white ones, is illustrated by Landon Carter's astonished fury at learning that runaways had been hiding in his own kitchen cellar after he had called out the militia to comb the countryside.[51]

Most freestanding eighteenth-century Chesapeake kitchens had a single main room with an unfinished loft above. Williamsburg mayor Thomas Everard's cook worked in such a kitchen behind the house on Palace Street. At night, the cook and other workers climbed a ladder stair from the earth-floored workroom to sleep in the attic space, which was floored and provided with a fireplace but otherwise little finished (Fig. 8.5). Some wealthy planters and successful townspeople doubled the kitchen, leaving the chimney on the partition to provide fireplaces for two workrooms or a cookroom and first-floor lodging. This solution was used in Williamsburg by tavern keeper Henry Wetherburn in the 1740s and tradesman James Geddy some twenty years later. Lydia Broadnax, George Wythe's favored cook, probably occupied the small heated space beside the cookroom near Palace Green.[52] Other owners added unheated end rooms or rear sheds to expand occupiable space. The former could result in two attic rooms if flooring was laid on the joists, though the second loft space was often reached through its neighbor rather than by a second stair, limiting privacy.

Lack of intense development pressure in colonial Chesapeake towns allowed the rich to acquire multiple adjoining lots even in the best locations so that their domestic service buildings spread out to resemble plantation patterns. Peyton Randolph's 1750s service building, later called a "kitchen, laundry, quarter," was unusual in being large enough to contain three rooms on the main floor (see Fig. 7.9). Two large workrooms flanked its internal chimney with oversized fireplaces. A third heated room was probably used for lodging and perhaps gathering space, most distant from the house. In 1776, twenty-seven slaves occupied three upstairs rooms, the lower three rooms, and the parts of the stable, as well as makeshift corners in the Randolphs' house. They worked in an adjoining fenced yard and served the house both through an enclosed "covered way" and across the yard to the house's passage and dining room.[53]

By the third quarter of the eighteenth century, some of the richest Virginians and their high-status workers, white and black, made secondary spaces around large kitchen buildings into separate lodgings. The varied interior quality of such spaces reveals the status of their intended occupants in the eyes of the owner, while the competing requirements of enforcing economy while cultivating genteel views governed their exterior form. An intact kitchen quarter at Marmion in King George County provides an unusual opportunity to see the results of repeated adjustments to provide modest heated rooms at the center of a substantial plantation (Fig. 8.6). While not quite a formal flanker, substantial construction

Fig. 8.5. Kitchen loft, Thomas Everard House, Williamsburg.

and placement of the kitchen represented part of an effort to bring visual order to planter William Fitzhugh's mansion. A dairy and smokehouse framed the front of the 1758 house, and the kitchen and a store were positioned symmetrically in the rear, where Fitzhugh's best room and a full-length porch faced the yard. A brick chimney was built in the kitchen by 1770, which had a work fireplace for a sizable cookroom and a heating fireplace for a smaller plastered rear room used as sleeping quarters.

As at the Randolph House, Mount Vernon, Harewood in Jefferson County, West Virginia, and elsewhere, the cookroom was located closer to the house, with the secondary space further away, suggesting that the latter was living space, not a servants' hall planned for easiest access. From the smaller room, a stair rose through a boarded lobby to one of two attic rooms, both with undersized fireplaces. The small room was finished with lapped boards and brown plaster, which was omitted from the uneven brickwork of the chimney stack (Fig. 8.7). Some residents walked through this space to reach a larger inner room, sheathed with riven clapboards, over the cookroom. In short, people living in the kitchen occupied at least three rooms beyond the cookroom, with those in the only private space having to pass through the other two residential rooms to reach their attic lodging. Occupants repeatedly repaired the space with unfinished and recycled wood and limited amounts of plaster, indicating a long life in active use.

Fig. 8.6. Kitchen, Marmion,
King George County, Virginia.
(HABS, 1936)

Fig. 8.7. Lodging room, Marmion kitchen, King George County, Virginia. The room is reached
from a stairway in the roughly enclosed lobby on the right.

Fig. 8.8. Attic lodging room, 1764–65, John Ridout House, Annapolis, Maryland. Residents walked through unfinished attic space to reach two rooms that were plastered and trimmed.

0   15
FEET

EXTENDED GENTRY HOUSEHOLDS

Marmion illustrates a common practice among gentry plantation ensembles in which better service buildings might be outwardly refined to suit the view from the owner's house but divided and variously finished to reflect the status of the work and workers inside.

Space for both white and black household staff in the homes of the richest landowners is found in service wings and flankers of their grand houses, reflecting owners' increasing investment in the machinery for a well-served gentry. Beyond the provision of cooking, such flankers in the Chesapeake could be flexible extensions of household space.[54] George Washington exemplified the flexibility of flankers by building one in 1775 that he intended to use as housing for servants of visiting elites, but his manager assumed it would be a laundry. He later assigned it as housing for an overseer and his family with little alteration.[55] The Governor's Palace in Williamsburg set a new standard for visually and functionally supporting the central residence, with flankers built in the scale of substantial landowners' houses. Mann Page I and his brother-in-law John Carter soon led the pack when creating rooms in L-shaped flankers at Rosewell and big two-story dependencies at Shirley, one of which provided a better-lighted kitchen and laundry and removed cooking from under Carter's entrance hall.[56] The best of the rooms in such buildings is a plastered but unpainted space upstairs in the kitchen flanker of Blandfield (1769–72), Robert Beverley's lavish plantation house in Essex County. Beverley's superior lodging room was 20 feet square, lighted by four windows, and provided with a fireplace much like the upper rooms in the Shirley dependencies. The room was trimmed with simple and unpainted architraves and a respectable little mantel, clearly marking it as better than the cookroom below it and other spaces in the flanker, which were finished with the most basic of plain facings. Smaller counterparts include

two plastered and wood-trimmed residential rooms within the otherwise unfinished attic of the 1764–65 John Ridout House in Annapolis (Fig. 8.8). Like three plastered and heated rooms in the 1720s cellar at Rosewell and two well-finished cellar rooms at Prestwould (1795), these were available to house white household staff—a tutor, housekeeper, bookkeeper, or other paid members of the household.

The accommodation of white family and staff members in secondary buildings is illustrated by tutor Philip Fithian's description of a clerk and steward named Mr. Randolph, who occupied two downstairs rooms in the schoolhouse at Nomini Hall while he and three Carter boys slept in two finished rooms upstairs.[57] Similarly, indentured tutor John Harrower enjoyed the comfort of a plastered room—in his case, the single-room schoolhouse at William Daingerfield's Belvidera, which he shared with an educated overseer. Fithian was treated as a genteel member of the household who conversed comfortably with family members and presided over dinner when Colonel Carter was absent from the table. Still, Carter and Daingerfield viewed both tutors as staff who should share sleeping quarters with other males outside the great house.

Comparable to Harrower's accommodation is one of the two small single-room flankers at Tuckahoe called a schoolhouse. Like Harrower, a tutor at Tuckahoe would certainly have slept as well as taught in the room. Beyond the small flankers is a larger, center-chimney house with two rooms both on the main floor and in the attic. Usually interpreted as one of four duplexes for slaves, it originally had an interior doorway and plastered rooms, indicating it was built as relatively high-quality housing for the likes of a valued tutor or respectable overseer. When such superior lodging rooms were placed upstairs in what might appear to be work buildings, they were normally provided independent access. Stairs to the second floor were contained in passages at the corners of the flankers at both Blandfield and Mount Airy and in center passages at Shirley and Brandon, allowing their

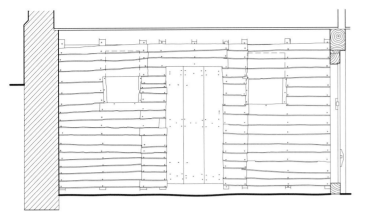

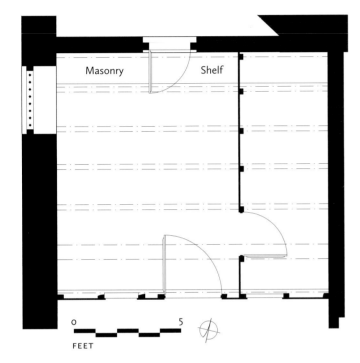

Masonry Shelf

0   5

FEET

Fig. 8.9. *Cellar apartment built with riven clapboard partitions, Bowling Green, Caroline County, Virginia.*

ified by workers within existing subsidiary spaces. Landon Carter suspected that "the servants that lay in [the] house" had stolen a butter pot from his dairy in 1770, and he sent overseer Billy Beal "to search all their holes and boxes," unintentionally drawing a parallel to subfloor pits with which field-workers modified their agricultural quarters.[60] Easily overlooked, the lodging spaces exist from cellar to attic, and their ad hoc quality demonstrates the absence of any standard for size, light, or finish. James Madison Sr. included a small heating fireplace in the large unpartitioned south room at the end of his cellar at Montpelier in 1763, making it usable for full-time occupation by domestic workers who would be close at hand. It was accessible only from the outside and to the bedchamber above by way of a ladder and trapdoor in the chamber closet. The space was completely unfinished, with unwhitewashed brickwork, exposed framing, and a clay floor. Two small windows in the foundation provided what little light there was.[61] If not for the fireplace and archaeological evidence, it would resemble the storage rooms elsewhere in the cellars. Landon Carter's son-in-law Robert Beverley included two separate 20-foot-square lodging rooms in the cellar of Blandfield, which were likely reserved for high-status black servants. Both had modest amenities, including a fireplace and small glazed windows. They had earthen or paved floors with exposed brick walls and a rough board ceiling. Both reached the outside through a shared passage to a cellar entrance.

A remarkable example of a room roughly carved out from an existing secondary space is in the unheated cellar of a 1743 plantation house called Bowling Green in Caroline County. It is a double-pile brick house with a cellar originally divided by a longitudinal brick wall. The front half of the cellar was made accessible later in the eighteenth century by adding an interior service stair that descends discreetly from a rear lobby. There, a substantial clapboarded wall divides a small space from a 16- by 12-foot outer room, the latter with a plastered ceiling, which may suggest occupation by house servants. A heavily secured door divided this room from the rear cellar. Originally accessible from the outside, the rear space was initially undivided until, less than ten years after initial construction, a resident created a small, unheated, two-room apartment at one end. The occupant built two spindly partitions with riven studs lapped to sills and to the joists overhead. The partition was cut by a short door hung on wood hinges, which led into a 9½- by 8½-foot room (Fig. 8.9). This, in turn, led to a smaller inner room. After the

residents to reach the superior upper rooms without passing through low-status workspaces.[58]

Though some white tutors, overseers, and favored slaves clearly were provided with separate sleeping spaces offering varying degrees of comfort and quality, these arrangements were exceptional, reserved for individuals of high status on the richest plantations. Most slaves had to make do on the margins, in kitchens and outbuildings and in the dwellings of their masters. Such spaces have survived because owners wished to hold the enslaved staff close at hand, seldom because the workers' superior status called for quality. Indeed, those who were most physically associated with their owners' lives within their houses were pushed into the corners by the owners' ambivalent attachment—desiring segregation while demanding constant service. House slaves commonly slept in passages, closets, and owners' bedchambers, where the physical and written evidence is often difficult to recover.[59]

Relatively unspecialized accommodation was sometimes visibly built into elite houses and, more often, crafted or mod-

single unglazed exterior window was blocked, both rooms were lit only by small shuttered openings in the partition, borrowing light from a distant cellar window.

In the absence of fireplaces, areas commonly occupied by domestic workers can now be virtually indistinguishable from storage space, except for ephemeral fragments of evidence like doors that lock from inside and multiple layers of whitewash. Such evidence appears in the ancillary space in a house Robert Carter III occupied from 1761 to 1773 in Williamsburg. This was the Robert Carter who employed Fithian at Nomini Hall and who, imbued later with New Light faith and Revolutionary ideology, freed all of his nearly 500 slaves in 1791.[62] In his Williamsburg house, the low unheated and unlit attic was divided by a rough stud partition to form two distinct spaces. Occupants would walk from the second-floor stair into the first room and through a locked doorway in the partition to reach the larger room. The partition was built to favor the inner room, with wood lath and a brown coat of plaster roughly applied to that side and subsequently twice whitewashed. In order to reach the private room, residents had to duck under internal gutters and roof beams 5 feet above the floor.[63] Living in the unventilated Carter attic would have provided neither comfort nor relative independence, with Carter bedrooms and a parlor just below. The owner's priority was efficient service economically provided.

POST-REVOLUTIONARY CHANGE

The post-Revolutionary era brought significant changes for slave housing in the Chesapeake. Improvements in accommodation were part of a broader pattern of selectively confronting the harshness of slavery without eliminating it, though some toyed with the idea during the economic slump of the late eighteenth century. Figures as prominent as George Washington struggled with the ethical concept and practicalities of freeing his workforce. Manumission increased to the point that 8.5 percent of the black population in Queen Anne's County, Maryland, was free in 1790.[64] Some denominations such as the Methodists and the Baptists welcomed black residents into their churches. Abolition remained a distant hope, while the Revolution and succeeding decades expanded the discourse on the ethics of slavery. Slavery was such a metaphor of Revolutionary rhetoric that owners were forced to construct arguments in its defense. Increasingly, they found the eyes of the world upon them. Everyday treatment of slaves became a central topic of discussion among slaveholders, many of whom argued, like Joseph Ball, that slaves who had "a good master" were not thoughtlessly exploited. Although the broad questioning of slavery in the Revolutionary era did not explicitly address housing, improved accommodations for enslaved workers allowed planters to claim amelioration in ways that fell well short of manumission. Housing became a matter of more consequence.[65]

The enslaved population was almost entirely native born by the 1780s. Multiple generations had learned ways of negotiating with the masters, and family connections were increasingly influential in the process. Slaves' resistance to owner coercion is difficult to now recognize, in part because their strategies were often covert and left little trace in the physical record. As Neiman has argued, their influence can best be recognized as indirect in architectural change owners carried out as countermeasures.[66]

Thomas Jefferson's 1790s reworking of the housing at Monticello exemplifies the shift from predominantly barracks housing to more private quarters for domestic workers and tradespeople made by the small group of planters who owned significant numbers of nonagricultural slaves. Jefferson demolished remnants of a two-room, 34- by 17-foot building he called the "Negro quarter," built around 1770, and replaced it with a 16- by 10½-foot house and three 12- by 14-foot houses on Mulberry Row. Each of the smaller houses had log walls, a board roof, a wooden chimney, and a single sizable storage pit. Here lived tradesmen and domestic workers with families, including the Hemingses, rather than unrelated individuals (Fig. 8.10).[67] Neiman argues that the parallel change to agricultural quarters with fewer pits at Monticello reflects diversification from tobacco to crops and trades requiring more personal initiative, which, in turn, offered negotiating power in choice of household formation, including single-family houses.[68] A 1798 plat of Sir Peyton Skipwith's holdings in Mecklenburg County shows as many as nine houses at the Prestwould home farm quarter and from four to seven at all outlying quarters. In 1787, Skipwith owned 144 people, 135 of them in Mecklenburg County.[69] The one surviving house among these is a 16- by 12-foot frame building, with a wood floor and clapboard-covered walls, superior in quality to Jefferson's three matched houses but possibly with a wooden chimney (see Fig. 2.8).

Owners of some moderate-sized labor forces relied on a mixture of housing that provided separation for certain families. A relatively well-housed group of twenty-two slaves occupied four buildings on the plantation of St. Mary's orphan Sarah Ann Caroline Fenwick in 1805. The four to six potential family groups lived in a small kitchen, a secure 20- by 16-foot quarter, and an old 30- by 12-foot, center-chimney quarter in bad repair, for an average of 36 square feet per per-

Fig. 8.10. Reconstruction of "Building S," one of three identical houses Thomas Jefferson had built for domestic workers and tradesmen at Monticello, c. 1793.

0   15

FEET

son. By comparison, an overseer occupied a 320-square-foot house on the same property. Two years later, St. Mary's County orphan Daniel W. Campbell owned twenty-three people in three to five family groups, whom he provided with 42 square feet per resident, in a 30- by 18-foot quarter in good repair, presumably with two rooms, and an old 16- by 12-foot house "past repair."[70]

Surviving buildings contribute to the picture of post-Revolutionary change, the extent of which is hard to measure. In eastern Virginia, evidence appears for slave owners' growing interest in segregating workers' sleeping space from that of production, especially from cooking. Small detached kitchens were built around 1800 behind two colonial houses in Williamsburg, the Grissell Hay House on Market Square and Bassett Hall at the south edge of town. In both, a second exterior door gave access to a stair rising to a bedchamber upstairs, which was not directly accessible from the cookroom. At the Hay House kitchen and at Cherry Walk in rural Essex County, entrance to the stair was discreetly placed at the rear so that residents could come and go as unobtrusively as possible.

The visibility of black bodies complicated the provision and location of quarters and serving spaces. In genteel settings, slave owners devised ways to control their workers' movements and to make them relatively unseen. Jefferson designed semi-subterranean passages that allowed his domestic slaves to move between work buildings, quarters, and the cellar of his rebuilt Monticello. Once inside the house, all but superior servants like Burwell Colbert hid themselves behind Jefferson's revolving service doors and below his dumbwaiter (see Fig. 12.18). Norfolk merchant Moses Myers connected a two-story kitchen quarter to his dining room with a louver-sided passage. Enslaved servants could deliver food to the dining room and wait in the exterior passage without being seen from outside. Builders in the town of Onancock, Virginia, incorporated a hidden passage allowing final preparation and delivery of food to merchant John Shepherd Ker's dining room without moving through either his entrance hall or rear doorway. Urban houses and stores built in Petersburg and Richmond placed kitchens and servant waiting areas in cellars and rear wings far more readily than had their Williamsburg and Annapolis predecessors.

Many older patterns, of course, persisted beyond the Revolution. Most notably, George Washington seems to have *increased* communal living space when he demolished an old two-story quarter at Mount Vernon measuring at least 55 by 35 feet and re-housed an estimated sixty of his slaves in two, single-story, 70- by 20-foot wings of a new greenhouse in 1792–93. Archaeologist Dennis Pogue suggests that a mixture of unattached adults, single women with children, and husband-and-wife families occupied four rooms.[71] Skilled male artisans may have predominated, but as in the old crowded Utopia and Kingsmill quarters, some Mount

Vernon families lived together without occupying spaces separate from others.

Cabins for Washington's agricultural workers were smaller and predominantly log walled, allowing many of them to be raised by their own residents rather than by skilled craftsmen, as Washington himself acknowledged. Fithian had observed slaves framing a small house on a Sunday afternoon in 1774 and remarked that Sundays were commonly given by Carter's slaves to "building & patching their Quarters or rather Cabins."[72] Owners increasingly employed this strategy of having slaves construct their own houses, much as the workers themselves fulfilled some of their dietary needs. As an economic calculation this allowed owners to avoid most carpentry costs, and it gave slaves more ability to create and defend separate kin-based residence groups. Neiman sees these mutual benefits, along with the regimen of wheat production, as coalescing in a preponderance of smaller log houses for the enslaved population of the Virginia Piedmont, especially after c. 1790.[73]

Nonetheless, as tax records from the turn of the century make clear, most slaves continued to be housed in the leftover corners of kitchens, principal dwellings, and work buildings, and many of those who did live in quarters found them to be just as crowded and cramped as their colonial predecessors. A 1785 tax list for Halifax County, Virginia, described the dwellings of 239 householders in this tobacco-dominated southern Piedmont landscape in which virtually everyone lived in small houses or outbuildings. Even the most successful planters occupied houses that were small by Tidewater gentry standards. Buildings called quarters ranged from 16 by 12 feet to 24 by 16 feet, which were similar in size to the houses occupied by most Halifax whites. The enumeration contained nine buildings listed as quarters on properties with a total of 68 slaves. Historian Michael Nicholls found that 165 enslaved blacks lived on 20 properties with separate kitchens or secondary houses presumably available to slaves or overseers. The list suggests that the remainder of Halifax County's enslaved African Americans, or 60 percent of the total, occupied parts of their owners' houses and farm buildings rather than kitchens or separate quarters.[74] Those who were housed in quarters were given roughly 35 to 40 square feet per person.

The 1798 Federal Direct Tax lists survive for a number of Tidewater counties in Maryland, providing a detailed enumeration of real estate, including the type and size of buildings. Orlando Ridout V has closely analyzed the 1798 tax lists for Queen Anne's County and matched the information about residents with the 1800 census records. As in Piedmont Virginia, this Eastern Shore county had few quarters. In a county with 7,315 whites, 525 free blacks, and 6,475 enslaved blacks, 60 percent of white households owned slaves. Yet only 18 plantations, or 12.5 percent of the 143 properties enumerated, had buildings specifically identified as quarters. Small secondary houses that may have housed slaves appeared on another 18 properties. Overseer houses appeared on only 11. Separate kitchens housed other workers, yet such kitchens were present on three of every four farms and for only one in five houses in town. Most enslaved domestic workers in the town of Centreville and the village of Abingdon lived in cellars, cellar kitchens, and attics.[75]

The Queen Anne's tax and census lists permit some estimation of housing for specific groups of workers, including those owned by successful middling planters as well as the gentry. On a 320-acre farm in Wye Hundred, 22 people owned by the heirs of Mary Nicholson occupied a 20- by 16-foot quarter and a kitchen. In a persistent pattern, 21 slaves occupied a 24- by 22-foot quarter and a kitchen on 615-acre Providence plantation, in the same district. William Helmsley's 30 to 35 enslaved people occupied only two buildings specifically called quarters, one 20 by 18 feet and the other 15 feet square. In all, quarters in Queen Anne's County ranged from 12 by 16 feet (192 square feet) to 30 by 28 feet (840 square feet), with most between 234 and 432 square feet. Based upon the tax records, Ridout estimates that most Queen Anne's County slaves were allotted 40 to 60 square feet of space, with 48 square feet as the mean, slightly more than those in Halifax County.

Most contemporary Orphans' Court records reinforce the evidence of people crowded into relatively small buildings, often with limited opportunity for separation by family group. They also confirm the point that many people occupied odd corners of outbuildings and their owners' houses rather than their own domestic space. Improvements in some ancillary buildings did not fundamentally alter the inferior quality of buildings primarily associated with slaves. Between 1781 and 1808, log walls were recorded twice as often as frame ones for kitchens on the properties of St. Mary's County orphans, and quarters were four times as likely to be log as frame. In the same sample, white owners and tenants were three times more likely to reside in a wood-framed house than a log or brick one.[76] Log had become the principal choice for housing rural workers and cooking in much of the Tidewater as well as the Piedmont.

Earlier observers, like the Presbyterian tutors Fithian and Harrower, expressed little concern about the accommodation of enslaved workers who lived all around them. After the

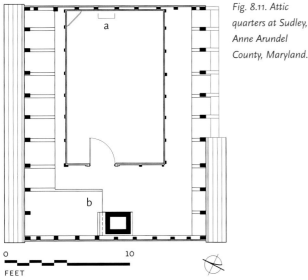

Fig. 8.11. Attic quarters at Sudley, Anne Arundel County, Maryland.

0   10
FEET

a. Location of original window
b. Location of original stair

war, outside travelers found slave housing to be a powerful embodiment of the contradictions inherent in the republic. Englishman J. F. D. Smythe described a Virginia house occupied by six enslaved workers and an overseer as a "miserable shell, a poor apology for a house, [which] consisted but of one small room, which served for the accommodation of the overseer and six negroes; it was not lathed or plastered, neither ceiled nor lofted above, and only very thin boards for its covering; it had a door on each side, one window but no glass in it; it had not even a brick chimney, and as it stood on blocks about a foot above the ground, the hogs lay constantly under the floor which makes it swarm with flies."[77] Johann David Schoepf wrote in the 1780s that dwellings for the enslaved on Virginia plantations were "commonly so many small separate, badly kept cabins of wood, without glass in the windows, of the structure and solidity of a house of cards."[78] As late as 1823, a correspondent confided that in Williamsburg servants "have to stay in the basement or the garret rooms," a condition that "you know cannot be very agreeable to [white] Virginians."[79]

Even carefully conceived quarters tended toward cheap execution and impoverished accommodation. Two small frame wings were added between 1790 and 1810 to an earlier eighteenth-century, hall-chamber house, Sudley, in Anne Arundel County, Maryland, which contained a well-finished chamber on the first floor and rough quarters above. In both wings, a ladder ascended from refined space to an unfinished attic lobby beside a chimney. Small board doors opened into unheated living spaces (Fig. 8.11). The rooms were cramped, with 5½ feet of headroom only at the center of the space be-

tween the kneewalls. Both had two coats of plaster, roughly troweled, above unpainted bases, and a small gable window. People continued to occupy the rooms well into the nineteenth century.

ANTEBELLUM PATERNALISM

In the four decades before the Civil War, workforce housing became a topic of debate as slave owners responded to the growing criticism of slavery and to calls to improve agricultural practices in the region. The model farm movement, which began in Britain and spread to the United States by the early nineteenth century, included discussion of housing strategies to enhance the welfare and productivity of free and enslaved laborers, while anti- and proslavery rhetoric prompted extensive debate about the treatment of bondspeople. Some proslavery advocates argued vigorously for better housing as a way to deflect criticism of the institution and to demonstrate the moral superiority of a system that could best look after the interests of those bound in servitude. Comparison to inferior accommodations for European workers was a popular position. A self-conscious paternalism replaced laissez faire management. What slave owners claimed were humane and healthy accommodations became a necessary piece of evidence for the legitimacy of the system. Correspondents to regional farm journals like *Farmer's Register* and *Southern Planter* called for better housing and debated the merits of various forms and materials. Many argued that healthier, better-housed workers were more productive. Planters since the time of Robert Carter and Joseph Ball had ostensibly sought a healthy workforce. By the antebellum period, improved productivity was tied to the health of a workforce that required salubrious housing. Farm journals reminded readers that it was not only their moral duty to build proper houses for their slaves but that increased productivity would improve their profit margins, sometimes acknowledging that the latter was more compelling.

The debate about housing was lively and invited numerous imaginative proposals for the arrangement of buildings and rooms, materials, and degrees of permanence. One slave-owning Virginia schoolteacher argued in 1840 for building a 20- by 16-foot central room with a stove, which would "comfortably" accommodate thirty-two people before they adjourned to eight adjoining bedchambers. The schoolteacher touted his design as an innovative means of control because it allowed a headman to maintain order and lock everyone in at night, thus improving health and productivity.[80] Such schemes echoed similar proposals for the education of poor city children derived from the thinking of reformer Joseph Lancaster.[81] Even in this age of supposedly benevolent paternalism, planters and reformers freely advocated approaches that favored undifferentiated, impersonal, barracks-style housing over strategies that nurtured, or even recognized, family groups.

In reality, such unusual architectural concepts were generally ignored. By the 1840s, slave housing in the Chesapeake and, indeed, in most of the South had become formulaic. The general model was the traditional Anglo-American single-room house developed in the region in the eighteenth century. Houses were usually about 18- by 16-feet in size, with a front doorway set off-center away from a chimney.[82] When freestanding, these houses generally had a gable-end exterior chimney, like the plank-walled 18- by 16-foot house Walter H. S. Briscoe constructed in the 1830s at Sotterley in St. Mary's County (see Fig. 10.16). It was said to have been one of five similar houses at his home farm. In the mid-1840s, the affluent Virginia planter William V. Fletcher built three brick slave dwellings with decorative corbelled parapets to ornament the view from his house, Ben Venue, in Rappahannock County.

A common economical approach to housing workers was to double the one-room plan by creating a house for two families who shared a central chimney. The form was used for two-room kitchen-quarters by the mid-eighteenth century in Williamsburg, and as we have seen, it appeared as well on home quarters at Kingsmill and Carter's Grove. Wealthy Chesapeake planters embraced the center-chimney plan and constructed it with varying degrees of quality. North Carolina congressman and state senator William Shepard directed his slaves to build "five negro houses about 36 feet long and 18 wide" on his Pasquotank County plantation.[83] Some rich planters employed professional builders to construct well-framed, expensive quarters on this model. About 1850, progressive farmer Hill Carter built a series of large, 40- by 20-foot center-chimney duplexes for agricultural workers at Shirley, each with nearly 10 feet of headroom, sizable glazed windows, and access to attic space (Fig. 8.12). About 1855–60, the owner of Wales in Dinwiddie County built a similar 34- by 16-foot center-chimney house for domestic slaves with a clear 10 feet of headroom, glazed windows, enclosed stairs to attic rooms, and no interior finish. The prominent reformer John Hartwell Cocke influenced his son to build substantial pisé (clay-walled) quarters on the same model at Four Mile Tree. William Ballard Bruce, perhaps with his vastly wealthy father, James C. Bruce, built a series of brick center-chimney quarters for field-workers along a farm lane below Morotock in Charlotte County about 1856. Each of them measured 30 by 18 feet. The Morotock quarters, like a well-built wooden

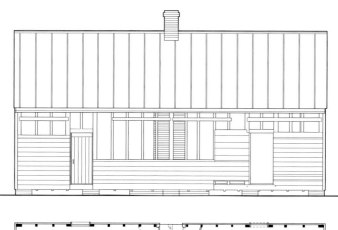

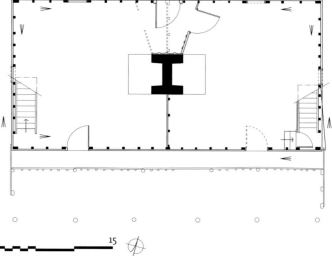

Fig. 8.12. Model slave quarters. Shirley, Charles City County, Virginia. Lobby and south shed are alterations.

duplex at Upper Brandon in Prince George County, were plastered inside. Generally, such larger, healthier rooms were intended for single families.

Both the greater number of slave quarters that survive from the 1820s through the 1850s and their character reflect changing standards of accommodation, with increased resistance to crowding and the mixing of kin groups.[84] It is especially noteworthy that some successful middling planters began to build home-farm quarters and work buildings that were durable and outwardly well finished within tidy farmyards. For these owners, a desire to create orderly plantations with ancillary buildings of a quality once confined to the settings of elite houses may have coincided with the necessity of building new structures to accommodate an increasing number of slaves whose population was expanding through natural reproduction and purchase within the region. One such respectable farmstead was that of Nathaniel Pruden, who owned 609 acres and seven slaves in 1820. That year, he built a prim hall-chamber house with minimally finished work space in the cellar and a single-room kitchen (Fig. 8.13). Some of his enslaved workers climbed exterior steps to reach

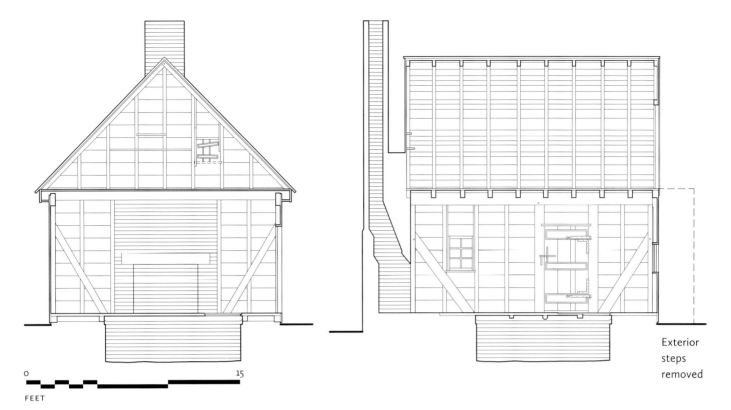

o ▬▬▬▬▬▬▬▬▬▬▬▬ 15

FEET

Exterior
steps
removed

Fig. 8.13. Pruden Kitchen quarter, Isle of Wight County, Virginia.

their unfinished attic space above the cookroom. About a decade later, Pruden constructed a quarter at the edge of the farmyard. It provided two separate rooms for slaves, one 17 by 16 feet and another 11 by 16 feet (Fig. 8.14). Both had raised wooden floors, and the larger room had access to a sizable brick-lined root cellar. The two rooms in the quarter were provided with small unglazed windows and large fireplaces in an off-center brick chimney. Both were open to the roof without an attic floor. The wall frame was left exposed without insulation or plaster. Pruden's plantation housing was similar to that of other farmers in the region who owned roughly 500 to 1,000 acres and six to a dozen people, who generally constructed kitchens, quarters, dairies, and smokehouses with well-made frames, raised on brick foundations, and finished with sawn siding and trim. Among these, dairies continued to be the best trimmed and most often plastered, reflecting the owners' household use. Still modest, the other structures represented a better-finished and more durable alternative to their eighteenth-century predecessors.

Of course, some well-off planters did not attempt to soothe their consciences or flatter their reputations so much as to improve their view. In Goochland County, in the 1850s, Ellen Bruce Morson and her husband, James, housed many of their seventy-eight slaves in four, center-chimney brick quarters that were built in an arc, framing what may have been an overseer's house. The ensemble was visible from their large and ornate house, called Dover. In contrast to

Fig. 8.14. Pruden Quarter, Isle of Wight County, Virginia.

their outward formality, these slave houses were relatively narrow, measuring 30 to 36½ feet in length and only 15 feet in depth. They had dirt floors and no interior finish or attics. An unusual form of cheap window featuring unglazed openings with bars below a sash with three panes of glass provided a modicum of light when shutters were closed against the cold. Each of the rooms in the smaller Dover quarters had one of these windows. The two larger buildings contained four windows, perhaps lighting four rather than two apartments per building.[85] Whatever the number of rooms, the

Fig. 8.15. Quarters, Dover, Goochland County, Virginia.

meager accommodation was intended to have a picturesque effect when viewed from a healthy distance (Fig. 8.15).

The embrace of model quarters was less than wholehearted in the Chesapeake, where even the largest and wealthiest slaveholders continued to house their workers in a variety of accommodations rather than with broad consistency. Despite a trend toward improvement, not all the old hovels were demolished, and miserable little shelters continued to be built alongside houses with glazed windows and plastered interiors. The Richmond manufacturer Edward Cunningham and his successors built a group of at least four two-family houses opposite two overseer or tenant houses at Howard's Neck in Goochland County after 1825. That nearest to the main house is a relatively well-built 36- by 18-foot frame house with beaded siding and brick filling in the walls. The brick but not the frame was plastered, creating a wall surface that could be kept clean, even though it was uneven. Two of the other houses are smaller with lower ceilings and are built of roughly hewn logs that were left exposed inside and out. Windows in the upper house were relatively large and well finished, with a pair of six-light sash lighting both rooms, while each room in the log houses was lit by a single small opening closed by a sliding shutter.

Whether offered model housing or not, enslaved workers increasingly expected some privacy for their families, including access without infringement on others' space. One southern planter in 1852 favored separate houses rather than double quarters, so there would be "no contention, as in the case of a double cabin, about the right of passage . . . each one having his own way and exercising his own control over everything in and around his house."[86] Bruce widely spaced his Morotock duplexes, but more planters focused on creating separate rooms for families than on their distance from one another.

The drive for separate habitations is evident in a scattered group of carefully conceived multifamily houses and work buildings with newly complex circulation patterns, including lobbies and stairs. At Bremo, in Fluvanna County, John Hartwell Cocke built pisé quarters with central lobbies that along with first floor doors provided separate access to two rooms on each of two floors (Fig. 8.16). About 1835–40, Humberston Skipwith, heir of Peyton and Jean Skipwith, built a well-finished loom house on the edge of the walled yard at Prestwould. It has three front doors, two that lead into first-floor workrooms and a central one, flanked by narrow windows, that opens into a lobby containing two ladder stairs rising to attic rooms. The upstairs rooms were warmed by a fireplace and lit by a single gable window (Fig. 8.17A). On a larger scale, a new kitchen-laundry at Strawberry Plain in Isle of Wight County had exterior steps to a second-floor lobby, opening into L-shaped rooms 17 feet deep (Fig. 8.17B). At Point of Honor, outside Lynchburg, the Cabell family built a brick office with two unheated attic rooms as quarters, one a 14- by 11-foot plastered room and the other a 14½- by 8-foot space with exposed and whitewashed framing, reached by two sets of exterior steps.

Concern for privacy is evident in modest remodelings as well as in new buildings. A second stair was added to the old kitchen at Marmion, giving independent access to the larger attic room. The room was slightly improved with a new cov-

Fig. 8.16. Bremo Quarter, Fluvanna County, Virginia. The lobby gave independent access to rooms for four groups of occupants.

A

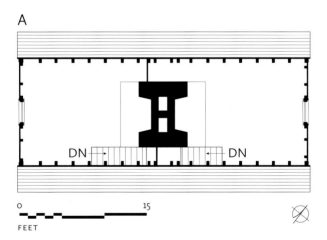

DN   DN

0   15

FEET

B

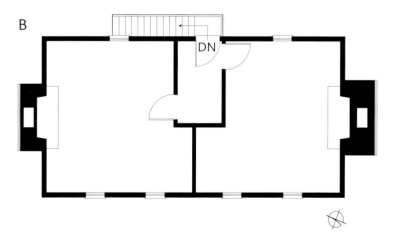

DN

Fig. 8.17. Second-floor quarters reached by interior and exterior stairs.
A: Prestwould Loom house, Mecklenburg County, Virginia; B: Strawberry Plain Kitchen laundry, Isle of Wight County, Virginia.

ering of rough-sawn boards, and the passage between rooms was replaced with a closet. An old detached kitchen at the Powers-Holloway House in the town of Port Royal was re-worked so that enslaved servants climbed a stair to a narrow second-floor passage separating two chambers of different size. Owners of Bacon's Castle enlarged a nineteen-year-old work or storage building in 1848 and eventually inserted a central ladder stair that rose to two separate attic chambers, both 16 by 14 feet and heated with small fireplaces.[87]

Archaeologist Larry McKee suggests that by providing a separate and secure house for each family group, owners sought to encourage productive and stable families in which the father or both parents assumed responsibility for controlling other family members, especially children. By assigning limited authority to parents, the private space of a quarter was intended as "a cradle of stable slave families," while physically reminding the residents of their inferior status to whites on the same properties.[88] The growing extent of separate accommodations suggests that parents took this as a useful bargaining position. Some owners believed that modestly improved private accommodations would increase the quality of labor from their workers. But there were other reasons to spend additional capital on housing, especially following the emancipation of slaves in English colonies in 1833 and the rise of abolitionism in the North. In the decades before the Civil War, planters who engaged in an international and regional argument over slavery incorporated ideas about workers' housing derived in part from the model farm movement and influenced by developing humanitarian concepts of minimal standards for all people.[89] Improved family-based quarters were investments, in this sense, not so much in the productivity of workers but in the slave system itself. That system offered a new route to profitability when Chesapeake slave owners increasingly sold their workers to cotton planters or moved them to their own new farms in the Deep South. So, just as material conditions improved for some slaves with model housing, the fates of individuals and families were at greater risk.[90]

The extent of model housing was far more limited than its survival now suggests. Most workers built their own small log houses from materials at hand, and even model farmers were inconsistent with their labor forces.[91] In 1852, Richard Eppes, a prominent Prince George County planter, spoke approvingly of the "very large and roomy" quarters that his fellow progressive farmer Charles Carter built at Shirley. Eppes styled himself as Virginia's most improvement-minded planter. He made adjustments to quarters when he thought his slaves "too confined" in old houses, and he agreed to alter steps to increase privacy for his man named George. Yet when rehabilitating a small structure for a favorite slave, he considered raising the ceiling so the man could stand erect inside but decided it was too costly. Such capriciousness characterized forced labor in general. Eppes found corporal punishment distasteful, but he severely whipped an eight-year-old cowherd who poorly followed orders.[92]

Some wealthy planters who were engaged in the discourse over proper plantation management made a case for cheap, temporary housing, arguing that the predictable unhealthiness of slave living habits made regular demolition and rebuilding a wiser housing strategy. Thomas Cameron, in Cumberland County, North Carolina, said as much to his brother Duncan in 1826, stating that the only way to prevent outbreaks of disease was to replace his slave houses every five to seven years. This was economical, he argued, because the cheap materials decayed so quickly.[93] Riding the train from Washington to Richmond in 1853, Frederick Law Olmsted saw no model slave housing. Rather, he observed "rotting log-cabins that you can see the light through the chinks of . . . scattered around a shabby board house without a tree or bit of grass near it."[94] From Richmond through the Deep South, Olmsted saw the results of those economic equations that left most people poorly housed and badly fed. It was part of a long legacy that had been established nearly two centuries earlier.

9 *Agricultural Buildings*

ORLANDO RIDOUT V

The story of farming in the Chesapeake watershed—a story about the region's many ordinary farmers—is most prominently written on the land itself, in the tilled fields, fence lines, and, here and there, surviving tobacco houses and granaries. Historians have been spoiled by a few exceptional great planters who, like Thomas Jefferson, left a "Farm Book" or, like Landon Carter, recorded agricultural experiments in a daily diary. Dirt farmers had neither time nor reason to favor posterity with such reflective chronicles. So, in their absence, researchers must glean what they can from buildings and landscapes and from the workaday records that farmers did write to make deals with their neighbors—or to take them to court when they broke those agreements.[1]

Much can be learned about the now almost invisible world of ordinary farmers in early Virginia and Maryland by parsing each line in numerous contracts and depositions recorded by officials of the county courts. Take, for instance, two documents from the "Isle of Kent," on the Eastern Shore of Maryland. From the first, a bond executed in November 1658, the careful historian discovers that tenant farmer John Raby received a loan from a neighbor, husbandman John Salter. By the following November, the borrower promised to repay the lender in "sound Merchantable Tob[acco] without ground leues [leaves] in Caske." For security, Raby pledged "all my Cropp of Tob, wch I shall plant or make this next ensuing yeare, and one Black Cow by name of black nann mrkt with a Cropp [a nick] on the left eare." Bonds were utilitarian documents in the extreme; thousands survive in county record offices. Yet these few lines from just this one agreement provide telltale clues to the small-scale enterprises of two seventeenth-century Maryland farmers—that successful planters might also be moneylenders to their poorer neighbors, that "merchantable" tobacco was the cash crop in the neighborhood, that it was harvested and packed("prized") into casks and was ready to sell by November, and that farmers' cattle were not pastured but were put out to forage in the woods and marshlands (hence the earmarks).[2]

The second document, a legally binding covenant, tells us more about the relationship between landowning farmers and their tenants. Salter obligated himself to provide Raby with land for planting tobacco and corn, housing for the crops, and "meat drinke & Lodginge." In addition to working the crops on equal shares and paying "six hundred pounds of Tob & Caske," Raby agreed to assist with fencing Salter's "Beaver necke" plantation, to "beate Corne for bread for himselfe John Salter his Wife & Child," and to undertake miscellaneous chores.[3]

Each passing remark in John Salter's covenant with John Raby offers a tantalizing clue to the principal benchmarks that characterized the early Chesapeake landscape. Yet for

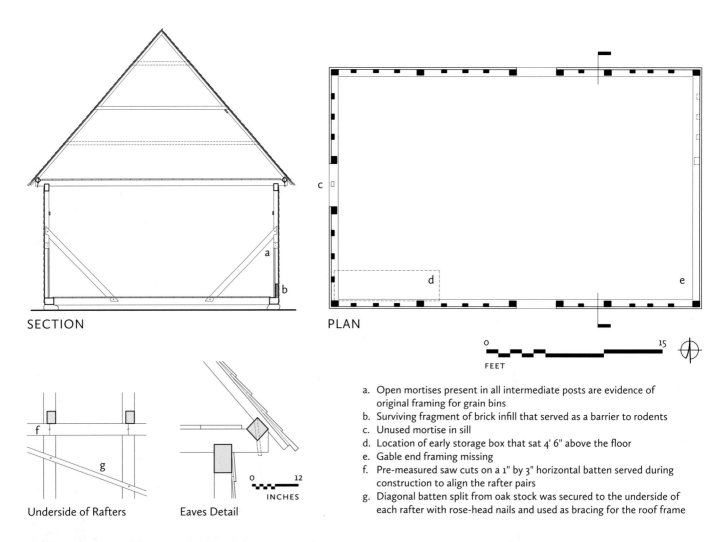

SECTION PLAN

0   15
FEET

Underside of Rafters   Eaves Detail

0   12
INCHES

a. Open mortises present in all intermediate posts are evidence of original framing for grain bins
b. Surviving fragment of brick infill that served as a barrier to rodents
c. Unused mortise in sill
d. Location of early storage box that sat 4' 6" above the floor
e. Gable end framing missing
f. Pre-measured saw cuts on a 1" by 3" horizontal batten served during construction to align the rafter pairs
g. Diagonal batten split from oak stock was secured to the underside of each rafter with rose-head nails and used as bracing for the roof frame

Fig. 9.1. Brome Farm Granary, 1758, St. Mary's City, Maryland. Dated by dendrochronology prior to disassembly, this frame granary is the earliest agricultural building that has been identified in the Chesapeake.

historians of the period, they raise equally troubling questions. What constituted the range of housing for the entire breadth of the Chesapeake population, and what buildings were necessary to support a farm family, whether a tenant struggling to make ends meet or a successful planter with indentured or slave labor? Previous scholarship on the colonial Chesapeake has mined a wealth of documentary sources to describe the evolving look of the land, and a more limited number of scholars have explored the evidence for early housing, but agricultural buildings have remained firmly fixed in the background. Interpretative work is hampered by remarkably poor survival rates for the defining features of that landscape. Old-growth forest has been nearly eradicated from the modern Tidewater, and traditional field patterns and cultivation practices have been obscured by modern farming methods and residential development. Of the earliest generations of buildings, a scant handful of dwellings survive from before the 1710s, and the earliest known agri-

cultural buildings date to the mid-eighteenth century and later (Fig. 9.1).[4]

Despite the dismally low survival rates for agricultural buildings from the colonial period, documentary and archeological evidence from the first two centuries of settlement may be combined with careful architectural fieldwork for post-1750 buildings to reconstruct the evolving nature of farming in the Chesapeake. In the process, it is possible to test a series of questions that have shaped much of the current scholarship on Tidewater Maryland and Virginia. Three themes in particular merit our attention. First, how did the first settlers adjust to agricultural opportunities in the Chesapeake, and how did that accommodation manifest itself architecturally? Second, as the colonial economy matured and agricultural choices evolved, how were those changes expressed in the built environment? Finally, to what extent can our efforts to reconstruct the agricultural practices and buildings of the Chesapeake offer insights into the lives and labors of Tidewater planters and their families, servants, and slaves?

To address these questions, it is first necessary to draw together the available evidence to reconstruct a sense of the agricultural landscape and trace the evolution over time of crop choices, methods of cultivation, and systems for storing, processing, and converting crops into food, material goods, and cash specie. Tobacco, corn, grain, and livestock each played a role, one that evolved over time, leaving markers in the landscape and the architectural heritage of the region.

TOBACCO HOUSES

Tobacco attracted the interest of the earliest explorers of the Chesapeake. In Virginia, tobacco gained recognition as a potentially valuable export within the first decade of settlement. From 2,500 pounds in 1616, annual tobacco exports from Virginia and Maryland grew to 15 million pounds in the 1660s and to 28 million pounds in the late 1680s. Challenging market conditions in the decades that followed slowed the expansion of tobacco production, but one source indicates that Virginia alone exported 70,000 hogsheads in 1758. Conservatively estimated at 1,000 pounds per hogshead, this represents 70 million pounds of tobacco, a crop that would have required thousands of tobacco houses to dry and cure.[5]

While it would be difficult to calculate the number and distribution of tobacco houses for any given year or county, two record groups offer some sense of the pervasive impact tobacco had on the Tidewater landscape. Orphans' Court valuations for Queen Anne's County, Maryland, reveal that tobacco houses were the most common agricultural building in that county prior to the Revolutionary War, appearing among the improvements on 80 percent of 163 property assessments spanning the years 1725–74. Tobacco production on the Eastern Shore peaked in the middle years of the eighteenth century, and by 1800 tobacco houses had all but disappeared from this part of Maryland and Virginia but remained commonplace in southern Maryland, as demonstrated by the 1798 Federal Direct Tax. In Prince George's County, a leader in Maryland tobacco cultivation, the 1798 tax enumerated more tobacco houses (829) than dwelling houses (759), while in Somerset on the Lower Eastern Shore, only two tobacco houses were identified in the entire county.[6]

Despite the thousands of tobacco houses that peppered the Tidewater landscape in the colonial period, not a single curing barn has been identified in this region that predates the Revolution, and only a few have been found that date

prior to 1800. Thus, to understand the fragmentary documentary descriptions that survive from the colonial period, it is necessary to look at post-Revolutionary tobacco houses and extrapolate back in time. It is also useful to briefly summarize the cultivation and processing of the tobacco crop (Fig. 9.2).

Tobacco culture has changed very little since the colonial period. Mechanization has eased some tasks, but it remains a labor-intensive process that follows a predictable annual cycle of planting, nurturing, harvesting, and processing of the individual plants for sale. Tobacco seed was sowed in the early spring in specially prepared and carefully tended beds. By early May, the young seedlings were hardy enough to be transplanted to the fields, where they were planted in individual hills formed by hoeing the soil into mounds aligned in rows, with regular spacing between the rows and the individual plants. As the plants grew, the field was cultivated with hoes to control weeds and the plants were tended by hand to remove suckers and the lower leaves, which diverted food from the most valuable parts of the plant, the middle and upper sets of leaves. When flowering tops emerged late in the growing season, these were pinched off, and in mid- to late August the tobacco plants were harvested.[7]

Colonial practice usually followed a very specific regimen that dictated the weather conditions in which to cut, the color of the leaves for optimum harvest, and the manner of treating the plants as they were cut. Rather than taking the plants directly to the tobacco house, they were laid along the rows in the field to wilt and begin to cure and often were then transferred to open-air hanging racks, known as "scaffolds." The purpose of this step was to advance the drying process while also exposing the leaves to the sun, referred to as "killing" the tobacco. To prepare the plants for drying, they were impaled on riven wood sticks 4½ to 5½ feet long, with ten or eleven plants per stick. The fully loaded sticks of tobacco could be hung on a prepared framework of forked poles set in the ground on regular intervals, or they might simply be propped against a split-rail fence at the edge of the field. After a brief period of open-air drying, the sticks of tobacco were hand carried to the tobacco house and hung up to cure there.[8]

Conditions in the curing barn were closely monitored, and each planter developed a skill for judging the condition of the curing plants. If the barn was packed too tightly, the plants would sweat and develop mold, in which case better air circulation was required, either by tinkering with the spacing of the plants (difficult in a fully loaded barn) or by opening the doors and selectively removing plants to create passages

Fig. 9.2. Tobacco House near Prince Frederick, Calvert County, Maryland. Tobacco houses were located on field margins scattered across the farm, often close to a "rolling road" for taking the filled hogsheads to market. (E. H. Pickering, HABS, 1936)

for air circulation. If the weather became too moist or foggy, the prescribed cure was to build small, smoldering fires across the earthen floor of the barn, using smoke and heat to reduce the moisture and provide an even temperature.[9]

Once the tobacco had properly cured, the plants were taken down and placed in heaps to sweat, in preparation for processing. A successful planter was expert at judging the proper time to "strip" and pack his tobacco. The leaves needed to achieve a particular balance of dryness and suppleness to be tied into hands and "prized" into the hogsheads that would carry the crop to market. The tobacco was packed using a simple mechanism called a "prize," which in the preindustrial period relied on weighted cantilever beams to press the tobacco into the hogshead. Tobacco hogsheads were simply large wooden barrels, measuring 2½ feet in diameter and 4 feet in height; when fully packed they typically

weighed from 800 to 1,100 pounds or more. Prizing, as with other steps in the process, had a specific regimen, and the placement and degree of loading were carefully monitored to ensure a tight, compact fit that would not spoil in transit (Figs. 9.3, 9.4).[10]

Fully packed hogsheads were transported by cart or bateau or by rolling them to the nearest deep-water landing. By the mid-eighteenth century, first Virginia and then Maryland had passed strict inspection laws to ensure quality and price thresholds for Chesapeake tobacco. Thus, tobacco bound for England had to be taken to an inspection warehouse, the hogsheads opened, and the tobacco subjected to a physical inspection. Once approved, it was repacked and ready for shipment. Inspection warehouses were established across the Chesapeake estuary, typically in a half-dozen locations per county. The few established port towns of the Chesapeake

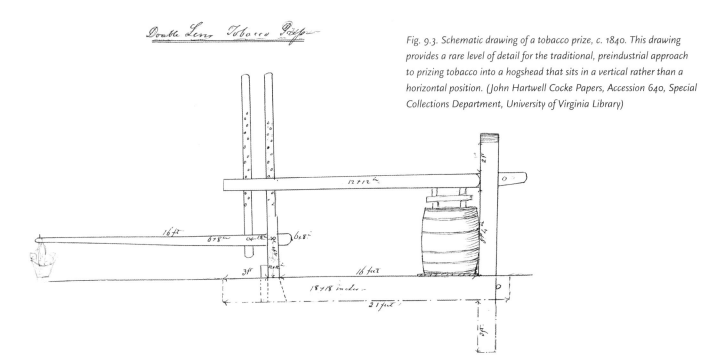

Double Lens Tobacco Prize

Fig. 9.3. Schematic drawing of a tobacco prize, c. 1840. This drawing provides a rare level of detail for the traditional, preindustrial approach to prizing tobacco into a hogshead that sits in a vertical rather than a horizontal position. (John Hartwell Cocke Papers, Accession 640, Special Collections Department, University of Virginia Library)

Fig. 9.4. Tobacco Prize, The Cottage, Upper Marlboro, Prince George's County, Maryland. By the third quarter of the nineteenth century, massive horizontal tobacco prizes had become common. The lever-and-cogwheel system offered far more leverage than the design portrayed in the Cocke drawing. (Jack E. Boucher, HABS, 1990)

served as locations for inspection warehouses, but most were landmarks unto themselves, sited for convenience of the planters on a particular estuary and known with appellations such as "Harris Clayland's Old-Field Landing" or "the Warehouse at Choptank Bridge."[11]

The curing barns that served as the most important step in this process were universally referred to as "tobacco houses" from the earliest recorded instances. Only as tobacco began to pass out of cultivation in parts of Maryland and Virginia did any confusion arise between "tobacco houses" and the more generic term "barn." A tobacco house differed in one important aspect from a traditional barn: it was designed to serve a single purpose—as a drying rack for the crop. The basic structural system provided a secure envelope from the weather, while the interior space was contrived for hanging the tobacco plants. The key to the latter function was the stick on which the plants were impaled and suspended. To efficiently fill a barn required a structural system designed to receive the sticks. The solution was to conceive of the tobacco house much like a loaf of bread, with each slice of the loaf representing one hanging bay for the tobacco. Each bay came to be known as a "room" of tobacco.[12]

In the seventeenth century and for much of the eighteenth, standard practice was to construct tobacco houses with 5-foot rooms, most likely driven by an array of factors, but most especially by the optimum loading of the individual tobacco sticks, combined with the common practice of cladding buildings with 5-foot lengths of split-oak clapboards. A tobacco house with 5-foot rooms was typically 30 to 60 feet long but could reach 90 or 100 feet in length. The most common widths for these buildings were 20 and 24 feet. For a 5-foot room system, the basic frame was organized in 10-foot structural bays, marked by heavy structural posts and interspersed by light studs set 2½ feet on center. Tie beams notched over the wall plates were set on 5-foot centers, and the roof was framed with common rafter pairs set on 2½-foot centers (Fig. 9.5).

To facilitate hanging the tobacco crop, the rafter pairs were of two types, which alternated over the length of the building. Aligned on the same 5-foot spacing as the tie beams were primary rafter pairs fitted with two, three, or four collar pieces, depending on the width and height of the roof. One of these collars would be required to ensure the structural integrity of the roof, regardless of function, but in a tobacco house the additional collars were needed to hang the crop. They provided further structural support to a roof frame that carried the substantial load imposed by the drying tobacco.

The secondary rafter pairs were just that, a pair of rafters joined at the ridge and secured at the base but lacking any tie

pieces at all, as collars on these rafter pairs would interfere with the 5-foot hanging bays. The sole purpose of these secondary rafter pairs was to provide intermediate support and nailing surfaces for the roof covering. The intermediate rafter pairs created a construction dilemma as well, but one that was easily resolved. Lacking a tie beam for direct structural support, the intermediate rafter pairs required a strong and rigid false plate that could carry the load despite a 5-foot span between the adjacent tie beams. Among extant early tobacco houses, the most common and practical solution was to use a square-section "raising" or "false" plate tipped 45 degrees and notched over the tie beams. This "tilted false plate" derived maximum structural benefit from the diagonal depth of the timber and provided a clean connection for the rafter, which was notched and spiked to the outside face. The alternative solution was to use a rectangular plate, typically laid flat but occasionally tipped 20 to 30 degrees toward the interior of the building, a blend of the two more common variants.

The 5-foot bay system formed by the tie beams and collar beams in the upper part of the tobacco house was duplicated in the main body of the structure by horizontal poles that ran across the width of the building, aligned directly below each of the tie beams and supported by horizontal rails along the outside walls and by vertical poles that bisected the building longitudinally. These horizontal layers were known as "tiers," and the height of the side walls of the building determined the number of tiers. Height in most colonial building descriptions is expressed as "pitch," referring to the height of the principal posts, extending from the top of the sill to the bottom of the wall plate. For tobacco houses, pitch was a function of the number of tiers, thus the most common pitch dimensions found in descriptions of tobacco houses are 8 feet (permitting two tiers) and 12 feet (three tiers). As a result, an alternate set of modifiers came into use. In 1759, Francis Jerdone entered charges for building two tobacco houses, one "double tier'd" and one "single tier'd"; and in 1758, Joseph Ball recommended building a tobacco house with "at least two tiers below the joists."[13]

Each horizontal layer of the tobacco house, whether defined by tier poles and tie beams in the lower part of the structure or by collar pieces in the roof, was positioned to create 3½ to 4 feet of vertical hanging space. The net result was a building that might provide from six to twenty bays of hanging space in 5-foot increments or rooms, with each room containing from five to eight tiers of tobacco suspended from 5½-foot tobacco sticks.

Tobacco houses were often supplemented by sheds that could be enclosed to provide additional space for hanging tobacco or left open for livestock shelter. Sheds were also

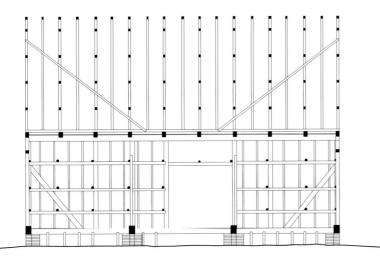

Fig. 9.5. *Tobacco House, Tracy's Landing, Anne Arundel County, Maryland. In plan and section, the tobacco house is divided into a series of 5-foot hanging bays, or "rooms," for curing tobacco.*

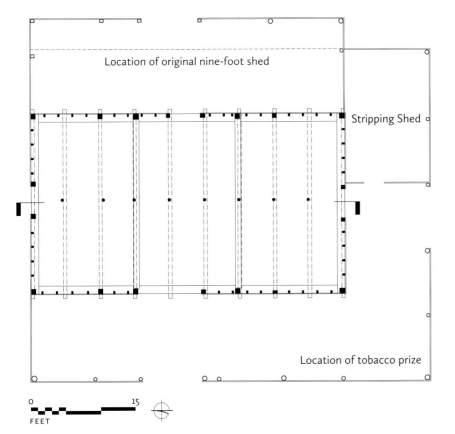

Location of original nine-foot shed

Stripping Shed

Location of tobacco prize

0   15
FEET

the preferred location for stripping and prizing tobacco. If twentieth-century practice is a guide, stripping occurred in a dedicated section at one end of a shed, partitioned off and crudely ceiled over to create a warmer, more protected space for the tedious task of preparing the crop for prizing.

"Prize sheds" and "prize houses" are noted in the documentary record, usually as a modifier to the description of a curing house. The improvements to a Virginia plantation in 1718, for example, included a "large new Tobacco house called ye press house," and the Ellenborough property in Maryland was improved in 1803 with a tobacco house with a "shed at one end for prizing Tobacco with two good posts

fixed."[14] In other cases, it seems clear that the prizing operation took place in a separate building. Joseph Ball provided specifications in 1744 for a prize house at Morattico in Virginia, wherein "the roof of the Prise house, and the shades [sheds] must be pulled off; and it must be new posted ... and Cover'd in the best manner and the floor a little rais'd. . . . I would have the door as Large as it is now, Easily to Roll a Hogshead of Tobacco out."[15]

Access and ventilation influenced the design of tobacco houses as well. Documentary clues are rare for these two features, but surviving buildings from the post-Revolutionary period provide a sense of the range of practice from the ear-

Fig. 9.6. Tobacco Barn, The Cottage, Upper Marlboro, Prince George's County, Maryland. By the late nineteenth century, form and plan had evolved significantly from the traditional model. Double doors centered on the gable ends created a longitudinal center aisle for the movement of wagons, and hinged vertical siding provided ventilation. (Jack E. Boucher, HABS, 1990)

lier period. In these extant buildings, door openings pierce each exterior wall of the core building, regardless of sheds. The gable door openings are centered on the opposing ends of the building and are usually 4 feet wide and 8 to 12 feet high, fitted with board-and-batten doors mounted on strap hinges or, less frequently, with cross-garnet hinges. On the long walls, door openings of 8 or 10 feet in width are positioned in the center structural bay, similarly fitted with a pair of doors that extend from sill to plate. Variations from this norm usually are driven either by the arrangement of structural bays or the choice of balancing a double door on one side of the building with a single door on the other.

Doors in all four sides of the tobacco house facilitated loading the tobacco into the barn and then were used to regulate ventilation. For both gable and long-wall door openings, the heavy sill members that form the base of the building are not interrupted, demonstrating clearly that carts and wagons could not be drawn into the building. This underscores the preference in that period to hand carry the loaded sticks rather than risk damage in a cart and is another reminder of the labor-intensive nature of this crop.

Once the tobacco house was fully loaded with tobacco, the doors became the principal means of controlling ventilation. In the seventeenth and eighteenth centuries, emphasis was placed on allowing adequate spacing between the hanging plants, and introducing extra air circulation was only considered a necessity if the plants showed evidence of overheating or too much moisture. Over the course of the nineteenth century, air circulation gained in favor, eventually leading to a significant change in the outer skin of the barn. The horizontal siding universally used prior to about 1800 gave way to vertical siding, facilitating the installation of hinges on intermittent siding boards. On clear days, the hinged siding boards could be propped open, allowing more evenly distributed ventilation to the hanging tobacco (Fig. 9.6).

The preceding description of the cultivation, curing, and processing of tobacco provides a basis for understanding the principal components of a tobacco house. What is not fully evident to this point is the degree of variation that occurred within this tradition. In the first decades of tobacco production, planters were forced to develop a building type that had little precedent. At first, tobacco was cured in piles, but air curing soon gained favor. One source states that air curing tobacco was first introduced in 1619 by a Jamestown planter who hung tobacco on lines. This method of curing appears in a Virginia court case in 1624, when a deponent alleged that George Yeardley's overseer at Flowerdew Hundred on the James River "did hang the Tobacco soe thick upon the lynes yt the lynes brake and the Tobacco fell to the ground . . . and soe by his faulte it was not merchantable." Other early references indicate that some planters hung tobacco in the lofts of their dwelling houses. However, as tobacco production ramped up in the decades after 1620, it is clear that a pattern of experimentation must have quickly coalesced around a well-defined set of core parameters.[16]

The basic model that developed for tobacco houses had much in common with the emerging model for housing—rectangular frame buildings clad with riven clapboards, with a structural system adapted to the length of the clapboards—5 feet in the seventeenth century and 4 feet later in the colonial period. This boxy, rectangular building could be built with continuous sills and wall plates or with principal posts set into the ground, and the joinery could be refined mortise-and-tenon work or faster and rougher "lapt work." Scattered references can be found in seventeenth-century records to "wall plate" tobacco houses, and as documentary sources expanded in the eighteenth century, the vocabulary became more varied as well. Descriptors used to differentiate the method of construction include "whole framed," "bastard framed," "post in ground," and several types of log construction. Exterior cladding materials include riven clapboards and sawn weatherboards, while roofs are covered with clapboards and other types of board roofing, wood shingles (short, long, featheredge), and even thatch.

However, the most common nomenclature referred only to size, and often only to length. The implication was that everyone knew what was meant by a 40-, 50-, or 60-foot tobacco house—they might vary in wall height or the width of the building but generally within well-established parameters. The most important changes that occurred over time were the dominance of double-tiered tobacco houses over single-tiered ones, and the gradual shift from 5-foot rooms to 4-foot hanging bays. The first trend can be inferred from scattered documentary references and the extant post-Revolutionary buildings, while the shift in room size can be quantified and suggests differing trends geographically.

Turning once again to the Maryland Orphans' Court valuations, it is possible to compare room size for tobacco houses in three counties. In Queen Anne's County, nearly 300 valuations have been located from the eighteenth century. A review of tobacco houses described in these valuations demonstrates that while 4-foot rooms may have been used in the first half of the eighteenth century, the 5-foot room was clearly dominant. Through the third quarter of the century, 5-foot rooms were still the preferred standard, but with a sharp rise in the use of 4-foot rooms. By the last quarter of the eighteenth century, the decline in the overall numbers signaled the rapid decline of tobacco cultivation in this Eastern Shore county, but 4-foot rooms had emerged as the favored module for tobacco houses.

In Dorchester County, farther south on the Eastern Shore, the sample is smaller, numbering 133 valuations spanning the years 1727–86. Of sixty-six tobacco houses with known dimensions, fifty are divisible solely by 5 feet, and just one is divisible solely by 4 feet. Here, the 5-foot room was still favored into the 1780s, at least. In southern Maryland, the St. Mary's County valuations show a different trend. Of eighty-five valuations from the period 1780–1807, forty-two tobacco houses were described in sufficient detail to analyze room size. Only three are solely divisible by 5 feet, and twenty-nine are divisible only by 4 feet. Data is not available to determine how early the 4-foot room came into common use in this county, but the change had certainly occurred by the end of the colonial period.[17]

CORN HOUSES

Maize, as corn was known in the early years of Chesapeake settlement, was a staple food for the Native Americans encountered by the first settlers at Jamestown and St. Mary's City, and it was quickly adopted as the central element of the newcomers' diet. Corn was well suited to this role. It was relatively easy to plant and cultivate, proved to be hardy and well adapted to the hot, sultry summer weather of the Tidewater, and provided high yields for the quantity of seeds planted (Fig. 9.7).[18]

As settlement matured and expanded along the shores of the Chesapeake, further advantages of the native maize became apparent. Whereas tobacco grew best in freshly tilled land and required fresh planting ground every three or four years, corn was well suited as a following crop. It also mixed well with other crops in the same field. Tidewater farmers planted squash, pumpkins, or peas between the rows of corn and could "double-crop" a cornfield by planting wheat, oats, or rye late in the season for harvest the following year. As

Fig. 9.7. Corn House, Habre de Venture, Charles County, Maryland. A rare example of the larger, broader form used for corn storage in the eighteenth century, with the door centered in the long wall.

corn production expanded, it became a means to supplement the diet of livestock, both as regular feed for draft horses and oxen and as part of a "fattening" process prior to slaughter of hogs and beef cattle. Livestock was fed corn that had cured on the cob, as well as "blades" and "tops" from the corn plants.[19]

The annual crop cycle for corn began in the late winter and early spring. As soon as the ground was dry enough, farmers began plowing or "listing" the fields. Corn was planted in early May, laid out in a grid pattern of hilled mounds formed with a hoe. Rows were typically spaced 6 or 7 feet apart, and the corn plants were spaced anywhere from 2 to 6 feet apart in each row. Four kernels were planted in each hill to ensure at least one good plant, and once the seedlings were of sufficient size, most farmers thinned the field to a single plant per hill.[20]

The crop required periodic cultivation to restrain competing weeds over the course of the summer, and in early September the first steps in the harvest process began. The blades or upper leaves were gathered first, usually in mid-September when they still had color and moisture. Blades were tied into bundles and lofted for winter forage. The tops or tassels were harvested in late September and stored with the blades. Corn was left to cure on the stalk in the field and harvested in October or later. At this stage of the process, yield was expressed in barrels, although the corn was deposited in corn houses loose and still in the husk. Once harvested, the laborious task of husking and shelling the

corn from the cob could begin. When the crop was intended primarily for home consumption, the shelling process could be stretched out over the winter months, and only a small supply of shelled corn might be on hand at any one time. As corn grew in importance as a money crop, the shelling process gained importance, and a farmer would shell the market portion of his crop in a matter of weeks and pack it for shipping as soon as he had reasonable quantities in hand.[21]

Different as the two crops are, corn and tobacco shared one characteristic in common—they required curing in a dry, well-ventilated environment, as both were vulnerable to damage if overheated or exposed to excessive moisture. In the early years, planters stored unshelled corn in house lofts and shelled corn in barrels tucked into passages, kitchens, and outbuildings. As harvest yields increased and as the characteristics of the crop were better understood, the need for specialized storage accommodations became evident (Fig. 9.8).

The basic requirements for a corn house were fairly simple—a building strong enough to carry significant dead loads and resist outward pressure against the walls and with good ventilation throughout. A survey of extant early corn houses produces a portrait of heavy timber frame buildings, rectangular in plan, typically 12 to 20 feet wide and 18 to 30 feet long, with ventilation provided by vertical slats nailed to rails that are joined to the principal structural posts. A careful examination of these buildings reveals an array of structural details intended to accommodate weight and outward

Fig. 9.8. Corn House, Belleview, Fort Washington, Prince George's County, Maryland. This early corn house illustrates the trend toward a narrow rectangular plan with gable-end door while continuing to employ a fully exposed and substantially braced frame. (Jack E. Boucher, HABS, 1989)

pressure. Timbers were robustly proportioned, and principal members were braced and joined with carefully carpentered mortise-and-tenon joints, floor joists were closely spaced and generously proportioned, and flooring was often 2 inches thick. The tie beams that supported the roof plates and spanned the width of the building were notched over the wall plates and pinned, and in some cases these joints employed a full dovetail rather than a plain notch. The dovetail caused a joint to tighten rather than shear as outward pressure was applied to the wall.

Among extant frame corn houses, ventilation was accomplished by sheathing the building either with vertical slats applied to rails or with horizontal siding offset to create a gap between each course (Fig. 9.9). If slats were used, typically they were nailed to the interior face of the rails, which were mortised into the principal posts. This arrangement ensured

that the pressure of the corn worked against the strongest elements of the frame and created an odd and immediately recognizable aspect to the building, since the frame was fully exposed. Horizontal siding applied to the exterior surface of the frame is less common among surviving corn houses but offered several advantages. This siding is usually 4 to 5 inches wide by a full inch thick, and both the top and bottom edges are cut at an angle, a detail known as "ciphered" siding. This joint detail is used for wide weatherboard siding across the Chesapeake and was the preferred system for roof sheathing in eighteenth-century Virginia. In these uses, ciphered boards were laid tight, but in a corn house, the siding was installed with a gap of about 1 to 1½ inches. Viewed from a distance, the gaps are barely perceptible, yet they allow free air movement to the stored crop and offer protection to the structural frame of the building. By the mid-nineteenth cen-

tury, vertical slat sheathing had become almost universal, and the slats were more likely to be applied to the outside face of the frame.

A search through documentary sources yields scattered examples that are consistent with the extant buildings, but a more rigorous examination of the records suggests that a significant part of the story is missing from the modern landscape. Maryland Orphans' Court records from three counties indicate that roughly half of rural properties included a corn house and that a substantial proportion—more than half in Dorchester County—were of log construction, including "rough," split, hewed, sawed, "squared and dovetailed," and round log buildings.[22]

Dimensional data for corn houses from the same sources in these three counties is remarkably diverse but reveals a clear pattern. In Queen Anne's County, seventy-nine corn houses with known dimensions were in twenty-seven different sizes, but 80 percent were from 6 to 8 feet wide and 91 percent were 12 to 20 feet long. In Dorchester County, the favored dimensions among sixty-six examples were 6 to 10 feet by 10 to 20 feet; in a sample of forty-four examples from St. Mary's County, the favored dimensions were 8 to 12 feet by 12 to 20 feet. The median size for corn houses also fell within a tight range: 7 by 16 feet in Queen Anne's

County, 8 by 15 feet in Dorchester County, and 8 by 20 feet in St. Mary's County (Fig. 9.10).

Random descriptions from Virginia property ads and other sources reinforce what the more extensive Maryland property valuations make clear: corn houses were frequently of log construction, and they tended to be relatively narrow in proportion to length, optimizing air flow across the breadth of the building (Fig. 9.11). Log construction was widely used for secondary buildings throughout the Tidewater, and a single pen of logs left in the round made a quick and efficient container for corn storage and curing. Speed and cost are evident in a series of entries in the Virginia diary of Francis Taylor. A carpenter named Charles Leathers, assisted by "M. Biggers," commenced work on a log corn house on Monday, November 10, 1794. The logs were in place on Tuesday, and by Thursday they were hauling in rough-sawn slabs from a local sawmill to use as flooring. On Saturday, they raised the roof frame and began to cover it. They did not work on Sunday, but as Leathers finished the roof on Monday, the farm crew "begain to put corn in New Corn house." Leathers was paid 2 shillings and 6 pence a day, or less than a pound for seven days' work.[23]

The Orphans' Court records offer insights into two other characteristics of pre-Revolutionary corn houses. These were

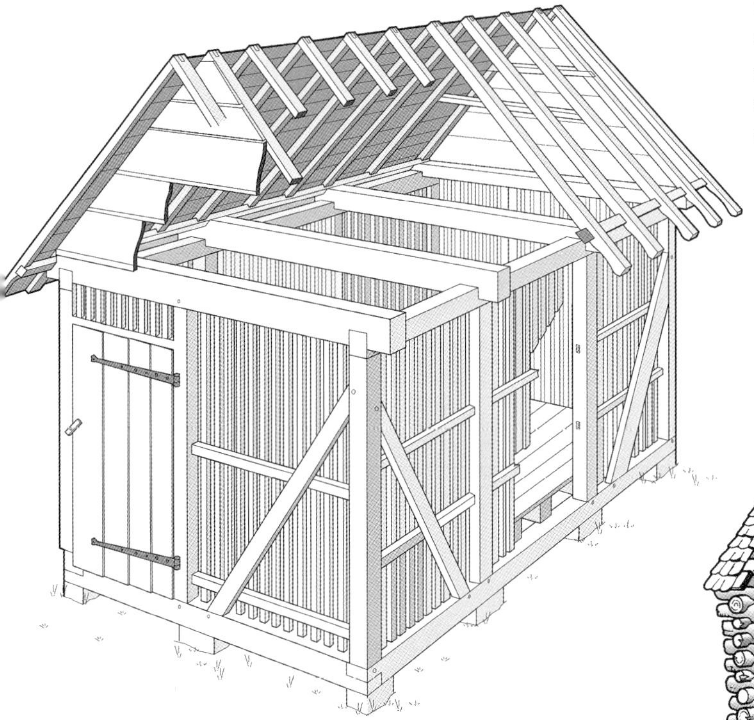

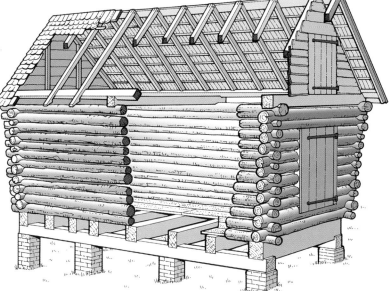

Fig. 9.10. *Corn House, Chaney Farm, Anne Arundel County, Maryland. An example of what became the prototype for well-built corn houses by the late eighteenth century, limited to 8 or 10 feet in width, with vertical slats nailed to the inside of the frame and the door located in the gable end.*

Fig. 9.11. *Corn House, White Farm, 1810s, Isle of Wight County, Virginia. Rarely found today, single-pen log structures were widely used for corn storage, in this case with canted walls and a gable-end door.*

usually stand-alone buildings rather than part of a larger multiuse structure, and the double-crib form with a central aisle had not yet come into widespread use. Among more than 300 pre-Revolutionary valuations from two Eastern Shore counties, just two examples were found of paired corn houses explicitly described as "double corn houses," and a third description clearly followed this form. Appraisers in Queen Anne's County recorded "one very old double corn house 24 feet by 20" on the Blakeford tract in 1768, and in 1772 they found "one double corn house of sawed poplar logs 24 feet square in middling repair" on the lands of Edward Harris. A 1773 valuation from Dorchester County included "two corn houses and a stable in between them." Half a dozen more properties can be identified, which include pairs of corn houses with matched dimensions, such as the "two 15 foot corn houses old and indifferent" appraised in Queen Anne's County in 1747 or the "two old log corn houses 16 by 8" in Dorchester County in 1770. Two references from the early nineteenth century allude to the value of the double-crib form. The Griffith property in 1801 included "two log corn houses 12 feet by 12 with a cart house between, the whole covered with feather edged oak shingles in good repair." In 1814, the improvements of another property included "one framed House 30 by 20 sheded on two sides,

wherein there is 2 corn cribs, one Carriage House below & a very fine granary above."[24]

Whether single or double, corn houses were occasionally supplemented by sheds on one or more sides. When a functional notation was included in the descriptions, the most common use was stabling. Of the more numerous unspecified sheds, many must have served as storage space for carts, harrows, harness material, barrels, and lumber, while simultaneously adding protection to the exposed timber frame of the core building.

The Orphans' Court valuations demonstrate as well that corn houses can be tied to shifting patterns of agriculture in the Tidewater. In pre-Revolutionary Queen Anne's County, tobacco was still a major crop, and tobacco houses outnumbered corn houses in both frequency of occurrence (66 percent versus 45 percent) and sheer numbers (210 versus 124). By the first decade of the nineteenth century, 80 percent (67 of 84) of property valuations in the county included at least one corn house, while only two had tobacco houses. The

Fig. 9.12. Granary and Corncrib, John Cannon Farm, near Centreville, Queen Anne's County, Maryland. This early nineteenth-century granary incorporates a corncrib, easily recognized by the slatted siding at left. This combination of functions encouraged the use of the term "crib" over "corn house."

1798 Federal Direct Tax confirms the subservient role of corn houses in tobacco-growing counties such as Anne Arundel and Prince George's and the complete dominance of corn over tobacco in counties such as Baltimore and Somerset.[25]

One final issue can be explored through the valuations and the 1798 Federal Direct Tax—the use of the term "crib." In Maryland, this term was not part of the agricultural lexicon until the end of the eighteenth century, and then it gradually gained wider usage throughout the nineteenth century (Fig. 9.12). The earliest firmly dated use of the term among the records examined for this study occurs in an Orphans' Court valuation dated November 20, 1798. In the same year, the federal tax assessment of four Maryland counties recorded 1,392 corn houses and just six corncribs. The Maryland evidence is in contrast to Virginia, where the term can be found as early as 1739 and appears in vestry minutes and newspaper property descriptions more than a dozen times through the 1750s and 1760s. Of these various references, the few that include size or material notations offer no evidence that a "crib" was in any way different from a corn house. More likely, the term came into use as a subtle acknowledgment that one of the most common forms for corn houses was a single pen or crib of logs. This connection can be demonstrated in one early entry. In 1767, the vestry of Elizabeth City Parish in Virginia "ordered that a Corn Cribb be built on the Glebe Land with good white oak sides and ends clear of Sap three Inches thick [that is, sawed logs]: The Roof to be lathed and well shingled the Cribb to be 14 feet long ten wide and five feet high."[26]

The Orphans' Court valuations for Queen Anne's County provide an opportunity to track the expanding use of the term "crib" over time and suggest a gradual evolution in meaning. Following the first use of the term in this county in 1798, it did not appear again in the valuations until 1814. Subsequently, it was used sporadically through the late 1810s and then with steadily increasing frequency. By the 1850s, "crib" was nearly at parity with the older term "corn house." As the term broadened out into wider usage, it was often used to describe corn storage spaces within a larger building. In 1815, for example, a Kent Island farm included "one barn thirty feet square, containing therein two corn cribs and one granary, and sheded on two sides."[27]

GRANARIES AND GRAIN STORAGE

Wheat, rye, oats, and barley were grains familiar to the first British settlers of the Chesapeake, yet these crops were poorly adapted to a frontier environment. All four were best suited to flat open fields that could be worked with a plow, and they were more susceptible to drought and had a lower yield ratio in comparison to maize. Harvesting these grain crops was labor intensive, as was the process of extracting the grain from the plant and turning it into flour. Given these constraints at each step of the process, corn was a clear choice, so long as local consumption was the primary end market. With tobacco filling the role of market crop, there was little incentive to pursue grain production on a grand scale in Maryland and Virginia throughout the seventeenth century.[28]

By the early eighteenth century, conditions were growing more favorable for grain production. Field systems were well established, market conditions were more favorable, and trade opportunities were expanding for both grain and livestock. Corn remained a staple for home consumption, as livestock feed, and for export to the West Indies, but Chesapeake farmers could now explore an alternative market crop at a time when the fresh, uncleared land that tobacco favored was in decline. Export figures for wheat climbed steadily through the middle years of the eighteenth century for both Maryland and Virginia, and by the 1760s tobacco was losing its central position in the agricultural economy of much of the Chesapeake, with the exception of southern Maryland.[29]

The annual crop cycle for wheat differed from corn and tobacco, and this made it easier for planters to venture into wheat with minimal risk. Corn and tobacco were planted in late April and early May; wheat was planted in late July or early August. Tobacco was harvested in mid- to late August; corn fodder was harvested in September; the corn ears' harvest was in October and November; and that for wheat was in late June and early July. Equally important, Chesapeake farmers were accustomed to planting corn in rows 6 or 7 feet apart, which made it possible to plant wheat, oats, or barley midway between the corn rows. The interplanting of crops was thought by some planters to reduce the corn yield, but double cropping and even triple cropping removed much of the risk from the venture.[30]

Economic risk was lessened, but the addition of another crop increased the labor burden and could create conflicts in harvest schedules and crop storage. Labor needs were modest for the wheat crop until harvest time, but when the crop reached maturity in late June, all available hands were diverted to the wheat fields. The skilled tasks of cutting and cradling the wheat were often accomplished using hired hands or were assigned to the most accomplished members of the plantation labor force, either slave or free. Landon Carter and William Daingerfield recorded charges for harvest hands in the 1770s. At Mount Vernon in the 1780s and 1790s, construction activity came to a halt during harvest as the carpenters and masons stepped into this key harvest role.[31] Field hands gathered the wheat and bound the stalks into sheaves and the sheaves into shocks. If the field was devoted solely to wheat, the shocks could be left scattered across the field until there was time to begin the laborious business of separating grain from the plants. If the field was double cropped, the shocks were gathered in pens in the farmyard or at the field margins. Landon Carter described this process

in early July 1775: "Wheat all cut down here at home, and my spelt almost down; but my gatherers have not as yet finished binding up the Saturday's Cuttings. My carts are bringing it in, and we intend to stack it in long racks and then thatch it over with rafter poles fastened at head and lying across at every 4 feet and thin laths tied across and so thatched."[32]

No sooner was the wheat harvested than preparations began for the next year's crop. In a detailed chronology of the wheat harvest on William Daingerfield's plantation in 1774, John Harrower reported that the harvest began on June 20, that cutting was completed on July 16, and that on August 19 the colonel "finished his wheat harvest by getting the last of it brought home and stacked." Three days later, the process of sowing the new crop began in fields of corn that were then approaching maturity. Sowing wheat proceeded sporadically through the fall, alternating with harvesting the corn, and the last of 260 bushels of seed was planted on November 1.[33] On July 26 of the following year, Harrower described "bringing hom and stacking the Colos. [Colonel's] Wheat haveing 18 Stacks of 100 Bushels each by Computation besides a Large Barn fill'd up to the roof."[34]

Once harvested, the grain had to be separated from the stalks. This was a tedious process that could be accomplished by several methods. The most labor intensive was to beat the grain out with wooden flails, best performed on a wood "threshing floor." As wheat crops grew in size and outstripped the labor available for flailing, it became common practice to use horses or cattle to tread the wheat. A few progressive farmers took pains to build circular, open-air treading floors to provide a clean surface for this activity, and George Washington built a sixteen-sided barn specifically designed for treading. The more universally accepted method, however, was to lay out a circular treading ground of hard-packed earth, which, combined with the use of livestock, must have lent a texture and subtle bouquet to colonial bread unknown to modern tastes.[35]

Once the grain was separated from the stalks, it still required winnowing, a process that separated the edible kernels from the rough husks or chaff. The traditional manner of winnowing wheat was to take the freshly flailed wheat and cast it up in the air in a light breeze. The heavy kernels fell back to the threshing floor, while the breeze carried away the lighter husks and chaff. Prior to threshing, wheat could be stored almost anywhere—in stacks in the field and farmyard or in any available building. Landon Carter routinely stored unthreshed grain in his tobacco houses and then fretted over the need to finish the threshing before the tobacco was ready for harvest. As wheat crops grew in size and importance, Chesapeake farmers found reason to build new and special-

Fig. 9.13. Brome-Howard Barn, St. Mary's City, Maryland. Dated by dendrochronology to 1785, this barn retains evidence that it was constructed originally as a tobacco house and was later converted to use as a granary.

ized structures to accommodate the processing and storage of grain (Fig. 9.13).[36]

A survey of early records from the Chesapeake reveals only scattered references to the term "granary" prior to 1750. The earliest listing of a granary in the Queen Anne's County valuations occurs in 1751, and the term becomes more frequent over the ensuing decades. By the first decade of the nineteenth century, about 30 percent of valuations in that county included a granary. Among a smaller sample of valuations for Dorchester County, only five listed granaries, all dating to the 1770s. The earliest mention of a granary in the valuations for St. Mary's County occurred in 1802. Based on crop production data, these references understate the importance of wheat but do conform to regional patterns of crop selection. Wheat culture in the Maryland Chesapeake was encouraged by mercantile interests in Philadelphia and Baltimore, and planters in Kent, Queen Anne's, and Talbot Counties were among the first to turn their efforts from tobacco to wheat, while tobacco remained the dominant crop in St. Mary's.[37]

The early granaries that have survived to the present day vary in size and material, but they share certain key characteristics (Fig. 9.14). The grain could be transported in bags or barrels, but it needed to be stored loose in a dry place and in a fashion that would not lead to overheating. Granaries were constructed on piers or blocks to ensure protection from ground moisture, and loose grain was stored in specially constructed bins that rarely exceeded 4 to 6 feet in width or length. The bins were built of closely fitted horizontal planks constructed against the perimeter walls of the building, which also were lined with interior sheathing boards.

Granaries were sometimes part of a larger, multipurpose building. One design that is widely found consists of a frame building perhaps 20 feet wide and 30 feet deep, of frame construction, with doors centered in the gable ends and fittings for grain processing and storage on the main floor and in the loft (Fig. 9.15). The interior walls are lined with horizontal sheathing, and a steep ladder stair ascends to the upper story (Fig. 9.16). Shed lean-tos line both side walls of this building type and serve a myriad of purposes. A variation on this arrangement places the granary in a spacious loft above a pair of corn houses with a central drive-through.

Documentary records yield abundant supporting evidence for these multipurpose designs but indicate that a much more diverse range of buildings were in use. Of thirty-six granaries described in the eighteenth-century Orphans' Court valuations for Queen Anne's County, twenty-four included material specifications. Fifteen of these were log, two were hewed log, and seven were frame. Dimensions were provided for an equal number of buildings, representing eighteen different sizes, ranging from 10 by 12 feet up to 26 feet square. As with other building types, the extant sample is representative of part of the original range, but time and attrition have removed all but a few of the log examples, as well as most of the small and lightly crafted structures.

The contraction in diversity for this building type over time is not surprising, but the relatively modest frequency of occurrence for the term "granary" in a county such as Queen Anne's (thirty-one of eighty-seven for the period 1800–1809) merits further consideration. By the end of the eighteenth century, wheat was the dominant market crop in this county, and one would expect to see grain storage represented on a majority of county farms. A careful review of this group of valuations is revealing. Seventeen of the eighty-seven valuations represented town lots or unimproved rural properties. Of the seventy properties that show evidence of active farm-

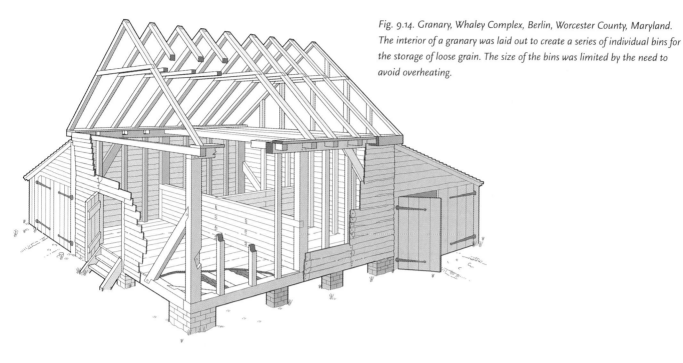

Fig. 9.14. Granary, Whaley Complex, Berlin, Worcester County, Maryland. The interior of a granary was laid out to create a series of individual bins for the storage of loose grain. The size of the bins was limited by the need to avoid overheating.

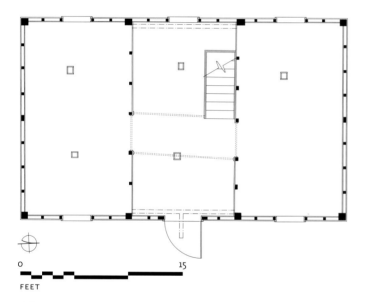

O   15

FEET

(left) Fig. 9.15. Plan, Granary, Shepherd's Delight, Kent County, Maryland. Built in the early nineteenth century, this granary is a full two stories, with a three-bay interior plan.

(right) Fig. 9.16. Granary interior, Shepherd's Delight, Kent County, Maryland. The interior of a granary is easily identified by the tightly fitted horizontal board sheathing used to line the exterior walls and for constructing the interior storage bins.

ing, thirty-one (44 percent) included granaries and another twenty-four (34 percent) mentioned a barn; the remaining eighteen were improved solely with corn houses. Not every barn included grain storage, but many certainly did.

Further insight into the role of granaries may be gained by looking more carefully at the disposition and sale of the crop. Wheat was susceptible to damage and loss at each step of the process. If harvested too soon, the kernels would not ripen fully; if too late, they were easily loosened from the stalk. More losses occurred during threshing, particularly if done by treading on open ground with livestock. Once securely in the granary, wheat could overheat, grow too moist and sprout, or be consumed by a destructive insect known as the "hessian fly." The longer the wheat crop remained in the planter's hands, the greater the risk of loss. Thus farmers were anxious to move their grain to market as quickly as practicable.

In most cases, wheat was sold as unprocessed grain, delivered either to a local gristmill or to a wholesale merchant. Newspapers from the 1750s and later routinely included advertisements for commercial enterprises with large granaries. In 1751, the *Virginia Gazette* offered for sale a lot in Fairfax County "in Belhaven, very convenient to a Landing, upon which is a Warehouse, 36 feet long and 24 wide, 4 Divisions below, 2 Granaries above, and a Cellar."[38] In 1769, John Ballendine placed an ad in the *Maryland Gazette* for a large mill and commercial complex "at the Landing" near "Falls of Potowmack," including "two large Graneries, 36 Feet by 30, on each Side the Mill."[39] At the end of the century, grain production at Tappahannock along the Rappahannock River in Virginia supported an enterprise that contained "a wharf extended at least 100 yards from the bank and 40 in width, which is in good order lately having undergone a thorough repair. On the wharf is an excellent granary, 60 by 20 feet, 3 stories high; the first is a cellar with three divisions, the second floor is divided into three bins for the reception of grain; the third into 6 bins, and the floor above being flush makes it suitable for a sail loft."[40]

The most prosperous among the planters were those who controlled more than one step in the process. By the late 1790s, George Washington relied entirely on his own labor to plant, cultivate, and harvest the crop; the wheat was threshed in his specially designed treading barn; and the grain was hauled to his own gristmill. There it was ground into flour, which could be loaded directly into pirogues for transport to merchants on the waterfront in Alexandria. At times, he even sold directly to ships passing by Mount Vernon on the Potomac. Meanwhile, encouraged by a Scottish overseer to establish a distillery, Washington expanded his production of rye but became a net buyer of that crop to feed his stills. The slop from the distilling process was delivered to hog pens, adding another dimension to the lucrative benefits of grain farming.

BARNS, STABLES, AND LIVESTOCK SHELTER

Chesapeake planters found little need for large, multipurpose barns until well into the eighteenth century. Tobacco and corn required specialized and distinctly different storage structures, and livestock either ranged in woods and marshes or were housed in very basic shelter. As grain supplanted tobacco, however, crop processing and storage needs changed, and horses and cattle were afforded better stabling. These trends encouraged the consolidation of needs into larger buildings that afforded specialized spaces for each part of the farm operation.

The term "barn" covers a broad range of building types and functional characteristics, but in the colonial Chesapeake, the most consistent term found as a modifier to "barn" was "floor" (Fig. 9.17). These descriptions vary in detail, but the floor often carries further descriptors that may relate to purpose, extent, thickness, and the type of fasteners. A rare early example from Virginia is typical of the most basic description. In a Northampton County marriage contract dated 1666, Alexander Fleminge agreed to "new Cover the Barne with Clapboard & the Loft & threshing flore with plank."[41] A 1730 order for construction of a 32- by 20-foot glebe barn in King and Queen County, Virginia, provides further details about the organizational plan. It called for the walls to have a "ten foot pitch underpinned three bricks high with brick and brick & half broad to be shingled with good Cyprus Shingles, fourteen foot ye length & the whole breadth to be floored with good white oake plank of inch [and a] half thick, the Studs Rafters Winbeams and braces to be sawed & to be weatherboarded with good white oake boards, one folding door and one single one opposite."[42]

The 10-foot pitch of the walls, continuous brick foundation, and wooden floor all make clear that this was not a tobacco house. The instructions regarding the size of the floor (14 by 20 feet) suggest a central threshing floor with two opposing doors to provide the cross-draft necessary for winnowing. Threshing floors took a good deal of punishment, and construction contracts often included instructions for the thickness and manner of fastening the planks. One-and-a-half or two inches was the preferred thickness for threshing floors, and the planks were either nailed down or "trunneled" to the joists with wood pins or "treenails." A 1773 order for a glebe barn in Fairfax Parish in northern Virginia describes

Fig. 9.17. Barn, Clay's Hope, Talbot County, Maryland. This barn bears evidence of use at various times for hanging tobacco, for storing grain and hay, for the stabling of livestock, and for the storage of implements.

a hierarchical approach to flooring that confirms a central threshing bay and tacitly acknowledges the added wear to a threshing floor. The building was to be 32 by 20 feet with 10-foot walls. The frame was "to be sawed out of white oak, the sides and ends to be weatherboarded with clapboards clear of sap, the roof to be covered with featheredge shingles got out of red oak timber and clear of sap 12 feet in the middle of the floor, to be laid with 2 inch white oak plank and spiked down, the rest to be laid with inch [plank] and nailed with 20d nails, the whole to be well fraimed with proper doors, locks & hinges." Other work included a "Stable 24 by 16."[43]

The flooring in the pair of 10- by 20-foot bays that flanked the threshing floor indicate that the rest of the building would be used for crop storage rather than livestock, an assumption reinforced by the order for construction of a separate stable. Based on available evidence, this was probably the most common type of barn found in the Chesapeake throughout the eighteenth century. An alternative arrangement is suggested by a 1780 advertisement for a farm in Prince George's County, Maryland, which included "a convenient frame barn, 30 feet wide, and 40 feet long, with a stable at one end that has stalls for six horses; a cow-house at the other end, with stalls for ten cows, and a threshing floor in the middle, 22 by 30 feet, through which a wagon may drive and discharge its load into the loft."[44] The flank-

ing stable bays presumably were ceiled over with elevated loft floors so that crops could be stored above (Fig. 9.18). The central drive-through was another characteristic absent from tobacco barns but occasionally noted in grain barns. A farm near Annapolis was described in 1786 as improved by a brick barn 52 feet long by 20 feet wide, "through which a loaded cart drives."[45]

A threshing floor required a substantial amount of space and cross-ventilation, characteristics better suited to a barn than a granary, but the grain, once threshed, could be stored in the barn or moved to a more secure and separate building. Barn descriptions sometimes noted that granaries were included but rarely offered any clue to the size, placement, or design of that space. Lacking good eighteenth-century examples among extant buildings, we must draw inferences from barns that postdate 1800. In these buildings, grain bins or "garners" were constructed along a side access aisle that opened onto the threshing floor. This section of the building was ceiled over with a loft floor so that wheat straw or hay for the livestock could be stored above.

Building contracts and real estate advertisements offer a sense of barn plans and functional arrangements but provide limited insights as to numbers and frequency in the Tidewater landscape, particularly over time. The Maryland Orphans' Court records are useful for establishing this context.

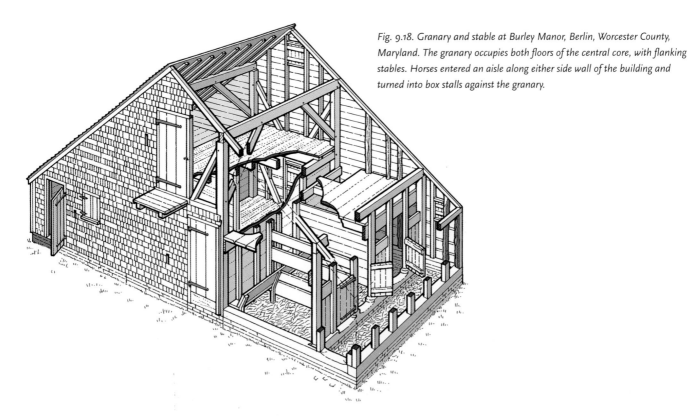

Fig. 9.18. Granary and stable at Burley Manor, Berlin, Worcester County, Maryland. The granary occupies both floors of the central core, with flanking stables. Horses entered an aisle along either side wall of the building and turned into box stalls against the granary.

In Queen Anne's County, barns were included in just two of fifty-seven estate valuations from the first half of the eighteenth century, but they appeared in 15 to 18 percent of property descriptions for each decade from the 1750s through the 1780s. Frequency jumped to 42 percent for the 1790s and was 36 percent for the first decade of the nineteenth century. Dimensional data is available for ninety-one barns from this assemblage, and three-quarters of the buildings fell within a range of 600 to 1,000 square feet. Despite a wide array of individual sizes, this sample demonstrates a clear preference for certain proportions. Eighty of the barns (88 percent) were 20 to 24 feet wide, and seventy-two (79 percent) were from 30 to 40 feet long. Building materials were specified for thirty-eight of these buildings, and among these, six were log and thirty-two were frame, including single examples of whole frame, bastard frame, and post-in-ground.

The Queen Anne's County valuations offer as well a sense of the functions most likely to be incorporated into a barn. Some descriptions are specific on this point. The 1795 valuation for the 100 acres of Bachelors Plains included just one agricultural building, a "barn containing stable, corn house and granary." This was an unusual combination, however, as demonstrated by a survey of eighty-three valuations that included at least one barn. Of these, seventy-two also featured a separate corn house, while just nineteen included a granary and twenty-eight had a separate stable. Corn, needing ventilation, was a poor fit within a larger, enclosed building.[46]

Stable needs could be met with more flexibility than corn

or grain, and this is reflected in the range of solutions alluded to in the various record sources. As used in documentary sources, the term "stable" primarily referred to shelter for horses and less frequently to cattle and oxen. The quality of stabling usually reflected the number and value of the animals. Through the first century or more of settlement, all but the wealthiest Chesapeake planters made do with a few draft animals and, if they could afford it, a riding horse or two. Over the course of the eighteenth century, numbers and diversity broadened to reflect increasing specialization and growing economic stability. A wealthy planter would own draft animals for farmwork, carriage horses to pull a chair, chaise, or carriage, "saddle horses" for business and pleasure, and, among a small elite, racehorses for sport (Figs. 9.19, 9.20).

Early descriptions of stables were usually of three types: stables for rural plantations and farms, stables to accommodate parish or county court needs, and commercial stables serving the customers of inns, taverns, coffeehouses, and, in the nineteenth century, hotels. A typical rural stable held four to ten horses, while a tavern stable may have contained spaces for from thirty to sixty or more. Considerable variation was found among all three types.

At the most basic level, a small stable was likely to be of log construction and encompass less than 300 square feet. In 1758, for example, the Dorsey's Chance property included "a log stable 10 feet square," while in 1766 Holbourn was improved with "one logged stable 15 by 12."[47] A 10-foot-square

(top) Fig. 9.19. Stable, Upton Scott House, c. 1762, Annapolis. Built as one of two flankers for a refined town house, this brick stable is a rare pre-Revolutionary survival.

(bottom) Fig. 9.20. Plan of stable, Upton Scott House, Annapolis. Horses were brought in through a door facing the courtyard, and they then turned either left or right into stalls that flanked a central aisle.

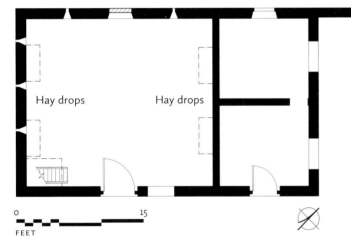

Hay drops   Hay drops

0   15
FEET

stable would have provided space for just two horses and may not have included any interior separation of space. At 15 by 12 feet, the Holbourn stable was probably intended for three horses and may have included simple stall separations and an aisle along one long wall. These assumptions are based upon evidence that the preferred size for horse stalls ranged from 4 to 5 feet in width and 8 to 9½ feet in length, while 4 feet was the preferred minimum for aisle widths.[48]

As stable buildings increased in size, the descriptions were more likely to include some reference to the number or configuration of stalls. In 1761, a stable for the president of the College of William and Mary was ordered, to be "thirty-two feet Long and twenty feet wide, with a partition taking off 12 feet at one end for a carriage and at the other a door leading into four stalls on each side."[49]

In 1766, a Virginia parish ordered a 16- by 20-foot sawed log stable for the glebe with "eight stalls with a passage be-

tween."[50] These two examples indicate stalls measuring a nominal 4–5 feet by 8 feet, flanking 4-foot central aisles. This formula of about 32 to 40 square feet per stall (and 40 to 50 square feet per animal if aisles are included) appears repeatedly in records for both Maryland and Virginia. Shed stables followed the same formula for width, but aisle space was only necessary if the outside walls were enclosed. A property advertised in the *Virginia Gazette* in 1783, for example, was improved by a kitchen with a 32- by 8-foot "shed Stable for 8 horses," indicating a row of 4- by 8-foot stalls with no aisle and hence no siding on the long wall.[51]

Stalls within a stable might be defined in a variety of ways, generally reflecting the duties, value, and temperament of the horses. Based on extant stabling in nineteenth-century barns, draft animals may have had minimal physical separation, perhaps consisting of one or two light rails to define the individual stalls. More valuable saddle and carriage horses were separated by "partitions," the term used most frequently to describe stall divisions (Figs. 9.21, 9.22). "Box stalls," the modern term for large and fully segregated stall spaces, were only used for the most valuable horses, or sometimes as a foaling stall for an expectant mare. A Maryland property to be sold at public venue in 1767, for example, featured "a commodious good Stable, with Nine complete Stalls, Two of which are close, for running horses." In 1776, John Harrower noted that work had begun on a "house to the Stallion," to measure 10 feet by 12 feet.[52]

A standard feature regardless of size and quality of indi-

Fig. 9.21. Stable, Mount Airy, Richmond County, Virginia. (HABS, 1936)

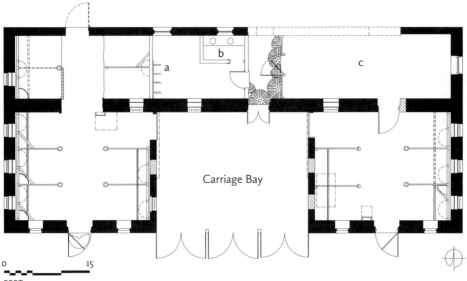

Carriage Bay

0   15
FEET

Fig. 9.22. Plan, Stable, Mount Airy, Richmond County, Virginia. Generously proportioned stalls flank a central carriage bay, indicating that this building sheltered valuable riding horses and possibly racehorses, while draft animals for the farmwork would have been quartered in much plainer stabling elsewhere.

a. Wooden pegs for tack storage
b. Space fitted out in late nineteenth century as a privy
c. Space altered for use as a dairy in the twentieth century

vidual stalls were "racks" and mangers for corn, blades, tops, and hay. These were mounted across the inner end of the stall, and, if the stable included a loft, a band of loft flooring was often omitted above the mangers as a "hay drop," greatly simplifying the process of feeding. The basic diet could be supplemented with oats and corn ground into meal, and for this feed each stall required a wooden box or tray, which was supplied from a grain storage box that resembled a crude and oversized blanket chest. Feed of this type was most easily provided from a "feeding aisle," a feature primarily found

in nineteenth-century stables large enough to accommodate paired bays of stall space served by a central aisle. Other features and fittings associated with stables included space for storing harnesses, saddles, curry combs, and the like. Wooden pegs for harnesses were a common feature on the passage walls of draft horse stables, and smaller tools and accoutrements were hung or shelved almost anywhere. Documentary descriptions mention "saddle rooms," "a Room for Harness Saddles & Bridles," and "a Room for Corn, and Horse Furniture."[53]

Commercial stables are generally identifiable by size as well as their connection to a tavern or similar enterprise (Fig. 9.23). A property offered for sale in Fredericksburg in 1789 included a coffeehouse and a stable for thirty horses. In

1795, "that well known Tavern and Stage-House," the Indian Queen, was offered for sale in the *Alexandria Gazette*. Improvements included "an elegant brick Stables, store-room, &c. 36 feet by 83 feet, capable of containing 50 horses, and 20 tons of hay." In 1812, the *Maryland Gazette* advertised for sale the City Tavern in Annapolis, improved with a "stable sufficient for fifty horses."[54]

For much of the colonial period, cattle were allowed to range freely in the woods and marshes, identifiable as to owner by the marks on their ears, which were recorded from time to time in the county court records. William Byrd disparaged free-range management of cattle, observing that because owners allowed "their cattle [to] wander in the runs all winter long... they grow very thin, and remain small, which does not happen if they are given hay and kept in stables."[55]

Despite the lack of care, cattle grew in number from an estimated 500 in Virginia in 1620 to 20,000 or more by the mid-seventeenth century. The Maryland Tidewater was equally suitable for cattle, particularly the lower Eastern Shore, rife with salt marshes and small islands that provided secure pasturage. As agricultural activity increased and tobacco depleted cropland, the value of dung encouraged planters to bring their cattle under tighter control. A favored solution was to create temporary fences around a section of field in need of replenishment in order to concentrate the cattle dung where it would provide the most benefit. The disadvantage of this practice was that penned cattle required feed. One solution was to pen the cattle in cornfields with the stalks left standing. If feed and provender were readily available, cattle could be gathered in more permanent pens and fed marsh grass, corn blades, tops and stalks, or even hay.[56]

Over time, references to cow houses, sheds, and stables appear in the records. Landon Carter considered shelter only necessary "for the care of weak Cattle in the winter" and as a way to gather dung for his fields. George Washington viewed these structures as part of a well-managed plantation and recorded the construction of cow houses on each of his Mount Vernon farms. Descriptions rarely offered more than the overall dimensions, and size alone suggests they were usually open, earthfast sheds, often roofed with thatch composed of rye straw or corn shocks. Milk cows required more control and better care than cattle intended for slaughter, and these animals were presumably the primary beneficiaries of cow stables. Cows were afforded less space than horses, with stall dimensions generally ranging from 3 to 3½ feet in width and 5½ to 8 feet in length (Fig. 9.24).[57]

Hogs were well adapted to the Chesapeake landscape and also were allowed free range, but not without some inherent problems. Hogs were as hard on crops as they were on mast in the woods and were difficult to outwit with fences, a point that underscores the role of fences for much of the colonial period. Initially, fences were necessary to keep animals out of cultivated fields rather than to protect livestock from predators. Fences needed to be tall enough to rebuff deer and tight enough to foil hogs. The usual solution was a split-rail fence laid in a zigzag pattern eight to ten rails high, secured at the top with a single or double "rider." The first step on a developing plantation was to create a perimeter or "outside" fence to protect the cultivated portion of the property; later this could be supplemented with "cross" or "inside" fences to create separation between individual fields. The principal purpose for fencing individual fields was to facilitate releasing cattle into a single field to fertilize it with dung.[58]

the accounts of Justinian Snow included charges "for 50 dais work in building 10 hogsties which were left imperfect and planking them within" and "for 10 daies work in railing in the hog-court." A Maryland court case relating to events in 1646 listed among the accusations that "the sd Rebells fyred a Tob. Howse & . . . a hogstey att Kent howse." Later references use the terms "hog sty" and "hog house" to suggest the distinction between open pens and structures that offered at least nominal shelter from the elements.[60]

While most Chesapeake farmers continued to adhere to the traditional cycle of free-range and pen-fattened hogs, by the late colonial period some plantation owners were testing new methods. In December 1774, pressured by the threat of British trade restrictions, Landon Carter acknowledged the advantages of food products over tobacco. He intended to increase his "hog raising scheme as food will always be wanted and the Cheaper we can raise them, the better, especially as the business of . . . raising hogs . . . in the woods is almost destroyed by the encreasing of the inhabitants and their settling in these backlands where these hogs used to be raised."[61]

Carter's heightened interest in pork production must have shaped the look of his Sabine Hall plantation in several ways. His proposed solution to lowering the cost of hog production was to plant peach trees—nearly 3,000 as an opening gambit. Equally important, Carter committed to raising hogs in pens rather than the woods, necessitating increased requirements for feed. Peaches would be part of the solution, but tobacco doubtless gave way to increased corn production as well.[62]

By the mid-1780s, George Washington was tightening up his management of hogs. He complained in November 1785 that since "the Hogs . . . [are] running in the Woods after the Mast, no account could be taken of them." Summarizing hog management and slaughter weights for the years 1785 and 1786, Washington concludes with these instructions: "Hogs—To be fatted for Bacon in a close pen, with a planked floor, sheltered by a roof to have properly contrived Troughs to feed them in, and running water always passing by them." By the late 1790s, Washington had gone into the distilling business and was fattening hogs on the residue from the manufacture of rye whiskey, employing a system of drains to deliver the mash directly from the distillery to the hog troughs. These hogs doubtless entertained few dreams of returning to the forest.[63]

Hogs foraged in the woods and marshes for much of the year and were branded in similar fashion to cattle. Where lands were especially suitable for hogs and little else, the affinity was imparted in the landscape with names such as "Hog Marsh Field," "Hogg Quarter," or "Hogg Harbor." Free-range hogs were vulnerable to a variety of predators, including wolves (for which bounties were paid), "rogues" from neighboring plantations, and members of the landowner's labor force.[59]

In the fall, hogs were gathered from the woods and placed in pens to be fattened with corn prior to slaughter. In early December, or with the advent of cold weather, the hogs were slaughtered and the meat was processed for curing and storage. From an early date, documentary records include references to hog pens, sties, and houses with a few hints as to both their purpose and construction. In 1639, for example,

LANDSCAPES OF CHANGE

Melding together these four principal products—tobacco, corn, grain, and livestock—and tracing their cultivation and exploitation over time, it is possible to detect a series of common themes that profoundly influenced the evolving look of the Chesapeake landscape. In the first decades of settlement, newly arrived immigrants tested new crops and carved rough fields from the forest. Lacking established models for housing tobacco and corn, they quickly developed a vocabulary of building methods and models that answered their needs. Casting aside conventional husbandry learned in a fully cultivated country, they set their animals loose in the woods and marsh and learned to fence their livestock out rather than in.

By the middle years of the seventeenth century, a Chesapeake course of farming was well established, and much of the next hundred years was spent refining the details of that system. Planters in Virginia and Maryland cleared a few acres of uncultivated land each year to support a fresh round of tobacco planting and worked old tobacco fields with corn, before abandoning them for twenty years of rest and reforestation. Livestock was left to forage on the land, and when shelter was offered it was modest in the extreme. Through the first half of the eighteenth century, shifting economic conditions and declining tobacco yields encouraged grain production. As wheat ascended to replace tobacco as the chief market crop, the Chesapeake landscape entered a period of pervasive change. The small 3- and 5-acre plots typical of tobacco culture were replaced with 40- to 80-acre fields of grain and corn.

Grain production required new buildings for crop processing and storage. As tobacco production declined, the distinctive curing houses could be adapted to new uses. Most were probably abandoned, however, as they were scattered across the plantation, sited for convenience to the crop and now ill suited to become the heart of a busy farmyard. Initially, grain crops could be accommodated in small frame and log granaries that took their places near corn houses and perhaps a rough stable or hog house. But as demand for threshing floors, better livestock stabling, and storage space for wheat, rye, and hay increased, large, multipurpose barns began to appear in growing numbers. On large, carefully managed farms, the barn became the central focus of an increasingly specialized array of support buildings. Storage spaces were needed for carts, wagons, and farm implements such as plows, harrows, seed drills, and wheat fans. Stabling was needed for draft horses, oxen, milk cows, and, eventually, mules. Property inventories increasingly included poultry houses for chickens, geese, ducks, and turkeys. Sheep pens and the occasional loom house hint at one form of home industry, and stills and cider houses identify another.

In the years after the Revolutionary War, a nascent movement to promote scientific agriculture gained momentum, and by the early nineteenth century the most conscientious Tidewater farmers were forming agricultural societies. The rise of what is often called "progressive agriculture" was both forward looking and a subtle signal of distress. Two centuries of unrelenting agricultural expansion had taken a toll on Chesapeake soil, and by the early nineteenth century Chesapeake farmers were facing stagnant yields and a time of reckoning with the natural carrying capacity of the land. Their salvation would prove to be the piecemeal arrival of the Industrial Revolution, first manifested by the rapid growth of urban centers in Baltimore, Washington, and Norfolk. The development of regular steam transportation on the Chesapeake in the late 1810s and 1820s opened up new markets for Tidewater farmers and created demand for vegetable crops, fruit, and dairy products, which previously would have spoiled before reaching market. The introduction of lime and guano fertilizer in the 1830s and 1840s and the rapid development of manufactured farm implements in the 1840s resurrected agricultural productivity across eastern Maryland and Virginia.

Industrialization brought a new vitality to tired Tidewater farms and simultaneously sowed the seeds of destruction for certain aspects of the region's agricultural traditions and buildings. Sidney George Fisher, a gentleman farmer on Maryland's Eastern Shore, marveled in 1847 at the ease with which he could now travel to and from Philadelphia and laid plans for a new farm complex anchored by an overshot forebay barn of a type favored in eastern Pennsylvania but rarely seen in Tidewater Maryland. Queen Anne's County farmer William Roe raised corn in much the same way his great-grandfather had, but rather than lofting the corn in a crib, his diary records the shelling and delivery of the crop to a wharf on the Chester River with the price realized each day upon delivery.[64]

Other changes were coming for Chesapeake farmers, and each generation subsequently has made adjustments to markets, technology, and labor. As we look across the fields, forests, and salt marshes of the modern Chesapeake landscape, markers of past practices are discernible for those who take the time to unravel the layers of change. Buildings, fence lines, even the courses of secondary roads hold clues to the property boundaries, field systems, farming practices, and crop management that formed the familiar world of earlier generations.

Materials

10 _Timber Framing_

WILLIE GRAHAM

Every house frame is a practical solution to an engineering problem or, more often than not, to a combination of problems.[1] A history of timber framing in the Chesapeake can therefore be written as a history of structural problem solving by generations of house carpenters working in the region. Their challenges arose from circumstances that made the colonies a different place from the homelands of the builders and their clients. Differences ranged from unfamiliar materials, inflated labor costs, and the special needs of homesteaders, to the quest for affordable gentility in the eighteenth century and the impact of new technologies on the building trades after 1800. When told this way, the history of timber-frame engineering in Maryland and Virginia is a chapter in a much larger story about the transformation of American society and how one of the trades employed in house building adjusted to these new ways of living.

Every new settler on every new frontier had to start from scratch. In the short run, getting plantations launched was more important than building well. Newcomers, therefore, had good reason to take whatever carpentry practices they remembered from England as starting points for experiments that took advantage of the prodigious timber resources in the colonies to develop inexpensive and practical technologies for building anew. The intent of these experiments was always to the same purpose: to save time and money until newcomers got their plantations up and running. Eventually, farmhouses and work buildings could be rebuilt using longer-lasting materials and more workmanlike construction techniques. By then, the much-improvised "Virginia house" had so thoroughly altered traditional carpentry practices that vernacular buildings in Maryland and Virginia never again resembled their British progenitors or functioned in quite the same way.

Excavations at the original 1607 fort on Jamestown Island have brought to light structures that open the story of building technology in British North America. Some of the earliest were raised on lightweight frames sandwiched in-

side thick earthen walls. Another one, a row house, was also timber framed but stood on a light masonry footing.[2] These present-at-the-creation buildings are significant because they represent contemporary English practice transplanted directly to the New World. Too little time had passed for experimentation to produce new forms.[3] Yet, easy as it is to assume that these earliest-of-all structures were English born and bred, their antecedents are not readily apparent from what has survived in Britain. Their ancestry, instead, is an ancient one, rooted in the lightly framed dwellings that were common to medieval peasants' cottages, structures also frequently raised on slight frames encased with clay.[4] Captain John Smith describes the first semipermanent church at Jamestown, built in 1607, as being of similar construction, noting that it was "a homely thing like a barne, set upon Cratchets [forked poles], covered with raft[ers], sedge [reeds], and earth; so was also the walls."[5] Smith's description applies just as accurately to the buildings adjacent to the church, buildings whose structural posts were so haphazardly aligned that they could not have been covered with boards. Instead, as earthen lumps found in the excavations suggest, they too were walled with clay (see Fig. 6.2).[6]

The Jamestown leaders were simply continuing a military tradition of constructing structures inside forts using readily collected local materials in this ancient way. Often these materials were nothing more than the small trees, clay, and reeds that Smith observed. It was a building system that required minimal preparation and assembly. A military expedition could not waste precious cargo space on building materials. Expedition leaders much preferred to recruit semiskilled "makers of mudwals," like those who accompanied Sir Walter Raleigh's New World voyage in 1584, than have ships filled with bulky supplies.[7]

The most important feature of these early fort structures that inspired later building practices was the upright posts that were set up in holes and backfilled to make the frame rigid. These hole-set posts did double duty as foundation and as the principal structural members of the wall frame. Post-in-the-ground, or earthfast buildings, as they have come to be called, have been discovered throughout the Chesapeake, with variations lingering into the nineteenth century (Fig. 10.1). During the first hundred years, newcomers and seasoned colonists alike relied on an array of earthfast construction methods for houses, barns, and, frequently, churches and public buildings.[8] Various trial-and-error experiments created novel building systems, which combined technologies from early fort structures with other carpentry practices remembered from home, all with an eye to making good use of locally available timber resources. Archaeologists working in Maryland and Virginia have recorded the extraordinary diversity of these experiments. They have brought to light pit houses, houses with earthfast posts standing on subsurface floors, and clay-walled structures with no supporting framework below the eaves. Still others were raftered buildings that were all roof and no walls and mud-clad cottages infilled with wattle and daub applied to wickerwork panels or, alternatively, a mixture of clay and plaster laid up on vertical staves "mud-and-stud" style (see Figs. 6.1, 6.2). The most complicated were carefully carpentered, timber-frame structures with sills laid directly on the ground or even some with masonry foundations used in combination with earthfast posts.[9]

As late as the 1660s, colonists still did not always equate these rudimentary framing methods with makeshift beginnings or poverty. A party of nonconformist Virginians who

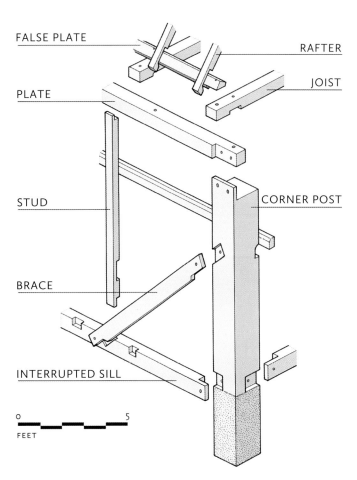

Fig. 10.1. *Virginia house framing details, Burrages End Tobacco House, 1780s, Anne Arundel County, Maryland.*

founded a settlement at Providence in southern Maryland built frontier houses with the homesteader's conventional mud walls, but they could also afford to glaze the windows, tile the roofs, cover the floors with green and yellow pavers, and decorate the best rooms with blue-and-white delftware fireplace tiles.[10] Nonetheless, these structures marked the end of the era of mud walling as a common house-building convention. Elsewhere, house carpenters had already discovered shortcuts that were to prevail throughout the Chesapeake region in the second half of the century. The newly invented "Virginia house" achieved a more uniform appearance than the mud cottages that preceded it, but, like them, it maximized easy-to-obtain construction supplies while minimizing the work involved to raise it.

A few newly arrived colonists wanted better accommodations than what these more ephemeral building methods afforded. They chose a familiar but more complicated route that bypassed the expeditious shortcuts in favor of a conventional English framed house with full masonry foundations, continuous sills, and an expensively carpentered timber frame. Thomas Cornwaleys, a prominent leader in the colonization of Maryland, had such a house in mind when he

Fig. 10.2. Close-studded box frame, St. Peter's Church, early fifteenth century, Melverley, Shropshire, England.

explained in 1638 that "I am building of A house toe put my head in, of sawn Timber framed A story and half hygh, with A sellar and Chimnies of brick, toe Encourage others toe follow my Example, for hithertoe wee liue in Cottages."[11] Brick was another, more permanent option, yet almost no one constructed dwellings or even churches or public buildings entirely of brick until the 1660s, despite its widespread use in Britain at this time. Brickmaking in quantity made little practical sense in a place where the forests held inexhaustible supplies of timbers for frames and coverings. Raw materials were cheap. It was the skilled labor necessary to burn bricks, saw planks, dress timbers, cut sophisticated carpentry joints, and raise chimneys that was so expensive. "The building of a good house to you there, will seem insupportable," one unhappy Virginia immigrant wrote back to England, "notwithstanding [here] we have timber for nothing but the felling & getting in place."[12] He reckoned that labor costs ran three times higher in the colony. To most newcomers, therefore, it was prudent to build as inexpensively as possible at first until they could get their feet on the ground. Anything more lavish, even by those who could afford more, was deemed "sillie" and "unnecessarie." That is how John Smith described the

"pallas in the woods" erected by John Ratcliffe, president of the Council of Virginia, "to fulfill his follies," Smith said, after Ratcliffe had squandered the colony's precious stores.[13] His reproach went to the heart of the lesson that every new arrival needed to learn—that extravagance put an entire enterprise at risk, be it a new plantation or, as at Jamestown in 1608, the colony itself. A later pamphleteer distilled the wisdom of what was by then long experience: "Ordinary beginners," he wrote, are strongly advised that "a mean way of Building" is "sufficient and safest" at the start.[14]

What "mean ways of building" eventually proved to be "sufficient" for beginners? Carpenters in due course selected for further development two strands from the many English building traditions they tested in the first three or four decades of settlement. They combined them to create what thereafter became known as the "Virginia house," a shorthand term for a highly successful, hybrid building system that spread throughout the region. This native engineering solution with a distant English ancestry would shape the development of the Chesapeake house for many generations to come and define domestic construction well into the nineteenth century.

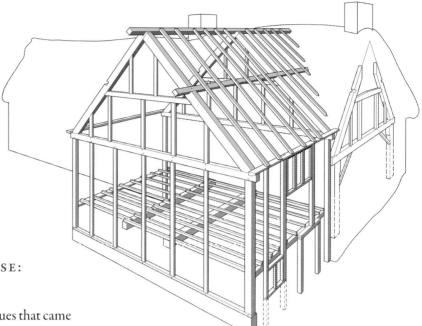

Fig. 10.3. *Slight-framed addition to Weylands, Kingsbury, second half of the sixteenth century, Somerset, England. A principal rafter roof was required to span the depth of this wing, but its walls were lightly framed using joinery efficiencies that minimized the amount of material and labor required for its erection. Note that the first-floor frame is not well integrated into the walls, with the joists bearing on ledgers that simply butt and are spiked to the studs. A false-plate-like timber carries the feet of the common rafters and doubles to catch the top of the studs.*

INVENTION OF THE VIRGINIA HOUSE: WALL SYSTEMS

The two starting points for the framing techniques that came to dominate the region were the close-studded box frame and a form of cheaper and less complicated timberwork that British architectural historians now call "slight framing." The English box frame was an assembly of vertical and horizontal timbers—posts, sills, plates, and beams—joined and pinned together and often braced at the corners. This self-supporting structure, usually elevated on a masonry foundation, was strong enough to bear a framework of roof trusses that was integral to the house frame underneath. There were many ways to assemble a box-frame building. One, close studding, seems to have developed as the standard way of structuring buildings in those parts of Britain where the practice of timber framing remained dominant into the seventeenth century. Close studding began as a conspicuously expensive way to embellish a half-timbered house by installing closely spaced (and structurally redundant) vertical studs between heavier wall posts. By the seventeenth century, carpenters tended to spread the studs farther apart, use smaller scantling, beef up the corner bracing, and increasingly hide the building's carcass underneath cladding of one kind or another.[15] This slow evolution led to the eventual demise of ornamental timberwork and foreshadowed its ordination as purely functional framing.

The box-frame model with secondary studs offered Chesapeake builders two advantages. First, it was made to order for a region rich in timber, and, second, by treating the wall framing and the roof separately, it allowed for separate development of each. Yet box frames had two disadvantages for settlers. Their many pieces required complicated joinery to assemble and were therefore time consuming and expensive to erect. Additionally, heavily carpentered frames had to be raised off the ground, usually on masonry footings, to pre-vent rotting. Brickwork was never cheap. On the other hand, slight frames often had no foundations. Builders of wattle-and-daub and mud-clad cottages treated light scantling as mere scaffolding to carry the roof. Uprights embedded inside clay walls acted as fasteners for the wattles or staves, to which the mud was then applied as a wall covering. Additionally, the uprights in slight-frame buildings could be earthfast, and, therefore, little time or money was needed to prepare the foundation to receive the building (Fig. 10.3). The obvious downside to the slight-frame cottage, though, was its flimsy nature and inherent short life.[16]

Besides being quick and easy, colonists soon learned that slight framing saved money, especially if, by borrowing and adding elements from the box-frame tradition, they could replace clay walls with a substitute covering made of wooden boards. Box framing inspired the use of more stout and regular framing members, which gave a greater degree of permanence and created surfaces true enough to receive siding. By midcentury, Chesapeake carpenters merged these two technologies into an amalgamated system that combined simplified joinery, earthfast construction, and cladding for roofs and walls made from short lengths of split clapboards, sometimes weatherproofed with a coating of pine tar. The resulting "Virginia house," as they called it, was a masterful engineering solution to the ordinary settler's need to manage his risks. It was indeed a simple way to fabricate and assemble the parts of a timber frame, skin the structure quickly and cheaply, and provide hearth and heat for a dwelling at considerably less expense than crafting a more sophisticated box frame and burning a kiln load of bricks for foundations and

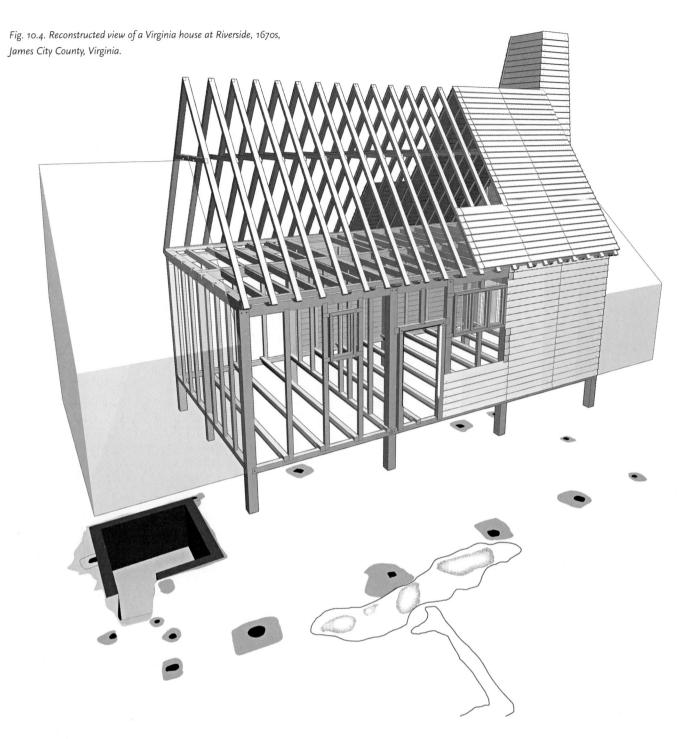

Fig. 10.4. Reconstructed view of a Virginia house at Riverside, 1670s, James City County, Virginia.

a chimney. So chimneys, too, were wooden affairs—timber framed, parged with clay for fireproofing, and often weatherized with the same riven boards used to cover walls and roofs (Fig. 10.4).

Box-frame construction was not unfamiliar to the first carpenters in Virginia. Not even all structures built inside early fortifications were lightly framed, even those raised on earthfast posts. The church rebuilt inside James Fort in 1608, for example, was a substantial structure, with 11-inch diameter posts set out at about 12-foot intervals and sunk 7 feet or more into the ground. The great width of the building—24 feet, considerably wider than its neighbors—must have re-

quired a significant spanning truss. One official mocked the mariners who raised it, declaring that they "might say they built such a golden church, that we can say the rain washed it to nothing in fourteen days."[17] Robust as its frame may have been, the walls and roof of the church were likely covered with the same clay and reeds as were other fort buildings. The Jamestown church was not the only early structure to stand on a heavy frame of earthfast posts. Sir George Yeardley's house at Flowerdew Hundred was another (see Fig. 6.6). Built in 1619, its foundations, made of ballast stones and salvaged bricks, did not support the weight of the main frame. Earthfast posts, hewn square and set between evenly

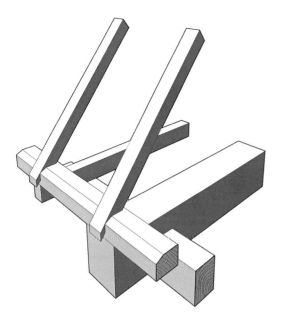

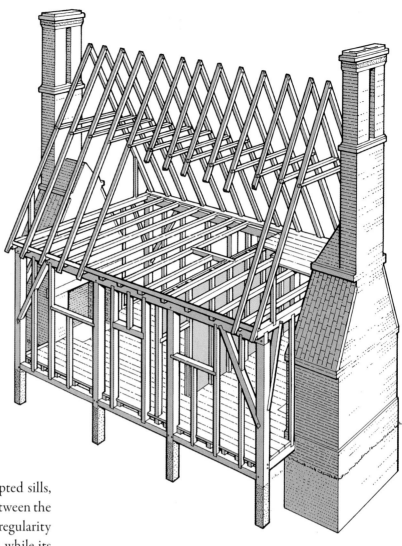

(left) Fig. 10.5. Eaves detail of the first phase of Sotterley, 1703–4, St. Mary's County, Maryland, showing the simplified joints typical of Virginia house construction.

(right) Fig. 10.6. Matthew Jones House frame and chimneys shown restored to their original, c. 1720, appearance. Newport News, Virginia.

spaced bays, did that. Besides supporting interrupted sills, this masonry work may have served as the filling between the bay posts that gave the building its enclosure. The regularity of this frame shows its DNA link to box framing, while its earthfast elements must have allowed for a simplified carpentry that probably required no braces and few complicated joints. These early, heavy-frame, earthfast buildings seem to have been tentative experiments with a hybrid that eventually led to a merger between the slight- and box-frame traditions.

Timberwork in the Virginia house was greatly simplified compared to conventional English box framing. Timbers were minimally prepared by either hewing, splitting or just peeling the bark off logs. Cutting simple lap joints and securing them with nails saved time and money. By contrast, mortise-and-tenon joints of the English box frame required neatly sawn material, careful laying out, prefabrication, and complicated fitting of parts. Frames raised in side-wall units became the preferred assembly method because it helped simplify joints at plate level.[18] With no bricks to fire or scantling to saw, and with less time needed to dress timbers and split the clapboards to sheath it, a Virginia house could be finished in a matter of weeks, thereby leaving planters more time and resources to spend on other pressing needs (Fig. 10.5).

The beauty of this simple but flexible system was its ver-

satility. It could be used to build a house of any size, plan, or chimney placement, as long as the width of the structure did not exceed about 20 feet. Posts were commonly set on 10-foot centers and were usually aligned between front and back walls. They were no longer joined from side to side in bents. Posts were half lapped and pegged to a top plate, creating a single side-wall unit. Interrupted sills, running between the post bays, carried the feet of light, in-between studs. The studs themselves were then quickly and easily fastened to the sill below and the plate overhead with bevel-lap joints. Once the side walls were reared, joists could be dropped in place to tie the building together and to provide a seat for the roof structure. If a solid attic floor was needed and the building had sufficient width, a summer beam could be added to break the span of the joists. The walls and roof were then dressed in boards. From there, carpenters and clients could make many different choices: where to locate doors, windows, and partitions, whether or not to cover the floor with sawn boards, how to fit in a staircase, and whether to pack the walls with clay filling (Fig. 10.6) (see Fig. 13.5).

Fig. 10.7. Clapboard roof used as a base for shingles, Benjamin Waller House, c. 1749, Williamsburg. (Loring J. Turner, Colonial Williamsburg Foundation, 1950)

VIRGINIA HOUSE COVERINGS: CLAPBOARDS

The use of riven clapboards precipitated the rapid development of building technology in the Chesapeake colonies more than anything else. The clapboard was a strong, lightweight, tapered slat, which was rived (split) quickly and easily, usually from straight-grained oak timbers that had been precut into standard lengths. The board's thin upper edge and feathered ends, cut with a few strokes of a drawknife, made it easy to overlap with adjoining clapboards to form a weather-tight, light, durable surface, which was nailed to the framing members. The costs of imported nails and semi-skilled American labor were not negligible, but clapboards, like plywood today, opened carpenters' eyes to other economizing innovations. Clapboard work not only superseded mud walls, half timbering, and other traditional walling materials used to enclose and weatherproof buildings on the exterior. It became the preferred alternative to thatch, tiles, and slate as an inexpensive roof covering (Fig. 10.7). Documents mention clapboards frequently only after midcentury, although archaeological evidence of ever-more-regular building frames in the 1640s and 1650s suggests that clapboard use coincided with the emergence of the Virginia house.[19]

Indeed, it was more than just coincidence. Clapboards both defined the Virginia house and made it affordable. The 5-foot board was an early standard for a modular framing system that builders could expand or contract to suit their needs. Regardless of function, buildings were generally laid out in a series of 10-foot bays, each two clapboards long.[20] Ranks of overlapping clapboards were nailed to lightweight riven studs (borrowed from the slight-frame tradition), which were typically set out on 2½-foot centers between heavier, load-bearing posts (from box-frame work) that formed each bay. The secondary studs were, in essence, non–load-bearing scaffolding needed simply to carry the clapboard sheathing and create the enclosure.

So integral to the structural system were clapboards that they gave buildings much of their rigidity. That function is seen most clearly in the Chesapeake roof frame, specifically the development of a distinctive truss design. Roofs in England were variously raised on a framework of principal and secondary rafters, with heavy, horizontal timbers, called "purlins," that connected the principal pairs, all usually fitted together with complex carpentry joints. The joints required for a single pair of principal rafters connecting it to a collar, a pair of purlins, and a tie beam could require nine tenon joints, all but one of which had to be cut on an angle. Roofs of clay tiles, stone and slate shingles, and even a proper thatch covering were tremendously heavy and thus mandated strongly built trusses for support (Fig. 10.8). By contrast, lightweight clapboards minimized the complexity. They freed Chesapeake builders to improvise an inexpensive roof frame constructed entirely of common rafters that were joined by collar beams simply lapped and nailed in place. The rafters themselves could be very small-dimensioned timbers, and some Maryland houses were spanned with rafters no more than 2 inches square in cross section.[21] Still, they adequately covered buildings 16 to 20 feet wide. Without braces or connecting purlins, such rafter pairs were not stable enough to stand upright by themselves until the final clapboard covering provided the diaphragm action that gave a finished roof frame its structural rigidity. In other words, clapboards did double duty, as protection from the weather and as the bracing system that held the roof aloft, all at a fraction of the cost of roofs in England that relied on heavy timbers, complex joints, and sawn lumber applied as an underlayment on which to hang tiles or slates. Clapboard work in the southern colonies was the ingenious matchmaker that arranged a marriage between earthfast slight framing and box construction, a union so close that the terms

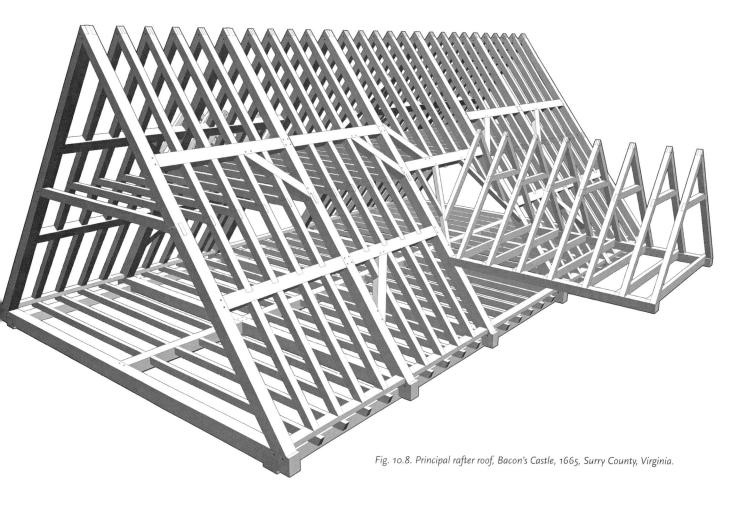

Fig. 10.8. Principal rafter roof, Bacon's Castle, 1665, Surry County, Virginia.

"Virginia house" and "clapboard work" were soon used synonymously.[22]

EMERGENCE OF THE FALSE PLATE FOR THE VIRGINIA HOUSE

Chesapeake builders borrowed one more element from English carpentry practice to complete their invention: the false plate. Box-frame construction required sophisticated joinery, most notably in the need to align the heavy, load-bearing, principal rafters with their associated tie beams—those spanning timbers that held the front and back walls together (often called "joists" in common work). Precision-made mortise-and-tenon joints were cut and fitted on an angle to tie the roof and walls together. Typically, then, major wall posts underpinned these rafter pairs in an orderly transfer of loads from roof to foundation. By contrast, builders erecting simplified frames employed differing methods to stand roofs on the tops of walls without regard to the structure underneath, thereby much simplifying the assembly process. A solution brought from the west of England that was favored in the Chesapeake colonies was to set a horizontal timber called a "false plate" on top of the joist ends.[23] Here, they devel-

oped it further as a complement to the common-rafter roof. Throughout the second half of the seventeenth century, this secondary plate was a thick board that typically lay on top of or lapped across the joist ends and was securely fixed to them with wooden pegs. The upper face was notched to receive the feet of the rafters, thereby eliminating any need for a more complicated tenon joint between rafters and joists. The laborsaving false plate became a hallmark of Chesapeake framing and continued in use in various forms until the early twentieth century.

This system of a post-set frame with a common-rafter roof set on a false plate, all covered with clapboards, defined ordinary building practice throughout the second half of the seventeenth century. Many social and economic factors conspired to perpetuate this type of building by repairing and rebuilding them across the region. Historians highlight the relentless demands of a volatile tobacco market, a high male-to-female sex ratio that forestalled normal family formation, a disease-ridden environment that broke up families prematurely and frustrated the orderly transfer of wealth and property from one generation to the next, and the influx of immigrants, which continually renewed English customs and practices. Toward the end of the seventeenth century,

Chesapeake society grew more stable and predictable as the trade in African slaves increased, the flow of indentured servants declined, and the economy became more diversified. Planters responded by investing in better-built, longer-lasting structures. The earliest surviving dwellings and farm buildings across the region consistently date from the decades when farmers began growing and marketing grains as well as tobacco. By then, the incessant repair and replacement of impermanent buildings going back two or three generations had long ago turned what had once been experiments and novelties into standard building practices everywhere from the Upper Chesapeake Bay to the Albemarle Sound.[24] Everywhere throughout the region, the legacy of a clapboard-inspired framing system held sway for another 150 years or more. Behind the sawn and painted weatherboard siding that dressed up the appearance of merchants' houses in prim-and-proper Williamsburg, and underneath the round-butt shingles that roofed handsome plantation houses in the countryside, were the descendants of the box-frame, the slight-frame, and the common-rafter roof. Generations of experimenting carpenters had learned lessons that Chesapeake builders never forgot.

TOWN AND COUNTRY INNOVATIONS

Tried and true as the Virginia house system had become by the end of the century, it never completely hardened into place. Chesapeake carpenters revisited it in the opening decades of the eighteenth century and borrowed from it freely to develop solutions to engineering problems that arose in response to the changing cultural, social, and economic realities of a new age. A rising generation of genteel clients made demands on house builders that surpassed their repertoire of time-honored craft practices. Because people after 1700 were generally healthier and wealthier than their predecessors, they no longer placed a premium on the inexpensive, quick-and-easy advantages of the Virginia house system, with its post-in-the-ground framing and riven clapboard coverings. Structures carpentered the old-fashioned way did not disappear overnight or altogether, but they tended to persist in areas settled by poorer planters and people with few genteel aspirations. Earthfast posts and clapboard walls also continued to serve well enough for barns and back buildings. Meanwhile, a flurry of new building activity in frontier settlements in the Piedmont and infill settlements in older areas across the region hastened the spread of new architectural innovations, most thoroughly in towns and cities, but throughout the countryside too, although differently.

Three innovations in the character of building frames appeared around the turn of the century. Each owed something to earlier carpentry traditions in the region. The first, termed "flush framing," was an engineering response to a growing market for houses built and finished in a genteel fashion. Flush frames were built so that the principal timbers in the house—the posts, studs, plates, and beams—were dimensioned to conceal their presence beneath a smooth skin of respectability. With the exception of a few country gentlemen, it was town-dwelling merchants, professionals, and gentry who first insisted on politeness in their houses. Those who lived in the new Virginia capital at Williamsburg and its immediate environs became the region's trendsetters.

Eventually and inevitably, the rural gentry sought to show off their own architectural sophistication. Being more conservatively disposed, though, they favored buildings that took the framework of a house as the organizing aesthetic to achieve the genteel appearance they desired. Instead of hiding structural members, as townspeople did, they accentuated them by deliberately articulating and elaborating their separate parts. Country carpenters often employed the same refined finish work found in town houses: plaster walls, chimneypieces, showcase stairs, and, at times, wainscoting and cornices. Yet the visual effect was somehow different, although not so unfamiliar that its meaning was unintelligible to visiting townsfolk and genteel visitors from abroad. All the same, the articulated frame was always distinctive enough to signal to other country families that the house owner held tradition in high regard.

A third walling type that gained popularity in the eighteenth century was log construction. Swedes and other Northern European newcomers who settled in the Upper Chesapeake during the second half of the seventeenth century brought with them a tradition and knowledge of log building that idled there until it gained traction on the expanding frontier in the opening decades of the eighteenth century. Soon it became the commonplace frontier alternative to the earthfast Virginia house. Logs provided an easy way to raise substantial walls. Materials preparation was kept to a minimum and foundations were unnecessary, two advantages the form shared with the Virginia house. Clay chinking made walls weather tight, and the logs themselves served as enclosure, with no need for siding. These three structural systems—flush frames, articulated frames, and log walls—served as subregional variations across Maryland and Virginia well into the eighteenth century, and flush frame and logs continued in use as dominant types through the antebellum period. An efficiency all three shared was the common-rafter roof. Such simplified roofs remained structurally independent of the frame or log walls over which they stood because each wall system bore its rafters on false plates carried on common joists, a practice borrowed wholesale from the Virginia house of the previous century.

TOWN BUILDING: FLUSH FRAMING

Flush framing has a pedigree older than Williamsburg itself. The earliest known flush-framed dwelling is the Nelson-Galt House, built in 1695, four years before Middle Plantation replaced Jamestown as the new capital city of Virginia and changed its name to Williamsburg. For twenty-five years, the neighborhood had attracted some of the wealthiest planters in the colony. Their influence was decisive in locating the new college at Middle Plantation in 1693 and moving the seat of government there soon after. The move set Williamsburg on the course it followed for the next seventy-five years as the avatar of Georgian fashionableness in the region. Its leading residents had a keener eye than gentlemen elsewhere for visual refinements, which became trademarks of the modern taste in architecture. They were the first of the gentry set, save for a handful of the provincial officials and country elite, to appreciate and to pay for an architectural aesthetic that replaced the post-and-beam construction of seventeenth-century buildings with broad, flat, smooth walls, ceilings, and eaves to which plaster, paint, paneling, moldings, and eventually wallpaper could be applied, regardless of the structural framing members that carried them. All surviving gentry houses built in Williamsburg after 1695 are constructed with flush frames. Yet, not far away, carpenters building a glebe house in 1708 had to be instructed that "all ye: fframe [was] to be sawn & fframed flush, as ye new way of Building is."[25] Patrons in the other Chesapeake capital city, Annapolis, were slower to demand this new look. Although Thomas Larkin's tenement (the Poe House) and the ambitious dwelling of Charles Carroll, the barrister, were both newly built in the 1720s, the Annapolis craftsmen who prepared their framing timbers sized the posts and plates as they always had, that is, as large enough to remain exposed.[26] Builders in the Maryland capital dared not reduce the dimensions of these bearing members until the 1730s, a full generation after Williamsburg led the way.

Flush framing was a direct descendant of the heavy, expensive, fully braced and tenoned English frame. Because the streamlined look they sought required hiding the structure inside wall finishes, the town's flush-frame builders turned back to English carpentry practices to borrow and then adapt four features that lent themselves to a strong but slender frame. Masonry foundations and continuous sills were one; scantling sawn (not riven or left rough hewn) to uniform dimensions was another; bracing was a third; and finally was a system that located principal posts independently wherever they were needed along the walls, not in the strict, regular bays required in the Virginia house. The flush frame was, in effect, an Americanized variation on the English frame: not a twin but a cousin.[27] Regardless, its Old World ancestry was remembered as late as 1737 when the frame of a glebe house in Fairfax County, Virginia, was specified "to be well sawed, and neatly & well set together, after the manner of English building."[28]

Investigation of houses in Williamsburg has revealed how their slimmed-down appearance was achieved. Corner and intermediate posts were made slenderer and studs deeper so that the interior faces of the uprights aligned to make a smooth, unbroken plane on which to apply finishes. Wall posts were no longer set on regular bay spacings but were located where needed at corners, door openings, and major partitions and wherever a stretch of wall was deemed too long to go unsupported. Generally fabricated as down braces, tension bracing reinforced corner posts, some intermediary posts, and partitions in larger buildings. At first, only sills and wall plates were left large, as if early carpenters were uncertain that they could be slimmed down and still bear their intended loads. Sills, of course, were hidden under the floor, so they did not interfere with creating smooth planes for finishes. However, plates remained a problem when they projected into the room just below the ceiling. The immediate solution was to conceal them behind a classical cornice, as was done at John Brush's house in Williamsburg, although eventually builders learned to accept narrower plates as well. Sometimes they might cheat out their dimensions just enough to match the thickness of the lath-and-plaster walls below the plates. They were then roughed up with an ax to receive the plaster, thereby eliminating the extra thickness of lath applied to the studs below. This remained a common expediency across Maryland and Virginia well into the nineteenth century.

The way flush frames were intended to work structurally was quite different from the Virginia house system. The new method made the whole wall load-bearing, instead of point loading the bay posts.[29] No longer were studs merely nailers for cladding. They therefore had to be mortised and tenoned to the horizontal timbers—the plates and girts—they supported. The quick-and-easy lap joints common to the Virginia house were unequal to the task. Load-bearing walls

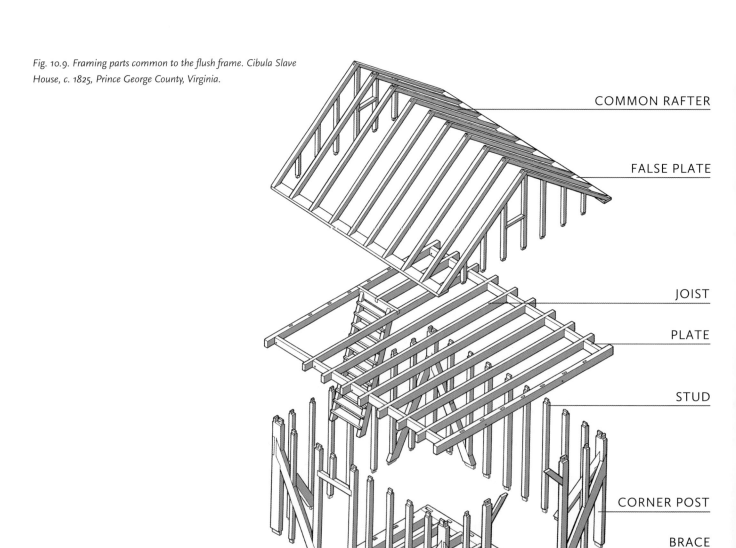

Fig. 10.9. *Framing parts common to the flush frame. Cibula Slave House, c. 1825, Prince George County, Virginia.*

COMMON RAFTER

FALSE PLATE

JOIST

PLATE

STUD

CORNER POST

BRACE

SILL

JOIST

GIRDER

were a prerequisite for the nonbayed structure of the flush frame. They also helped to make the frame a nonornamental part of the building (Fig. 10.9).

Sawn scantling replaced hewn or riven timbers, thereby creating more consistent dimensions, which were critical to the success of the refined house. Uniformity aided in the preparation of interchangeable tenon joinery. Although tenon joints took longer to make than bevel laps, a carpenter could quickly lay out mortises in the plates and sills on regular 20 to 24 inch centers, making adjustments as he went along for wider post tenons and for studs that framed window openings whose spacing did not match the prescribed

centers. Finish carpenters reaped an additional time- and cost-saving advantage from the use of sawn framing materials with trued surfaces (Fig. 10.10). They could install paneling, mantels, and door and window trim with less fitting and greater evenness. Sawing the structural timbers created a more predictable carcass, which allowed for standardization of parts and more control over its cladding.

The most far-reaching benefit of timbers sawn to size was the homogeneity it brought to carpentry. As flush framing gradually spread beyond Williamsburg and later Annapolis, craftsmen learned to cut stock for studs to a standard 2¾ by 3¾ inches (nominally 3 inches by 4 inches), whether for long

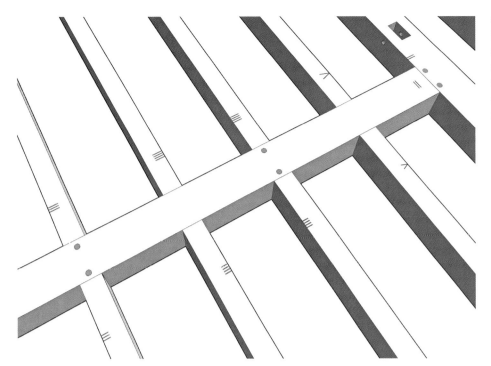

Fig. 10.10. Attic floor framing, Peyton Randolph House, Williamsburg, showing carpenter's assembly marks. By alternating which side of the timbers these marks were inscribed and their size, the carpenter could minimize just how many distinct numbers were needed to create discrete identification for all the framing members.

walls, gables, or interior partitions. Even scantling for rafters and collars in small houses tended to conform to these dimensions by the 1730s. Larger framing members, such as posts, braces and plates, were typically cut in 4-inch thicknesses. Standardizing dimensions allowed sawyers to mass-produce framing material all to regular sizes. Common dimensioned timbers simply needed to be cut to length and fitted with mortises and tenons to be ready for use almost anywhere for walls and roofs.

The practice of stockpiling building materials in lumberyards on the outskirts of towns further encouraged standardization. Tree-ring analysis reveals that by the opening decades of the eighteenth century, builders in Williamsburg assembled precut materials from supplies that had been sawed and stored sometimes three or four years before they were used.[30] Unlike for New Englanders, who were routinely served by water-powered mills from the seventeenth century onward, southerners were slower to replace labor-intensive pit-sawing and invest in mills. Mills had little impact on the supply of lumber until just before the Revolution, and even then it remained a secondary way to cut framing and finish material until the nineteenth century. The shift to milled timbers came first to towns, especially those along the fall line, in the opening decade of the nineteenth century. Country carpenters were slower to change. Not until the 1810s and 1820s did lumber cut at mills finally become the principal source of supply everywhere, although pit-sawn framing continued to be used well into the antebellum era. Hand production by

the nineteenth century simply could not compete with milling, either in uniform sizing of planks and scantling or in the cost of their production.

An invention largely of towns, flush framing took decades to make its way into the countryside. There were a few exceptions among the county gentry who built this way. William and Mary Randolph, for example, built Tuckahoe in 1733 with fully paneled interiors and no exposed framing. It was only a matter of time, though, before most country houses were modernized; most had made the change by the third quarter of the century. As the practice of flush framing spread west and south after 1750, other refinements gained in popularity. Guttered corner posts were the principal improvement made to the flush frame as it matured. A 1799 contract for building a house in Rowan County, North Carolina, described the procedure: The corner posts were "to be hewed nine Inches Square [then] guttered," which meant cutting the forward corner back into the center of the post to create an upright with an L-shaped cross section.[31] While examples of guttering showed up in Williamsburg as early as the 1750s, it was never as widespread in the eastern counties as it was in the Piedmont, where it was popular from the 1780s to the 1820s. Guttered corner posts were a highly engineered solution to a problem created by making flush-framed gable and side walls the bearing walls (Fig. 10.11). L-shaped corner posts provided a perpendicular surface to which lath could be nailed. More importantly, this shape allowed the posts to simultaneously carry the load of the side-wall plate and the

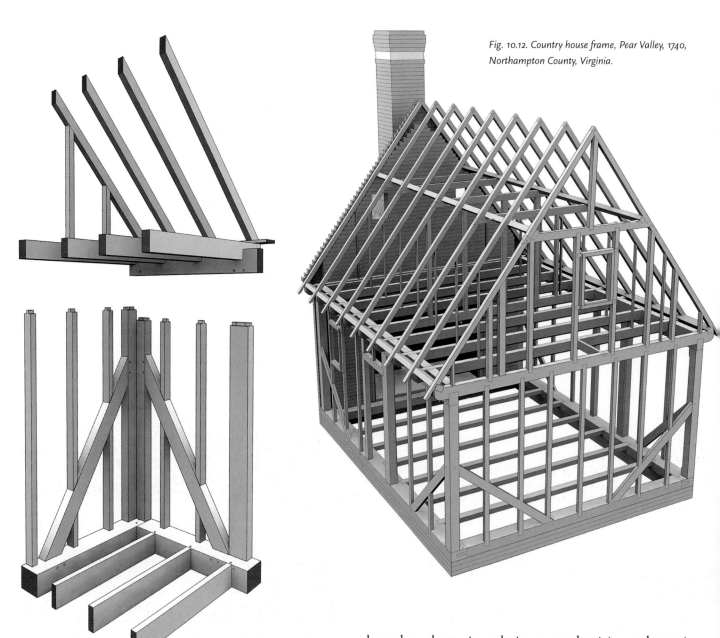

Fig. 10.12. Country house frame, Pear Valley, 1740, Northampton County, Virginia.

Fig.10.11. Guttered corner post, Springdale, 1810s, New Kent County, Virginia.

gable-end tie beams. For similar reasons, intermediate posts were often guttered into a T-shape on load-bearing partitions. Nonetheless, guttering was labor intensive, expensive, and ultimately unnecessary. Normal studs and posts were more than adequate to carry the gable-end weight without wrapping the posts around the corner. Flush framers farther west were reluctant to give up the practice, and guttering can be found there as late as 1840. In the long run, the trend toward lighter framing and simpler joinery led to its extinction.

COUNTRY PRACTICE: ARTICULATED FRAMES

Urban flush framing spread slowly into the Chesapeake countryside, partly because rural builders had already em-braced an alternative solution to modernizing and gentri-fying old-fashioned, seventeenth-century house-building practices (Fig. 10.12). Their engineering innovation was the articulated frame, a modern term for a system that exposed to view the principal structural members of the walls, ceil-ings, and roof—the posts, plates, summer beams, joists, and principal rafters and collars. Often their surfaces were fin-ished to give these refined country interiors their own dis-tinctive and stylish appearance. The exposed faces of posts, beams, and joists in early timber houses such as Pear Valley and Brandy, or brick houses like Lynnhaven, Weblin House, and Criss Cross, were smoothly planed and their leading edges were chamfered or molded with shallow cymas, ovo-los, or beads. Stops were carved at the ends of chamfers and moldings where they intersected other timbers or surfaces. In this respect, the articulated frame carried on a decorative tradition inherited from earlier generations of carpenters whose handiwork survives now only at Bacon's Castle. Even

so, country gentlemen and their builders were not blind to the attention that artisans elsewhere were increasingly paying after 1700 to larger, plainer wall surfaces and uncluttered ceilings. While corner posts and plates still stood proud of plaster walls in articulated-frame houses, smaller dimensioned framing members—studs, braces, and trimmers (the period term for headers) over window and door openings—were more likely to be concealed. Exposed timberwork on these country houses, neatly planed and molded and overlaid with Georgian finishes, integrated refinement with framing in a way that set them apart from the superficial skinning of the flush frames that were transforming towns.

Whereas flush frames looked back to English box-frame carpentry practices, the articulated frame was only half a step removed from the homegrown combination of the light and heavy mix of framing typical of the Virginia house. At first, the two systems were almost identical, except that most articulated-frame houses stood on continuous sills kept dry on masonry foundations. Earthfast posts aside, the family resemblance to the Virginia house system was unmistakable—point loading on the major uprights; non-load-bearing studs bevel-lapped and nailed to plates without mortises and tenons; exterior walls and sometimes partitions covered with clapboards; common-rafter roofs, often with riven boards used as a base for a roof covering of shingles; and finally retention of a heavy false plate to separate wall frames from roof frames (Fig. 10.13). All were frequently replicated in the earliest articulated-frame houses built after 1700, though not invariably. Three early survivors—Cedar Park, Sotterley, and the Matthew Jones House—are reminders that some substantial plantation houses were still raised on earthfast posts, however temporarily (see Fig. 10.6).[32]

Inside, the articulated frame was still proudly shown off and celebrated by gentlemen planters. Refined finishes were usually applied to the secondary frame, finishes that often featured expanses of whitewashed plaster applied on laths attached to the studs between the posts (Fig. 10.14). Planters were almost as quick as their city cousins to install sash windows, classical architraves around door and window openings, decorative chimneypieces, and freestanding staircases with turned balusters and molded handrails. Thus, rural buildings played to two audiences. On the one hand, the forthright presentation of articulated frames exhibited the socially conservative values of country people by explicit association with a respected architectural ancestry. At the same time, its elaboration announced planter families' aspirations to be numbered in the second group, the universal company of ladies and gentlemen.

As the eighteenth century progressed, country carpenters adopted refinements from the vocabulary of city building—sawn secondary timbers, more tenon joinery and fewer lap joints, weatherboard walls and shingled roofs instead of clapboards, and chimney stacks of brick where formerly many had been made of wood and clay. Earthfast posts were increasingly relegated to farm structures, where they continued to be useful well into the nineteenth century. Alternatively, they were replaced altogether with log construction in inferior buildings. This country approach to genteel building should be regarded as the dominant strain in the region through the 1740s, with the flush framing of Williamsburg the exception. Even towns some distance from Williams-

Fig. 10.14. *An elaborate country house frame, Belle Air, Charles City County, Virginia. The hall is elaborated with exposed, chamfered corner and window posts, summer beam, and end girts. The photograph was taken during renovation of the house in the 1950s.*

burg were slow to adopt the newer refinements. Articulated frames remained popular in Annapolis, for instance, through the 1720s; carpenters did not start erecting flush frames in the Maryland capital until the 1730s.

LOG CONSTRUCTION: ARCHITECTURE OF THE FRONTIER

"Hee spoake to me in giles glouers loged hows and hee bid mee speak too my wife that shee should giue Consent to fulfill his lust."[33] So goes a brief but salacious tale of sex, jealousy, and intrigue that unfolded in Giles Glover's Charles County, Maryland, home in May 1663. It was the mention of the house of logs that gave veracity to the aggrieved husband's story. Everyone in court would have recognized it as Glover's, because there were few others in the community who lived in such an exotic dwelling. Glover's house likely cost him no more or no less to erect than did the rough-frame, clapboard-covered boxes more familiar to his neighbors. Instead, it was simply another of those experimental building forms, like so

many of the earthfast variety, that had Old World antecedents and that were tried out in the New World in the seventeenth century in search of architectural solutions to the challenges of living on the frontier. Continental Europe, not England, was the source of log building. With hindsight, no one now doubts that log-building technologies were tested in Virginia and Maryland as they were in other American colonies. But a log house in the Chesapeake region was a very new thing in 1663. No one could have guessed that it would become a major rival to the ubiquitous post-in-the-ground Virginia house.

Since building with logs was unknown to Englishmen, just where Glover got the idea for the unusual house is anybody's guess. Documentary evidence suggests that horizontal log walling was introduced to America by Swedes and other Northern Europeans who settled the Delaware Valley in the middle of the seventeenth century. Log-building conventions in the mid-Atlantic colonies were further reinforced by later-arriving immigrant groups from Northern and Central Europe. By then, though, the practice may already have mi-

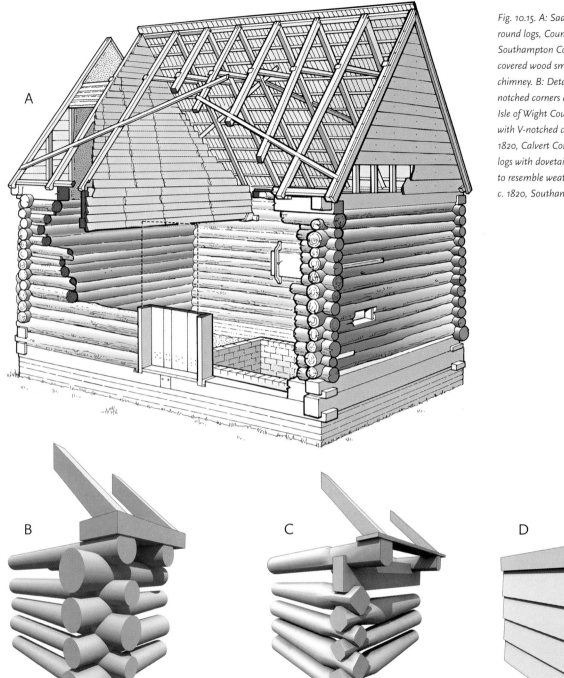

Fig. 10.15. A: Saddle-notched building with round logs, Council Kitchen, c. 1800–1810, Southampton County, Virginia. A clapboard-covered wood smoke hood served for a chimney. B: Detail, round logs with saddle-notched corners at Pruden Corncrib, c. 1840, Isle of Wight County, Virginia; C: Round logs with V-notched corners, Wilson Tobacco Barn, 1820, Calvert County, Maryland; D: Hewn logs with dovetail corners, here oddly canted to resemble weatherboards, Porter House, c. 1820, Southampton County, Virginia.

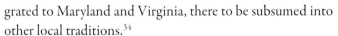

grated to Maryland and Virginia, there to be subsumed into other local traditions.[34]

Had log technologies shown up before the invention of the Virginia house, they might have prevailed. Logs were an efficient engineering solution, one that did not require foundations or siding. Log-building joinery was spare and uncomplicated, and it capitalized on the abundant timber supply everywhere in the Chesapeake region. When logs did become the preferred building material for houses and outbuildings, they were valued not just for sturdiness but

also because log structures were simple and cheap to put up. Log houses became a mainstream carpentry tradition in the eighteenth century only after the efficiencies of the Virginia house roof frame were married to the equally streamlined technology of interlocking log walls (Fig. 10.15).

Several considerations weighted in favor of log construction for ordinary buildings, especially on sparsely settled backcountry frontiers. Logs required little preparation, and log walls did not need siding. A log dwelling could therefore be raised even faster than a Virginia house. Furthermore, they were less perishable. There were disadvantages that had to be considered. The Virginia house-building system accommodated structures of almost any length, but log houses were most manageable if small and limited to one or two rooms. Consequently, log-built farmsteads tended to remove kitchens and service functions to separate structures, leaving behind a one- or two-room house, which soon became the norm throughout the backcountry.[35] Not only did small-scale log houses ease the handling of heavy timbers, but their frequent lack of masonry foundations removed the need for much excavation—a particularly welcome shortcut in the rocky Piedmont region. With few exceptions, such as the earthfast house that James Madison Sr. built at Mount Pleasant in Orange County, the Virginia house could not compete with the efficiency of logs outside the Tidewater region, and it was soon abandoned by settlers on new frontiers.[36]

A sense of just how much cheaper it was to erect walls of log instead of frame is evident in the bill Benjamin Harrison charged Thomas Baughan's estate in 1837 for construction of a gate and a nicely appointed 18- by 20-foot log house near Farmville. The expense totaled $93.49. Of that amount, only $4 was assessed to square the logs for the walls, notch their corners, and raise them into walls. In contrast, just to make and hang the gate and hew its two posts cost Harrison $1 more. Note that the roof frame—likely no more than sawn, 3- by 4-inch common rafters, cost more than the log walls, at $6.26.[37] By this date, log walls simply were a very cheap and sturdy way to create volume. It was rare for log houses to be more than 20-feet deep, and so common joists without summer beams could easily span the depth. The usual solution, then, was to cover the building with a common-rafter roof set on false plates, the roof system having been borrowed from the Virginia house. Most often, too, the gables above the log walls were framed. These could be covered with riven clapboards, or if especially well finished and of more recent date, could be fitted with weatherboards. The Baughan account suggests just how efficient it was to build in log, a powerful reason the form caught on so well on the developing frontier.

William Byrd, in 1728, called log building "the architecture . . . of North Carolina."[38] By that time, it was already well established on the Upper Eastern Shore. Log buildings are consistently present in the more than 1,200 buildings mentioned in the management records of orphans' estates each decade from 1711 to the end of the colonial era for the counties of Dorchester and Somerset. A similar trend can be found for Upper Western Shore counties in their orphan's records. In Baltimore County, for instance, they are mentioned as early as 1703. This document group indicates that log was

TABLE 10.1. Wall Materials for All Building Types, Dorchester and Somerset Counties, Maryland, Orphan Court Records, 1710–1782

MATERIALS	NUMBER OF BUILDINGS	PERCENTAGE
Unknown	640	51.6
Brick	21	1.7
Frame	140	11.3
Frame or post-in-ground	21	1.7
Post-in-ground	8	.7
Log	411	33.1
TOTAL	1,241	100.1

TABLE 10.2. Wall Materials for Kitchens, Queen Anne's County, Maryland, Orphan Court Records, 1708–1797

MATERIALS	NUMBER OF BUILDINGS	PERCENTAGE
Unknown	29	28.4
Brick	2	2
Frame	17	16.7
Frame, brick gable	1	1
Post-in-ground	2	2
Log	51	50
TOTAL	102	100.01

TABLE 10.3. Wall Materials for All Building Types, Bates's Tax List, Halifax County, Virginia, 1785

MATERIAL	NUMBER OF BUILDINGS	PERCENTAGE
Unknown	65	30.7
Brick or stone	0	0
Frame	4	1.9
Post-in-ground	0	0
Log	76	35.9
Cabin	67	31.6
TOTAL	212	100.1

contending for middling house forms in the opening decades of the eighteenth century and was soon deemed appropriate for all but the best of outbuildings, having quickly overtaken earthfast construction for these purposes (Tables 10.1, 10.2). Log makes up a third of the total known and unknown wall systems in Dorchester and Somerset, while post-in-the-ground and frame buildings together account for fewer than 14 percent. The 1798 direct tax, for which documents covering several Maryland counties survive, gives a more nuanced view of how log buildings were distributed. The record for

Fig. 10.16. *Log Slave House, Sotterley, 1830s, St. Mary's County, Maryland. A regional peculiarity of southern Maryland was to use earthfast posts pegged to the logs to keep them in alignment instead of the more conventional internal pegs.*

Baltimore County shows that 71 percent of all dwellings that were listed—those with values over $100—were log, while only 15 percent were of frame construction, which might also include earthfast buildings. But if the four westernmost hundreds that eventually formed Carroll County are separated, a staggering 92 percent of their buildings are log. Clearly, by this time, log was simply the idiom of eighteenth-century frontier architecture.[39]

The direct tax list also survives for some of the older established eastern counties, such as Prince George's. Here, only 22 percent of the dwellings are made of log, while 52 percent are noted as frame and 18 percent are listed ambiguously as "wood." Although log was creeping in, it did not take over in the same way as on the Upper Eastern Shore and in the newly expanded regions of the Piedmont.

Documentary data of this type is thinner for Virginia. Certainly, building in log was rare in towns and common in Southside and the Piedmont. One surviving record group with building descriptions is that collected by James Bates for his tax district in Halifax County in 1785, in which he distinguished between frame, log, and cabin construction—a pejorative term for structures of inferior quality in build and material, no matter their walling type.[40] There were no masonry structures listed, and a mere 2 percent were framed. The rest were nearly evenly divided between log, cabin, and undesignated. The Bates material suggests a similar pattern to what was revealed north of the Potomac River, that remote areas of Virginia also placed a heavy reliance on log instead of earthfast construction for ordinary buildings by this late date (Table 10.3).

Building a log house began with the selection of trees and the fashioning of them into usable timbers. Pine is the most common material found in surviving nineteenth-century buildings, although occasionally hardwoods such as oak were

used. The trees were dressed into usable logs by one of several methods. In ascending order of complexity, they included logs left round with the bark on, debarked logs, timbers split into two, trees hewn or sawn on the two vertical faces, and ones hewn on all four faces. End conditions also varied, from rough ax cuts made at the time of the trees' felling to the ends sawn neatly in a straight line after the walls were assembled. The various methods of preparing the logs allowed farmers to select degrees of refinement and simplicity to fit their budget and functional needs (see Fig. 10.15).

If not hewn square, the logs were laid with the butt and top ends alternating back and forth from one end of the building to the other in order to keep the wall relatively level. The corners were locked tight with one of a large selection of ways to notch them. Notching differences were selected as a way to regulate expense and elaboration, but they were also limited according to how the logs were prepared. For instance, saddle notching was a common, inexpensive choice for round logs, while a form of dovetailing only worked well with squared logs. V-notching could be used for either.[41] In addition to corner notching, walls need secondary reinforcement to keep them in alignment. In some areas, earth-

fast posts, tied into the horizontal logs, provided additional strength (Fig. 10.16). The most common solution was to lock them together with vertically set pins that tied one course of logs to the next (Fig. 10.17). Wall stability was also vulnerable to the insertion of doorways, windows, and fireplace openings. These cuts were generally treated by pinning or spiking a stout plank about 2 inches thick and as broad as the thickness of the wall to the ends of each cut log. These planks could also double as the jambs for doors, shutters, and sash openings. A quite rigid system was created by using spiked planks, running pegs vertically through the wall, and by stiffening the corners with interlocking joints.

Buildings were usually chinked in some fashion, except for those agricultural buildings that required gaps between the logs, such as tobacco barns and corn houses. Small scraps of riven boards, or pieces of stone in regions where they were available, could be wedged into large interstices, which narrowed the expanse that needed filling. The filling was then usually completed with a clay mix not unlike that used to fill walls and pack eaves in the Virginia house. Most often, these troweled joints became the final wall finish, both inside and out, unless they were additionally coated with whitewash.

Log construction was an unrefined building convention, born of rustic European traditions and used principally throughout this era for secondary structures and storage buildings or for dwellings that housed both master and slave when there was no pretension of politeness. Eventually some aspiring farmers pushed to create a local version of the genteel house in log, particularly in the nineteenth century. The house William Baynham had built about 1840 at Springfield in Essex County is one example. Its logs are neatly squared; it has a wooden floor raised on wooden piers; and it has a framed center passage flanked by two neatly finished rooms, each constructed as separate log pens (Figs. 10.18, 10.19). In the same tradition that neighbors embraced in their frame houses, Baynham's had a heated entertaining parlor on one side of his passage and an unheated chamber on the other. A nicely joined staircase rose to the attic story, which included two more chambers, one with a fireplace, the other with none. Baynham was no country bumpkin. His wealth placed him in the top third of property owners in this old Virginia county. When he built the house while still early in his wealth-building years, he was taxed on twenty-three slaves, four horses, and a "coachee."[42] Others with social aspirations found different ways to add respectability to their log houses. Some clad them with clapboards, thereby masking the rudeness of the wall body. One particularly energetic builder erected his dovetail log house with the timbers canted ever so slightly to give the semblance of tapered weatherboards. In spite of those refinements, log continued in the nineteenth century as a dominant rural convention that was a cheap substitute for frame building, rarely rising to a degree deemed genteel.

ROOF FRAMES

Common-Rafter Roofs

Several aspects of seventeenth-century carpentry traditions carried over to the new century virtually unchanged. One was the depths of buildings. It was almost as unusual for a Chesapeake house to be more than 20 feet deep in the eighteenth century as it had been before 1700. Of 328 houses, outbuildings, barns, and other structures recorded in Bates's Halifax County survey, only two buildings were deeper than 20 feet—a 28- by 42-foot dwelling and a large barn.[43] From an engineering point of view, such narrow buildings meant

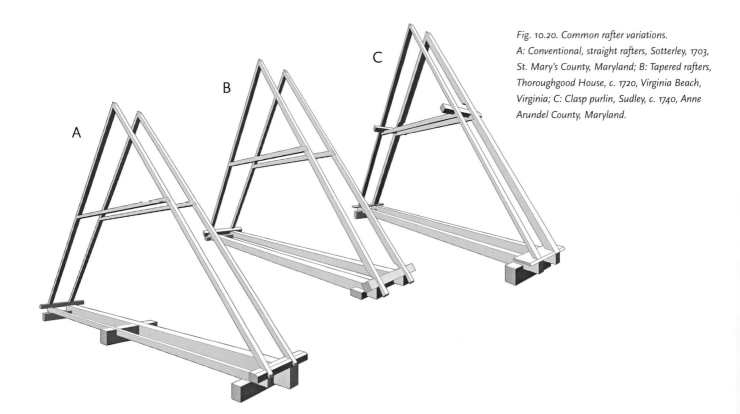

Fig. 10.20. Common rafter variations.
A: Conventional, straight rafters, Sotterley, 1703,
St. Mary's County, Maryland; B: Tapered rafters,
Thoroughgood House, c. 1720, Virginia Beach,
Virginia; C: Clasp purlin, Sudley, c. 1740, Anne
Arundel County, Maryland.

that the common-rafter roof continued to work just as well in this new era, despite the greater number of architecturally and socially ambitious houses. The lower ends of common rafters could be exposed or shaped and chamfered for country taste or boxed behind a classical cornice for city folk. Inside, rafters and collar beams could be lathed and plastered to hide them from view. Rafter scantling on eighteenth-century houses continued the earlier convention of being small and lightweight. Rafter pairs were merely joined at the ridge, nailed to false plates at their feet, and linked together by a collar beam that was either half lapped, dovetail lapped, or, on rare occasions, tenoned and pinned to the rafters.

Convention did not prevent some innovation, and the common-rafter roof system underwent a few improvements in the eighteenth century. Rafters in smaller buildings were often still half lapped at the ridge and either nailed or pinned, probably reflecting a close link to their Virginia house frame ancestry. More surviving examples, though, are joined with an open mortise and tenon or bridle joint and are pinned. Rafters in fine buildings were sometimes tapered from approximately 5 inches in depth at their feet to about 3 inches at the ridge. The Thoroughgood House in Virginia Beach (about 1720) is an early example. Tapering had been a common way to treat the principal rafters in heavier roofs, but by the late 1710s the convention carried over to some common-rafter roofs as well. Whereas a few builders experimented with clasp-purlin roofs in which common rafters were supported by horizontal purlins without principal trusses, as

were frequently seen in simple buildings in England, they proved to be an unnecessarily complicated engineering solution for Chesapeake carpenters. These variations, however, did little to change the general character of common rafter roofs, which remained a mainstay of Chesapeake construction through the nineteenth century (Fig. 10.20).

The sudden popularity of shingles around 1700 gave rise to various roof underlayments. Clapboards could serve as a base for shingles and still provide the lateral stability they had long given seventeenth-century houses. They were frequently used that way through the middle of the eighteenth century.[44] Yet, almost from the start, carpenters charged with hanging shingles had other more practical covering solutions. They often sheathed the roofs of finer houses with wide boards, especially in Virginia. These they sometimes ciphered (creating tight-fitting bevels on adjoining horizontal edges); other times they simply butted them together. Both techniques required the pit-sawing of large planks, a laborious task, but one that left an even surface on which to nail the shingles. This was not a new idea. New Englanders had long been laying sawn planks as a substrate for shingles. Officials in Billerica, Massachusetts, ordered a house to be built in 1667 with a roof to be "covered with bords, chamfered [ciphered] and after shingled."[45]

Board roofs made sense in a region where mill-sawn stock came readily to hand. Sawmills were scarce in Virginia and Maryland, and pit-sawn lumber was expensive. Consequently, Chesapeake carpenters looked for alternatives.

Shingles hung on laths were one. Made from either riven stock or narrowly sawn planks, the smaller dimensions of laths reduced the cost of construction. In all cases, laths or sheathing continued to provide the lateral bracing for the roof that clapboards once did. The stiffening was frequently reinforced with a lightweight wind brace, usually run on a long angle and either let into the upper surface of the rafters before the laths were installed or nailed to their undersides.

The growing preference for shingle coverings affected roof pitch and the spacing of the rafter pairs. Water that wicked up where clapboards overlapped had been a chronic problem in the roof coverings on the Virginia house. Carpenters' favored solution was to pitch the roof steeper, from 47 to 52 degrees, if early nineteenth-century clapboard roofs can be used as a guide. Shingles tolerated a gentler slope. A 45-degree rake became the preferred choice for polite buildings in town and country throughout the eighteenth century and remained the standard for many rural buildings well into the nineteenth century. This lower slope still provided dwellings of sufficient width with a habitable upper floor, one with ample headroom, which encouraged the use of attic chambers.

Clapboards, whether they were the primary covering or an underlayment for shingles, needed narrowly spaced rafter pairs for support. Rafters were often set on 20-inch centers to accommodate the standard 5-foot clapboard, compared to the more generous spacing—2½ feet—between the studs to which wall clapboards were nailed. The closer space on the roof was an advantage since it minimized the tendency of the underlayment to spring back and forth when workmen hammered on the shingle nails. The spacing could be widened when laths or sheathing were put down first. Sawn boards could be of any reasonable length and depended less on uniform rafter spacing. Moreover, there was little significant play in these boards, which were usually about 1 inch thick. The 24 inches that became the standard measure between stud centers for weatherboarded walls soon extended to roof frames and the spacing between rafters. Needless to say, such regularity could be adjusted to make room for chimneys and dormers. While more time and attention was given to the joinery of the collars and ridge, the trade-off that made these new roofs affordable was that less material was needed to cover the same square footage.

The false plate was the one element in the roof frame that was greatly altered by the spread of fashionable architecture. The desire for classically inspired ornament focused attention on the visual connection between roof and wall frame. That led to less obtrusive treatments of the false plate, still a key structural element in supporting a roof frame. A handful

of early eighteenth-century buildings chronicle its development. At Cedar Park, in Anne Arundel County (1702), a crown molding runs along the foot of the rafters; the false plate was beveled to make a better seating for that member. Nonetheless, the country carpenter who built Cedar Park saw no reason to hide the joist ends or the bottom of the false plate, and they remained uncovered. A decade and a half later and, most importantly, a carpenter working in town in the new flush-frame mode also beveled the false plates to take a crown molding on a tenement that he was building for William Robertson in Williamsburg (which later became the Peyton Randolph House). In this case, though, the client wanted a proper boxed cornice, complete with fascia, soffit, bed mold, and modillions, and the bottom of the false plate was simply squared off. The false plate and the eaves assembly were thereby completely concealed inside this classical feature. This cover-up solution to the problem of hiding the rafter ends, ingenious as it was, lacked the novelty and sophistication that carpenter James Morris achieved a few years earlier at nearby Bruton Church (1714–15). Morris had the bright idea to set the feet of the common rafters on a false plate that was nothing more than a thin board, notwithstanding the large span of the roof. Soon the lesson learned at Bruton—that common rafters needed no more bearing than a board false plate seldom more than 1 inch thick—spread to other professional carpenters working in town and eventually to the countryside. There it became compulsory for polite buildings with boxed eaves. By the nineteenth century, few structures except for farm buildings were framed with anything other than a board false plate (Fig. 10.21).

Country gentlemen were less inclined in these early years to hide their eaves than were city folk. Even though they too desired some type of ornamentation, they preferred to express the frame on the exterior just as it was inside. The novel solution was an abstract version of the eaves treatment at Cedar Park. The joist ends, which jettied over the wall, were rounded and sometimes lightly chamfered and stopped on the edges as highlights. The crown molding was eliminated, and the false plate was made square in cross section but set on the diagonal, creating what architectural historians now call a tilted false plate. It was innovation purely for delight. The earliest known example survives in a new room added to Sotterley in 1715. That one is neatly planed, chamfered, and stopped on the underside between each joist bay. Country builders relished the use of these tilted false plates, until finally flush framing superseded the conventional articulated frame in the third quarter of the century. By then, their clients had begun insisting on boxed eaves anyway. Thereafter,

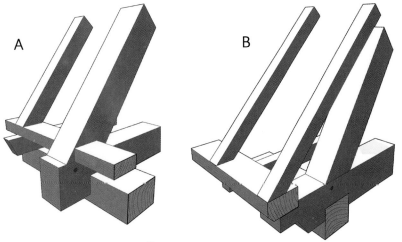

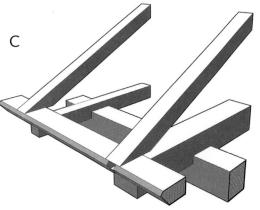

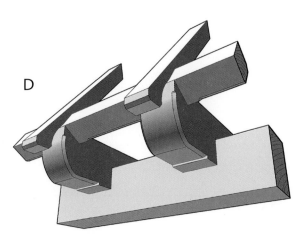

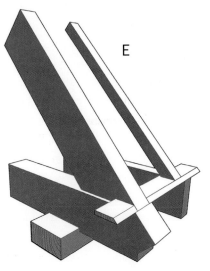

Fig. 10.21. Stylistic evolution of the false plate. A:Heavy board false plate, Bacon's Castle, 1665, Surry County, Virginia; B: False plate shaped abstractly as a crown molding, Cedar Park, 1702, Anne Arundel County, Maryland: C: False plate beveled to serve as a solid seat for a classical crown molding, William Robertson's Tenement (Peyton Randolph House), 1715–18, Williamsburg; D: Decorated tilted false plate, Period II wing, Sotterley, 1715, St. Mary's County, Maryland; E: False plate reduced to a thin board for the common rafters, Bruton Parish Church, 1714–15, Williamsburg.

tilted false plates were relegated more and more to outbuildings and barn construction.

Girt Roofs

Seventeenth-century roof framers had two ways to span houses deeper than about 20 feet. A principal-rafter roof system was one; an M roof was the other. Bacon's Castle, a substantial brick house 25 feet deep, was framed with a principal-rafter roof, often called a "girt roof" in period literature. Although it differed little from similar trusses in large houses in England and New England, the roof at Bacon's Castle incorporates some refinements peculiar to Chesapeake engineering. The large rafter pairs, trussed with collar ties, were arranged in regular bays about 10 feet apart. The principal rafters taper from 9 inches at their feet to 5½ inches at the ridge in order to lighten the roof and limit deflection along the lengths of the rafters. Horizontal purlins joined the sets of principal-rafter pairs together and interrupt the run of common rafters that filled the spaces in between (Fig. 10.8). New England carpenters had a ready supply of mill-sawn planks that they placed on roof slopes, setting them vertically over multiple purlins and thereby eliminating the need for common rafters altogether. Chesapeake carpenters did not always have that luxury. Instead, they married the region's common-rafter roof system to the girt roof, which allowed for spaced laths.

To carry the common rafters, the typical trussed roof included a single row of purlins that were staggered from one bay to the next. Purlins efficiently transferred the roof load carried by the common rafters to the principals. That load was then borne by the mass of the walls below in masonry buildings like Bacon's Castle. For early frame buildings, the weight of the roof was generally concentrated on the posts since they were the only wall members designed for such compressive loads. The complicated connection of rafter to tie beams could not be avoided in this truss design, and so

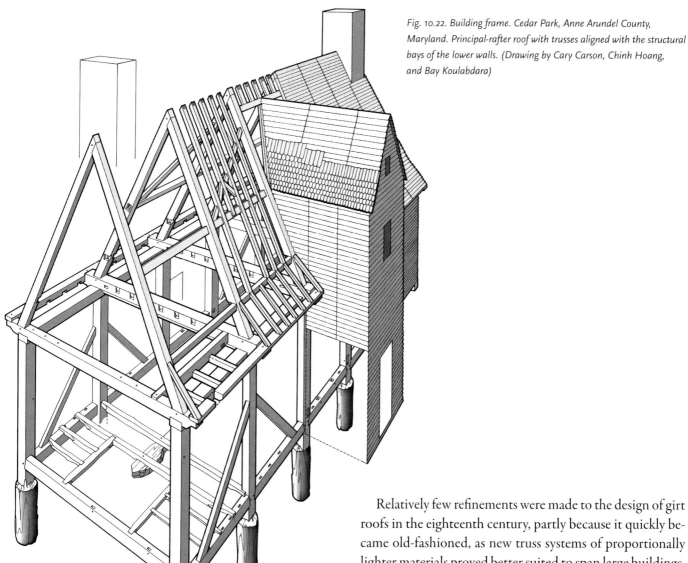

Fig. 10.22. Building frame. Cedar Park, Anne Arundel County, Maryland. Principal-rafter roof with trusses aligned with the structural bays of the lower walls. (Drawing by Cary Carson, Chinh Hoang, and Bay Koulabdara)

the principals were tenoned and pinned to them. Notwithstanding, Chesapeake framers usually ran false plates along the upper ends of the common joists between the principals as a seat for the secondary rafters. Structurally, these common rafters were superficial in much the same way early wall studs were. Heavy wind braces that connected principal rafters to purlins had been all but forgotten in Britain by this time, but here carpenters could not trust lightweight clapboards or even sheathing to keep heavy roof frames from racking. Consequently, braced roofs can be found in Virginia and Maryland structures until girt roofs ceased to be built at the end of the eighteenth century (Fig. 10.22).

Relatively few refinements were made to the design of girt roofs in the eighteenth century, partly because it quickly became old-fashioned, as new truss systems of proportionally lighter materials proved better suited to span large buildings. One small improvement was the use of bent or "kneed" principals, an engineered solution popularized in Britain. Joseph Moxon illustrates the bent principal in his frontispiece of *Mechanick Exercises or the Doctrine of Handy-Works* in association with a king-post truss. It translated well to girt roofs because it placed roof loads directly on the wall plates and not on cantilevered joists.[46] Classical cornices could easily be boxed off, and short rafter spurs could be used to draw the roof covering down over the cornice without shifting significant loads to the ends of the joists. That had been a concern when carpenters first jettied eaves to receive the addition of newfangled cornices. An early set of bent principals spans the roof over Bruton Church in Williamsburg at the gables to accommodate now-missing parapets. Occasionally, they were used to construct trusses for dwellings as well. Sweet Hall, in Virginia, and Cloverfields and Ocean Hall, in Maryland, all dating to the 1730s, are surviving examples. The problem was that bent principals required excessively large timbers to haul to the saw pits and were an awkward shape to cut. Since carpenters already built houses of comparable

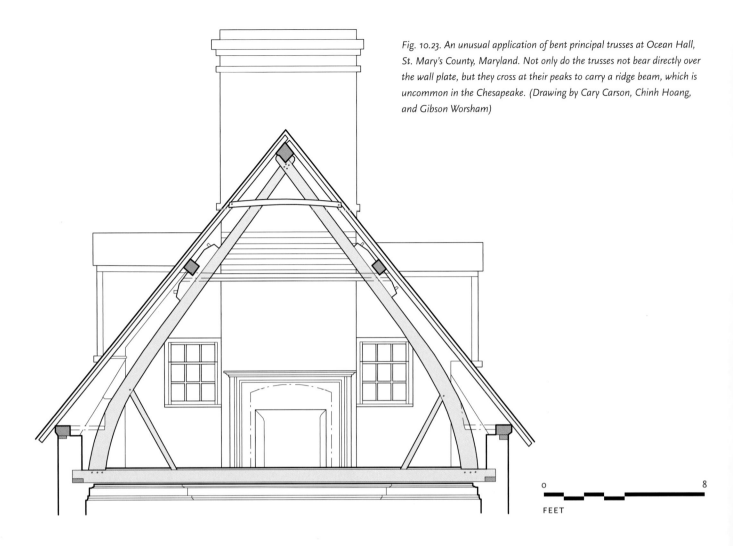

Fig. 10.23. An unusual application of bent principal trusses at Ocean Hall, St. Mary's County, Maryland. Not only do the trusses not bear directly over the wall plate, but they cross at their peaks to carry a ridge beam, which is uncommon in the Chesapeake. (Drawing by Cary Carson, Chinh Hoang, and Gibson Worsham)

0   8
FEET

size without such kneed rafters, this variant form was soon abandoned (Fig. 10.23).

House builders made a second improvement to the principal-rafter system in the eighteenth century that better suited the new age of larger houses, center passages, and asymmetrical plans. Instead of arranging trusses in regular bays and standing them over wall posts, the newer practice aligned them with cross walls regardless of their intervening spans. Gable ends and the two walls that formed the passage were usual places for these truss locations, an improvement that carried over to other new truss forms. This scheme provided the tie beams with extra support from below, which was especially important in double-pile houses. Additional trusses might be needed between them in long buildings, but even they were usually additionally supported by the lower floor partitions. Girt roofs lingered in the repertoire of country builders, who sometimes dressed up exposed primary timbers with planed surfaces, chamfers, and stops through the middle of the eighteenth century, as upstairs chambers assumed greater importance than they had had before.

M Roofs

M roofs were the other traditional option that eighteenth-century builders used to cover very large spans, especially those over double-pile dwellings. A 1683 sketch of Governor William Berkeley's Green Spring Plantation appears to show a house roofed with multiple gables, a widely accepted way to cover houses throughout Britain for centuries (see Fig. 6.20). M roofs had the advantage of requiring smaller and lighter rafter pairs, each covering a shorter distance than a girt roof did. Two or more sets of common-rafter pairs were joined to create an "M" silhouette. Their weight was transferred from the valleys of the intersecting slopes to the partitions that divided front and back rooms in double-pile houses. For eighteenth-century builders in Williamsburg, they were a convenient answer to early double-pile buildings like Robertson's tenement and Robert Carter's house on Palace Green. These M roofs created engineering problems that builders needed to resolve. The worst was their tendency to leak along the valley between the interior slopes. In the case of Robertson's tenement, wooden gutters inside the attic collected water from the valleys and ejected it through lead

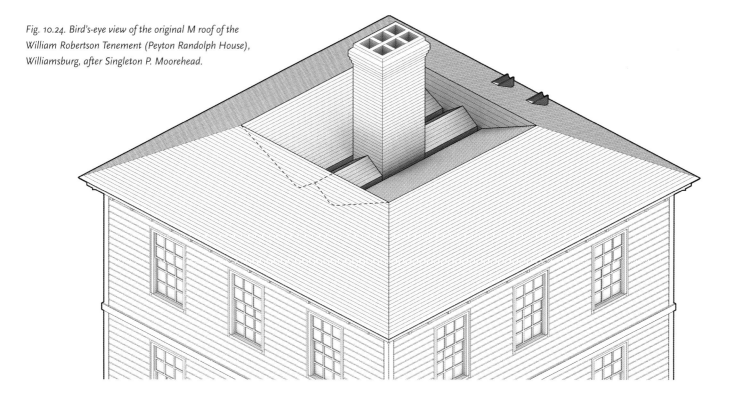

Fig. 10.24. Bird's-eye view of the original M roof of the William Robertson Tenement (Peyton Randolph House), Williamsburg, after Singleton P. Moorehead.

drainpipes that extended through the hips at the ends of the roof. Still, a heavy downpour could easily overflow the gutters and damage finishes in the rooms below. Carter's builders tried something else. They lined the valleys with sheets of lead—a smarter idea to be sure—but rainwater was still directed through the attic before it was discharged outside. Before long, both houses were retrofitted with supplemental roofs built over the valleys to correct this design flaw (Fig. 10.24).

King-Post Truss Variations

A bigger problem than leaky valleys was the greater distance roof framers were trying to span. The ambition to build ever-larger churches and public buildings and grander double-pile houses stretched girt roofs to and beyond their limits. Even M roofs could not make up the difference. The answer was another kind of roof altogether, something that trade books like Moxon's *Mechanick Exercises* called a "king-post" truss. Carpenters raised king-post trusses in Britain and in New England years before builders adopted them in the Chesapeake colonies. The earliest recorded example in this region is the roof of Ware Church, tree-ring dated to 1718–19.[47] The king posts there were not as fully developed as they soon would be, but even so, their longevity attests to their success.

King posts extended the span of tie beams farther than had ever before been practical (Fig. 10.25). Many trusses were made of yellow poplar, a lightweight wood that was strong in tension. Angled struts tenoned to haunches set low on the king posts themselves served as compression members to underpin rafters halfway along their length. The rafters were tenoned and pinned to the peak of the king post, which also was tenoned to the tie beam to help reduce deflection along its length. Otherwise, such trusses resembled a girt roof: the rafters were tapered; they were mortised into tie beams; purlins carried common rafters; and they in turn sat on false plates. Likewise, heavy wind braces strengthened the rafter-and-purlin connections, and rafter pairs were spaced relative to the plan, just as other principal-rafter roofs were doing in the second half of the eighteenth century (Fig. 10.26).

The king-post system introduced one novelty that became standard practice for simple roofs in the nineteenth century—the use of ridge boards to join common-rafter pairs at their upper ends. Builders of principal-rafter roofs had always insisted on a bridle joint. The new thinking questioned whether a carpenter's time was well spent carefully fashioning ridge joints if common rafters were of lesser structural importance. This same logic was soon applied to small secondary roofs such as those used to frame pediments and occasionally dormers. The efficiency of ridge boards was not lost on builders of common-rafter roofs. A carpenter working for John Brice III tried it sometime between 1766 and 1775 when he built a low-pitched common-rafter roof with a ridge board that ran the length of his Annapolis house. Generally though, it was too much to expect this innovation to supersede a tradition more than 100 years old of joining rafters at their peaks, and ridge boards remained rare for non-

Fig. 10.25. King-post truss roof, Brockenbrough House, 1778, Port Royal, Caroline County, Virginia.

trussed roofs until lightweight metal coverings that put less stress on the ridge connection came into regular use in the middle of the nineteenth century.

The king-post truss was a good fit for large gentry houses of Virginia, but its limitations required ever-more-ingenious engineering solutions to make it work for sophisticated dwellings in and around Annapolis. Those newly built in the 1760s and 1770s gave special importance to the second story. The most cosmopolitan of these houses featured upstairs drawing rooms, unlike the ground-floor entertaining rooms typical of even the best gentry mansions south of the Potomac. Fashionable upper-story public rooms pushed servants' chambers and storage into garrets in ways that multistoried Virginia houses did not (see Fig. 8.8). Older-style

king-post trusses obstructed movement through these spaces and needed a new solution to create a large open space.

Moreover, these great Maryland families often built larger houses than those owned by their Virginia cousins. So, in addition to providing enough unobstructed attic space for quarters and storage, roof framers in Maryland were challenged to span enormous double-depth houses. The solution was a queen-post roof, or, in extremis, a king-and-queen post combination. A pair of queen posts were fitted below the collar on each principal-rafter pair to open the lower roof, while the king post and its supporting struts stood on top of the collar to help extend the practical depth of the truss system. Carpenters had to have had considerable expertise to build these ever-more-complicated roofs, but they were not

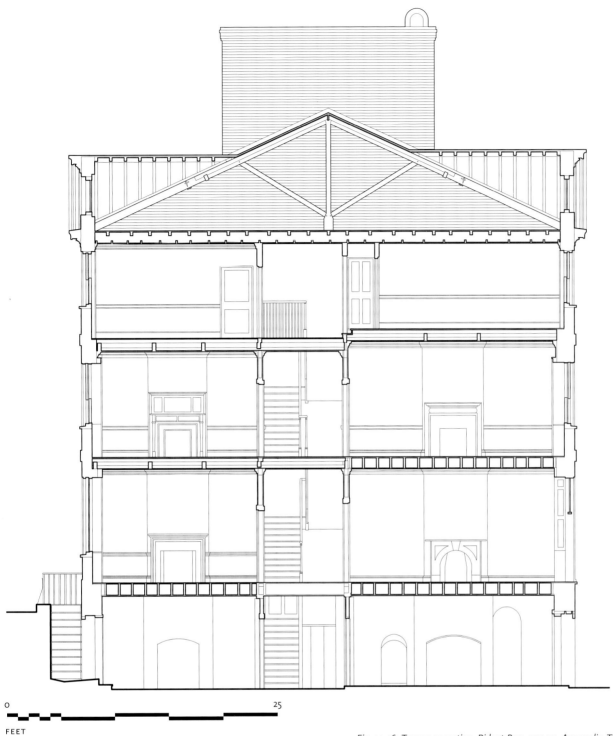

O   25

FEET

Fig. 10.26. Transverse section, Ridout Row, 1773–74, Annapolis. The framing supporting the secondary rooms consists of smaller joists with light timber hangers to carry the ceiling beneath them and to hide the summer beams, whereas the joists supporting the floors in the principal entertaining rooms are carried on full-depth joists. This more complicated system of sizing joists was intended to save on material and was more common in Maryland than in Virginia. A king-post truss was used to span the excessive depth of this town house.

inventing these new solutions by themselves. Similar trusses were illustrated in architectural books, and builders in other regions of America had already used them. Annapolis carpenters simply saw that the king-post/queen-post combination would not only work for them but was a logical extension of what they already knew. Producing the infill framing, adding the wind bracing, and including a false plate for the common rafters was already part of the regional repertoire. It simply carried over to this more complicated structure (Fig. 10.27).

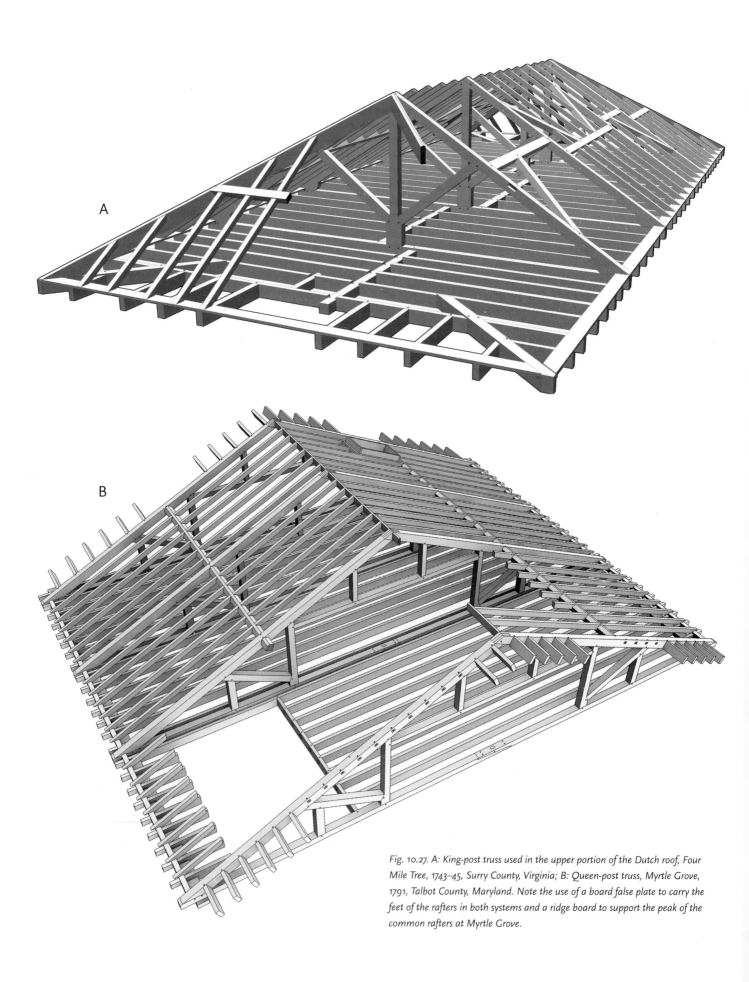

A

B

Fig. 10.27. A: King-post truss used in the upper portion of the Dutch roof, Four Mile Tree, 1743–45, Surry County, Virginia; B: Queen-post truss, Myrtle Grove, 1791, Talbot County, Maryland. Note the use of a board false plate to carry the feet of the rafters in both systems and a ridge board to support the peak of the common rafters at Myrtle Grove.

Fig. 10.28. Dutch roof, Pemberton Hall, 1741, Wicomico County, Maryland.

Dutch Roofs

Leading Annapolis householders may have assigned more exalted importance to their upper floors than others in the region, but everywhere in Maryland and Virginia, families sought greater comfort and privacy in their own lodgings as well as in the accommodations they offered to guests. Single-story houses still dominated, but ladies and gentlemen learned to give themselves more headroom in upstairs chambers by covering a one-story house with a Dutch or gambrel roof (Fig. 10.28). A roof built of two levels with the lower slope steeper than the upper combined with dormers to make a generous and well-lit chamber floor at less expense than a full two-story house. At first, Dutch roofs tended to be used on larger houses that were two rooms deep.[48] By the 1780s and as late as the 1820s, they were a common alternative for even modest single-pile dwellings.

"Dutch roof" was the term used locally until Chesapeake builders borrowed "gambrel" from northerners in the early nineteenth century. The form can be traced to southeast England, where Low Country influence in the seventeenth century gave rise to roofs double pitched on all four elevations. In Britain, it was commonly called a "mansard roof," after the French architect François Mansart, who popularized it.[49] Dutch roofs in Virginia and Maryland tended to be double sloped on the two long elevations and not on their ends, although some did have jerkin head or clipped gables,

as seen, for instance, at Four Mile Tree in Surry County. Shirley, another country seat in Virginia, was given a rare and voluptuous double-pitched roof in the mansard style in 1738 (see Figs. 15.16, 7.17).

The Sands House in Annapolis has an unusual Dutch roof and may have been built in the 1730s, if not earlier.[50] It appears to represent an experiment by carpenters before a regional engineering solution was fully developed. It was built with principal-rafter pairs along the lower slope, each tenoned to an associated tie beam. But unlike all other known examples, common rafters were omitted in favor of multiple purlins on this level. The purlins at the Sands House were most likely intended to carry side-lapped shingles without using a sheathed underlayment, making it quite different from what became the Chesapeake convention.[51]

The Sands House frame may owe its unusual features to its early date. Yet another early Dutch roof house at Rural Plains, tree-ring dated to 1724–26, more closely resembles the system that became dominant throughout the region from the late 1730s into the 1750s.[52] Its Dutch roof was a modified version of the common-rafter roof, a system that included a trapezoidal framework to form the lower roof tier. Often, as was the case here, the frame was made of common rafters, to which a top chord was then tenoned. The set of lower rafters was nailed to a false plate. Ashlers, the period term for knee wall studs, buttressed the rafters near the eaves

Fig. 10.29. *Roof, Callander Croft House, 1852, Accomack County, Virginia. True story-and-a-half frames in which the loft floor joists are dropped lower than the plate are rare in the Chesapeake. Although known from the eighteenth century, most were built in the second quarter of the nineteenth century and appeared more frequently in the Piedmont.*

for additional support. The upper roof, also made of a series of common rafters, typically sat on a second pair of false plates that ran across the top chords of the lower roof. What kept the trapezoid framework from collapsing was stiffening from attic partitions, gable-end studs, roof sheathing, and what little reinforcement the upper trusses could add to keep the whole roof in place.

FRAMING IN THE NINETEENTH CENTURY

Country carpenters continued building roof frames much as they had at the end of the previous century. Conservatism led to replication of earlier forms, particularly the joined, common-rafter roof set on board false plates. Roof types for agricultural buildings had their own trajectory. Features once deemed stylish for dwellings were eventually refashioned for

use in corn houses, granaries, and barns. New technologies entailed risks and therefore costs associated with them that did not need to apply to secondary buildings. One was the common practice of using tilted false plates for work buildings from the end of the colonial era into the nineteenth century.[53] Once rural builders gave up the false plate as a decorative element in favor of boxed eaves, it lost its association with refined taste and was appropriated for utility. It remained a tried-and-true technology, one that could clearly bear the weight of roofs, even in heavily laden tobacco barns, for instance. It was so successfully integrated into farm building design that tilted false plates were still being used in barn construction as late as the 1820s and 1830s, a half century or more after being given up for common house use.

Steeply pitched roofs are another example of conservatism that persisted into the nineteenth century in agricul-

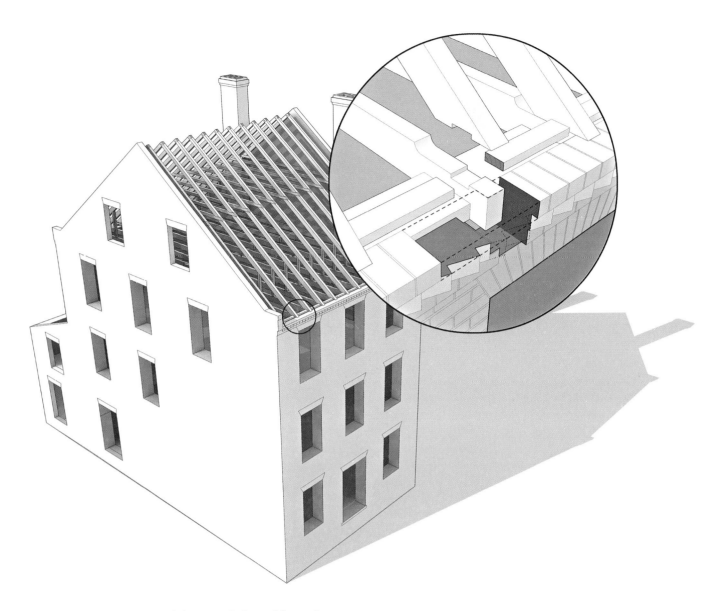

tural buildings. Lower roofs became fashionable in the second quarter of the nineteenth century as builders and clients fell under the sway of Greek forms and as new roof materials made lower pitches possible. Barns and outbuildings were generally left out of this development. Style was costly, and although metal roofs were said to be as competitively priced as shingles, the metal itself and the labor to install it were still more expensive.[54] Moreover, spacious roofs were often needed for storage in agricultural buildings. Therefore wood—usually shingles but also clapboards—remained the dominant choice for agricultural and service buildings. Old-fashioned styles, materials, and technologies were acceptable solutions to everyday building problems as their former social and cultural associations lost their original connotations.

While building in the countryside remained conservative, carpenters in towns were quicker to embrace novelties like metal roofing and readier to turn the carpentry trade into a profession (Figs. 10.29, 10.30). Agricultural journals and building-trade publications promoted truss forms that made

Fig. 10.30. 8 Old Street, 1815–16, Petersburg, Virginia. Common-rafter roofs were stretched in the nineteenth century to cover buildings as deep as 40 feet. Tapered rafters slightly larger than earlier ones and false plates clasped to the feet of the rafters were strategies used to extend the span of the common-rafter roof system. Since it was unreasonable to cover the 40-foot depth without breaking the lengths of the joists, two pieces were used for each truss pair. These crossed at the center bearing wall and a small timber set perpendicular to them was trenched into their tops to lock the assembly together and to keep them from spreading. Solid roof sheathing further stiffened the roof, making it capable of carrying heavy slates and pantiles, which were increasingly common coverings for these town buildings. The inset shows the clasped connection between the rafter feet and the false plate.

use of milled stock from lumberyards and architectural trim from sash-and-blind factories. To master this flood of architectural literature and drawings made new demands on ordinary house carpenters. And yet despite these changes, most houses continued to be roofed and framed much as they had been since the late eighteenth century.

The demise of the building frame as ornament in the eighteenth century was the first in a series of steps that eventually led to and merged with a nationwide carpentry form called "balloon framing." Balloon framing was a structural system that used small but standard dimensioned lightweight scantling and relied on butted and nailed joints instead of tenon and lapped joinery. It became the common way to frame houses after the Civil War, although it was certainly used sporadically in the decade before it. Once Chesapeake builders hid their house frames from view, their appearance lost importance and the trajectory toward balloon framing slowly began. Complicated roof frames, like the king-post and queen-post trusses, taught builders that secondary members need not be elaborately (and expensively) joined. Soon they applied that same lesson to the common-rafter roof, although it took carpenters until the mid-nineteenth century to feel comfortable joining them with ridge boards. Metal roof coverings further reduced reliance on complex trusses and ridge joints. Mill-sawn lumber provided the base for tin roofs, and their regularity contributed to ever-more-standardized material. Despite these advances, vestiges of Chesapeake tradition remained. Regional conservatism encouraged the continued use of tenon joinery for corner posts, intermediate plates, and braces. Larger stock was still preferred over the growing practice among balloon-frame builders to put smaller scantling together to make posts and plates. The most obvious traditional hangover was the use of the board false plate to manage the connection between wall and roof frame, still a superior solution to the balloon-frame technique of bird mouthing rafters by cutting a concave joint in the rafter ends to fit the inside corner of the top plate. The simplification of traditional framing practices had been the hallmark of Chesapeake timber framing for two centuries. By the middle of the nineteenth century, the nation adopted that concept that had been so integral to Virginia and Maryland framing since the middle of the seventeenth century. Exterior cladding and interior sheathing gave modest frames structural integrity. That engineering principle is one of the key elements of modern house framing and can be traced directly to those experiments that led to the creation of the Virginia house in those first decades following the settlement of Jamestown.

11 *Brickwork*

CARL R. LOUNSBURY

Over the course of several generations, Chesapeake brickwork developed distinctive patterns that distinguished it from other regions. Building practices changed dramatically over the two centuries between the settlement of Jamestown and Jefferson's death. This transformation was not driven by new technology. The methods employed by brickmakers during this period for turning clay and lime into bricks and mortar continued to rely upon a laborious repetitive process that was fraught with imprecision and waste. The mechanization of brickmaking occurred only in the second and third quarters of the nineteenth century, making the manufacture of brick less precarious and resulting in a more uniform product. The differences in brickwork from the seventeenth century through the early nineteenth century were not in the nature of brickmaking but in the style of bricklaying and in the increasing popularity of its use. From bonding patterns to the use of shaped elements, brickwork reflected broader patterns in Chesapeake design, moving from an exuberance of decorative surface patterns to a more restrained "neat and plain" aesthetic based on classical design principles.

THE PATTERN OF BRICK BUILDING

Masonry construction provided a visual, structural, and symbolic counterpoint to the wooden buildings that dominated the Chesapeake landscape in the seventeenth and eighteenth centuries. The absence of building stone throughout most of Tidewater Virginia and southern Maryland meant that brick was the only alternative to wood as a building material.[1] Deposits of brick clay were plentiful throughout the region, but the skills and cost involved in making bricks and tiles limited their use throughout the colonial period. Many areas of the Chesapeake suffered a shortage of good brickmakers and bricklayers, which drove up the cost of their services.[2] Lime mortar, manufactured from the burning of oyster shells in lieu of limestone, sometimes proved a scarce commodity and could disrupt a construction project when supplies were ex

hausted. Brick building, therefore, became a symbol of permanence and the material of choice for those who wished to make a statement about their status in this plantation society (Fig. 11.1).

Just as Chesapeake carpenters and joiners developed a regional timber-framing tradition, bricklayers improvised on the visual subtleties and structural features of masonry construction to produce distinctive methods and aesthetic patterns that set their work apart from stylistic details found throughout Britain and the other American colonies. Flemish bond, gauged work, segmental jack arches, molded water table bricks, and decorative glazing could be found in gentry houses in East Anglia, Anglican parish churches in South Carolina, and row houses in Philadelphia. Out of this commonly understood but flexible vocabulary, Chesapeake builders adapted a number of these features and combined them in novel ways that became standard practices, mark

239

Fig. 11.1. Thomas Nelson House,
1730, Yorktown, Virginia.

ing them as characteristic of the regional or even subregional pattern.

As a building material, brick provided resourceful brickmakers and bricklayers with a rich variety of design choices. Brickmakers molded bricks into different sizes and shapes; uncontrollable clamps and inconsistent kilns produced bricks of uneven colors, shapes, and density; and carving, cutting, and smoothing selected low-fired bricks, termed "rubbed bricks," added to the profusion of textures and shapes. By bonding these bricks in different patterns with mortar joints of varying sizes, colors, and finishes, craftsmen erected buildings that often contrasted widely in appearance—from richly articulated dwellings of the most stunning precision to humble utilitarian structures of rudimentary workmanship. Despite these variables, there was a chronological and regional consistency to masonry architecture. Brick building skills, which passed from one generation of masons to the next through the apprenticeship system, tended to reduce experimentation in favor of tried methods. Most clients and their builders preferred to follow traditional forms, choosing to copy the features of known local examples. Rarely did contracts specify the type of bonding that would be used, the width of a mortar joint, or the shape of an arch, leaving these decisions to the craftsmen, who would have negotiated with the client any alterations to long-standing practices. For the most part, bricklayers built "in the usual manner" commonly understood to be appropriate for particular building types or features. They understood the cryptic language of contracts, which called for "neat and plain" brickwork, to mean a sliding scale of decorative detailing for apertures, wall surfaces, and chimneys. Change required explicit instructions. As in most construction matters, these discussions rarely appeared on paper but rather arose and were resolved on the building site.

Across most of the Chesapeake, bricklayers worked with the same structural rules and decorative vocabulary. Differences in the workmanship of a competent bricklayer in Charles City County, Virginia, and his counterpart in Charles County, Maryland, in the 1760s, for example, would rarely appear in the shape of a mortar joint, jack arch, or water table profile but in the manner in which these details were amalgamated. Individual craftsmanship may account for some differences, though it is very difficult to distinguish the idiosyncratic details of a particular bricklayer compared to those of a wood-carver. Though most of the Chesapeake followed similar standards, there were subregional differences in the use of a number of features and in the combination of details. Certain areas can be distinguished for concentrations of unusual bonding patterns, while in others bricklayers fashioned compound-molded stretcher water table bricks, which they laid on edge rather than horizontally. At the upper end of the Chesapeake, features common to Philadelphia and the Delaware Valley appear in bonding patterns and decorative detailing. For example, one-to-three bonding (a course of headers alternating with three courses of stretchers) in secondary walls could be found as early as the third quarter of the eighteenth century in Maryland but did not appear in the Virginia Tidewater until the end of the century (see Fig. 11.7E). At the southern edge of this vast region, much of the early brickwork in eastern North Carolina is indistinguishable from the patterns found along the James River. Some variations from Tidewater forms emerged in western Virginia, where there was a propensity to eschew some of the decorative devices such as jack arches in favor of rowlock courses above secondary apertures. Thicker clays

in the Piedmont also produced bricks of deep red tones. It is easy to overlook these subtleties when so much else was shared in common.

BRICKMAKING

From archaeological evidence and standing structures, Chesapeake brickwork resembled contemporary English forms in terms of size, color, bonding, and decorative details. At the most elemental level, handmade English and American bricks are nearly indistinguishable. The size of English bricks had been standardized in the late sixteenth century and varied little afterward.[3] Seventeenth- and eighteenth-century Chesapeake bricks display a similar range of sizes to those used in England. The average size of a Chesapeake brick was approximately 8½ inches in length, 4 inches in width, and 2⅝ inches in height, making it somewhat shorter in length than the English statute brick but slightly taller. Occasionally, Chesapeake builders worked with smaller bricks, especially imported hard-fired yellow or Dutch bricks used for hearths and paving, but there was little change in the size of bricks over time.[4] Although there were no chronological differences in brick dimensions, there were regional variations. The average size of bricks made farther north in the Delaware Valley, the Hudson Valley, and New England was slightly smaller in length, narrower in width, and shorter in height than those made in the Chesapeake and the Carolinas.[5] Visually, the reduced length and width of northern bricks is barely discernible, but when the shorter height is compounded over several courses, the difference is quite evident. For example, four courses (with mortar joints) in most New England, Hudson Valley, and Delaware Valley buildings measure between 9 and 10½ inches in height, while the same number of courses in most Chesapeake buildings runs between 11¾ and 13½ inches. There are variations within regions, but on the whole, this discrepancy in size between North and South is pervasive through the end of the eighteenth century. Once the pattern had been established, brickmakers kept working in the established tradition (Table 11.1).

The color and quality of Chesapeake bricks stemmed from the individual nature of the raw materials and the abilities of the brickmakers. Brick clay was plentiful throughout the Chesapeake, and brickmakers had no trouble finding raw materials nearby for their projects. Bricks ranged from orange and pinkish red to dark reddish purple, due to the mineralogical composition of the clay, the amount of iron oxide present, the quality of the sand, and, perhaps most important, the temperature and consistency of heat used in firing the bricks—in temporary clamps that were established

TABLE 11.1. Comparative Brick Sizes by Region

LOCATION	GENERAL RANGE	AVERAGE	STANDARD DEVIATION
Length			
North of the Delaware	7¾–8½	8⅛	.359
Chesapeake	8¼–9	8½	.335
Width			
North of the Delaware	3⅝–4	3⅞	.228
Chesapeake	3⅞–4¼	4	.211
Height			
North of the Delaware	1⅞–2⅜	2⅛	.232
Chesapeake	2⅜–2⅞	2⅝	.214

Fig. 11.2. Brickmaking in rural Virginia, c. 1900. Although brickmaking had been fully mechanized in some locations by the second half of the nineteenth century, many bricklayers continued to rely on age-old methods well into the twentieth century, as this illustration exemplifies. Laborers excavated brick clay from shallow pits. A horse-drawn pug mill mixed the clay, water, and sand into a malleable paste. The brickmaker placed the mixture in wooden or iron molds, and children carried the green bricks to open drying beds before they were fired in a temporary kiln. (Chappell Collection, Colonial Williamsburg)

on the building site or in more permanent kilns in brick-making yards located near towns or watercourses for ease of transportation.

Brickmaking depended heavily on chance and the experience of workmen to mitigate many of the uncertainties inherent in the production process. After the clay had been excavated, it was sometimes left exposed during the winter months so that frost could break it up to make it more workable. A brickmaker and his assistants removed intrusive elements such as stones and sticks, tempered the clay with sand and water, and kneaded the mixture into a malleable paste. Once the clay was the consistency of stiff mortar, the crafts-man placed it into rectangular wooden or iron molds that were sanded or wetted to lessen sticking. Laborers removed the green bricks from their molds and laid them out to dry in the open in a sanded bed or under a partially covered open-sided storage shed called a hack. At this vulnerable stage, wet weather could ruin much of the batch before the unfired bricks were clamped or placed in a kiln to burn (Fig. 11.2).[6]

More problems could appear when the bricks were fired in a clamp or a kiln. Clamps were temporary structures erected on or near the building site and were composed of the raw bricks themselves, which were sealed with an exterior coating of mud, fired, and taken down after the bricks

(left) Fig. 11.3. Brick kiln. Colonial Williamsburg.

(right) Fig. 11.4. Lime burning. Colonial Williamsburg.

had been burned and were allowed to cool. Kilns were more permanent structures that were reused on a regular basis in a brickyard, consisting of previously fired bricks that formed part of the structure in which the green bricks were arranged (Fig. 11.3). They contained a series of channels and corbelled arches at the base to allow for a more even distribution of heat. The skills of a brickmaker were tested during the firing. He had to raise the level of heat to modulate the release of steam from the burning bricks and then regulate the temperature of the kiln over several days by keeping it fed with the appropriate amount of fuel and by adjusting the flow of air in the openings. Generally, the longer a clamp or kiln was fired at sustained high temperatures over a period of a few days the denser the bricks became and the better their structural quality. Even among the best brickmakers, wastage was very high—many bricks were underfired, producing soft "semels" or "samels" (half-burnt), or overfired, creating brittle, dark red or purplish clinkers. As late as the antebellum period, when pug mills and other mechanical operations allowed for greater control over the process, a brickmaker considered a burnt kiln an operational success if he lost only a quarter of the total.[7] Colonial bricklayers used many of these wasters in less-exposed areas in a brick wall, either internally or on the inside face, where they were less subject to the harmful effects of weathering. Builders also salvaged the poorly fired bricks and fragments, or bats, using them as infill or, on occasion, as pavers for floors and walkways.

Well-fired kilns helped create hotter temperatures that produced more durable bricks, as well as numerous ones with vitrified or glazed surfaces. Seventeenth-century kilns in the Chesapeake seem to have produced a larger proportion of glazed bricks per kiln than English ones. This was partly due to the fact that English bricklayers began to rely on coal to fire their kilns, which altered the chemical reaction in the firing process. Wood-fired kilns produced potash, an essential element in natural glazing. Compared to contemporary English examples, early Virginia buildings have far more random glazing on their wall surfaces.

If access to hardwood timbers in the Chesapeake set colonial brickmaking on a different course from English practices, further modifications occurred in the production of mortar. The absence of natural limestone in the Tidewater forced masons to turn to oyster shells as an alternative source of lime. The bay abounded in oysters and shell middens, created by centuries of consumption by Indians, manifest in the many places with names referring to oyster shell point or oyster shoals. Oysters were also a staple in the colonial diet, which also increased the supply of shells for lime burners.[8] Bushel loads were carted off to supply the makeshift kilns used to fabricate lime mortar (Fig. 11.4). The origins of the lime is evident in many early buildings, where fragments of shells protrude from mortar joints, yet another subtle

Fig. 11.5. Mortar joints. A: Unfinished joint. Often used below ground, inside, and in areas where it would not be seen; B: Scribed joint. The most common decorative joint from the seventeenth century through the beginning of the second quarter of the nineteenth century; C: V-joint. The form and its variants appeared from the 1790s through the 1840s; D: Tuck point. This most expensive finish often had higher lime content.

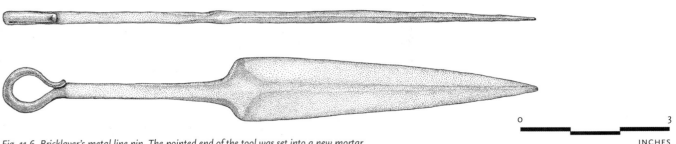

Fig. 11.6. Bricklayer's metal line pin. The pointed end of the tool was set into a new mortar joint at the corner of a building, with string attached through the projecting end loop so bricklayers could align new brick courses. This tool was found in the south pavilion attic at Monticello, Albemarle County, Virginia.

indication of the influence of the environment on building practices.

Bricklayers often varied the amount of lime in a mortar mix, using more of it where there was a concern for strength. For example, the mortar in two of the units in Structure 144, a block of row houses erected at Jamestown in the 1660s, was carefully blended so that there was a greater percentage of lime in the outer joints. This provided greater durability against the elements. Less lime was used in the mortar inside the walls and inner face, where weathering was less of a concern, a practice that continued through the next century

and a half.[9] On exposed exterior surfaces, bricklayers finished the mortar joints with decorative pointing (Fig. 11.5). From the seventeenth century through the first few decades of the nineteenth century, they used an iron tool to scribe a ⅜-inch indentation in the middle of the joint to create the illusion of horizontal and vertical regularity against the irregular edges of the bricks (Fig. 11.6). By the late eighteenth century, this detail began to be superseded by a V-shaped joint that formed an outward projecting ridge. The mason formed this by striking the upper and lower edges to create a sharp point in the center of the joint. The most expen-

Fig. 11.7. Bonding patterns. A: English bond; B: Flemish bond; C: Flemish bond with glazed headers; D: Header bond; E: One-to-three bond; F: One-to-seven bond.

sive finish was a tuck point, which consisted of applying a projecting hard lime mortar layer over the regular mortar and finishing it with either a scribed line or a flat face with rounded edges.

EARLY BRICKWORK, 1660–1750

Changing aesthetics slowly transformed the appearance of Chesapeake brickwork between the seventeenth century and the early nineteenth century. Compared to the late colonial and early national periods, early brickwork tended to be laid with less regularity, though often with bolder flourishes. As in England, these early bricklayers and their clients were less concerned with precision of details or regular

bonding patterns than their counterparts would be in the late seventeenth and eighteenth centuries. They generally gave little consideration to tightly laid walls. The bonding pattern was often irregular, with numerous stretchers and clipped bricks set into rows of headers laid in wide mortar joints that sometimes reached a thickness of over an inch. English bond was the most common decorative pattern in the early Chesapeake, though there were a few notable examples of Flemish-bond buildings as early as the second half of the seventeenth century (Fig. 11.7). In the Jamestown building boom of the early 1660s, bricklayers finished the interior and exterior walls of the cellar of Structure 19 A/B in Flemish bond. Newport Parish Church (c. 1682) has walls of Flemish bond, though the buttresses supporting the body

(left) Fig. 11.8. Glazed headers created a tessellated effect when light reflected off the thin sheen of glazing. The decorative use of glazed headers was popular in the Tidewater during the first three-quarters of the eighteenth century.

(right) Fig. 11.9. Bricklayer's tools, Joseph Moxon, Mechanick Exercises (London, 1703). 1: Brick trowel; 2: Brick axe; 3: Saw; 4: Rubstone; 5: Small square; 6: Bevel; 7: Iron treenail; 8: Float stone; 9: Ruler; 10: Banker; 11: Brick pier to lay rubbing stone on; 12: Grinding stone; 13: Line pins; 14: Plumb rule; 15: Level; 16: Large square; 17: Ten-foot and five-foot rod; 18: Jointing rule; 19: Jointer; 20: Compass; 21: Hammer; 22: Rammer; 23: Crow.

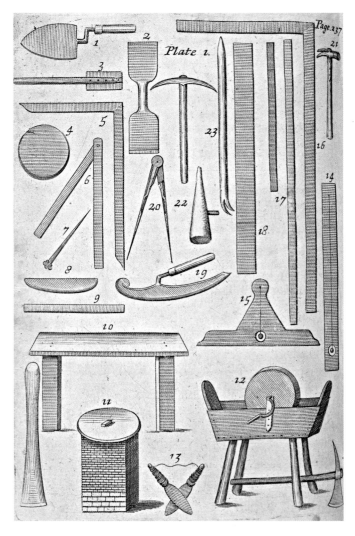

of the church are laid in English bond. At the end of the century, Carvill Hall, c. 1695–1709, was built with walls laid in Flemish bond below and above its water table. Increasingly, after this date, Flemish bond became the most common bond for principal walls and above the plinth and chimneys. English bond was generally relegated to secondary facades, plinths, and interior walls through the end of the eighteenth century.

As if fashioning a giant mosaic, bricklayers often took advantage of the variegated colors of individual bricks to create striking patterns, especially through the selection of glazed bricks, which reflected light with a shimmering brilliance. Flemish bond, with its alternating pattern of headers and stretchers, readily lent itself to tessellated designs (Fig. 11.8). Fully developed glazed header walls did not appear in the Chesapeake until the end of the seventeenth century; the foundations, walls, and massive stacks at Fairfield (1694) in Gloucester County are among the earliest examples. The builders of Carvill Hall also used glazed headers to offset the red stretchers of the Flemish-bond walls, as did the brick-

layers at the Newbold-White House (1730) in northeastern North Carolina.

Chevrons, diapering, and diamonds provided no less dramatic decorative designs, especially in gables and chimneys. An early example of decorative patterning appeared at Malvern Hill in Henrico County (now destroyed), which may have dated to the beginning of the eighteenth century (see Fig. 13.14). A framed house, later encased in brick, the original chimney had a series of diamond patterns of glazed headers. The south porch at Yeocomico Church (1706) has glazed headers rising along the rake of the gable with a glazed diamond pattern in the center of the gable. Perhaps because of its proximity to the Delaware Valley, parts of Maryland have buildings with highly expressive glazing patterns.[10] On the Eastern Shore, the walls of Genesar (c. 1730) and the Fassitt House (c. 1730–40) are decorated with chevrons, while at Makepeace (c. 1725–50) and Beauchamp (c. 1710–30), bricklayers chose a laced diapering of glazed bricks on the gable ends.[11] The penchant for patterning extended south into northeastern North Carolina. The Sumner-Winslow

(left) Fig. 11.10. Some shaped bricks were cut and sawn after being fired in a kiln to create molded shapes.

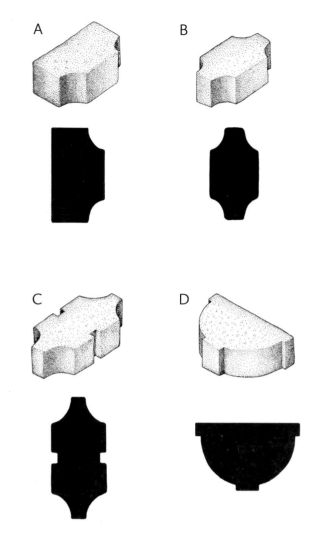

(right) Fig. 11.11. Shaped, cut, molded mullion and jamb bricks. A: Jamb, House 5, Structure 144, c. 1663, Jamestown; B: Mullion, Catholic Chapel, c. 1667, St. Mary's City, Maryland; C: Mullion, Church, c. 1677, Jamestown; D: Mullion, Newport Parish Church, c. 1682, Isle of Wight County, Virginia.

House (1744) has chevrons in its surviving colonial gable end, while the now-demolished Walton House had a series of graduated interlocking diamond patterns laid in glazed headers.[12]

Later Tidewater Virginia examples of bold glazing appear at Brooke's Bank (1751), where the stacks are festooned with large, solidly glazed diamonds, and at Marmion (c. 1754), which has a solid field of blue-glazed headers set within red brick corners in the upper part of the original stack. These two midcentury examples mark the end of this type of decorative motif in the Tidewater, though it survived outside the area into the early nineteenth century. Along with glazed-header walls, it flourished in the period between the 1690s and the 1750s, with the height of fashion for glazed surfaces peaking around the middle of the century, though a number of examples can still be found from the late colonial and early national periods. After midcentury, builders seem to have eschewed their use in favor of more monochromatic surfaces in more ambitious structures.

Most early shaped bricks used for water tables, parapets, and mullions were cut to profile from burnt bricks with a tin saw, brick ax, and other cutting and abrasive tools (Fig. 11.9). Saw and ax marks remain visible on these bricks, indicative of the cutting process (Fig. 11.10). The shapes of these bricks often appear uneven and rough, found on the few surviving seventeenth-century buildings such as Newport Parish Church. Given their fullness in the archaeological record, cut molded brickwork seems to have been very common on the best buildings through the early eighteenth century. The saw marks that run across the mortar between the ovolo bricks in the water table of the 1731 Northampton County, Virginia, courthouse is a late, but good, example of applying the finished shape to the bricks in situ.

The fashion for vigorously carved and molded brickwork with projecting window and door surrounds, cavetto and ovolo brick mullions, and curvilinear gables flourished in England from the 1630s and in the Chesapeake in the second half of the seventeenth century, appearing in a variety of building types as diverse as gentry houses, taverns, churches, and almshouses (see Figs. 2.10 and 6.20) (Fig. 11.11). Termed "artisan mannerism" by historian John Summerson, this bricklaying style used molded and carved brick to create wall surfaces and gables embellished and punctuated with projecting or recessed forms such as balls, pilasters, hearts, cartouches, channels, and niches.[13] These rich surfaces used many of the same forms that appeared in decorative wood-work. Many of these elements were inspired by classical de-tails—plinths, pilasters, and cornices—but were used in a way that simply disregarded the rules of classical ornamenta-tion and proportion, not out of ignorance but with a sense of zest.

The prevalence of artisan mannerism in the Chesapeake in the seventeenth century is difficult to measure, given the pau-city of documentary evidence and standing structures. The excavations of Jamestown, St. Mary's City, and a few other sites have revealed a number of shaped bricks that may have been used in a decorative manner as part of a curved gable, cornice, or window surround, but determining the original context for these features from long demolished buildings is often difficult. A molded torus and cavetto corner of what appears to be a pilaster base was discovered in 1901 in the ex-cavation of the 1670s Jamestown Church, where it had been turned upside down and reused as paving in the central aisle. It may have originally been used as part of a molded frontis-piece that was demolished when the tower was added at the end of the seventeenth century.[14] The many shaped bricks found at the site of John Page's 1662 dwelling at Middle Plantation suggest that the structure may have had shaped parapets or some other artisan mannerist feature, while the ball-shaped bricks discovered in the churchyard at Abingdon Church may point to decorative gate piers or some feature on the earlier church that stood south of the present building (see Fig. 6.22). The first brick church of Bruton Parish also had a double set of curved gables on its west and east facades, with a ball, perhaps similar to the one found at Abingdon, crowning the apex of its churchyard gate.

A rare and celebrated survivor of this style, Bacon's Castle, features twin curvilinear gable parapets with diagonally set chimney stacks and molded eaves, projecting flat-headed window surrounds, a stuccoed and pulvinated stringcourse, and the rudiments of a pedimented frontispiece above the front doorway (see Fig. 2.10). Though rebuilt, Newport Parish Church originally had an impressive series of gables with short stepped battlements on its west and east ends, reminiscent of earlier English ecclesiastical structures such as the Elizabethan St. Michael, built in Woodham Walter, Essex, in 1563–64. Bacon's Castle, Newport Parish Church, and Yeocomico Church also have decorative pedimented or arched entrance porches with projecting brick decorations.

Fig. 11.12. Scribed line on the side of rubbed cornice brick, St. John's Parish Church, 1734, King William County, Virginia. During the repair of the frontispiece in 2011, restoration mason Raymond Cannetti discovered the layout line made by a colonial bricklayer used to cut the cyma profile on one of the bricks that formed the rubbed and gauged frontispiece.

The Yeocomico doorways were built with pilasters that ter-minate with a pyramid capped by projecting ball-shaped ele-ments flanking the south entrance and chancel entry, though the balls have disappeared from the latter.

The popularity of shaped gables followed English trends—fashionable in the third quarter of the seventeenth century but eventually eclipsed by buildings with hipped roofs and classical cornices by the beginning of the next century. Even so, late examples of stepped and curvilinear gables could be found at St. Peter's Church in New Kent County and possibly the present Bruton Parish Church in Williamsburg (1713–15).[15] Though they went out of fashion in the Chesapeake by the second quarter of the eighteenth century, shaped gables did not disappear entirely from co-lonial America. They continued in use in Charleston and the Lowcountry of South Carolina through the American Revolution.[16]

Gauged and rubbed work emerged in the late seventeenth century as a major decorative treatment. Gauged work be-came very popular in London in the 1670s during the re-building that followed the Great Fire and spread rapidly through the southeastern counties in the ensuing decades and can be found in the Chesapeake by the end of the cen-tury.[17] Brickmakers molded soft bricks of a uniform color, which were then baked rather than burnt; they then cut the bricks to precise shapes and smoothed them with an abra-sive tool or material (Fig. 11.12). Rubbed bricks were used to accent certain parts of a facade, especially the water table, stringcourse, cornice, corners or quoins, as well as the arches

Fig. 11.13. A: Rubbed-and-gauged west frontispiece, c. 1732–35, Christ Church, Lancaster County, Virginia. The stonework was from the Aquia quarry in Stafford County, Virginia; B: Detail of the entablature; C: Detail of putty joint with red wash on mortar.

and jambs of apertures (Fig. 11.13A). In some instances, these rubbed bricks were laid with regular mortar joints, as was the case for the water table, jambs, and oval openings in the tower of Newport Parish Church, perhaps the earliest surviving example of this practice. Rubbed corner and jamb bricks, described in England as "rubbed and edged," were often laid with regular joints.[18] However, in certain locations such as stringcourses, water tables, and especially arches and frontispieces, gauged and rubbed bricks were set in very thin joints measuring between $\frac{1}{16}$ and $\frac{1}{8}$ inch, filled with lime putty mixed with fine sand mortar (Fig. 11.13C). The virtuosity of the bricklayer's art was evident in precisely laid jack arches and stringcourses that contrasted the uniform color of these features with the variegated background of the wall. Rubbed and gauged work became the hallmark of Chesapeake bricklaying in the late colonial period. It was far more common in the region than elsewhere in America, and the high quality of its workmanship was rarely matched.

The treatment of apertures varied widely (Fig. 11.14). Flat-headed openings appear as early as the 1660s, such as those with the stuccoed lugged surrounds in the second-story windows at Bacon's Castle, but were more prevalent in the following century.[19] Segmental arches set off by headers or stretchers or a combination of the two were perhaps one of the most common forms in the Chesapeake. However, by the second quarter of the eighteenth century, they had been increasingly relegated to subsidiary openings on more pretentious buildings, which were generally flat headed with splayed arch bricks.[20] The influence of classical design led to the widespread use of compass-headed or rounded windows and doorways in English public buildings in the last half of the seventeenth century. Circular-headed openings were more expensive because they required more labor and skill and were generally limited to the best buildings.[21] By the 1670s and 1680s, Chesapeake builders began to use these forms in ecclesiastical architecture, and at the beginning of

Fig. 11.14. Arched openings. A: Flat jack arch. Straight-headed openings became the most common form for principal apertures in the eighteenth century; B: Segmental arch. Perhaps the most common form for modest buildings, they were primarily used for secondary openings in cellars, side and rear facades, and service buildings; C: Compass-headed. The most expensive form of arched openings appeared principally on public buildings and Anglican churches and occasionally to light stair landings in gentry houses.

the eighteenth century they adapted them for civic buildings as well.[22] Two Virginia churches from the 1680s had compass-headed windows—Newport Parish Church and the first brick Bruton Parish Church. The former has round arched openings with ovolo Y-tracery in the body of the church and lower stages of the west tower, while the third-story openings have rounded arches without tracery (see Fig 11.11D). Bruton had compass-headed windows and a flat arch over its west door.

Beyond its ambitious scale, the construction of the College of William and Mary at Middle Plantation from 1695 to 1697 represents the culmination of a century of brickwork in the Chesapeake (see Fig. 2.1B). The east front facade has five to eight courses of Flemish bond above the water table before it reverts to English bond in the upper sections of the building. This may have simply been the unintended result of a misunderstanding between the bricklayers and the client or evidence of a change order made by the college building committee, who were perhaps unready to accept the novel treatment. The rather sloppy manner in which they were laid recalls the indifferent quality of earlier brickwork. Yet many of the decorative features represent a departure from seventeenth-century practices and herald the beginnings of a new aesthetic, which would reach exquisite refinement in the coming decades in the large plantation houses, courthouses,

and churches. Though there are earlier examples of rubbed work, the bricklayers used it profusely to decorate the corners, water table, stringcourse, and jack arches. Set with thin mortar joints of lime putty and sand, the rubbed and gauged stringcourse and the flat-headed jack arches on the first and second stories set the standard for the future. Along with the use of rubbed segmental arched windows in the cellar and gauged and rubbed compass-headed openings of the hall in the north wing, the college bricklayers established the vocabulary for hierarchical ornamentation that would be followed for most of the next century.

England had a long history of using color washes on masonry buildings to enhance their appearance and to disguise poor brickwork, a practice that continued in the Chesapeake.[23] Workmen applied pigmented red limewash on the walls of Bacon's Castle as well as on the end unit of Structure 144 at Jamestown at the time of their construction in the 1660s (Fig. 11.15A).[24] The cartouche of the Page House had applied washes, as did parts of the walls of Arlington (1674–75), in Northampton County, Virginia (see Figs. 6.23 and 6.25).[25] Red wash covered just the joints at the Mount, a Taliaferro family house, which was built in the last decade of the seventeenth century. The practice became commonplace in the eighteenth century. At Shirley (1738), red wash covered the scribed mortar joints of the Flemish-bond, glazed

or without a base coat also appeared throughout the Chesapeake and across the country from utilitarian buildings and perimeter walls to pretentious dwellings and public structures (Fig. 11.15B).

LATER BRICKWORK, 1750–1840

By the beginning of the eighteenth century, the artisan mannerist style of decorative brickwork lost favor in provincial England and the Chesapeake and was replaced by a more restrained approach to ornamentation. Brick bonding became more regular, and mortar joints ranging from ⅜ to ½ inch thickness became standard. English bond remained the most common method of laying interior face bricks and retained a degree of acceptance for plinths through the end of the eighteenth century. However, it went out of fashion as a finish bond for the principal facades. As in England and other American colonies, Flemish bond became the predominant pattern for exterior walls, foundations, and chimneys by the early eighteenth century. It remained the prevailing pattern for principal facades in the region until the 1840s, when common bond consisting of three-, five-, or seven-stretcher courses for every course of headers or an all-stretcher bond surpassed it in popularity (see Figs. 11.7E, 11.7F).

Indicative of the new aesthetic that transformed Chesapeake brickwork in the first half of the eighteenth century, craftsmen pared back ornamentation, indentations, and undulations so that the wall plane was an unbroken surface. Bricklayers modulated the textures and colors of the wall surface to produce decorative accents. Features that had appeared at the end of the seventeenth century—Flemish-bond walls with glazed headers, rubbed and gauged work, molded water tables, flat, segmental, and compass-headed arches—became the means by which bricklayers exercised their decorative skills.

These standard conventions gave the brickwork of the region a visual coherence, and within the circumscribed range of options there was a clearly articulated hierarchy of treatments. As one of the most costly features in the bricklayer's repertoire, rubbed and gauged work set the standard of elaboration. At the very minimum, splayed, gauged, jack-arch

header walls of the main house. Montpelier, the Madison house in Orange County, has several generations of red wash on its brickwork, dating from the 1760s through the time of its enlargement by the president some forty years later.[26]

Workmen also applied a red wash over the small putty joints of gauged work. The effect was an illusion of uniformity, giving a monolithic appearance to these features.[27] Faint traces of the original color wash are still evident on the rubbed frontispieces at Christ Church, Lancaster County, and at Abington Church (see Fig. 11.13C). By the last decade of the eighteenth century, the practice of applying color washes on joints or on the entire brickwork and the use of penciling as a contrast became quite fashionable, as the penchant for color uniformity and regularity may have inspired its widespread use. Evidence of white penciling appears at the Matthew Jones House, an earlier framed building encased in brick in the late 1720s, where the scribed joints were penciled with a fine white plaster.[28] Continuing the pattern found at the Jones House, scores of later eighteenth- and early nineteenth-century buildings retain traces of penciling. A variety of thick limewashes were penciled over finished mortar joints. Sometimes a thin limewash of red or ocher or other color was put on the mortar before a second, thicker and narrower coat in a similar color or contrasting white (or red) was applied over top.[29] Red and white pencil joints with

Fig. 11.16. Carter's Grove, 1751–55,
James City County, Virginia.

bricks, rubbed to a uniform color, bonded together with thin putty joints, and often coated with a red wash, could be found on the principal openings of the main facade of many dwellings from the 1720s and 1730s through the 1780s and 1790s. In more ambitious buildings, gauged and rubbed work extended to other elements such as shaped water tables, paneled aprons, stringcourses, and, in Virginia, frontispieces. Because of the expense of this level of brickwork, only the largest houses, best churches, and a few public buildings contained all of these elements.

In the early 1750s, at Carter's Grove, Nathaniel Burwell's plantation near Williamsburg, bricklayer David Minitree embellished the two-story brickwork with delicately attenuated gauged and rubbed jack arches in every aperture on the building, from the cellar to the second story (Fig. 11.16). The aperture openings on the two main stories were identical in size and maintained a two-to-one ratio of height to width. The craftsman lightly rubbed the jambs on both stories. He emphasized the hierarchy of the stories by building shorter

jack arches on the cellar apertures, which also blended more closely with the color of the plinth bricks. The rich red bricks of the second-story jack arches extend four courses in height, compared to the five courses of the main story. Typical of many craftsmen in the region, Minitree created the angle of the splay of the voussoirs of the jack arches by measuring from a point below the center of the opening that was equal to its width. This method resulted in a splay roughly 63 degrees at the end of the flat arch.[30]

He capped the plinth with a three-course molded water table. A Flemish-bond cavetto course sits atop a double row that forms a torus, all of which are rubbed and laid in wafer-thin, limed putty joints. However, Minitree muted the contrast between the water table and the walls by choosing bricks of a similar color range. The precision of the water table is matched by a three-course rubbed stringcourse with the same narrow joints. The stringcourse stops short of the lightly rubbed corners. The entrances on both the land- and the river-sides of Carter's Grove are marked by pedimented frontispieces whose gauged bricks are rubbed a deep red and whose thin joints were covered with a red wash. Minitree's work represents the epitome of late colonial workmanship.

Yet, within a generation, the contrast coloring at Carter's Grove was beginning to lose favor. After the Revolution, fewer patrons chose to augment their buildings with gauged and rubbed stringcourses, water tables, and frontispieces. However, rubbed arches remained a staple of the bricklayer's art through the second or third decade of the nineteenth century, and the uniform color of the brick walls became the new aesthetic cynosure. In the 1790s, V-shaped joints began to supersede scribed ones as the preferred decorative mortar finish, a gradual switch that occurred over the next thirty years (see Fig. 11.5C).

Because far more buildings survive from the late colonial and early national periods, there are a number of recognizable differences in the bricklayer's art in Virginia and Maryland. This geographic division is not rigid, however, as brickwork in some areas of Virginia that border the Potomac River and the Eastern Shore display certain affinities with patterns that became common in Maryland. Conversely, the brickwork in sections of southern Maryland appears nearly indistinguishable from that of its southern neighbor. As was probably true of the previous century, much more united the work on both sides of the provincial boundaries than divided it. Yet distinctions did appear, and one of the most discernible is in the treatment of secondary or subsidiary walls. In that respect, Maryland and Virginia began to part ways sometime in the second quarter of the eighteenth century.

The use of different bonds on different facades for dramatic purposes appeared much later in the Chesapeake than in England and other regions of America. In the seventeenth century, English bricklayers had used Flemish bond on principal facades while laying secondary facades in English bond and other variants. This hierarchy of bonds appeared in the Chesapeake by the beginning of the eighteenth century, if not slightly earlier. Many buildings also took advantage of the glazing patterns inherent in Flemish bond to further accentuate the differences between primary and secondary facades. One of the earliest surviving examples is at Yeocomico Church, where the main south wall is laid primarily in Flemish bond with glazed headers, while secondary walls are laid in English bond with random glazing. At the Adam Thoroughgood House in Virginia Beach, a dwelling once thought to date from the 1630s but now dated by dendrochronology to the early 1720s, the principal facade is Flemish bond with glazed headers, while the other three sides are English bond. At the nearby Weblin House, a much-altered dwelling of a

similar date, the principal facade was laid in Flemish bond with glazed headers. That decorative pattern continues on the east gable end up to the point where the massive exterior chimney juts out from the wall. On the other side of the chimney, the bonding of the gable-end wall is English bond, which matches the pattern on the rear wall.

Maryland bricklayers developed a flair for varying bonding patterns on different walls to emphasize the importance of entrance facades. In Annapolis and in certain parts of the central Eastern Shore, workmen and their clients developed a partiality for all-header bonding, which flourished from the 1740s through the 1780s (see Fig. 11.7D).[31] Clearly a demonstration of virtuoso skills, elite houses, fashionable taverns, and Anglican parish churches often had tightly laid header bonding on their principal facades, while the subsidiary walls were decorated in English bond or Flemish bond.

In seventeenth-century England, bricklayers sometimes reworked English bond to include multiple stretcher courses, a technique that required less intricate bonding and fewer bricks. The bond initially may have been sloppy brickwork or evidence of skimpiness. Yet, by the late seventeenth century, it appears more deliberate, whereby masons laid secondary facades that contained header to stretcher ratios of one-to-two, one-to-three, and one-to-five (see Fig. 11.7E). This outgrowth of English bond, often called common bond and laid in many variant ratios, first appeared in America in the first decades of the eighteenth century. Among the earliest examples are the Pierce-Hichborn House in Boston (c. 1712), where the side walls are laid in one-to-three bond. The slightly later MacPheadris-Warner House in Portsmouth, New Hampshire (1716), has a similar arrangement, where the Flemish-bond front contrasts with the one-to-three bond of the side walls.

By contrast, the use of multiple stretcher courses does not appear in the Chesapeake until late in the colonial period. The earliest examples appear in Maryland in the second quarter of the eighteenth century and probably derived from the practices of Delaware Valley masons working in and around Philadelphia. For example, Caulk's Field and Stanley's Hope, both built in Kent County in 1743, have one-to-three bonding in secondary walls.[32] Virginians turned to common bond relatively late, not using it on secondary walls and chimneys until the 1790s.[33] One of the earliest extant examples appears inconspicuously on the plinth of the clerk's office (1799) in Smithfield.

Besides variations in bonding patterns, bricklayers also distinguished primary and secondary facades by the use of glazed headers, raised impost blocks, and keystones. During

Fig. 11.17. South frontispiece, Aquia Church, 1757, Stafford County, Virginia. The nearby Aquia quarry supplied the sandstone used to construct the three frontispieces of the church. The design was loosely based on several examples found in contemporary English architectural books.

windows have no arches at all. Impost blocks and keystone bricks in compass-headed apertures were sometimes accentuated by being raised beyond the wall surface or rubbed, glazed, or molded, according to their location. At St. Mary Anne's, North East, Cecil County (1743), the principal entrance facade on the south side is finished with glazed headers, a stringcourse, and raised keystone bricks at the apex of the compass windows. The stringcourse carries around the secondary entrance on the west facade and the east end, and the apertures on these walls are also marked by keystone bricks. However, there is no decorative glazing on them. The back wall is plainly treated with no glazing, stringcourse, or keystones.

Few Chesapeake brick buildings after the 1730s display any embellishments except pilastered walls and pedimented frontispieces, which derived from standard classical forms used in a manner that adhered to or approached codified rules of proportion and detail (Fig. 11.17). These forms are less pervasive but distinctly regional. A few Maryland clients and their builders chose to embellish the walls of their houses with integral brick pilasters.[34] The timber-framed Cedar Park in Anne Arundel County was encased in brick in the 1740s. The east elevation of this one-story house was laid in header bond, accentuated at the corners by brick pilasters executed in the Doric order. A much more dramatic use of pilasters appears on the garden facade of Mount Clare, a five-bay dwelling erected around 1757 by Charles Carroll. Doric pilasters ascend two stories from the plinth at the corners and in the middle of the building at the second and fifth bay to frame a three-bay pediment (Fig. 11.18). With sharply rubbed corners and blue glazing in the center, the pilaster bricks contrast with the header bond of the walls.

William Buckland treated giant pilasters in a slightly different manner on the garden facade of the Hammond-Harwood House (1774) in Annapolis (see Fig. 7.25). Four pilasters define the central three bays of the building and support the full entablature of the central pediment. The pilasters have molded dados that stand upon the building's plinth. The vertical thrust of the two-story Doric pilasters is counterbalanced by the three-course, rubbed stringcourse that projects and wraps around them as it runs across the facade. A simpler method of creating this visual distinction appears at Larkin's Hills, a one-story, gambrel-roof dwelling built in Anne Arundel County about 1753. On the all-

the first three decades of the eighteenth century, Virginia and Maryland bricklayers used glazed headers to accentuate primary facades, while randomly glazing secondary walls. The plinth and main walls on the south and west sides of Christ Church, Middlesex County, Virginia (1714), are Flemish bond with glazed headers. These sides contained the main entrance on the west and the south chancel door. Maryland bricklayers followed the same rules in a number of early Anglican parish churches—glazing the principal facade and perhaps the apse, while leaving the rear walls unglazed, as at St. Luke's (1731) in Queen Anne's County. Marking principal facades with glazed headers while leaving the rest of the walls unglazed or with random glazing went out of fashion in most of Virginia by the 1730s but continued in Maryland through the late eighteenth century.

In addition to decorative glazing and bonding patterns, Maryland bricklayers treated other elements in a similar hierarchical fashion. For example, the apertures on the entrance facades of St. John's, Broad Creek, Prince George's County (1766), are capped with segmental jack arches, while the rear

Fig. 11.18. Mount Clare, c. 1757–60, Baltimore.

header-bond front facade, vertical bands of glazed headers that imitate pilasters appear at the corners and between the apertures, a decorative treatment found in a number of English buildings in the first half of the eighteenth century.

Rather than bold pilasters or glazed vertical strips, the epitome of brick craftsmanship in Virginia was the gauged and rubbed classical doorway, such as David Minitree's fine examples at Carter's Grove (see Fig. 11.16). Instead of modulating the bonding or smaller decorative elements to accentuate the hierarchy of different facades, bricklayers and their elite clients in Virginia choose to accentuate principal entrances through pedimented frontispieces. Though many houses and other buildings had wooden frontispieces, brick ones were reserved for grand gentry houses and parish churches. The earliest appear in the late 1710s and continued through the Revolution before they lost favor. Among the most elaborate, with full entablatures of molded bricks, were those erected at Rosewell in Gloucester County (begun c. 1726) and Christ Church, Lancaster (c. 1732–35), which has three doorways—two secondary entrances with trian-

gular pediments and a segmental pediment in the main west entrance. The west frontispiece at Christ Church is further accentuated by molded Aquia sandstone bases, surbases, Doric capitals, impost blocks, and the fluted keystone of the compass-headed door opening, while the two side doorways have only stone bases and capitals. Despite their popularity among the Virginia gentry, brick frontispieces never made it north of the Potomac River, either in a domestic setting or in an Anglican parish church.

BRICK AS A STATUS MATERIAL

For more than two centuries, residents of the Chesapeake recognized brick as a status material. Because of their durability, the survival of so many brick buildings from the colonial period has habitually led many historians to overestimate their historical presence. At no time during this period did brick-walled structures constitute anything more than a small presence in the countryside.[35] In a landscape dominated by wooden dwellings, outbuildings, fences, and public structures, a brick building or even the more modest use of brick in foundations and chimneys provoked comment and invited respect. Place-names and dwellings described in documents and noted on maps simply as "brick house" speak of the rarity of such buildings in the countryside and in villages in the colonial period. Long before Bacon's Castle came to be known by its historical association with the rebellious turmoil of 1676, the inhabitants of Surry County referred to the dwelling as "Arthur Allen's brick house" (see Fig. 2.10). Even buildings with brick underpinnings and brick chimneys stood out where log houses, post-in-the-ground construction, and wooden chimneys were the norm. William Byrd described most of the houses he encountered on his survey of the border between Virginia and North Carolina in 1728 as being constructed entirely of log, including the chimneys. Byrd contemptuously dismissed the quality of the forty or fifty houses in Edenton, North Carolina, as "small and built without Expense. A Citizen here is counted Extravagant, if he has Ambition enough to aspire to a Brick-chimney."[36]

If the absence of brick exemplified the rawness of the frontier and the indolence of its inhabitants in Byrd's mind, the presence of brick suggested just the opposite to some contemporaries. English traveler William Hugh Grove, who visited Virginia in 1732, took notice when he came upon a house where "2 brick Chimbles shew there is a spare bed and lodging and Welcome." Hospitality was associated with gentility, and brick was one of the most visible symbols of a homeowner's genteel status.[37] George Washington made a similar comparison some sixty years later on one of his presidential journeys. Traveling through Charlotte County in Southside Virginia in 1791, Washington observed that "the Houses (tho' none elegt.) are in genl. Decent, & bespeak good livers; being for the most part weatherboarded & Shingled, with brick Chimnies."[38]

In towns and cities where the hazard of fire led to the banning of the construction of wooden chimneys, wood remained the material of choice in the colonial period. A visitor to Yorktown in the early 1730s reckoned that out of the thirty or so dwellings in the small port, there were "about 10 good houses, not above 4 of Brick, the rest of Timber."[39] Yorktown may have had more brick houses per household than other towns in the Chesapeake since it had attracted a number of rich merchants, such as Thomas Nelson, who could afford to undertake the construction of sizable brick houses (see Fig. 11.1). In more typical Chesapeake communities, brick was extremely rare, as an English traveler who visited Snow Hill, the small courthouse village in Worcester County, Maryland, discovered in 1746. He observed that "the Church and all the Houses are built of Wood, but some

of them have Brick Stacks of Chimneys." Amid the many post-in-the-ground dwellings, puncheon houses, and log buildings that filled the lots of Snow Hill, the Anglican minister lived in "the only Brick-House in Town."[40]

By the end of the eighteenth century, wooden buildings continued to dominate the streets of most cities and towns, punctuated here and there by more substantial brick residences of merchants and professionals and their associated brick outbuildings, particularly kitchens. Despite the construction of a number of sizeable brick houses in the late colonial period, which still define the architectural perception of early Annapolis, the Maryland capital was still mostly a wooden city. In 1798, timber-framed structures made up more than half the standing buildings. Nearly 40 percent of the 211 dwellings enumerated in a tax list were one-story wooden houses, most of which have long since disappeared, while only a quarter of the residences were the two-story brick structures that so dominate the remains of the town's colonial architecture.[41] Wood dwellings were even more ubiquitous outside of town in the countryside of Anne Arundel County, where less than a fifth of the dwellings were made of brick. In neighboring Prince George's County to the west, where tobacco fields still dominated this rural landscape bordering on the new federal city, only 10 percent of the farmhouses had masonry walls, according to the federal tax survey.[42]

Those who erected brick structures worked against a regional tradition that had been charted early. Archaeological evidence from scores of early tobacco plantation sites across eastern Virginia and southern Maryland suggest that brick buildings were unusual.[43] Jamestown may have had a number of brick cellars or foundations and a few brick-walled buildings, but after a half century of settlement the town was still scarcely more than an unkempt collection of timber-framed taverns, dwellings, and storehouses. The straggling, impermanent nature of the capital was brought to royal attention, prompting provincial officials to sponsor legislation to create a brick city. In the early 1660s, a massive building program underwritten by public money created a series of two-story brick row houses. At least three, and probably a few more, two-, three-, and four-unit row houses rose along the banks of the James, mirroring the form of many of the rows that were being erected in London following the Great Fire of 1666 (see Fig. 6.16). The scheme never transformed Jamestown into an urban center, and the torching of the town by Nathaniel Bacon in 1676 left many of the units of the brick row houses in permanent ruins.

Those who had the desire and the money could always build well. Governor William Berkeley erected the earliest part of Green Spring, his plantation, just outside of James-town in 1645 (see Fig. 6.20). In the early 1660s, John Page of Middle Plantation erected a brick and tile kiln on his plantation and proceeded to construct a one-story brick residence, kitchen, and other service buildings (see Fig. 6.22). In 1665, Arthur Allen, a first-generation immigrant from Worcestershire, built the two-story Bacon's Castle, the lone surviving substantial brick house erected in seventeenth-century Virginia (see Fig. 2.10). Ten years later, John Custis oversaw the construction of a three-story, double-pile mansion at Arlington on the Eastern Shore (see Fig. 6.24). These were the exceptions, and almost all of them were first-generation immigrants who probably believed that residence on the fringe of empire should be no deterrent to replicating the housing standards of the provincial English gentry. Far more immigrants and native-born planters chose not to build brick houses, even though they may have had the wherewithal to do so. William Byrd II of Westover, the bane of North Carolina, may well have lived in a wooden house, albeit with flanking brick wings.

Byrd rose to be president of the council of Virginia before his death in 1744. A few of the great planters who served with him in the first decades of the eighteenth century lived in frame houses, although the double-pile brick Governor's Palace in Williamsburg set the pattern that Virginia's elite began to replicate. By the time William Byrd III took his father's place on the council in 1754, a new, two-story, brick Westover had replaced the old family house (see Fig. 3.7). For those who served on the council with the younger Byrd in the third quarter of the eighteenth century, a masonry building was nearly a prerequisite for membership. Thomas Nelson of Yorktown, Richard Corbin of Laneville in King and Queen County, Philip Ludwell III of Green Spring, John Tayloe of Mount Airy in Richmond County, Philip Ludwell Lee of Stratford in Westmoreland County, Robert Carter III of Nomini Hall in Westmoreland County, George William Fairfax of Belvoir in Fairfax County, Ralph Wormeley III of Rosegill in Middlesex County, John Page Jr. of Rosewell in Gloucester County, and Gawin Corbin of Peckatone in Westmoreland County either built or dwelled in brick or stone houses that signaled the pinnacle of architectural ambition in colonial Virginia.

The elite's growing allegiance to brick in the middle decades of the eighteenth century is evident in public buildings. There were only a handful of brick churches and courthouses in Maryland and Virginia at the beginning of the eighteenth century, but by the last decade before independence few parishes or counties in the oldest settled regions were without an imposing masonry building. Frame churches still far out-numbered brick ones in the Anglican parishes of Virginia at the end of the colonial period, but this was partly the result of the church expanding westward into new territories and the construction of frame structures in new parishes.[44] Most Anglicans in the Tidewater could worship in at least one brick church in their parish. In some of the wealthier parishes, vestries had undertaken the replacement of secondary wooden chapels with brick ones until the disestablishment of the church and its taxing privileges following the Revolution resulted in a dramatic collapse of the traditional ecclesiastical landscape, leaving many Episcopal churches bereft of funds, rectors, and parishioners. The same pattern appeared in Maryland, though on a smaller scale. Older parishes bordering the bay had at least one brick Anglican church, and some had even built a second or even a third one by the end of the colonial period.[45] Civic building mirrored the pattern of the established church. There was a slow but inexorable replacement of wooden buildings with brick ones. This began in Virginia in the 1720s and 1730s, and by the time of the Revolution, not one county that had been established in the seventeenth century retained its old frame courthouse. Some counties even began to build brick prisons, though these were far fewer, since they were still seen as utilitarian structures designed for short-term use.[46]

The Revolution deflated the power of the tobacco planters of the Chesapeake, leaving many deeply in debt and unable to build on the scale that had been buoyed by the credit British merchants previously had extended to them. Tobacco no longer proved the road to riches. The power of the Anglican Church had collapsed in both colonies, and the Baptist and Methodist congregations that reaped the rewards from the wreckage had neither the wealth nor the desire to build substantial places of worship in the late eighteenth century. Only the county courts came through unscathed from the old triumvirate of power bases embodied in imposing brick buildings. New brick courthouses with classical pedimented porticoes, inspired by Jefferson's design for the new state capitol in Richmond, spread across Virginia and parts of Maryland, but they signaled a more democratic spirit in public discourse, one less associated with the deferential old order.

If the nature of brick building changed in the Chesapeake in the late eighteenth and early nineteenth centuries, it did not disappear with the eclipse of the old gentry. Across the region, brick marked the ending of the frontier or the movement of a family, community, or region into a more settled and prosperous stage of farming or commercial development. The passage from frame or log to brick, or occasionally stone, was never straightforward or even, but the trend was inevitable. Many farmsteads that had brick dwellings

Fig. 11.19. *James House, 1810s, Surry County, Virginia. An example of the increasing use of brick for foundations and chimneys among more modest houses in the early nineteenth century.*

contained rude post-in-the-ground work buildings. Within sight of the west portico of Monticello stood a line of log and frame service buildings and slave quarters (see Fig. 8.10). Though most people never lived in brick houses, shopped in brick stores, drank in brick taverns, or worshipped in brick churches, by the early nineteenth century far more of them dwelled in houses that had masonry chimneys, foundations, cellars, and floor paving (Fig. 11.19). In 1810, an inhabitant of eastern North Carolina described the process. He observed that "the first Inhabitants of Duplin and Sampson Counties built and lived in log Cabbins and as they became more Wealthy, some of them Built framed Clapboard Houses with Clay Chimneys; at present there are many good Houses, well

Constructed, with Brick Chimneys, and glass lights; there are no Stone or Brick Walled houses, nor any that can be called Edifices in the County."[47]

The transformation in the housing stock in which brick became a much-more-pervasive element may have varied in timing and detail but was equally compelling to contemporaries in eastern Virginia and southern Maryland who recognized improvements in the landscape. For every imposing two-story plantation dwelling, hundreds of smaller brick-walled buildings and timber-framed farmhouses with masonry chimneys and foundations survive from the first decades of the nineteenth century, the unheralded testaments of a revolution in housing standards.

12 *Hardware*

EDWARD A. CHAPPELL

Hardware holds buildings together. Nails, spikes, pins, and screws are fasteners, pure and simple. Hinges, latches, and bolts open, close, and lock. Jacks, cranes, hooks, and spits lift, swing, hold, and spin. For centuries before the first European house carpenter opened his toolbox in Virginia, architectural metalwork had provided solutions to structural and mechanical problems involved in building buildings. Between the late 1600s and the early 1800s, much changed. With each passing decade, increasing numbers of householders expected hardware to do more than function efficiently. Like paint, wallpaper, architectural moldings, and even brick and stonework, the hinges, locks, latches, doorknobs, and assorted other architectural hardware became accessories to and evidence of the good life. Some increasingly gave delight to the eye; others retreated into decorous invisibility; virtually all hardware used in elite houses broadcast visual messages about the function of the rooms in which they appeared, the importance of those rooms in relation to adjoining spaces, and the intended circulation of specific people through the rooms. Most metal hardware used in the Chesapeake region came from England, and so did the rules that governed its use. Boatloads of both arrived year after year. This, then, is the story of hardware's transformation from useful tools to social arbiters.

THE BEHOLDER'S EYE

Gentility was as much an outlook on life as a way of life in the seventeenth and eighteenth centuries. Its emphasis on refinement and visual order changed the way British and American men and women of all ranks, but especially the wealthy, perceived the world around them, including architectural hardware. Like the clothes they wore and the dinner dishes that set their tables, the hardware they encountered in dwellings and public buildings engaged their several senses. Door and window fittings were for show—or not. Their surfaces were pleasing to the touch—or not. They permitted

graceful movement—or not. Hardware increasingly came in an assortment of materials, forms, and qualities, priced accordingly. Utility remained a consideration for each buyer, but as the eighteenth century wore on, matters of placement and status guided householders' decisions more and more.

Hiding the working elements of a house emphasized graceful use over household operations, whether the parts were servants or functioning pieces of a door lock. Architecturally, the evolution of hardware in the Chesapeake is part of a larger story of shifting attention from the structural and mechanical elements of construction to a more orchestrated visual unity. Almost everywhere in the English-speaking world, eighteenth-century builders increasingly concealed

259

the mundane jobs being done by features like chimney flues and structural framing. They both simplified the look of such working elements and, in the case of luxury hardware, diverted the eye by enriching the parts that users touched. In large houses, people employed a new generation of hardware to communicate messages about status, circulation, and function. Door fittings especially reinforced the legible messages of woodwork and provided the observer with information not fully evident in room trim and color.

Pursuit of refined life and visual order among elites and successful middling residents of the Chesapeake, Britain, and its other colonies changed the way architectural metalwork was perceived in the eighteenth century. Hardware reveals that refinement was measured by multiple senses—by what wealthy people felt and saw and by what they smelled and heard. Refinement involved provision of luxury materials and exclusion of low-status materials, forms, and people. The most important reason for the variation in kinds of hardware used in the eighteenth-century Chesapeake was the social nature of the setting and the intentions as well as wealth of the building owners, to a degree unknown in the previous century. In polite houses, directing movement and purveying a sense of refinement usually outweighed the desire to protect people and property when selections were made.

Coordinated gentry use of status-conferring architectural metalwork stands in stark contrast to how everyone had used hardware earlier in the Chesapeake. Latches from Robert Carter's Corotoman (which burned in 1729) seem a world away from door handles used by his grandchildren's generation. Carter's fingers turned a roughly wrought iron ring that pivoted a rudimentary cam or rocker bar to push up a latch bar against an L-shaped spring, all exposed on a plate nailed to the face of a prominent door (Fig. 12.1B). English smiths emphasized a sharp bend in the spring by filing alternating edges, and they often ornamented the latch bar by cutting indentations and punching circles. Workmen gave special attention to decorating the outer end of the latch bar, which dropped into an iron keeper visibly supported at Corotoman by an ornamental rattail, driven and tacked to the face of the doorframe, further drawing attention to the mechanical action (Fig. 12.1A). Such combinations of carefully finished working elements and roughly forged iron came to be dismissed later as unrefined. In 1772, grandson Charles Carter installed new interior doors at Shirley using mortise locks that hid every element but their smooth brass handles, which were mounted on gracefully nonfunctional brass escutcheons (Fig. 12.2).

Such expensive Georgian hardware was unaffordable for ordinary people, who fitted out modest dwellings well into the age of Jefferson. Ironmongery is nearly absent in the earliest surviving buildings and remained scarce for those at the lower end of the social scale. Nearly two decades of excavation at the Jamestown Fort (1607–20s) have uncovered a rich array of high-status accoutrements but little building hardware beyond nails and padlocks. Findings at later seventeenth-century sites often follow the settlement-era pattern of limited hardware where the residents were relatively poor. The poorer the building, the fewer the number of nails found. The archaeological record of the dwelling of Thomas Atkinson, a relatively minor slave owner in James City County (c. 1680–1710), produced hundreds of nails and two iron hinges; his adjoining slave quarter left almost none. A nearby tenant's house or slave quarter from the first half of the eighteenth century also left many nails, while the associated tobacco house left virtually none.[1] Nails were needed to secure roof coverings and wall siding. Building with logs lessened the need for nails, and a handful of Virginia houses retain evidence that their builders laboriously whittled pegs and drilled holes in roof lath as an alternative to nailing shingles (Fig. 12.6A). In 1728, William Byrd II remarked on the absence of metal in the log houses that he observed along the border between Virginia and North Carolina. He noted that "their doors, too, turn upon Wooden hinges and have wooden Locks to secure them, so that the Building is finisht without Nails or other Iron-Work."[2] Some modest Chesapeake houses have survived to the present with wood hinges and bars or pegs used to wedge doors closed from the inside (Fig. 12.3). They are the last remnants of once-common strategies for living with limited ironwork. Relying on wooden pins, hinges, and locks reduced the amount of skilled labor required for a building, employed cheaper materials, and avoided the problem of relying on imported metalwork (Figs. 12.4, 12.5).

By the late eighteenth century, English hardware catalogs illustrating the range of forms and sizes available indicate how prices reflected minor variations in quality. But the complex choices that contextual meanings brought to the selection of hardware for a large gentry house or a slave quarter were subject to the vagaries of acquisition, whether buyers ordered directly from Britain or purchased imported hardware from limited stocks available in Chesapeake stores. Inventories of major Annapolis merchants like Daniel Dulaney and Edward Dorsey show that consumers could buy nails, screws, a small number of medium-value hinges, and simple iron locks locally but none of the more unusual hinges and other hardware. Smiths working in the region produced and repaired some hardware, but their known products were limited in variety and quantity. The assortment of mismatched

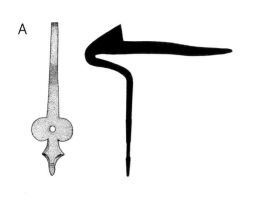

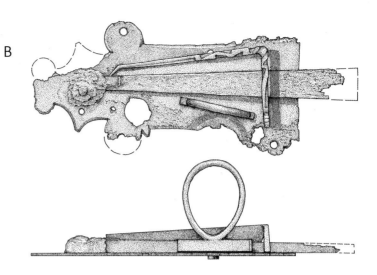

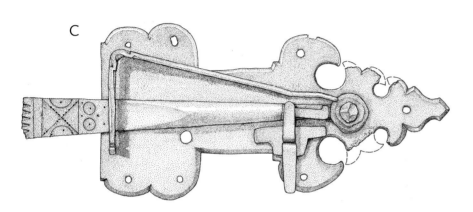

Fig. 12.1. Seventeenth-century latches from Virginia archaeological sites. A and B: Latch keeper and latch, Corotoman, burned 1729, Lancaster County; C: Rich Neck, James City County; D: Latch bar from Structure 17, Jamestown; E: Plate lock from Yeardley House, Flowerdew Hundred, Prince George County; F: Plate lock from Structure 144, Jamestown.

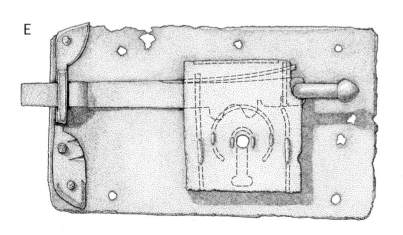

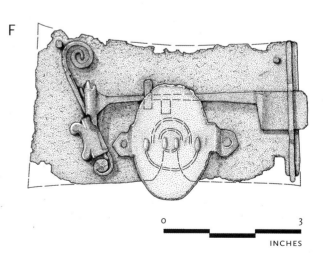

0   3
INCHES

(clockwise from top left)

Fig. 12.2. Mortise lock with brass escutcheons and handles, 1774, Hammond-Harwood House, Annapolis. This hardware was installed on all the doors of the house, except that leading from stairwell to private passage upstairs. Around 1772, Charles Carter installed similar locks on leaves in the first- and second-floor doorways at Shirley.

Fig. 12.3. Door hung on wooden hinges, Walnut Valley, Surry County, Virginia.

Fig. 12.4. String latch, Woodlawn, Essex County, Virginia.

Fig. 12.5. Slide bolt, cellar, Bowling Green, Caroline County, Virginia.

hinges and right-hand or left-hand locks turned upside down to make do, even in locations like the entrance hall at Shirley, illustrates the problems of supply. Virginians were forbidden by a 1645 act from burning their buildings to recover nails, and as late as 1781 certain decayed houses and farm buildings in St. Mary's County, Maryland, were valued only for their salvageable nails.[3] Importation remained high even as domestic iron production grew after the Revolution. In 1822, builder John M. Perry made the point explicitly to his client, Supreme Court justice Philip Pendleton Barbour, when he submitted a list of nails, screws, hinges, and locks as "the foreign materials that you will want" for his house, Frascati in Orange County.[4]

FASTENERS

Even the choice of nails and screws indicates the selective nature of construction and the broadening distaste for rusticity or constructional expression in the preindustrial Chesapeake. Appearance and methods of production for nails changed relatively little from the sixteenth century until the 1780s. English and Chesapeake blacksmiths and nail makers hammered a taper into the end of long pieces of square iron "nail rod," cut off the upper end, and finished the head. The point could be made sharp, as part of the gradual taper on all four sides, or flat and thin, created by a single hammer strike on the tip, depending on intended function and somewhat on size (Figs. 12.6D–G). Small, sharp-pointed nails were commonly used to secure plaster lath to walls and ceilings, while slightly longer flat-point nails attached shingles to roof lath or sheathing, without splitting the wood. Larger flat-point nails secured those surfaces to the rafters and the siding to vertical framing. Oversized nails were used to secure simple lapped connections between framing members that lacked more complex joinery, which was generally pegged. Earlier and cheaper framing could in fact call for more iron fasteners than the best quality eighteenth-century framing, which relied heavily on chiseled and sawn mortises and tenons.

Heads of common nails were finished with four hammer blows. The result was a small, imprecisely faceted top, or "rose-head," which stood above the surface into which the nail was driven. Rose-head nails fulfilled most architectural needs for metal fasteners in the seventeenth- and early eighteenth-century Chesapeake, but their broad use was curtailed by a growing perception among the elite that such nails were too crude for finish work. They were increasingly relegated to rough carpentry and to hidden framing, lath, and shingles, as well as to certain jobs where sizable nail heads helped secure siding and hinges. Their use in refined interior

woodwork was becoming rare when a joiner used them on the walnut staircase at Tuckahoe in the 1730s.

Joiners achieved cleaner appearances by hiding fasteners. English smiths made common finish nails by flattening the head on opposite sides, creating a folded T-shape that could be driven completely into the wood, leaving only a thin surface visible (Fig. 12.6H). Builders made these the standard for wood trim and floors by the mid-eighteenth century and even for weatherboards on some good quality buildings late in the century. The term "clasp nail" was sometimes applied to them but could also refer more narrowly to nails with peaked narrow heads, used for flooring. Alternatives for finish work included L-headed and headless brads, often made with sharp points and used most often for expensive wood flooring (Fig. 12.6J–L). A more expensive method for better floors was "blind" or "secret-nailed" work, in which craftsmen took pains to edge-nail fasteners, hiding them from view completely.[5] Joiners employed by William Byrd III minimized the need for finish nails by hanging the best paneling at Westover on heavy iron holdfasts hidden behind chair boards and bases (Fig. 12.6EE). Builders used holdfasts in securing heavy finish to masonry in other expensive construction, such as classical pediments over exterior doorways at the President's House, College of William and Mary, and marble fireplace facing at Blandfield (Figs. 12.6DD, 12.6FF).

Hinges presented a challenge, as many of them were visibly secured on the doors of parlors and chambers with rose-head nails, often driven through small square pieces of leather as washers, a practice called "botching" (Figs. 12.10I, 12.10K). Rivets, dome-headed "dog nails," and "clout nails" with wider and flatter heads were usually reserved for the heaviest hinges in the Chesapeake (Fig. 12.6M–O, S).[6] Flat-headed and round-headed screws became alternatives to nails for H and HL hinges, despite the greater expense incurred in turning or filing their threads (Figs. 12.6T, 12.6U). A 1760 English patent for lathe-turning screws used drawn wire rather than hand-forged blanks, thereby streamlining production by the 1790s. The holding capacity of screws and later their mass production made them the normal means of securing butt hinges; by the 1830s, machine fabrication resulted in economy as well as in more regular heads and sharp points. When finish carpenters installed box locks in the eighteenth century, they preferred screws to nails and bolts for refined doors to create a clean appearance and to avoid damaging the metal locks. Iron screws were consistently used for attaching other superior door hardware such as brass escutcheons for keyholes and mortise locks and the occasional knocker. They were likewise the standard choice for delicate window hardware, such as metal casings for sash pulleys and for latches.

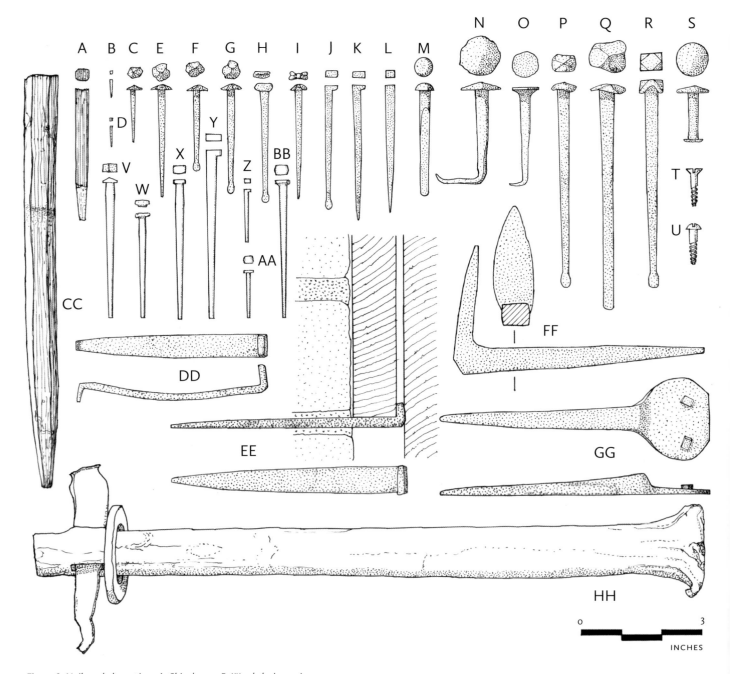

Fig. 12.6. Nails and alternatives. A: Shingle peg; B: Wood glazing sprig.
C–R Wrought iron nails. C: Glazing sprig; D–E: Rose head nails with
sharp point. F–G: Rose head nails with flat point; H: T-head nail;
I: Clasp-head nail; J–K: L-headed brads; L: Headless brad; M: Die-headed
dog nail; N: Dog nail with hammered head; O: Clout nail; P–R: Spikes;
S: Rivet; T: Flat-headed screw; U: Dome-headed screw. V–BB Cut nails.
V: Hand-headed cut nail; W: T-headed cut nail; X: Early machine-headed
cut nail; Y–Z: L-headed cut brads; AA: Early cut lath nail; BB: Mature
cut nail; CC: Framing peg; DD: Holdfast securing marble fireplace facing,
Blandfield, Essex County, Virginia; EE: Holdfast supporting wainscot,
Westover, Charles City County, Virginia; FF: Holdfast supporting exterior
door pediment, President's House, College of William and Mary,
Williamsburg; GG: Holdfast securing doorframe to masonry, residential
wing, Mount Airy, Richmond County, Virginia; HH: Riveted pin holding
paired summer beams together in entrance hall, Blandfield, 1769–72.

Machine-made nails also reduced the range of fasteners by
making conventional heads less visible. Builders began using
them on city houses in the region, including Georgetown
and Baltimore, beginning in the mid- to late 1790s. They
became commonplace after 1810. The heads were initially
hammered by hand, creating a recognizable two-faceted
silhouette (Fig. 12.6V). The introduction of machine-cut
nails soon offered stiffer competition in the 1810s, when the
heads, too, began to be produced by machines (Fig. 12.6X).
Early cut nails were sheared from iron plates, the plate being
flipped over by hand. These display burrs on adjoining corners, helpful in dating buildings in which they are used, most
often in the period between 1800 and 1815.[7] Nevertheless,
carpenters in the Chesapeake continued using rose-head

wrought nails through the middle of the nineteenth century for rough hinges and to construct board-and-batten doors. Manufacturing the rod aligned the grain with the length of the bar, making for nails that were stronger than those that were chopped from iron plates and imparting flexibility for clinching.

HINGES

Prestige-conscious eighteenth-century elites' quest for visual refinement is more dramatically evident in the evolving character of hinges. The disappearance of decoration from strap hinges and their declining status illustrate how craftsmanship changed in the eighteenth century. The most rugged and common among surviving hinges, iron straps were made as a single long bar with an eye wrapped around an L-shaped hook, or pintle, that was set into a frame. The period names were "hook-and-eye" or "hook and hinge."[8] Straps had been used since the Middle Ages to support heavy doors. In 1688, Randle Holme considered what he called "Hook and Hinge, or a Hinge for a Hook" to be so ubiquitous for the doors "of Houses, Barns, Stables, Gates of Towns and Cities, Parks and Fields, & c.," that he simply referred to it as a "Door Hinge." Tellingly, Holme noted the freedom with which seventeenth-century smiths decorated them, "made and adorned at the ends, and on the sides, *according to the fancy and pleasure of the maker*, with Flourishes, Caroses, Scrolls, heads of Flowers de lis, and such like."[9] Decoration was used to embellish strap hinges throughout the British Empire as late as the 1730s, including in the Chesapeake colonies.

The principal entrance at Yeocomico Church (1706), in Westmoreland County, Virginia, is a two-part door hung on straps. It has a small inner leaf, or wicket, hung on cross garnets—strap hinges with flat stationary arms pinned at the joint—nailed, here, into the larger leaf. The Yeocomico examples combine a heavy appearance with enrichment in the form of terminals hammered into a large fleur-de-lis (Fig. 12.7B). Builder Patrick Creagh used a similar set of cross garnets to hang a thick, out-swinging door to the Treasury building on State Circle in Annapolis in 1735–37. Another pair reused on a Dinwiddie County smokehouse expresses the fancy of their maker in a raised grid of squares and a crease running toward the terminal point (Fig. 12.7A). Strap hinges with fleurs-de-lis were a common sight on medieval European churches, and they remained a popular choice for rural English churches throughout much of the seventeenth century, but they fell from favor for elite British buildings well before the 1730s. They are largely absent, for example, from large urban churches and houses beginning

in the 1670s. Such assertive heavy hardware would disappear from new Chesapeake buildings within a decade or two after the Treasury building, and ultimately the use of strap hinges would have as much to do with their low-status setting as with strength and security.

Blending weight and decoration became so unfashionable that certain once-common choices of hardware eventually disappeared from the Chesapeake. A seemingly arcane detail of strap hinges found archaeologically at the Jamestown fort and late seventeenth-century Jamestown houses makes the point (Figs. 12.7E, 12.7F). Among strap hinges still in place on Chesapeake doors, the barrel or gudgeon was formed by rolling the bar out and around a drift pin equal in size to the hook, and the hinge's sloping face was often given a modest finish, like countersunk holes and chamfered edges (Fig. 12.7G). Some of the seventeenth-century Jamestown hinges have their bevels or countersinking on the flat, opposite face of the bar—the face that one would normally expect to be hidden. A small Jamestown example has scrolled terminals outlining the shape of a robust heart, suggesting use in a prominent setting. Such hinges were mounted in reverse, so that the eye hugged the frame of doors without rebates. As with surviving archaic doors in Britain, Bermuda, and the Caribbean, the door leaf was larger than the opening, and it closed against the frame rather than being carefully sized for nestling into a recess often finished with classical moldings. Alternately, sandwiched layers of sheathing were used to create rebates on the leaf closing against a square frame. Either way, the resulting thickness of the leaf inside made use of reverse hinges necessary. Reverse-mounted strap hinges disappeared from Chesapeake buildings other than barns by the mid-eighteenth century.

The simplicity of hook-and-eye hinges illustrates their perceived low status from the 1740s onward, particularly when compared to flamboyant choices made elsewhere. Those in what now seem old-fashioned pre-1750 dwellings, like the Powell-Benston House in Somerset County, Maryland (Fig. 12.7C), and the Lynnhaven House in Virginia Beach, are plain in appearance, with only a spade terminal in place of the more extravagant motifs typical a few decades earlier. Thereafter, Virginians in pursuit of refinement usually relegated the hook and eye to storage spaces and outbuildings. As early as 1801–9, Jefferson's blacksmiths omitted even the simplest of finials in favor of plain, tapered straps (Fig. 12.7H). The growing preference for plainness made rat-tail reinforcements of the pintles, called "stay hooks," much rarer there than in the Northeast. Pintles were simply too large and unseemly for a refined Chesapeake setting.[10]

Cross garnets were acceptable for passage doors when

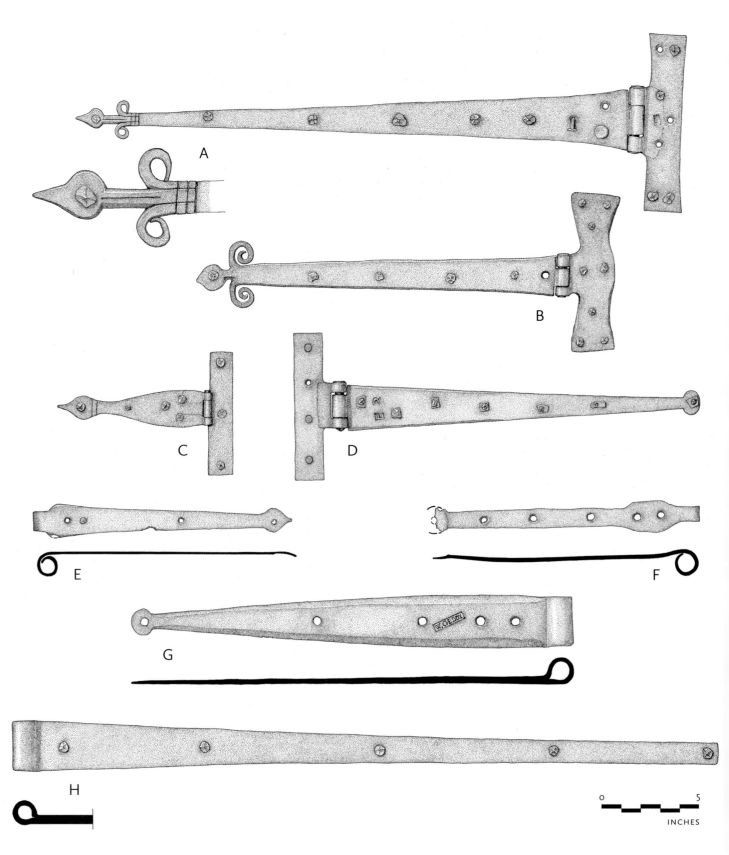

Fig. 12.7. Cross-garnet hinges. A: Reused on smokehouse in the early nineteenth century, Wales, Dinwiddie County, Virginia; B: Door, Yeocomico Church, 1706, Westmoreland County, Virginia; C: Closet door, Powell–Benston House, c. 1730, Somerset County, Maryland; D: Smokehouse door, late eighteenth century, Hillsborough, King and Queen County, Virginia. Strap hinges. E: Structure 110, Jamestown; F: Probably Governor's House, c. 1611–17, Jamestown; G: Hinge with mark of Williamsburg smith William Geddy, James City County, Virginia; H: Smokehouse, Monticello, Albemarle County, Virginia.

concern for strength overcame taste late in the eighteenth century. These hybrid straps with flat stationary arms shaped like half an H or dovetail were considered superior to straps hung on hooks. They were slightly more expensive and did not require spiking into a solid frame. They were often well made and are the principal variety of wrought hinge found to have stamped marks identifying the English maker and size (Fig. 12.7D). Builders for the very rich John Tayloe used a substantial set on the unusually heavy door to his secondary residential wing at Mount Airy about 1760, and John Robinson ordered six pairs of "x-garnets" for paneled doors in his York County houses in 1770, while ordering more HL hinges for both doors and shutters, all from London merchant John Norton.[11] The Neville family from Virginia employed a foliated set on a front passage closet at Woodville when they moved to western Pennsylvania. Generally though, cross garnets were plain and mostly used for unrefined locations. Long gone were the days—in 1716—when a North Carolina merchant-planter ordered even a dozen "good" pair of cross garnets "for inner room dores for my house."[12]

Even hook-and-eye hinges and cross garnets represented an investment. There were less-expensive choices. Pairs of small iron staples, or eyes, hooked together, were used as hinges on the tops of eighteenth-century chests. Occasionally these were used as an inexpensive means of hanging doors in the Chesapeake. Three were driven into the jamb and clinched in the edge of the leaf on all the doors along the backstage route from cellar to garret rooms at Bowling Green (c. 1743), which contrasted with the more expensive hinges on every other first-floor and garret door (Fig. 12.8). More common for low-status doors were wooden straps turning on wooden pintles nailed into the doorframe, as in the rudest cellar room at Bowling Green (see Fig. 12.3).

A simple variety of small hinges called "dovetails," with butterfly-shaped leaves, were employed for lighter work than straps were used for, and they followed a similar decline in status and ornament. Butterfly hinges were used on the face of fine late seventeenth-century Virginia and Massachusetts cupboards and could be filed "bright" to appear more finished. The best eighteenth-century butterfly hinges were given gracefully curved sides and tapered bevels with stops, as found on an early pair from the Governor's Palace in Williamsburg, perhaps installed in 1710–20, and on another from the next decade at Corotoman (Figs. 12.9A, 12.9B). By the 1750s, plain examples and simple rectangular "back-flap" hinges with one leaf roughly square and the other longer were commonly used to hold the inner flap of interior shutters—such a modest function that precise workmanship was inappropriate (Figs. 12.9E, 12.9F). Dovetails and back-flap hinges (resembling table hinges but mounted in reverse) were generally combined with plain offset or conventional H hinges on the larger leafs. Indeed, dovetail hinges were interchangeable with small H hinges for the outer face of cupboards, the backs of shutters, and little casement windows. Normally, they were painted along with the woodwork where they were attached.

Like dovetail hinges, surface-mounted hinges of more or less H-shaped— called "H hinges" or "side hinges" in the period— worked best when the opening had rebates and the leaf closed flush with the frame. Such required more carefully fashioned joinery to achieve an orderly appearance. English and continental smiths produced side hinges with decorative silhouettes long before American settlement. At their most elaborate, arms were hammered and cut into curvilinear shapes, which are now called "cock's-head" hinges for their sometimes birdlike terminals, popular in the second quarter of the seventeenth century. The plainest heads faced one another, while better-dressed cocks seemed in retreat, showing that the designs had more to do with the play of baroque "C" and "S" curves than with a zoomorphic reference. Smiths lavished care on cock's-head hinges, selectively beveling their edges, filing their faces smooth, and often adding a tinned surface intended to resist rust and make the arms stand out as decorative elements in mid-seventeenth-century rooms, like those at Walter Aston's house in Charles City County, Virginia, and at Councilor Samuel Mathews's house downriver in Warwick County (Figs. 12.10A, 12.10B).

Structures from the 1660s building boom at Jamestown employed simpler H hinges, with sharp-pointed, concave, and cyma terminals, as a substantial step away from labored

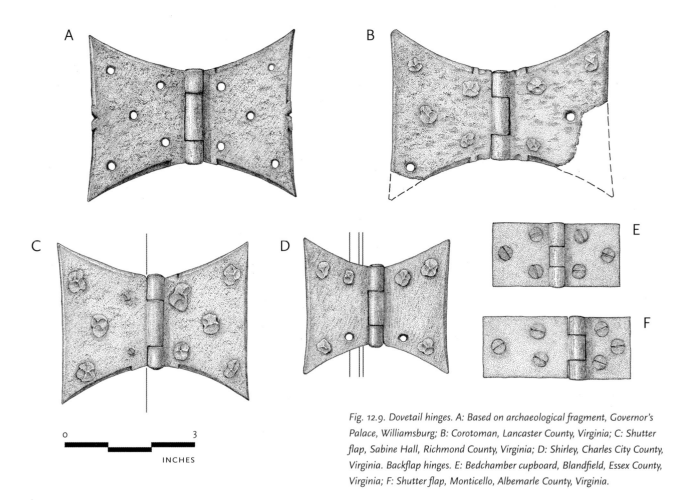

A

B

C

D

E

F

0   3

INCHES

Fig. 12.9. Dovetail hinges. A: Based on archaeological fragment, Governor's Palace, Williamsburg; B: Corotoman, Lancaster County, Virginia; C: Shutter flap, Sabine Hall, Richmond County, Virginia; D: Shirley, Charles City County, Virginia. Backflap hinges. E: Bedchamber cupboard, Blandfield, Essex County, Virginia; F: Shutter flap, Monticello, Albemarle County, Virginia.

cock's-head shapes. Similar ones survive in place at the Fairbanks House in Dedham, Massachusetts (1641). Comparable time-consuming workmanship can be seen in ordinary side hinges with terminations worked into round, trefoil, or foliated shapes, often set off from the straight hinge arms by parallel lines and triangular nicks (Figs. 12.10D, G, I). These were filed into their surface after it had been carefully smoothed, both to make the hardware look highly finished and to increase its contrast with colored or unpainted woodwork, not unlike glazed headers in a brick facade. Delicate file-work also involved beveling the edges, usually stopping the bevels short of the ends, in a tiny echo of exposed and chamfered ceiling frames.

Such artisanal quality has often been interpreted as evidence for a seventeenth-century date. In fact, most foliated hinges in the Chesapeake colonies were installed after 1700. Archaeologists have recovered crude pairs with round terminations as well as plain face hinges from the cellar of Corotoman, along with an oversized plain pair with iron finials on the barrels. Quaker planter Abraham Sanders used shaped face hinges when building a hall-chamber brick house in Perquimans County, North Carolina, in 1730. In the late 1730s, Landon Carter used them on at least his interior shut-

ters at Sabine Hall, and Dr. Charles Carroll used them on both floors when building or remodeling a lobby-entrance Annapolis tenement. Such decorated H and HL hinges remained a conventional choice for Virginians into the middle of the eighteenth century. Thereafter, they were increasingly used in secondary spaces where their appearance was of little value. The inner shutter flaps installed in a simple domestic space when William Beverley II remodeled the south wing at Blandfield between 1801 and 1805 was one such location (Fig. 12.10H), as was a floor hatch hidden in a stair closet at Farmer's Mount in King and Queen County around 1810. Builders at Wales in Dinwiddie County (c. 1750s) used foliated hinges on exterior shutters—visible only when the shutters were closed—and plain face hinges inside.

While Chesapeake builders continued to use decorative face hinges well past their prime popularity, taste shifted toward conventionalized and less fussy iron hardware for polite spaces. Unlike Yeocomico Church, the main doors to Christ Church, Lancaster County (1732–35), the finest church in Virginia, were hung with completely plain HL and face hinges, as were doors to the pews. Builders did likewise with virtually all surviving later eighteenth-century Anglican churches in the region. The same is true of London

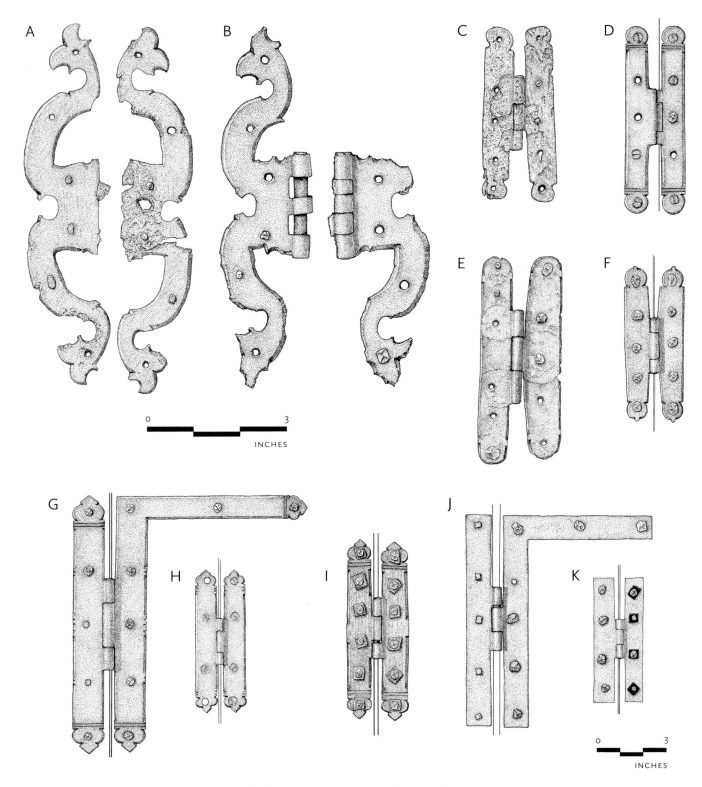

Fig. 12.10. *Cock's-head hinges. A: Walter Aston's House, Charles City County, Virginia; B: Two fragments from Mathews Manor, Newport News, Virginia. H and HL hinges. C and E: Corotoman, Lancaster County, Virginia; D: Interior shutter, Sabine Hall, Richmond County, Virginia; F: Domestic Wing, Mount Airy, Richmond County, Virginia; G: Chamber door, Sweet Hall, King William County, Virginia; H: Interior shutter, domestic wing, Blandfield, Essex County, Virginia; I: Thomas Everard House, Williamsburg, Virginia; J: Door to upper room, Bacon's Castle quarter, Surry County, Virginia; K: Knee-wall closet door, Pleasant Shade, Prince Edward County, Virginia.*

churches. By the 1680s, London church builders were using HL hinges that have simple rounded terminals or no elaboration at all. Decoration was focused elsewhere, on the larger elements of wood and masonry, not on fanciful blacksmith's work. Likewise, affluent Chesapeake builders came to prefer understated "neat and plain" work by the 1730s, rather than the rustic handiwork still beloved by merchants and farmers in the Connecticut River Valley and Germanic Pennsylvania.

Some of the shift can be read in Ruskinian terms as a decline in the care and individualized expression ironworkers were permitted to lavish on everyday wares. Most eighteenth-century H and HL hinges show signs of hasty fabrication; they lack even plain bevels or much attention to regularity of shape, let alone decorative finish (Figs. 12.10J, 12.10K). Weld marks created by folding the barrels into the arms were often left visible as products of quick production rather than being entirely hammered or filed away. Part of the reason was the accelerated pace of production. Staffordshire and London smiths produced tens of thousands of such hinges for the Georgian rebuilding at home and for export to Britain's colonies abroad. In the eighteenth-century Chesapeake and Carolina Lowcountry, builders and clients made side hinges the hardware of choice for refined spaces. Functional varieties developed for specialized uses, like "rising joint" hinges with offset barrels to allow clearance for doorjambs, shutters, and railed gates (Fig. 12.10D). Likewise, "raising," "rising," "worm," "screw," or "skew hinges" were made with a beveled bearing surface in the barrel or a threaded pin to raise a door leaf above carpets, stone paving, and other obstacles. Both elaborations increased the price by a quarter or more.[13] H-shaped hinges with especially long horizontal arms adjoining the barrel and short vertical extensions, called "shutter hinges" and "Parliament hinges," were principally used for exterior shutters.

But visual elaboration—what Joseph Moxon called "curious" work—largely disappeared from side hinges.[14] Whatever role increased production played, the refined taste of elites in Georgian Britain and the Chesapeake disdained the visual celebration of a building's structural or mechanical parts. Lacking interest in the decorative possibilities of side hinges, most builders of expensive houses preferred working hardware to be invisible after installation. Tuckahoe in Goochland County provides an early illustration. In the early 1730s, William Randolph's skilled joiners hung walnut doors upstairs on unfiled HL hinges with the stationary arms hidden behind the classical architrave. By the 1750s, builders constructing houses for successful Williamsburg tradesmen and lawyers often hid their fixed arms behind architraves in

the best rooms and set their movable arm flush in the face of door leafs. They were then painted over, leaving only seams and bumps to reveal their presence. HL hinges used when Charles Carter remodeled Shirley were primarily handled in this way, with exposed parts painted off-white to match the doors.[15]

The growing eighteenth-century preference for clean woodwork unencumbered by working hardware is illustrated by the alternatives employed in the refined rooms of the best Chesapeake houses. Rich men hid their hinges differently in different locations. One costly means was to use face hinges with polished brass plates that clipped into sockets on the functioning hinge arms, which were recessed into the face of leaf and frame. Such fittings expressed elite taste for bright materials and created a sense of refinement and play by drawing attention to the hinges while hiding their actual shape and means of attachment. In 1733, Randolph's builders used these on walnut doors opening into both first-floor rooms at Tuckahoe. Sometime after 1750, Philip Ludwell Lee installed pairs of them on a suite of bookshelf closet doors, further elaborating the grand entry hall his father had built at Stratford in 1738–39. He attached plain iron HL hinges on the two large doors leading into the passages. Soon-to-be-governor George Plater III employed them only on the mahogany door to his best reception room when he remodeled the rambling old wooden house called Sotterley in St. Mary's County, Maryland, in 1762–63 (Fig. 12.11). The alternative of making H hinges entirely of brass was advertised in English hardware catalogs into the nineteenth century, but they were never as popular with gentlemen in Virginia and Maryland as they were with West Indian planters. The handful of exceptions include Samuel Washington's use of them in the best room at Harewood (now Jefferson County, West Virginia) and Charles Carter's placement of them along the processional route from hall to river view at Shirley.

Beginning in the 1750s, wealthy house builders found a novel way to conceal the mechanics of door opening. A superior hinge had a heavy iron or brass arm of dovetail shape mortised and wedged into the edge of the leaf and a stationary arm of the same shape or of rectangular or T-shaped form screwed and hidden inside the doorframe, leaving only the barrel visible. Iron mortise hinges cost at least twice as much as HLs of comparable strength, and the delicate workmanship they required raised the cost of installation higher still.[16] In 1771–72, Robert Beverley, then probably the second-richest man in Virginia, used plain iron "Mortise Dove Tail hinges with screws" in all the room doors on both main floors of Blandfield in Essex County, while using

(top) Fig. 12.11. Hinge with snap-on brass plate on the door to George Plater III's best room at Sotterley, St. Mary's County, Maryland.

(bottom) Fig. 12.12. Mortise hinge used on the doors in John Randolph's best room at Tazewell Hall, Williamsburg.

side hinges in the cellar, attic, and kitchen wing.[17] Two years later, Fielding Lewis followed the same pattern when building his Fredericksburg house, using plain iron mortise hinges on every room and closet door except those to the cellar stair and the attic stair and within the cellar. There, HLs sufficed. Charles Carter was less enamored with mortise hinges, using them exposed and flush-mounted only on three first-floor doors at Shirley.

Inspiration for English mortise hinges probably came from the Continent, where tall brass versions with long decorative barrel caps and offset arms were a frequent choice for princely French and Italian buildings by the 1660s. Variants of this form became common for rebated doors in Central Europe before 1700. Hinge barrels could not be hidden, of course, and superior English brass mortise hinges had polished barrels that sprouted beefier decorative brass caps screwed onto both ends. This appealed to the profligate William Byrd III, who installed brass mortise hinges with such finials—tiny, carefully executed essays in classical form—on all principal doors in the main block of Westover about 1751. These were graduated in size, the largest confined to the pair of superior first-floor rooms and the smallest in lesser second- and third-floor chambers. They represent the most lavish use of such eighteenth-century hinges surviving in the region, installed by a Virginian who lived well beyond his means. Peyton Randolph settled instead for eight pairs of comparable brass mortise hinges on walnut doors for public spaces and his bedchamber when he enlarged his parents' old Williamsburg house in 1754–55, leaving the less-important painted pine doors with HL hinges. His brother John used large ones in front-stage spaces in his grand house nearby (Fig. 12.12). As late as 1809, Jefferson placed six sets of fine brass mortise hinges on the four passage doors opening into the entry hall at Monticello and on two doors opening into his bedroom, marking the status of the two-story hall and chamber. Brass mortise and face hinges favored show over durability, as their bearing surfaces wore down more rapidly, with the result that doors eventually dragged on the floor.

H and HL hinges remained the normal choice only as long as builders continued to believe that hinges with extended arms were required to firmly grip the leaf. About 1765, carpenters at the John Ridout House in Annapolis used H hinges mounted like butt hinges but screwed into the edge

(top) Fig. 12.13. H hinge mounted on the edge of a door leaf and jamb on third floor, Ridout Row, 112 Duke of Gloucester Street, 1773–74, Annapolis.

(bottom) Fig. 12.14. Cast-iron butt hinge secured with wrought nails to closet door at Myrtle Grove, 1791, Talbot County, Maryland.

of door leafs and rebates. Workmen did the same at Ridout's adjoining row houses, the neighboring Adams-Kilty House, and Wye House on the Eastern Shore in the 1770s and 1780s (Fig. 12.13). As the eighteenth century drew to a close, the variety of hinges narrowed, owing primarily to the advent of a versatile cast-iron butt hinge secured with flat-head screws. Although butt hinges, often of wrought iron, had been used on furniture and buffets since the 1720s and 1730s, technological improvements in the 1770s and 1780s allowed the production of sturdy cast-iron butt hinges that could carry heavy loads.[18] Aesthetics and economics contributed to the rapidly rising popularity of this hinge. With short rectangular arms set flush and screwed to the edge of the door and to the rebate of the doorframe, only the barrel remained fully exposed. Thus the butt hinge approximated the clean appearance of a mortise hinge and could be more easily installed.

Practical-minded George Washington bought raising butt hinges in Philadelphia for the interior and exterior doors of his new large dining room in 1788, a decade after he mounted iron mortise hinges on doors in the best first-floor rooms and installed HL hinges upstairs.[19] In the same year, the magistrates in Prince William County, Virginia, directed that a paneled door between the jailer's two rooms be hung "with common HL or butt hinges."[20] Builders hung a door on butt hinges with wrought nails and others with screws at Myrtle Grove in Talbot County, Maryland, in 1791 (Fig. 12.14). Carpenter John Inge installed fifty-four pairs of raising hinges at Prestwould in 1794–95; forty-two were wrought butt hinges.[21] At first, the use of butt hinges on doors remained experimental among well-off consumers, who thought of them in hierarchal terms. For his fine Norfolk house of 1796, the merchant Moses Myers selected raising butt hinges that had large and flashy polished brass barrels, steel bearing surfaces, and steel pins for all but one door on the first floor; cast-iron raising butts for the second-floor doors; and cast-iron nonraising butts for those on the third floor. Jefferson, by contrast, chose plain cast butt hinges for most doors on the three floors when he remodeled Monticello from 1796 to 1809. By 1820, butt hinges had become the most common form in the Chesapeake, but H and HL hinges were still used selectively into the second quarter of the nineteenth century, particularly in out-of-the-way locations.

Fig. 12.15. Mid-nineteenth-century stock lock mounted upside down, Tulip Hill, Anne Arundel County, Maryland.

LOCKS AND EARLY LATCHES

Locks and latches tell a comparable story and more clearly illuminate the growing preference for hiding the working elements of the mechanisms. They also illustrate that the different choices available by the third quarter of the eighteenth century were judged by the degree of their visual and tactile quality. Because people both saw and touched the handles of door locks and latches, these features became more important elements of refinement. The eventual ubiquity of shiny brass knobs in the region indicates that wealthy families preferred brass to iron, even though brass cost twice as much. Wood handles came in a distant third.

Archaeology has yielded a scant handful of seventeenth-century locks and latches, among them English-made locks with embellishments on the working parts. The row houses known as Structure 144 at Jamestown (1662–63) and the contemporaneous Rich Neck at Middle Plantation had wrought-iron spring latches with plates featuring decorative outlines of lobes and cymas and round holes, fitted with an ornamented bar (Fig. 12.1C). Oversized latch bars from Structure 17 at Jamestown and Mathews Manor likewise have picturesque outlines, rich bevels, and incisions done with straight, curved, and V-shaped files and chisels, all without any reference to a classical vocabulary (Figs. 12.1D). The latest known example was found in the cellar of Corotoman. Latches on iron casement windows excavated at Jamestown and Corotoman had thin iron ring handles used to pivot decoratively shaped catches into slots in the window jambs. The catches were mounted on guard plates with more elaborate silhouettes, one from Jamestown shaped as a fleur-de-lis and baluster.

The mechanism that operated most seventeenth-century plate locks was not complicated. Much like keyless latches, spring-loaded bars mounted on the open iron face were operated from inside the house or room by an iron arm or a lever and from outside by a key. Only the wards (projecting obstructions that allow only a key with matching notches to turn the bolt) and engaging part of the bolt were boxed. The other elements were exposed and could be decorated, as the keeper was shaped and filed on one installed at Abraham Peirsey's house (c. 1626) at Flowerdew Hundred on the south bank of the James River. The spring was scrolled and ornamental on a later and simpler plate lock at Structure 144 in Jamestown (Figs. 12.1E, 12.1F).

Chesapeake property owners increasingly selected locks over latches. By the second quarter of the eighteenth century, the shift away from emphasizing working parts resulted in a preference for locks contained in plain metal (rim lock) or wood (stock lock) cases, which householders used in both refined rooms and storage spaces. Many of these proved quite durable and still survive (Fig. 12.15). Stock locks generally have oak cases, often cut from riven planks and unevenly planed. Some seventeenth-century English-made stock locks have better-finished oak cases decorated with zigzag lines and C-shaped punches, similar to the embellishments found

Fig. 12.16. Brass rim lock and keeper, both with hidden means of attachment, on first-floor door at Westover, 1751, Charles City County, Virginia. An iron plate screwed to the door has hooks that engage with tabs cast into the brass case.

on ironwork from the same era. The cheapest of these locks were called "plain stock locks" or "Banbury locks," as many came from Banbury, Oxfordshire.[22] Lock makers nailed or screwed the works directly to the wooden case and sealed them with two small iron plates. Keepers for stock locks were often only an oversized iron staple driven into the doorframe. The vast majority of rim locks had iron cases. They generally came with a matching boxed keeper, which was screwed to the doorframe. Although boxed, this keeper often retained the old name "staple." Like plain face hinges, iron locks in conspicuous locations were usually painted to match the doors.

Most brass-cased locks used in Chesapeake houses date from late in the eighteenth century or from the first decades of the nineteenth. They were luxury items designed to impress visitors to the finest houses. Early in the 1750s, William Byrd III selectively used brass locks at Westover that are reminiscent of hinges with snap-on brass plates. These have works assembled in a polished brass outer case that hooked onto an iron plate, thereby hiding the screws. A thin brass plate also clipped onto the face of the keeper in order to create no visible means of attachment (Fig. 12.16). Charles Carter installed more conventional brass locks only on the two axial doors that had brass hinges at Shirley. At Prestwould, in 1794–95, the Skipwiths installed brass locks throughout the first-floor rooms and installed iron ones up-

stairs. In 1809, Michael Hancock placed them on the first- and second-floor doors of his fashionable Richmond house. Hancock followed common genteel practice in mounting flashy brass locks on the most visible side of his doors and modest iron locks on the rear of the door leaves, inside closets, and in service passages.

As with other late eighteenth-century hardware purchased in the Chesapeake, plain shiny surfaces trumped both mechanical displays and nonclassical ornament. Buyers chose locks that confined elaborate shapes and showy materials to the handles, keeper edges, and keyhole escutcheons. English brass founders smoothed away rough casting marks more carefully than their blacksmith brethren finished the ironwork. Most knobs on rim locks were round or oval, invariably brass, and adorned with classically inspired rosettes. Some buyers ordered a more costly type, with elegant, rococo-patterned pierced handles, which were called "lock rings," in reference to their plain iron predecessors, which turned easily when engaged by graceful hands.[23] Moses Myers had drop-handle rim locks installed throughout the first- and second-floor rooms of his house. Even wealthy householders chose handleless locks for lesser rooms and closets, where a key offered the only grip. Myers used these on his third-floor rooms. The Skipwiths placed them on a second-floor closet and all the cellar doors.

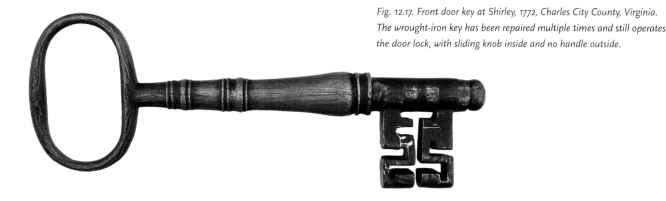

Fig. 12.17. Front door key at Shirley, 1772, Charles City County, Virginia. The wrought-iron key has been repaired multiple times and still operates the door lock, with sliding knob inside and no handle outside.

Keyholes were often left as cut from the door or stock case; better ones were finished with iron or preferably brass plates, usually oval. Keys continued to be made of wrought iron for the sake of durability until the declining price of brass, rising cost of labor, and improvements to the tumblers in the 1830s and 1840s made cast-brass keys practical. Georgian keys were nevertheless made more elegant by shaping the eye to receive two fingers comfortably and by turning the shaft with well-positioned classical moldings (Fig. 12.17).

The taste for hidden mechanism is evident by the 1760s in the most expensive security device chosen by very wealthy house builders, one that is analogous to mortise hinges—namely, mortise locks. These mechanisms, generally ¾ inch to 1¼ inches thick and roughly 5 to 7 inches long, were designed to slide into recesses carefully chiseled in the door edge. Many came with neat brass escutcheons designed to be applied to both sides, and each was treated as a simple composition in neoclassical oval, circles, and concave piercings (Fig. 12.2).[24] Mortise locks allowed keys to be smaller. A brass plate covered the iron outer edge of the lock. Bolts appeared only as small iron rectangles that slid smoothly into carefully sized holes in a brass plate discreetly attached to the doorjamb without breaking the lines of its classical architrave. When the door was closed, no bolt or keeper was visible, only the escutcheon and handles. Even keyholes were deemed unsightly, so manufacturers added pivoting three-dimensional keyhole covers.[25]

Such refinements cost dearly. George Wythe expected to pay from 7 shillings and 6 pence to 16 shillings and 6 pence each for the various mortise locks he ordered from John Norton in London in 1771.[26] The installation of mortise locks was time consuming and cost homeowners three to four times the amount charged for a common lock.[27] Purchasers were the owners of the Chesapeake's most expensive houses, and they used the locks selectively. Charles Carter installed them on most first- and second-floor room doors, but not on the third floor. Matthias Hammond created a subtle distinction between the public and private spaces in his Annapolis house, using smaller mortise locks with escutcheons on the sides of doors facing second-floor chambers and their passage but not that between (public) stair passage and (private) chamber passage. Richmond banker John Wickham used mortise locks on doors to first-floor rooms and the three best second-floor chambers but employed iron rim locks elsewhere in his town house (1811–13).

Many affluent house owners worried about the appearance of such details. George Washington thought using mortise locks on two exterior doors in the new dining room at Mount Vernon would "make the room more uniform," and he ultimately added them.[28] Jefferson decided to use mortise locks when rebuilding Monticello, in a characteristically complex way. In September 1805, he counted that he had ten mortise locks in hand but needed sixteen more for twenty-six doors. By the time the last of the doors were hung in about 1809, his workman had installed four varieties of mortise locks, numerous iron rim locks, and a few stock locks on the three refined floors of the house. In addition, the workman also positioned iron rim locks on doors to closets, privies, and lesser chambers. As a result, several kinds of locks or handles were often visible within a single space, particularly in the passages, offering the visitor a quick guide to the relative status of the room behind each doorway.

On exterior doors in even the best houses, rim locks could be reserved for front openings well past 1800, when rear and side doors were secured with wood bars that were dropped into an iron staple and bracket called a "bolt." In 1772, the St. Mark's vestry specified for a new glebe house: "One of the passage doors to have a strong spring lock[,] the others to be fixed with staple hook and barr."[29] Some exterior door locks, such as at Skipwiths' Prestwould, at Carter's remodeled Shirley, and at John Tayloe's Octagon in Washington, D.C., had only an interior handle, so anyone outside needed either a key or someone on the inside to open the door. Economy was not the issue. Control was. Guests had to wait until they were invited inside. At Shirley, a servant could stand unseen at the top of the cellar stairs and watch the porch. When someone approached, the servant could step into the hall, open the door from the inside, and disappear under the stair when the job was done. The Octagon had a porter's closet that more gracefully contained the same point of surveillance.[30] At Prestwould, a servant simply waited in the entrance hall.

Locks were an obsession for Chesapeake property owners in general. Tutor Philip Fithian recorded a nighttime intrusion by slaves into their owner's bedchamber in 1774 and reported "I sleep in fear too, though my Doors & Windows are all secured!" Several nights earlier, an intruder reached the Carters's nursery by tampering with the lock on its door.[31] Virtually all rooms and closets in expensive houses had them. Like drawers in chests, such spaces were probably locked when not in use, although junctions between circulation spaces were both unlocked and usually doorless. In a small house, a stair rising to a garret passage might remain open, but one rising directly into the garret chamber would have a door and often a lock.

That said, not all middling slave owners saw the need to lock every room or space. Planter Nathaniel Pruden, for example, owned seven slaves and 609 acres in Isle of Wight County when he built a four-room house there in 1821–22. Pruden never installed a key-operated lock between the hall and first-floor chamber, or between a second-floor lobby and at least one upper chamber. When he added a superior two-story wing fifteen years later, no locks were put on the new chamber doors or the entrance to a well-finished attic. At most, only two of eight rooms were locked before the end of the nineteenth century.

GEORGIAN LATCHES, SLIDING BOLTS, AND CHEAP LOCKS

Privacy within rooms could be attained through a variety of means, including installation of spring latches. These were neater in appearance by the 1740s, provided with brass knobs or ring handles and free of outdated ornament, but they did have exposed workings. The improved spring latches often came with a night latch so that a chamber door could be locked from the inside when occupied. They found acceptance in eastern Maryland in the decades after the Revolutionary War, but never to the degree that they were used in Britain for chamber and closet doors. Thumb latches were a half to a third the price, but they too found only a limited market among Chesapeake builders.[32] Most wealthy eastern Virginians and Marylanders judged them to be inferior to locks with knobs. The combination of a latch and separate lock was seen as ungainly after 1750, and these were usually relegated to rear doors on low-status spaces.

Cheaper still were wooden sliding bolts and string latches, easily made with everyday tools and mostly used for interior doors (Figs. 12.4, 12.5). Both commonly have beveled wooden staples and keepers of a form consistently seen in Britain, the Chesapeake, New England, and elsewhere. Except for the bevels, they were unornamented. String unceremoniously passed through a hole in the door stile or boards and was pulled to serve like a thumb lever, lifting the bar over the keeper. Large numbers of wooden latches still found in small houses and in low-security backstage spaces in expensive buildings suggest they were once extremely common.

Wide double doors generally marked major openings; their scale and symmetry enhanced the drama of arrival at genteel houses. Locking them required "slide bolts" or "staple bolts," as did double doors in public buildings. When the doors needed to be secured, a flat or rectangular bolt with a scrolled handle or round knob was slid through staples on the stationary leaf of the door and into staples in the door head.[33] Lower bolts were usually shorter and slid into a mortise in the doorsill or floor. A cased lock on the active leaf was then engaged with a keeper on the stationary one. These top-of-the-line examples also illustrate a shift from old artisanal decorative work to the plain aesthetic with classical form and best material confined to the handles. Charles Carter had a full ensemble, with brass knobs on long upper bolts and short lower ones, installed on all three axial first-floor doors at Shirley. They too marked the route from landside entry through the hall and parlor to the river-side door (Fig. 12.18A).

Taste and technology toward the end of the century favored hiding the bolt inside the door leaf, in the manner of mortise locks. Rich Virginians and Marylanders could then use "sunk bolts," with only a brass knob sliding above an iron or brass cover plate. By 1800, a clever mechanic could mount threaded bolts entirely hidden in the leaf. The bolt was operated by the spindle attached to an oval brass knob. This allowed users simply to turn the knob, which they could do more easily than shoving the bolt up or down. Builders Dinsmore and Neilson's 1804 installation of a spring-loaded bolt inside a stile of Jefferson's chain-geared doors between the hall and parlor at Monticello was the extreme expression of the Chesapeake gentry's fascination with graceful access to formal spaces. Jefferson then had his workmen mount imported iron door closers backward on the exterior parlor doors, so that the leaves would swing open automatically when their bolt was released. The two sets of mechanisms gave the inveterate design experimenter an effortless means of ushering guests along his processional route—from a hall hung with Indian relics, into the parlor occupied by portraits

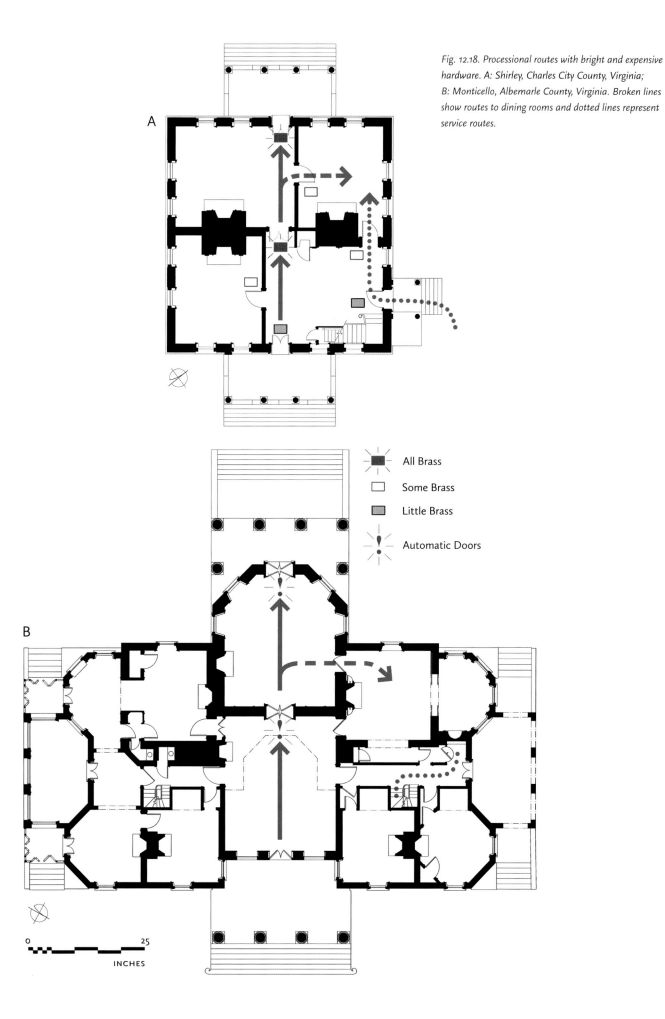

Fig. 12.18. Processional routes with bright and expensive hardware. A: Shirley, Charles City County, Virginia; B: Monticello, Albemarle County, Virginia. Broken lines show routes to dining rooms and dotted lines represent service routes.

All Brass

Some Brass

Little Brass

Automatic Doors

0   25

INCHES

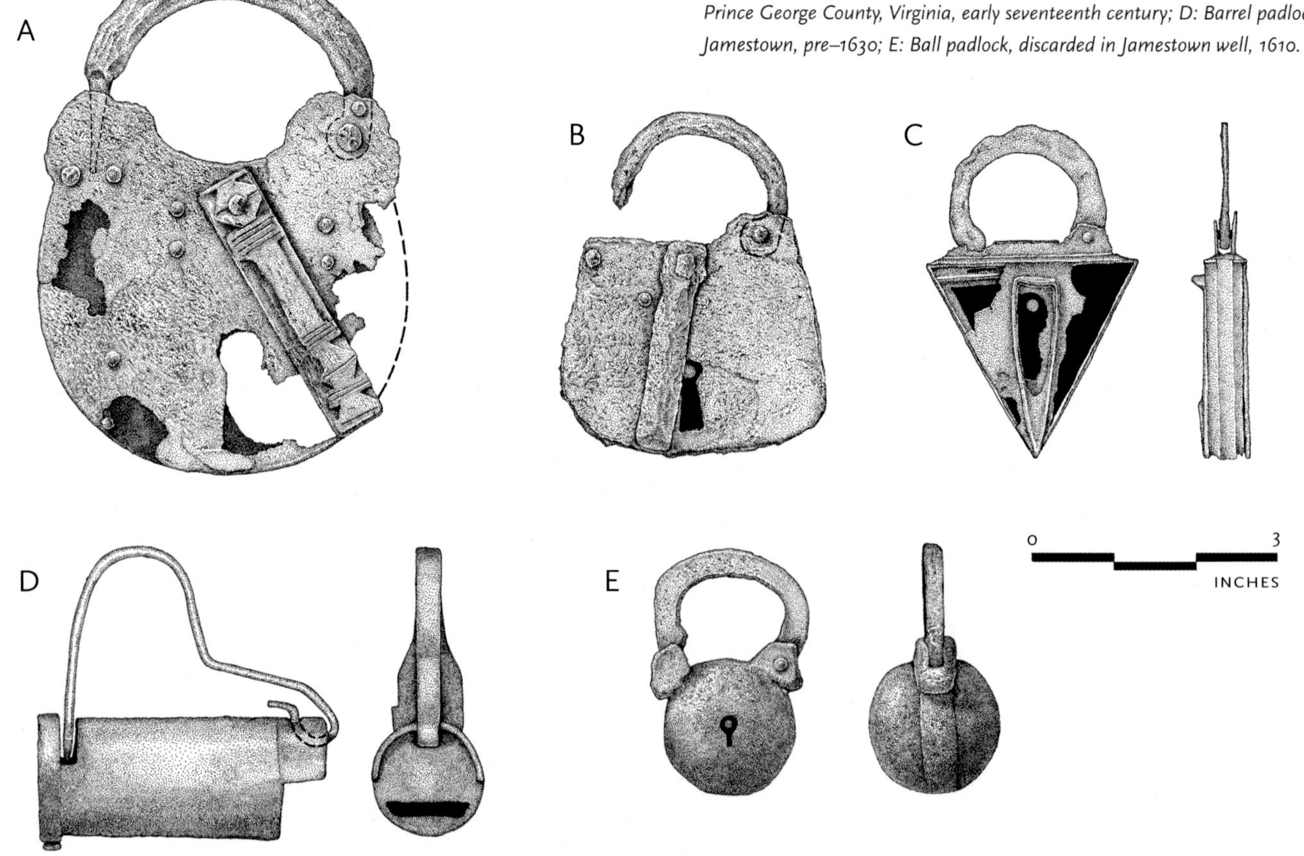

Fig. 12.19. Padlocks. A: Public Gaol, Williamsburg, early eighteenth century; B: Chiswell-Bucktrout House, Williamsburg, c. 1750; C. Flowerdew Hundred, Prince George County, Virginia, early seventeenth century; D: Barrel padlock, Jamestown, pre–1630; E: Ball padlock, discarded in Jamestown well, 1610.

of worthy men, and out to a lofty view of the Virginia countryside. It was the Carter sequence enlivened with wizardry (Fig. 12.18B).

By contrast, plain iron sliding bolts were applied horizontally to the inner faces of doors to rooms occupied by people of modest status. They provided a means of securing a room without a mechanical lock. Domestic workers used them in a plainly finished attic room at the Ridout House in Annapolis.[34] Wrought-iron hasps secured to staples with a padlock were a common alternative to box locks for storage and workrooms. Residents of another roughly plastered room in the attic at the Ridout House used a hasp attached to the frames on both sides of their door so they could lock the room when outside or inside without the use of a fixed lock.

Padlocks have been low-status fetters since the early seventeenth century (Fig 12.19). More than sixty have been found at the Jamestown Fort, all plain.[35] Early excavators found a large, 6½-inch padlock with filed geometric surface decoration on the keyhole cover at the Williamsburg jail, a singular exception to the dozens of completely plain, modest padlocks found elsewhere in the eighteenth-century town. By 1800, hasps and padlocks were used more commonly than

case and rim locks on corncribs, barns, and other backstage buildings.

Cheaper still was a locking method used by Chesapeake slaves to secure doors when inside their rooms. The surviving slave quarter at Prestwould and a detached kitchen (c. 1820) on the Pruden farm have holes drilled diagonally into the inner doorjamb. Occupants wedged a peg into such holes to prevent the doors from being pushed open from outside. When this was the sole means of locking, it represented protection of body more than property; otherwise a second lock was necessary outside. This contrasts with simply pegging closed a second exterior entrance, much like wood bars set in staples and brackets. Owners of the Roper-Carden House in New Kent County (c. 1800) had two doors opening into their single first-floor room. One was secured with a small rim lock, the other with a hefty peg, still today the only means for locking what has become the front door.

WINDOW HARDWARE

Window fittings, like door hardware, illustrate the pattern of comfort and conspicuous display, on the one hand, and utility and economy, on the other. In the mid-eighteenth

(top) Fig. 12.20. Sliding shutter closing a low rectangular window, Amos Council Kitchen, Southampton County, Virginia. The shutter is supported by wooden brackets and a wrought nail is its only handle.

(bottom) Fig. 12.21. Sash pulleys. A: Wetherburn's Tavern, Williamsburg; B: Walthoe's storehouse, Williamsburg; C: Montpelier, Orange County, Virginia. Boxwood wheels were set directly into window jambs at the storehouse in 1750 and into oak casings at Wetherburn's Tavern in the 1750s. Brass wheels were set in iron housings with polished brass covers in the 1809–11 wings at Montpelier.

A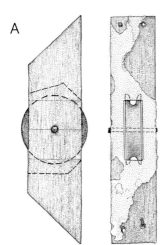

B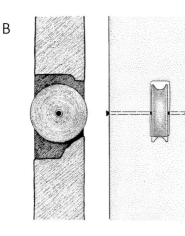

C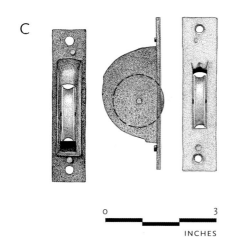

0   3

INCHES

century, spaces primarily occupied by slaves generally had small windows without glass. The best cellar cookrooms and quarters had low horizontal sash that swung up on face hinges and hooked overhead, as in the cellar rooms at Shirley and in Nathaniel Walthoe's storehouse in Williamsburg (1750). But most had only hinged or sliding wooden shutters at best. There was no means of closing the one exterior window in the occupied cellar room at Bowling Green. Improved cellar kitchens were increasingly fitted with movable glass sash after the American Revolution, but as late as the 1840s, board shutters in cheap accommodations were built to slide in crude wooden tracks, with one or two nails used for handles as the only hardware (Fig. 12.20).

By the second quarter of the eighteenth century, houses of the wealthy and the most respectable taverns had sizable glazed windows with vertically sliding sash. Sash windows were made more easily manageable and also more expensive by counterweighting, a technique that used lathe-turned hardwood wheels to raise and lower lead weights attached to ropes and set in the adjacent hollow window jambs. William Byrd II was promised pulleys for his windows at Westover in 1709.[36] The best early "frame pulleys" or "framed pulleys" had wheels in wood (usually oak) housings, which were in turn tacked into the upper tracks (Fig. 12.21A). Plainer ones had wheels pinned directly into the frame (Fig. 12.21B).[37] Both were superseded by metal frame pulleys and cast-iron weights at the end of the eighteenth century. Jefferson paid 42 shillings for six pair of brass pulleys in iron frames in Philadelphia in 1775.[38] James Madison preferred the brass variety when expanding Montpelier in 1809–12 (Fig. 12.21C).

Like most eighteenth-century hardware, use of window weights was selective.[39] The majority were used for windows in first and full upper stories but almost never in dormer or outbuilding windows. They were usually confined to the lower sash of each window, as at Tuckahoe in 1733 and in James Geddy's House, Wetherburn's Tavern, and Walthoe's storehouse, all midcentury Williamsburg buildings. Robert Beverley spent lavishly on Blandfield in 1769–72, and he

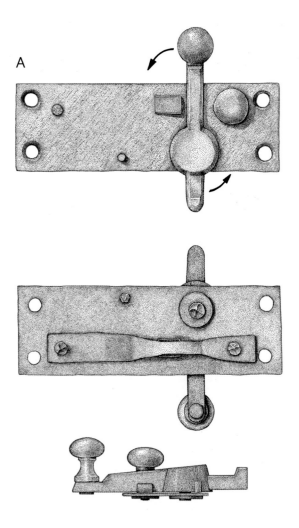

A

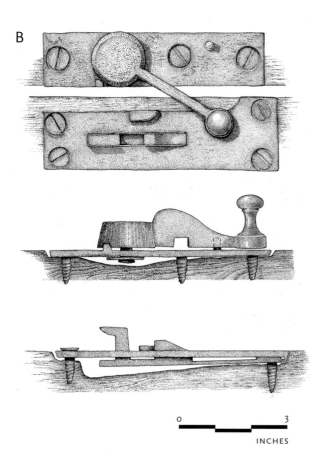

B

0   3
INCHES

counterweighted upper and lower sash on both main floors of the central block, but not the sash in the wings or the hyphens connecting them. Occupants there relied on stick props or wooden turnbuckles screwed or nailed to the window jambs.

Though Beverley was unconcerned about convenience for those who occupied lesser spaces on his plantation, he, like many other wealthy householders, did pay attention to security. The rooms that opened on the first-floor passage in his kitchen had locks on their doors and interior bars resting on wrought-iron keepers to secure their shutters. Charles Carter had similar concerns when he remodeled Shirley. He installed wooden brackets to hold wooden bars behind nearly every window from first to third floor and behind some of the cellar sash as well, notwithstanding that close-set iron bars were fixed permanently in these cellar windows. John Ridout fitted out the first-floor windows in his Annapolis house and three adjoining row houses with iron bars that pivoted on a bolt and rested on a catch in a diagonal position to keep the shutters closed against the sash. A pin could be pushed through the catch to lock the bar in place. The windows in John Tayloe's Williamsburg house were secured by

slide bolts with long plates that extended across the shutters and wrapped around the rebate for the sash, so the shutters were doubly locked in place when the bottom sash were lowered. Wealthy city dwellers seem to have been particularly concerned about break-ins. Ground-floor windows in John Wickham's Richmond house had slots in plastered jambs into which a loose horizontal bar was set behind closed shutters. To secure triple-sash rear windows, brackets helped hold horizontal iron bars in place, securing both upper and lower shutters. Wickham's family could more discreetly hook the shutter together using small metal arms and keepers, both of which pivoted and locked together with simple finger movements.

At Mount Vernon, in 1787, George Washington installed delicate "sash fasteners" on the windows in his two best rooms—the large dining room and the west parlor.[40] On each window, a small classical knob pivoted an arm mounted on one meeting rail until it engaged with a keeper on the other rail. The brass latch was locked in place by a tiny spring-loaded catch made of iron (Fig. 12.22A). Merchant John Wharton installed similar fasteners on all first-floor sash when building a well-finished Accomack County

Fig. 12.23. Bell slide applied to the side of a doorframe, Prestwould, Mecklenburg County, Virginia. When pulled, the device rang a bell mounted on the side of the Skipwith house nearest the kitchen.

plantation house in 1808–9 (Fig. 12.22B). Such fasteners were fragile, unlike Ridout's and Wickham's hefty bars, and would have thwarted few energetic burglars. Their primary purpose was to hold movable upper sash in place.

Assorted hardware allowed householders to open and close their paneled interior shutters with ease and grace. To preserve fingernails and dignity, Charles Carter put plain brass rings attached to brass-capped iron screws on all the shutters, from first floor to third floor at Shirley. Landon Carter installed three dozen shutter rings "to pull [shutters] out of their warmest [swollen] linings" at Sabine Hall.[41] The Skipwiths chose small brass knobs for this use and more expensive and comfortable drop handles for latching the inner leaves at Prestwould. Matthias Hammond included drop handles on all shutters in the main block of his house, with second handles on the rear face of first-floor shutters.

SERVANT BELLS

At the end of the eighteenth century, notions of refinement involved excluding slaves from public spaces as well as acquiring the appropriate equipage for entertainment.

Imported bell systems summoned domestic workers only when they were wanted. Increasingly, masters wished to control precisely when and where they encountered their serving staff. Owners and chosen guests in reception rooms and chambers used pulls, commonly called "slides" or "sliders," to call for help. The pulls themselves were attached to copper wires that moved around corners with the aid of "cranks" and passed through small holes in walls at the far end to ring brass bells mounted on springs. Beginning in England in the 1740s, such "house bells" were used to summon servants working or waiting below stairs. Chesapeake bell systems reflect the presence of slaves working outside the house, generally in a kitchen but sometimes perhaps in a detached servants' hall. Jefferson sought bells, cranks, and wire for Monticello in 1769, after Washington installed bells within earshot of the detached kitchen at Mount Vernon.[42] In the 1780s and 1790s, house bells became more common in the Chesapeake. Some were arranged to ring inside kitchen wings and cellar kitchens.[43] In 1795, the Skipwiths ordered "2 House Bells with Scrowl Springs . . . 3 doz. Bell Cranks . . . 1 doz Bell slides" and associated parts for Prestwould.[44] Six years later, in 1801, John Tayloe III paid $150 to have a "bell hanger" install a system at the Octagon in Washington, D.C. That same year, a bell system was ordered for the President's House, at John Adams's insistence. The bell hangers were called in from Baltimore.[45] Elaborate brass slides and levers appealed to the English market, where silently calling a servant was a celebrated act. In contrast, surviving bell hardware in houses in Virginia and Maryland is usually plain, although the cranks were always made of brass with iron spikes. Examples of variations in quality included cranks that were burnished and lacquered. The slides at Prestwould have decorative brass plates intended for display, but, positioned on the sides of doorframes in reception rooms and chambers, they are all but invisible (Fig. 12.23).[46]

HARDWARE FOR WORK AND STORAGE

Hardware in domestic work spaces and storerooms in the Chesapeake contrasted sharply with that in refined spaces in affluent households. Unlike early New England kitchens and especially those in Rhenish-American houses, Chesapeake workrooms as well as quartering spaces were virtually devoid of decorative hardware. The poorest level of cooking was with a single pot—the utensil owners most often provided slaves for the workers' own meals. Cooks used wrought-iron hooks and chains to hang cast-iron pots and kettles from straight iron or wood trammel bars set horizontally into the inner side walls of fireplaces. Cooking cranes allowed easier move-

Fig. 12.24. Plain iron cooking cranes in the fireplace at Blandfield, 1769–72, Essex County, Virginia.

ment and more flexibility when preparing multiple dishes. The crane's vertical post pivoted in two iron gudgeons set into the fireplace masonry and carried the working arm with help from a diagonal brace.[47] A grand house like Blandfield might have a pair of cranes in the cooking fireplace. Even the most substantial Chesapeake cranes have little visual elaboration, unlike those in regions where the kitchen was at the core of the owner's house, which were favorite elements for decoration (Fig. 12.24).

Roasting offered a means of refining food. Iron spits carried by stationary hooks on the face of andirons could be turned by hand or, expensively, by a mechanical clock jack driven by lead weights. Robert Beverley ordered a "spit to roast meat on" for his kitchen at Blandfield.[48]

Twenty-nine eighteenth-century York County inventories mentioned spit jacks. These include inventories of Williamsburg tradesmen, like armorer John Brush in 1727 and gunsmith James Geddy in 1744, as well as tavern owners and wealthy merchants. Among these successful tradesmen and elites, the value assigned to their spits, jacks, andirons, and sometimes a dripping pan ranged from £2 to £6, depending on quality, age, and number of pieces. The implication is that the majority were plain, without the brass or iron ornament lavished on many surviving jacks in England.[49] Most expensive were heat-driven smoke jacks turned by heat rising

through the chimney flue. A "Smoak Jack and 3 Iron Spits" in Governor Robert Eden's Annapolis house were valued at £15 in 1776.[50] Jacks were less commonly used in the Chesapeake countryside, where trammels and cranes were deemed sufficient, even in most wealthy households.

The prevalence of specialized equipment for tending wood or coal fires in domestic rooms reflects an ambition by middling folk to live politely in new post-Revolutionary parlors and chambers with the aid of ornamental fittings to hold tongs and shovels. Wooden pegs used for hanging garments and hats were confined in well-built houses to passages and closets, in contrast to showy brass pins employed to hold curtains and hang pictures in the finest rooms. Armorer John Brush confined hanging pegs to a lobby at the rear of his Williamsburg passage. Peg strips on the walls of back stair passages at Bewdley in King and Queen County and Wales in Dinwiddie County are more representative than those in the splashy entrance hall at Ker Place in Onancock. Affluent and middling residents increasingly stored textiles on closet shelves and in freestanding furniture. Poor householders lacked specialized fireplace equipment and refined storage containers. Many eighteenth-century slaves stored belongings in subfloor pits. Nails were the poor person's most durable means of ready storage. In kitchens, separate quarters, and occupied attics, dozens of wrought and early cut nails methodically driven into the sides of joists, rafters, and collars show where food, tools, and apparel were hung overhead.

❖ Changing taste in hardware, like the demise of ornamental framing and the growing popularity of uniform brickwork, contributed to the development of the polite Chesapeake house. The change was gradual, but it accelerated most in the second quarter of the eighteenth century. Georgian hardware was seldom more functional than its predecessors. Excellence of appearance rather than improved operation accounts for much of its selection by affluent house owners. Beyond fulfilling needs of accommodation and security, new locks, latches, and hinges were used alongside masonry and carpentry for calculated architectural effect. In small ways, they served as signals for movement through the largest gentry houses. More commonly, they contributed to spaces that genteel residents constructed as settings for acting out roles aimed at asserting or demonstrating one's rightful place in a wider community of ladies and gentlemen.

Variations in hardware were used to fine-tune gradations of quality no less than was woodwork, wallpaper, and other finishes. The greatest contrast was between refined entertaining spaces and unrefined work and storage areas. Distinctions between these rooms remained particularly conspicuous into the 1850s and 1860s, when mechanized production of building materials began to transform basic qualities of finish and light and the region's principal workforce was at least statutorily freed. Mass production of hardware happened sooner, including cast butt hinges and rapid assembly locks, along with fully machine-manufactured nails and screws. The greater availability of these products extinguished much of the evident range in quality that had characterized Chesapeake hardware in the second half of the eighteenth century.

Both the purchase of British wares and the binary distinction between refined and rough, respectable and otherwise, characterized early hardware in other regions with staple-producing economies, notably the Carolina Lowcountry and the British Caribbean, as well as Britain and the Chesapeake. Variations in the use of hardware among the substantial slaveholding regions were subtle. Greater differences stemmed from the impact of craft traditions and aesthetics that lay outside the British Isles, particularly regions that had sizable populations whose origins were European. Successful mid-Atlantic farmers favored heavy strap hinges for exterior and even some fine entertaining room doors well into the nineteenth century, as did wealthy urbanites for outside shutters and cellar doors. Rhenish-American smiths executed for Germanic-speaking households decorative versions of hinges with wriggling serpentine shapes or with the outline of snakes having eaten eggs or dividing hydralike into multiple arms.

Decorative strap hinges and alternatives with circular arms were common in Portuguese- and Spanish-settled areas of America well into the mid-nineteenth century, sometimes with pintles hammered and filed into fancy shapes that a British smith or Virginia house builder would have thought ridiculous. Continental nationalities shared affection for certain flamboyant and nonclassical shapes, Rhenish-Americans also using circular and other wide, compact arms. Germanic, Dutch, and French smiths in America all combined these rounded nailing plates with straps, more for show than for strength. Such work was not purely non-British. Connecticut Valley smiths created showy iron latches that complemented outrageously overdrawn frontispieces on merchant houses. Connecticut smiths worked with joiners to match strap hinges to the shape of curved door rails. The observer would look in vain for such collaboration in the Chesapeake, where builders and property owners ordered conventional metal hardware or bought it off store shelves. New England smiths, in general, supplied more hardware with regional folk qualities. The smaller amounts of local ironmongery in the Chesapeake followed plain British models, to the degree that most pieces were unrecognizably regional. Strap hinges stamped with the name "Geddy," a blacksmith family in Williamsburg, are otherwise identical to hinges from the English Midlands (Fig. 12.7G).

At the root of these regional contrasts was the perception of labor. Drudgery's association with slave labor created in the Chesapeake a division between areas of refinement and those for workers and service that was even more stark than the upstairs-downstairs divisions of elite British households. Rhenish and Dutch households in North America, as well as English-speaking households in New England, were different, even at the most elite level. The fact that artisanal ornament on hardware existed at all in these other regions into the early nineteenth century and could be found there in kitchens and butteries can be seen as an expression of a more socially integrated society. Hardware in Virginia and Maryland reveals genteel house owners' keeping an eye on distant metropolitan models, but it more significantly illustrates the profoundly segregated nature of life in the early Chesapeake.

Finishes

13 Exterior Finishes

WILLIE GRAHAM

Among early American builders, the word "workman-like" covered a multitude of expectations left unspoken. It appeared frequently in building contracts as a catchall phrase for work not specified but still required.[1] This all-encompassing term can be vexing to architectural historians looking for explicit evidence of house-building practices in the Chesapeake colonies. But the shorthand word had its uses, too. As Carl Lounsbury notes in chapter 5, "workman-like" served as a marker that separated those parts of a building that builders and clients took for granted from others that could not be and had to be spelled out. It drew a line between much that was traditional and commonplace and aspects that were novel and required explanation to ensure that all parties understood each other's intentions (Fig. 13.1).

That difference runs like a bright line through this chapter on finish work applied to the outside of houses and the treatment of interior finishes in the next chapter. Both describe carpentry work in the centuries before postbellum sash and blind factories supplied ready-made building materials. While the heyday of finish carpentry predated factory-made finish work by almost two centuries, the fundamentals of its character can be traced to the second half of the seventeenth century. It was then that "workmanlike" was used to cover a set of firmly entrenched building conventions to create the so-called Virginia house. Yet, sometime in the 1690s, the term began covering less than everything that house builders needed to know. Carpenters were increasingly confronted with names and descriptions of architectural features that until then had little place in the vernacular building traditions of the region, words like "cornice," "modillion," "architrave," and "mantelpiece." Their abrupt appearance in the space of two or three decades indicates that something was changing what owners wanted their houses to look like. As a consequence, they altered the instructions to the workmen they hired. Traditional dwellings acquired moldings, turnings, and other decorative elaborations that owed little to folk conventions. Instead, this new work had genealogies

that ran back, albeit many times removed, to Renaissance renditions of classical antiquity. An aesthetic revolution redefined finish carpentry from that time forward. In the process, it challenged house builders to add cabinetmaker's skills to their repertoire of age-old carpentry practices.[2]

One result of this revolution is the proliferation of decorative elements that are described in the following catalogue raisonné. Another is the formal composition of many architectural features, such as a balanced disposition of windows and doors. A third goes to the very meaning of finish work. The surfaces of eighteenth-century houses were literally given a finish—a skin-deep appearance—that masked the framework underneath. Eaves were boxed, architraves were applied to door and window frames, lath-and-plaster walls were brought forward, and ceilings were lowered to hide

Fig. 13.1. West St. Mary's Manor, St. Mary's County, Maryland. (Frances Benjamin Johnston, 1930s, Library of Congress)

structural posts and beams. Likewise, floorboards were blind nailed, walls were paneled, hardware was concealed, fireboxes were plastered, and their openings were framed with decorative tiles and trimmed with chimneypieces. Painters, and before long paperhangers, finished the makeover, all to the purpose of creating appearances and conveying meanings that were more complex and distinct from those embodied by an earlier generation of dwellings.

The difference was not simply the introduction of ornament where none had been before. Traditional buildings had at times been enriched, too, but a different principle had governed this use of ornament. Structural elements of earlier houses were themselves embellished, not concealed behind faux surfaces. Their posts and beams were edged with chamfers, plank partitions were planed with shallow moldings, and nail heads were formed into decorative patterns on doors. In contrast, Renaissance-inspired finish work reached for an altogether different effect. The new idiom was both the basis for and the coordinator of wall treatments, ceilings, staircases, window and door openings, and built-in storage cabinets, in short, all the architectural elements needed to create a theatrical setting, a stage with scenery, as it were, for performances that took place in genteel parlors, dining rooms, and chambers. Trimmed-out reception rooms became performance spaces for activities that began in this period to distinguish ladies and gentlemen from their rustic neighbors who still followed an older-fashioned way of life

(Fig. 13.2). From the early eighteenth century forward, craftsmen employed in the finishing trades were expected to create formal facades and refined interiors to provide their aspiring clients with appropriate settings for the serious business of leading refined and genteel lives.[3]

Eventually, the term "workmanlike" came to encompass these formal architectural features, as they, too, became commonplace. Novelties and innovations gradually entered the vocabularies and working traditions of house carpenters, joiners, plasterers, and painters throughout British America, but not everywhere at once. Usually, it took some major building event—an urban building boom, for instance—to codify a developing custom, which then, going forward, gave buildings throughout the region a family resemblance. This new finish work, whether influenced by London, Boston, Philadelphia, or someplace else, was comprehensible to anyone versed in the classical language of architecture. Still, each city and its hinterland developed its own architectural dialect. Maryland and Virginia were no exception.

The neat-and-plain look of Chesapeake buildings (for so it was called) owed its initial impetus to the founding of the two relocated colonial capitals at Williamsburg and Annapolis in the first decade of the eighteenth century. The swarm of artisans who assembled there to build the statehouses, churches, official residences, and other public and private buildings in those two cities established basic heavy-frame carpentry conventions that soon spread to the countryside

(top) Fig. 13.2. The drawing room as it was rebuilt in 1768–70, Sotterley, St. Mary's County, Maryland.

(bottom) Fig. 13.3. Eppington, Chesterfield County, Virginia. The house was built in stages, starting soon after the builder, Francis Eppes, reached his majority in the late 1760s, but it was not completed until 1802, near the end of his life.

and prevailed for the rest of the century. A second building boom replaced much of the housing stock a generation later in Williamsburg and two generations later in Annapolis. Each rebuilding set the mold for the refined finish carpentry that prepared many new or remodeled houses in Virginia and Maryland to enter, quite literally, into polite society.

Field research undertaken in the last thirty years has made a special study of trim work throughout the region. Researchers can now explain how carpenters and clients expanded the meaning of "workmanlike," from the clapboard-covered vernacular houses the term had once described into the theaters of good manners that it eventually came to signify. The scene setting and the drama began on the exterior—the subject of this chapter—before moving inside, where genteel performances were acted out in full—as described in the next chapter (Fig. 13.3).

EXTERIOR CLADDING MATERIALS

It should come as no surprise that the construction materials of early frontier dwellings built outside of Jamestown had wall finishes similar to the simple ones used in the colonists' first forts and the modest clay and thatched dwellings their builders remembered from back home. William Strachey, one of the early secretaries of the Virginia colony, reported that, from the start, buildings had been "pargeted and plastered with bitumen or tough clay."[4] Clay was an expeditious choice because supplies were easily collected and its application required no great skill to master. At its best, a thin coating of plaster or whitewash weatherproofed both the underlying frame and the mud panels in between.[5] By midcentury, though, the practice of either building with solid earthen walls or parging daub on panels of wooden armatures was mostly confined to start-up settlements or cheaply built secondary structures (see Fig. 6.5).[6]

Whereas clay had been a common traditional wall material in many parts of Great Britain, riven clapboards, an American novelty, eventually replaced it as the covering of choice for walls. It doubled for roofs and was even used on interior partitions and for attic floors in the Chesapeake houses by the middle of the seventeenth century.[7] Little attempt was made to ease the roughness of these short boards and their conspicuous vertical columns of nail heads when used as wall and roof coverings. Clapboard siding required no corner boards or bargeboards. Instead, the boards on gables were scribed to those on the long walls, which in turn were carried an inch or two beyond the corners to make the seal as watertight as possible. Often a coating of pine tar pro-

vided additional weatherproofing to walls and roofs, however much it coarsened their appearance.

While it is known that clay and clapboards covered the walls of virtually all earthfast structures in the second half of the seventeenth century, it is less certain how better-built timber structures were treated. Most likely, many so-called English frame houses were also clapboarded. A good indicator is the persistence of clapboards applied to walls and roofs of many gentry houses as late as 1750, even in the style-conscious towns of Annapolis and Williamsburg.[8] Despite their use of old-fashioned siding, these town houses frequently sported boxed cornices, sash windows, concealed framing, and other refinements shared with nearby dwellings covered with more up-to-date sawn-and-planed weatherboards. Occasionally in the eighteenth century, and more often in rural Maryland than in Virginia, split clapboards were themselves carefully planed and fitted, the joints staggered to minimize their visual impact, and sometimes they were even beaded to look more like sawn weatherboards once they received a coat of paint. These knockoffs employed traditional splitting technology to achieve stylishness on the cheap.

Dwellings and farm buildings raised on a crib of interlocking logs rapidly replaced the hole-set Virginia house among ordinary builders as the eighteenth century wore on, especially in the backcountry, but here and there in the longer-settled Tidewater counties as well (see Fig. 10.15).[9] Not all log buildings received the same degree of finish. They ranged from makeshift cabins to better-built structures, such as a story-and-a-half, two-room parsonage the churchwardens of Augusta Parish, Virginia, wanted built. The wardens instructed carpenters to square logs and dovetail them at the corners for the parsonage, directing them to roof it with side-lapped shingles, and install wooden floors throughout.[10] The popularity of this new walling system meant that many ordinary buildings of the eighteenth century traded one type of coarseness—clapboard work—for another—logs that were rough hewn, sawn, or left in the round. Although clapboards continued to see service into the nineteenth century, particularly for secondary structures, sawn weatherboards were used on more and more dwellings and other frame buildings intended for show after the turn of the eighteenth century. Weatherboards were often planed on their exposed face and beaded on their bottom edge, but variation did exist. Savings were afforded by eliminating planing (left "in the rough"), and occasionally field research turns up unbeaded boards. Ovolo moldings, perhaps inspired by buildings farther south, occasionally substituted for beads, especially in Southside Virginia and eastern North Carolina

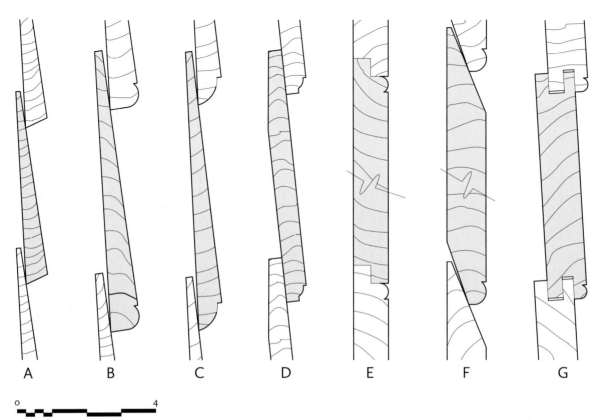

A   B   C   D   E   F   G

0   4

INCHES

Fig. 13.4. Clapboard and weatherboard profiles. A: Clapboard, Holly Hill, Anne Arundel County, Maryland; B: Beaded weatherboard, Strawberry Hill, Petersburg, Virginia; C: Ovolo-molded weatherboard, Wales, Dinwiddie County, Virginia; D: Weatherboard molded with ovolo and fillet, Bragg House, Petersburg, Virginia; E: Beaded flush-board sheathing, Myrtle Grove, Talbot County, Maryland; F: Beaded cyphered sheathing, Sotterley, St. Mary's County, Maryland; G: Beaded tongue and groove siding, Bowman Farm, Frederick, Maryland.

from the 1780s through the 1810s. Even greater differences can be observed from region to region in the width of weatherboards—6-inch exposures were conventional throughout most of Virginia, generally with a 1½- to 2-inch overlap, and these boards were invariably tapered or "feathered" in cross section.[11] In contrast, Virginia buildings immediately south of the Potomac River and north into Maryland were usually clad with wider boards, often with 8- to 10-inch exposures; they could be untapered and simply given a short bevel at their top, nestling the front of one board against a back bevel at the bottom of the course above it. Alternatively, beaded solid sheathing was sometimes shiplapped, especially on the Upper Shore after the middle of the eighteenth century. No matter what their exposure, long, sawn weatherboards gave exteriors a regularized appearance and provided more substantial covering than clapboards in this new age that most respected orderliness, refinement, and durability (Fig. 13.4).

Like clapboards, weatherboards capitalized on the abundance of timber everywhere in the region. All the same,

their preparation was more labor intensive and therefore more costly. The payoff came in their overall appearance, weather resistance, and longevity. The greater length of sawn boards, the uniformity of planed surfaces, a shadow-catching bead running along each board's lower edge, and staggered joints—all conspired to trick the eye. Their finish gave these broad planes the appearance of unbroken, uniform rows that contrasted with the roughly textured surfaces and staccato effect of many short clapboards. Both features, weather tightness and regularity, made weatherboards an ideal covering for gentlemen's houses from this time forward.

New circumstances influenced builders' choices of wall coverings after the Revolution and into the early nineteenth century. More clients could afford nicely trimmed, longer-lasting houses than ever before.[12] Consequently, traditional building materials and finishes such as clapboards, tar, and wooden chimneys gradually fell from the house carpenters' repertoire. Before long, growing numbers of water-driven sawmills supplied builders with less expensive weatherboards, which spread their popularity. At the same time, though, many ordinary farmers in the older and now poorer areas of settlement tended to build small but often well-constructed houses and outbuildings that, while less well finished than such farmhouses had been a generation earlier, still compared favorably with smaller gentry townhouses of that earlier era. The beads on weatherboards were often smaller than they had been before the Revolution, and moldings around openings and along cornices were now

Fig. 13.5. Clay filling in the partition that separates the hall from the passage, Mason House, 1729–30, Accomack County, Virginia. Clay filling and brick filling (brick filling was called "nogging" in the nineteenth century) were used for insulation from the weather and as soundproofing in the more public rooms of houses.

frequently cut with neoclassical profiles. Still, these country houses were essentially conceived as Georgian boxes. The persistence of their conservative trim work often led earlier generations of historians to mistake them for structures built before the Revolution (see Fig. 11.19).

EAVES

Field researchers can only speculate about the finishing of eaves on those seventeenth-century houses known only from archaeological excavation. The rafters on most houses probably stood directly on the walls below with little to no overhang, as does the massive roof frame at Bacon's Castle. As discussed in chapter 10, on framing, earlier Chesapeake roof systems did not require the over-sailing floor joists to which boxed cornices were so conveniently attached.[13] Their introduction came the other way around. Specifications for "jettied roofs" show up with growing frequency at the turn of the eighteenth century, indicating that overhangs were,

if not completely novel, at least not yet routine. It was the fashion for classical cornices that finally made an overhang a necessity. With or without an overhang, eaves that lacked the protection afforded by a cornice resulted in drafty interiors. Seventeenth-century documents indicate that the problem could be fixed by packing the walls and eaves with clay (Fig. 13.5).[14] Surviving physical evidence for such expedients is slight; it may be assumed from later examples that carpenters also inserted short clapboards between the joist ends to stop drafts at the eaves in the Virginia house.

Fully developed cornices appeared first on churches, public buildings, architecturally ambitious plantation houses, and, soon after, town houses. Classically inspired cornices on such edifices as the College of William and Mary and even the remote Yeocomico Church, Westmoreland County, prove that such newfangled ideas had reached the gentlemen who commissioned and oversaw these projects by the turn of the century. They lost no time rehabbing or rebuilding their own houses with similar improvements. Cornices were rou-

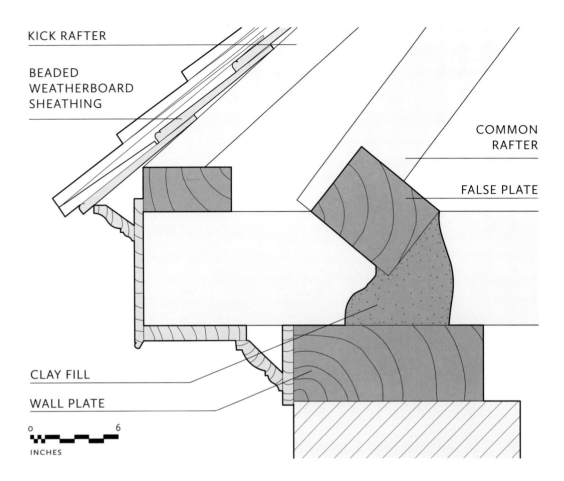

KICK RAFTER

BEADED
WEATHERBOARD
SHEATHING

COMMON
RAFTER

FALSE PLATE

CLAY FILL

WALL PLATE

0   6

INCHES

Fig. 13.6. Kick rafters and boxed eaves at the Mason House, 1729–30, Accomack County, Virginia. Although Mason wanted a boxed cornice on this early country house, his carpenters nonetheless employed a tilted false plate to carry the rafter feet, and thus repurposed it simply as a functional structural element.

tinely installed on all types of fashionable buildings in town, as well as on many civic and ecclesiastical structures in the countryside. By the 1720s and 1730s, even most two-story country houses were likewise fashionably corniced.

The tradition of the feet of rafters seated directly atop wall plates (and not on the ends of jettied joists) persisted a while longer as carpenters got used to the idea of boxed cornices. In these cases, the joists overhung the wall plate, to which the cornice was then secured. Short kick rafters extended the roof beyond the plane of the wall. These kicks piggybacked on the tops of the main rafters to create a sweeping sculpted roof profile, a design treatment consistent with a baroque taste, which was quickly superseded in the Tidewater by a more severe neat-and-plain aesthetic as the fashion for kick rafters waned (Fig. 13.6).

Wooden houses from the turn of the eighteenth century suggest that the practice of boxing the overhanging eaves with fascias and soffits came later to moderate-size plantations. Exposed rafter ends and decorative false plates were the norm on rural houses until the middle of the eighteenth century, and these came later still to more remote parts of the region. The citified notion that structural elements should be decorously hidden from view made little sense to most country gentlemen, and they even delighted in showing off exposed eaves construction, often by rounding and chamfer-

ing the joist ends and giving pleasing shapes to rafter feet. Rural builders only came round to adding formal cornices gradually when they adopted sawn weatherboards and other exterior refinements. Little by little, the finished appearance of houses in town and country became more alike.

Whereas simple classical cornices with and without modillions held sway over much of the region, Annapolis builders at the pinnacle of their trade began installing more elaborate cornice treatments beginning in the 1760s, as did carpenters working on large country houses influenced by Annapolis tastes and standards. Some presented full entablatures. Others flaunted Georgian conventions in unorthodox and fanciful inventions that foreshadowed the imaginative and often whimsical cornices that became commonplace in the neoclassical era. A taste for revival forms in the 1830s and 1840s heralded a return to plainer cornices when architectural fashion embraced ancient Greek models.

CORNER BOARDS, BARGEBOARDS, AND END BOARDS

Walls sheathed with sawn weatherboards were neatly trimmed with corner boards and roof rakes for both practical and aesthetic reasons. Corner boards, used to protect the end grain of weatherboards, were usually about 3 inches wide,

Fig. 13.7. Cibula Slave House, c. 1825, Prince George County, Virginia.

with a bead on the outside corner. Nailed to each corner of the two long walls, they ran from sill to the bottom of the cornice or eaves framing (Fig. 13.7). They were sufficiently thick for the weatherboards to fully terminate against them. A common alternative was to wrap the corner board onto the gable elevations with a bead or an ovolo molding applied to the corner of the two pieces. Bargeboards also helped protect the ends of weatherboard courses in the gables where they met the roof. They followed the slope from the eaves to the ridge, tapering an inch or more in width in order to create a perspective illusion that the roof was steeper than it really was. An occasional variation included the addition of a backband at the top of the rake, thereby making a more prominent feature of the board. Bargeboards on frame buildings sat on top of the weatherboards, and at the eaves they were terminated by an end board that capped the cornice, if one existed. If not, the bargeboards were simply cut off, either square or in some decorative manner. End boards were decorative, too, and usually cut to the shape of the cornice, except that they often projected about a half inch beyond the cornice profile to create a sharp shadow line. These trim pieces—bargeboards, corner boards, and end boards—did double duty by neatly framing each wall in a way that was visually pleasing while at the same time protecting vulnerable parts of the weatherboards and the cornice from direct exposure to the weather.

ROOFING MATERIALS

Before clapboards, thatch must have been the most common roofing material for all buildings outside of Jamestown.[15] Thatch was made of dried vegetation, usually straw, reed, or marsh grass, gathered into bundles and lashed to a light framework of crosspieces secured to the rafters. The first dwellings at Kecoughtan in present-day Hampton were described in 1610 as "thatch'd cabins." A century-and-a-half later, Landon Carter thatched a pair of tobacco barns he repaired in Richmond County.[16] Thatch was probably a common roof covering as long as clay walls remained dominant. Once carpenters came to appreciate the cost efficiency of clapboards for walls and roofs alike, the use of thatch declined and was relegated to a few secondary structures and homestead structures in the backcountry.[17]

The most complex and expensive roof materials of the seventeenth century were clay tiles and stone slates. They were occasionally used on the best early buildings, notably those erected at public expense. Ceramic tiles and slates from the second quarter of the seventeenth century have been found on a few archaeological sites, where excavators

Fig. 13.8. A: Recovered pantiles from Rich Neck, c. 1665, James City County, Virginia; B: Flat roofing tile from Robert Beverley's lot, last quarter of the seventeenth century, Jamestown (Courtesy Jamestown Rediscovery, Preservation Virginia).

recovered both flat tiles and S-shaped pantiles (Fig. 13.8). Slates and flat tiles were nailed in place. Pantiles usually had lugs molded on their underside from which they were hung on laths. Sometimes they were additionally reinforced with a thin bed of mortar laid between each course. Always they were a minor alternative to thatch and eventually wooden coverings, except at Jamestown.

Tile roofs gave this first Virginia capital, such as it was, a vaguely London look. Three-fifths of almost forty seventeenth-century building sites explored by archaeologists have produced pantile and flat tile fragments or pieces of imported slate. Fully three-fourths of the brick buildings in Jamestown were originally covered or repaired with tiles or slates, and so were more than half the known timber structures.[18] The abundance of tile roofs in Jamestown and their rarity elsewhere mark one of the conspicuous differences

Fig. 13.9. Round-butt shingle roof, Bowling Green, 1743, Caroline County, Virginia. Shingles were "combed" at the ridge and fanned in the valleys.

between town and country building until the end of the seventeenth century.[19]

This was less true a few years later, when the Virginia capital moved to Williamsburg. By then, slates and tiles were giving way to wooden shingles. The Governor's Palace, begun in 1706, was covered with slates. Yet, three years later, the roof needed repair—tradesmen complained that no one remembered how to lay a slate roof and so they substituted shingles.[20] As Robert Beverley noted, "They have Slate enough in some particular parts of the Country and as strong Clay as can be desired for making of Tile, yet they have very few tiled Houses."[21] The problem was not supply. Dutch merchants had sold tiles by the shipload to buyers in Maryland before the Navigation Acts curtailed the trade. Some wealthy planters ordered them directly from England, and at least two brickyards in eastern Virginia produced tiles for the local market. One was the brick-and-tile works that John Page operated on the outskirts of Middle Plantation, later renamed Williamsburg.[22] Tile and stone roofs, despite some advantages, impeded the tendency to streamline the carpenter's art. The heavy roofing timbers and the sophisticated joinery they required meant that such roofs ultimately stood little chance in competition with the lightweight Virginia house roof frame. Nor could the time-consuming manufacture of tiles and slates compete with the prodigious timber resources in the colonies and the easy fabrication of

wooden shingles. Carpenters learned that a well-laid shingle roof could last seventy-five years or more, and that was good enough for most builders after 1700.[23]

Wooden "Shingell[s] for Tyle" were used in the region as early as 1649.[24] However, because they were still not yet part of the workmanlike lexicon when specifications were drawn up for the replacement of tiles on the statehouse in St. Mary's City twelve leaky years after the building was first constructed in 1676, their manufacture and installation had to be carefully explained in specifications that called for them to be "good Ciprus Shingles twenty four Inches in length[,] in thickness one Inch[,] and in breadth from Six to nine Inches[.] the same to be well Jointed [on their edges] and close Laid, and well nailed with Six peny Nailes."[25]

Much variety existed in the making and installation of shingles by the eighteenth century, and some of it can be traced back to seventeenth-century practice. The unusually long and extra-wide shingle made for the statehouse at St. Mary's City may have been an experiment quickly abandoned. More typical of eighteenth-century shingles was the kind ordered in 1701 for St. Peter's Church, New Kent County: 20,000 "Good Sound sipres [cypress] shingles" were to be "18 inches in Length, and none to be more than 5 inches in breadth, or narrower than 3 inches, and not to be lesser then ½ an inch or more than ¾ of an inch thick, and all to be well rounded" (Fig. 13.9).[26] Round butts, mimick-

TABLE 13.1. Butt Shapes and Finishes on Shingles Recorded in the Field, 1684–1850

	MARYLAND		VIRGINIA	
	NUMBER	PERCENTAGE	NUMBER	PERCENTAGE
Round butt	7	41	100	84
Square butt	9	53	17	14
Unknown shape	1	6	2	2
Total	17	100	119	100
No paint	9	53	60	50
Paint or tar	3	18	52	44
Unknown paint or tar	5	29	7	6
Total	17	100	119	100

ing pantiles, were an incremental improvement known to have been used as early as the 1680s from a surviving shingle reused as a shim at Third Haven Meetinghouse, Talbot County, Maryland (1682–84). By the early eighteenth century, carpenters could choose from round-butt, square-butt, or side-lap ("long") shingles, and they pegged and/or nailed them to a subsurface of riven or sawn lath or clapboards or to a solid covering of wide, sawn boards. Some variants seem to have started as independent regional developments, but most, perhaps with the exception of pegging, soon became common alternatives throughout the mid-Atlantic colonies. Once established, a great deal of this diversity persisted through the middle of the nineteenth century.[27]

Roofs of gentry houses by the opening decades of the eighteenth century were increasingly being covered with shingles like those specified for St. Peter's Church. Usually made of cypress or Atlantic white cedar, common shingles were split from 18- to 20-inch log cants, draw-knifed to a wedge shape, and usually jointed on their edges. Although the butts could be cut off straight, rounded ends were by far the most common. Round-butt shingles were chosen for Cedar Park in 1702, and thereafter they account for more than 80 percent of the shingle roofs across the region where physical evidence has been recorded. After installation, roofers often painted or tarred them to enhance their durability. Sometimes they were painted red or orange to simulate the clay tiles they sought to emulate.[28] Alternatively, and mostly after the middle of the eighteenth century, some shingle roofs were colored black or shades of gray intended to mimic slate, even though these, too, were most often finished with rounded ends.[29]

The tradition of shingle use formed and hardened at an early date in Virginia, and consequently carpenters there were resistant to change. Marylanders followed a somewhat different path, where those with genteel aspirations soon

turned from Williamsburg and Norfolk and looked more and more to Philadelphia for architectural inspiration, especially late in the colonial period. By the time of the Revolution they were preferring shingles with square butts that more closely resembled slate. Wood shingles had become such an economic, durable and ingrained part of the carpentry tradition that slate had little chance of replacing them, but that did not mean the gentry did not desire the less parochial look of slate. Photographs taken on the eve and during the Civil War suggest that square-butt shingles were finally preferred in Virginia as well (notwithstanding contradictory field evidence that should be excused for being limited and mostly rural). Shingles made by machines were largely produced with square butts. The advent of this technology on the eve of the Civil War resulted in cheaper prices and made the shingles accessible for all types of buildings, including agricultural structures. The plainer appearance of manufactured square-butt shingles was not unappreciated, since the plainness and regularity of their shape were increasingly favored by builders working in the Greek style (Table 13.1).

Side-lapped or long shingles were a secondary variety of a wooden covering used in the eighteenth and nineteenth centuries. They became standard for barns, secondary structures, modest rural houses, and buildings of the backcountry (Fig. 13.10). Resembling short clapboards, they were laid up vertically in rows, each row turned sideways like a clapboard wall. The thick side of these shingles overlapped their neighbor's thin edge, and each row higher up covered the top of the one below it. Side-lapped shingles appeared in the Chesapeake around 1700. They were contemporary with or predated similar coverings in the Germanic settlements of Pennsylvania, western Maryland, and the Shenandoah Valley.[30] This was one of several incremental improvements carpenters made to the clapboard roof. Unlike pegged shingles, which were an isolated evolution of the Lower

Eastern Shore, mid-priced side-lap shingles spread throughout the region as a whole. Shingles, generally, including the side-lapped variety, formed a more waterproof roof covering than did clapboards. Those were better suited to temporary coverings, as an alternative base for shingles, and for use on farm buildings, where water tightness was less of a concern.

Since the adoption of clapboards, wood, however fashioned, remained the covering of choice until the close of the Civil War. Nevertheless, the growth of towns after the Revolution, particularly along the fall line and the rapid industrialization of building supplies and materials, created a rising demand for new roofing materials, which challenged the reign of wood. These challenges were at first modest. Records of the Mutual Assurance Society of Virginia reveal that more than 98 percent of the buildings documented in policies issued between the years 1796 and 1800 were covered with wood. Eventually, concern for fireproofing town buildings provoked interest in other roofing materials.[31] A revival of slate was one such solution particularly favored for row houses and large commercial buildings in downtowns. Slate roofs represented nearly 17 percent of all coverings noted in the insurance record by 1820, and the use of slate continued to expand through the remainder of the antebellum era. Native sources of slate were nearby, including the Buckingham quarry in Virginia and the Peach Bottom area of Maryland and southern Pennsylvania. Quarrying began in both deposits in the early nineteenth century.[32] Yet despite these local sources, most slate was imported from Wales, which boasted a superior product and sold at lower prices than the local material. The success of a native slate industry had to await improved transportation, Welsh investors, and skilled immigrant workers who took over local production beginning in the 1840s and made a better product. This and lower transportation costs eventually made local slate affordable, which helps account for its use on nearly 30 percent of buildings listed in the insurance records for Chesapeake towns by 1845.[33]

Although pantiles never covered more than 4 percent of buildings after 1800, they too were revived as fireproofing for the same buildings for which slate was deemed appropriate. Tile was actually slightly more popular than slate through the mid-1810s. The problem with pantiles was their weight. They were too heavy to be carried on the improved common-rafter roof of the nineteenth century. Moreover, those manufactured in this country were often too carelessly produced to work as they were intended. The cost of importing them from foreign sources and the additional labor needed to properly mortar a pantile roof to keep it dry was not worth the effort, and so slate increasingly became the

Fig. 13.10. *Side-lap shingles installed on the Bowman Farmhouse, 1800, Frederick County, Maryland.*

principal urban alternative to wooden shingles in the opening decades of the new century (Fig. 13.11).[34]

Metal was another roofing material used to solve a host of problems that other traditional coverings could not. Metal coverings were not new. They simply had not been cost effective until the nineteenth century. Furthermore, eighteenth-century metal products were not well adapted to building needs. Lead had been tried, for instance. It was used to weatherproof the flat deck on the Governor's Palace in Williamsburg in 1709, at Rosewell in the 1720s, and at the new capitol in Richmond in 1784 (where it failed and was soon replaced). Copper sheeting was used to crown the dome on the Maryland Statehouse in 1788, and it was in-

Fig. 13.11. Brick building in Petersburg, Virginia, dating from about 1820, with a pantile roof damaged by shell fire. Photograph, April 1865. (Library of Congress)

stalled at Homewood in Baltimore to repair vulnerable M roof valleys where shingles failed to keep out rain and snow. Generally, though, local builders did not like to work with lead, partly because it tended to sag and fail on steep roof pitches and partly because it was expensive relative to other materials. They also frowned on copper since it was expensive and took special skills to install. It took the construction of an iron-rolling mill in Philadelphia at the end of the eighteenth century to encourage innovators like Thomas Jefferson and Benjamin Latrobe to experiment with a new metal covering: sheets of iron. Jefferson believed this covering could last a hundred years or more.[35] Soon an industry grew up for tin, zinc, and terne-plated iron and steel. Even so, sheets of these materials became widely available only late in the antebellum period.

Metal sheets for roofing first appear in insurance records for Alexandria and Richmond at the beginning of the nineteenth century. Their use slowly made their way to Norfolk, and by the 1830s metal sheets were being used sparingly in Lynchburg and other Piedmont towns, including Petersburg and Fredericksburg. Metal roofs did not supersede wood until after the Civil War. By then, roofers had overcome technical problems associated with their installation, and carpenters and their clients had finally recognized their efficiencies (Table 13.2). *The Richmond and Alexandria Builders' Price Book* of 1820 explained that money saved in framing

TABLE 13.2. Roof Coverings as Recorded in Mutual Assurance Society of Virginia Policies, 1796–1866.

YEAR	WOOD	METAL	TILE	SLATE	OTHER	UNKNOWN	NUMBER	% TOTALS
1796–1800	98.86	0.03	0.49	0.37	0	0.26	3,506	100.01
1801–5	98.64	0.07	0.13	0.47	0.11	0.58	8,762	100
1806–10	96.97	0	1.57	1.23	0	0.27	2,109	100.04
1811–15	93.51	0.07	3.29	2.69	0.09	0.38	4,439	100.03
1816–20	79.30	0.42	2.54	16.71	0.25	0.78	5,232	100
1821–25	75.37	0.52	3.90	19.03	0.36	0.81	5,790	99.99
1826–30	68.02	0.60	3.47	26.29	0.45	1.18	5,165	100.01
1831–35	66.91	4.75	0.41	27.76	0	0.16	1,221	99.99
1836–40	68.76	1.77	1.51	27.52	0.30	0.15	6,098	100.01
1841–45	64.02	4.21	0.73	30.63	0.33	0.08	6,340	100
1846–50	56.69	11.18	0.12	31.06	0.58	0.37	3,265	100
1851–55	58.80	15.53	0.58	24.19	0.76	0.15	5,519	100.01
1856–60	53.25	16.41	0.44	28.20	1.62	0.09	6,898	100.01
1861–65	36.65	26.70	0	31.75	4.90	0	633	100
1866	26.67	41.03	0	24.62	3.60	4.10	195	100.02

Note: These data are almost exclusively from town buildings and largely represent new construction or remodeling of existing buildings for which owners were willing and able to pay for insurance.

costs compensated for the greater expense of buying and installing metal roofs. It noted that metal roofs "require but a slight frame, this kind of cover being light itself, and may be made nearly flat to walk upon."[36] The light weight of tin and other metal coverings other than lead eventually led to simpler and cheaper roof frames that omitted ridge joinery, widened the spacing of rafter pairs, and required less lath material, while at the same time permitting gentler roof slopes. This was a winning combination: labor and material savings in roof frames and the appearance of lower-pitched roofs favored by Greek Revival aesthetics. Advances in metal roofing materials made this practical after midcentury.

FLASHING, CRICKETS, AND WATERPROOFING

Edges of roofs and valleys and penetrations by chimneys required special attention to prevent leaking. The simple way to seal chimneys was the application of a mortar wash where the shingles abutted the stack. Its disadvantage was a constant need for renewal.[37] Lead flashing lasted longer. Remnants of lead are often recovered from seventeenth-century archaeological sites, and traces are sometimes found in surviving eighteenth-century buildings. Notwithstanding, the expense of lead and the expertise and tools needed to install it encouraged roofers to find ingenious ways to lay shingles in hips and valleys and along the rakes of gables so as to minimize the amount of flashing required for a job.

It took careful planning to install a complicated shingle roof with as little flashing as possible. Raising the underlayment at the edges of gables by lifting the bargeboards slightly and by adding cant strips against dormers and sometimes even against chimneys were two tricks builders employed to divert water away from these vulnerable locations. A cricket was another device designed to shed rainwater and prevent leaks (Fig. 13.12). Sloping roofs behind large chimney stacks and the valleys of M roofs were sometimes given small A-frame crickets covered with shingles to prevent water from collecting in these pockets. Because shingles were easy to trim, they could be cut into trapezoidal shapes and then laid fanlike to wrap the main roof shingles into the crickets in a continuous sweep across the valleys. Doing so eliminated the need for additional flashing. This sweeping of the shingles also worked to eliminate flashing from the hips and valleys of larger intersecting roof planes. All the same, despite flashing, fanning, sweeping, and triple lapping, even the best of eighteenth-century buildings leaked to some degree, at least before the shingles were swollen tightly with rainwater to create a more secure seal.

Fig. 13.12. Tarred, square-butt shingles were used to sweep the valleys of the cricket, Ringgold House, c. 1743, Chestertown, Kent County, Maryland.

DORMERS

The growing practice of accommodating masters, mistresses, family members, and guests in upstairs chambers increased demand for more comfortable quarters. Warmer, brighter, better-ventilated bedchambers were desirable, whether people lived in two-story town houses or in old-fashioned one-story farmhouses. Fireplaces to heat garrets became more common in this era, and finishes were improved. Dormer windows completed the makeover. They provided more light, better air flow, and additional headroom. A dormer was a separately framed structure with a window in front and roof overhead. The sides were fitted with narrow studs, often no more than thin boards turned flat to maximize interior space. The triangular sides could be sheathed outside with

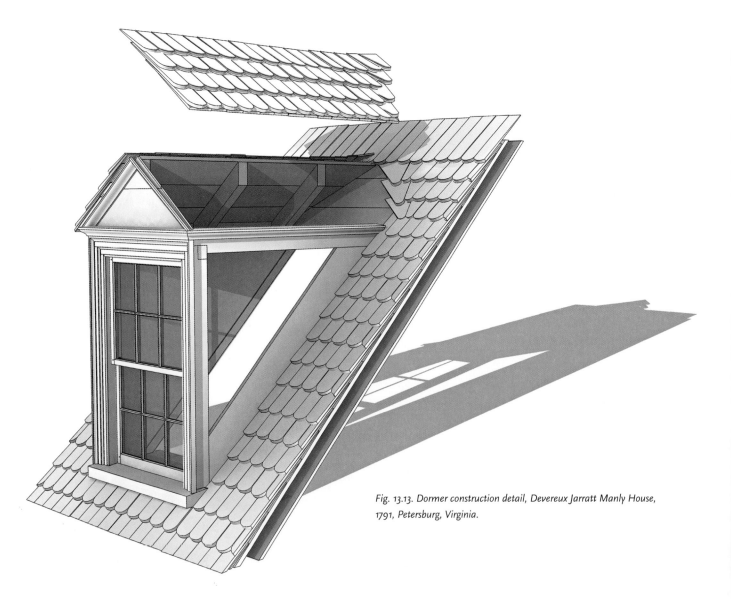

Fig. 13.13. Dormer construction detail, Devereux Jarratt Manly House, 1791, Petersburg, Virginia.

horizontal boards, weatherboarded, or, on rare occasions, shingled. A crown molding usually supplied a transition to the roof. These could be pedimented or hipped or, in rare cases, built shedlike. Like crickets, the dormer valleys were generally swept where they met the main roof, giving them a distinctive and sculpted appearance (Fig. 13.13).[38]

PORCHES, PIAZZAS, AND PORTICOES

Porches on Chesapeake buildings underwent a great change from their first appearance in the seventeenth century to their widespread use in a completely different form 125 years later. The earliest porches were enclosed entries attached to the fronts of buildings. Sometimes they stood two stories tall, even on single-story buildings. The room above the entry was often called the "porch chamber." Such porches were derived from English precedent and appeared in Virginia during the third quarter of the seventeenth century. Their popularity peaked in the 1710s and 1720s but was never a dominant

form.[39] Enclosed porches were first used on public buildings and the best houses, Bacon's Castle in Surry County and Carvill Hall in Kent County, Maryland, being two notable examples (see Figs. 2.10 and 7.4). By the early eighteenth century, fashion-conscious people had increasingly come to regard this style of porch as a blemish on the facade of houses with pretentions to stylishness. It made a poor fit, especially in towns where the new classical aesthetic made its earliest appearance. With a few exceptions, enclosed porches were confined to country houses by the 1710s and 1720s. Country gentlemen—better than townspeople—accepted a hybrid blend of earlier forms and new, refined, classical detailing (Fig. 13.14). The introduction of a center passage in the early eighteenth century rendered porch appendages obsolete. Enclosed porches fell out of favor in Britain and the colonies at about the same time. The Chesapeake was no exception.

This old-fashioned enclosed porch was superseded by a structure that had open sides. Termed "piazza," it evolved

Fig. 13.14. "View of the Malvern House or 'Wyatt House' on Malvern Hill, Virginia." Watercolor by Robert Knox Sneden, July 1, 1862. (Virginia Historical Society, Mss5:1 Sn237:1 v.3 p.210B)

from the earlier style enclosure by adding open railings on the ground story. Contract specifications for a courthouse in Dorchester County, Maryland, in 1686 called for a "large Porch att the end of the house with rails and Bannisters about it."[40] The capitol in Williamsburg made a bigger step in 1701. It was to have porches "built circular fifteen foot in breadth" and was to "stand upon cedar columns."[41] The capitol model was a novelty as far as Chesapeake carpenters were concerned. It may have originated with the enclosed entry, but it was now transformed into a different kind of space altogether, one with a more modern look. From now on, the open porch was looked upon as an appended classical portico, an idea that prepared it for eventual domestic use by the colonies' forward-looking grandees.

It took longer before the open porch was finally adopted by ordinary house builders. The essential architectural elements of the open porch, however freely local builders applied them, were intrinsically classical. A portico at Holly Hill demonstrates that the builder there understood the classical reference to antiquity that his newfangled porch was supposed to make. Known now only from a period painting, the porch took the form of a shed, which was likely added to the older house in the 1720s (Fig. 13.15). Although it sat awkwardly on the facade, it had tall columns rising atop freestanding plinths. These formal architectural elements—such as plinths, turned Ionic columns, a cornice (although

Fig. 13.15. Detail of painting, "Samuel Harrison's Land Near Herring Bay," Holly Hill, Anne Arundel County, Maryland, painted before 1733. Holly Hill became quite modern when the 1698 frame house was enlarged and improved in 1713 and again in the 1720s. It is shown in this painting with brick walls, sash windows (which replaced its original leaded casements), dormers, a round-butt shingle roof, and a shed porch with columns and a central pediment over the front door. Oil on wood. (Courtesy of Brooke Clagett)

not a full entablature), and a pediment—together make up the classical imagery the porch presented. The one at Holly Hill was a rarity because of its date. Not until the middle of the eighteenth century did open porches become commonplace additions to elite houses and genteel taverns. By then, they were invariably called "piazzas."

The shed roof of the Holly Hill piazza was an oddity that was more typical of taverns than house fronts in the colonial era. Piazzas on grand houses—they appeared mostly on very ambitious dwellings until after the Revolution—were usually represented as classical "porticoes" with columns supporting an entablature and a pedimented roof. Acknowledging their classical origins, clients and carpenters were describing them as porticos by the 1770s. Thus, a distinction was made between a "piazza" and a "portico" on a house sold in 1807 near Wilmington, North Carolina, which was described as having "piazzas to the east and south, and [a] portico to the west."[42] Unlike the shed-roof piazza, single-bay porticoes were regarded as frontispieces rendered in three dimensions. Columns in the front corners with perhaps pilasters on the rear wall were used to carry an entablature or cornice, which in turn supported a pediment.

What is striking about porches in the Chesapeake region were the liberties builders took to improvise on designs they might have seen in architectural books. John Ridout's carpenter fitted an otherwise fine Doric portico on the garden facade of his Annapolis house with the columns grossly out of proportion to prescriptive norms. Otherwise, he followed the rules to the letter when he placed the Doric order below a Venetian window and a cornice rendered in the Ionic order. The garden porch demonstrates that Ridout and his builder fully understood the architectural conventions of the age. Yet, on the street front, they felt freer to mix the orders in unconventional ways, not out of ignorance—the garden elevation proves they knew better—but because enlightened tastes in the Chesapeake colonies never required a strict adherence to classical dictates. The street elevation was spare; the garden front less so. Ridout's frontispiece transgressed further. There the Ionic entablature was mismatched to its column, which may have had an Ionic base but was certainly crowned with a Doric capital. Furthermore, the principal cornice on this street facade was rendered in the Doric order but stripped of enrichment and inferior to the Ionic detailing of the frontispiece. Published architectural books frowned on the ungrammatical use of the orders and their ill proportions, but to Marylanders and Virginians it was enough simply to use them at all and to create a hierarchy among them. That alone made a genteel building genteel.

Eighteenth-century porches mediated between the in-

doors and the out-of-doors. Despite their openness, wall surfaces under early porches were often finished in the manner of interior space. Some were sheathed with horizontal boards, in contrast to weatherboarded walls, as an indication of their transitional status. Sometimes even more explicit interior references were made. For example, workmen created plastered walls with an applied base and chair board typical of a refined interior room beneath porches that were added to Shirley in 1771. These finishes served as an appropriate backdrop when the Carters and their guests used the porch as a summer sitting room (see Fig. 7.17).[43] All refined interior finishes were fair game for such porches—even wainscot was installed under the river-front portico at Tuckahoe (see Fig. 7.31). Treating piazzas as rooms links them back to their enclosed porch ancestry. That identification gradually faded in the nineteenth century as they shed the architectural artifices that connected them to the interior. Gone by then were the baseboards and chair boards, plaster and sheathed walls, and paneling. Instead, exterior wall finishes such as siding or brickwork were simply allowed to run unbroken from one end of a porch to the other (Fig. 13.16).

Beyond the use for show, for protection of an entry, or for contemplating views of a garden, by the late colonial period, some were also associated with service. These were plainer than their front-stage counterparts and were more likely to have a shed roof. The one on the rear of Marmion is a good example, which, if not part of the original building in the 1750s, had certainly been added by 1797.[44] It was more workaday than the front porch at Holly Hill since it overlooked a work yard flanked by a kitchen with quarters upstairs on one side and a storehouse on the other. The porch posts were heavily chamfered, forming an octagonal cross section with lamb's-tongue stops that transitioned the shaft to square stock at the top and bottom. Porch posts so treated were often associated with service and secondary spaces in other contexts, such as in the cellar of Four Mile Tree. They were also used in stores and warehouses. Its presence on the rear piazza at Marmion—still hung with its service bells to summon slaves who labored in the nearby service buildings—suggests that the porch was indeed intended for menials.

Piazzas increased in popularity after the Revolution in both town and country; they became one of the democratizing elements in the emerging landscape of the early republic. Their detailing changed as well (Fig. 13.17). Some, such as those at Montpelier and Monticello, were consciously academic in their design. More common were porches that responded to this neoclassical age with fanciful trim work and attenuated columns, which were frequently capped with whimsical cornices. Cabinetmakers increased their produc-

(top) Fig. 13.16. Porch at Prestwould, Mecklenburg County, Virginia. The porch was built soon after the house was constructed by Lady Jean and Sir Peyton Skipwith in 1794–95.

(bottom) Fig. 13.17. Front porch, Burley Manor, 1832, Berlin, Worcester County, Maryland.

Fig. 13.18. Pedimented porch on the garden side of the Upton Scott House, 1762–63, Annapolis.

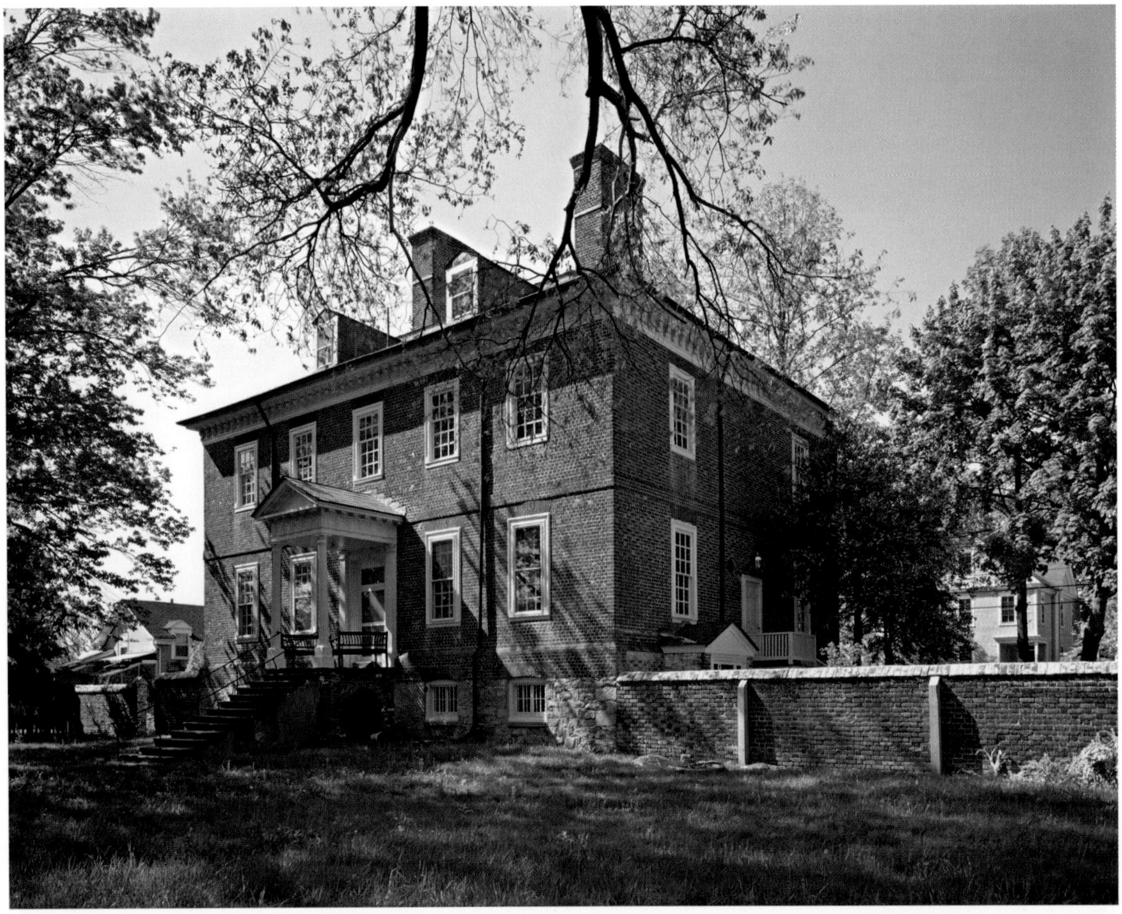

tion of turned columns to meet a growing demand for porch posts. At the same time, heavily chamfered posts, once relegated to secondary structures and commercial use, became popular additions to more modest dwellings.[45] The larger size of shedded piazzas, used for both taverns and dwellings by the late eighteenth century, created more generous space for sitting and strengthened their connection to the outdoors. William Martin recorded a typical scene on one of these tavern porches in Halifax County when he noted in his journal that "it was now morning, & many of the young people . . . were seated or walking for their amuzement in the cool shade of a long piazza, enjoying the morning breezes."[46]

DOORWAYS AND THEIR SURROUNDS

House carpenters in the Chesapeake seldom embellished exterior door openings with more than architraves before the early nineteenth century. The gentry generally preferred restrained, unadorned, neat-and-plain entrances. Applied pediments could be seen here and there, but they were far less common than they were, for example, in New England. Frontispieces of any kind at this time were rare and generally confined to masonry buildings. As noted in chapter 11, the earliest were of gauged-and-rubbed brick and limited to a few Virginia mansions and churches (see Figs. 11.13A, 11.16). None appeared north of the Potomac. Masonry frontispieces, even in Virginia, had run their course by the time of the Revolution. Those carved of imported Portland stone for William Byrd III at Westover in the mid-1760s were among the last.[47] They disappear about the same time that the leading gentlemen of Annapolis began constructing large brick houses in a new style, one with less sculptured facades but adorned with applied wooden embellishments to a degree absent in the region until this time. This new work was often distinguished by ornament crafted by highly skilled joiners. Elaborate cornices, Venetian windows lighting stair landings fitted with orders and entablatures, and large, intricate cornices set Annapolis houses and those they influenced apart from the more somber dwellings of their Virginia counterparts. Often their principal doorways were treated differently on the two main facades, with a classically detailed wooden frontispiece on the street side and a single-bay portico overlooking the garden. A striking example is Upton Scott's house on Shipwright Street of 1762–63, which has a Doric frontispiece to signal entry on the front and a portico of the same order to protect guests and family when they sat to gaze across Dr. Scott's garden on the rear (Fig. 13.18).

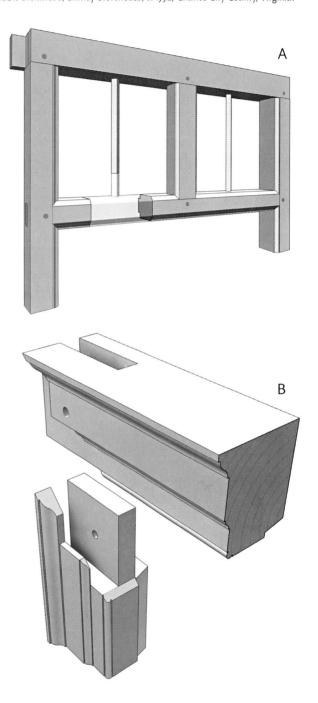

(left) Fig. 13.19. Frontispiece, Bragg House, 1823, Petersburg, Virginia.

(below) Fig. 13.20. A: Detail of door head and transom mullion made of solid timbers, Brandy, 1720s, Anne Arundel County, Maryland; B: Solid doorjamb built in the form of a double architrave, Shirley Storehouse, c. 1772, Charles City County, Virginia.

There were only a scattering of houses with frontispieces in the two colonies until the early nineteenth century (Fig. 13.19). Otherwise, doorjambs on refined houses tended to follow one of two paths. If early or rural, and therefore conservative and old-fashioned, the jambs were usually molded from a single piece of wood, perhaps with an ogee or ovolo on the interior corner and tenoned and pinned to both the head and the sill (Fig. 13.20). They followed an older tradition of chamfered and molded jambs presumably typical of the best work in seventeenth-century houses. These earlier practices were relegated to cellar openings in genteel houses in the eighteenth century. It was not long after the rise of the refined house at the turn of the century that doorframes in well-finished houses were being trimmed with applied architrave surrounds and often fitted for a transom, especially when the front door opened into an otherwise dark passage. The architrave might be reduced to a plain board with a simple corner bead in more modest houses, for back doors, and in many outbuildings. But single and double architraves became standard in gentry houses and gradually were applied

to apertures in secondary structures in domestic yards (usually as single architraves) at the beginning of the nineteenth century. Even then they were typically limited to buildings in the immediate vicinity of the house (Fig. 13.20B).

Documents indicate that workmanlike doors in seventeenth-century houses were plank, or what has since been called board-and-batten (Fig. 13.21B). None has survived from that century, but a few rare examples from early eighteenth-century houses indicate they resembled

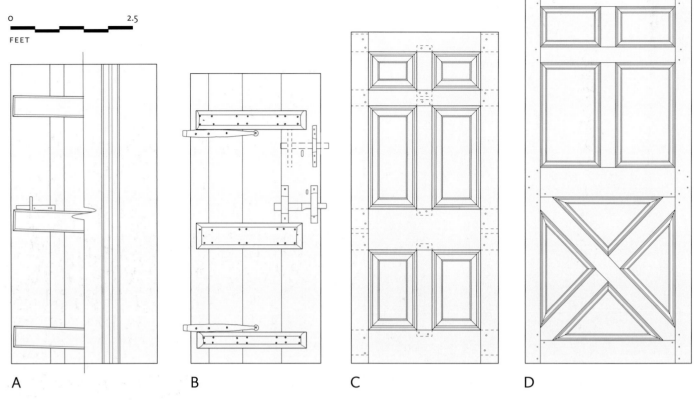

A   B   C   D

Fig. 13.21. A: Rear plank-and-panel door, Powell-Benston House (Tilghman House), c. 1730, Somerset County, Maryland, now in the Museum of Southern Decorative Arts, Winston-Salem, North Carolina; B: Board-and-batten (plank) door, Everard Kitchen, c. 1730, Williamsburg; C: Six-panel door, Walthoe's Storehouse, 1749–50, Williamsburg; D: Architectural pattern book–inspired door to second-period hyphens at Wales, 1780s, Dinwiddie County, Virginia.

seventeenth-century doors known from England and New England. A plank door dating to 1696 in the attic of the Wanton-Lyman-Hazard House in Newport, Rhode Island, for instance, is not unlike surviving doors from the Chesapeake. It is made with two vertical boards joined by three spaced, horizontal battens nailed to the back. Eighteenth-century batten doors are very similar, but there are differences that tell them apart. Instead of shallow-cut molded edges running along three sides of the battens, later battens are most often chamfered on all four edges. Another variation survived as a hall door in the William Benston House of about 1730. There, three vertical boards molded with ovolos and rabbets clasp two raised panels between them. This faux panel work required no rails. Instead, three ovolo-molded battens were again nailed to the reverse of the leaf to hold the boards together (Fig. 13.21A). Documents indicate that more conventional joined panel work—"wainscot" in the seventeenth-century parlance—was occasionally used in the late 1600s before it became the standard for polite houses by the beginning of the eighteenth century.

Most wainscot doors were composed of a series of rectangular and square panels (Fig. 13.21C). Exotic variations appear here and there throughout the region, notably the diagonal cross panels inspired by published sources at Tuckahoe

around midcentury, two that were used in the hyphen additions to Wales in the 1780s, and the arched-headed front and rear doors at Four Mile Tree (Fig. 13.21D). Making wainscot doors with more or fewer panels and molding them more or less elaborately were variables that carpenters could adjust to a client's purse. Double-sheathed doors were one final variety known in the period. Some were used on houses; more often they were specified for buildings that needed additional security, such as storehouses, lumber houses, public buildings, and churches.

WINDOWS

Archaeological excavations are the source of most information about the use of casement windows in early Chesapeake buildings. Pieces of window glass called "quarrels" and the lead strips known as "cames" or "turned leads," which secured individual panes into framed casements, have come to light on many early sites in Maryland and Virginia.[48] Excavated cames sometimes bear the makers' names and dates imprinted into the soft metal inside the crease. When marked, they provide useful dating information concerning the construction of buildings, later renovations, or the replacement of windows (Fig. 13.22B).

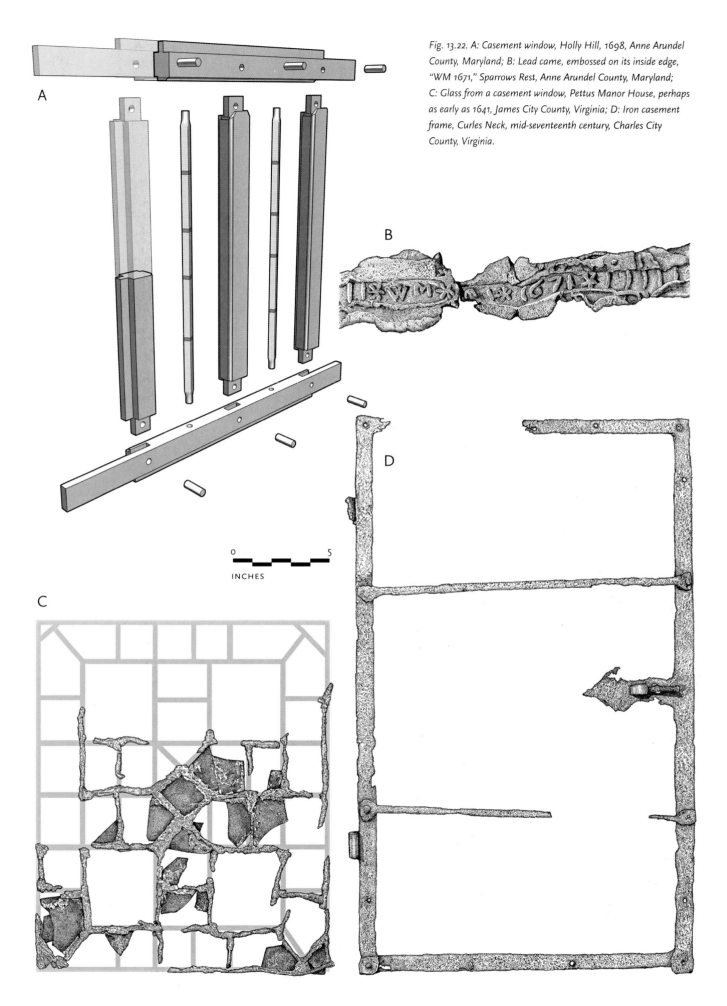

Fig. 13.22. A: Casement window, Holly Hill, 1698, Anne Arundel County, Maryland; B: Lead came, embossed on its inside edge, "WM 1671," Sparrows Rest, Anne Arundel County, Maryland; C: Glass from a casement window, Pettus Manor House, perhaps as early as 1641, James City County, Virginia; D: Iron casement frame, Curles Neck, mid-seventeenth century, Charles City County, Virginia.

A

B

C

D

0   5
INCHES

Glass quarrels recovered by archaeologists are most commonly lozenge shaped and are seldom larger than 5 by 6 inches. Occasionally, excavators find other shapes, such as square or rectangular panes. Five-sided quarrels recovered from the site of John Lewger's 1638 house at St. Mary's City came from an elaborately patterned casement that probably lighted a large parlor, one that also served as an assembly room for the colony's early lawmakers.[49] Whatever their shape, individual panes were set into rectangular window frames formed with ribbonlike turned leads fitted around each piece of glass and soldered at their intersection to hold the unit together. Fixed casements were set directly into wooden frames, secured with small sprigs driven into the jambs like glaziers' points, and wired to wooden or iron bars for stiffening. A surviving casement frame at Holly Hill preserves evidence of all these fasteners (Fig. 13.22A). Hinged casements presented a different problem. They were often set in rigid iron frames, which swung on hooks (pintles) driven into wooden jambs and then held shut with catches (Fig. 13.22D). Vertical wooden mullions divided large frames into multiple lights; exceptionally large window apertures, the kind found in public buildings such as the Third Haven Meetinghouse, used a horizontal mullion to further subdivide windows into four casements—two small ones above and two larger ones below. Whether hinged or stationary, leaded-glass casements fit into window openings formed by solid wooden frames or, in masonry structures, by molded brick surrounds (Fig. 13.22C).

The earliest recovered lead cames in the region come from excavations at Martin's Hundred, a fragile settlement that had barely recovered from a devastating Indian uprising three years earlier than the 1625 dated fragments.[50] The first to show up in excavations at Jamestown date to the John White Store lot from the 1640s.[51] Thereafter, nearly all excavated Chesapeake sites have produced evidence of glazed windows. Seventeen of twenty excavated seventeenth-century sites in Anne Arundel County, Maryland, for instance, yielded casement window fragments.[52] The same is true for Virginia. There, window glass and bits of lead were found on most sites occupied after 1640, even plantations as modest as yeoman farmer Humphrey Tompkins's farmstead on the Bennett tract in York County, built about 1640.[53] The typical Virginia house, according to an eyewitness writing in 1656, is usually "daubed and whitelimed, glazed and flowered [floored]."[54]

Those not having glazed windows, the same observer continued, were fitted with "shutters which are made very pritty and convenient." Wooden shutters were one alternative to leaded casements, as they sometimes were later for sash windows. Shutters dating to the seventeenth, eighteenth, and early nineteenth centuries rarely survive. Those few that have been found, mostly in Southside Virginia, swing on hinges or slide vertically in wooden tracks, the latter an innovation learned from sash window construction and popularized early in the nineteenth century.

The regular manufacture of crown glass and the sash frames that mounted these new improved "crystal" panes soon banished old-fashioned casements to secondary locations in attics, cellars, and outbuildings and other out-of-the-way places.[55] Joseph Kidd and Joshua Kendall, two Williamsburg plumbers, as workers in lead were known, advertised that they still made leaded windows as late as 1769.[56] William Porter's fine brick house built on Kent Island was fitted with casement windows in the upper gables when it was built on the eve of the American Revolution.[57] Benjamin Latrobe's watercolor sketch of Green Spring Plantation in 1797 shows a large, four-light, diamond-pane window still in use in a ground-floor back room he identified as a nursery. Casements may have ceased to answer most gentlemen's expectations decades earlier, but their dusky illumination was sometimes still good enough for closets, attics, and workplaces inhabited by slaves, servants, farmhands, and nursemaids well into the eighteenth century.

Counterbalanced sash windows were an English invention of the early 1660s. At first, their use was confined to royal apartments and great country houses.[58] They were slow to catch on in the colonies, until the turn of the eighteenth century, when suddenly "sash windows are the newest Fashion" from Boston to Williamsburg.[59] One of the first buildings constructed with new sash windows was the College of William and Mary, which was under construction by 1695. Masons supervised by an overseer brought from England to manage them left a void for a casement-sized window as they laid up the cellar walls.[60] A change order was issued before the work proceeded further. Workers were instructed to resize the opening to match the proportions of new-styled sash windows intended on the floors above. The windows themselves, ordered from England, were not installed until 1700.[61] Not long after, other public building projects followed suit—the new capitol in 1701, for instance, and St. Peter's Church, New Kent County, in 1701–3.[62]

New as the city itself was in 1700, Williamsburg immediately became the trendsetter in Virginia, and sash windows led the way. Written records and paint research confirm that large single- and double-hung sash windows, raised and lowered on weights and pulleys, graced many houses in the Virginia capital by the 1710s. Bruton Parish Church followed the fashion in 1715 with large compass-headed sash windows.

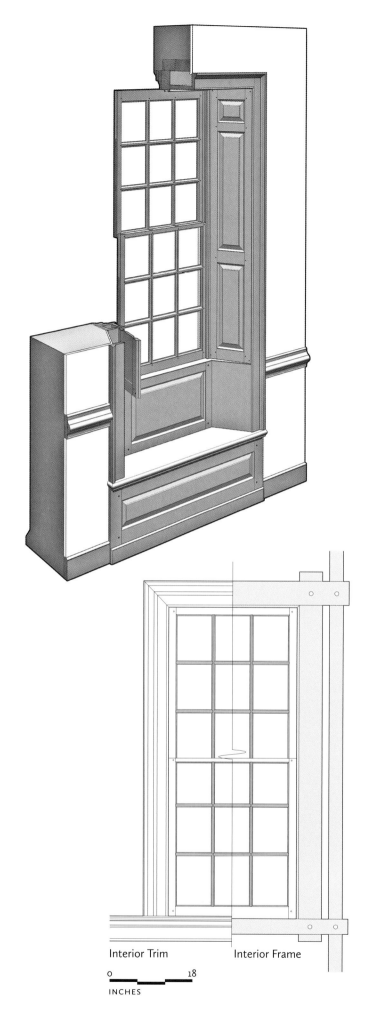

(top) Fig. 13.23. Window with seat, Four Mile Tree, 1745, Surry County, Virginia.

(bottom) Fig. 13.24. Sash window with solid jambs, Myrick House, c. 1820, Southampton County, Virginia.

Interior Trim   Interior Frame

0   18

INCHES

A block away, William Robertson used double-hung sash to light a fine tenement house, and even the modest one-room house of William Timson was built with sash windows.[63] English influence was seen first in the countryside among the colonies' grandees. Did Lewis Burwell II always intend to install sliding sash across the formal front of the sophisti-cated house he built at Fairfield in 1694, just a year before the college builders switched from casements to sash frames (see Fig. 6.21)? No such doubts attend William Byrd II's reno-vations at Westover; he ordered double-hung sash windows from his London agent in 1709 and engaged a local trades-man "to make me some [pulleys] for my windows."[64] Else-where in the countryside, though, it took another decade or two before their use became widespread. Even then builders cut corners to make sash windows affordable. As late as the early nineteenth century, many planters lived in houses in which the top sash was fixed and the lower one had to be propped open without the benefit of counterweights.

Sliding sash with large sheets of crown glass flooded so-cial spaces with the sunlight and fresh air that conventional casements rationed (Fig. 13.23). That was their special appeal. They also contributed to the overall cleaner look of modern buildings. Their proportions conformed to the new classical ideal, their uniformly rectangular panes replaced the fussi-ness of cames and quarrels, and they eliminated the cluttered appearance of hinges, latches, and hooks by hiding their own apparatus of cords, pulleys, and weights inside the jambs. Carpenters molded or applied separate architraves to the ex-terior face of window units, disguising the joinery employed in their making. In its simplest form, a solid joined frame of sash windows resembled a casement window. Stout jambs were mortised and tenoned into a sill and header, with the ex-tended ends of the sill and head anchoring the window unit to masonry walls; alternatively, they were lapped and nailed to flanking studs in frame buildings. Solid jambs could be hogged out to form a chase for counterweights where hung sash were desired, especially if only the lower one moved up and down. The exterior face of solid window units was fin-ished in one of three ways: by running moldings directly on the timber frame, by applying a separate architrave (increas-ingly common as the century progressed), or by beading the header and jambs and applying a square-stock backband to create a rabbet for a shutter. The latter was much favored in Williamsburg but a bit more arcane in the countryside for frame houses, where shutters were often mounted to applied

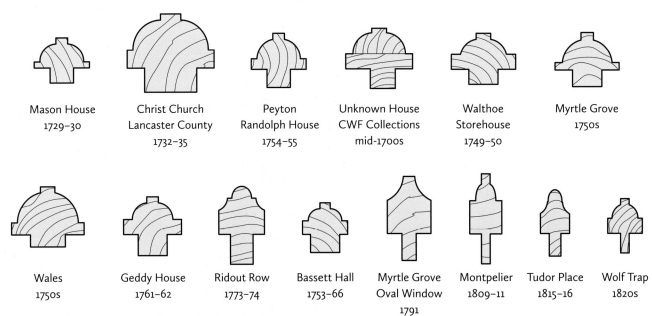

Mason House
1729–30

Christ Church
Lancaster County
1732–35

Peyton
Randolph House
1754–55

Unknown House
CWF Collections
mid-1700s

Walthoe
Storehouse
1749–50

Myrtle Grove
1750s

Wales
1750s

Geddy House
1761–62

Ridout Row
1773–74

Bassett Hall
1753–66

Myrtle Grove
Oval Window
1791

Montpelier
1809–11

Tudor Place
1815–16

Wolf Trap
1820s

Fig. 13.25. Sash muntin profiles (profiles reproduced at half scale).

architraves (Fig. 13.24). However styled, these new sash windows assisted greatly in the overall transformation of architecture from the emphasis on its many parts, so favored in the seventeenth century, into a harmonious composition of the whole.

Changing aesthetic and mechanical innovations from the last quarter of the eighteenth century through the 1830s and 1840s combined to make window openings larger, glassier, and airier. Internal sliding dividers, promoted in *The Carpenters' Company of the City and County of Philadelphia 1786 Rule Book* to separate sash weights and prevent them from tangling, were used at Montpelier and Poplar Forest.[65] A more sophisticated system of weighting windows, apparently developed in England and adopted by the builders of fine town houses in the Chesapeake by the 1820s, enabled both upper sash and lower sash to be operated in tandem. As the bottom sash opened, the top one descended.[66] Window openings in larger neoclassical houses sometimes extended to floor level; the lower sash of these invariably opened onto a piazza. Glass panes grew ever larger as the muntins that held them in place slimmed down almost to invisibility in the 1820s and 1830s (Fig. 13.25). These bigger windows created splendid exteriors and at the same time brightly lit what were increasingly lavish interiors.

At first, such novelties appeared at different times in different places. New ideas debuted and reached their apogee in the colonial capitals. Eventually, they spread to the countryside, where they settled into the region's building conventions, despite later improvements. For example, many of the most elegant buildings in Annapolis during the city's effervescence in the third quarter of the eighteenth cen-

tury employed the latest window treatment, featuring large panes with muntins as thin as 1 inch. Builders in Virginia paid no heed. Outside Williamsburg, clients still preferred the smaller pane sizes and stouter muntins that had been the fashion 60 years earlier, when the burgeoning Virginia capital was the style setter. Williamsburg, for its part, did favor large panes as early as midcentury, but muntin profiles remained robust until the end of the century. Outside the town, such refined carpenter's work awaited the opening decades of the nineteenth century.

❖ A larger truth rests beneath these regional variations. The capital cities, first Williamsburg and its environs and later Annapolis and its hinterland, were forcing grounds for architectural innovations from the moment of their blossoming. Both were paragons of classicism in their respective colonies. Street- and garden-facing windows showed off urban modishness like nothing else. They became exceptionally large, not just those that lit dwelling houses in Williamsburg but window openings in the town's taverns and storehouses as well. The result was a handsome prospect all around, as oversized sash windows encouraged looking at, looking out, and looking in. A Russian traveler to Williamsburg in 1779 was so impressed with "Mr. Reeds store" across the street from his lodgings that he drew its portrait inside the cover of his diary, not failing to emphasize the huge front windows (Figs. 13.26, 13.27).[67] He appears to have made the sketch while sitting at another large window inside a tavern opposite the store. Glazed street-level apertures invited window shopping, the commercial kind, and, after dark, the curiosity

of passersby. City folk throughout the British Empire under-stood that modern eighteenth- and early nineteenth-century towns were gathering places where private entertainments often deliberately courted public spectacle, even if the spec-tators were strollers who lingered before unshuttered win-dows. Where "every curtain, and every shutter of every win-dow" was left agape, the revealed "apartments [were] all in a blaze of light," said a French-American visitor to England, who could just as well have been describing the social scene along the fashionable Duke of Gloucester streets in either Williamsburg or Annapolis. "This custom," he reported, "is so general" that servants often leave "the windows thus exposed, thinking, no doubt that [any evening gathering of five or six persons] was a rout after our fashion."[68] Servants and slaves adjusted the scenery for these private-public en-tertainments, but the spectacle went on only because sash makers and glaziers had already turned ordinary dwellings into theatrical showcases.

14 Interior Finishes

WILLIE GRAHAM

The theatrical allusions that carpenters and masons built into the outside appearance of formal house facades by the middle of the eighteenth century—the symmetry and center-stage centrality of quite ordinary plantation houses and prosceniumlike porches, elaborate frontispieces, and matching advance buildings stage-right and stage-left seen in the grandest gentry houses in the region—were overtures to the full-fledged productions that finish carpenters created indoors.[1] Listen to an awestruck visitor to William Byrd's plantation house at Westover: "The front door leads thru' a very wide entry, beautifully adorned with pictures and furniture and an elegant staircase, very high and stuccoed at the top. The first room, with fourteen black & gilt framed pictures, wainscoted (as all the rooms are) to the ceiling. . . . The furniture [in the drawing room] . . . is more rich, being of silk damask and in the other room a yellow stuff with red and white cases to the chairs."[2] Affluence and aspirations to gentility were preconditions to such displays of architectural sophistication, prerequisites beyond the means and ambitions of most freedmen in Virginia and Maryland. Knowledgeable finish carpenters were also essential. Some regions had none to hire at any price. Benjamin Latrobe, in a rare generous moment for this famously acerbic observer, reflected on the difficulty of living like a gentlemen in the backcountry of Virginia: "In Amelia I could have again fancied myself in a society of English Country Gentlemen . . . had not the shabbiness of their mansions undeceived me. Of the latter I do not mean to speak disrespectfully. It is a necessary consequence of the remoteness of the country," where, he explained, able workmen "can [not] at all times be had. An unlucky boy breaks two or three squares of glass. The glazier lives fifty miles off. An old newspaper supplies their place in the *mean time*. Before the *mean time* is over the family gets used to the newspaper & thinks no more of the glazier."[3] Town living and country living had their differences, access to skilled tradesmen being only one of them. Yet the aspirations of the families of both places were often much

the same. Whether city residents or their country cousins, it was remarked that "they live in the same neat manner, dress after the same modes, and behave themselves exactly as the gentry in London."[4] Carpenters, glaziers, plasterers, painters, and paperhangers set the stage, and among them, finish carpenters were first and foremost.

Nothing gave finish carpenters greater scope for their specialized skills than the fittings they installed in public buildings and fashion-conscious private dwellings, especially those built in the region's larger towns and on great planters' country estates. Increasingly, throughout the eighteenth century, their work transformed town houses, large-

Fig. 14.1. Wainscoted parlor in the original section of Sotterley, St. Mary's County, Maryland, remodeled by Rebecca and George Plater II in 1732. As part of the new finishes, some of the posts and summer beams were paneled, but they continued to project into the room.

scale public buildings, and substantial plantation houses into edifices that little resembled ordinary buildings in the countryside. A principal difference was the effort to hide the framing of a genteel house on the inside as thoroughly as weatherboards and cornices masked it from without (Fig. 14.1). Another was the trim applied to rooms, passages, and staircases to indicate their relative social importance and thus to signal to users of those spaces where they belonged and how to get there, depending on their rank and the business that brought them into the building. Both qualities— refinement and hierarchy—became more elaborate in urban buildings and country houses as the eighteenth century wore on. Eventually, but slowly and unevenly, these fashionable improvements also showed up in farmhouses and backstreet city buildings. As a distinctively main street urban architectural style, it was first seen at Jamestown after 1662. Afterward, it flowered in Williamsburg, Yorktown, Annapolis, and Norfolk. And finally it carried all before it everywhere in the Tidewater region by the opening decade of the nineteenth century.

WALL SURFACES AND CEILINGS

Rooms trimmed in Georgian finery gave carpenters a new way to achieve the two goals that their work was expected to accomplish—masking a building's frame and providing visual clues to the relative importance of interior spaces. Carpenters needed to understand society's hierarchical rules in order to create the physical spaces and visual signposts that made living and working in buildings predictable. For centuries, the most important rooms in British buildings were typically larger, taller, more brightly lit, and better finished than secondary spaces. The placement of doorways, passages, and staircases further adjusted the social dynamics of room use. The new Georgian aesthetic did not replace that older system. It simply layered another set of signaling devices on top and introduced ladies and gentlemen to a refined language of moldings, forms, and ornament to communicate the messages that made buildings work the way they were supposed to. Accordingly, important social spaces became ever-more-complex collections of features that told the acutely class-conscious users of eighteenth-century houses who should be where and who should be someplace else. The best spaces received the most up-to-date paneling and the most sophisticated architraves, chair boards, cornices, and chimneypieces. Secondary spaces necessarily made do with less elaboration, more out-of-date trim, and simpler finishes. Almost every visible element in a well-appointed room presented builders with another opportunity to display its rank in relation to adjacent rooms and spaces (Fig. 14.2).[5]

Fig. 14.2. Section through Eppington, c. 1768–1802, Chesterfield County, Virginia. Francis Eppes IV spent most of his adult life building, remodeling, and finishing this house. The degree of elaboration of each space reflects the date of its completion and its relative importance.

Each feature contributed to this calculation, with the wall and ceiling treatments being the foundation for this new work. Carpenters working in the region's best houses had always treated the exposed framing members themselves as decorative elements—posts, plates, ceiling beams, joists, rafters, and collars. They followed ancient English custom in that respect, and also in their practice of easing the leading edges of such visible timberwork with decorative chamfers or simple moldings such as an ovolo or an ogee (Fig. 14.3). Sometimes wall posts and the lintels over fireplaces became showcases for extra elaboration, date panels, or the owner's initials. Lime plaster applied to split laths infilled between these posts and lintels. Yet whole rooms, even into the early nineteenth century, could at times be left altogether unfinished, except for a possible coating of whitewash lightly brushed over posts, studs, and the backside of the exterior cladding visible in between.

Dwellings with exposed framing eventually became an anathema to builders, who took their cue from English architectural refinements that emerged in the second half of the seventeenth century. Walls and partitions became more than simple divisions covered with plaster or clapboards. Instead, they served as canvases for architectural possibilities unimag-

Fig. 14.3. Inscribed date "1716" on the center wall post. Woodward-Jones House, Suffolk, Virginia.

ined by a previous generation of builders. Their vacant expanses were soon organized into the parts and proportions of a classical order, starting with a plinth made of three parts: a base along the floor, a dado (wainscot), and a surbase (chair board). Above all and across the top ran a classically inspired entablature, or at least one stripped down to a cornice or crown molding. In such an ideal scheme, structural posts and studs disappeared completely behind the visible wall

Fig. 14.4. Reconstructed view of Pear Valley as it appeared when first built in 1740, Northampton County, Virginia. Although their sizes are known, the design of the mantel, window, and doors is conjectural.

surfaces, and plates and beams disappeared behind cornice moldings, if not already hidden by deepened wall studs and raised summer beams. Not surprisingly, the earliest elements in this architectural masquerade have come to light at Jamestown as archaeological fragments of plasterwork cornices, pargeted ceiling ornaments, and decorative chimneypieces installed in quasi-public buildings erected about 1680.[6]

This radically new treatment of interior spaces followed the provincial capital to its new home in Williamsburg after 1699 and to the dwellings of the greater planters, merchants, and officials who had an association with these two places. From there, it spread gradually and imperfectly into the countryside. Beyond Williamsburg's immediate sphere of influence, country house builders were slower to adopt the idea of hiding the frame—inside or out. If anything, their lingering fondness for articulated frames reached new heights in the 1720s, 1730s, and 1740s, in a lavish use of chamfers at such

smaller plantation houses as Pear Valley, for instance (Fig. 14.4), or a tighter spacing of joists to indicate the superiority of the hall over the adjoining chamber at the Matthew Jones House (see Fig. 10.6). As late as 1755, when Henry Darnell erected a new dwelling at Portland Manor, he settled on a design that reflected a cross between older country ways and flush framing. On the first floor, corner posts were allowed to project and the ceiling of the inner room was exposed, while that in the hall and stair passage were plastered over for a more modern look.[7] Chambers were usually finished conservatively, and here Darnell's carpenter proudly planed, chamfered, and stopped the chamfers on the underside of the principal rafters. This finely tuned mix of old and urbane fashions was a clever way to define private and public areas at a time when articulated frames were becoming obsolete, even for country folk. Still, as late as the 1810s, builders of some country houses left parts of the framing uncovered. One cau-

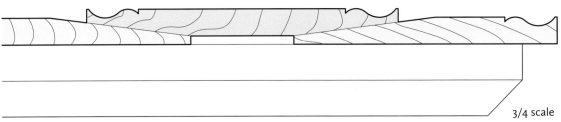

3/4 scale

Fig. 14.5. Detail of the board-and-batten door to the staircase in the John Hill Kitchen, Southampton County, Virginia. The door and stair enclosure is made of planks molded with an early style of shallow-molded cymas.

tious farmer building his house in rural North Carolina in 1818 wanted "the inside of the whole building to be Ceiled all that is exposed to view." Yet he realized that traditions died hard and thus agreed that "the timbers that are exposed to view are to be plained and beaded if required."[8]

Virtually all aspects of interior elaboration in the new, refined style were employed in enough houses, churches, and public buildings across the Chesapeake by the early eighteenth century that builders and their clients had ready-made examples to copy. Nonetheless, decoration of this type was not used indiscriminately. Hidden framing covered with plaster and perhaps a baseboard sufficed for countless parlor, passage, and dining room walls in many a gentry house through the first half of the century. Gradually, though, carpenters long accustomed to the workmanlike traditions of their ancient craft felt pressured by clients to make new things that pattern books, tradesmen trained in England, and traveling merchants and gentleman called by unfamiliar names.

One simple improvement over coarse clapboards for partitions and as wall coverings was the installation of planed, vertical planks. Plank walling originated in the seventeenth century, but so few dwellings survive from then that it can only be surmised what the range of configurations may have been used to sheath the many fireplace walls, staircases, and occasionally entire rooms in better houses. Perhaps craftsmen followed the common practice in both old and New England of running a shallow molding along the edges of such planks to call attention to their joints. Some later examples of this type survive. The enclosed stair in the John Hill Kitchen (1810s), for instance, is sheathed with reused shiplapped boards molded with shallow ogees, similar to the reused boards masking the wall framing under the stair at Four Mile Tree in Surry County (1745) (Fig. 14.5). Perhaps these boards did not originate in the seventeenth century, yet in both instances the moldings are of the style of pre-Georgian work and indicate the persistence of this tradition into the age of refinement and classicism.

Another option often seen in houses dating to the first half of the eighteenth century was a hybrid of panel work

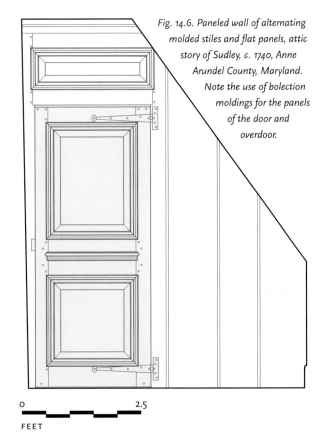

Fig. 14.6. Paneled wall of alternating molded stiles and flat panels, attic story of Sudley, c. 1740, Anne Arundel County, Maryland. Note the use of bolection moldings for the panels of the door and overdoor.

0   2.5

FEET

made of vertical ceiling-height walling that eliminated the horizontal rails normally used to tie more elaborate wainscoting together. This type of paneling had the appearance of conventional wainscot without horizontal rails but with narrow panels—either flat or raised—that ran uninterrupted the full height of the wall (Fig. 14.6). At some point, perhaps by the second quarter of the eighteenth century, plank walls were built with less modulation across their surfaces. They were increasingly replaced with beaded shiplapped and tongue-and-groove boards, which remained a standard wall covering well into the nineteenth century.

Plank walling in all its varieties became one way to help manage costs and establish hierarchical order throughout a house. Sawing logs into boards remained expensive until the early nineteenth century. Nonetheless, planking, despite its more laborious production, was a common finish for utilitarian structures throughout the colonial era, such as for

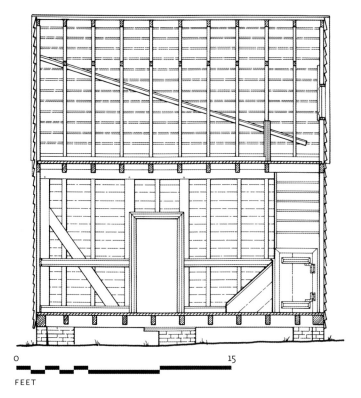

O   15
▬▬▬▬▬▬▬▬▬▬▬▬▬▬
FEET

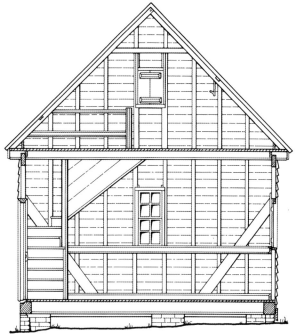

Fig. 14.7. Bryant-Deloatche House, early nineteenth century, Southampton County, Virginia. The interior was trimmed with base and surbase, but the walls never received plaster.

stores and warehouses, and at times it sufficed for kitchens and other work buildings. The association of planking with utility recommended it for domestic use. Secondary spaces in better houses, the attic story in the Paca House in Annapolis, for instance, cellar divisions, service spaces, and walls and partitions in modest dwellings were obvious places for its application. The popularity of plank walls peaked in the early nineteenth century when mills produced enough sawn material to force more competitive prices for wide boards.

That change was significant enough that by 1820, when the *Richmond and Alexandria Builders' Price Book* was published, plank was cheaper than plaster for wall material. A client in these two cities could be expected to pay $7.56 for two coats of plaster on a 9- by 18-foot wall, including materials, lath, and labor, and $9.00 for three coats. To cover that same wall in planed tongue-and-groove boards, Richmond craftsmen received only $6.48 and an Alexandria carpenter earned a mere $4.86.[9] Mechanization made plank partitions an economical alternative for modest houses in the early nineteenth century, allowing their occupants a degree of refinement that might not otherwise have been affordable. Thus, over several decades, the use of plank evolved from heavily contoured surfaces suitable for early gentry walls, to smoother walls more in keeping with notions of refinement but often reserved for secondary and service rooms, to a cheap and respectable alternative for partitions and wall coverings in ordinary dwellings in the early nineteenth century.

The amount of trim used to regulate the relative refinement of a room started with the base, generally known as a washboard or mopboard. However, a washboard was not required, especially in early houses. Plaster walls could run uninterrupted to the floor, as was done on the upper floor of the Mason House in Accomack County. There a faux base was painted on the wall where none existed. In contrast, by the nineteenth century, baseboards had become an important element in the definition of space and were sometimes used where no wall finish was present, not even lath and plaster. An example is the base and surbase nailed to the framing of the Bryant-Deloatche House, a small one-room dwelling in Southampton County, where the walls have never been plastered and the framing remains exposed to this day, whether intended originally or not (Fig. 14.7). There is no doubt that the loft over the wing of the Hillsman House was left unplastered on purpose; its base was fitted tight to the eaves and would have disappeared altogether had the roof been plastered. If surbase, cornice, or wainscot was to be used, a base was invariably present.

Other wall embellishment typically included a chair board, which sometimes had a molded surbase planted on top of it. The chair board was often beaded on its top and bottom edges and was set at the height of a low wainscot cap, whether or not wainscoting was present. The chair board could be elaborated with the addition of a projecting bolection molding. Although bolection moldings applied to pan-

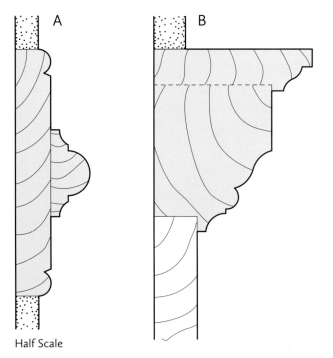

A

B

Half Scale

Fig. 14.8. Surbase profiles. A: Beaded board with bolection, third–floor passage, Shirley, 1772, Charles City County, Virginia; B: Pedestal-style chair board, Hammond-Harwood House, 1774, Annapolis.

eling and architraves largely disappear by 1750, they adorned surbases until the end of the century. Bolections were a clean way to resolve the intersection between the surbase and adjoining door, window, and mantel architraves because they could be returned against the chair board just short of the architraves. Beaded boards and bolections served poorly as a cap for wainscoting. Instead, the usual profile was a simple molding with a torus and cavetto profile about the same size as stair tread nosings. More complex surbases known as pedestal caps that copied the form of classical plinth caps appeared in town houses and large country houses beginning in the 1750s (Fig. 14.8). With a surbase in place, a cornice could be added, be it simply a crown molding, a full cornice, or an extended entablature. While the surbase became standard trim for gentry interiors in the eighteenth century, they mostly disappeared from dwellings constructed after 1830, once the massing of large, unbroken planes of plaster became the preferred interior treatment for private and public rooms alike. Eventually even cornices were eliminated.

Besides simple coordination of moldings (a classical base worked better with a pedestal surbase, for instance), the profile of one element often had implications for the selection of others in the same room. A principal concern was how far a molding projected from the wall, especially if it intersected other moldings, as bases and surbases routinely ran into door architraves, chimneypieces, and window trim. Occasionally, cornices abutted windows and chimney fronts. A cornice might project over and around these elements, but bases and surbases had to be cut off. Usually an effort was made to hide the end grain of the horizontal timbers by projecting enough

of an architrave backband to hide them. If bases and surbases stuck out too far, the proud parts were either simply cut off or sometimes beveled on their ends to eliminate sharp corners. Either way, they looked awkward not by completely terminating against the mantels and architraves. Better-resolved work pulled the architraves off the openings sufficiently into the room to stop at least the vertical planes of these members. The molded parts of the surbase could then be neatly mitered and their ends returned against themselves before meeting the architraves. This careful treatment of trim work at the corners was part of the same aesthetic that was applied to exterior work; both eliminated unresolved ends and visible end grain.

Wainscot was used to create the most refined work of the eighteenth century. "Wainscot" was a term for wooden panels loosely fixed inside a framework of vertical stiles and horizontal rails. In this region, it was first associated with door construction, there being little opportunity for its application as a wall treatment until the late seventeenth century. It was also an alternative term for oak, the material from which most early paneling was made, doors and paneled walls alike. Use of wainscoting increased in the last quarter of the seventeenth century in public buildings and for pew boxes in churches. Although it occasionally covered walls in fine gentry houses in the first quarter of the eighteenth century, it was not common in domestic settings until the 1730s. After that, it became the standard finish for the most genteel rooms in both public and private buildings for the next several decades. By then, paneling was so closely associated with social pretensions that no great house was without one style of it or another until the end of the colonial era.

One of the earliest wainscoted interiors is noted in the sale of an unfinished dwelling, Moores Lodge, to the Lord Proprietors of Maryland for use as the Charles County Courthouse in 1674. The transaction required the "lower roome to be well wainscoted, the upper room to be well daubed & scaled [sealed] with mortar white limed & sized" (see Fig. 1.7).[10] If the few surviving pieces of locally made seventeenth-century paneled furniture are any indication, this wainscoting probably resembled traditional English paneled walls.[11] Such early work had shallow moldings cut along the edges of the stiles and rails. Wainscot wall finish of this type was divided into many small rectangles, in contrast to the larger scale panels so common later.

New-style Georgian wainscoting always ran modern

moldings along all four sides of each enlarged panel. The panel-work itself could run floor to ceiling, and usually did, before midcentury. The lowest panel usually rose to the height of the surbase, and a longer one stretched from there to the cornice. Panels varied in width, based on the spacing of other architectural features. They also were differently detailed, usually according to the dates of construction. Bolection paneling, a rare early type, consisted of a projecting molding surrounding a raised, fielded panel. It was short lived in the mid-Atlantic colonies, perhaps for two related reasons. First, wainscoted interiors were unusual here until the second quarter of the eighteenth century, by which time bolection moldings were out of date in London.[12] By the time local carpenters began making wainscoting with regularity, they and their gentry clients had their eye on London fashion, at which time plainer wainscot was in vogue. Second, most Marylanders and especially Virginians preferred the neat-and-plain style that eschewed excessive ornamentation. Anything that suggested baroque exuberance, as did robust bolection molds, was to be avoided. Nonetheless, some bolection paneling appeared here and there in the first half of the century, mostly for overmantels on the Upper Eastern Shore and in rural parlors such as at Sudley in southern Anne Arundel County, a dwelling that was otherwise covered with beaded, riven clapboards.

The plainer, more classical style of wainscoting included a raised, fielded panel floated in a groove cut into a grid of lightly molded stiles and rails (Fig. 14.9). Unlike a bolection molding that was attached to the face of the framework, the moldings on all other Georgian wainscot were planed directly on the edges of the stiles and rails (most often an ovolo), or else those members were not molded at all. Fielded panels were typically raised with only a fillet to separate the beveled sides from their top flat surface. Simple as it was, such paneling could be manipulated for a variety of effects. Differences were exploited in part to produce refined order throughout a building. The degree of elaboration was also used to set apart the finest dwellings in the region from lesser neighbors. An example in Williamsburg uses a small cyma added above the conventional ovolo molding on the panels in the front door on Walthoe's storehouse, and the fielded panels were raised with an additional astragal below the fillet to indicate which of the two front doors led to the more elegant apartment (see Fig. 13.21C). This same embellishment worked for wainscot moldings, interior doors, and chimneypieces to distinguish superior interior work. Another device was to give the upper panels arched heads, like those seen in the parlor at the Hampton farmhouse and on the exterior doors at Four Mile Tree. One more trick was to highlight ordinary wainscot walls with a few choice bolection panels, such as turning them diamond-wise over a fireplace. The more baroque among these contrivances—the selective

Fig. 14.10. Dining room, Salubria, 1757, Culpeper County, Virginia. In order to expose plaster on upper walls, Virginians began reducing the scale of wainscot in the 1750s to become two boards high, with short upper panels set above the conventional level for the surbase. This style reached the height of its popularity in the 1780s.

use of bolections and arched panels—were outliers and had largely run their course by the 1750s. Wainscoting for most houses generally did not include additional ornamentation. Instead, the trend emphasized simplicity. One increasingly frequent choice was to not raise the panels at all and leave the fields flat. Known as square paneling, it became common after the Revolution. It was certainly used much earlier, since restraint was a genteel trait favored at this time. Conformity and uniformity were most prized through the middle of the eighteenth century, leaving little room for excessive variation in most gentry house interiors.

Floor to ceiling paneling remained popular in Virginia through the 1750s. It lingered on in Maryland even longer, through the 1770s in the form of decorative plasterwork paneling above flush-board wainscoting. Although used before midcentury as a secondary treatment, chair-board–height wainscoting with plaster walls above soon became a preferred installation. Confining panel work to the dado left large expanses of brightly finished plastered walls, which were often papered after the late 1750s. By the late colonial period, full-height wainscot ran its course. It was overly textured and was dismissed as old fashioned. A transitional variety, favored by some, was wainscoting mounted two-panels high, which raised the surbase to chest height, thereby leaving room for some plaster above and at the same time show-

ing off extensive panel work (Fig. 14.10). This was a popular choice in Virginia from the late 1750s until the 1790s but seems to have been too parochial for Marylanders, who were already turning away from Norfolk and Williamsburg as paragons and looking toward Philadelphia and London for their architectural inspiration. Their preferred newer style was less staid and parochial, and instead favored a more flamboyant and ornate rococo look.

One way to embellish wainscoted rooms was to add pilasters and, occasionally, engaged columns. They were a natural fit, since the proportioning of rooms was roughly based on the orders. One of the earliest and most ambitious uses of orders may have been the hall at Rosewell, built by Mann Page I between 1725 and 1730. It was reportedly encircled with pilasters fashioned in the Corinthian order, or (as surviving fragments suggest) the Ionic order.[13] Another early installation was the engaged Corinthian columns that flanked the fireplace and principal openings in the dining room of Thomas Nelson's 1729–30 Yorktown house. His parlor was a more modest room where pilasters were confined to the fireplace wall and where the capitals were omitted to achieve a plainer effect. The orders in Nelson's dining room were even more awkward than those in the parlor. The capitals were oddly carved and the engaged columns were too tall for anything more than a cornice; a mere wisp of a pulvinated frieze

Fig. 14.11. Dining room, Nelson House, 1729–30, Yorktown, Virginia. Engaged Corinthian columns flanked the fireplace and all the openings in Thomas Nelson's best entertaining room.

set above the windows between the columns suggested an Ionic entablature. One might excuse the mixed orders and awkward columns at Nelson's house as the work of carpenters new to such refinements, but in many ways it anticipated trim not uncommonly produced in Virginia over the next seventy-five years (Fig. 14.11).[14]

By the late 1730s, Corinthian capitals were a rarity, as the plainer—and easier to fabricate—Doric and Ionic orders became near universal. That was partly due to a weak carving tradition in Virginia before midcentury and partly due to Virginians' fondness for the neat-and-plain style. Most pilasters were made by joiners working solely with molding planes, not carving tools, planes that could shape fluting and even occasionally stop fluting but could not cut elaborate capitals. That quickly ruled out the Corinthian and Composite orders. The Tuscan order found little favor in the region, at least for interior work. That left either the Doric, easily made with molding planes, or an alternative for the

Ionic order assembled from molded profiles resembling impost blocks. The pilasters William Byrd III installed in the southeast drawing room at Westover, for instance, are fluted with an Ionic base and with a capital that is a cross between an impost profile and a Doric capital. The pilasters carry a full Ionic entablature, but one with a pulvinated frieze in which conventional modillions are replaced with dentils. Strange as it appeared, carpenters in Maryland and Virginia mixed and matched assorted parts from different orders to create a facsimile of classicism in which architectural book rigor was less important than its overall effect. Jefferson said as much in describing the two-story portico of the capitol in Williamsburg. The Ionic order of the upper story, he observed, was "much too small for that on which it is mounted, its ornaments not proper to the order, nor proportioned within themselves. . . . Yet, on the whole, it is the most pleasing piece of architecture we have."[15]

Pilasters came to be used differently in the late colonial

period. The gradual decline of the neat-and-plain style set the change in motion. This was most noticeable in and around Annapolis, but the change appeared in Virginia, too, after the Revolution. The use of the orders to ornament a room was not common in Annapolis, but skilled carvers and decorative plasterers occasionally made sumptuous rooms that included Corinthian decoration. Governor Horatio Sharpe chose it for the door surround in the hall of his country estate, Whitehall (Fig. 14.12). Even in the more modest Pleasant Hall in Virginia Beach (1779), Corinthian was selected for the pilasters to flank the dining room fireplace. Just as wall paneling was shrunk to become chest-high wainscot and chimneypieces, the orders were also diminished so that they could be integrated into other parts of room elements in the late colonial period. Completed in the mid- to late 1750s, the parlor at Marmion was one of the last full-height pilastered rooms in the region (see Fig. 15.15). At first reducing the orders simply meant that such pilasters were limited to the flanking of doorways and fireplaces, but even they gave way to smaller ones used as part of window surrounds and overmantels (Fig. 14.13). Examples include the pilasters flanking interior doors at Gunston Hall, the overmantel at Elmwood, and the engaged columns on the Venetian window at the stair landing of the Chase-Lloyd House. Reduction of pilasters continued after the Revolution, not only in overmantel treatments, as at Strawberry Hill, but even more frequently as pilasters, engaged, or as freestanding columns on the chimneypieces themselves. What the diminution of the orders accomplished was to open larger expanses of walls to plaster and make it easier to wallpaper.

By the late colonial period, the use of full-height orders, along with raised paneling, had gone out of fashion. Modern wainscot, or flush paneling, was a popular alternative to raised and square paneling. This change was intended to smooth out the wall surfaces as craftsmen sought ever-more aggressive ways to reduce textured surfaces in house interiors. It first emerged in the 1750s in the best rooms of the grandest houses as part of the new rococo interiors in Annapolis and in the more neat-and-plain rural mansions of Virginia. It was made of a framework of unmolded stiles and rails with flat panels fitted flush to it. When used in conjunction with raised panels, modern wainscoting was always set below the surbase with raised panels above. This treatment appears at Carter's Grove, Elmwood, and the Carlyle House. Annapolis tradesmen replicated this pattern in plaster, with a modern wainscoted dado below and raised panels in the upper part of the wall. Cast and run-in-place plaster allowed for a degree of enrichment not seen before in Chesapeake buildings. One of the most expert executions in this style was the drawing room of the James Brice House. Modern wainscot was used to accentuate the most important spaces, leaving inferior rooms to be fitted with more ordinary raised paneling.

By the last quarter of the eighteenth century, the stiles and rails of modern wainscot were often eliminated altogether and were replaced by a plain dado made of long horizontal boards. One extremely wide or two glued-up horizontal boards formed a chair-board height plinth that often ran unbroken the length of the room except where it was interrupted by doorways and windows (see Fig. 15.21). As an aesthetic advancement, the plain dado was a good fit for the rising middle class of the early nineteenth century. It was stylish and cheap, and complemented an emerging style that rendered architectural trim a mere canvas on which to paint decorative faux finishes.

An updated version of square paneling appeared in the best neoclassical houses in the first quarter of the nineteenth century. Instead of stiles and rails with heavy ovolos, characteristic of the colonial period, this new wainscoting incorporated delicate quirked moldings. The carpenter's accounts for work on Mrs. Riddell's house in Baltimore called this "framed & paneled Weanscoating fancy."[16] "Fancy" was a new decorative style that relied on delicately molded woodwork ornamented in a creative, spirited, and fanciful way. Elaborate faux finishes covered plain dados and flat paneling with quirked moldings, whose broad surfaces lent themselves to this new craze. Like flush wainscoting, these dados were plain enough to be grained, and many of them were fanciful interpretations of a variety of woods. Wooden chimneypieces were often marbleized in contrasting patterns and colors, and walls were hung with multicolored wallpaper designs. Windows, floors, and furniture were covered with patterned curtains, carpets, and upholstery in a riot of patterns that reached its zenith in the 1830s.[17]

Decorative plaster appeared in only a few of the best houses in the late colonial period. The plaster paneling that builders installed in Annapolis and a few Maryland country houses was borrowed from a contemporary London convention (Fig. 14.14). Still, almost all gentry houses had some relatively smooth plastered walls and perhaps ceilings. These surfaces required a layer of split laths, or sawn ones after circular saws became commonplace in the early 1850s, which were nailed to the wall and ceiling framing. Plasterers then applied a scratch coat made of sand, clay, lime putty, and, usually, animal hair to spaced wooden lath. The scratch coat would ooze into the small gaps between the laths. This first layer was often scored on its surface to assist in the bonding of the next layer, which in eighteenth-century work was most typically also the top coat. In better, three-layer plastering,

(top) Fig. 14.12. Doorway framed by Corinthian pilasters and pediment, Whitehall, 1765, Anne Arundel County, Maryland.

(bottom) Fig. 14.13. Raised panel end wall, Wilton, 1763, Middlesex County, Virginia.

(left) Fig. 14.14. A mixture of elaborate plasterwork and joinery in the drawing room of the James Brice House, 1767–73, Annapolis. Modern wainscot woodwork was used below the surbase, with raised panels rendered in plaster applied above.

(right) Fig. 14.15. Cornice and ceiling plaster, dining room, Kenmore, 1776, Fredericksburg.

the second "brown coat" contained the same ingredients as the first one, and then a third or finish coat was applied. The finish coat had a higher lime content, lacked clay and hair, and could be made with finer sand for a smoother finish. Yet, as standard as this three-coat system became in the nineteenth century, it was actually rarely so finely produced in the colonial era. Even the finest work, represented by the ornamental panel plasterwork in Annapolis, frequently lacked a smooth finish coat.

Ornamental plaster played a minor role in the decoration of the Chesapeake house, except for a few notable exceptions, including the rococo ceilings at Westover and the extravagant mantels and ceilings at Kenmore (Fig. 14.15). This work, which was equal to the better plastering in Britain, in-

dicates that it was cost rather than an unsophisticated understanding of the craft that restricted its popularity. Decorative plastering simply could not replace a tradition where the carpentry and joinery trades predominated. Nonetheless, it did impress a few wealthy and knowledgeable individuals, such as George Washington and his brother-in-law Fielding Lewis, who could afford it.

The Adams-Kilty House in Annapolis, built between 1773 and 1786, has particularly fine plaster cornices and a splendid ceiling, which was perhaps executed by John Rawlings and James Barnes, who had been in Annapolis since 1771 and had been responsible for the interiors at the Chase-Lloyd House. The craftsmen installed a Gothic cornice in the entry, along with a rococo ceiling and Corinthian modillion cornice in the dining room, similar to the one in the Hammond-Harwood House.[18] These moldings were run in place where practical, but components like the modillions required casting. To make a simple run, a plasterer used a "horse," which was made in the shape of the desired molding, and dragged it with fresh plaster across the brown wall coat as a way to trowel it to shape. Once the first molded run had set, it was then finished using the same tool. If the walls and ceilings were to have a finished white coat, the moldings were usually the last to be troweled on, in order to help lock them in place.

Cast ornament was then applied to cornices, like those in the Adams-Kilty House, and sometimes was added to enrich the walls and ceiling. Wooden molds carved for each element were filled with a special plaster mixture. The plaster ceilings and chimneypieces at Kenmore, for example, included lime or chalk (calcite), hide glue, brick dust, and sand. Workmen pressed metal armatures into the mix while it was still wet to hold a string of pieces together to create long sections of floral designs. They used an adhesive of calcite and hide glue to attach the cast ornament to the flat plaster surfaces. Headless brads driven into the plaster walls provided additional reinforcement to secure the delicate floral elements of the overmantels.[19] Although the fashion for ornate plastered interiors ended shortly after the Revolution, it left a tradition, albeit a modest one, of using plaster for cornices and medallions that continued into the middle of the nineteenth century.

FLOORS

Flooring exemplified the Georgian obsession of using materials and workmanship to reflect the social order of buildings. Its variety reveals the subtlety that homebuilders employed to express the relative significance of a space and control the cost spent on fabrication and installation. Wood flooring presented many choices that represented more than just a matter of personal preference. Wood species, the character of the grain, board lengths and widths, the manner in which head and side joints were treated, and fastening methods contributed to the relative expense of a floor. Each factor was carefully considered to adjust the relationship between one space and another.

Flooring methods had not always been as complex and sophisticated as they became in the eighteenth century. When a Norfolk County house carpenter was asked in 1666 "to laye a floore of plank," the intention was to use sawn boards to create a regular finished surface. In contrast, many residents of earthfast dwellings simply walked on bare hardened earth. Their lofts and upper garrets or "cocklofts" were frequently

Fig. 14.16. Underside of the cockloft fitted with riven clapboards, c. 1730, Cloverfields, Queen Anne's County, Maryland.

finished with riven, wedged-shaped clapboards that overlapped like siding. Well into the eighteenth century, cocklofts in otherwise refined houses were finished with clapboards; the cockloft in Cloverfields in Queen Anne's County was built about 1730, and the one in Hedgelawn in Chesterfield County was constructed about fifteen years later (Fig. 14.16). As rudimentary as clapboard floors were, they remained a viable alternative for secondary spaces through the first half of the eighteenth century.

The vast majority of plank floors in this region were made of pine. Yellow poplar was an occasional and cheaper alternative in secondary spaces but did not wear well for use in public rooms. The main attic floor of Cloverfields—that under the cockloft—was made of pit-sawn poplar. Red and white oak were other minor alternatives used occasionally for stair treads, especially in early country dwellings like the Mason House on the Lower Eastern Shore and the service stairs at Riversdale (1807) in Prince George's County, Maryland. The best floors were made of southern yellow longleaf pine, often referred to as "heart pine." The Tidewater area of the James River was roughly the northern and western limit of this species. Use of the timber outside the area entailed significant transportation costs. A common substitute for heart pine was one of a number of local species that were softer, less durable, and paler in color. Thomas Jefferson had problems acquiring good flooring, which led him to write to his enslaved joiner, John Hemings, that "considering how dear and distant heart pine is, you had better lay the floor of the office terras with oak, which is as good and can be had at

Butted boards, face nailed

Splined and face nailed

Doweled and secret nailed

Tongue and groove, secret nailed

Fig. 14.17. Range of flooring joinery common to the region.

home."[20] In general, the quality of pine floors diminishes the farther north a house is located. Cheaper grades of pine and wider boards appeared more frequently in Maryland than in southern Virginia. Even so, southern Virginia material was typically less desirable than flooring in the Carolinas.

Boards were graded by size and grain. Builders preferred narrower boards, denser edge-grain material, and longer lengths. Clients in the early nineteenth century paid more than a 10 percent premium for boards that ranged from 3 to 5 inches over those that averaged 5 to 6½ inches.[21] Typically, then, carpenters laid the widest boards the farthest from the entertaining rooms. John Ridout's builder selected dense heart pine boards, 5½ to 8 inches wide, for the entertaining rooms of his speculative row and used shortleaf pine up to 21 inches in width for the attic. The added expense and greater desirability of narrower boards lay in both the extra labor required to fabricate and install them and the greater exposure of quarter-sawn (or edge-grain) surfaces.

Carpenters faced numerous decisions that affected floors' appearances and final costs. The selection of floor material and the manner in which it was laid tended to get better through the eighteenth and into the nineteenth centuries, even, oddly enough, when some rooms received wall-to-wall carpeting in these later years. William Brown relaid the floor in the parlor of Four Mile Tree in 1796 so that the boards would run uninterrupted from one end of the room to the other. If not immediately, this floor was soon carpeted, hiding what was otherwise exquisite material. Unless rooms were small or on those rare occasions when long boards were

procured (more than about 16 feet was considered dear), carpenters laid the best floors so that the head joints were staggered from one row to the next as a way to minimize their presence. Some early eighteenth-century houses (and continuing later for some second-story floors and those in secondary spaces) ran the head joints of a handful of boards in a line before staggering and repeating the pattern across the room, which visually emphasized the joints in a way that was quite old-fashioned for midcentury taste.

Careful attention to surface treatment extended to the manner in which flooring was fixed in place. Headless brads were available at least from the time of the construction of Bacon's Castle in 1665. Brads and T-head fasteners were used to face nail flooring in fine spaces. The heads were set flush and aligned with the direction of the grain as a way to downplay their presence. Carpenters often secured ordinary floors with common rose-head nails, which were used in secondary buildings and the attics of early houses, such as the upstairs of the Matthew Jones House (c. 1720). Better still were blind- or "secret"-nailed floors, which completely eliminated fasteners from view, except for where T-heads were necessary along the perimeter of a room to secure the ends of boards in a way that would keep them from splitting. Subtle workmanship appeared in the joining of edges. They could simply be butted, as most face-nailed boards were, or for a tighter fit they could be joined with either a spline or a tongue and groove. The best floors, though, were doweled. Workmen drilled holes in the edges of otherwise butted boards, in which they inserted a series of horizontal wooden (or occasionally iron) pins every foot or so to connect one board to the next. The flooring was then secret-nailed in place. The *Builders' Price Book* listed the cost of the "Best doweled floors" at $8.50 per square, five-and-a-half times more expensive than the widest, face-nailed, "square" joint (butted) flooring. Such a price disparity meant that only a few rooms in the best of houses had doweled flooring. Introduced in the second quarter of the eighteenth century, it was abandoned by the end of the colonial era long before the *Price Book* was published (Fig. 14.17).[22]

Until mill-sawn floorboards became common in the early nineteenth century (the first decade for most towns and by the 1820s in the countryside), the production of floorboards was a laborious task, which represented a significant investment in time and money. Sawyers generally produced boards that ranged from 1-inch- to ¾-inch-thick or more as finished stock (that is, with one planed face). The top face and the edges were jointed square, but the bottoms were left rough, unless intended to be exposed in polite space, in which case it, too, was often planed. In order to ensure a level floor, carpenters gauged and undercut the boards to create an even surface. They first planed rabbets on both edges to "gauge" the boards, making each precisely the same thickness on their sides, usually about 1 inch.[23] Next, they cut the boards to length and placed them upside down over the joists. Finally, they used an adze to cut away (or "undercut") any excess wood that extended below the gauged edges, ensuring that once flipped, each board was level on the surface to the board beside it. Mill-sawn timber produced more regularly dimensioned framing and flooring, which eventually led to the end of the heavy handwork of gauging and undercutting. Nonetheless, the gauging and undercutting of flooring survived into the 1850s in more backward places.

DOORWAYS AND WINDOWS

Molded architraves defined the importance of a room and accentuated its features. In polite houses, doorways marked entrances into rooms, window trim framed views to the outside, and chimneypieces formed the centerpiece of decorated interiors. Architraves served as visual signposts to movement throughout a house. Those on doorjambs routinely received different treatments on their room and passage faces. There was no contradiction between using more elaborate trim to lead guests into a better-finished room and having the plainer side of the doorway show them out. Slight differences in the moldings applied to raised panels on opposite sides of the same door reinforced the message broadcast by the trim. These social-sorting traffic maps were posted for

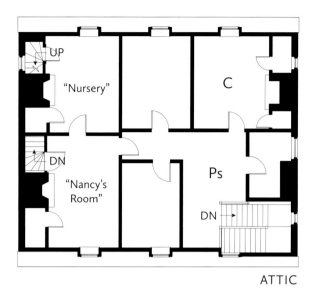

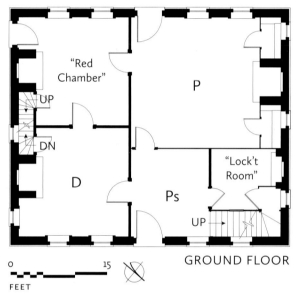

Fig. 14.18. *Restored ground- and second-floor plans, Judge John Brice House, 1739, Annapolis. Room names reflect usage in a 1768 probate inventory.*

everyone who could be expected to know the rules of the road, guests and family alike.

A useful example of this hierarchical ordering is the set of second-floor directional markers that Judge John Brice had fitted into his Annapolis house when it was constructed in 1739. They were used to usher guests in one direction, while directing Brice's wife, Sarah, and perhaps her nursemaid in another (Fig. 14.18). The upper-floor openings had plain jambs made of old-fashioned solid timbers, which were left plain on one face and had an applied beaded board on their better side. According to custom, the different sides of the jamb signaled the ordained direction of travel. All openings were set so their beaded side faced outward into the passage, except a doorway at the end of the passage, which opened into Sarah's room and was reversed. Guests and older children used the main stair to get to their chambers and knew to avoid the one to Sarah's room because of its plainer, reversed jamb. While the judge slept downstairs, his wife retired to her own space on the second floor, which she entered by way of a back stairs through a small door in the judge's bedchamber. At the head of this stair was another plain opening with the beaded side turned into the stairway—in other words, in Sarah's expected direction of travel to her upper-story room. Once there, she could go into the adjoining nursery through a doorway whose trim was oriented to lead her in. She could also move from her room into the rest of the upstairs through the one doorway in the passage that was seen in reverse by all others. Formalizing the direction of travel at the time of construction for guests and family through these jambs brought order to the upper floor, marking it as an extension of polite space. The signposts may have been subtle, but early in this new era of refinement it was necessary to make them distinct.[24]

Within a generation of the advent of the polite house, it became less important to signal direction, not that hierarchical treatment of jamb and door faces disappeared altogether. Brice's upper-floor trim was executed in an old style in terms of the explicitness and simplicity of its message, but the public rooms downstairs reveal the beginnings of a more nuanced treatment of signals. The two principal rooms there were entered from the passage—the dining room and a parlor. The doorways to both were framed with single architraves, which were superior to the simple beaded jambs of the upper-story doors. The best entertaining room, the parlor, was divided from the passage with a partition of full-height wainscoting that was paneled on both the passage and room faces. Since this is the only wainscot wall in the passage, it left no doubt as to what lay beyond. Unlike the upper story where architraves signaled direction, those on the entertaining floor were used to reinforce the quality of the rooms. The entry side was fitted with a single architrave, while the parlor side was doubled to enhance this more-refined space.

Increasingly, the signposts of hierarchical treatment only made sense in the context of the rest of the house. The big houses, after all, had servants to welcome guests at the front door and a passage to wait in, and unused doors were locked. The earlier overt expressions of circulation made less sense in these later houses. Hierarchy depended on knowing what was beyond, since ornamentation was about relative degrees of refinement, which could only be assessed and understood once trim everywhere in the house was revealed. In a more socially sophisticated household, doors and their trim were treated en suite with the rest of the room decoration, like what Brice was suggesting in his parlor. George Mason's parlor at Gunston Hall was decorated with Chinese and Gothic motifs. Its doorjambs were made of unusual, asymmetrical

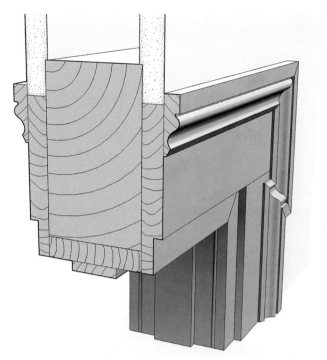

Fig. 14.19. Section through doorjamb, Stirling Castle, 1839, Petersburg, Virginia.

rococo forms (see Figs. 7.21A, 14.40). Trim on the passage side of the parlor doorway was in stark contrast, made of large, bold ovolos and fillets, which were intended as part of a more severely classical treatment of the entry. Likewise, the moldings in the other first-floor rooms—those in the dining room, the little parlor, and the chamber—were each designed in their own distinctive style. Since all door moldings in the passage were the same, there was nothing architectural in the space to inform a guest which rooms were public and which were private, and where guests were welcomed and where not. Mason's house had one further obstacle in the passage that guests had to maneuver—a blind door to balance a doorway opposite, which led to a secondary passage. Visual order within a space was now taking precedence over directional hierarchy. With all indications of the relative importance and function of each room stripped from the passage, Mason depended on house servants to guide those calling on the family as they sat in his passage waiting to be announced. Distinctions in trim between spaces began to erode in the nineteenth century, so that by the 1830s and 1840s, doors and their casings were often treated uniformly, the same on both sides throughout a given floor (Fig. 14.19).

The emphasis on en suite room finish in the late colonial period is reflected in the rise of more elaborate door treatments, especially overdoors. The retrimming of Shirley in 1771 included broken pedimented tabernacles on top of the door architraves in the dining room. Still within the bounds of the neat-and-plain style, they are more subdued than the scrolled pedimented overdoors that merchant John Carlyle

Fig. 14.20. Parlor, 1772, Shirley, Charles City County, Virginia.

used in his northern Virginia house (Fig. 14.20). Carlyle's doorways are a robust, bold interpretation of Abraham Swan's designs in *The British Architect*, an indication that the gentry no longer strongly revered the simple clean interiors of the previous age but looked outside the region's traditions for new ideas, especially newcomers such as Carlyle. Annapolis builders took their overdoors a step further by enriching them to a degree Virginians never did. Those at the Chase-Lloyd House, the Hammond-Harwood House, and Governor Horatio Sharpe's Whitehall outside of town included everything from carved architraves, cornices and consoles, ramped crossetted architrave bases, and rococo ornament applied to friezes, to pediments supporting tabernacle frames, a level of ornament and finery never seen before in the two colonies.

As voids to be framed, windows were treated much like doorways, except there was no ambiguity about trim to mark their status. Windows typically were fitted with an architrave surround that defined the importance of their associ-

ated space regardless of what type of architrave trimmed the doors. Occasionally, windows were given a decorative frieze or cornice overtreatment, but these were generally limited to late colonial or later two-story houses where their heads could be sufficiently dropped from the ceiling to make room for them. One particularly ornate form that also emerged at this time is the Venetian window, a three-part opening made of a central window flanked by sidelights. Venetian windows often have square heads, but some, like that at the Chase-Lloyd House, incorporate a rounded head for the central bay flanked by square-headed sidelights. Another advance in window treatments in brick houses was the creation of a seat. Early dwellings tended not to have them, but they became common after midcentury. They were created by extending the jamb architraves to rest on a board that formed the seat. Often the front below the bench was paneled, as were the back and sides of the seat area. These side panels usually aligned with paneled interior shutters that neatly fit into pockets above the window sill. The shutters were often of insufficient width for the pair to meet in the center. To address this problem, a third unadorned leaf was attached to one of the two outer shutters that was wide enough to fill the gap between the two. When closed, it simply folded away behind the shutter to which it was attached.

Window seats ceased to be built into houses at the beginning of the nineteenth century, but their decline started earlier in Annapolis. Some of the late colonial houses used jib doors as openings to garden piazzas. Without seats in any of the windows overlooking the garden, jib doors could be made less obvious by appearing to be yet another window whose trim extended to the floor. Windows that extended to floor level in neoclassical houses also omitted interior shutters. The growing popularity of exterior Venetian blinds (as louvered shutters were called) made interior shutters redundant. The presentation of windows in the nineteenth century became more focused on curtains that hung about them than the architectural trim of seats, paneling, and interior shutters. Hanging interiors with curtains and wallpaper, ornately painting the trim, and fitting the floors with carpets increasingly led to the simplification of architectural trim.

CHIMNEYPIECES

Chimneypieces were one of the main focal points in the eighteenth-century genteel house, but it had not always been that way. The plainness of the Virginia house had no place for such features. Fireplace openings in these earlier dwellings required a simple span of the hearth made with a large wooden lintel called a "manteltree." Decoration was integral to this structural piece on those rare occasions when it was included at all, which took the form of chamfers or moldings with decorative stops carved on its lower edge, as was done at Bacon's Castle. If in a masonry chimney, the manteltree sat on "tassels"—the secondary wooden timbers that ran along the upper inside corners of the fireplace perpendicular to the lintel that rested on them. Manteltrees measured as much as 15 inches in height and almost as deep, except that the back face was cut off on a diagonal to guide rising smoke into the flues. This heavy chamfering on the rear terminated just short of the masonry jambs to allow for adequate support at both ends.

Manteltrees alleviated the need to construct large brick arches over the firebox openings. But they were not limited to wider fireboxes. The upper-floor chambers of the Keeling House (1735), for example, also used manteltrees as an inexpensive way to support brickwork above its fireplaces. Segmental and flat brick jack arches were increasingly used in the eighteenth century as the hearth opening decreased in size, eliminating the need for a manteltree. After 1770, iron lintels were increasingly used in combination with these brick arches. Although wooden lintels became less common, they were still used to span large openings in the early nineteenth century in service areas such as kitchens and in slave houses, until they were given up completely by the 1820s and 1830s.

The earliest chimneypieces (or "mantelpieces," as they were alternatively called) were usually brought flush with the inside corners of fireplaces to clean up their openings, in much the same way as doors and windows were treated, and were usually sufficient to hide the manteltree. Delft tiles had been used to decorate fireplaces as early as the 1640s. By the early eighteenth century, they were often used on the face of the fireplace opening, thereby pushing out the chimneypiece about 5 inches. Even without tiles, it soon became fashionable to create exposure between the mantel and the opening. If not lined with tiles, the brick jambs could be plastered or left exposed, with either neatly rubbed-and-gauged work or simply with common bricks.[25]

The earliest of these surrounds were made of large bolection moldings used like architraves, often capped with a small frieze and crown molding to resemble an entablature (Fig. 14.21). Presumably that is what was intended when an order was given in 1680 for the Talbot County Courthouse to be fitted up "with two chimney pieces for the lower rooms."[26] Bolection chimneypieces were used as late as the 1730s and 1740s, mainly in the countryside, in dwellings like the Powell-Benston House on the Upper Shore and the Keeling House in Virginia Beach. By the time the Reverend John and Lady Butler Brayne Thompson installed one in 1757 in the parlor at Salubria in Culpeper County, virtually all of their Tidewater contemporaries had moved on to more classically inspired surrounds (Fig. 14.22).

Architrave surrounds on which an entablature might sit became the basis for mantels by the second quarter of the eighteenth century (Fig. 14.23). The architrave was a natural building block to elaborate the trim around the opening. Even more so than with bolections, an entablature was a natural addition to the architrave surround, since the two were paired in formal architecture. One common way to expand this mantel type was to plant the architrave on three flat boards that were tenoned together. The upper crosspiece was treated as a frieze of the entablature, and the whole was capped with a cornice, which could serve as a shelf. To further dress the upper board, the frieze might be decorated in a number of ways—with fretwork, by pulvination, or fitted with trusses, which were flat blocks applied to the face of the frieze at its two ends. A tablet, which was another board

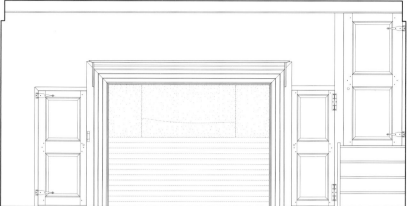

Fig. 14.21. Fireplace wall with bolection mantel, Powell-Benston House (Tilghman House), c. 1730, Somerset County, Maryland. The stair is tucked into a closet-like space to the right of the fireplace.

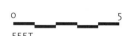

0   5

FEET

Fig. 14.22. Bolection mantel in the drawing room, 1757, Salubria, Culpeper County, Virginia.

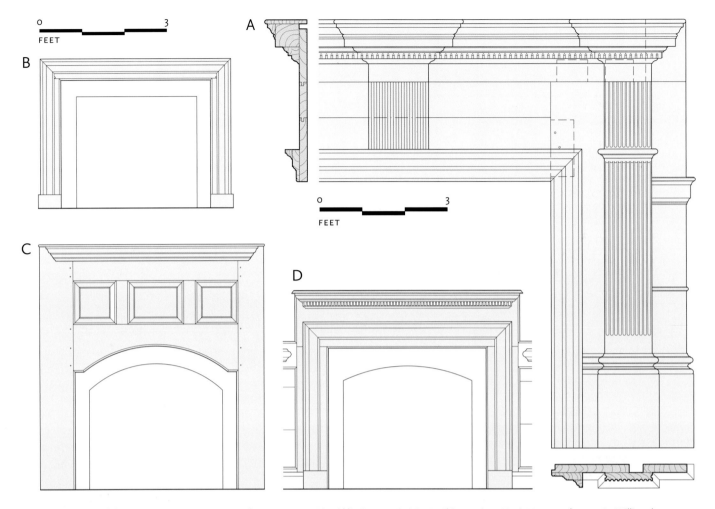

Fig. 14.23. A: Detail of chimneypiece construction, Seward House, c. 1815, Dinwiddie County, Virginia; B: Chimneypiece, Travis House parlor, c. 1765, Williamsburg; C: Chimneypiece, Pasteur House saloon, c. 1769–70, Williamsburg; D: Chimneypiece, St. George Tucker House chamber, 1788–92, Williamsburg.

centered on the frieze, was an additional feature that could be used with or without the trusses. More elaborate still were mantelpieces that had applied consoles (or brackets) in place of the trusses supported by pilasters that flanked the architrave of the jambs. An architrave could be reduced to a simple beaded board, especially in later mantels, as other components became more important than the architrave. These basic elements were expanded or contracted and occasionally enriched with carvings to create the appropriate level of embellishment for a given space.

A common alternative to the architrave mantel was a wainscoted wall that filled the chimney end of the room, at times with only a bead run along the inside corner of the paneling to surround the firebox. A variation regularly used in Williamsburg was to diminish that panel wall to simply become a large chimneypiece, which was envisioned as a wainscoted-end room complete with a crown molding reduced to frame the fireplace. This was the likely form of those in a Queen Anne's County house whose deed noted that "the partitions and mantel pieces" were "wainscot."[27]

Overmantels further elaborated the importance of the fireplace as the centerpiece of a room. One way to highlight the area above the opening if the fireplace wall was wainscoted was to treat it differently, such as with diagonally set panels used to suggest framed hatchments. This can be seen in a few Upper Shore houses. Another focal overmantel treatment was a long panel painted as a "landskip," depicting fictional or real landscapes, like the one at Holly Hill (see Fig. 15.11). These earlier overmantel forms were superseded in the 1750s by more sophisticated treatments, which were typically made with backbands that had crossettes in the corners and astragal offsets that defined a band around a plain inner field. This basic overmantel could then be embellished in a number of ways. One was to add fretwork or carving between the backband and astragal. Another was to flank the overmantel with additional ornament, such as pilasters, and cap the whole with an entablature or pediment to create a tabernacle frame (Fig. 14.24). A number of ostentatious late colonial houses in northern Virginia and Maryland had enriched tabernacle carved with rococo ornament. Reaching

Fig. 14.24. Chimneypiece with overmantel, Strawberry Hill, Petersburg, Virginia, c. 1795.

a crescendo by the time of the Revolution, overmantels faded from use by the turn of the nineteenth century in favor of plainer wall surfaces.

As fireplace walls lost most of their embellishment in the early nineteenth century, their elaboration was concentrated on the chimneypiece itself. Early nineteenth-century mantels could be richly layered with fine carving, drillwork, reeding, and other profusions of ornamentation that were suggestive of new forms. Yet underneath the surface was usually the same basic mantel construction that was used in their eighteenth-century counterparts, just enriched with new moldings and in different ways. It was common, for instance, to create pi-lasters or colonettes to carry the frieze, with tablets breaking out over the columns and perhaps the addition of a center tablet. The frieze of these mantels could be further enriched, some with reeding or fluting, others carved or applied with paterae to the trusses and tablets. The addition of a shaped shelf—sometimes supported by a bed molding and other times simply breaking out over the tablets and consoles—was a way of reimagining the plainer chimney treatments of earlier times. As late as the 1830s, reeding, fluting, and sur-face texture were so in vogue that they could be profusely applied to almost any part of a chimneypiece, and, indeed, at times, to other decorative woodwork. Pilasters might be

Fig. 14.25. Rococo enrichment, Chase-Lloyd House, 1769–74, Annapolis.

would ship the parts to a joiner who would apply it. The material closely resembled the cast plasterwork at Kenmore, but with two principal exceptions. First, the formulas differed, and, second, composition ornament tended to be made in shops for purchase and not by the installer. Because of the variety of styles and relative cost, this type of ornament became a common alternative to carving in neoclassical houses of the early nineteenth century. A distributor in Baltimore in 1797 offered a selection of American-manufactured "Composition Ornaments for Chimney pieces, Frontispieces, Pilasters, &c. among which are the following articles—viz. Landscape tablets, with rich flower festoons, Vase tables, with wheat festoons, Eagle do. with vine and ivy festoons, Flora do. and festoons, Figures of Apollo and Flora with pedestals. Do. of husks, pine apple, war trophe, wheat trophe, music trophe, liberty cap, fruit baskets, &c. The above are far superior to any imported and much cheaper."[28] The rich assortment of scenes and elements expressed in this advertisement was echoed in the opulence of its combination and use in the mantelpieces they decorated.

Composition ornament created decoration that was less robust and of shallower relief than the rococo plaster chimney and ceiling treatments of the late colonial period. Compo makers eschewed the asymmetry of the rococo, more tightly controlled its design, made it more delicate, and gave it a lighter appearance (Fig. 14.25).[29] The mantelpiece frieze was the most common place to apply this ornament, but it was occasionally found on the face of chair boards and cornices, and on frontispieces. Although it was a good fit as a surface treatment with the elaborated fancy interiors, it was already going out of style in the late 1810s, when the notion of fancy was taking off. Composition ornament was never more than a secondary option in the Chesapeake, and it did not reach the level of popularity it gained in some of the larger American cities, such as Charleston and Philadelphia, or in smaller ports, like cotton-rich Beaufort, South Carolina.

STAIRCASES

Function and ornament are two useful ways to track the evolution of staircases, the importance that was placed on them, and the changing character of where they led (Fig. 14.26). A staircase was the most expensive decorative architectural feature in better eighteenth-century houses. It was often the first thing a visitor saw upon entering a dwelling, and its prominent position and degree of elaboration suggested for whom it was intended and what might lie beyond (Fig. 14.27). Two

fluted, with stop fluting if literally interpreted. But often they were reduced to a reeded face and then elongated to fit the light and attenuated style of the neoclassical era. Reeding, too, could either be applied to the architrave surround or used as an elaborate way to finish the opening. Joiners carved, gouged, and applied decorative features in the most imaginative manner, with a zestfulness that was unrivaled in earlier or later periods. All of this embellishment, along with the use of neoclassical quirked moldings, gave mantelpieces of this era an air of the fancy.

Sometimes mantels were enriched with composition ornament, a new decorative material that appeared in the late eighteenth century and became popular among those looking for novel ways to create elaborate, delicate centerpieces (see Fig. 3.19). Made of resin, linseed oil, glue, and whiting, which was mixed to a stiff paste and then pressed into a mold, composition ornament was typically ordered from a dealer, who

Fig. 14.26. Open-string staircase, Four Mile Tree, 1743–45, Surry County, Virginia.

Fig. 14.27. Chinese lattice stair with Gothic design at landing, Battersea, 1768, Petersburg, Virginia.

houses built within a decade and a half of each other illustrate the dramatic transformation of stair design and placement in the early part of the eighteenth century. Not long after receiving his inheritance in 1733, Thomas Williams, a successful planter and merchant in rural Somerset County, Maryland, built a three-room-plan brick dwelling called Williams's Green (see Fig. 7.2). Williams fitted the business end of his hall with a wainscoted wall that included a bolection mantel and overmantel, a closet tucked to one side, and a short string of stairs leading to a door on the other side of the hearth. He constructed a winder staircase behind the door, which wrapped tightly against the side of the chimney on its rise to the attic floor. Relative to the finery of the brick shell and the woodwork of the first story, Williams's stair was quite unremarkable and undoubtedly similar to common stairs of

the previous century. Yet, not long before, John Brush, an aspiring tradesman, had had a more innovative solution for the frame dwelling he completed around 1720, next door to the new governor's house in Williamsburg. Brush also built a dwelling with three ground-floor rooms, but his featured a very generous center passage. Instead of tucking his staircase in a hidden corner the way Williams did, he erected a very public and elaborate one in the passage, which was revealed as soon as the front door was opened. Why the difference between the two houses? Williams did not plan for polite guests to visit the second floor, and so his tight, darkly lit staircase ascended to a sparely finished unheated attic that was reserved for servants, children, and perhaps storage. In contrast, Brush's stair beckoned his family and guests to a second story that was divided into two neatly trimmed and

Fig. 14.28. Closed-string staircase, Mason House, 1729–30, Accomack County, Virginia.

heated chambers on either side of a passage, making them more comfortable accommodations.

The open-well and dogleg stairs that were inserted in the passages of genteel dwellings in the eighteenth century had pedigrees that extend back to the 1660s. Towers on the backs of houses built by John Page at Middle Plantation (1662) and by Arthur Allen at Bacon's Castle (1665), and several dwellings in Jamestown each contained open wells with flights of stairs rising against their respective wall enclosures. So, too, did the 1680 Talbot County Courthouse, which had "a fayre open well stare Casse."[30] A few early staircases probably even filled the ends of passages. That was the likely position of the one at Arlington, the imposing house John Custis II built about 1676 on the Lower Eastern Shore (see Fig. 6.24). Custis's reason for a grand ascent was to enhance the route his guests followed to reach an entertaining room on the second floor, the space he called the "greate Parlour."[31] What these early stairs undoubtedly had in common was that they were constructed with closed strings—a row of turned balusters that rested on a stringboard that hid the ends of the treads and risers. The closed-string staircase persisted well into the middle of the century, though the baluster, handrail, and newel-post profiles would differ significantly from the ones of Custis's era (Fig. 14.28).

One reason the closed-string stair remained a part of regional building practice for so long was that the initial development of Williamsburg and Annapolis began before open-string stairs—those with exposed riser ends and nosing returns on the treads—had a chance to gain much traction. After all, it was a new form in England as well. The first reported use of an open-string stair there was one made at Kensington Palace in 1691.[32] Through the middle of the next century, then, closed strings remained the dominant form of staircases in Chesapeake houses, save for a few large plantation houses and an experiment here and there in the capitals. One of the first of these was executed at John Brush's house, whose structural timbers were cut in 1719.[33] Although nicely finished, the stair had a number of construction flaws. Knowing just how to work out the alignment of balusters, railings, and nosings to the newel posts, how to properly curve the railing above its curtail step (a lower step that scrolls on its end), and how to seat the balusters on the treads took careful calculation and an intimate knowledge of the art of stair building. Despite the carpenter's naïveté in open-string conventions, the result was spectacular, especially when compared to what his neighbors were building. Instead of an open-string stair, most carpenters working through the middle of the century fabricated ones with closed strings

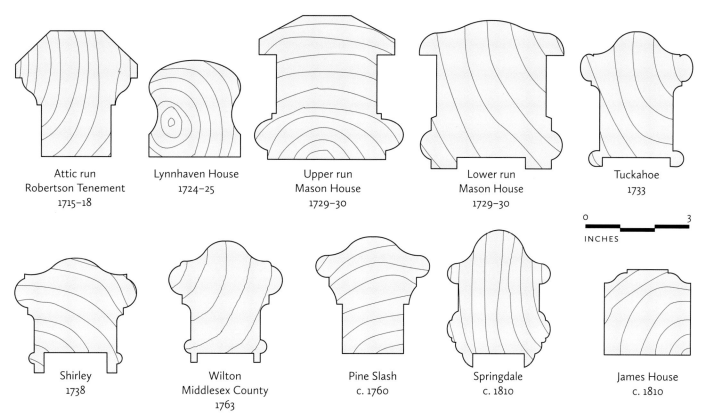

| Attic run Robertson Tenement 1715–18 | Lynnhaven House 1724–25 | Upper run Mason House 1729–30 | Lower run Mason House 1729–30 | Tuckahoe 1733 |

0 — 3
INCHES

| Shirley 1738 | Wilton Middlesex County 1763 | Pine Slash c. 1760 | Springdale c. 1810 | James House c. 1810 |

Fig. 14.29. Handrail profiles from Virginia closed and open-string staircases.

but stripped away some of the baroque heaviness that was inherent in earlier versions—large, squat, turned balusters, usually symmetrical about their midpoint, heavy handrails, and bolection moldings in the skirt were replaced with features in the lighter neo-Palladian taste. It is in this form that the closed-string stair persisted for the next 100 years, some being built as late as the 1810s.

Joiners working for leading families in both Maryland and Virginia generally began building open-string staircases in new houses by the 1750s, although their reasons for the selection differed. Most Virginians, from the elite downward, reserved their upper floors solely for bedchambers. A passage at the top of the stairs was sometimes used as a summer sitting room, but there were no formal living spaces on this floor. With ever-increasing frequency, the Virginia gentry moved their principal chambers upstairs, which resulted in better-finished rooms on this floor, but they still expected the second story to be private. Thus, nicely appointed open-string stairs reflected the modernity of the householder and indicated better-appointed upper-floor chambers than in generations past.[34] With few exceptions, these stairs were much plainer than those that appeared in Maryland, in terms of carved enrichment, stylish handrails, baluster profiles, newel-post designs, and the manner in which their undersides were treated (Fig. 14.29). Virginia open-string staircases tended to use more conventional Georgian handrails with symmetri-

cally molded sides and a double-cyma cap; balusters with turned classical elements; simple, though sometimes carved, stair brackets; and an architrave rake to trim the underside of each run. The effect was restrained, yet it was able to imply that the upper floor contained important rooms beyond the public entertainment sphere of the ground story.

Maryland houses followed a different trajectory. Until the mid 1750s, stairs in that colony were generally more workmanlike and even old-fashioned when compared with those in Virginia. An extraordinary example is the staircase in Charles Carroll's large brick mansion, built between 1749 and 1751 on Duke of Gloucester Street in Annapolis. It is quite modest, considering that Carroll was one of Maryland's wealthiest merchants. His dwelling was built in the new Maryland style, with paired rear entertaining rooms replete with decorative plaster wainscoting, and overlooked a garden on Carroll Creek. His second-floor spaces were every bit as large as those on the first, but these rooms were likely used as private chambers rather than for entertaining, as was soon to become fashionable. In this context, the modestly finished, closed-string flight of steps that rose from a small entry to the second story should not be totally unexpected (Fig. 14.30). However, the stair could not have been clumsier, given its date. Its handrail profile is of the same Georgian tradition found in Virginia at this time, and yet it is massive and lacks a common astragal along its lower edge and would

(left) Fig. 14.30. Closed-string staircase, Charles Carroll of Annapolis House, 1749–51, Annapolis.

(right) Fig. 14.31. One of the first grand staircases in Annapolis of the 1760s, that at the Upton Scott House, 1762–63, incorporates square-section balusters, an asymmetrical rococo handrail profile, and minimal newel posts.

not have looked out of place in late seventeenth-century England. The balusters are turned with a classical column seated on an urn and spool but are thicker than most contemporary ones. What is so striking about this staircase is how ill fitting it seems, when compared to what neighbors built just a few years later.

Governor Horatio Sharpe's clever management of the proprietary Maryland bureaucracy brought untold wealth to Annapolis with the ending of the French and Indian War. This fueled a building boom that lasted more than a decade. The profits from lavish spending on luxury goods lined the pockets of merchants, whose prosperity spread to those who worked for them. The provincial bureaucracy generated wealth for a number of professionals, who flocked like others to Annapolis, which had now become a booming entrepôt for this economic bonanza. Many of these lawyers and merchants and those who benefited from the public largesse

and patronage built luxurious homes, for which Annapolis is now so well known.[35] These houses expanded the trends first evident in the Carroll House, with elaborately finished interiors. The staircase became the showpiece of the houses of the wealthy.

As the war drew to a close, the first of these houses was built in 1763 by Dr. Upton Scott, who came to Maryland from England as part of Sharpe's entourage and profited from that association. Unlike houses that soon followed, Scott's stair, like Carroll's, simply led to a chamber floor (Figs. 14.31, 14.32). Yet Scott's bedchambers were lavish enough to warrant an equally impressive means of ascent, and several improvements devised for him became the model for this new generation of Maryland houses. First was the open string with delicately carved brackets at the ends of each tread. The handrail profile was new to Maryland—sensually curvilinear in cross section and asymmetrical, inspired by florid, rococo

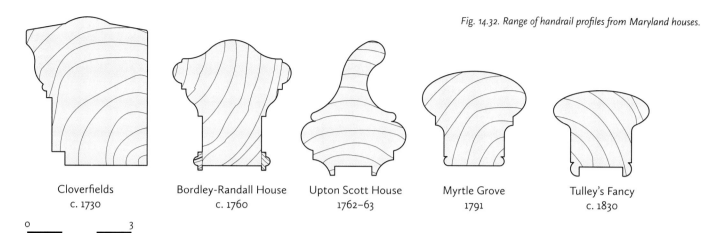

Fig. 14.32. Range of handrail profiles from Maryland houses.

Cloverfields	Bordley-Randall House	Upton Scott House	Myrtle Grove	Tulley's Fancy
c. 1730	c. 1760	1762–63	1791	c. 1830

0   3
INCHES

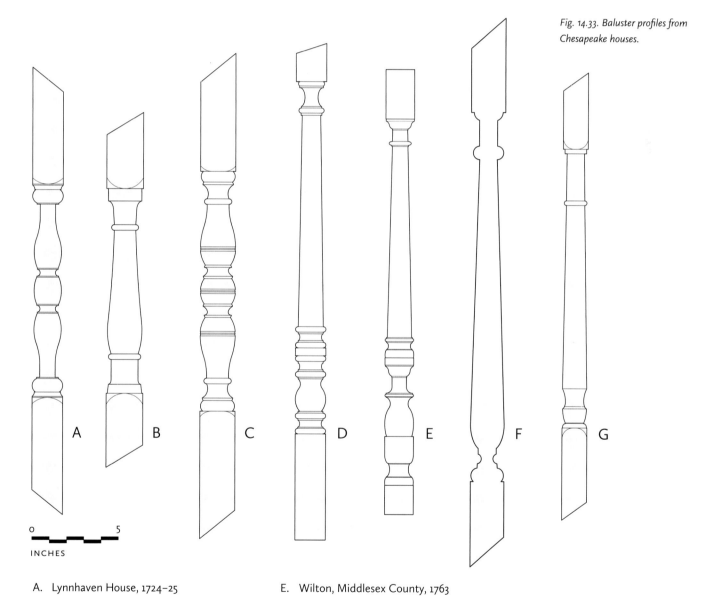

Fig. 14.33. Baluster profiles from Chesapeake houses.

A   B   C   D   E   F   G

0   5
INCHES

A. Lynnhaven House, 1724–25
B. Charles Carroll, Barrister, House 1724–27
C. Mason House, 1729–30
D. Marmion, 1750s

E. Wilton, Middlesex County, 1763
F. Wales (splat baluster), 1780s
G. Springdale, c. 1810

design sources. The railing rose from a curtail step on the first floor, twisting itself out of a tight knot that eliminated the need for a prominent newel. The balusters were perhaps another first for the region—square in cross section instead of turned (Fig. 14.33). They not only served as an immediate prototype for nearby mansions but eventually became the standard form in the early nineteenth century up and down the eastern seaboard. Scott's simple balusters and carved, scrolled, stair brackets were intended to evoke the iron railings and marble steps that were illustrated in midcentury architectural pattern books, which reflected the kind of staircases built in contemporary English country houses. To accomplish all of this, Scott needed a craftsman with more than conventional joinery skills. He undoubtedly commissioned a cabinetmaker with knowledge of English work, as he set the standard for ones that soon followed.

Although more refined bedchambers may have been the initial reason for more elaborate staircases, creating more important and increasingly public rooms upstairs soon followed. There was now quite sufficient reason for sumptuous means of ascent, and cabinetmakers were hired to make more refined and complicated stairs. John Ridout may have fashioned a grand chamber at the head of his stair in 1764–65 for the use of Governor Sharpe when he was in town, and William Buckland's 1774 design for the Hammond-Harwood House included a very fine second-floor drawing room.

The stairs in these houses had elements of the new form, but none as grand as that executed under the direction of William Buckland for Edward Lloyd IV, who completed a house that Samuel Chase had started in 1769 but could not finish (Fig. 14.34). Lloyd's stair rose centrally behind a screen of columns in his passage, splitting to become two separate runs to the upper floor. The railing curved without newels at the transition to the upper run, an amazing feat for its day. The soffit of the stair was made with individual scrolled pieces conceived as extensions of the brackets, thereby making them appear as if each step was carved of stone, one stacked on the other seemingly without any means of support. The scrolled soffits were not completely new to the region; in 1738, brothers John and Landon Carter each built similar soffitted stairs at Shirley and Sabine Hall, respectively. Yet Buckland's design was used in combination with square balusters, a curving rail without landing newels, and an elegant rococo handrail. It most successfully conveyed in three dimensions what the pattern book designers intended—a staircase that appeared to be free floating, built with cantilevered stone steps and thin iron balusters. None of which, of course, was true.

Lloyd's stair rose to an elaborate Venetian window at

Fig. 14.34. The staircase at the Chase-Lloyd House, 1769–74, Annapolis.

its landing, which was finished with delicate plasterwork overhead, and it arrived at a second-story doorway that was flanked by arched niches, as if a very important room lay just beyond that door. The room, though, turned out to be anticlimactic. It was fitted no better than the other chambers upstairs. Perhaps it was Chase's vision to have a grand second-floor drawing room, which Lloyd more reasonably reclaimed as a bedchamber. If that was the case, it is a puzzle that the height of the upper floor was almost two feet shorter than the first. Builders of other Annapolis houses with second-floor entertaining rooms found ways to increase the ceiling heights upstairs for at least the public rooms, to create a more conventional *piano nobile*. Whatever the reason that Lloyd limited the public spaces to the first story, he nonetheless

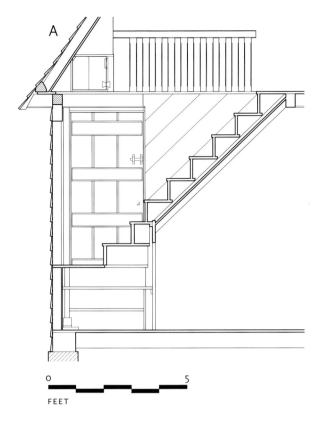

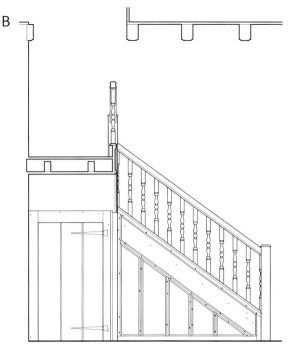

0   5

FEET

Fig. 14.35. A: Section through enclosed stair, Rochester House, 1745, Westmoreland County, Virginia; B: Stair, Lynnhaven House, 1725, Virginia Beach, Virginia.

now had the most magnificent stairway built to date in either of the two colonies.[36]

As exotic as it was at the time of its construction, the staircase of the Chase-Lloyd House looks restrained compared to what Benjamin Latrobe introduced in his 1796 design for William Pennock's house in Norfolk (see Fig. 5.2). Its sweeping, curvilinear lines contained the stair within a passage that had a rounded end and a second-floor passage that was finished with an undulating, railed balcony overlooking the staircase. Alexander Parris's design of 1811 for John Wickham's Richmond house was similar but visually more successful. By housing it within a circular room, Paris was able to create a more elegant sweep, which more successfully gave the illusion of a floating staircase without support. This type of ascent no longer used the scrolled soffits common in Annapolis but instead smoothed its underside into a continuous arc of plaster that was uninterrupted from one floor to the next. The framing was also diminished to the extent that the stair appeared to have none. Grand and impressive as these gracefully curving stairs were, they were built for an elite clientele and were very much outliers to the more restrained and boxy staircases that even most wealthy clients in Maryland and Virginia continued to prefer.

If gentry houses were filled with elaborate open staircases, those erected by most families followed a different path, especially when their upper floors were of little consequence. If the stair rose in the main room as in one- and two-room houses, it was expected to be separated from the room by a wall. This was frequently solved by casing the stair, as had been done at Williams's Green. Increasingly, though, the stair was moved opposite the fireplace wall, since it was cumbersome to run against the fireplace when chimneys were located outside the house, or there was simply not enough room for a gentle ascent. These stairs tended to be plainly cased, with a few advanced steps set in front of a door, not unlike the closet-chimney model. Once inside the door, a landing or a short set of winders led to a straight run that terminated near the center of the roofline in the attic story, ensuring sufficient headroom at the upper landing. These stairs were usually nestled in a corner of the hall and enclosed on their room side with sheathing fitted in the triangle formed by the door post, ceiling, and the bottom of the stringer (Fig. 14.35A). When the stair rose to a passage instead of a chamber, the enclosure could be eliminated. A variation of this type was constructed in the hall at the Lynnhaven House, which is open below and rises into a tight passage with doors securing chambers on either side of it (Fig. 14.35B). Old-fashioned or not, boxed stairs remained common for modest houses through the 1820s and for slave houses into the 1850s.[37]

Another means of ascending to the upper story in the houses of poorer folks, as secondary stairs, and in outbuildings was by way of a ladder stair, a type used as late as the Civil War. Purely functional and bereft of most ornament,

Fig. 14.36. Ladder stair, Holeman
Kitchen, 1820s, Isle of Wight County,
Virginia.

of a pair of stout stringers that received their saw-tooth–like shape by nailing cleats to their sides, to which the treads and risers were then nailed. Stringers cut to the profile of the stairs supersede this older construction method in the early nineteenth century.

Stairs lost some of their cachet as the major showpiece by the second quarter of the nineteenth century. That role was taken up by furnishings and interior decoration. Architectural trim work increasingly served as the background for these. Moreover, Marylanders gave up on the idea of the second floor as a *piano nobile* when it became a refuge for the family and not a place to parade guests. To emphasize just how private the upper floor was intended to be, stairs were made less showy. More focus was placed on the newel post, which reflected new architectural styles, but otherwise the stair was fairly plain, most often with handrails round in cross section and balusters that were usually square or unadorned turnings. The combined effect no longer had the exotic feel that made the pre-Revolutionary staircases seem so different. What offset the simplicity of the design was the costliness of the materials, as many of the newel posts and handrails in the best houses were made from imported hardwoods, primarily mahogany.

MOLDINGS

Carpenters and joiners used molding planes, gouges, chisels, and drawknives to finish the edges and shape the faces of many separate elements used to cover, trim, and build houses. They applied moldings to everything, from heavy posts and beams, to door and window jambs, to chimneypieces and panels, and even to weatherboards and occasionally clapboards. Moldings dressed up early buildings and made carpentry work look finished. Another practical purpose was to blunt prominent edges that were otherwise easily nicked or broken. Eventually, moldings were put to additional tasks that required a modicum of book learning by knowledgeable carpenters and knowing users. From the late seventeenth century forward, shapes borrowed first from Roman and later Greek architecture helped craftsmen create appropriate habitations for fashionable gentlemen and gentlewomen, embellish the public spaces where they received and entertained their peers, and fit out the private spaces to which they retired. The relative richness of moldings in one room or another performed the added function of steering sophisticated guests to and through the social spaces intended for their use. Moldings themselves were only an assortment of astragals, beads, reeds, flutes, frets, fillets, dentils, ovolos, ogees, and cavettos (see Portfolio II). But intel-

ladder stairs have a long genealogy, dating to medieval English prototypes. One of the earliest to survive in Virginia is located in the second-floor passage at Blandfield, which was built to reach an unfinished attic. Ironically, this is one of the most lavish houses to be erected in all of eighteenth-century Virginia. The name "ladder stair" comes from its lack of risers. It was fashioned with stringers that were usually slotted to receive the treads. Most of the treads were nailed in place through the stringers into their end grain, but usually two treads, one near the top, the other near the bottom, were tenoned in some fashion to provide additional rigidity. Except for the plainest of ladder stairs, the treads were often returned on their ends with a cyma or a bevel where they projected from the stringer (Fig. 14.36).

The structure supporting early stairs could look quite casually assembled. Constructing winders was to some degree a jerry-rigged affair, usually with cleats nailed to the wall framing to carry them and with the risers toenailed to the newel post around which they wrapped. The framing for most eighteenth-century stairs in the Chesapeake consisted

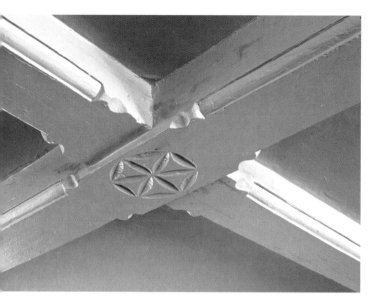

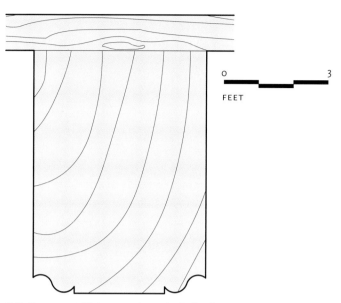

(left) Fig. 14.37. Molded summer beams in the first-floor parlor, Bacon's Castle, 1665, Surry County, Virginia.

(right) Fig. 14.38. Shallow-cut cymas were run on the underside of the first-floor ceiling joists in the Lynnhaven House, 1724–25, Virginia Beach.

ligently combined and strategically deployed throughout a structure, they functioned as a visual communication system that became more complex over the course of the eighteenth century.

The development of moldings can be grouped into three general stages from the seventeenth century through the second quarter of the nineteenth century. The earliest planters' houses in Maryland and Virginia offered builders few opportunities to finish interiors with refined surface ornamentation. Running a molding plane along a piece of stock required straight, smooth surfaces. Those were few and far between in the typical "Virginia house" where split and hewn work deliberately kept costs low. Moreover, ordinary plantation houses made no room for the kind of polite accommodations that molded surfaces gentrified. Only a few great country houses built after 1660 and some dwellings repaired or rebuilt at Jamestown following Bacon's Rebellion in 1676 boasted finished interiors in which refined moldings distinguished best rooms from second best. In these cases, chamfered or simple molded edges were the standard and age-old finish applied to beams and posts (Fig. 14.37). Flat chamfers were carefully cut with a drawknife; ovolos and cymas were made with molding planes. Planes were also used occasionally to incise shallow moldings along the edges of smooth planks used for vertical sheathing on walls, partitions, and stair stringers. These shallow-cut moldings often employed two separate planes, termed "hollows and rounds," the one to gouge out a "cavetto" (or quarter round shape) and the other to form its inverse. If combined they created a shallow, pre-classical ogee. When shallow cut, the molding might be rolled back to such an extent as to inadvertently create a "quirk" or a grooved channel (Fig. 14.38).

After about 1690, a few genteel families began paying closer attention to antique classical architecture, which led to the second stage in molding development. Increasingly, they expected the carpenters and joiners they engaged to fit out their domestic interiors with architectural features modeled, albeit loosely, on Roman sources, the kind of fittings that have already been described in this chapter. Increasingly, too, they instructed tradesmen to hide the structural parts of new or refurbished houses behind smoothly planed boards and expanses of lath and plaster. Classically inspired moldings aided and abetted both ambitions: they were integral to the design and finish of cornices, chimneypieces, columns, pilasters, buffets, and balustered staircases; likewise, beads and ovolos gave a dressy look to trim used to conceal structural members, as wainscot did to wall frames, chimneypieces did to manteltrees, and architraves did to door and window frames. Baroque-inspired bolection moldings were among the earliest Roman forms to make a limited appearance in the region, usually as firebox surrounds and occasionally as architraves. Ubiquitous in English building after 1670, bolections were composed of large, complex moldings that stood proud of the surfaces to which they were applied. They were not as fashionable in the Chesapeake colonies as they had been in old and New England and in South Carolina. House builders in Maryland and Virginia were slow to embrace fully joined interiors, and when they did, in the 1710s and 1720s, the fashion for bolection moldings was nearing an end in England. Their use in the Chesapeake colonies, however limited, all but disappeared from the repertoire of regional builders by the 1730s and 1740s, except for chair

boards and in the more conservative Piedmont, where they hung on for chimneypieces through the 1750s.

Molding planes came in relatively few profiles until the 1690s. Planes for flat surfaces and blades with curved edges based on the geometry of circles met the need for most molded contours (Fig. 14.39). But finish carpenters needed shaped blades in more than one size, because the new emphasis on classical proportions required that ovolos (convex shapes), cavettos (concave shapes), ogees (S-shapes), and fillets (straights) be sized according to their contexts. These planes were typically imported from England, with the same profiles used throughout Britain and the colonies. Novelty was therefore to be found more in their use than in their profile.

A few genuinely new molding shapes were introduced in response to the brief popularity of a florid rococo style, especially among fashion-conscious Maryland builders before the American Revolution. They were inspired by architectural books and were deliberately asymmetrical, flowing patterns that looked strikingly different from conventional Georgian woodwork. Combined with more orthodox moldings, they were used to make unusually large backbands for architraves around doors and windows (Fig. 14.40). Another version revamped the shape of handrails, as seen in a few fine

Annapolis town houses and in the Maryland countryside as far away as the Wye House on the Upper Eastern Shore and Sotterley along the Patuxent River. A third form inspired by pattern books was a quirked molding used to highlight mantelpieces. Quirks of this age differed from those of the seventeenth century, when the form had simply been the accidental result of cutting shallow moldings and rendering their profiles nearly flat. The quirks of late colonial Annapolis were deliberate and aggressive neoclassical forms. They took the first step toward what would become an all-encompassing way to treat trim work at the turn of the nineteenth century. These rococo and chinoiserie profiles were as short lived as they were exotic. They had largely disappeared by the time of the Revolution.

But they left behind the asymmetrical quirk molding that became the hallmark of a third era in the development of molding styles. The neoclassical aesthetic took its inspiration not from Roman sources but from Greek. Although quirked moldings could be found in the vocabulary of ancient Roman builders, they had seldom been quoted by the Renaissance masters and were largely ignored by their imitators in the southern colonies before 1800. Thereafter, they became the dominant molding profile used in sophisticated trim work for the next three decades. Their popularity spread widely and rapidly in carpenters' handbooks, such as those published by Asher Benjamin. His *American Builder's Assistant* (1797) and *American Builder's Companion* (1816) gave carpenters not only profiles to copy on the job site but also a new-model philosophy to match. No stranger to the hand plane himself, Benjamin explained that he had cut many a Roman ovolo and ogee molding in his time, but "I do not generally use them in practice" any longer. He had converted to Greek in the meantime: "The bending, or turning inward, of the upper edge of the Grecian, or quirk ovolo, when the sun shines on its surface, causes a beautiful variety of light and shade, which greatly relieves it from plane surfaces."[38] Neoclassical taste and neoclassical moldings were all about creating a lightness and clarity that contrasted with the heavy, rigid, strictly Roman look that had reigned for most of the eighteenth century. Quirked moldings of the nineteenth century, with their complex elliptical shapes, deeply incised beads, and accentuated fillets, were deemed superior to old-

Fig. 14.40. Deeply molded rococo trim surrounding the parlor doorway at Gunston Hall, 1755–59, Fairfax County, Virginia.

fashioned moldings, because they cast well-defined shadow lines that gave woodwork a crisp visual coherence, that "variety of light and shade" that Benjamin admired.

As did his contemporaries. So much so, that carpenters could not resist the temptation to exaggerate the playful qualities of neoclassicism, the light and lively look that matched the ebullient optimism of the new republic. Joiners quickly turned away from the bold simplicity of the ancient Greek muses and piled on quirk moldings, layer upon layer. Fluted columns were condensed into ceremonial fasces complete with binding ribbon; reeding was spread thickly across the length and breadth of mantelpiece friezes; paterae rosettes popped up like dandelions wherever trim carpenters could squeeze them in (Fig. 14.41). All contributed to what became known as "fancy" decoration. Soon the name referred to the moldings themselves—the phrase "quirk or fancy mouldings" acknowledged their shared lineage. References in price books and building contracts to "doors fancy moulding double raised," "fancy base & surbase," "Elliptical Double Architrave fancy Bands"—all allude to the whimsical makeover of neoclassicism that overtook the decoration of interiors in the 1810s.[39]

Moldings played an essential role in defining the function and quality of spaces in the Chesapeake house for nearly two centuries. This was true in the second half of the seventeenth century, when few surfaces received any ornamentation and those that did assumed special meaning. It was even more so in the eighteenth century, when social elites learned the language of classicism and used it to cue behavior among their status-conscious peers. Moldings never lost this power in the years encompassed by this study. More complicated are the many factors that came into play in a carpenter's selection of moldings. The date of a project influenced his choices, of course, but so did the nature of the client he worked for. Was he or she a town merchant, an elite planter, a widow, or a yeoman farmer? Geography was another consideration. Trim appropriate to frontier dwellings was different from the moldings needed to finish a house built in the longer-settled Tidewater counties. On any one site, the selection of moldings also varied—from those used to trim the main house to those good enough for work buildings and secondary structures. Finally, the relationship between important and less-important rooms within any given house governed the degree of refinement expressed in molding selections for

Fig. 14.41. An 1810s chimneypiece from the Dunlop House, Petersburg, moved to Stirling Castle in the 1920s or 1930s.

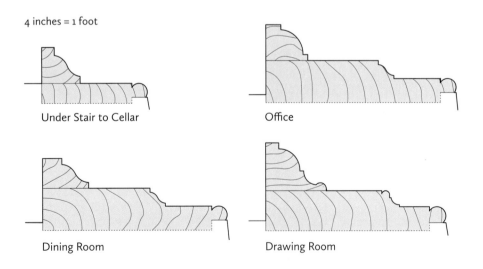

4 inches = 1 foot

Under Stair to Cellar

Office

Dining Room

Drawing Room

Fig. 14.42. Architrave profiles finely regulated to reflect the character and importance of the rooms in which they were used. Ground floor, Ridout House, 1764–65, Annapolis.

each. So many variables produced the many different decorative schemes that field-workers encounter throughout the Chesapeake region, despite a relatively limited repertoire of shared design ideas at any one time (Fig. 14.42).

REGULATING WORKMANLIKE EXPECTATIONS

Traditional practices prevailed among finish carpenters in Maryland and Virginia beyond the period covered in this book. Eventually, factory-made building materials and mechanized transportation eroded the time-honored way of putting buildings together. Yet the process of creating traditional architecture was governed by the relationship between carpenters and their clients, which changed little until after the Civil War. What should not be forgotten were the particular needs of different clients and therefore the different instructions they gave to their craftsmen. The great variety of dwellings in Maryland and Virginia reflect the varied expectations that a new house was supposed to fulfill. Men and women who sought to improve their economic opportunities by moving to the region's expanding frontiers favored an approach to building that helped them deal with the many uncertainties they encountered. Those shortcuts and innovations led to the rise of the Virginia house, with its roughboard cladding, in the seventeenth century, and it ushered in a long era of log building thereafter. Once frontiers became more settled and predictable, clients began asking carpenters for something better and longer lasting. By the eighteenth century, gentlemen and gentlewomen throughout the region took for granted improved living standards and sought lifestyles that their parents could have scarcely imagined. Gentry families living in Chesapeake towns came to express their sense of refinement somewhat differently from those who were seated in the country.

At the heart of traditional work was a shared notion about what made a house a house at any given time and place. This was the part of the carpenter-client relationship that both parties called "workmanlike"—their consensus that certain craft practices could be taken as a matter of course. Those expectations were sometimes disappointed, as in the case of two plasterers ordered by the court to review the work of a third such tradesman, who, it seems, "had not in a workmanlike manner" plastered an interior, with the result that "a great deal had fallen downe." But "workmanlike" meant more than just performance. It embodied a mutually agreed-upon set of ideas about the amount of finish work to be delivered. Such assumptions were often moving targets, sometimes expanding hastily as construction practices developed in response to the rapid spread of good taste and genteel manners. By the 1730s, most carpenters knew what a classical cornice looked like, but what could produce disagreement was its degree of elaboration. Did "cornice" imply a "plain cornice" or a "mundillion" one? The vestry of Bristol Parish called in a professional to arbitrate such a dispute. Ultimately, the conflict was not over how well the work was executed but over how to regulate workmanlike expectations when the world was changing rapidly around the craftsman and his client.

PORTFOLIO II *DNA in Moldings*

What makes regional architecture regional? Are there recognizable attributes that define the architecture of a place? Why do early houses in Maryland and Virginia look different from those, say, in New England, New York, or the Carolinas? Builders everywhere in British North America used the same English-made tools and imported the same hardware, paint colors, and wallpapers. They consulted the same British architectural books, read London newspapers and magazines, and employed specialized craftsmen who had been trained abroad. Even the colonists themselves, those who settled in English communities, shared a common culture. To a certain extent, that included British architectural traditions. So why did the houses they and their American-born descendants build in the Chesapeake colonies end up looking recognizably different? Elsewhere, this book answers that complicated question by reference to the social, racial, economic, and environmental conditions immigrants encountered in Maryland and Virginia. Those are background explanations. They fail to account for the visual attributes that distinguish Chesapeake houses from those outside the region.

For that, architectural historians must pay close attention to the myriad trials and errors that drove a process of improvisation from which a new regional architecture evolved over several generations from the traditions that builders either remembered from home or inherited from their English forebears. Moldings—or more accurately carpenters' extemporized use of moldings—carry a line of DNA evidence that records that process of experimentation. So do other architectural elements—plan types, for instance, or roof framing methods. But for every one of those, there are dozens of moldings. A close study of trim work provides a prolific sample from which to track the development of the region's architectural personality. Only when we see moldings in combination as parts of a whole do we begin to detect attributes that might be interpreted as regional.

The drawings in this Portfolio are reproduced at half scale unless otherwise noted.

LEXICON OF CHESAPEAKE MOLDINGS

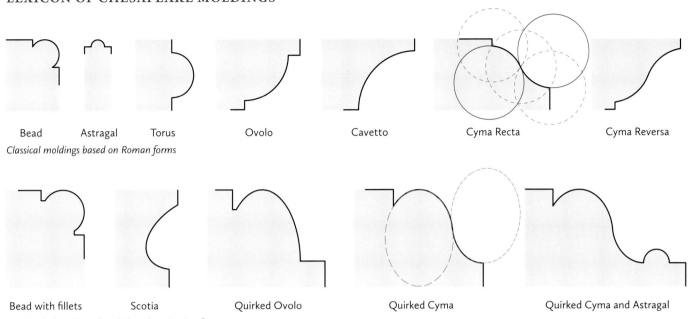

| Bead | Astragal | Torus | Ovolo | Cavetto | Cyma Recta | Cyma Reversa |

Classical moldings based on Roman forms

| Bead with fillets | Scotia | Quirked Ovolo | Quirked Cyma | Quirked Cyma and Astragal |

Neoclassical moldings loosely based on Grecian forms

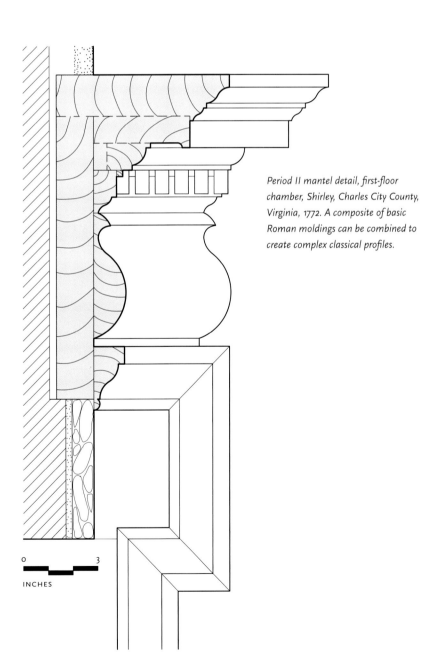

Period II mantel detail, first-floor chamber, Shirley, Charles City County, Virginia, 1772. A composite of basic Roman moldings can be combined to create complex classical profiles.

0   3

INCHES

Pre-classical, Seventeenth Century

The history of moldings used in the Chesapeake begins unremarkably with embellishments that were commonplace throughout the English-speaking world in the seventeenth century but used sparingly by cost-conscious carpenters in Maryland and Virginia. Early sheathing with pre-classical, shallow-cut moldings is now rarely found in situ but occasionally turns up reused in later buildings in out-of-the-way places, for example, under staircases. Large-scale moldings in the seventeenth century were invariably cut with simple planes, called hollows and rounds. This solid doorjamb was so molded to resemble an architrave—an early attempt at classicism.

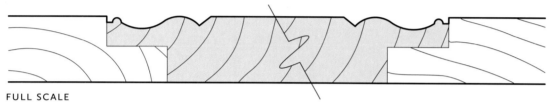

FULL SCALE

Re-used sheathing, Four Mile Tree, Surry County

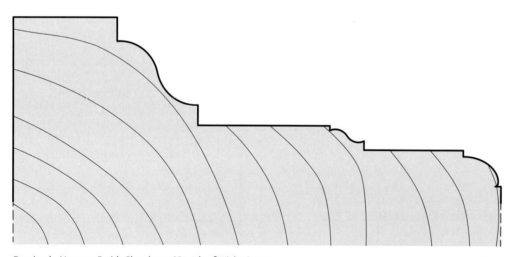

Doorjamb, Newport Parish Church, c. 1682, Isle of Wight County.

Early Classical

Although classical moldings based on ancient Roman forms supplanted shallow-cut moldings by the early eighteenth century, Chesapeake carpenters sometimes applied these forms in novel ways that stood out from prescribed rules and conventional practice. One reason was the conservative taste of many country clients. Wanting new or improved houses that were more modern than those of their forebears and yet not wishing to forsake tradition altogether, they often settled for up-to-date profiles used in old-fashioned ways. A door casing might include applied trim finished with a cyma but be turned over so the molding faced away from the doorstop, sometimes used in seventeenth-century work. Likewise, as in earlier work, it was often the frame itself that received moldings and not a separate board used to conceal the framing.

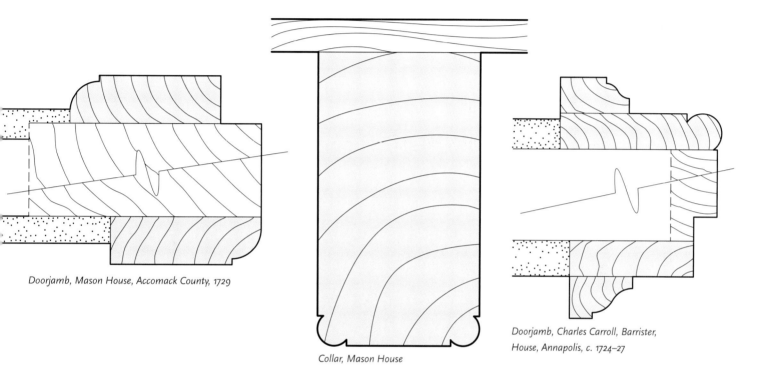

Doorjamb, Mason House, Accomack County, 1729

Collar, Mason House

Doorjamb, Charles Carroll, Barrister, House, Annapolis, c. 1724–27

A second expression of regionalism in early Georgian work is the occasional use of bolection moldings. Although similar to those found elsewhere in Britain and its colonies, they were used sparingly in the Chesapeake region. They tended to enframe prominent fireplace and door openings, and then almost exclusively in the countryside. By the time the gentry families in Maryland and Virginia began instructing carpenters to build well-appointed interiors, bolection moldings had fallen from English fashion. They were only deemed appropriate for Chesapeake houses when joiners were attempting to evoke a sense of tradition and immutability

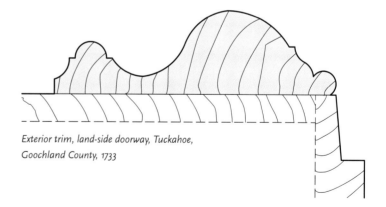

Exterior trim, land-side doorway, Tuckahoe, Goochland County, 1733

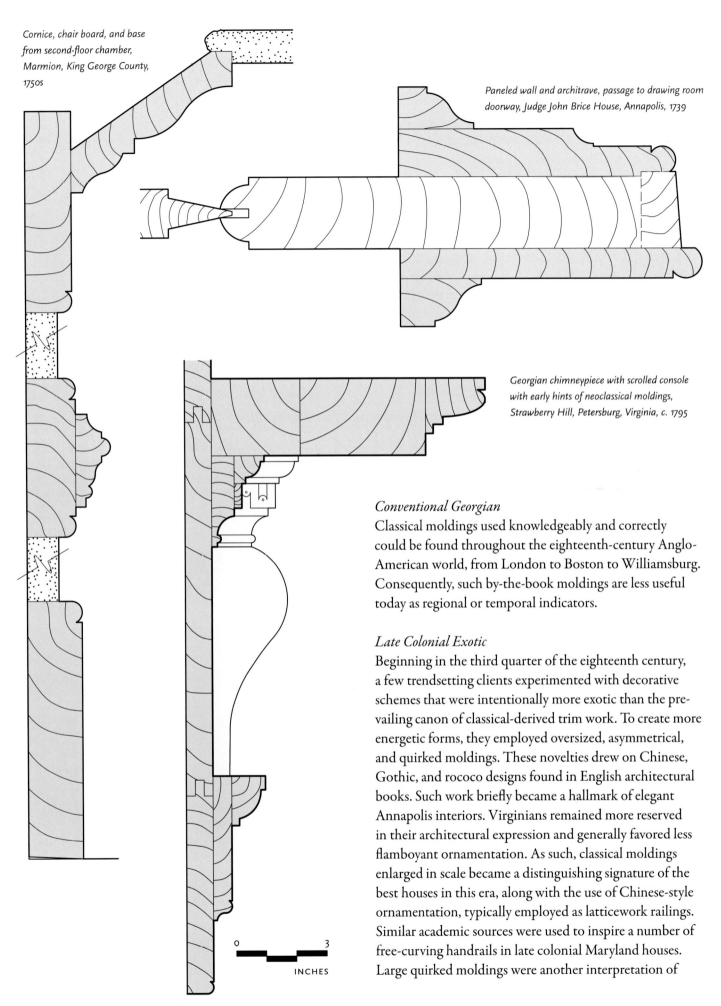

Cornice, chair board, and base from second-floor chamber, Marmion, King George County, 1750s

Paneled wall and architrave, passage to drawing room doorway, Judge John Brice House, Annapolis, 1739

Georgian chimneypiece with scrolled console with early hints of neoclassical moldings, Strawberry Hill, Petersburg, Virginia, c. 1795

0   3
INCHES

Conventional Georgian
Classical moldings used knowledgeably and correctly could be found throughout the eighteenth-century Anglo-American world, from London to Boston to Williamsburg. Consequently, such by-the-book moldings are less useful today as regional or temporal indicators.

Late Colonial Exotic
Beginning in the third quarter of the eighteenth century, a few trendsetting clients experimented with decorative schemes that were intentionally more exotic than the prevailing canon of classical-derived trim work. To create more energetic forms, they employed oversized, asymmetrical, and quirked moldings. These novelties drew on Chinese, Gothic, and rococo designs found in English architectural books. Such work briefly became a hallmark of elegant Annapolis interiors. Virginians remained more reserved in their architectural expression and generally favored less flamboyant ornamentation. As such, classical moldings enlarged in scale became a distinguishing signature of the best houses in this era, along with the use of Chinese-style ornamentation, typically employed as latticework railings. Similar academic sources were used to inspire a number of free-curving handrails in late colonial Maryland houses. Large quirked moldings were another interpretation of

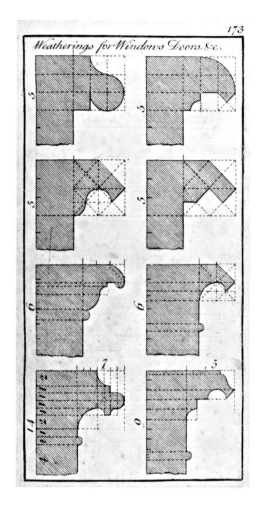

"Gothick
Weatherings
for Windows
Doors, &c.,"
Batty Langley,
The Builder's
Director, 1751

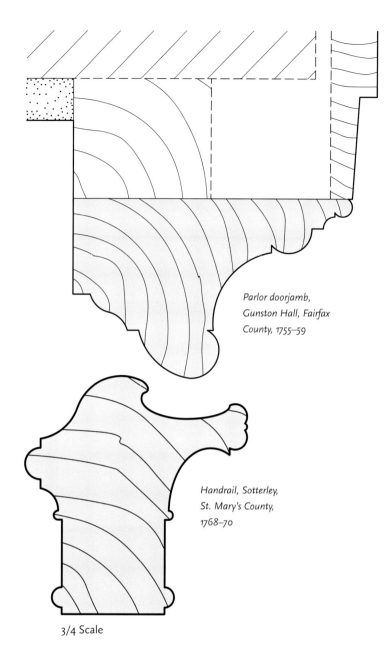

Parlor doorjamb,
Gunston Hall, Fairfax
County, 1755–59

Handrail, Sotterley,
St. Mary's County,
1768–70

3/4 Scale

these pattern-book profiles that appear occasionally in
Maryland houses. Unlike the quirked moldings that would
come to dominate nineteenth-century trim work, these late
eighteenth-century variants were more robust, with profiles
that were derived from circles and not ellipses like their
neoclassical successors.

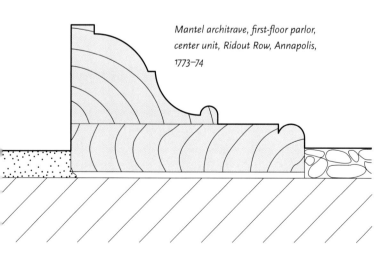

Mantel architrave, first-floor parlor,
center unit, Ridout Row, Annapolis,
1773–74

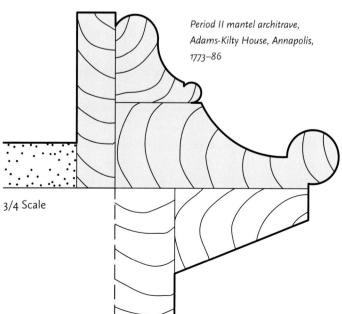

Period II mantel architrave,
Adams-Kilty House, Annapolis,
1773–86

3/4 Scale

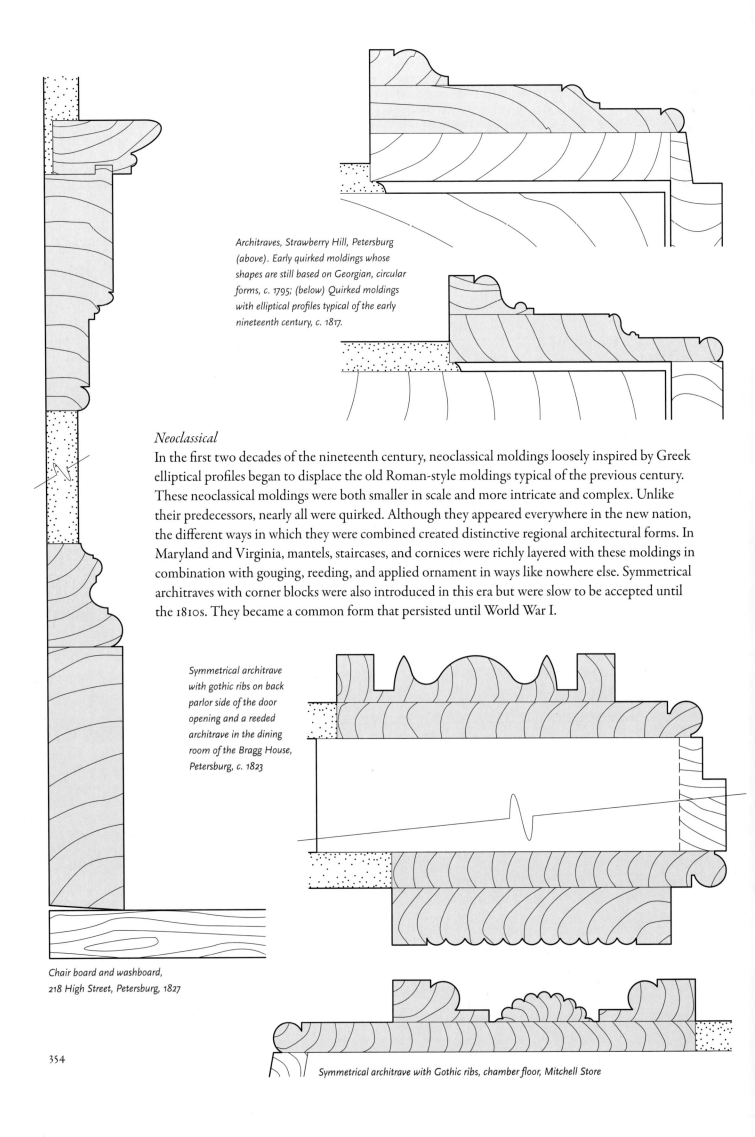

Architraves, Strawberry Hill, Petersburg
(above). Early quirked moldings whose
shapes are still based on Georgian, circular
forms, c. 1795; (below) Quirked moldings
with elliptical profiles typical of the early
nineteenth century, c. 1817.

Neoclassical

In the first two decades of the nineteenth century, neoclassical moldings loosely inspired by Greek elliptical profiles began to displace the old Roman-style moldings typical of the previous century. These neoclassical moldings were both smaller in scale and more intricate and complex. Unlike their predecessors, nearly all were quirked. Although they appeared everywhere in the new nation, the different ways in which they were combined created distinctive regional architectural forms. In Maryland and Virginia, mantels, staircases, and cornices were richly layered with these moldings in combination with gouging, reeding, and applied ornament in ways like nowhere else. Symmetrical architraves with corner blocks were also introduced in this era but were slow to be accepted until the 1810s. They became a common form that persisted until World War I.

Symmetrical architrave
with gothic ribs on back
parlor side of the door
opening and a reeded
architrave in the dining
room of the Bragg House,
Petersburg, c. 1823

Chair board and washboard,
218 High Street, Petersburg, 1827

354

Symmetrical architrave with Gothic ribs, chamber floor, Mitchell Store

Country Conservative, Early Nineteenth Century

Despite the abundance of molding planes that flooded Maryland and Virginia markets in the early nineteenth century, these new profiles were not adopted for all applications. At Monticello and in other projects influenced by Jefferson, craftsmen continued to run Roman moldings. In the countryside, many a farmer still trimmed his house with eighteenth-century-style moldings applied in old-fashioned ways. Often smaller in scale than they had been (that much a concession to the new aesthetic for lightness), this retardataire trim nevertheless retained its Roman-molding origins. Exposed framing was also commonly employed, by now largely limited to ceiling framing.

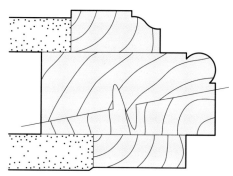

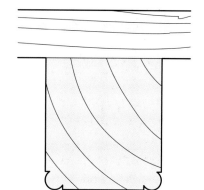

Molded collar, James House

Door architrave, James House,
Surry County, c. 1810

15 *Paint*

SUSAN BUCK AND WILLIE GRAHAM

Paint and other surface treatments put the finishing touches on the Chesapeake house. Their availability and use reflected the economic and social conditions of the region. At first, finishes were primarily functional and were used to protect vulnerable surfaces, generally with natural tar-based coatings that provided a measure of weatherproofing but not much more. Gradually, changing expectations and the increasing supply of a wider range of pigments, binders, and varnishes allowed for a host of new ways to protect and decorate the houses of the colonies' wealthiest residents. Gentry householders used them by the early eighteenth century as one more means to signal the importance of a fashionable house for those who aspired to and assumed political authority in the region. All the while, cultural meanings associated with their more refined schemes continued to shift, requiring new palettes to satisfy increasingly sophisticated demands. Eventually, families further down the social scale were able to enliven their houses with a touch of color, many for the first time.

There is a long history of research into interior and exterior finishes applied to buildings in Maryland and Virginia, much of it spurred forward by the restoration of Colonial Williamsburg after 1927. Early on, Walter Macomber, Colonial Williamsburg's first resident architect, questioned the initial assumption that most buildings in the restored town should be painted white. He wrote to the organization's interior designer, Susan Higginson Nash, in the summer of 1930: "I would like very much to render friendly protest against the use of white paint for the exteriors of so many of our restored buildings." Nash's study of historic paints had relied on rudimentary scrape tests that revealed early paint colors, which she then rendered in watercolor. Her work had indeed uncovered a variety of colors other than white. Macomber, who was undoubtedly aware of her findings, pressed his complaint, noting that "we have discussed this several times, and I am quite sure we all feel certain colors were used quite extensively on the outside, as well as the inside, in the pre-

Revolutionary period."[1] The issue of accurate historic colors continued to bedevil Nash during her tenure at Williamsburg. Two years later, she addressed the concerns about her preference for a very limited exterior palette by identifying the presence of white lead in the paint on some of these buildings and by calling to witness a late eighteenth-century visitor to Williamsburg who observed that "the houses stand at convenient distances apart, have a good exterior, and on account of the general white paint, a neat look."[2]

Subsequent research over the next eighty years has led to a larger and more nuanced body of information about architectural finishes than the evidence that was available to

Fig. 15.1. *Stair, Wilton, 1763, Middlesex County, Virginia. The brackets and balusters were originally coated with pigmented shellac while the paneling was painted a red-brown.*

Macomber and Nash. Today's knowledge of the visual appearance of paint extends beyond colors to the raw materials used in their preparation and the variety of techniques used to apply them. It is also now evident that social factors, date, and location had a great bearing on the choices painters and their clients made.[3] The evolution of paints and finishes, from the earliest protective coatings to the complex faux finishes that were common by the early nineteenth century, can be gleaned from newspaper advertisements, diaries, recipe books, and other period documents and from surviving paint evidence itself.

Most seventeenth-century dwellings and later secondary structures such as outbuildings and farm buildings used, at best, low-grade finishes. By the 1690s, there was a rising interest in fine finishes associated with an exclusive group of planter, merchant, and professional families that wanted to set themselves apart from ordinary folks in a bid to consolidate their social and political control of Virginia and Maryland. They used architecture as a way to establish their hegemony, adopting a style of building new to the region that had a classical pretense loosely based on contemporary practice in England. Generally, it was more elegant and polished than what the colonists had previously built. A concern for gentility affected how this group of people planned their houses and—particular to this discussion of paint—how they chose to present them. The application of sophisticated finishes turned gentry houses into showplaces.[4] The new craft of architectural painting required skilled artisans to make and apply finishes and necessitated new materials to meet the increasing demand in the eighteenth century for decorative treatments that reflected the affluence and taste of their customers. The history of architectural paints and finishes in the Chesapeake mirrors contemporary changes in construction, design, and furnishings in the buildings of this region (Fig. 15.1).

THE SEVENTEENTH CENTURY: SCARCE RESOURCES ON THE FRONTIER

So few buildings survive in the Chesapeake from the seventeenth century that they alone cannot reliably tell the story of how colonists used paint, finishes, and color to preserve and decorate them. Recipe books, such as John Smith's 1687 *The Art of Painting in Oyl*, describe the paint craft that was practiced in England at the time and that would have informed settlers in Maryland and Virginia who wanted to use oil and distemper paints (a mixture of pigments bound in diluted hide glue) to enliven their dwellings.[5] Research into finishes used on the colony's seventeenth-century domestic furniture indicates a frequent use of linseed oil–based paints made of inexpensive pigments such as lampblack, red lead, red ocher, yellow ocher, and a range of siennas and umbers. Extrapolating from this furniture evidence suggests that any oil-based finishes applied to buildings would have been no more sophisticated. The best information about the nature and extent of early house painting in the colonies is found in documentary records.

The unrefined surfaces of timber-framed, clapboard-covered buildings in seventeenth-century Maryland and Virginia relegated paints and finishes to the role of preservatives. The least expensive and most readily available material for

coating exterior wooden surfaces was pine tar, a by-product of turpentine production.[6] When applied to riven clapboard walls and roof coverings, the viscous brown pitch extended the life of the Virginia house very considerably. Colonists applied it to public buildings as well. Petsworth Parish vestry spent 400 pounds of tobacco in 1680 to tar its church in Gloucester County and thereafter yearly recoated it, into the 1690s.[7] Its tarred clapboards would have contrasted markedly with the elaborate plastered interiors where walls or ceilings were rendered with drawings of cherubs. The importance of tar to seventeenth-century builders cannot be overstated. It was the universal preservative, plugging potential water leaks and staving off rot, which otherwise threatened common wooden buildings.

The Petsworth Parish church interior was an outlier. Walls inside most buildings, including other churches, public buildings, and private dwellings, were at best finished with a simple coating of plaster. The little trim that did exist was rarely painted. Instead, colonists found limewash to be a quick, inexpensive way to brighten interiors and freshen dirty walls and ceilings.[8] Limewash was made by mixing slaked lime with water. The consistency could vary depending upon the formula for the amount of water or the quality of the slaked lime. Some diluted washes were as thin as milk; others approached the thickness of cream or paint. Either way, it was thinly applied and frequently renewed.[9] Limewash was also called "whitewash" in period documents, al-

though the latter term also referred to a mixture of whiting (calcium carbonate or Spanish white) in water or whiting in a distemper paint (whiting mixed with diluted hide glue). Limewash was used to seal a finish coat of plaster, or more frequently until the late eighteenth century as a substitute for the white coat, accomplished by brushing the limewash directly onto a brown plaster base. Exteriors could also be whitewashed. It worked well for clay walls, protecting their exposed face from the elements. Occasionally evidence is found for the limewashing of weatherboarded buildings. That said, if the documentary record is a reliable gauge, tarred exteriors were much preferred to limewash until well into the nineteenth century.

In England, it was the plasterer who was expected to apply limewashes; the work of "painters" was generally limited to finishes with pigments that were mixed in both oils and distemper.[10] In the Chesapeake colonies, where there were fewer trained craftspeople and less specialization early on, carpenters, masons, and plasterers were enlisted to tar, paint, and limewash buildings. This helps explain why the St. Peter's vestry in New Kent County sent away to England in 1701 for "Ironwork, Glass for Sash Windows, and paint for the aforesaid Church according as the Carpenter shall Give Directions."[11]

Evidence for anything other than tarring or limewashing is scarce before the end of the seventeenth century, but certainly a few of the painters in the region had knowledge of the trade in England and tried to replicate it here. For instance, Colonel Philip Ludwell was charged with enclosing the yard of the statehouse at Jamestown in 1685 "with railes and banisters of locusts and cedar laid double in oyle."[12] Superior paintwork was undoubtedly part of William Sherwood's scheme for remodeling the Jamestown residence that he leased to Lord Effingham, partly as lodgings and partly as meeting room for the Governor's Council shortly before 1682 (Structure 138/53) (Fig. 15.2). This top-of-the-line rental property had a decorative plaster overmantel and one or more elaborate ceilings that were picked out in colored distemper paint. Most of the plasterwork, including three-dimensional figures, foliage, and architectural elements, was limewashed overall before the painter accentuated the focal elements with splashes of color. The palette consisted of a brilliant blue verditer pigment (a copper-based blue), red ocher, and orange made from red lead. Pink was also made by mixing white with the red to resemble a flesh color. The effect must have been striking in a colony that was otherwise bereft of brightly colored interiors, even though it had a coarseness, owing to a lack of attention paid to the edges of the elements being painted.[13]

Given the rough-and-tumble living conditions in the region, the limited evidence for painting in oil and distemper throughout most of the seventeenth century is not surprising. The Virginia house was a competent and efficient form of building, one that reduced the amount of labor required for its erection. It was also one with little in the way of trim, and its pre-classical, vernacular appearance did not lend itself to genteel finishes. Interior framing members were generally unplaned, so they, too, would not take paint well; limewash sufficed for coating exposed posts, beams, and joists in the best of these buildings. Painting in oil was costly. Moreover, there were few men trained to grind pigments, properly mix colors with oil, and apply it. Oil paints were rare, even on the plaster and joinery of English frame and brick buildings in this period. Except for exposed frames, fireplace lintels, and staircases, there was little to decorate in buildings. Virginia houses were described in 1656 as "contrived so delightful, that your ordinary houses in England are not so handsome, for usually the rooms are large, daubed and whitewashed."[14] Although the pleasantness of these houses is probably overstated, the level of their finish is not.[15]

THE RISE OF CLASSICISM AND THE SPREAD OF GENTILITY

The rise of a consumer society at the end of the seventeenth century and the genteel culture it encouraged were the impetus for much renovation and rebuilding by families that laid claim to it. Paint was one of the visual indicators they used to distinguish their houses from those of their less genteel neighbors. Demand for color and more sophisticated finishes required artisans with new skills. Within a short time, a specialized profession arose to meet that need.[16]

One of the earliest documented projects that employed skilled painters was the Lancaster County, Virginia, Courthouse. The 1699 specifications called for a classical modillion cornice and exterior trim painted in oil, "and ye King's Arms to be left to ye descretion of ye undertaker."[17] As a recipe book of the period explained, pigments for this sort of work had to be ground in oil, a process more complicated than making the distemper paints used in Sherwood's house at Jamestown. The advantage of oil paint was that it was more durable than distemper, tar, and limewash, and thus it provided a longer lasting and elegant coating for both

Fig. 15.3. A: Fragment of woodwork with original spotted decoration intended to resemble ray flecks common to quarter-sawn oak, Ocean Hall, St. Mary's County, Maryland; B: Fragment of grained woodwork from a second room at Ocean Hall.

interior and exterior work. By the beginning of the eighteenth century, church construction and public projects such as courthouses were being overseen by gentlemen who were themselves beginning to construct new houses. Robert "King" Carter, one of the most powerful men in the colony of Virginia, had charge of the Lancaster Courthouse project. He commanded the resources and skilled labor to ensure the success of the paint scheme. Men like him quickly turned to paint as a way to weatherproof their buildings, while at the same time giving them an architectural distinction that other gentlemen recognized and respected.

Williamsburg builder Henry Cary needed old skills and new ones to fulfill his contract for work on the new capitol in 1705. Tarring the roof was one job. The contract spelled out another, very different task: The "wanscote and the Wooden Work on the first & Second ffloor in that part of the Building where ye General Court is to be painted Like Marble and the wanscote and the other wooden work on The two first floors in the other part of The Building shall be painted like Wanscote."[18] Painting the rooms inside the building not only required specialized knowledge to grind pigments and mix them in oil, but it also assumed acquaintance with the art of marbleizing and graining. Experienced painters who came to America to assist in these public projects must have been men who had previous experience painting gentlemen's houses in England. Instead of tarring the exterior trim at Ocean Hall,

Fig. 15.4. Wetherburn's Tavern, Williamsburg. Re-creation of its red-brown linseed oil paint with red lead and Spanish brown pigment.

Fig. 15.5. Everard House, Williamsburg. Re-created original lead white exterior.

Fig. 15.6. Reconstruction of Charlton's Coffeehouse, Williamsburg. Paint research from surviving fragments shows that its trim, siding, and woodwork was entirely painted red-brown, inside and out, when first constructed as a storehouse in 1750, but that it was repainted a light yellow ocher when it was remodeled into a coffeehouse in the 1760s.

the builder selected a red-brown oil-bound paint, the same that he used for interior work. This scheme may seem uncomplicated in retrospect, yet the technology of laying on oil was much more difficult than painters had been used to. Subsequently, the interiors at Ocean Hall were repainted with a scheme of even more sophistication requiring greater skill to execute. Some of the trim was grained in imitation of a delicate black, burl-like wood, while other woodwork was dabbed with fanciful white spots on a dark yellow background (Fig. 15.3).[19] As rare as these more elaborate projects were, the expertise necessary to produce them stood painters in good stead, preparing them to do even routine work with more precision and greater skill.

Even the plainest paint schemes for woodwork required consistent preparation to ensure that the top coat looked right. Best practice called for multiple coats of paint, starting with a primer. Modern paint analysis has discovered that this ideal was not always followed. Instead, the usual treat-

ment for both interior and exterior work was to prepare the wood with an application of a resinous material to seal the surface. Shellac, or some type of resinous sealant, is so routinely discovered in the course of paint research that analysts who study eighteenth-century Williamsburg are surprised when it does not show up on paint cross sections under reflected ultraviolet light. Oil paints tend to "flash" or lose their sheen in streaks when absorbed into wood, especially near joints, where the end grain can siphon off oil from the surface. Sealers limit flashing and allow paint to sit on the surface of trim work, giving it a more even, glossy finish than could otherwise be achieved. Contrary to assumptions historians have made about the introduction of shellac into the colonies in the late 1730s, fieldwork has demonstrated its consistent presence as first-layer prep coatings in the earliest houses where paint evidence survives. It shows just how quickly good craft practices were adopted by Chesapeake artisans (Figs. 15.4, 15.5, 15.6).

Despite a growing demand for refined paints and finishes to embellish gentry houses, many ordinary dwellings never came close to achieving the Georgian ideal, not to mention the cabins and clapboard cottages inhabited by slaves, servants, the poor, and the laboring class or run-of-the-mill farm buildings. That is not to say that all these buildings were always crude and unpainted. Gentlemen frequently treated quarters and ancillary buildings as formal elements in a controlled landscape that emphasized the regularity and uniformity of the grounds immediately surrounding the house.[20] It was the contrast between coarseness and refinement, and various degrees of refinement in between, that gave polite architecture its meaning.

One way to achieve these differences was simply to not paint a building at all. There remain a number of houses in Southside Virginia, for example, that have never been painted on the interior. A few never had paint or whitewash applied to their outside walls, and still others were painted only once in the eighteenth century and then allowed to weather significantly before another coat was applied, by which time virtually no paint was discernible (see Fig. 14.7). The wood trim on Robert Beverley's house, Blandfield, the home of one of Virginia's richest families at the time of its construction in 1772, did not receive a second coat of paint until it was remodeled some seventy years later, and by that time, even molding profiles on wood jambs were wearing badly.

Tar continued to be used as well as a way to regulate these relationships. Even otherwise genteel buildings often had tar applied on their shingled roofs and walls.[21] Most physical evidence for the study of pine tar comes from eighteenth- and nineteenth-century contexts because so little architectural fabric survives from pre-Georgian times in the Tidewater region. Its weatherproofing qualities were so well regarded that it was continuously used for shingle roofs and to protect wooden gutters on sophisticated structures well into the nineteenth century. With few surviving examples, the formulations for seventeenth-century tar recipes have to be interpolated from early eighteenth-century contexts. A mixture used to waterproof the modillion cornice on Yeocomico Church in 1706 and the clapboard walls of the 1713 addition to Holly Hill suggests that early concoctions were devoid of pigments and made of pine pitch heated with linseed or fish oil.[22] Eighteenth-century directions for making tar corroborate the recovered physical evidence that indicates that pine pitch and oil were cooked together with the addition of pigments, typically Spanish brown and red lead, the latter pigment used to hasten drying, limit ultraviolet damage, and give the finish some color.[23] The pine pitch they used may have been little better than the dregs left over from tar production, resulting in a finish that was dark and glossy and degraded rapidly upon exposure to the elements.[24]

Although pine tar continued to be used as a protective coating, change occurred in the practice of its application. Documents suggest that tar persisted as the coating of choice for roofs and walls on both primary structures and outbuildings through the first few decades of the eighteenth century. Oil-bound paint still remained rare. Finally, after about 1720, the use of tar on major buildings began to decline, lingering on in poorer houses, secondary buildings, roofs, and fences to the end of the century. Specifications for two churches in Spotsylvania County in 1732 called for doors, windows, and the cornices to be "well painted and laid with white lead," while everything else was to be well tarred.[25] A similar scheme was discovered at Linden Farm from a building campaign that dates to the middle of the eighteenth century, when its clapboard walls were tarred and the trim was coated with yellow ocher linseed oil paint. The decline in tar usage after 1720 paralleled a sharp rise in orders for paint supplies, a material better suited to the new age of refinement.

COLOR CHOICES AND THE PREDOMINANCE OF RED-BROWN IN THE PRE-REVOLUTIONARY PERIOD

As oil paints saw wider use in the first half of the eighteenth century, colors were often selected for their literal association with conventional building materials. Mention has already been made of faux marbling and wood graining specified for the capitol. Painters did not always have to resort to these special effects to suggest an association with wood, stone, or stucco. Color was often applied to represent building materials in a more general way. John Harrower noted, for instance, that roofs in Fredericksburg were "all covered with wood made in the form of slates about four Inches broad, which when painted blew you wou'd not know it from a house sclated with Isdell sclate."[26] It was even more common to paint round-butt shingles on roofs a red-brown or orange in imitation of clay tiles (Fig. 15.7).[27] Gray was used to mimic stone on the paneled and pilastered walls of the Great Hall at Stratford in Westmoreland County (Fig. 15.8). Names assigned to common colors often referred explicitly to the material they were intended to replicate, such as "walnut," a common color for doors and baseboards, and "wainscot" color, used to recall

Fig. 15.7. Red painted and tarred shingles. Left: Round-butt shingle from Shirley, 1738, Charles City County, Virginia, painted red-brown; Right: Small tarred square-butt shingle from the M roof of William Robertson's Tenement (later the Peyton Randolph House), c. 1718, Williamsburg.

the color of oak (wainscoting in seventeenth-century England was usually made of oak). St. George Tucker instructed Jeremiah Satterwhite to paint the lowest few weatherboards on the sides and rear of his Williamsburg house "of the dark brick Colour, nearly approaching to a Chocolate colour" to match the brick foundations with which they aligned on the front facade.[28]

Occasionally, gray, often referred to as "lead" or "stone color," or off-white was selected for exteriors because of their perceived association with the classical architecture that gentry houses were designed to recall. Henry Cary's work at the capitol shows that colonists understood this association well. He was ordered to paint the outside trim work white as part of its construction in 1705.[29] Sometimes early houses used white for the exterior trim and siding, such as the one John Brush built on Palace Green in 1718 (see Fig. 15.5). Yet despite these few early white exteriors and a growing assortment of colors available in the first half of the eighteenth century, most painted buildings that were not tarred were colored red-brown. Often made with a Spanish brown pigment mixed with red lead, it was described in Smith's 1723 edition of *The Art of Painting in Oyle* as "generally used as the first or priming color, that they lay upon any kind of work, being cheap and plentiful."[30] But Smith also noted that Spanish

Fig. 15.8. The Great Hall, Stratford, 1738–39, Westmoreland County, Virginia. The room was recently repainted with hand-ground, linseed oil–based paint to replicate its appearance in 1760. Evidence was uncovered for gilding the stop fluting and moldings of the capital and base of one pilaster as if the gilding were a decorative test sample treatment that was ultimately not chosen for the room.

brown could be mixed more thickly to serve as a finish coat and it was in that form that it was commonly used in the Chesapeake.

Spanish brown, red ocher, or similarly colored earth (clay-based) pigments mixed with red lead were extensively used on the siding and trim of respectable buildings, inside and out, for the first fifty years of the century. William Robertson built a tenement in Williamsburg between 1715 and 1718 and painted the exterior with red lead, giving it an orange cast. It was a surprisingly unclassical choice for a building otherwise full of Georgian features, including weatherboard siding, a modillion cornice, and sash windows.[31] As much as a century later, St. George Tucker specified that the roof of his house be painted with "Spanish brown, somewhat enlivened, if necessary, with red Lead, or other proper paint." Similar recipes were used to coat the walls and trim of scores of buildings across the region, including dwellings like the Palmer-Marsh House in Bath, North Carolina, Nathaniel Walthoe's Storehouse in Williamsburg, and the newly remodeled Sotterley in southern Maryland in 1732.[32]

Several factors help explain the popularity of red-brown for early painted buildings. One was the ready availability of the pigments. Paint materials were imported from England, where red-brown had a long tradition of use. In the Chesapeake colonies, the color carried a useful connotation for gentlemen's houses and for the public buildings where their social and political authority was displayed. Clapboard plantation houses of the previous century, however commonplace, rarely survived long. By contrast, brick epitomized durability. It was the building material preferred by the gentry as a symbol of its dominance, prosperity, and social status. Red paint in its various shades can be seen as an attempt to give otherwise well-finished frame buildings the same aura of permanence that brickwork offered. An explicit example associating red-brown with brickwork is Tuckahoe, built by William Randolph in Goochland County in 1733. Its beaded weatherboard siding, doors, windows, and cornice, and an unusual wooden stringcourse running between the first and second stories were all protected with a finish of red-brown oil-bound paint. Stringcourses were a common feature of brick structures, and in such rare cases as Tuckahoe, when applied to wooden houses, they intentionally mimicked this masonry detail. The exterior, then, painted red-brown and punctuated by a stringcourse, was an overt reference to neighboring brick buildings. Once the polite house debuted in Virginia and Maryland, it was quite distinct from ordinary roughly clapboarded dwellings, and red-brown paint was an exclamation point to emphasize its permanence and refinement.

A telling example of the fondness colonists had for this color is the Williamsburg house rebuilt by Peyton Randolph, whose political career was on the rise at midcentury. He remodeled and enlarged William Robertson's earlier tenement as a place to entertain and conduct business when he became attorney general and soon thereafter Speaker of the House of Burgesses. The renovation of this frame town house included a large addition to expand the available entertaining space and to create a generous master bedchamber suite upstairs. All but three rooms in the remodeled house had full-height paneling. If ceiling height wainscoting was a bit stodgy by the 1750s, it was offset by stylish wallpaper in two rooms and a grand marble chimneypiece in a new dining room. Randolph filled his dining room with some of the most elaborate furnishings then available in the colony. The color Randolph chose to paint his splendid new house was red-brown—that is, every stick of wood, inside and out, that required oil paint (Fig. 15.9). Red-brown woodwork may seem oddly out of place to modern sensibilities, a strange complement to the papered walls and an incongruous livery for the lavish dining room with its marble mantel and four gilt mirrors. How, too, one wonders, could Betty Randolph have hung the two beds in the master chamber suite to blend with the dark red-brown walls, especially considering that they were among the most elaborate bed set-ups in all of Virginia?[33] Although not a classical color, red-brown continued to resonate with the gentry for its symbolic meaning. It became an integral part of the early polite house form and was a mark of respectability that set houses so colored apart from the tarred unpainted clapboards that covered outbuildings and the houses of unrefined neighbors.[34]

One explanation for the monochrome color schemes typical of the first half of the eighteenth century was the sheer novelty of paint. Using it at all created an elegant embellishment to polite buildings far more spectacular than what preceded it. The color chosen for the body of a house could suffice just as well for trim, doors, and sash, and often for shingles. In a few cases when attempting to be strictly classical, this was white and sometimes gray, but red-brown was far more common. It was not only suited to frame buildings, but it also covered the trim on brick buildings, whether public or private, giving them a similar consistent and monochromatic appearance (Fig. 15.10). A prime example is Bruton Parish Church in Williamsburg. Painted this color inside and out when initially built in 1715, it retained its red-brown exterior color for the next one hundred years.[35] All one would have seen was dark red brick, red window sash and trim, red doors, and a red modillion cornice. Single-color schemes reinforced the neat-and-plain look cherished by the Chesapeake gen-

Fig. 15.9. Chamber over the library, Peyton Randolph House, Williamsburg. When Randolph expanded his house in 1752, he painted the trim and siding inside and out a red-brown.

Fig. 15.10. North storehouse, Shirley, probably 1772, Charles City County, Virginia. Paint analysis indicates that exterior trim on this brick building was originally painted red-brown.

Fig. 15.11. *Landskip, Holly Hill, Anne Arundel County, Maryland.*

try. House builders may not have been fully engaged in the London fashion that eliminated wooden trim on exteriors of buildings following the Great Fire in 1666, since large town fires were less of a concern in the Chesapeake. But the style for less-articulated facades that resulted from omitting trim in urban England was often reflected in a single color when painting frame houses and in the fondness for brick-colored trim on masonry buildings on this side of the Atlantic.

NEW PAINT MATERIALS AND MORE SOPHISTICATED PALETTES

Monochromatic color schemes had become such a distant memory by the late colonial period that polite households no longer compared their dwellings to those from ancient times. Fashionable house builders in this new age demanded more complicated decoration, which in turn required the services of skilled painters from England or apprentices they trained in the colonies.[36] Their paint schemes were often multicolored, some requiring complicated glazes and dazzling pigments, the likes of which had not been seen until now. Varied decoration was itself not a new concept to these colonists; early attempts had already been made to use a more diverse palette inside: the polka-dotted and exotically grained woodwork at Ocean Hall, the unusually grained paneling and "landskip" overmantel treatments at Holly Hill, and the gilding test on the stop fluting and base and

capital moldings of a pilaster at Stratford are but a few examples (Fig. 15.11). Paintwork in churches (particularly the specialty painting required of altarpieces) and public buildings and the budding trade of coach and sign painting prepared painters for the more sophisticated demands clients made after midcentury, a time when gentlemen were looking for decoration that made their houses different and more elaborate than those of their fathers.

A wider range of paints was also needed to produce the varied schemes typical of the second half of the eighteenth century. Most paint supplies were purchased from abroad. William Beverley's 1739 order of 10 gallons of linseed oil, a half quart each of white lead, Spanish brown, and red lead, and "as much paint of a deep olive color ready ground with linseed oil as will paint 200 yds wainscot" came from England.[37] Yet documents tell only part of the story about the importation of desirable pigments. Paint studies demonstrate that imported pigments, Prussian blue and verdigris, for instance, reached Chesapeake painters long before they appeared for sale in newspapers. Although Prussian blue was initially synthesized in Berlin in 1704 and was commercially available in Europe for artists' colors by 1710, paint historians think this pigment was not in widespread commercial use for architectural applications in Europe or America until much later.[38] The first evidence of its use in England is 1729, when Lord Burlington had it applied to his drawing room at Chiswick House just west of London.[39] It was expensive

Fig. 15.12. A: Sash brush reused as a wedge during construction of the Mason House, 1729–30, Accomack County, Virginia. Prussian blue paint was discovered in the stiff fiber bristles of this crudely made brush. It was placed in the wall cavity of the house. B: Articles recovered in archaeological excavations that were used by painters in eighteenth-century Williamsburg. Clockwise from top left: Bladder that once held red lead pigment, James Wray site, 1740s; Broken bottle fragment from Bassett Hall that was used to hold a small quantity of paint for touch-up work; Oyster shell from the Walthoe Storehouse site, also used to hold paint for touch-up work, third quarter of the eighteenth century; Paint spatula, James Wray site, 1740s.

and not readily available in the colonies until much later. In Virginia, for instance, it was first advertised in 1746. But "readily available" is the operative phrase, since this same pigment was discovered in a paint layer trapped in the fibers of a small, coarse sash brush recovered from the Mason House in Accomack County. This worn-out brush had been reused as a wedge and hidden behind plaster during original construction of the house in 1729–30, thereby suggesting that interior woodwork of some Eastern Shore building had been painted a remarkable sky blue by the late 1720s, almost the same time that Burlington first used it in London (Fig. 15.12).[40] Clearly, the limited paint palette used by the first generation of refined house builders in the two colonies was not based solely on the availability of materials, since even the rarest of pigments could be had. Instead, it can be argued that the early schemes were a process of discovering which colors and materials worked for this genteel group and how to contextualize them.

Despite the presence of a few skilled craftsmen and exotic colors for those with the means to acquire both, it was only after 1750 that assorted paints in a variety of colors were regularly stocked on merchants' shelves. Only then could rooms be routinely painted different colors in the colonies. The trend for variety paralleled contemporary fashion in England. A skeptic attending an entertainment held at Norfolk House in St. James Square, London, observed in 1748 that "there were in all eleven rooms Open, three below, the rest above, every room was furnished with a different colour, which used to be reckon'd absurd, but this I Suppose is to be the Standard."[41] Many Chesapeake painters followed this fashion in a more modest way, as recorded in probate inventories, where rooms were increasingly designated by color. References to "the red room" or "the blue room" might have, of course, referred to fabrics, but by midcentury such descriptions could have also referred to paint. William Reynolds's Annapolis tavern, inventoried in 1777, gave names to chambers that corresponded to the color of their woodwork.[42] For the avant-garde, the monochromatic red-brown of the past half century was being replaced by brand-new colors using a broader palette and requiring ever-more sophisticated skill to apply (Figs. 15.13, 15.14).

Painting rooms different colors added another dimension to the distinctions used to create spatial hierarchies as a way to reflect their relative social importance. At Marmion, a 1750s house in King George County, Virginia, secondary first-floor spaces were painted red-brown, which by now was growing quite old fashioned. The public rooms were decorated with a more sophisticated palette, using a stylish blue (Prussian blue and white lead) in the passage and parlor and an even more fashionable deep yellow in the drawing room. Fashion required novelty, and to give the drawing room a fresh appearance, it was repainted in a handsome graining and marbling scheme about the time George Lewis bought the property in 1785 (Fig. 15.15).[43] Remodeling of Four Mile Tree in Surry County, Virginia, produced another of these varied interior schemes. Initially, when the house was completed in 1745, the trim inside and out was painted red-brown (Fig. 15.16). This was much too plain for builder

(top) Fig. 15.13. Everard House, Williamsburg. Light yellow ocher woodwork and reproduction of wallpaper discovered in the dining room. The interior was later restored to its 1770s appearance.

(bottom) Fig. 15.14. Everard House, Williamsburg. Re-created green verdigris glaze on the woodwork in the parlor.

(top) Fig. 15.15. Drawing room, Marmion, King George County, Virginia, as re-erected in the Metropolitan Museum of Art, New York. The skillfully painted landscape, marbleizing, faux bois, and still-life images were applied as a second-generation finish on top of the original deep yellow monochromatic paint scheme. (The Metropolitan Museum of Art, Rogers Fund, 1939 (39.175), Image © The Metropolitan Museum of Art)

(bottom) Fig. 15.16. Four Mile Tree, 1743–45, Surry County, Virginia. The porches were added and the exterior stuccoed in 1835–36.

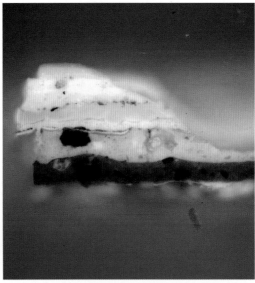

Fig. 15.17. Photomicrographs of cross-section paint sample from the raised paneling in the passage, Four Mile Tree. Samples taken under visible light, left, and ultraviolet light, right, at 100x magnification. The original paint on this paneling is quite coarsely ground, with chunky, irregularly mixed verdigris pigments, suggesting the paint was originally a brilliant green and also grainy and heavily textured.

William Brown's heir, William Jr., who updated the house in 1796 with new colors to help define how he intended to use the house. He had the passage and the chamber behind the parlor repainted with a coarsely ground, brilliant green, verdigris-based paint on top of a gray primer (Fig. 15.17). This bright green had the effect of drawing the chamber into the suite of public spaces, thereby elevating its importance. The drawing room was completely retrimmed and then painted a subtle cream color, with the decorative elements, such as the mantel plinth blocks, picked out in light gray.[44] The dining room was also newly wainscoted and its woodwork was painted blue, a color more old-fashioned by this time than the white of the parlor or the bright green of the passage and chamber, but one whose age and heritage was appropriate for this masculine space. This new fashion for multiple colors—adding new hues and using new color combinations—was intended to both dazzle guests and serve as a visual cue to room functions. By the eve of the Revolution, paint had shifted from simply contributing a degree of refinement to a house to becoming one of the principal organizing signals of the modern house plan.

Yet varying colors was only one way that decorators could create meaningful interiors in these late colonial gentry houses (Fig. 15.18). Another, more closely associated with the neat-and-plain aesthetic, used paint to emphasize the refinement and simplicity of the classical nature of Georgian trim. These interiors used a dominant color everywhere for wainscoting and trim (typically off-white or light yellow ocher, colors more closely associated with classicism) and often combined it with walnut-colored baseboards and doors that were either grained or painted to match the baseboard. Architectural ornament in these houses was intended as a backdrop for a decorating scheme that increasingly featured patterned

wallpaper, curtains, bed hangings, carpets, and upholstered furniture, which assumed predominance as indicators of room status. The off-white selected for woodwork in Matthias Hammond's Annapolis house in 1774 was a different color but in the same mode as George Wythe's redecorating scheme for his Williamsburg residence about 1770. Wythe used a light yellow ocher as the dominant color, and he added walnut color for the doors and baseboards. Two rooms, however, were painted differently. Wythe's study was painted blue and varnished to make it stand out from the other rooms. And to make it clear that the bedchamber over the study was the least important space in the house, it was painted an old-fashioned gray. These exceptions aside and with little difference in the woodwork and paint, it was left to patterned wallpapers to express intended room functions and not the more conventional use of colors and distinctions in molding profiles (Fig. 15.19).[45]

Exteriors were not immune to the late colonial fashion for using new colors. Since red-brown and gray were considered ordinary by then, they were relegated to secondary spaces and to buildings of inferior importance. White lead in linseed oil soon eclipsed these drabber colors as the most common exterior paint. Williamsburg, which had been largely a town of red-brown dwellings as late as 1750, had taken on a new look thirty years later. In 1784, a visitor noted that the capital's public buildings were "built of brick, but the generality of houses are of wood, chiefly painted white."[46] A sampling of masonry public buildings and churches in the region revealed a similar pattern. Trim on brick churches and courthouses built before midcentury was originally painted red-brown, but during the quarter century leading up to the Revolution these buildings were generally repainted an off-white. Those newly built after midcentury were universally

(top) Fig. 15.18. Grained and marbled chamber, Holly Hill, Anne Arundel County, Maryland. Paint analysis indicates this to be a third-generation finish to the room. It appears to replace an earlier faux treatment.

(bottom) Fig. 15.19. View from the parlor through the passage with the dining room in the background. Wythe House, Williamsburg. The decorative scheme is a re-creation of its appearance about 1770.

off-white, confirming the movement toward contrasting trim and brickwork.[47] The growing fashion for lead white and, to a lesser degree, yellow ocher—colors associated with a more strict classicism—paralleled the more academic execution of woodwork in late colonial buildings (see Figs. 15.5, 15.6).

Restriction on the importation of English-made paint materials prior to the American Revolution had some impact on regional paint practices. Among the materials enumerated in the 1767 Townshend Duties were painters' colors and the staple pigments of white and red lead. This was directly aimed at architectural painting since white lead in linseed oil was the base material for virtually all colors except browns and reds. Red lead was commonly used as a drier for oil paints.[48] The Virginia House of Burgesses voted in 1770 to repeal the duties on a number of imported materials "for more effectively preventing the running of Goods in the said Colonies and Plantations, as relates to the Duties upon Glass, Red Lead, White Lead, Painters Colours, Paper, Paste-Boards, Mill-Boards and Scale-Boards of the Produce of Manufacture of Great Britain, imported into any of his Majesty's Colonies in America."[49] William Allason of Falmouth wrote his brother-in-law five years later that "white Lead is not to be had for Love or Money; what you have make go as far as you can."[50] Despite the scarcity and high cost of red and white lead during these troubled times, some gentry still wanted them and found ways to obtain these scarce materials. John Page Jr. of Rosewell was one of these. He placed an order with a London merchant in 1771 for 100 pounds of white lead and 5 pounds of red lead, along with substantial amounts of yellow ocher, linseed oil, and Venetian red (an iron oxide red).[51] Likewise, in 1774, painters used white lead–based paints to finish the interior trim of John Ridout's Annapolis row house. There was no acceptable opaque white pigment to substitute for white lead until zinc white became a common alternative in the middle of the nineteenth century. In contrast to Page and Ridout, there were those like Speaker Randolph who simply did not paint during this period. Painted in 1752 after extensive remodeling, the outside of his Williamsburg house was not recoated until after his death twenty-five years later, at which time so little finish remained that it appeared to be unpainted.[52]

By the time of the Revolution, oil-based paints were being applied in a much more complex way than they had a century earlier, and the connotations and cultural meaning of particular colors had shifted. Red-brown and gray had initially been used for their literal association with building materials and were used to convey a sense of durability and elegance. Now that these colors were cheaper, they were in-creasingly limited to where conservative choices made sense. These colors were relegated to secondary use, while lead white was becoming the new exterior color of fashion. Like the neat-and-plain interior treatment, white emphasized the consciously classical aspect of exterior detailing.

THE TOWN AND COUNTRY DIVIDE IN THE EARLY NINETEENTH CENTURY

Less research has been done on paint patterns and trade practices in the half century following the Revolution. The distinctiveness of the era can be sketched from documentary records, the few buildings that have been analyzed, and the record of later paint layers sampled in earlier buildings. From this limited work, several trends appear. Foremost, the quality of craftsmanship showed marked improvement. Those in the profession built on a century of experience, and many began to specialize in certain aspects of the trade, in which they employed more tools to meet the demanding complexity of their work. Professionalism of this homegrown talent meant that there were more choices at the high end of the paint market. However, painters continued to cater to a traditional market as well. In many places, there was hardly a break in the manner in which older colors were allocated to buildings and spaces. Yet there was also a growing divide between how houses in town and those in the countryside were painted and decorated. Generally, town houses and some of the grander country dwellings followed the more popular trends that were affecting American cities up and down the eastern seaboard, while most modest country houses tended to be more conservatively finished, albeit often in interesting ways.

The growth of cities and towns along the Maryland and Virginia fall line created a huge market for paint services, and the profession developed specialties. By 1797, a theater scene painter worked in Petersburg. John Badger abandoned a career as a portrait painter in Charleston to move to Petersburg, where he focused solely on carriage and architectural work. Agreements of the late eighteenth and early nineteenth centuries reveal a greater knowledge about paint by those who commissioned building projects, more intricacy in their desires, and increased skills demanded of those who contracted to paint them. Paint contracts became more complicated. St. George Tucker's agreement with painter Jeremiah Satterwhite in 1798 specified how all interior and exterior parts of the building were to be finished and who would supply the materials, down to who would contribute the brushes and the pot for boiling the linseed oil. In this contract, even the composition of the colors, and in some cases the manner in

Fig. 15.20. St. George Tucker House, Williamsburg. The paint scheme is a re-creation of that specified in the contract between Tucker and Satterwhite in 1798. The painted roof colors were based on the results of microscopy analysis and on replication of the tar-based paints for color matching, using the contract specifications as guidelines.

which they were to be mixed, was spelled out (Fig. 15.20). Painting had become so complex by this time that the profession required reference manuals to assist the practitioners in their craft. Although no recipe books were published in the region, American authors wrote some of the most influential ones of the early nineteenth century.[53] Books had the effect of bringing uniformity to the practice of painting and of standardizing the methods by which building fabric was coated.

The contrast between country and town painting habits continued. Country folk retained their more conservative ways—from the colors they chose to the continued reluctance of some to apply any finish at all on many of their structures. By the early nineteenth century, even they were abandoning tar. In cities and towns, on the other hand, home owners applied paint more generously and in more complex ways. More and more exteriors, whether in town or in the countryside, were painted lead white. However, houses were not as monochromatic as their colonial counterparts. In contrast to Thomas Everard's all-white exterior in Williamsburg, or the dozens of completely red-brown exteriors found

elsewhere in the colonial period, doors and shutters of early nineteenth-century houses were most often picked out in a color different from the siding. Louvered shutters replaced paneled ones and were commonly painted green, while doors were painted dark colors or were often grained (see Fig. 7.18). It was the complexity of these exteriors as much as a near-universal use of white for siding and trim work that subtly distinguished them from earlier houses.

The colonial trend of ascribing meaning and relative value to new colors continued. An interesting example is Tudor Place in Georgetown, a five-part formal house that was started in the 1790s but not completed until William Thornton redesigned it in the early 1810s.[54] As part of the earlier work, a green verdigris glaze was applied to the woodwork in a second-floor bedchamber of the kitchen wing. This was a fine room, but it was neither a public space nor one of the principal chambers of the house. Fashionable when it was so grandly displayed at Four Mile Tree and in Thomas Everard's Williamsburg parlor twenty to fifty years earlier, bright green was now simply used as one of several common finishes to add variety to the second-story private

rooms. The use of even older, less-fashionable colors held on in some parts of the countryside in houses whose families continued to venerate tradition. The James House, a small, well-built dwelling in Surry County, was erected in the 1810s with a traditional hall-parlor plan, and it was framed with exposed and beaded ceiling joists and collars, details that had been long abandoned in city dwellings. Its woodwork was painted red-brown, most likely not as a money-saving effort, since lead white was no more expensive, but to give the house an earlier aura. Red-brown conveyed a sense of timelessness to the owner of the James House, a far different association attached to the color when it was used a century earlier to express novelty in the first of the region's refined houses.

Although faux finishes had been around since the beginning of the eighteenth century, their use a century later became more commonplace and sophisticated. It was a trend common in the large towns from Boston to Charleston and in Maryland and Virginia, as well. In particular, doors were grained, often in imitation of mahogany, with simulated inlay work that either accentuated raised panels or decorated flat panels on both sides of doors. Sometimes baseboards and mantels were marbleized, but it was not unknown to faux paint entire rooms. Much of this work was finely done. The graining that Thomas Jefferson commissioned for Monticello was typical of the refined work of this era, as it was a very literal and convincing copy of figured mahogany with inlay work.

The graining and marbleizing of country houses reached its zenith in the 1820s and 1830s and could be so extensive that faux finishes were used to cover wainscoting, door and window trim, and mantels—almost any and all painted surfaces. Instead of the strict replication of wood grains and inlay of the more academic work, these country examples were freer in their interpretation of wood grain and patterned stone. An early example is the rich graining and marbleizing at Prestwould in Mecklenburg County (Fig. 15.21). When overlaid with exotically flamed veneered furniture, patterned carpets, bed dressings and curtains, and, at times, wallpaper, these rooms became the embodiment of the style called "fancy" by contemporaries. This rich patterning, too, ran its course and was replaced by a more restrained style near midcentury.

Paint contracts after 1825 reveal more complicated pricing structures for different types of materials and their application, an example of the higher expectations clients held for painters with the training and tools to produce them. An 1837 contract between the Mutual Assurance Society of Virginia and George Roche for painting the Richmond dwelling owned by the society specified prices for painting per square yard of work.[55] The cheapest was "one coat work," at 7 cents per square yard. Two coats cost twice as much, and "imitation work" (faux finishes) cost 50 cents per yard. The contract specified two coats on the house exterior and inside the principal story and one coat on the second-floor woodwork. The second-story doors were to be "Mahogany Imitation," while the doors in the principal story were to be "in imitation of Mahogany, Oak, or some other fancy colour, as may be determined on—the outside of the Doors exposed to the weather to be of Green." Graining doors mahogany color was a common treatment earlier in the century, and this contract shows that it was beginning to be eclipsed, for it was relegated to the upper floor, as oak graining, the newest novelty, was introduced to passages, parlors, dining rooms, and libraries.[56]

As this contract suggests, there was an implicit understanding that the painter would provide all tools and supplies necessary to complete the work in a "substantial and workmanlike manner." At the beginning of the century, a range of tools equipped tradesmen for the growing complexity of their jobs. Roche would have had access to many of these—feathers, natural sponges, cork, a short grainer's tool with stiff leather to create ray flecks or the wavy pattern of mahogany, special flat brushes, grainer's combs with teeth

of varying widths, and grainer's tools with tufts of hog's hair set at unequal distances—all to produce figured wood patterns. And, whereas Satterwhite's work in 1798 would have required round brushes for his oil paints and thick, long-handled, flat or round brushes for whitewash, Roche was able to purchase a broader range of specialized tools to create much finer finishes. By the mid-nineteenth century, the greater variety and availability of paint and varnish materials, tools, trained and competent painters, and painting guidebooks meant that the sophisticated decorative finishes formerly commissioned solely by the gentry had now become an accepted idiom for paint decoration of more ordinary households, or indeed, of commercial premises, such as the offices of the Mutual Assurance Society. Stylish paint treatments were finally available to those of modest means, thus significantly changing the painted architectural landscape and expanding the expectations of consumers.

REPLICATING HISTORIC PAINTS

The aged, degraded coatings examined on seventeenth-, eighteenth-, and early nineteenth-century buildings must be deciphered to understand how structures first appeared when freshly painted. Hand-ground paints made with stone or glass mullers on stone slabs and linseed oil and natural resin varnishes cooked in iron pots over open flames approximate these early decorative materials, replicating what has been found under the microscope. Although it is possible to identify the components of aged paint coatings and reconstruct how they were formulated, the raw pigments available today are generally more finely ground and their particles more consistent in size than the imported dry pigments of the colonial period. Moreover, modern pine tars, natural resin varnishes, and linseed oils are usually more highly processed. Therefore, most hand-ground paint replications have greater purity to their colors and are less three-dimensional in texture than the originals. Despite these shortcomings, attempts at re-creating period coatings provide the best means of recapturing an understanding of the visual qualities and tactile experience of an early Chesapeake house, which the documentary and physical evidence can only suggest.

16 *Wallpaper*

MARGARET BECK PRITCHARD

The consumer revolution introduced people on both sides of the Atlantic to a new universe of household goods and behaviors. The pursuit of these things was closely allied to the idea of "gentility," a social concept that transformed how a select group of American colonists carried and dressed themselves and how they adorned their dwellings. During the second quarter of the eighteenth century, gentility also produced a new kind of house in the Chesapeake colonies, a physically refined dwelling, adapted to the daily pursuits of an emerging gentry class. Among the most visible attributes of this new house were the colors and patterns that eventually embellished its walls and the ornaments that occasionally enriched its ceilings. Most of the documentary evidence illustrating how Virginians used interior decoration to define their environment is limited to the accounts of the wealthiest inhabitants and through recent architectural investigations of their houses. However, once the gentry began to incorporate the most up-to-date English and French fashions within these newly defined spaces, a decorative formula was established that the middle-class householders were able to adapt and emulate, owing in no small part to the increasing availability of a wide variety of affordable decorative wallpapers.

THE EVIDENCE

The study of early wall treatments in the Chesapeake is complicated by the paucity of evidence. As styles changed, wall hangings, fabrics, and papers were usually removed and replaced with something more up-to-date. Even when existing treatments were allowed to remain, those pasted directly on to plaster or wood deteriorated more quickly in southern regions than in cooler, less humid parts of the country. As a result, few early wall hangings survive. The documentary record is equally troublesome. Unlike most household furnishings, wall treatments were rarely recorded in probate inventories. Once affixed to the walls, they became a part of the house and so passed out of the appraiser's purview. Consequently, they remain less visible in written records than is the case for other sorts of furnishings. The dearth of information from probate records is partly compensated for by local advertisements, orders, and invoices. These shed light on the handful of early papers that *do* survive. In addition, analogous evidence from beyond the Chesapeake—English as well as American—forms a broader context for their use and allows us to formulate some general observations about early Chesapeake wall treatments. Most of this evidence is limited to the accounts of the wealthiest inhabitants and the results of recent architectural investigations of their houses.

TEXTILE AND LEATHER HANGINGS

Fixed textile wall hangings became fashionable in England in the second half of the seventeenth century. Many types of fabrics were used to cover walls. The wealthiest English householders upholstered their walls with silk velvets, damasks, brocades, satins, and tapestries. Woolen fabrics were a much-less-expensive alternative to silk and could be woven or stamped to resemble a variety of more costly fabrics. A small handful of wealthier Chesapeake householders followed English taste in hanging the best rooms of their dwellings with fabric as well.[1] The 1692 inventory of Elizabeth Diggs listed a "yellow roome," a "large roome over against ye yellow roome," and a "red roome."[2] In general, room names were often keyed to the color, pattern, or fabric type used as specialized wall treatments. Aside from an occasional subordinate element, nothing in the contents of these rooms explicitly incorporated the colors mentioned. The only reference to yellow in the "yellow roome," for instance, was in the description of the lining of the bed valance. Clearly, the terms "red" and "yellow" for these rooms derived from the color of the walls.

Curiously, as seen in the above-mentioned inventory, the room most frequently given the name of a specific color in the first half of the eighteenth century was the bedchamber, a space associated by a long tradition in English houses with tapestries or wool hangings. Over fifty years later, the 1747 inventory of planter John Tayloe identified a bedchamber as "the green room," even though none of its furnishings were described as having upholstery in that color. Instead, appraisers listed "a Chints standing bed and window curtains, a white Callico Field Bed, a set of dammask Bottom'd Chairs, a dammask Couch."[3] Since wallpaper does not appear evident in the region until the second half of the eighteenth century, it is most likely that fabric hangings were used more frequently than previously thought.

The English fashion for hanging rooms with tapestries seems to have made its way to the American colonies as well.[4] In 1679, the inventory of Colonel Francis Eppes listed a "suit of tapestry hangings" at 18 pounds, 17 shillings, 0 pence, and in 1683, William Fitzhugh of Stafford County requested that his London correspondent "procure for me a suit of Tapestry hangings for a Room 20 Foot long, 16 foot wide and nine high." Four years later, Fitzhugh described his house: "With 13 Rooms in it, four of the best of them [are] hung."[5]

Fig. 16.1. "Captain Ulrich or Greed Deceived," showing a room hung with gilded leather. Cornelis Troost, 1738, Holland. (Royal Cabinet of Paintings, Mauritshuis, The Hague)

Tapestry wall hangings persisted into the eighteenth century. An antebellum description of Rosewell, seat of the Page family in Gloucester County, noted that the "old hall is a superb room: around the panelling are some antique hooks, on which the tapestry hangings were suspended. The tapestry was still preserved there a few years ago."[6] William Burnet Browne, who lived at Elsing Green between about 1763 and 1784, reportedly owned a set of Gobelin tapestries that had been presented by William of Orange to his grandfather, William Burnet, governor of New York.[7] Several years after the royal governor, John Murray, Lord Dunmore, fled Virginia, in 1775, he filed a schedule of losses to cover the objects that had been left behind, which included "valuable Tapestry."[8]

Painted and gilded leather offered an alternative to textile wall hangings for important rooms. Although the use of leather hangings seems to have been very limited in the colonies, the fashion for them was persistent. While serving apprenticeships in Holland, where leather hangings were then being produced and used in great quantity, Virginians William Byrd II and John Custis IV, Byrd's brother-in-law, would certainly have observed numerous rooms outfitted in this fashion (Fig. 16.1). Their experience may have prompted one or the other of these men to suggest gilded leather hangings for the best reception room at the Governor's Palace, the Upper Middle Room. Whether or not the Virginia Council was prompted by Byrd or Custis, in 1710 it submitted a proposal "that the great Room in the second Story be furnished with gilt Leather hangings, [and] 16 Chairs of the same."[9] In Annapolis, the 1776 inventory of Maryland governor Robert Eden indicates that one room in his residence was hung with gilt leather. The appraiser's denomination of this space as the "Gilt Leather Parlour" was clearly derived from the treatment of its walls, since none of the upholstered furnishings were covered with leather. The chair bottoms were horsehair and the curtains were "Crimson Stuff Damask."[10]

WALLPAPER

Wallpaper had already enjoyed a long history of use in England when it first began to appear in the Chesapeake colonies in the middle of the eighteenth century. London paper stainers had established a lucrative trade in wallpaper by the end of the seventeenth century.[11] From about 1710, paper hangings became readily available in New England but were slower to appear in the Chesapeake.[12] There is a recorded example of wallpaper in the region as early as 1700, but it was not until the 1750s that it became a popular alternative to textile hangings.[13]

British and American consumers readily adopted the fashion for wallpaper, often contrasting its merits against outdated rooms hung with textiles or fully wainscoted. An English publication of 1763 observed that wallpaper was "not only a cheap, but an elegant part of furniture, and saves the builders the expense of wainscoting: for which reason they have brought it in vogue, and most of the new houses lately erected are lined throughout with paper."[14] Americans also remarked on wallpaper's growing ascendancy over the heavier, more formal look of wainscot or textile treatments. In planning his new house at Blandfield, Robert Beverley wrote to his London agent that he was "desirous of fitting it up in a plain neat Manner, I w^d willingly consult the present Fashion, for you know that foolish Passion has made its way, Even into this remote Region. I observ'd that L^d. B. [Lord Botetourt] had hung a room with plain blue paper & border'd it with a narrow stripe of gilt leather, wch I thought had a pretty effect." Clearly, the "foolish Passion" that Beverley referred to was the "present fashion" of upholstering the walls with paper.[15]

METHODS FOR HANGING TEXTILES AND WALLPAPER

The installation of each of these forms of wall treatments—tapestry, gilt leather, textiles, and ultimately wallpaper—

Fig. 16.2. A mock-flock wallpaper fragment was located in a second-floor parlor in the Robert Carter House, Williamsburg. This fragment corresponds to an order for paper that Carter placed with his London agent in 1762. (Colonial Williamsburg Foundation, 1976-88)

was one of the primary responsibilities of an upholsterer. London-trained upholsterers worked in the Chesapeake during the first half of the eighteenth century, and descriptions of the services that they performed suggest that they were familiar with each branch of the upholstery trade. As early as 1737, Samuel Bowler announced in the *Virginia Gazette* that he "performs all manner of Upholdsterers Work," and in 1745, Richard Caulton, an upholsterer from London, informed Virginians that he "doth all Sorts of Upholsterer's Work, after the newest Fashion."[16] Nearly a quarter century later, upholsterer Joseph Kidd, newly arrived in Virginia, advertised that he hung rooms with paper as well as damask.[17]

Several methods were employed for affixing hangings to the walls. In brick or stone houses, wooden furring was sometimes applied directly to the masonry to provide a nailing surface for the fabric. An alternative was to cover the interior walls with flush boards or wainscoting, which provided a measure of insulation in addition to a ground for nailing up wall hangings. Usually, a scrim or canvas was tacked in place around the room, often with a lining paper pasted to the canvas to provide an additional dust barrier, before the outer layer of fabric or wallpaper was attached. Evidence from two Williamsburg houses confirms the existence of wooden rails and stiles, which were probably used in the attachment of wall hangings. An upstairs chamber at the Peyton Randolph House was outfitted with wooden stiles and rails in the mid-1750s. One of the surviving upper rails retains tack holes that suggest an early textile or wallpaper installation. A similar grid of rails at the Robert Carter House,

Fig. 16.3. The reconstructed ballroom of the Governor's Palace in Williamsburg is hung with plain blue wallpaper, re-created to correspond to Governor Botetourt's order for wallpaper supplies, which was shipped to Virginia in 1768.

adjacent to the Governor's Palace, provided attachments for each of the four wallpaper patterns that Carter ordered in 1762. A small section of the fabric backing, paper lining, and fragment of the printed paper was discovered still adhering to one of these stiles (Fig. 16.2). There were no nail holes in the wooden member; the backing had been glued to the wood and perhaps to the plaster as well. The lining paper had been taken from a page in a 1755 edition of the Virginia laws, a discovery that helped narrow down the date of the wallpaper.[18]

In 1768, the royal governor, Lord Botetourt, used the same method to attach wallpaper in the ballroom of the Governor's Palace. The surviving order for supplies—"50 lb of the best Verdeter," "24 lb of prusian blue," "2 Ream of fine large Elephant paper," and 10,000 tacks—suggests that Botetourt decorated that room in the up-to-date fashion of covering the walls with plain paper, painted in situ. To achieve the effect, coarse, unbleached linen called oznaburg was tacked to the wooden stiles and rails in order to provide a protective barrier between the paper and the wall surface. Sheets of elephant folio–sized cartridge paper was pasted to the fabric and then painted over with distemper pigments (Fig. 16.3).[19]

Nailing the hangings to wooden stiles rather than pasting them in place would have facilitated its removal for cleaning, or for repairs of the sort mentioned in connection with the ballroom hangings. Several months after Lord Botetourt's paper was installed, upholsterer Joseph Kidd charged for "Mending Paper in the Ball Room."[20]

The practice of pasting papers over canvas gradually diminished as other methods came into favor. Paperhangers began to nail paper directly to wooden surfaces. The procedure went like this: All four sides of the first length of paper were tacked down first. Hangers then attached subsequent panels along the top and bottom and on *one* vertical side, the other being pasted over the tacked edge of the preceding sheet. This method would later influence the manner of pasting papers directly to the wall. As in the tacking of paper, only one side was usually trimmed, this being lapped over the untrimmed edge of the preceding sheet.

By the 1770s, gluing paper directly to the wall was the most common method of installation. Whether on canvas or not, virtually all surviving examples of paper from the Chesapeake colonies were pasted directly to the wall. In some cases, such as at Rock Castle in Goochland County, the substrate

(left) Fig. 16.4. Wallpaper fragment adhered to newspaper used as a backing to line the walls, 1797, probably American, Brandy, Anne Arundel County, Maryland. (Colonial Williamsburg Foundation, 2009-73)

(right) Fig. 16.5. Festoon wallpaper border stamped on reverse with the maker's mark, Anthony Chardin, c. 1795, Philadelphia, removed from the walls of Pendleton House, Elizabeth City, North Carolina.

was wood.[21] During the restoration of the Nicholson Shop in Williamsburg, large fragments of lattice-pattern wallpaper were discovered attached directly to flush-board wall sheathing. Prior to pasting wallpaper directly on to sheathing at Brandy in Anne Arundel County, narrow strips of linen and newspaper were pasted over the joints on the wall to protect the paper from tearing as the boards shrank and swelled with humidity (Fig. 16.4).[22]

While pasting paper directly to wooden sheathing provided minimal challenges, plaster and whitewash presented numerous difficulties for the paperhanger. Joseph Dickinson, who practiced in Philadelphia, noted that "having considered the nature of this climate and the texture of the walls, which have too generally been whitened with lime, insomuch that if care is not taken, the paper will start and sometimes affect the colours of the paper."[23] The practice of omitting the white or finish coat of plaster in rooms to be papered was probably intended to address this problem. Physical evidence for omitting the last coat of plaster has been found at Kenmore and Montpelier.[24]

BORDERS

Decorative borders originated as the means for hiding the tacks that fixed textile hangings in place. Gimps (twisted thread with a cord running through it), tapes, and braids were commonly used, as well as carved and gilded wooden fillets. Since most early wallpaper installations were mounted on linen and tacked to wooden battens or sheathing, borders were a necessary component of the overall scheme. Separate patterns were designed for borders that could be printed on paper to paste over the nail holes. As the eighteenth century progressed, borders of varying widths were produced

to fulfill several functions. Narrower patterns, usually 1 to 2 inches wide, were used as edging papers. These surrounded door and window architraves and were placed above wainscot paneling or chair boards. Wider designs were created to place below cornice moldings or, in some cases, in lieu of moldings altogether. Ultimately, these borders became a decorative element in their own right, incorporating elaborate festoon swags or other decorative drapery treatments (Fig. 16.5).

A more costly alternative than printed paper borders for covering tacks involved gilded or colored moldings made of wood or papier-mâché. Carved wooden borders were often the choice of the wealthy English gentry, costing as much as

Fig. 16.6. Portrait of Eleazar Tyng showing a gilded papier-mâché border outlining plain green paper hangings. John Singleton Copley, 1772, Boston. (Courtesy of National Gallery of Art, Washington, D.C.)

£5 per yard.[25] The only three-dimensional borders known to have been used in the colonies were made of papier-mâché (Fig. 16.6). Included in the supplies that Lord Botetourt ordered to redecorate the ballroom and supper room of the Governor's Palace was "500 foot of Gooder oun [gadroon] Gilt moulding" to cover the tacks.[26] Two entries in the 1770 inventory of the Governor's Palace—"Oznabrigs intended to paste the Paper on in the Supper Room" and "a long box of Gilt bordering intended for the supper Room"—suggest that it was intended to be hung in a similar manner as the ballroom.[27]

Robert Beverley of Essex County wrote enthusiastically of the look that Governor Botetourt achieved in his ballroom. Perhaps this was Beverley's first view of a gilded papier-mâché border, for he mistakenly identified it as "a narrow stripe of gilt leather."[28] Several factors suggest that Botetourt's border was papier-mâché rather than leather or wood. First, it is unlikely that the term "moulding," as it was described in Botetourt's account book, would have referred to a pliable leather border, nor would such borders have been stored in the long boxes mentioned in the inventory. Significantly, the

price that Botetourt paid for his borders correlates precisely with charges recorded by Thomas Chippendale and others for papier-mâché borders.

Other Virginians besides Beverley commented on the pleasing combination of blue paper and gilt borders. In 1784, George Washington wrote to his agent, Clement Biddle: "I have seen rooms with gilded borders; made I believe, of papier Maché fastned on with Brads or Cement round the Doors and window Casings, Surbase &ca.; and which gives a plain blew, or green paper a rich and handsome look."[29] Jefferson was undoubtedly familiar with the plain blue wallpaper in Lord Botetourt's ballroom. Within months of its installation, he noted his intention to order supplies to install a plain blue paper in his dining room at Monticello. Preferring a more neoclassical look, he planned to outline his paper with a white papier-mâché border rather than a gilded one.[30] While surviving colonial references imply that solid-colored papers were most often adorned with gilded borders, plain white papier-mâché borders, such as those Jefferson described in 1769, were also fashionable in New England and in Europe.[31]

CEILING TREATMENTS

Papier-mâché borders designed to hide tack holes on wall hangings were not the only type of three-dimensional ornament fabricated from paper found in houses in Maryland and Virginia and farther south. Just as many wallpaper patterns were designed to imitate more expensive textile hangings, paper was molded in sculptural forms designed to replicate wooden or plaster decoration of the type used on walls and ceilings by the middle of the eighteenth century. There is ample evidence that ceiling ornaments made of paper were used in southern houses. Miles Brewton procured at least two papier-mâché ceilings for his house in Charleston, South Carolina, one for the south parlor and another, molded as the head of Apollo, for the cove ceiling in the stair landing.[32] At Belvoir, in 1763, George William Fairfax ordered "paier mashe Ornaments for Ceiling agreeable to drawing for room."[33] The 1774 inventory of the estate of builder William Buckland included "2 Ornamented Ceilings of Paper" valued at £10.[34] In 1757, George Washington ordered six patterns of wallpaper for Mount Vernon. To adorn the ceiling of his dining room, he specified "a Set of best painted ornaments for a Ceiling" and "a Set of Papier Mache for ditto."[35] Washington's ceiling ornamentation is somewhat more difficult to decipher since he ordered both painted ornament (presumably a flat printed pattern) and papier-mâché for his dining room.

Despite the infrequent survival of early wallpapers in Chesapeake houses, documents leave no doubt that by the 1760s they were as prevalent there as in New England and the middle colonies. Although no wallpaper pattern books seem to have survived from the eighteenth century, it is clear that colonists in the Chesapeake occasionally referred to such books in making their selections. Robert Beverley certainly consulted one in 1771 when he ordered wallpaper for his new house, Blandfield, referring to the patterns by number. While many wealthier home owners ordered papers directly from their English merchants, early newspaper advertisements reveal that local upholsterers stocked a wide variety of patterns. In 1761, merchant Charles Digges of Alexandria had on hand imported "stain'd Paper for Rooms, in the *Gothic* and *Chinese* Taste."[36] Williamsburg upholsterers Joseph Kidd and Joshua Kendall offered "A CHOICE COLLECTION of the most fashionable PAPER HANGINGS, for rooms, ceilings, staircases."[37]

The adoption of wallpaper vastly expanded the visual richness and expressive power of domestic interiors. Yet colonists did not choose from an unlimited range of options—nor were their choices a simple matter of whim. Until the time of the Revolution, most papers in Chesapeake houses were imported from England, and thus they reflected the tastes of the British market. Indeed, Americans relied heavily on overseas merchants to acquire papers in the most up-to-date styles and colors. A 1757 letter from George Washington to his London agent contains one of the region's earliest wallpaper orders. He requested "Paper for 5 rooms . . . the paper differing in their colours; also a paper of a very good kind and color for a Dining Room 18 by 16 above Chair boards ye pitch of the Room is 11 feet."[38] That the proprietor of Mount Vernon could leave such an important matter as the selection of individual colors and patterns to the discretion of an agent suggests that his correspondent was familiar with Washington's taste and furnishings and that his merchant could be trusted to procure suitable patterns. He required the agent to exercise not only "Judgment in the Materials, but Taste in the Fashions," looking always for "Skill in the Workmanship."[39]

That is not to say that colonists entirely relinquished their prerogatives. Some were quite specific in their requests, describing which patterns and colors they preferred. In 1762, Robert Carter ordered "Paper to hang 3 Parlours . . . The 1st Parlour a good Paper of Crimson Colour—The 2nd Parlours a better Paper, a white ground wth large green leaves. The 3rd Parlour Best Paper a blue ground wth large Yellow flowers."[40] In reply, his London merchant included "a small piece of blew & yellow Paper which ive sent as a Sample, there being none but that to be had in town, as they are Colors that can't be made lively on Paper[;] they have never been in demand here. I have sent a sufficient Quantity of another kind which is reckon'd very genteel, however will immediately on receiving yr Orders again, have some blew & yellow made and shipt by the first Ship."[41] Curiously, Carter seems to have maintained closer touch with current fashions than his London merchant did. Surviving wallpaper fragments suggest that blue and yellow actually were a popular color combination at the time.

Numerous eighteenth-century descriptions of wallpaper sold by merchants or requested by clients indicate that the choice of wallpaper patterns was often governed by the distinctive attributes ascribed to various categories of rooms. There were specific patterns that properly expressed the character of passages, for example, but were considered inappropriate for parlors. When Benjamin Bucktrout advertised wallpaper for sale in Williamsburg in 1771, he noted different sorts that would be suitable for staircases, rooms, or ceilings. Patterns falling into those three categories were described as "embossed, Stucco, Chintz, striped, Mosaick, Damask and common."[42] But how did each of those patterns evoke unique characteristics prescribed by eighteenth-century room usage? Which type of pattern was considered appropriate for one type of space but not for another? Clearly, these consumers possessed a shared understanding of the specialized nature of individual types of patterns and their appropriateness for specific contexts—subtleties that may be more elusive to modern eyes.

Fortunately, a few advertisements, such as that placed by Moses Grant in the *New-England Palladium* in 1809, provide greater clarification for how different sorts of patterns should be used: "Draperies with match top and bottom Borders, for Drawing Rooms; pillar, column and marble Patterns, suitable for Entries; neat stripes, vines and set Figures, for Chambers, with Borders new and suitable."[43] Was Grant's understanding of the individual nature of room treatments consistent with the way in which rooms would have been decorated fifty years earlier in the Chesapeake? To form a more complete picture requires dissecting each surviving order for wallpaper, particularly those for which other types of information relating to the house survive. Robert Beverley's order for Blandfield provides a good example, for his invoice listed five separate wallpaper patterns. Like most orders, it made no mention of the individual room for which each paper was intended, but by examining other information relating to his household furnishings it is possible to determine how Beverley intended to use some of his patterns.

Fig. 16.7. "An Interior with Members of a Family," showing a room hung with an architectural paper. Attributed to Strickland Lowry, c. 1770s, Ireland. (Courtesy of National Gallery of Ireland)

In a later invoice, he noted that he wanted "3 Yellow Damask Window Curtains of stuff [worstit or workt] with Pullies to draw up to the Top of [torn page] Window, 11 Feet high & 4 Feet six Inches wide, the Colour to be the same as the ground of the rich yellow Paper as I directed."[44] These curtains, as well as a set of twelve mahogany chairs, also to be covered with the same yellow wool damask, were intended to match the "Large yellow Pattern mixed with stucco Colour."[45] Examining the other furnishings that Beverley ordered suggests that the yellow damask set was intended to be used in the parlor.[46] Another clue found in this order suggested where the parlor was located in the house. The order mentioned curtains for three windows—there is only one room on the first floor with that number of openings.[47]

PASSAGES AND STAIRCASES

Like other kinds of household objects, wall treatments were used expressively, with a full appreciation of the ideas and associations they embodied. For this reason, textile or paper hangings offer a means by which to recover the social meanings attached to domestic spaces. Numerous pre-Revolutionary references to papers described as being suitable for passage, staircase, or entry for houses in the Chesapeake indicate that specific types of papers were called for in this location. Robert Carter's 1762 order for wallpapers to adorn his Williamsburg house included one pattern "proper to hang a Passage & Staircase."[48] The notion of a paper peculiarly suited to entries was shared so widely that Carter's English correspondent could be counted on to fill the request. Carter's neighbors were equally familiar with this idea. In 1769, Nathaniel Lyttleton Savage, a resident of Virginia's Eastern Shore, received "8 pieces of paper hanging suitable for a passage."[49]

The most distinctive of all of the types of patterns available in the eighteenth and early nineteenth centuries were large-scaled architectural patterns, such as those that Moses Grant described as "pillar, column and marble Patterns suitable for Entries" (Fig. 16.7). Among the salient attributes of grander English halls of the early eighteenth century were their walls of stone, which were often enriched with ornaments carved in high relief. Often these adornments were highly architectural, sometimes consisting of columns and arched niches, the latter for the display of freestanding stone sculptures.[50]

(left) Fig. 16.8. "Domestick Amusement: The Lovely Spinner," showing a room hung with a paper imitation of wainscot, published by John and Carington Bowles, c. 1760, London. (Colonial Williamsburg Foundation, 1975-307)

(right) Fig. 16.9. The stair hall of the Jeremiah Lee House, Marblehead, Massachusetts, showing wallpaper painted en grisaille after engravings by Vernet, 1760–70, London.

In lesser houses, these ornaments could be executed in stucco to simulate the appearance of stone. In either case, the typical entry was cool, imposing, and monochromatic.

In England, papers depicting architectural treatments—galleries of marble columns and arches, ashlar stonework, or faux representations of wooden paneling—had been available since the 1690s, when the trade card of Edward Butling advertised "Paper in Imitation of Irish Stitch, of the newest Fashion, and several other sorts, viz. Flock work, Wainscot, Marble, Damask, Turkey-Work."[51] At this early date, "wainscot" generally consisted of a joined grid of rails and stiles to which flat panels were secured with bolection moldings. Such work, usually executed in oak, was a staple of architectural interiors, including entries, at the end of the seventeenth century.[52] Papers printed to imitate wainscot were still associated with entries nearly a century later. In 1789, Boston paper stainer William May announced that he sold "Architecture-Papers for entryways" and "Pannel Papers to imitate Wainscotting" (Fig. 16.8).[53]

Stucco ornament was fashionable for halls and entryways, and this treatment was eventually adopted for paper for hangings as well. To imitate the stone entries of grand English houses, paper stainers produced galleries of arches and faux stucco ornaments, all reduced to two dimensions and printed *en grisaille*. One of the papers that Robert Beverley ordered for Blandfield was "No. 10 Stucco Colour large Patterns of Pillars & Galleries 600 yds at 3½."[54] George William Fairfax ordered "8 Pieces of Painted Stucco [and] 8 Doz Borders" for the passage of Belvoir in 1763, which in all likelihood was a printed architectural pattern.[55]

In the Chesapeake colonies, the relationship between the exterior and the interior that existed in the passage or entry was frequently expressed in its furnishings and other appointments as well as in the decoration. In 1790, Thomas Jefferson ordered twenty-two rolls of paper in a pattern representing brickwork, clearly intended for his entry or "hall" at Monticello, consciously creating a relationship between this space and the exterior. Among the contents of the room were twenty-eight Windsor chairs, a form strongly associated with the passages of large houses. Lightweight and easily portable, these chairs generally had no upholstery and were frequently carried outdoors for use. The significance of the Windsor chairs that Jefferson chose for his hall was reinforced by his decision to paint the floor grass green in 1805. To even the most unsophisticated visitor, Jefferson's attempt to "call in the outdoors" must have been perfectly clear.

While wallpapers designed with architectural motifs dominated passages and entrance halls throughout the eighteenth century, by the beginning of the nineteenth century scenic papers were also used as another means of emphasiz-

Fig. 16.10. *"Les Rives du Bosphore," in the back passage of Eyre Hall, Northampton County, Virginia. Dufour, c. 1816, France.*

ing the communication with the outdoors. The rigid and structured ordering of architectural elements gave way to a more open expression, reflected by the ideals of neoclassicism and Americans' growing interest in landscape painting. This expression is perhaps first seen in the passage and staircase paper at the Jeremiah Lee House in Marblehead, Massachusetts. In this installation, large scenes of classical ruins based on paintings by artists such as Giovanni Paolo Panini were surrounded by painted "frames" in imitation of stucco (Fig. 16.9).[56]

Decades later, French wallpaper manufacturers found a welcome market for their large-format panoramic papers on this side of the ocean, as American interest in neoclassic ideals shifted toward romanticism. Scenic papers, "Well calculated for Halls and Passages," were advertised by S. P. Franklin in Washington, D.C., in 1825 and soon became prevalent in North America, including those manufactured by the firms of Zuber and Dufour.[57] Although scenic papers

of the nineteenth century were hung in dining rooms and parlors as well, those adorning the walls of entrance halls were the most effective. At Eyre Hall, on Virginia's Eastern Shore, Dufour's "Les Rives du Bosphore" (c. 1816) hung in the rear portion of the broad stair passage—a summer sitting room that overlooked the garden (Fig. 16.10). The bold colors and scale of these scenic papers displayed in this setting defied the boundaries of the house, uniting its interior with the landscape beyond.

Francis Regnault of Richmond provided three such papers for Prestwould, in Clarksville, Virginia, in 1831. Among these was "Le Parc Français," which adorned one wall of the Saloon. Like passages in other houses, this Saloon opened directly to the outdoors (Fig. 16.11). During the warm and humid Virginia summers, the doors at either end would have been opened to allow greater airflow, and this is certainly the space where the family would have congregated. The three remaining walls of the Saloon were hung with a

Fig. 16.11. "Le Parc Français," by Jacquemart et Bénard, and a floral paper were hung on the walls of the Saloon at Prestwould, Mecklenburg County, Virginia, 1831.

large-scale "French Green leaf" paper, again creating the interior association with nature. At Prestwould, as at Eyre Hall, the paper treatment amplified the "doors-open" aspect of this summer sitting room. Whether scenic or architectural, whether French or English, the wallpaper of the Chesapeake planter's entry embodied functions and meanings that were *locally* important, in this case, the passage as summer sitting room, waiting room, and transition point between inside and outside.

PARLORS AND DRAWING ROOMS

Whereas passage papers were typically architectural or scenic, specific patterns described in advertisements as being suitable for drawing rooms and parlors are more illusive. However, Moses Grant's 1809 advertisement, identifying parlor or drawing room papers as those designed to imitate "Draperies with match top and bottom borders" is reminiscent of the earlier tradition of furnishing the primary entertaining spaces with expensive textile hangings. Architectural historian John Cornforth recognized that the fashion for upholstering rooms with textiles in English houses corresponded with the desire to amass large picture collections.[58] Damask and cut-velvet hangings provided a visually appealing backdrop upon which to display paintings in gilded frames. Additionally, hanging a large quantity of framed objects was easier to manage on a flat surface than on a three-dimensional paneled wall. Consequently, by the beginning

of the eighteenth century, formal reception rooms and long galleries in English houses, where painting collections were displayed, were most often hung with monochromatic textile hangings.

Although colonial Americans rarely amassed large picture collections of the type represented in English country houses, those who did own paintings, primarily family portraits, followed English precedent by placing them in the most formal reception room of their houses, the parlor or withdrawing room. In Chesapeake houses, the parlor was the space where the primary social functions aside from dining—card playing, musical entertainments, and tea drinking—took place. Brilliance, articulation, and refinement were the characteristics that defined the parlor. Chairs that were used in parlors and drawing rooms were often richly carved and covered with figured damask that frequently coordinated with the wall treatments, visual qualities that captured and expressed the elegant nature of the space. The large-scale flamboyance of damask patterns was well suited to the amplitude of public gesture and performance, and the long repeats of these papers connoted expense. The textured richness and exotic overtones of costly fabrics served to elevate the importance of the parlor over other rooms in the house.

Certainly one of the most elegantly appointed parlors known in Virginia during the colonial period was to be seen at Gunston Hall. The more ornate southwest room likely served as the parlor during George Mason's lifetime. Nail patterns, paint residue, and other markings on the sheathing

Fig. 16.12. Threads trapped beneath early tacks suggest that George Mason's Palladian Room may have originally been hung with a crimson textile. View of the room restored with reproduction paper. Gunston Hall, Fairfax County, Virginia.

strongly indicate that the room was originally hung with a textile. Early tacks are still evident beneath the woodwork, suggesting that it was upholstered prior to the final installation of the carved woodwork (Fig. 16.12).

Once wallpapers became a fashionable alternative to textile hangings, the patterns chosen for important rooms in English houses were those printed in imitation of cut velvets. These same designs adorned the walls of parlors and drawing rooms of the Chesapeake region as well. Flocked papers, often called "embossed" during the period, and mock-flock patterns were purchased by Virginians such as George Washington in 1757, Robert Carter in 1762, and Robert Beverley in 1771. Fragments of a green flocked floral pattern were found on the parlor walls of Kenmore in Fredericksburg.

Color, as well as pattern selection, could also be used to elevate the status of a particular room. Although green and blue were occasionally used in the most formal spaces, the conventional color was crimson. In 1688, English genealogist Randle Holme noted that "this colour Vermilion, or Red, is the chief amongst colours, . . . none should bear this Colour but Persons of Noble Birth and Rank, and Men of Special desent; for it signifyeth Dignity."[59] Not only was crimson the most expensive color; it was considered the most suitable background for the display of paintings in gilded frames. Robert Carter selected the color for the best room at Nomini Hall, his plantation house in the Northern Neck. In 1773, he ordered three papers with borders, including "20 Ps of plain Crimson paper Hanging; gilded Border for Ditto of Pappia Marche; 20 Ps plain yellow paper Hangings; Border for Ditto yellow ground with a Darker shaded figure; 20 Ps Plain blue Paper hangings well finished; Border for Ditto with, blue figured with Chineese rail."[60] The hierarchy in the importance of these papers is evident in Robert Carter's request for an expensive papier-mâché border to accompany the crimson paper, versus printed paper borders for the plain yellow and blue papers. Clearly, the crimson paper was to be used in Carter's best room.

There is reason to believe that Jefferson hung crimson paper in his parlor, based on an order he placed in 1790 for papers for Monticello.[61] Although he did not identify which rooms he intended each paper for, the argument for his intention to use the crimson paper in the parlor is supported by the description of the textiles he used there. While in France he had acquired a set of twelve armchairs upholstered in crimson damask, which he earmarked specifically for this room. In 1808, moreover, he provided a sketch for parlor draperies, directing that they be made of "crimson damask silk lined with a green and a yellow fringe."[62] The crimson color would have served as an appropriate backdrop for the fifty-seven works of art, many of them mounted in gilt frames. Not only was Jefferson's parlor studded with gilt-framed works of art, but this principal reception space also included a keyboard instrument, a pair of large mirrors, and even a Campeachy chair.[63]

DINING ROOMS

Since dining rooms did not become an essential element of Chesapeake houses until the 1720s, they had no decorative tradition. Initially, it is likely that most dining rooms were fully paneled or wainscoted, since textile hangings would have absorbed strong food odors. The choice of seating furniture confirms this notion as well. Unlike the damask or cut-velvet stuffed chairs that were more typically found in parlors, dining room chairs were often covered with leather or horsehair. Not only would they have retained fewer odors, but spills would have been easier to clean.

Once wallpaper became fashionable in the region, shortly after the middle of the eighteenth century, some type of it was hung in dining rooms as well. Unfortunately, no newspaper ads have yet come to light that describe which patterns were suitable for this space. Even as late as the nineteenth century, Moses Grant described papers designed for entries and drawing rooms but made no specific mention of papers suitable for dining rooms. Nevertheless, orders suggest that consumers initially chose the same type of patterns for dining rooms as they did for parlors. In Washington's 1757 wallpaper order in anticipation of enlarging Mount Vernon, it appears that he planned an embossed, or "flocked," paper for his new dining room. Robert Carter specified paper for three parlors for his Williamsburg town house in 1762. Judging from the description of the patterns in his order, it is likely that one of those was a dining parlor, in which case it would

have been hung with a damask pattern. Thomas Everard of Williamsburg hung his dining room with a yellow mock-flocked floral pattern about 1770 (see Fig. 15.13).

It could be suggested that dining rooms acquired a more unique decorative character with the introduction of the neoclassical style. As discussed earlier, Governor Botetourt installed plain blue paper in the ballroom of the Governor's Palace in 1768. From that time, plain papers became the most prevalent style for dining rooms in Chesapeake houses. Within months of Botetourt's installation, Jefferson expressed his intention to install plain blue paper outlined with a white papier-mâché border in his dining room at Monticello. His notation further revealed that he also contemplated ornamenting the ceiling of his dining room with papier-mâché, though recent architectural investigations suggest that he never actually installed the blue wallpaper.[64]

A very small fragment of a surviving blue paper that had been used in the dining room was discovered at Kenmore. Moreover, owner Fielding Lewis not only omitted the final coat of plaster in the dining room in anticipation of installing wallpaper, but he incorporated decorative cast plaster moldings around the room that created twelve distinct panels. The most likely conclusion to draw is that the paper that Lewis installed both within and surrounding the panels was a plain blue. Lewis's combination of white plaster and blue paper and Jefferson's intention to furnish his dining room with plain blue paper outlined with white papier-mâché borders reflects the same neoclassical aesthetic achieved by Josiah Wedgwood, who was simultaneously producing large quantities of blue and white jasperware (see Fig. 3.16).[65]

Virtually from the time of their inception, dining rooms had assumed a male character, and the room's architectural appointments often expressed this. This notion was probably related to the banishment of women after meals and to the interlude of drinking, smoking, and male fellowship that followed. At Monticello, Jefferson built the decorative scheme of his dining room around the Doric order, which had been likened to "a certain masculine and natural beauty."[66] Under the sway of this Vitruvian lore, Richard Neve had recommended the Doric order in settings where "Strength, and a rough, but noble Simplicity are particularly required . . . having been composed in Imitation of a naked Man, nervous and robust as an Hercules."[67] Jefferson is certain to have formulated the decorative program of his dining room with a full appreciation of these meanings. In the Doric ornaments and massive detailing of this space, he crystallized the contemporary notions of maleness and its association with the meal.

The furnishings of the public rooms at Monticello provide an excellent case study to begin to understand the contrast between parlors and dining rooms. The bold simplicity of the architectural character of the dining room, with its Doric entablature, massive arches, and flush wainscoting, was echoed in the furnishings and extended to the very floor, which consisted merely of conventional pine boards. Even with the added light from north-facing windows in Jefferson's tea room, the single window in the dining room was never sufficient to dispel shadows completely from this space.

Jefferson's parlor, on the other hand, was brilliantly illuminated by a polygonal bay of three west-facing windows. A full-height Corinthian entablature, studded with acanthus-covered modillions and delicate, richly detailed frieze ornaments, adorns the space. Added to these enrichments were silk damask upholstery, the carved and inlaid articulation of lavish furniture, and the vivid richness of numerous portraits in their gilded frames. Under all was the polished surface of a parquetry floor fashioned from cherry and beech. The contrast between the parlor and the dining room must have been striking indeed. One was simple, tectonic, and dowdy; the other was articulated, brilliant, and refined. This visual distinction expressed a deeper social contrast, grounded in the gender associations of each space.

CHAMBERS

Until the second half of the eighteenth century, the chamber occasionally functioned as a quasi-public sitting room where guests were often received and entertained. In 1710, William Byrd visited the governor's niece at the Governor's Palace, noting in his diary that "after dinner I went to make a visit to Mrs. Russell in her chamber and drank some tea with her. Then we went down and played at piquet."[68] There is no record of how Mrs. Russell's chamber at the Governor's Palace was decorated at the time that Byrd paid his visit, although, following the tradition of hanging state bedchambers with elaborate tapestry or other textile hangings, it is possible the walls of her chamber were treated in such a manner. Once wallpaper became a fashionable alternative to the more expensive textile hangings, the most common patterns used for chambers were those that were flocked to imitate cut velvet. For example, in George Washington's first wallpaper installation at Mount Vernon, he chose a blue flocked paper to adorn the walls of the room likely used as the principal chamber in the house.[69]

As the eighteenth century progressed, the public visibility of the chamber began to diminish, and what was once a semi-public space was now off-limits to all but family members or close associates. Perhaps it was this growing aspect of privacy

Fig. 16.13. This wallpaper fragment, printed in a lattice design, was discovered in the Nicholson Shop in Williamsburg. The French paper dates to about 1790. Jefferson chose the same pattern for the walls of the North Octagonal Room at Monticello. (Colonial Williamsburg Foundation, 1938-223)

and quietude—the absence of public performance—that explains the shift in decorating chambers, from patterns more closely associated with formal reception rooms to softer, more delicate designs.

The 1809 Grant advertisement mentions a variety of patterns appropriate to specific locations, including "neat stripes, vines and set Figures for Chambers, with Borders new and suitable."[70] Although the simple and less-expensive character of Grant's "neat stripes" was undoubtedly a factor in their use for rooms of modest importance, the small scale and repeat of these patterns were well suited to the social and spatial intimacy of the chamber. Designs that incorporated aspects of nature, from small sprigs of greenery to abstracted natural forms borrowed from chintz textiles, provided a staple of chamber decoration.

Thomas Jefferson ordered wallpaper to hang in five rooms at Monticello in 1790. One of the patterns from this order, "22. rouleaux of lattice or treillage," can clearly be identified as the pattern that Jefferson intended for one of his chambers, since an offset image of the design was uncovered on the plastered walls of the North Octagonal Room.[71] The ghost of the paper on the wall at Monticello exactly matched paper discovered during the restoration of the Nicolson Shop in Williamsburg (Fig. 16.13). The lattice pattern represents only a portion of the original treatment, however, since Jefferson also ordered a border printed to imitate festooned drapery, which was to have been placed directly beneath the cornice. Additionally, for each of the eight angles of the room,

Fig. 16.14. A: A fragment of foliate rococo paper on a blue ground was discovered on the walls of the first-floor chamber of the Everard House. The English paper dates to about 1760 (Colonial Williamsburg Foundation, 1951-351); B: Bedchamber as restored with the reproduction of the original paper.

A

he ordered "corner papers," described as "stamped with the representation of curtains hanging in furbelo."[72] While the completed treatment would have resembled the lavishly upholstered tent rooms popular in France at the time, it is likely that Jefferson's combination of drapery and lattice was intended to create the impression of a garden house—to provide the occupant with the impression of sleeping in a gazebo. The octagonal form of the room almost certainly suggested this decorative program and surely enhanced the overall effect. Although Jefferson's scheme would have been considerably more dramatic than most treatments typically used in chambers, the naturalistic motifs convey the more tranquil aspect of the room, reflected in the growing separation between the public and private spheres of domestic life in the second half of the eighteenth century.

Conforming to the sense of intimacy that had become characteristic of bedchambers, "India" and "Chintz" designs were also fashionable choices to decorate the walls. Hand-painted Chinese papers depicting naturalistic motifs, often described as "India papers," were prohibitively expensive and generally adorned only the walls of chambers and closets in grand English country houses. To complement these papers, Chippendale would have recommended that the room be furnished with chairs designed in the Chinese taste, for he wrote that they were "very proper for a Lady's Dressing Room: especially if it is hung with India Paper."[73]

To respond to the taste for chinoiserie patterns, English, French, and American paper stainers created block-printed imitations of oriental motifs that were more affordable. These papers, described in orders and advertisements in American newspapers as "India-figured" or "mock India" patterns, were most often used in chambers, closets, dressing rooms, and other remote areas of American houses. In addition to creating oriental designs that were referred to as India papers, paper stainers also copied the beautiful floral designs that were hand-painted on cotton in India, known as Indian chintzes. These imitations were most often referred to during the period as chintz papers. Not only were they a pattern of paper stocked by craftsmen such as Benjamin Bucktrout in Williamsburg, but customer orders reveal that colonists were ordering them from their London merchants as well. In 1757, Richard Washington shipped "96 y.ds India figurd Paper" and "96 y.ds Chintz paper" to George Washington.[74] The price that Washington paid for these papers identifies

B

them as English adaptations of the more-expensive Indian chintzes and Chinese hand-painted papers. In fact, Washington's "India figurd" and "Chintz papers" cost less than each of the other four English flocked patterns that made up the rest of the order.

In general, the most prevalent patterns for bedchambers were also the most affordable. These were the simple stripes, most often used in combination with loose meandering floral motifs, or modest rococo foliate designs, such as the pattern that was discovered during the restoration of the Thomas Everard House, adjacent to the Governor's Palace in Williamsburg (Fig. 16.14). About 1770, Everard remodeled the interior of his house by adding new woodwork, paint, and wallpaper. This rococo foliate and scroll fragment from the first-floor bedchamber would have been relatively inexpensive to produce, requiring only one woodblock, since the depth in the design was created by printing both the black and the white with the same block. After the ground was painted blue, the yardage was printed with the foliate design in black distemper and then overprinted with white pigment, slightly slipping the registration of the block.

THE DOMESTIC ENSEMBLE

Having explored the role of wall hangings in expressing the distinctive attributes of individual rooms, we should consider how varied treatments coexisted within the arrangement of entire houses. The first and most important observation in this regard is that individual rooms were conceived as distinct environments. This assertion is based in part on physical evidence that the doors between rooms remained closed most of the time. Indeed, the current practice of holding open every interior door would have seemed alien in the eighteenth century. The planter's house was an aggregation of separate environments, each with its own character and purpose, to be experienced sequentially and more or less in isolation from one another. As a result, there was often no discernible relationship between the painting and papering of adjacent rooms. However, this had not always been the case. Earlier interior spaces were treated more or less uniformly, possibly because the individual rooms were regarded as subordinate parts of an integrated domestic setting.

Thomas Everard's Williamsburg house illustrates the trend away from undifferentiated interiors toward a collection of independent scenes. Initially, the 1740s interior woodwork was painted reddish brown throughout, and it is likely that all plaster was whitewashed. Over time, the unity of this scheme broke down. About 1770, Thomas Everard altered and refinished the entire house, painting and papering

every room differently. Having evolved from the purely mental divisions of the one-room house to the intimately compartmentalized interiors of the second half of the eighteenth century, the planter's conception of "house" had changed in a fundamentally important way—and this change was not unique to the Chesapeake but was common in Britain as well. George Washington's 1757 paperhanging scheme for Mount Vernon included six rooms, each with "Paper differing in their Colours."[75] The diverse range of colors he received included blue, green, yellow, and crimson.[76]

Once wallpaper became fashionable, it quickly dominated the decoration of dwellings, often covering as much as three-fourths of the interior wall surfaces.[77] In 1767, Edward Scott advertised the sale of his Chestertown house, describing it "as completely finished as any House in Maryland, with Eight genteel Rooms, Six of which are papered with most elegant Paper."[78] Rawleigh Downman of Morattico wanted to have "the walls below Stairs . . . cover'd."[79] Others also preferred papering all of the first-floor rooms within a house, such as the one advertised for sale in Williamsburg in 1777, which had "4 handsome Rooms below neatly papered, and a Fire Place in Each, with 3 Closets and 6 Rooms above."[80]

References such as these provide a general impression of the aesthetic that home owners in the Chesapeake were attempting to achieve. Fortunately, a clearer understanding of where specific patterns and colors were used within a single dwelling can often be determined by examining the orders for other household furnishings. While a varied range of colors and patterns were combined to establish a hierarchical progression throughout the house, correspondence from Chesapeake planters indicates that there was a conscious effort to create harmony within the rooms themselves. They clearly sought unity between the wall treatments, bed furniture, window curtains, and seating upholstery within individual spaces.

Subsequent correspondence that Washington wrote concerning furnishings for Mount Vernon provides some indication of which papers in the 1757 order were intended for specific rooms. He wanted, for example, "one doz'n strong Chairs of about fifteen Shillings price the bottoms to be exactly made by the Inclos'd Dimensions and of the three different colours to suit the paper of three of the bed chambers."[81] Since Washington ordered blue and white bed curtains and he wanted them to match the paper, the blue embossed pattern would have been intended for the walls of a bedchamber. Similarly, the yellow embossed paper was intended to accompany the yellow silk and worsted damask for bedhangings.[82] Comparing the quantities of wallpaper shipped for each room with the room dimensions that Washington had also provided suggests that the dining room was to be papered with the crimson embossed pattern. Since the front parlor and the first-floor chamber were paneled, it seems likely that what today is called the little parlor on the first floor was papered with the green embossed pattern, leaving the Chintz and India papers for the remaining two bedchambers on the second floor. Similarly, Robert Beverley of Blandfield had requested that the color of the damask for his parlor window curtains "be the same as the ground of the rich yellow Paper."[83]

From the 1760s through the first decades of the nineteenth century, a significant number of choices in wallpaper patterns and colors were available to home owners in Virginia and Maryland. Wallpaper provided many of them an affordable means of imitating what was fashionable in the homes of English and European gentry. Documents and fragmentary surviving evidence leave little doubt that the formulas they applied to their wall treatments were universally understood. The large quantity of patterns used within a single dwelling suggests that Americans, like their English counterparts, were also striving to create a progression through their houses. While someone like Robert Carter of Williamsburg ordered wallpaper "proper to hang a Passage & Staircase," less-affluent tradesmen and planters could also purchase stocked papers off the shelves of local stores identified as being appropriate "for Staircases, Rooms, and Ceilings." They too, appreciated the distinctions that wallpaper provided.

Ladies and gentlemen in the colonies were also eager to integrate their papers with the other furnishings of individual rooms, taking care to adhere to the basic formula that the type of room required. Just how decoration was used expressively to articulate the hierarchy of a particular space is probably best seen by comparing the parlors of Thomas Jefferson and James Madison. Both were hung with paintings in gilded frames. Each room was furnished with a keyboard instrument, mirrors, and a Campeachy chair. Both rooms appear to have been furnished with crimson wallpaper and textiles, the color that "signifyeth Dignity."

Conclusion

17 The Demise of Traditional Building Practices

CARL LOUNSBURY

Industrialized technology radically transformed many building practices in the second half of the nineteenth century. The application of steam-powered machinery to the production of building materials displaced many of the traditional tasks performed by brickmakers, sawyers, carpenters, and joiners in the construction process. Industrial goods steadily replaced handmade materials and fundamentally reshaped the manner in which buildings were assembled. Skilled craftsmen found much of their handiwork rendered redundant by machinery that could fabricate items such as sash, doors, blinds, mantels, newels, balusters, handrails, paneling, moldings, and other components faster, more cheaply, and in greater volume than the old methods (Fig. 17.1). The unvarying regularity and limited choice of standardized factory goods supplanted the specialized custom work and local materials that had been the heart of regional diversity.

The displacement of skilled labor from the job site had a profound impact on the manner in which contemporaries expressed the importance of a building, space, or room. In traditional building, most common materials were relatively inexpensive compared to the cost of the skilled labor necessary to transform them into finished components.[1] Joining a paneled door, carving a bracket, or planing a sawn board to create a double architrave took the time and hand tools of a skilled craftsman. Steam-power machinery eliminated most of the skilled labor necessary in their fabrication. As a result, more and more buildings could be fitted with components that hitherto had been limited to a much smaller number of structures or installed primarily in more public spaces within a building. A nicely carved mantel no longer signified a client's capacity to pay for labor or bore the mark of a craftsman's creativity. In the age of industrial building, the old subtle gradations of elaboration lost currency. Not that the homes of a wealthy businessman and a common laborer could be mistaken for each other, for the scale and a host of new manufactured materials ensured that there was a substantive difference between them. However, it was the

quality and variety of materials, not the degree of workmanship, that provided visual clues to spatial hierarchies.

The beginning of industrialized building took root in parts of the Chesapeake ten to fifteen years before the outbreak of the Civil War. However, it grew rapidly in the chaotic decades following the cessation of hostilities, when so much of the physical fabric of the region had to be rebuilt. The Civil War had also destroyed slavery and the social and economic foundations on which the plantation societies had been established. After the war, planters readjusted their agricultural practices to accommodate wage labor, experimented with new crops, and found novel ways to market their produce. Improvements in transportation—wagon roads, turnpikes, and railroads, which connected most of Maryland and Virginia with regional and national routes by the end of the

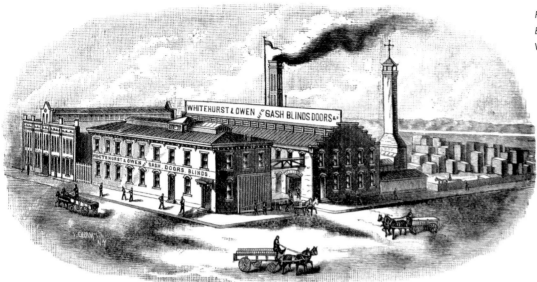

Fig. 17.1. Whitehurst & Owens Sash, Blind, and Door Works, Richmond, Virginia, 1889.

century—provided better access to markets and became the conduit for the introduction of manufactured goods and materials into rural areas. Virginia had 1,771 miles of railroad track in 1860. By the end of the century, that number had nearly tripled, and all but the remotest counties in the state were within easy reach of a main or branch line.[2]

Although postbellum farm families still produced many of the things they needed, they purchased a steadily increasing amount of household and personal goods from neighboring stores, which sold everything from crockery to clothing and guano to galvanized sheet metal. At the beginning of the nineteenth century, rural and village stores offered many domestic goods, but by 1900 a far greater variety of manufactured items from all parts of the nation lined their shelves, turning once exotic luxuries into daily necessities. If an item was not at the local emporium, it could be ordered through the mail and delivered at home. The growing stock of manufactured food, drink, and clothing lessened the need for a meat house, cider mill, and loom house in the farmyard. The lines of transportation, which facilitated the distribution of household goods and necessities across the country, also made it possible for bulky building materials such as bricks, stonework, slate shingles, and other items produced in distant yards, quarries, and factories to appear with growing regularity on new building sites in cities and the countryside. The use of cast iron, pressed metal ornament, sheet metal roofing, cooking stoves, plate glass, and machine-pressed brick manufactured in Richmond and Baltimore or in more distant factories in northern and midwestern cities increased with the spread of rail lines.

Such far-reaching innovations in the manufacture of materials and the organization of the building trades are often easily overlooked in the field. Consider the construction of

two dwellings in Southside Virginia—Snow Hill, built in Surry County in 1836, and the Stevenson House, erected in Southampton County around 1886. The home of the Booth family, Snow Hill was the center of a 500-acre plantation, with many outbuildings flanking it. These included a detached kitchen and other service structures—a smokehouse sat just behind the dwelling house, with slave quarters located a few hundred yards away on the edge of fields of tobacco and corn (Figs. 17.2, 17.3). Charles Stevenson built his farmhouse in the midst of a rural tract of cotton and peanut fields a half dozen miles west of Ivor, a small depot established in 1858 on the Norfolk and Western Railroad (Figs. 17.4, 17.5).[3] In the early twentieth century, his descendants added a complement of agricultural and service buildings to the home lot.

These two houses bear a strong resemblance to one another in terms of their massing, symmetry, decorative details, and plan. Both are two-story, single-pile, frame structures built as the principal dwellings on farms. They sit on brick foundations and have symmetrically arranged windows and a central doorway on the ground floor. Wood weatherboards and shingles originally covered the exterior walls and gable roofs. Both had porches on their front facades. Exterior, gable-end brick chimneys vented the fires that warmed the main rooms on the first and second floors. The front door of each house opened into a center passage, which gave access to the rooms on either side as well as to a wooden staircase that rose to the second-floor bedrooms. The interiors were finished with wide pine floorboards, wood trim around the apertures, decorative wooden mantels, and plaster walls.

In the half century separating their construction, much had happened to transform domestic life in Virginia, especially on farmsteads, where most people still lived. If less iso-

(top) Fig. 17.2. Snow Hill, 1836, Surry County, Virginia.

(bottom) Fig. 17.3. Plan, Snow Hill, Surry County, Virginia.

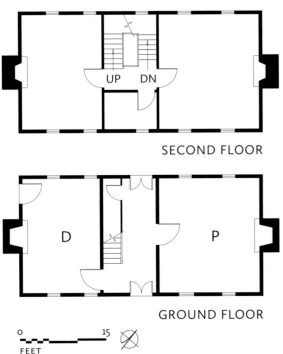

SECOND FLOOR

GROUND FLOOR

0   15
FEET

dining room. By the end of the nineteenth century, food was increasingly prepared in an adjacent kitchen and cooked on a cast-iron stove rather than in a separate building over an open fire. The new technology, coupled with the abolition of slavery, accelerated the movement of the kitchen into the main body of the house, often to a rear wing. Except for the attached one-story kitchen and dining room wing, which was added about a dozen years after the main house, the plan and function of Charles Stevenson's farmhouse replicates the pattern at Snow Hill. Their resemblance suggests a strong continuity in domestic architecture, one that historian Fernand Braudel characterized as "an enduring thing," which "bears perpetual witness to the slowness of civilizations, of cultures bent on preserving, maintaining and repeating."[4]

The form and plan of Snow Hill and the Stevenson House do indeed testify to the conservative nature of house building in the Chesapeake region. Prominent planters constructed similar dwellings as early as the second quarter of the eighteenth century on Tidewater plantations such as Genesar in Worcester County, Maryland, and Tuckahoe in Goochland County, Virginia. They could also be found as far north as the Delaware Valley, and they derived from late seventeenth-century English prototypes. By the beginning of the nineteenth century, the house type appeared on the farms of prosperous planters and in cities and towns as residences of merchants and professionals. As the century progressed, the form spread in popularity as it descended the social scale.

lated, rural life still revolved around the farmhouse, which had changed little in its form and use. Antebellum planters set aside one of the ground-floor rooms as a parlor to entertain their guests. The larger and more decorative east room at Snow Hill served as the Booth family's parlor. At mealtimes, the family gathered around a dining table in the smaller room opposite the parlor. Slaves brought food prepared in the detached kitchen through the back door of the passage into the

(top) Fig. 17.4. Charles Stevenson House, c. 1886, Southampton County, Virginia.

(bottom) Fig. 17.5. Plan, Charles Stevenson House, Southampton County, Virginia.

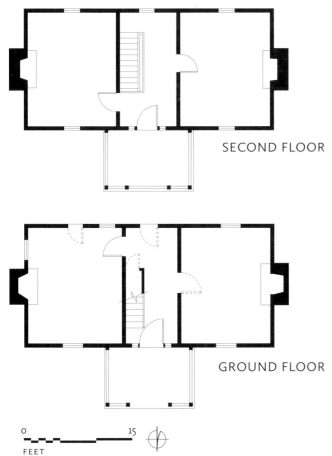

SECOND FLOOR

GROUND FLOOR

0   15

FEET

The Stevenson House is representative of this trend. It is a modestly finished dwelling of cramped proportions at the center of a family-run farm. It measures 34½ feet in length and is 16½ feet deep, compared to Snow Hill, which is 42 by 20 feet, with larger and more elaborately trimmed rooms and an impressive staircase in a broad passage.

The two-story, single-pile house continued to be a popular choice among farmers in many parts of the Chesapeake, but it also accommodated laboring families in mill villages and in new suburban developments in the decades following the Civil War. Though long associated with the Chesapeake, the house type spread westward with settlement, across the mountains into the uplands of Kentucky and Tennessee and the Northwest territories. So ubiquitous were such farmhouses in the Midwest in the early twentieth century that cultural geographer Fred Kniffen christened the form the "I" house in recognition of its omnipresence in Indiana, Illinois, and Iowa.[5] By the time Charles Stevenson erected his farmhouse, the Chesapeake pedigree was no longer recognizable, as the form had migrated into a building type that had become popular across a broad stretch of the country.

If the form of the Stevenson House had lost its regional distinctiveness, the manner in which the materials were fabricated and assembled on the building site was completely severed from the traditional practices used at Snow Hill. There was little that was timeless in the construction of the Stevenson House. The framing members, bricks, woodwork, and other materials that were used to build the Southampton County house were manufactured by semiskilled machine operators in factories and assembled by a crew of workmen on site in a manner that saved time and reduced the dependence on skilled labor.[6] The application of steam power to sawing and the improvement in sawmill technology in the last quarter of the century, especially the increase in the size of the carriage to accommodate larger and longer timbers and more efficient circular saws, dramatically reduced the cost of dimensional lumber for framing, flooring, and sheathing. Rather than selecting trees in a nearby forest to fell and prepare for the principal framing members, as the carpenters did at Snow Hill in 1836, the builder of the Stevenson House purchased pre-sawn lumber from a supply on hand at the local sawmill in Ivor, which by the early 1890s was shipping several million feet of local lumber to regional and national destinations, or, perhaps, from a building supply company located along the Norfolk and Western line, in Petersburg 36 miles to the west or in Norfolk 45 miles to the east.[7] Prefabricated materials from one of these regional suppliers would have been shipped to Ivor and then carried in wagons from the depot to the building site.

No longer did carpenters carefully lay out framing members on the ground, measure lengths and angles, and fashion joints to fit the specific pieces together like a jigsaw puzzle in a highly structured sequential order. Instead, from their stock of pre-cut dimensioned lumber, they sawed studs, joists, rafters, plates, and sills to their appropriate lengths and spiked them together with machine-made nails in a system that was known as balloon framing. Covering the frame with weatherboards and roof sheathing provided structural rigidity to this simplified framing, one that in many ways was the natural extension of efforts to reduce the laborious task of complicated joinery that Chesapeake craftsmen had initiated in the seventeenth century with the riven clapboard carpentry of the "Virginia house." Balloon framing eliminated the last elements of the old English tradition of securing differently sized principal members with mortise-and-tenon joints. Fastening pieces of a frame together with nails accelerated the pace of construction and abolished the need to employ highly skilled craftsmen. Raised piece by piece instead of in entire wall sections or roof trusses, the system reduced not only the level of skilled craftsmanship required but also the amount of labor. An advocate of this manner of building claimed that a man and boy could erect a balloon frame, whereas the assembly and raising of a heavy timber frame "required the combined force of a village."[8]

After the carpenters had erected the frame of the Stevenson House and enclosed it with weatherboards and shingles, they unloaded from their wagons and installed the windows, doors, mantels, newels, balusters, and other pre-assembled pieces that had been manufactured in one of the regional factories connected by the Norfolk and Western line. By the late nineteenth century, efficient, labor-saving machinery set up in mechanized millwork shops known as sash and blind factories had appeared in growing towns such as Petersburg, Suffolk, and Norfolk and even in smaller places along railway lines. These shops produced fully assembled building components, as well as thousands of feet of stock moldings and machine-planed floorboards and weatherboards.

Mechanization reduced the cost of production. In the old tradition, slaves probably hand sawed the heart pine floorboards and paneling that went into Snow Hill. Carpenters smoothed the face of the pit-sawn boards with a series of hand planes, used special molding planes to create straight sides with tongue-and-groove joints, and adzed off excessive thicknesses on their undersides where they sat across a joist. By 1870, this laborious process had been superseded, so that, as one trade journal observed, the "lumber can be planed and the edges matched so cheaply by machinery that it is far more economical to have all such work done at the planing mill than to have boards planed by hand."[9] In the 1880s, the S. A. Wood Machine Company of New York, Boston, and Chicago manufactured a fast-feed flooring machine that was capable of planing floorboards on both sides, as well as adding tongue-and-groove joints, at the rate of 100 feet per minute.[10] In building Snow Hill in 1836, two carpenters would have labored an entire day to produce a few hundred linear feet of molding. Over a matter of days, they would have shaped and installed more stylish quirked Greek Revival moldings in the passage and front parlor to reinforce the superiority of these spaces over the dining room and bedchambers, which were fabricated with a different set of molding planes, whose blades formed older, Roman-style moldings. In contrast, an unskilled laborer operating a power-driven machine could make several thousand feet of complex molding in far less time in the postwar era.[11]

Ready-made doors, windows, mantels, flooring, moldings—even entire houses—could be easily purchased at factories, at such a low cost that one farm journal advised its readers in 1887 that it was "not profitable to make them at the bench."[12] The use of machines that sawed, planed, turned, mortised, and tenoned wood in sash and blind factories became so pervasive by the last decades of the century that hand joinery rapidly disappeared. By the end of the nineteenth century, it was exceedingly rare to find any craftsman still turning balusters, running moldings, or making doors and windows with hand tools for a particular job. The eclipse of handmade, site-specific materials meant that Maryland and Virginia and indeed the entire nation were saturated with standardized building components. Thus the idiosyncratic mantel designs or stair brackets of an individual joiner, which could be found in so many early Chesapeake buildings, disappeared beneath the homogeneous shapes churned out in the mill.

The transformation of the manufacture of building materials began in the late 1840s and 1850s in large cities such as Baltimore and Richmond, where old joinery shops added woodworking machines to meet the growing demand for their products. Miles Ambler, a builder in Richmond, enlarged and mechanized his shop in the late 1850s to meet "the rapidly increasing demands for work in my line."[13] Despite the appearance of industrial machine shops such as Poole and Hunt in Baltimore and iron works in Richmond and an increasing reliance on steam machinery to power ships and railroads, grind agricultural produce, and turn engines in specialized industries, Maryland and Virginia lagged far behind northern states in the mechanization of the building trades before the Civil War. The 1860 census listed only nine sash and blind factories in Virginia, with products valued at $84,700. By contrast, there were 108 factories in Pennsylvania, while in New York the value of building materials produced in 212 mechanized shops far exceeded $1.5 million.[14]

More than a quarter of a century elapsed before the mass production of building components became commonplace throughout Virginia and Maryland. The application of steam machinery to the manufacture of building materials depended less on the development of new technology than on rail access to large markets and a shift in labor practices. Before the Civil War, southern capital was deeply wedded to unfree labor. Builders and suppliers of materials chose to use slaves to do much of the laborious handwork rather than invest in steam-powered machinery. Slave sawyers hewed and pit-sawed most of the timber used in antebellum buildings, whereas in northern states mechanical sawing had all but eclipsed sawing by hand. The end of the Civil War forced southerners to develop new labor systems that incorporated machine technology where it proved more cost-effective. The absence of large towns in many parts of Virginia and Maryland before the war had also deterred the investment in costly machinery. Without a large market, carpenters' shops could handle the relatively low volume of demand. Industrial development was also closely tied to good rail facilities, and following the Civil War the repair and expansion of lines

opened up regions that had long been isolated. New towns such as Roanoke grew up from forests and green pastures, and older cities expanded as increasing numbers of former farm laborers began seeking their fortunes in cities.

The rising demand for new buildings in the decades following the Civil War strained the resources and capacities of the building trades in many parts of the Chesapeake. The advent of a region-wide railroad network conveniently connected the sources of raw materials in forests, clay pits, and quarries with processing mills and steam-powered factories—and the building materials processed in these establishments with a more accessible and expanding market. Access to a plentiful supply of coal shipped from mines in Appalachia and reliance on steam power alleviated the necessity to locate manufacturing establishments along water routes. New sash and blind factories, planing mills, and brickyards operated conveniently at rail junctions and in cities and towns. Improved transportation systems also severed the old dependence upon local building materials, opening the way for the wholesale introduction of new manufactured materials, such as pressed brick, cast iron, stained glass, and other components. The pace was relentless. Between 1870 and 1880, sash and blind manufacturers in Baltimore alone more than quadrupled the value of their building products, from $145,000 to over $660,000.[15]

As more and more parts of a building, such as the framing and finish elements, were manufactured at sash and blind factories and shipped to sites across town or across the country, regional building patterns were lost to the standardized shapes of the mill. The enticing cheapness and ease with which mill-produced materials could be obtained led many clients and local craftsmen to abandon traditional building practices such as log construction in favor of the improved comfort of an inexpensive frame house. By the end of the nineteenth century, the industrialized building process had transformed the entire structure of the building trades and penetrated all but the most remote areas of the Chesapeake.

Industrialized building also improved housing standards by reducing the cost of building materials, to a point that many more poor home owners could afford to fill unglazed apertures with window sash, replace fire-prone wooden chimneys with masonry ones fabricated with machine-made bricks, and cover dirt floors and chinked log walls with floorboards and matchstick sheathing. Bracketed eaves, jigsaw work on porches, symmetrical architrave moldings, board-and-batten sheathing, and other Italianate-style features, which had once been found on only the finest houses in the region in the 1850s, festooned countless suburban dwellings

Fig. 17.6. Eaves brackets, scrollwork, and jigsaw balusters, Charles Stevenson House, Southampton County, Virginia.

and farmhouses, such as the Stevenson House, in the decades after the Civil War, not only because they were fashionable, but also because they were exceedingly affordable. On an otherwise plain exterior, Charles Stevenson's two-story pedimented porch and cornice are embellished with pairs of turned brackets, and the second-story porch is enclosed by flat pierced balusters, cheap products of a woodworking factory (Fig. 17.6). Symmetrical moldings with ornamental corner blocks had been a part of Chesapeake building since the second decade of the nineteenth century but had decorated only the most public entertaining rooms of the best houses before the Civil War. Afterward, sash and blind factories reproduced symmetrical moldings by the millions of lineal feet. No longer turned by hand, carved corner blocks cost but a few pennies apiece and were installed in hundreds of modest houses in towns and the countryside. By their ubiquity, they lost their social cachet. "So great have been the advances" in the factory production of building materials, one postbellum writer observed, "that the humblest and cheapest dwelling erected in the larger cities" such as Baltimore "will compare favorably in interior finish with the most gorgeous edifices of former times."[16]

Although many traditional indicators of social significance disappeared with industrial building, new ones arose and others changed. Wealthy planters, merchants, and professionals were among the first to adopt new household technologies. Before the construction of municipal gas houses, water supplies, and sewage systems, they built individual gas plants and pump houses and installed vents, pipelines, fittings, cisterns, and drains so that they could have running water, indoor plumbing, gas lighting, and cooking and heating systems in their homes. Materials too distinguished the quality of houses, but in ways that were different from earlier generations. In the Chesapeake in the colonial and early national periods, brick-wall houses had been few and far between and set off those with social aspirations and economic wherewithal from their neighbors. By the late nineteenth century, the mechanization of the brickmaking process, along with the ease of transporting bricks in bulk, meant that the material was no longer the preserve of the rich man but was used to build mills and mill houses as well. The level of production by antebellum standards had become staggering. In 1873, brickyards in Baltimore, which had been recognized as leaders in the production of high quality face or pressed brick for several decades, manufactured more than 100 million bricks annually to meet the expanding housing and commercial market. By the end of the century, the number had more than doubled.[17]

To distinguish their homes, the wealthy installed imported Italian marble and other foreign stone mantels, hearths, lintels, sills, and steps, marquetry and parquet floors, mahogany newels, railings, and balusters, and cast plaster ceiling medallions and furnished their rooms with acres of upholstered and oversized furniture, great folds of drapery, and swaths of carpeting. Architectural woodwork, once so prominent, receded into the background in these supersaturated environments as new materials came onto the market, which reshaped traditional cultural associations. Foundries branched out to manufacture decorative architectural ironwork, including columns, finials, fences, gates, and steps, as well as traditional items such as pipes, ventilators, stoves, and grates, which became more prevalent in postbellum housing. Machines could also produce concrete blocks molded to imitate rusticated stone, columns, and capitals; pressed metal to match the intricate design once the preserve of the plasterer; cornices stamped out of sheet metal to emulate the wood and plaster of earlier styles as well as explore expressive new forms; and linoleum flooring to replicate the feel and patterns of painted floor cloths.[18] Although imitation finishes and materials—rusticated siding, stucco, graining, composition ornament, and Coade stone—had been around for a long time, the rapidity with which new materials replicated or replaced old ones and their widespread use in all kinds of buildings throughout the country in the last decades of the nineteenth century disrupted familiar status markers.

In the old system of building, the value of labor had a direct correlation with a finished product. Every extra carving or molding represented the added amount of handiwork necessary for its fabrication. As this relationship was severed by the mechanized production of building materials, new ways of distinguishing the significance of a building, space, or room emerged. Given the rapidity of change, many of those visual signals may have been confusing to contemporaries, who had to learn their implications within a national rather than a regional context. With the same machine-made moldings in every room in buildings such as the Stevenson House in Southampton County, decorative trim lost much of its significance as an indicator of the relative importance of a space. Materials and workmanship in the industrial age took on new meanings. Historians who study late nineteenth- and twentieth-century buildings address a different set of cultural signifiers in ways that require new hypotheses and other research methods than the careful field analysis that marks the intellectual basis for the essays in this book.

* dendrochronological date
^ inscribed date
† not extant

DISTRICT OF COLUMBIA
Bowie-Sevier House, 1810s
The Octagon, 1799–1802
Tudor Place, c. 1795, completed 1815–16
The White House, 1792–1800

MARYLAND

Annapolis
Adams-Kilty House, c. 1773–86
Bordley-Randall House, c. 1760
James Brice House, 1767–73
Judge John Brice House, 1738–39*
John Brice III House, c. 1766–75
Charles Carroll, Barrister, House,
    c. 1724–27, enlarged c. 1740
Charles Carroll of Annapolis, House,
    1749–51*
Chase-Lloyd House, 1769–74
Hammond-Harwood House, 1774
Jennings-Eden House, c. 1735–50,
    enlarged 1770s
Ogle Hall, 1739–42, enlarged 1775–76
Paca House, 1763–65
Poe House, c. 1720, remodeled c. 1762
John Ridout House, 1764–65
Ridout Row, 1773–74
Sands House, c. 1725–40
Upton Scott House, 1762–63
Upton Scott House, Stable, 1760s
State House, 1772–79, dome 1785–88
Treasury Building, 1735–37

Anne Arundel County
Brandy, 1720s
Burrages End, Tobacco House, 1780s
Cedar Park, 1702*, remodeled c. 1745
Chaney Farm, Corn House, c. 1800–20
Coe Farm, Tobacco House, Tracy's
    Landing, 1804*
Holly Hill, 1699*, enlarged 1713*,
    enlarged c. 1723
Larkin's Hills, c. 1753
Portland Manor, 1755*
Sudley, c. 1740

Tulip Hill, 1755–56
Whitehall, 1764–65

Baltimore
Homewood, 1801–6
Mount Clare, 1757–60, portico 1768
Riddell House, 1810–11†

Baltimore County
Hampton, 1783–90
Hampton, Farmhouse, 1747*, enlarged
    1754*, enlarged 1773*
Hayfields, Barn, c. 1800–20

Calvert County
Cedar Hill, c. 1730
Wilson Farm, Tobacco Barn, 1820*

Cecil County
Rose Hill, mid-1790s, 1837
St. Mary Anne Church, 1742–43

Charles County
Habre de Venture, Corn House, 1830s
Trinity Church, 1752–56

Frederick County
Bowman House, late 18th century,
    enlarged 1800*

Kent County
Carvill Hall, c.1695–1709
Caulk's Field, 1743^
Providence Plantation, 1781^
The Reward, after 1742
Ringgold House, Chestertown,
    after 1743, enlarged 1771
Shepherd's Delight, Granary, c. 1820
Stanley's Hope, 1743^
Tulley's Fancy, c. 1830

Prince George's County
Belleview, Corn House, c. 1830
Bloomingdale, 1792^
Cannon Farm, Granary and Corn Crib,
    c. 1825–50
The Cottage, Tobacco House, early
    20th century
William Porter House, 1760s

Riversdale, 1801–07
St. John's Church, Broad Creek, 1767–68
St. Paul's Church, Baden, 1733–35

Queen Anne's County
Cloverfields, c. 1730, enlarged 1760s
St. Luke's Church, Church Hill, 1729–31

St. Mary's City
Leonard Calvert's Country House,
    c. 1635, enlarged by 1688†
Philip Calvert House, 1679†
St. John's, 1638, remodeled 1678†
State House, 1676, repaired 1688†
    (reconstructed)

St. Mary's County
Bayside Farm, 1790s–1815†
Bond-Simms Farm, Tobacco Barn, 1837,*
    enlarged c. 1840
Brome Farm, Granary, 1758*†
Brome-Howard Farm, Barn, 1785*
Dixon's Purchase, 1858*
Kingston Manor, 1760s–1780s
Long Lane Farm, c. 1750
Abraham Medley House, c. 1840
Ocean Hall, c. 1730
Resurrection Manor, c. 1725–50, enlarged
    1780–90†
St. Andrew's Church, 1766–68
Sotterley, 1703–4*, enlarged 1715*,
    enlarged 1732*, enlarged 1762–63*,
    enlarged 1768–70*
Sotterley, Slave House, 1830s

Somerset County
Beauchamp, c. 1710–30
Maddox Farm, Corn Houses, 1830s,
    1870s
Makepeace, c. 1725–50
Powell-Benston House (Tilghman
    House), c. 1730†
Williams Green, after 1731*

Talbot County
Clay's Hope, Barn, c. 1800
Myrtle Grove, c. 1750, enlarged 1791
Third Haven Meetinghouse, 1682–84,
    remodeled 1797–98

Wickersham, 1750
Wye House, 1786–87
Wye Town Farm, Corn House,
    c. 1800–1820

Wicomico County
Pemberton Hall, 1741^

Worcester County
Burley Manor, 1835
Burley Manor, Granary and Stable,
    1830s
Fassitt House, c. 1730
Genesar, c. 1732
Whaley Farm, Granary, c. 1800–20

VIRGINIA

Accomack County
Callander Croft House, 1852*
Timothy Hill House, c. 1815
Ker Place, 1799–1803
Mason House, 1729–30*
Wharton Place, 1808–09*

Albemarle County
Monticello, 1770–85, enlarged
    1796–1809
Solitude, last quarter of 18th century

Alexandria
Carlyle House, 1753
Fawcett House, 1772, enlarged 1784, 1797
Gadsby's Tavern, 1782–85, enlarged
    1791–92*

Amelia County
Hillsman House, c. 1780–1810, c. 1810–15
Wigwam, late 18th century, enlarged
    c. 1815

Bedford County
Poplar Forest, 1806–23, partially burned
    1845 (restored)

Caroline County
Bowling Green, 1738–43*, enlarged
    1790–91*
Brockenbrough House, Port Royal, 1778*
The Mount, c. 1696†
Powers-Holloway House, Port Royal,
    c. 1800
Town Field, Port Royal, 1790s, enlarged
    c. 1815

Charles City County
Walter Aston site, c. 1630†
Belle Air, c. 1725–40
Berkeley, 1726^
Curle's Neck, c. 1650†
Shirley, 1738*, remodeled 1772
Tomahund, c. 1750–80, enlarged
    c. 1841–47
Westover, 1750–51*

Charlotte County
Morotock, Slave Quarters, 1856

Chesterfield County
Eppington, 1768–1802
Hedgelawn, c. 1725–40

Culpeper County
Glebe House, St. Mark's Parish, 1772†
Salubria, 1755–57*, remodeled 1794

Dinwiddie County
Seward House, c. 1815†
Wales, 1750s, enlarged 1780s
Wales, Slave Quarters, c. 1855–60

Essex County
Belle Farm, c. 1770–85
Blandfield, 1769–72, altered 1801–5,
    altered 1847–48
Brooke's Bank, 1751^
Cherry Walk, c. 1795
Elmwood, c. 1774
Springfield, c. 1839–40†

Fairfax County
Belvoir, 1736–41†
Gunston Hall, 1755–59
Mount Vernon, 1734*, enlarged
    1758–59*, enlarged 1775–76*,
    remodeled 1787
Pohick Church, 1769–74

Fluvanna County
Upper Bremo, 1820

Fredericksburg
Kenmore, 1772*–1776

Gloucester County
Abingdon Church, 1751–55^
Belle Isle, c. 1775–1800 (moved)
Fairfield, 1694, enlarged c. 1704–20†
Kempsville, mid-18th century

Rosewell, 1726–37 (ruins)
Ware Church, 1719*

Goochland County
Dover, Slave Quarters, 1850s
Howard's Neck, Slave Quarters, after
    1825, 1850s
Tuckahoe, 1733,* enlarged 1750s

Halifax County
Berry Hill, 1842–44

Hampton
Elizabeth City Parish Church (St. John's),
    1728

Hanover County
Church Quarter, c. 1850
Gould Hill, Flankers, c. 1760
Pine Slash, c. 1760
Rural Plains, 1723–25*

Henrico County
Malvern Hill, c. 1700–25†
Wilton, 1750–53^ (moved to Richmond)

Isle of Wight County
Clerk's Office, Smithfield, 1799
Holeman Kitchen, 1820s
Jordan House, 1813*†
Newport Parish Church (St. Luke's),
    c. 1682 (after 1677*)
Pruden Farm, Corncrib, 1820s
Pruden Farm, Slave Quarters, 1820s
Pruden House, 1821–22
Strawberry Plain, Slave Quarters, 1850s
White Farm, Corn House, c. 1810
Whitley-Nelms Farm, Kitchen, c. 1820
Wolf Trap, 1820s†

James City County
Atkinson House, c. 1680–1710†
Bray Plantation, Slave Quarter, Kingsmill
    c. 1700–50†
Carter's Grove, c. 1751–55
Carter's Grove, Slave Quarter, c. 1750–
    75† (reconstructed)
Green Spring, 1643–45, enlarged by 1674,
    rebuilt before 1755†
Littletown (Pettus), Kingsmill, c. 1640†
Martin's Hundred, Wolstenholme
    Town and associated sites, 1620–22,
    c. 1625–45†; John Boyse House, Site
    H, Structure A, c. 1620–22†; Site A,

Structure C, 1625†; Site C, Company Compound, c. 1620†

Page House, Middle Plantation, 1662^†

Pettus Manor House, c. 1641†

Pettus, Utopia Quarter, overall 1675–1775; P.I: house, 1675–91†, P.II: 1700–25†, P.III: including barn converted to barracks, c. 1730–50†, P.IV: 3 log houses, 1751–75†

Utopia, Kingsmill, c. 1660†

Rich Neck, Middle Plantation, 1642, remodeled c. 1665†

Riverside, 1670s†

Jamestown

Church, 1640s, rebuilt after 1676†, (reconstructed 1907), tower 1690s

Harvey House, Structure 112, 1620s, remodeled before 1656, rebuilt c. 1665–76†

Kemp House, Structure 44, 1638–39†

Pit houses, 1607†

Sherwood House, Structure 138/53, 1653–58, enlarged 1673–76, rebuilt by 1682†

Structure 115, 1663, rebuilt c. 1681†

Structure 144, 1662–63, enlarged, partially rebuilt after 1676†

Structure 160, c. 1607–08†

Structure 165, c. 1608†

Structure 183, c. 1607–8†

King and Queen County

Bewdley, 1760s, completed after 1767

Farmer's Mount, c. 1810

Hillsborough, mid–18th century

Marlborough, 1805^

King George County

Marmion, 1750s

Nanzatico, 1801

King William County

Elsing Green, c. 1758

King William Courthouse, Stable, c. 1830†

Sweet Hall, c.1725–40

Lancaster County

Belle Isle, 1767*, wings, 1802*

Christ Church, c.1732*–35

Corotoman, 1726–27, burned 1729†

Morattico, Slave Quarters and agricultural buildings, 1720s–1750s†

Lynchburg

Point of Honor, c. 1815

Mecklenburg County

Prestwould, 1794–95, redecorated 1831

Prestwould, Slave House, 1780s, enlarged c. 1840

Prestwould, Loom House, c. 1835–40

Middlesex County

Christ Church, 1712–14

Hewick, mid-18th century

Rosegill, 1650s†, rebuilt c. 1715–20

Wilton, 1763^

Nelson County

Soldier's Joy, 1783–85, enlarged 1806

New Kent County

Criss Cross, c. 1725

Roper-Carden House, c. 1800

St. Peter's Church, 1701–03

Springdale, 1810s

Wilson Kitchen, c. 1850

Newport News

Matthew Jones House, c. 1720, enlarged 1729–30*

Mathews Manor, late 1630s, enlarged 1640s, c. 1650†

Mathews Manor, Earthfast House and Service Unit, c. 1650†

Norfolk

Moses Myers House, c. 1797, enlarged by 1818

Pennock House, 1796†

Elizabeth River Parish Church (St. Paul's), 1739^

Northampton County

Arlington, c. 1674–75†

Eyre Hall, 1759*, Wing, 1807*

Glebe House, Hungars Parish, c.1745

Pear Valley, 1740*

Sturgis House, c. 1725–50

Orange County

Frascati, 1822–23

Montpelier, 1762–63*, enlarged 1797–98, enlarged 1809–11

Petersburg

8 Old Street, 1815–16

John Baird House, 1784–85*

Battersea, 1767*

Bragg House, c. 1823

Devereux Jarratt Manly House, 1791*

Mitchell Store, 1816

Strawberry Hill, c. 1795, enlarged 1818

218 High Street, 1827

Pittsylvania County

Hunt House, c. 1820

Little Cherrystone, c. 1820

Prince Edward County

R. R. Moton House, 1745–46*, altered c. 1820–40, c. 1890

Prince George County

Brandon, Wings, c. 1750, Center Block after 1795

Cibula, Slave Quarters, c. 1825†

Abraham Peirsey House, Flowerdew, c. 1626†

Structure 4, Jordan's Point, mid-1620s†

Yeardley House, Flowerdew, c. 1619†

Upper Brandon, c. 1825

Rappahannock County

Ben Venue, Slave Houses, 1840s

Richmond

Capitol, 1785–92

Hancock House, 1808–09

St. John's Church, 1744*

Wickham House, 1811–12

Wilton (formerly Henrico County), 1750–53^

Richmond County

Courthouse, 1749–50

Grove Mount, 1787*

Indian Banks, 1738*

Linden Farm, 1760–61*, enlarged 1778*, enlarged 1803*

Mount Airy, 1760–64, partially burned 1844 and rebuilt

Mount Airy, Stable, 1760s

Sabine Hall, 1738*

Southampton County

Bryant-Deloatche House, c. 1810

Council Kitchen, c. 1800–10

Hill Farm, Kitchen, c. 1810†

Myrick House, c. 1820

Porter House, c. 1820†

Stevenson House, c. 1886

Stafford County
Aquia Church, 1751–57^
Eagle's Nest, 1680s†
Ferry Farm, c. 1725–40†
Marlborough, c. 1747–49†

Suffolk (Nansemond County)
Woodward-Jones House, 1716^†

Surry County
Bacon's Castle 1665*, remodeled
    before 1755, enlarged 1852–54
Bacon's Castle, Slave Quarters, 1829*,
    enlarged 1849*
Burrows House, c. 1770
Four Mile Tree, 1743–45*, remodeled
    1796, 1835–36
Four Mile Tree, Slave Quarters,
    1838†
James House, 1810s
Pleasant Point, 1765*
Smith's Fort, 1763*
Snow Hill, 1836
Walnut Valley, Small House, 1815*

Virginia Beach
Keeling House, 1734–35*
Lynnhaven House, 1724–25*
Pleasant Hall, 1779^
Thoroughgood House, c. 1720
    (after 1716*)
Weblin House, c. 1725–40

Westmoreland County
Clifts, c. 1670–85, enlarged c. 1705†
Hallowes, 1660s†
Nomini Hall, mid-18th century,
    altered early 1770s†
Rochester House, 1745*
Stratford, 1737–38*, remodeled c. 1795

Wilton 1742*, altered 1793*
Yeocomico Church 1706^, enlarged
    1730s

Williamsburg
Ayscough House, before 1768
Bassett Hall, 1753–66, enlarged
John Blair House, 1720–23*, enlarged
    1737*
The Brafferton, College of William and
    Mary, 1723^
John Brush House (see Thomas Everard
    House)
Bruton Parish Church 1713–15*, enlarged
    1752, tower 1769–71
Capitol, 1701–5, rebuilt 1752–53†
    (reconstructed)
Robert Carter House, c. 1747, remodeled
    c. 1760
Charlton's Coffeehouse (see Walthoe's
    Storehouse)
Chiswell-Bucktrout House, c. 1750
Coke-Garrett House, by 1762, enlarged
    1836–37
College of William and Mary, 1695–97,
    burned 1705, repaired 1709–16
Courthouse, 1771
John Crump House (Mr. Reed's store),
    c. 1750–75† (reconstructed)
Custis House, c. 1715–17†
Thomas Everard House (Brush House),
    1718–20*
James Geddy House, 1761–62*
Governor's Palace, 1706–22, enlarged
    1752–53† (reconstructed)
Harwood House, c. 1750–70†
Grissell Hay House, c. 1750
Ludwell-Paradise House, 1752–53*
Marot's Ordinary, c. 1705†
Nicholson Store, c. 1745–60

Nelson-Galt House (earlier Robertson
    House), 1695*, remodeled before 1718,
    remodeled 1750s
Orrell House, c. 1770
Palmer House, c. 1755
William Pasteur House (Finnie House),
    c. 1769–70
Benjamin Powell House, c. 1763
Powell-Hallam House, c. 1753
President's House, College of William and
    Mary, 1732–33
Public Hospital, 1773† (reconstructed)
Peyton Randolph House (earlier
    Robertson Tenement), 1715–18*,
    enlarged 1754–55*
George Reid House, c. 1790
Tayloe House, c. 1752–59
Timson House, 1715–16*, enlarged c. 1752^
Travis House, c. 1765, enlarged c. 1770–90,
    enlarged 1794*
St. George Tucker House, 1788–92
    (earlier Levingston House 1718*)
Waller House, c. 1749, enlarged 1750s
    or 1760s, enlarged by 1782
Walthoe's Storehouse, 1749–50*†
    (later Charlton's Coffeehouse),
    (reconstructed)
Wetherburn's Tavern, 1730s, enlarged
    c. 1752
George Wythe House, c. 1752–54

York County
Bennett House, c. 1640–50†
Dudley Digges House, Yorktown, c. 1744
Moore House, Yorktown, mid-18th
    century
Thomas Nelson House, Yorktown,
    1729–30*
Secretary Thomas Nelson House,
    Yorktown, 1765†

Notes

CHAPTER 2

1. An early version of this essay was presented as a keynote address to the annual meeting of the Vernacular Architecture Forum in Williamsburg, Virginia, in May 2002. Though unintended at the time, it opened what has become an ongoing debate in that lively organization about the value of field recording to the future of vernacular building studies. See Dell Upton, "The VAF at 25: What Now?" *Perspectives in Vernacular Architecture* 13 (2006/2007): 7–13; and running commentary in ensuing numbers of the *Vernacular Architecture Newsletter*, by Tania Martin (104), Warren Hofstra (108), Thomas Carter (109), and others.

2. Dell Upton, *Architecture in the United States, Oxford History of Art* (New York: Oxford University Press, 1998), especially chap. 2, "Community"; J. Douglas Porteous and Sandra E. Smith, *Domicide: The Global Destruction of Home* (Montreal: McGill-Queen's University Press, 2001); Edward Chappell, "Williamsburg Architecture as Social Space," *Fresh Advices*, supplement to *Colonial Williamsburg Interpreter* (November 1981): i–ii, vi. Architectural research at Colonial Williamsburg thus conforms and contributes to the foundation's overall educational philosophy, as explained in Cary Carson, ed., *Becoming Americans: Our Struggle to Be Both Free and Equal* (Williamsburg: Colonial Williamsburg Foundation, 1998).

3. See also Travis C. McDonald, "The Fundamental Practice of Fieldwork at Colonial Williamsburg," *Perspectives in Vernacular Architecture* 13 (2006/2007): 36–53.

4. Carl R. Lounsbury, "Beaux-Arts Ideals and Colonial Reality: The Reconstruction of Williamsburg's Capitol, 1928–1934," *Journal of the Society of Architectural Historians* 49 (December 1990): 373–89.

5. Nancy Halverson Schless, "Dutch Influence on the Governor's Palace, Williamsburg," *Journal of the Society of Architectural Historians* 28 (December 1969): 254–70; Barbara Carson, *The Governor's Palace: The Williamsburg Residence of Virginia's Royal Governor* (Williamsburg: Colonial Williamsburg Foundation, 1987); Graham Hood, *The Governor's Palace in Williamsburg: A Cultural Study* (Williamsburg: Colonial Williamsburg Foundation, 1991).

6. See William Seale, "Paul Buchanan and Architectural History," in *Paul Buchanan: Stratford Hall and Other Architectural Studies* (Stratford, Va.: Robert E. Lee Memorial Association, 1998): 1–53.

7. Carl R. Lounsbury, "Order in the Court: Recommendations for the Restoration of the James City County/Williamsburg Courthouse," unpublished report, Colonial Williamsburg Foundation, 1985; David Thomas Konig, "The Williamsburg Courthouse: Research Report and Interpretive Guide," unpublished report, Colonial Williamsburg Foundation, 1987; Carl R.

Lounsbury, *The Courthouses of Early Virginia: An Architectural History* (Charlottesville: University of Virginia Press, 2005).

8. Students of British buildings have asked similar questions: Cary Carson, "Segregation in Vernacular Buildings," *Vernacular Architecture* 7 (1976): 24–29; Mark Girouard, *Life in the English Country House* (New Haven: Yale University Press, 1978); Nathaniel W. Alcock, "Physical Space and Social Space: The Interpretation of Vernacular Architecture," in *Meaningful Architecture: Social Interpretations of Buildings*, ed. Martin Locock (Aldershot, England: Avebury, 1994): 207–30.

9. Jack P. Greene, ed., *The Diary of Colonel Landon Carter of Sabine Hall, 1752–1778*, 2 vols. (Charlottesville: University Press of Virginia, 1965), 2:495–96.

10. Fraser D. Neiman, "The Lost World of Monticello: An Evolutionary Perspective," *Journal of Anthropological Research* 64 (Summer 2008): 161–93, especially 174–80 for subfloor pits; Patricia M. Samford, *Subfloor Pits and the Archaeology of Slavery in Colonial Virginia* (Tuscaloosa: University of Alabama Press, 2007).

11. Lorena S. Walsh, *Motives of Honor, Pleasure, and Profit: Plantation Management in the Colonial Chesapeake, 1607–1763* (Chapel Hill: University of North Carolina Press, 2010), 381.

12. Susan Kern shows how social controls were built into man-made landscapes, in "The Material World of the Jeffersons at Shadwell," *William and Mary Quarterly*, 3d ser., 62 (April 2005): 213–42.

13. In antebellum Virginia, for example, by abolitionist sentiments and women's claims to domesticity, both ingeniously demonstrated in Clifton Ellis, "The Mansion House at Berry Hill Plantation: Architecture and the Changing Nature of Slavery in Antebellum Virginia," *Perspectives in Vernacular Architecture* 13 (2006): 22–48.

14. Reprinted in Stephenson B. Andrews, ed., *Bacon's Castle* (Richmond: Association for the Preservation of Virginia Antiquities, 1984), 84–92.

15. Cary Carson, "The Consumer Revolution in Colonial British America: Why Demand?" in *Of Consuming Interests: The Styles of Life in the Eighteenth Century*, ed. Cary Carson, Ronald Hoffman, and Peter J. Albert (Charlottesville: University Press of Virginia, 1994), 616–18.

16. George McDaniel, *Hearth and Home: Preserving a People's Culture* (Philadelphia: Temple University Press, 1982), 149–86; see also Michael Ann Williams, "The Little 'Big House': The Use and Meaning of the Single-Pen Dwelling," in *Perspectives in Vernacular Architecture, II*, ed. Camille Wells (Columbia: University of Missouri Press, 1986), 133–35.

17. Lounsbury, *Courthouses of Early Virginia*, 140–65; William Waller Hening, ed., *Statutes at Large; Being a Collection of All the*

Laws of Virginia, 13 vols. (Richmond, 1809–23; reprint, Charlottesville: University Press of Virginia, 1969), 1:302.

18. *Moreau de St. Méry's American Journey*, trans. and ed. Kenneth Roberts and Anna Roberts (New York: Doubleday, 1947), 65. Moreau de St. Méry made the observation on a visit to Portsmouth in May 1794.

19. Orlando Ridout V, *Building the Octagon* (Washington, D.C.: American Institute of Architects Press, 1989), 107–22; Edward Chappell, "Looking at Buildings," *Fresh Advices*, supplement to *Colonial Williamsburg Interpreter* 15 (November 1984): i–vi.

20. A singular exception is economic historian Hans-Joachim Voth's *Time and Work in England, 1750–1830* (New York: Oxford University Press, 2000). Modern sociologists and ethnologists have their own reasons to study time use, as explained in F. Thomas Juster and Frank Stafford, eds., *Time, Goods, and Well-Being* (Ann Arbor: University of Michigan Press, 1985).

21. Pat Gibbs, "Daily Schedule for a Cook in a Gentry Household," *Colonial Williamsburg Interpreter* 7 (May 1986): 1, 5–6; "Daily Schedule for a Young Gentry Woman," *Colonial Williamsburg Interpreter* 15 (November 1984): 1–4; "Daily Schedule for an Urban Gentry Housewife," *Fresh Advices* 2 (November 1981): iii–vi.

22. Voth, *Time and Work in England*, 106–18.

23. Paul Groth and Todd W. Bressi, eds., *Understanding Ordinary Landscapes* (New Haven: Yale University Press, 1997); Dell Upton, "Black and White Landscapes in Eighteenth-Century Virginia," *Places* 2 (1984): 59–72.

24. Margaret Wood, *The English Medieval House* (London: Phoenix House, 1965); Eric Mercer, *English Vernacular Houses* (London: HMSO, 1975); Matthew Johnson, *English Houses, 1300–1800: Vernacular Architecture, Social Life* (Harlow, England: Pearson Longman, 2010); Graham Connah, *African Civilizations: Precolonial Cities and States in Tropical Africa: An Archaeological Perspective* (Cambridge: Cambridge University Press, 1987), 97–120; Christopher R. DeCorse, *An Archaeology of Elmina: Africans and Europeans on the Gold Coast, 1400–1900* (Washington, D.C.: Smithsonian Books, 2001), 62–66, 71–102.

25. The published master plan by that title (see note 2 above) was the third in a series of curricular plans beginning in 1977. See Cary Carson, "Colonial Williamsburg and the Practice of Interpretive Planning in American History Museums," *Public Historian* 20 (Summer 1998): 11–51.

CHAPTER 3

1. William G. Perry, "Notes on the Architecture," in "The Restoration of Colonial Williamsburg in Virginia," *Architectural Record* 78 (December 1935); Walter Macomber to author, 1981.

2. Fiske Kimball, *Domestic Architecture of the American Colonies and of the Early Republic* (New York: Charles Scribner's, 1922); Thomas Tileston Waterman, *The Mansions of Virginia, 1706–1776* (Chapel Hill: University of North Carolina Press, 1945).

3. Henry Glassie, *Folk Housing in Middle Virginia: A Structural Analysis of Historic Artifacts* (Knoxville: University of Tennessee Press, 1975).

4. Dell Upton, "Vernacular Domestic Architecture in Eighteenth-Century Virginia," *Winterthur Portfolio* 17 (1982): 95–119; Dell Upton, "White and Black Landscapes in Eighteenth-Century Virginia," in *Cabin, Quarter, Plantation: Architecture and Landscapes of North American Slavery*, ed. Clifton Ellis and Rebecca Ginsburg (New Haven: Yale University Press, 2010): 121–39; Edmund S. Morgan, *American Slavery, American Freedom: The Ordeal of Colonial Virginia* (New York: W. W. Norton, 1975). Historian Rhys Isaac embraced and extended Upton's perspective of Virginia, in *The Transformation of Virginia, 1740–1790* (Chapel Hill: University of North Carolina Press 1982), a portrait of haves and have-nots that also drew on recent Chesapeake historiography in general. Cary Carson, Norman F. Barka, William M. Kelso, Garry Wheeler Stone, and Dell Upton, "Impermanent Architecture in the Southern American Colonies," *Winterthur Portfolio* 16 (1981): 135–78.

5. D. W. H. Miles and M. J. Worthington, "The Tree-Ring Dating of the R. R. Moton House, Pleasant Shade Kitchen-Quarter, Rice, Prince Edward County, Virginia," unpublished report, Oxford Dendrochronology Laboratory, December, 2006.

6. Mark R. Wenger was the first to recognize that Westover was built by William Byrd III, confirmed by a dendrochronology date for timbers cut in 1750. Camille Wells, "The Dream of Discovered Origins: Dendrochronology for the Colonial Virginia House," report to Jessie Ball du Pont Fund Grant, 2002. The date 1751 was found boldly written on a binding beam behind original paneling in the right rear second-floor chamber in 2007. Lucy Parke Byrd died in 1716, and her husband William Byrd II died in 1744.

7. Concerning a sawmill in truly low Tidewater, see Elizabeth City County Will and Order Book, 1684–99, 286, November 16, 1689.

8. Herman J. Heikkenen, "The Years of Construction for Eight Historical Structures in Colonial Williamsburg, Virginia, as Derived by the Key-Year Dendrochronology Technique," unpublished report, American Institute of Dendrochronology, April 1984.

9. Frank S. Welsh, "A Comparative Microscopical Paint and Color Analysis of Interior and Exterior to Determine the Nature and Color of the 1718 and 1756 Architectural Surface Coatings – Brush-Everard House, Williamsburg, Virginia," unpublished report for the Architectural Research Department, Colonial Williamsburg Foundation, July, 1991; Kirsten E. Travers, "Cross-Section Microscopy Report, Thomas Everard House – Interior," unpublished report for the Architectural Research Department, Colonial Williamsburg Foundation, March 8, 2012.

10. D. W. H. Miles and M. J. Worthington, "The Tree-Ring Dating of Staircase Timbers from the Brush-Everard House, Williamsburg, Virginia," unpublished report, Oxford Dendrochronology Laboratory, December, 2006.

11. Willie Graham, Carter L. Hudgins, Carl R. Lounsbury, Fraser D. Neiman, and James P. Whittenburg, "Adaptation and Innovation: Archaeological and Architectural Perspectives on the Seventeenth-Century Chesapeake," *William and Mary Quarterly*, 3d ser., 64 (July 2007): 451–522.

12. Frank S. Welsh, "Microscopic Analysis to Determine and Evaluate the Nature and Colors of the Original Surface Coatings, Blandfield Plantation," unpublished report at the Architectural Research Department, Colonial Williamsburg Foundation, April 6, 1984; Susan L. Buck, "Cross-Section Microscopy Report: Shirley Plantation, Charles City County, Virginia," unpublished report for the Architectural Research Department, Colonial Williamsburg Foundation, April 26, 2003.

13. Fredericksburg Will Book A, inventory available on George Washington Foundation website, http://www.kenmore.org/collections/documents/fielding_probate.html.

14. Frank S. Welsh, "The Historic Paints and Wallpapers of Kenmore," unpublished report, May 1, 1998; Susan L. Buck, "Cross-Section Microscopy Report, Kenmore, Fredericksburg, Virginia: Phase 1—First Floor," unpublished report, June 17, 2003; Susan L. Buck, "Paint Cross-Section Microscopy Report, Kenmore, Fredericksburg, Virginia: Phase 2—Second Floor," unpublished report, August 17, 2004.

15. Lund Washington's letters from October and December 1775 record "the stucco man's" connection with Fielding Lewis and his work in the small dining room at Mount Vernon.

16. Barbara Burlison Mooney, *Prodigy Houses of Virginia: Architecture and the Native Elite* (Charlottesville: University of Virginia Press, 2008).

17. Emory G. Evans, *A "Topping People": The Rise and Decline of Virginia's Old Political Elite, 1680–1790* (Charlottesville: University of Virginia Press, 2009).

18. Ian Hodder, *Reading the Past: Current Approaches to Interpretation in Archaeology* (Cambridge: Cambridge University Press, 2003).

CHAPTER 4

1. For general European migration, see John J. McCusker and Russell R. Menard, *The Economy of British America, 1607–1789* (Chapel Hill: University of North Carolina Press, 1985), chaps. 6 and 10; Henry A. Gemery, "The White Population of the Colonial United States, 1607–1790," in *A Population History of North America*, ed. Michael R. Haines and Richard H. Steckel (Cambridge: Cambridge University Press, 2000), 143–90; Aaron S. Fogleman, "From Slaves, Convicts, and Servants to Free Passengers: The Transformation of Immigration in the Era of the American Revolution," *Journal of American History* 85 (1998): 43–76; James Horn and Philip D. Morgan, "Settlers and Slaves: European and African Migrations to Early Modern British America," in *The Creation of the British Atlantic World*, ed. Elizabeth Mancke and Carole Shammas (Baltimore: Johns Hopkins University Press, 2005), 19–44; and Christopher Tomlins, "Indentured Servitude in Perspective: European Migration into North America and the Composition of the Early American Labor Force, 1600–1775," in *The Economy of Early America: Historical Perspectives and New Directions*, ed. Cathy Matson (University Park: Pennsylvania State University Press, 2006), 146–82. Estimates for the total number of European migrants to the mainland colonies are 160,000 (Gemery, "White Population of the Colonial United States");

161,000 (Tomlins, "Indentured Servitude in Perspective"); and 165,200 (Fogleman, "From Slaves, Convicts, and Servants to Free Passengers"). For Chesapeake migration, see Russell R. Menard, "British Migration to the Chesapeake Colonies," in *Colonial Chesapeake Society*, ed. Lois Green Carr, Philip D. Morgan, and Jean B. Russo (Chapel Hill: University of North Carolina Press, 1988), 99–132; James Horn, *Adapting to a New World: English Society in the Seventeenth-Century Chesapeake* (Chapel Hill: University of North Carolina Press, 1994), chaps. 1 and 3; and Lorena S. Walsh, "The Differential Cultural Impact of Free and Coerced Migration to Colonial America," in *Coerced and Free Migration: Global Perspectives*, ed. David Eltis (Stanford: Stanford University Press, 2002), 117–51.

2. Bernard Bailyn, *The Peopling of British North America: An Introduction* (New York: Alfred A. Knopf, 1986), especially 12–15; Horn, *Adapting to a New World*, 25–31, 52–61, 262–64, 421–24.

3. Henry A. Gemery, "Markets for Migrants: English Indentured Servitude and Emigration in the Seventeenth and Eighteenth Centuries," in *Colonialism and Migration: Indentured Labour Before and After Slavery*, ed. P. C. Emmer (Dordrecht: Springer, 1986), 33–54 (quotation, 48).

4. For the disease environment, see Lorena S. Walsh and Russell R. Menard, "Death in the Chesapeake: Two Life Tables for Men in Early Colonial Maryland," *Maryland Historical Magazine* 69 (1974): 211–27; Darrett B. Rutman and Anita H. Rutman, "'Now-Wives and Sons-in-Law': Parental Death in a Seventeenth-Century Virginia County," in *The Chesapeake in the Seventeenth Century: Essays on Anglo-American Society*, ed. Thad Tate and David Ammerman (Chapel Hill: University of North Carolina Press, 1979), 153–82; Darrett B. Rutman and Anita H. Rutman, "'Of Agues and Fevers': Malaria in the Early Chesapeake, *William and Mary Quarterly*, 3d ser., 33 (1976): 31–60; Darrett B. Rutman, Charles Wetherell, and Anita H. Rutman, "Rhythms of Life: Black and White Seasonality in the Early Chesapeake," *Journal of Interdisciplinary History* 11 (1980): 29–53; and Carville V. Earle, "Environment, Disease, and Mortality in Early Virginia," in Tate and Ammerman, *Chesapeake in the Seventeenth Century*, 96–125. For reproduction among Europeans, see Menard, "British Migration to the Chesapeake Colonies"; and Lorena S. Walsh, "'Till Death Us Do Part': Marriage and Family in Seventeenth-Century Maryland," in Tate and Ammerman, *Chesapeake in the Seventeenth Century*, 126–52. For Africans, see Russell R. Menard, "The Maryland Slave Population, 1658–1730: A Demographic Profile of Blacks in Four Counties," *William and Mary Quarterly*, 3d ser., 32 (1975): 29–54; and Allan Kulikoff, *Tobacco and Slaves: The Development of Southern Cultures in the Chesapeake, 1680–1800* (Chapel Hill: University of North Carolina Press, 1986), chap. 8.

5. Russell R. Menard, "From Servant to Freeholder: Status, Mobility, and Property Accumulation in Seventeenth-Century Maryland," *William and Mary Quarterly*, 3d ser., 30 (1973): 37–64; Lois Green Carr, Russell R. Menard, and Lorena S. Walsh, *Robert Cole's World: Agriculture and Society in Early Maryland* (Chapel Hill: University of North Carolina Press, 1991), chaps. 1 and 5.

6. David W. Galenson, *White Servitude in Colonial America: An Economic Analysis* (Cambridge: Cambridge University Press, 1981); Menard, "British Migration to the Chesapeake Colonies"; Gemery, "Markets for Migrants" (quotation, 49).

7. "Journal of a French Traveller in the Colonies, 1765, I," *American Historical Review* 26 (1921): 744 (quotation); Henry A. Gemery, "European Emigration to North America, 1700–1820: Numbers and Quasi-Numbers," *Perspectives in American History* 1 (1984): 283–342; A. Roger Ekirch, *Bound for America: The Transportation of British Convicts to the Colonies, 1718–1775* (Oxford: Oxford University Press, 1987).

8. Lorena S. Walsh, *Motives of Honor, Pleasure, and Profit: Plantation Management in the Colonial Chesapeake, 1607–1763* (Chapel Hill: University of North Carolina Press, 2010), chaps. 1–3; John C. Coombs, "Beyond the 'Origins Debate:' Rethinking the Rise of Virginia Slavery," in *Early Modern Virginia: Reconsidering the Old Dominion*, ed. Douglas Bradburn and John C. Coombs (Charlottesville: University of Virginia Press, 2011), 239–78.

9. Lorena S. Walsh, "Mercantile Strategies, Credit Networks, and Labor Supply in the Colonial Chesapeake in Trans-Atlantic Perspective," in *Slavery in the Development of the Americas*, ed. David Eltis, Frank D. Lewis, and Kenneth L. Sokoloff (Cambridge: Cambridge University Press, 2004), 89–119; Coombs, "Beyond the 'Origins Debate'"; Philip D. Morgan, *Slave Counterpoint: Black Culture in the Eighteenth-Century Chesapeake and Lowcountry* (Chapel Hill: University of North Carolina Press, 1998); Anthony S. Parent Jr., *Foul Means: The Formation of a Slave Society in Virginia, 1660–1740* (Chapel Hill: University of North Carolina Press, 2003).

10. Lois Green Carr and Lorena S. Walsh, "Economic Diversification and Labor Organization in the Chesapeake, 1650–1820," in *Work and Labor in Early America*, ed. Stephen B. Innes (Chapel Hill: University of North Carolina Press, 1988), 144–88.

11. William Byrd II to the Earl of Egmont, July 12, 1736, in *The Correspondence of the Three William Byrds of Westover, Virginia, 1684–1776*, 3 vols., ed. Marion Tinling (Charlottesville: University Press of Virginia, 1977), 2:488; Parent, *Foul Means*.

12. Carr et al., *Robert Cole's World*, chaps. 5–6; Kulikoff, *Tobacco and Slaves*, chap. 2.

13. J. P. Horn, "Moving On in the New World: Migration and Out-Migration in the Seventeenth-Century Chesapeake," in *Migration and Society in Early Modern England*, ed. Peter Clark and David Souden (London: Rowman and Littlefield, 1988), 172–212.

14. Walsh, *Motives of Honor, Pleasure, and Profit*, chap. 5.

15. Walsh, "Differential Cultural Impact of Free and Coerced Migration."

16. Lorena S. Walsh, "The Chesapeake Slave Trade: Regional Patterns, African Origins, and Some Implications," *William and Mary Quarterly*, 3d ser., 58 (2001): 139–70.

17. Lorena S. Walsh, *From Calabar to Carter's Grove: The History of a Virginia Slave Community* (Charlottesville: University Press of Virginia, 1997), chap. 3; Patricia Samford, *Subfloor Pits and the Archaeology of Slavery in Colonial Virginia* (Tuscaloosa: University of Alabama Press, 2007).

18. Morgan, *Slave Counterpoint*, 61; Walsh, "Differential Cultural Impact of Free and Coerced Migration," 144–51.

19. Fogleman, "From Slaves, Convicts, and Servants to Free Passengers."

20. Walsh, *Motives of Honor, Pleasure, and Profit*, chaps. 1–2.

21. Michael G. Kammen, ed., "Maryland in 1699: A Letter from the Reverend Hugh Jones," *Journal of Southern History* 29 (1963): 369–70 (quotation); George Alsop, "A Character of the Province of Maryland," in *Narratives of Early Maryland, 1633–1684*, ed. Clayton Colman Hall (New York: Charles Scribner's, 1910); Carr et al., *Robert Cole's World*, chap. 4.

22. Walsh, *Motives of Honor, Pleasure, and Profit*, chap. 3.

23. Lorena S. Walsh, "Summing the Parts: Implications for Estimating Chesapeake Output and Income Subregionally," *William and Mary Quarterly*, 3d ser., 56 (1999): 53–94; Carr et al., *Robert Cole's World*; Gloria T. Main, *Tobacco Colony: Life in Early Maryland, 1650–1720* (Princeton: Princeton University Press, 1982); Paul G. Clemens, *The Atlantic Economy and Colonial Maryland's Eastern Shore: From Tobacco to Grain* (Ithaca: Cornell University Press, 1980).

24. John W. Reps, *Tidewater Towns: City Planning in Colonial Virginia and Maryland* (Williamsburg: Colonial Williamsburg Foundation, 1972); Jacob M. Price, "Economic Function and the Growth of American Port Towns in the Eighteenth Century," *Perspectives in American History* 8 (1974): 123–85.

25. Philip D. Morgan and Michael L. Nicholls, "Slaves in Piedmont Virginia, 1720–1790," *William and Mary Quarterly*, 3d ser., 46 (1989): 215.

26. Russell R. Menard, "The Tobacco Industry in the Chesapeake Colonies, 1617–1730: An Interpretation," *Research in Economic History* 5 (1980): 109–77; Walsh, *Motives of Honor, Pleasure, and Profit*, chaps. 3–7.

27. Lorena S. Walsh, "Plantation Management in the Chesapeake, 1620–1820," *Journal of Economic History* 49 (1989): 393–406; Walsh, "Summing the Parts," 76–86; McCusker and Menard, *Economy of British America*, chap. 17.

28. Jacob M. Price, *France and the Chesapeake: A History of the French Tobacco Monopoly, 1674–1791, and of Its Relationship to the British and American Tobacco Trades* (Ann Arbor: University of Michigan Press, 1973); Walsh, "Summing the Parts," 76–86.

29. Walsh, "Plantation Management," 396–406.

30. Athanasius Fenwick, "Address to the Agricultural Society of St. Mary's County," *American Farmer* (September 10, 1819): 185; Philip D. Curtin, Grace S. Brush, and George W. Fisher, eds., *Discovering the Chesapeake: The History of an Ecosystem* (Baltimore: Johns Hopkins University Press, 2001).

31. Walsh, "Plantation Management."

32. Ibid.; Susan Dunn, *Dominion of Memories: Jefferson, Madison, and the Decline of Virginia* (New York: Basic Books, 2007).

CHAPTER 5

1. Edward C. Carter, ed., *The Virginia Journals of Benjamin Henry Latrobe, 1795–1798*, 2 vols. (New Haven: Yale University Press, 1977), 1:75–76.

2. John C. Van Horne and Lee W. Formwalt, eds., *The Correspondence and Miscellaneous Papers of Benjamin Henry Latrobe*, 2 vols. (New Haven: Yale University Press, 1984), 1:148.

3. For a detailed study of this commission, see Michael W. Fazio and Patrick A. Snadon, *The Domestic Architecture of Benjamin Henry Latrobe* (Baltimore: Johns Hopkins University Press, 2006), 211–21.

4. For a critique of this perspective, see Dell Upton, "Outside the Academy: A Century of Vernacular Studies, 1890–1990," in *The Architectural Historian in America*, ed. Elizabeth Blair MacDougall (Washington, D.C.: National Gallery of Art, 1990), 199–213.

5. Two of the most influential architectural histories of early American architecture written from this perspective are Fiske Kimball, *Domestic Architecture of the American Colonies and of the Early Republic* (New York: Charles Scribner's, 1922); and Thomas Tileston Waterman, *The Mansions of Virginia, 1706–1776* (Chapel Hill: University of North Carolina Press, 1946).

6. "The Plan of the Parlour Floor of a House Now Building by the Hon.ble Thos. Nelson Esqr. in York Town, Virginia, Designed by Himself," in an album of drawings of Thomas Hunt dated September 15, 1765. I would like to thank John Harris for bringing this drawing to my attention. For a full description, see Jill Lever, ed., *Catalogue of the Drawings Collection of the Royal Institute of British Architects, G–K* (London: Gregg International, 1973), 148–49.

7. Specification cited in Elizabeth Merrit, *Old Wye Church, 1694–1949* (Baltimore: Maryland Historical Society, 1954).

8. Willie Graham, Carter L. Hudgins, Carl R. Lounsbury, Fraser D. Neiman, and James P. Whittenburg, "Adaptation and Innovation: Archaeological and Architectural Perspectives on the Seventeenth-Century Chesapeake," *William and Mary Quarterly*, 3d ser., 64 (July 2007): 451–70.

9. Accomack-Northampton County Court Records, 1632–40, 63, September 29, 1635.

10. Surry County Order, Deed, and Will Book, 1645–72, 55, October 25, 1651.

11. Ibid., 96, January 28, 1657.

12. Ibid.

13. Upper Parish Vestry Book, 1743–93, 28, December 19, 1747.

14. *Virginia Magazine of History and Biography* 31 (January 1923): 67.

15. Charlotte County Court Order Book, 1784–86, 89, June 7, 1785.

16. For a study of courthouse fittings, see Carl R. Lounsbury, *The Courthouses of Early Virginia: An Architectural History* (Charlottesville: University of Virginia Press, 2005), 68–82, 128–65.

17. Christ Church Parish Vestry Book, 1663–1767, 4, September 26, 1665.

18. W. A. R. Goodwin, ed., *The Record of Bruton Parish Church* (Richmond: Dietz Press, 1941), 124.

19. Middlesex County Court Order Book, 1680–94, 200–201, February 3, 1685.

20. Northampton County Court Order Book, 1689–98, 33, May 28, 1690.

21. On this pattern, see also Lounsbury, *Courthouses of Early Virginia*, 182.

22. Louisa County Court Order Book, 1742–48, 32, April 11, 1743.

23. Norfolk County Court Order and Will Book, 1723–34, 60, August 19, 1726.

24. St. Peter's Parish Vestry Book, 1682–1758, 126–27, November 18, 1719.

25. Dell Upton, *Holy Things and Profane: Anglican Parish Churches in Colonial Virginia* (Cambridge, Mass.: MIT Press, 1986), 82.

26. George Washington to William Thornton, December 30, 1798, in Dorothy Twohig, ed., *The Papers of George Washington, Retirement Series*, 4 vols. (Charlottesville: University of Virginia Press, 1998), 3:300.

27. For the timing of the introduction of classical terminology in Chesapeake building vocabulary, see Carl Lounsbury, *An Illustrated Glossary of Early Southern Architecture and Landscape* (New York: Oxford University Press, 1994).

28. Batty Langley, *The Builder's Chest-Book; or a Complete Key to the Five Orders of Columns in Architecture* (London, 1727; reprint, Farnborough, England: Gregg International, 1971), iii.

29. Truro Parish Vestry Book, 1732–85, 94–97, February 4, 1766.

30. See Jefferson's critique of the public buildings in Williamsburg, in Thomas Jefferson, *Notes on the State of Virginia*, ed. William Peden (Chapel Hill: University of North Carolina Press, 1955), 152–53.

31. Dan Cruickshank and Peter Wyld, *London: The Art of Georgian Building* (London: Architectural Press, 1975), 21.

32. The ground-floor windows of the exceptionally well-proportioned Wythe House in Williamsburg are 4 feet in width and 7 feet 9 inches high, and those on the second story are 3½ feet wide and 6½ feet tall—the golden ratio. Although the diminution of the width of the second-floor windows is unusual, the reduced height was common among many but not all larger houses in the region. While no houses appeared with taller second-story windows, a number have apertures that are the same size on both floors. Such is the case of Carter's Grove near Williamsburg, where the apertures on both floors have a two-to-one ratio. The first- and second-story windows measure 8 feet 4 inches in height and are 4 feet 2 inches wide.

33. Kaitlyn Gardy, "Massachusetts, Philadelphia, and Virginia: How Window Measurements and Architectural Details Illustrate Regionalism," unpublished research paper, Architectural Research Department, Colonial Williamsburg Foundation, December 2008.

34. The results are based on a random sample of twenty-five buildings from Maryland and Virginia, frame buildings and brick ones (no variation), single story and two story, urban and rural. The English statistics are based on the measurement of an equal number of buildings in London, ranging from row houses to free-standing structures from the 1720s through the 1770s.

35. For a detailed analysis of the development of early Virginia churches, see Upton, *Holy Things and Profane*.

36. Blisland Parish Vestry Book, 1721–86, 53–55, December 11, 1733.

37. Edward Chappell and Julie Richter, "Wealth and Houses in Post-Revolutionary Virginia," in *Exploring Everyday Landscapes: Perspectives in Vernacular Architecture, VII*, ed. Annmarie Adams and Sally McMurry (Knoxville: University of Tennessee Press, 1997), 3–23.

38. George Washington to John Rawlins, August 29, 1785, in W. W. Abbot and Dorothy Twohig, eds., *The Papers of George Washington, Confederation Series*, 6 vols. (Charlottesville: University of Virginia Press, 1992), 3:442.

39. St. Peter's Parish Vestry Book, 1682–1758, 182, April 12, 1740.

40. St. Andrew's Parish Vestry Book, May 28, 1766.

41. *Maryland Journal or Baltimore Advertiser*, December 28, 1784.

42. *Maryland Gazette*, April 7, 1785.

43. Orange County Loose Papers, November 28, 1765, Library of Virginia, Richmond.

44. St. Paul's Parish Vestry Book, 1733–1819, October 10, 1733.

45. Ibid., October 27, 1742.

46. Trinity Parish Vestry Book, October 4, 1752.

47. *Virginia Gazette*, June 20, 1775.

48. Ibid., June 23, 1775.

49. Rosamond Beirne and John Scarff, *William Buckland: Architect of Virginia and Maryland* (Baltimore: Board of Regents, Gunston Hall, and the Hammond Harwood House Association, 1958), 142.

50. See, for example, advertisements for runaways from these places. Carpenter and joiner Richard Kibble ran away from master builder William Walker at Stratford. *Virginia Gazette*, July 6, 1739. At Shirley, bricklayer Charles Pickford fled the services of John Carter. *Virginia Gazette*, November 20, 1739. John Winter, "a very compleat House painter," worked for Colonel Washington at Mount Vernon but bolted from the services of John Fendall in Alexandria in 1760. *Maryland Gazette*, June 26, 1760.

51. Joiners John Ewen and Samuel Bailey twice fled Buckland's service while he was working in Richmond County, Virginia, in the late 1760s and early 1770s. Following his move to Annapolis in 1771, Buckland had further trouble with runaways. Thomas Hoskins, a bricklayer, Thomas Hall, a carver, Thomas M'Inerhency, an Irish joiner, Richard Sadler, an Irish plasterer, John Wakefield, a plasterer, and Croasdale Sprotson, a joiner, disappeared from various projects in the Maryland capital. *Virginia Gazette*, June 15, 1769, July 26, 1770, January 3, 1771, and August 1, 1771. *Maryland Gazette*, September 23, 1773, December 16, 1773, March 17, 1774, and April 7, 1774.

52. William Buckland to Robert Carter III, March 25, 1771, Carter Family Papers, Virginia Historical Society, Richmond.

53. Carl Lounsbury, "'An Elegant and Commodious Building': William Buckland and the Design of the Prince William County Courthouse," *Journal of the Society of Architectural Historians* 46 (September 1987): 228–40.

54. "Diary of William Beverley of 'Blandfield' during a Visit to England, 1750," *Virginia Magazine of History and Biography* 36 (April 1928): 163, 165, 168.

55. "Answer to Query, 1724," in *Maryland*, vol. 4 of *Historical Collections Relating to the American Colonial Church*, 5 vols., ed. William Steven Perry (Hartford, 1879; reprint, New York: AMS Press, 1969), 209.

56. Joan Dolmetsch, "Prints in Colonial America: Supply and Demand in the Mid-eighteenth Century," in *Prints in and of America to 1850*, ed. John D. Morse (Charlottesville: University Press of Virginia, 1970), 53–74; Timothy Clayton, *The English Print* (New Haven: Yale University Press, 1997).

57. *Virginia Gazette*, June 27, 1751, September 17, 1771, and December 12, 1771.

58. On the pervasiveness of English prints, see *Virginia Gazette*, November 28, 1777, and October 16, 1778; and "Narrative of George Fisher," *William and Mary Quarterly*, 1st ser., 17 (January 1909): 170.

59. Eileen Harris, *British Architectural Books and Writers, 1556–1785* (New York: Cambridge University Press, 1990); Helen Park, *List of Architectural Books Available in America before the Revolution* (Los Angeles: Hennessey and Ingalls, 1973); Janice Schimmelman, *Architectural Books in Early America: Architectural Treatises and Building Handbooks Available in American Libraries and Bookstores through 1800* (New Castle, Del.: Oak Knoll Press, 1999).

60. Bennie Brown, "The Ownership of Architecture Books in Colonial Virginia," in *American Architects and Their Books to 1848*, ed. Kenneth Hafertepe and James F. O'Gorman (Amherst: University of Massachusetts Press, 2002), 17–33.

61. See John Carter of Shirley to his brother Charles Carter in King George County about consulting a recently published *Builder's Dictionary* to gauge the validity of a workman's bill. John Carter to Charles Carter, August 26, 1738, Plummer-Carter Letterbook, Alderman Library, University of Virginia, Charlottesville.

62. The books were Edward Hoppus's *Repository on Architecture Displayed* (1738); William Salmon's *Palladio Londinensis* (1734 or 1738); Giacomo Leoni's translation of Andrea Palladio's *Four Books of Architecture* (1715, 1721, or 1742); and Batty Langley's *Workman's Treasury of Designs* (1740 or 1745). C. Malcolm Watkins, *The Cultural History of Marlborough, Virginia* (Washington, D.C.: Smithsonian Institution Press, 1968), 37–39. In another instance of a client purchasing a builder's book as he undertook the construction of a new house, in December 1751 Carter Burwell purchased a copy of William Salmon's *Palladio Londinensis* from the *Virginia Gazette* printing office in Williamsburg. He had just begun work on Carter's Grove, his James City County plantation. Marcus Whiffen, *The Eighteenth-Century Houses of Williamsburg*, rev. ed. (Williamsburg: Colonial Williamsburg Foundation, 1984), 265.

63. Batty Langley, *The City and Country Builder's and Workman's Treasury of Designs* (London, 1745; reprint, Farnborough, England: Gregg International, 1969), i.

64. Truro Parish Vestry Book, 1732–85, 121–22, July 8, 1771. Dell Upton has concluded from circumstantial evidence that the

altarpiece design might have derived from plate CX in Langley's *Workman's Treasury of Designs*. James Wren, the designer and undertaker of neighboring Falls Church in the late 1760s, used the plate for the church's altarpiece. Upton, *Holy Things and Profane*, 128, 132–33.

65. Cabinetmaker John Shaw of Annapolis borrowed a copy of Isaac Ware's *A Complete Body of Architecture* from James Brice sometime after 1767. Brice had purchased this primer on building from his London factor and probably used it as a guide during the construction of his new two-story brick house on East Street. The reason for the loan is not known. Orlando Ridout IV, "The James Brice House, Annapolis, Maryland" (master's thesis, University of Maryland, 1978), 60.

66. Beirne and Scarff, *William Buckland*, 149–50.

67. Quoted in Terry Friedman, *James Gibbs* (New Haven: Yale University Press, 1984), 259.

68. Van Horne and Formwalt, *Correspondence and Miscellaneous Papers of Benjamin Henry Latrobe*, 1:203.

69. Robert Dalzell, "George Washington, Mount Vernon, and the Pattern Books," in *American Architects and Their Books to 1848*, 36–37.

70. Truro Parish Vestry Book, 1732–85, 129, June 4, 1773.

71. Kimball, *Domestic Architecture of the American Colonies*, 55–56.

72. See, for example, Calder Loth, "Palladio in Southside Virginia: Brandon and Battersea," and William Rasmussen, "Palladio in Tidewater Virginia: Mount Airy and Blandfield," in *Building by the Book I*, ed. Mario di Valmarana (Charlottesville: University Press of Virginia, 1984), 25–46, 75–109; and Michael Trostel, "The 'Annapolis Plan' in Maryland," and Barbara Allston Brand, "William Buckland, Architect in Annapolis," in *Building by the Book II*, ed. Mario di Valmarana (Charlottesville: University Press of Virginia, 1986), 1–33, 65–100.

73. Waterman, *Mansions of Virginia, 1706–1776*, 253–56.

74. Waterman believed that *Vitruvius Scoticus* was published in 1750, but it did not appear in print until 1811. Harris, *British Architectural Books and Writers, 1556–1785*, 94–95.

75. Tayloe had corresponded with Edmund Jennings II, the former secretary of the colony of Maryland who was active in colonial politics in London, about designs for the house as early as 1754. Edmund Jennings II to John Tayloe II, June 9, 1754, Edmund Jennings Letterbook, 1753–69, 67–68, Virginia Historical Society, Richmond.

76. Ibid.

CHAPTER 6

1. "Reflections of the Life and Death of Thomas Fuller" (1680), in T. H. Breen, James H. Lewis, and Keith Schlesinger, "Motive for Murder: A Servant's Life in Virginia, 1678," *William and Mary Quarterly*, 3d ser., 40 (January 1983): 118.

2. Richard Beale Davis, ed., *William Fitzhugh and His Chesapeake World, 1676–1701: The Fitzhugh Letters and Other Documents* (Chapel Hill: University of North Carolina Press for Virginia Historical Society, 1963), 202–3.

3. *Information and Direction to Such Persons as Are Inclined to America, More Especially Those Related to the Province of Pennsylvania* (1682), in *Pennsylvania Magazine of History and Biography* 4 (1880): 335.

4. Ebenezer Cooke, *The Sot-Weed Factor: Or, a Voyage to Maryland* (London: D. Bragg, 1708), [1]; Cary Carson, Joanne Bowen, William Graham, Martha McCartney, and Lorena Walsh, "New World, Real World: Improvising English Culture in Seventeenth-Century Virginia," *Journal of Southern History* 74, no. 1 (February 2008): 31–88.

5. Susan Myra Kingsbury, ed., *The Records of the Virginia Company of London*, 4 vols. (Washington, D.C.: Government Printing Office, 1906–35), 3:257.

6. A "four years slave" was Ebenezer Cooke's cynical term for an indentured servant unlucky enough to call Virginia or Maryland his new home.

7. Cary Carson, Norman F. Barka, William M. Kelso, Garry Wheeler Stone, and Dell Upton, "Impermanent Architecture in the Southern American Colonies," *Winterthur Portfolio* 16, nos. 2/3 (Summer/Autumn 1981): 139–60.

8. Ivor Noel Hume and Audrey Noel Hume, *The Archaeology of Martin's Hundred, Part I: Interpretive Studies* (Williamsburg: Colonial Williamsburg Foundation, 2001), 128–34; William M. Kelso and Beverly Straube, *2000–2006 Interim Report on the APVA Excavations at Jamestown, Virginia* (Richmond, Va.: APVA, 2008), 17–30; William M. Kelso, *Jamestown: The Buried Truth* (Charlottesville: University of Virginia Press, 2006), 80–83.

9. Carson et al., "New World, Real World," 49–63.

10. Kingsbury, *Records of the Virginia Company of London*, 3:276, May 17, 1620.

11. Ibid., 3:441, May 1621.

12. Patricia M. Samford, *Subfloor Pits and the Archaeology of Slavery in Colonial Virginia* (Tuscaloosa: University of Alabama Press, 2007), 41–84.

13. Garrett Randall Fesler, "From Houses to Homes: An Archaeological Case Study of Household Formation at the Utopia Slave Quarter, ca. 1675–1775" (Ph.D. diss., University of Virginia, 2004).

14. Edward Williams, *Virginia: More Especially the South Part Thereof, Richly and Truly Valued in Tracts and Other Papers* (1650), in *Tracts and Other Papers Relating Principally to the Origin, Settlement, and Progress of the Colonies in North America, from the Discovery of the Country to the Year 1776*, 4 vols., ed. Peter Force (Washington, D.C.: P. Force, 1836–46), 3:36.

15. Ann Kussmaul, *Servants in Husbandry in Early Modern England* (Cambridge: Cambridge University Press, 1981), 97–119.

16. Philip T. Hoffman, David Jacks, Patricia A. Levin, and Peter H. Lindert, "Real Inequality in Europe since 1500," *Journal of Economic History* 62, no. 2 (June 2002): 322–55.

17. Timothy Nourse, *Campania Foelix* (London: T. Bennet, 1700), 213.

18. Cary Carson, "Segregation in Vernacular Architecture," *Vernacular Architecture* 7 (1976): 24–29.

19. Peter Earle, *The Making of the English Middle Class: Business, Society, and Family Life in London, 1669–1730* (Berkeley: University of California Press, 1989); J. H. Plumb, *The Pursuit of Happiness: A View of Life in Georgian England* (New Haven: Yale University Press, 1977); Richard L. Bushman, *The Refinement of America: Persons, Houses, Cities* (New York: Alfred A. Knopf, 1992); Keith Wright, *Earthly Necessities: Economic Lives in Early Modern Britain* (New Haven: Yale University Press, 2000).

20. Thomas Nairne, *A Letter from South Carolina* (London: A. Baldwin, 1710), 49–50.

21. William Hand Browne, ed., *Archives of Maryland, V: Proceedings of the Council of Maryland, 1667–1687/8* (Baltimore: Maryland Historical Society, 1887), 266.

22. Ralph Hamor, *A True Discourse of the Present State of Virginia* (London, 1615; reprint, Richmond: Virginia State Library, 1957), 19.

23. Noel Hume and Noel Hume, *Archaeology of Martin's Hundred, I*, 13–138. Structure C on the Harwood Plantation (Site A) is said to have been built in two or three phases, which field drawings do not differentiate. It is therefore illustrated here as one period.

24. Lorena S. Walsh, *Motives of Honor, Pleasure, and Profit: Plantation Management in the Colonial Chesapeake, 1607–1763* (Chapel Hill: University of North Carolina Press, 2010), 76–83; "Claiborne vs. Clobery," *Maryland Historical Magazine* 28 (1933): 180–87.

25. Norman F. Barka, *The Archaeology of Flowerdew Hundred Plantation: The Stone Foundation Site* (Williamsburg: Southside Historical Sites, Department of Anthropology, College of William and Mary, 1976); James Deetz, *Flowerdew Hundred: The Archaeology of a Virginia Plantation, 1619–1864* (Charlottesville: University Press of Virginia, 1993).

26. Garry Wheeler Stone, "St. John's: Archaeological Questions and Answers," *Maryland Historical Magazine* 69, no. 2 (1974): 146–68; personal correspondence with Henry Miller and Garry W. Stone, July 2, 2003.

27. Robert Winston Keeler, "The Homelot on the Seventeenth-Century Chesapeake Tidewater Frontier" (Ph.D. diss., University of Oregon, 1978).

28. David De Vries, *Voyages from Holland to America, 1632–1644*, trans. Henry C. Murphy (New York: New York Historical Society, 1857); Ivor Noel Hume, *Historical Archaeology* (New York: Knopf, 1969), 228–29; Edward A. Chappell offers an alternative interpretation of the plan. See Edward A. Chappell, "Architecture at Mathews Manor," unpublished report, Architectural Research Department, Colonial Williamsburg Foundation, 2011.

29. Cary Carson, Audrey J. Horning, Beverly A. Straube, and Ronald Fuchs II, *Jamestown Archaeological Assessment, 1992–1996: Evaluation of Previous Archaeology* (Williamsburg: Colonial Williamsburg Foundation for National Park Service, 2006), Structure 44. Quotation in William Noel Sainsbury, ed., *Calendar of State Papers, Colonial Series, America and West Indies*, 40 vols. (London: HMSO, 1860–1939; reprint, Vaduz: Kraus Reprint, 1964), 1:288.

30. David Muraca, Philip Levy, and Leslie McFaden, *The Archaeology of Rich Neck Plantation (44WB52): Description of the Features* (Williamsburg: Colonial Williamsburg Foundation, 2003); Maria Franklin, *An Archaeological Study of the Rich Neck Slave Quarter and Enslaved Domestic Life* (Williamsburg: Colonial Williamsburg Foundation, 2004).

31. Carson et al., *Jamestown Archaeological Assessment, 1992–1996: Evaluation of Previous Archaeology:* Structure 112, Period 1; Martha McCartney, *Jamestown Archaeological Assessment, 1992–1996: Documentary History of Jamestown Island*, 3 vols. (Williamsburg: Colonial Williamsburg Foundation for National Park Service, 2000), 3:157.

32. William T. Buchannan and Edward F. Heite, "The Hallowes Site: A Seventeenth-Century Yeoman's Cottage in Virginia," *Historical Archaeology* 5 (1971): 38–48.

33. Fraser D. Neiman, "Domestic Architecture at the Clifts Plantation: The Social Context of Early Virginia Building," *Northern Neck of Virginia Historical Magazine* 28, no. 1 (December 1978): 3096–128.

34. Henry M. Miller, "The Country's House Site: An Archaeological Study of a Seventeenth-Century Domestic Landscape," in *Historical Archaeology of the Chesapeake*, ed. Paul A. Shackel and Barbara J. Little (Washington, D.C.: Smithsonian Institution Press, 1994), 65–83.

35. Testamentary Proceedings 3: folio 127–59, Maryland State Archives, Annapolis.

36. Fraser D. Neiman, "Temporal Patterning in House Plans from the 17th-Century Chesapeake," in *The Archaeology of 17th-Century Virginia*, ed. Theodore R. Reinhart and Dennis J. Pogue (Richmond: Dietz Press for the Archaeological Society of Virginia, Special Publication no. 30, 1993), 251–83.

37. Robert Beverley, *The History and Present State of Virginia*, ed. Louis B. Wright (London, 1705; Chapel Hill: University of North Carolina Press, 1947), 290.

38. Russell R. Menard, "The Tobacco Industry in the Chesapeake Colonies, 1671–1730: An Interpretation," *Research in Economic History* 5 (1980): 109–77; Walsh, *Motives of Honor, Pleasure, and Profit*, 25–193. Tobacco prices fluctuated too rapidly to establish a correlation between recessions in the mid- to late 1620s, the late 1630s to the early 1640s, and the mid-1660s and any observable adjustments in the design of farmhouses and the accommodation of laborers.

39. Walsh, *Motives of Honor, Pleasure, and Profit*, 182–87.

40. Bartlett Burleigh James and J. Franklin Jameson, eds., *Journal of Jasper Danckaerts, 1679–1680* (New York: Charles Scribner's, 1913), 133; Walsh, *Motives of Honor, Pleasure, and Profit*, 381.

41. Henry M. Miller, "An Archaeological Perspective on the Evolution of Diet in the Colonial Chesapeake, 1620–1745," in *Colonial Chesapeake Society*, ed. Lois Green Carr, Philip D. Morgan, and Jean B. Russo (Chapel Hill: University of North Carolina Press, 1988), 176–99. Archaeological evidence from the two seventeenth-century Virginia sites that might have provided information about the diet of slaves—Utopia Quarter (James City County) and the Atkinson site (James City County)—was not collected systematically or remains unpublished. More is known

about feeding slaves on early to mid-eighteenth-century plantations. To some extent, those findings can be extrapolated backward to the late seventeenth century using Joanne Bowen and
Stephen C. Atkins, "Preliminary Report on Faunal Remains from
the Rich Neck Slave Quarter," appendix to Franklin, *An Archaeological Study of the Rich Neck Slave Quarter and Enslaved Domestic
Life*; and Maria Fashing, "Recognizing Variability in Eighteenth-
Century Plantation Diet through Pattern Analysis" (honor's thesis, College of William and Mary, 2005).

42. T. H. Breen, "George Donne's 'Virginia Reviewed': A 1638
Plan to Reform Colonial Society," *William and Mary Quarterly*,
3d ser., 30 (1973): 457.

43. Important early studies that dated the replacement to the
decades after 1660—Russell R. Menard, "From Servants to Slaves:
The Transformation of the Chesapeake Labor System," *Southern
Studies* 16 (1977): 355–90; and Anthony S. Parent Jr., *Foul Means:
The Formation of a Slave Society in Virginia, 1660–1740* (Chapel
Hill: University of North Carolina Press, 2003)—have since been
revised by John C. Coombs, "Building 'the Machine': The Devel-
opment of Slavery and Slave Society in Early Colonial Virginia"
(Ph.D. diss., College of William and Mary, 2003); and Walsh, *Mo-
tives of Honor, Pleasure, and Profit*, 138–44, 200–210.

44. Quotation from Warren M. Billings, John E. Selby, and
Thad W. Tate, *Colonial Virginia: A History* (White Plains, N.Y.:
KTO Press, 1986), 205; Bernard Christian Steiner, ed., *Archives
of Maryland, XLI: Proceedings of the Provincial Court, 1658–1662*
(Baltimore: Maryland Historical Society, 1922), 205.

45. Hugh Jones, *The Present State of Virginia*, ed. Richard B.
Morton (London: J. Clarke, 1724; reprint, Chapel Hill: University of North Carolina Press, 1956), 38.

46. William S. Perry, ed., *Historical Collections Relating to the
American Colonial Church*, 5 vols. (Hartford, 1870–78; reprint,
New York: AMS Press, 1969), 1:267, 283, 293 (quotation, 283).

47. Quoted in Thomas N. Ingersoll, "'Release Us Out of This
Cruell Bondegg': An Appeal from Virginia in 1723," *William and
Mary Quarterly*, 3d ser., 51 (October 1994): 781–82.

48. Lord Culpeper to the Lords of Trade and Plantations,
September 20, 1683, in *Documents Illustrative of the History of the
Slave Trade to America*, 4 vols., ed. Elizabeth Donnan (Washing-
ton, D.C.: Carnegie Institution Publication no. 409, 1931), 4:58.

49. Jasper Danckaerts and Peter Sluyter, *Journal of a Voyage
to New York, and a Tour in Several of the American Colonies in
1679–80*, trans. and ed. Henry C. Murphy (Brooklyn: Long Island
Historical Society, 1867), 173.

50. Durand de Dauphine, *A Huguenot Exile in Virginia; Or,
Voyages of a Frenchman Exiled for This Religion, with a Description
of Virginia and Maryland* (1687), trans. and ed. Gilbert Chinard
(New York: Press of the Pioneers, 1934), 119–20.

51. A pattern discovered by Coombs, "Building the 'Machine,'"
199–200.

52. Lord Effingham to Philadelphia Pelham Howard, April 1,
1684, in *The Papers of Francis Howard, Baron Howard of Effingham, 1643–1695*, ed. Warren M. Billings (Richmond: Virginia
State Library and Archives, 1989), 77.

53. Carson et al., "Impermanent Architecture," 157, 180; William M. Kelso, *Kingsmill Plantations, 1619–1800: Archaeology
of Country Life in Colonial Virginia* (Orlando: Academic Press,
1984), 76–80.

54. Beverley, *History and Present State of Virginia*, 290; Jones,
Present State of Virginia, 74. Donald Linebaugh marshals these
references and other historical and scientific evidence to make the
case for a climatic explanation, in "'All the Annoyances and In-
conveniences of the Country': Environmental Factors in the Development of Outbuildings in the Colonial Chesapeake," *Winterthur Portfolio* 29, no. 1 (Spring 1994): 1–18.

55. R. T. Gunther, *The Architecture of Sir Roger Pratt* (Oxford:
Printed by J. Johnson for the author at Oxford University Press,
1928), 27.

56. Carson et al., "Impermanent Architecture," 157, 180; Fesler, "From Houses to Homes," and personal correspondence with
author.

57. Nicholas M. Luccketti, "Archaeology at Bennett Farm [c.
1648–1702]: The Life Style of a Seventeenth-Century Middling
Planter in York County, Virginia" (master's thesis, College of William and Mary, 1990).

58. Neiman, "Temporal Patterning," 269–70.

59. Dell Upton, "Virginia Domestic Architecture in Eighteenth-
Century Virginia," *Winterthur Portfolio* 17, nos. 2/3 (Summer/
Autumn 1982): 95–103.

60. *Minutes of the Vestry: Truro Parish, Virginia, 1732–1785*
(Lorton, Va.: Pohick Church, 1974), 15.

61. Lower Norfolk County, Virginia, Court Records, 1646–52,
177; Inventory of William Stevens, 1688, Somerset County, Maryland, Maryland Prerogative Court, Inventories and Accounts,
1688–92, 56–60.

62. Marquis de Chastellux, *Travels in North America in the
Years 1780, 1781, and 1782*, 2 vols., ed. Howard C. Rice Jr. (Chapel
Hill: University of North Carolina Press, 1963), 2:441.

63. Cary Carson, Willie Graham, Carl Lounsbury, and Martha
McCartney, "Description and Analysis of Structure 144 [Ludwell
Statehouse Group]," unpublished report to Association for the
Preservation of Virginia Antiquities, Jamestown Rediscovery,
Williamsburg, Virginia, August 20, 2002; Carson et al., *James-
town Archaeological Assessment, 1992–1996: Evaluation of Previous
Archaeology*, entry for Structure 115; Carson et al., "New World,
Real World," 66–77.

64. Mark R. Wenger, "The Nelson-Galt House: A Preliminary Architectural Report," unpublished report, Architectural
Research Department, Colonial Williamsburg Foundation, 2003.

65. Davis, *Fitzhugh and His Chesapeake World*, 203.

66. Warren M. Billings, *Sir William Berkeley and the Forging of
Colonial Virginia* (Baton Rouge: Louisiana State University Press,
2004).

67. De Vries, *Voyages from Holland to America, 1632–1644*, 129.

68. Billings, *Sir William Berkeley*, 59n, sorts out the complicated history of patents and sales from which the governor assembled the Green Spring estate over a period of almost twenty years.

69. Richard Kemp to Sir William and Sir John Berkeley, Febru-

ary 27, 1645, Clarendon ms. 24, ff. 48–51, Bodleian Library, Oxford University, Oxford, England; Cary Carson, "Understanding William Berkeley's Green Spring Plantation: Documentation and Analysis," unpublished report, Architectural Research Department, Colonial Williamsburg Foundation, August 29, 2010.

70. Gervase Markham, *The English Husbandman* (London: T. S[nodham] for John Browne, 1613; 2d ed., London: Augustine Mathewes and John Norton, 1635), 33, plan 76.

71. Lady Frances Berkeley to Sir Abstrupus Danby, June 27, 1678, ms. letter, Cunliffe-Lister Muniments, bundle 69, section 11, Bradford District, West Yorkshire Archive Service, England.

72. Nicholas Cooper, *Houses of the Gentry, 1480–1680* (New Haven: Yale University Press, 1999), 190–94; Mark Girouard, *Life in the English Country House* (New Haven: Yale University Press, 1978), 104–8; Paula Henderson, "The Loggia in Tudor and Early Stuart England: The Adaptation and Function of Classical Form," in *Albion's Classicism: The Visual Arts in Britain, 1550–1660*, ed. Lucy Gent (New Haven: Yale University Press for the Paul Mellon Centre for Studies in British Art, 1995), 109–45.

73. M. Kent Brinkley, *The Green Spring Plantation/Orangery and the Probable Evolution of the Domestic Area Landscape*, unpublished research report, Colonial National Historical Park, National Park Service, 2003.

74. Cooper, *Houses of the Gentry*, 289–99; personal correspondence, Nicholas Cooper to author, June 8, 2005.

75. Davis, *Fitzhugh and His Chesapeake World*, 175. He was writing in 1686.

76. Cary Carson, "Consumption," in *A Companion to Colonial America*, ed. Daniel Vickers (Oxford: Blackwell, 2003), 334–65.

77. Stephenson B. Andrews, ed., *Bacon's Castle* (Richmond: Association for the Preservation of Virginia Antiquities, Research Bulletin 3, 1984), including inventories transcribed by Ronald Hurst.

78. Arthur Allen I died when his new house was only three years old. Therefore, the earliest inventory, though not compiled until 1711, really records the seventeenth-century furnishings, room uses, and lifestyle of Arthur Allen II.

79. A watercolor painting of Bacon's Castle, from about 1815, shows frames around the ground-floor windows as well as those upstairs (reproduced in Andrews, *Bacon's Castle*, 6), but careful examination of the lower window heads and jambs reveals no trace of bonded brick frames similar to those above.

80. "Agreement between Corbin, Lee, &c., to Build a Banqueting House," *Virginia Magazine of History and Biography* 8 (October 1900): 171–72.

81. Thane Harpole and David A. Brown, "The Architecture of the Fairfield Manor House: The Convergence of Wealth, Style, and Practicality," *Quarterly Bulletin of the Archeological Society of Virginia* 63, no. 3 (2007): 136–48; David A. Brown, "The 1694 Manor House at Fairfield: An Analysis Based on Six Surviving Late Nineteenth-Century Photographs," unpublished report, Fairfield Foundation, May 31, 2009.

82. Cary Carson, "Corotoman: Documentation and Analysis," unpublished report, Architectural Research Department, Colonial Williamsburg Foundation, October 2, 2010.

83. Howard Colvin and John Newman, eds., *On Building: Roger North's Writings on Architecture* (c. 1690) (Oxford: Oxford University Press, 1981), 32. Carter too never intended to remove his residence to the new banqueting lodge. His dwelling, built in 1685, stood immediately next door.

84. Arthur and Elizabeth Smith solved this problem by partitioning a center passage out of the hall sometime after Arthur Allen III's death in 1727.

85. John Metz, Jennifer Jones, Dwayne Pickett, and David Muraca, *"Upon the Palisado" and Other Stories of Place from Burton Heights* (Williamsburg: Colonial Williamsburg Foundation, 1998), 31–83; Dwayne Pickett, "The John Page House Site: An Example of the Increase in Domestic Brick Architecture in Seventeenth-Century Tidewater Virginia" (master's thesis, College of William and Mary, 1996).

86. Edward A. Chappell, "Arlington, c. 1674–76," unpublished report for the Arlington Foundation, Williamsburg, 2003; John C. Bedell and Nicholas M. Luccketti, "An Archaeological Assessment of Arlington, Northampton County, Virginia," unpublished report for James River Institute for Archaeology, Jamestown, Virginia, 1988; Nicholas M. Luccketti, "Archaeology at Arlington: Excavations at the Ancestral Custis Plantation, Northampton County, Virginia," unpublished report for Virginia Company Foundation and Association for the Preservation of Virginia Antiquities, Jamestown, 1999; Joe B. Jones, "Additional Archaeological Survey and Artifact Analysis: The Arlington Site (44NH92), Northampton County, Virginia," unpublished report for the William and Mary Center for Archaeological Research, Williamsburg, 2001.

87. James B. Lynch, *The Custis Chronicles: The Years of Migration* (Camden, Maine: Picton Press, 1992), 157–81.

88. Parke estate papers, no. 6077, Custis Family Papers, Virginia Historical Society, Richmond.

89. Will of John Custis II (1691), Northampton County Court Records, 1689–98, 356–59.

90. Beverley, *History and Present State of Virginia*, 289. Although the book was not published until 1705, it describes the colony as the author saw it and wrote about in the 1690s.

91. Archaeologists never found the detached kitchen. Nevertheless, a slander case documents its presence by 1693 when one of the litigants "came out of the Great house and into the Kitchen to light his pipe." Tithe lists and Custis's will show the changing racial makeup of his labor force in the last quarter of the century.

PORTFOLIO I

1. Building agreement between Thomas Wilford and Paul Sympson, December 2, 1654, Testamentary Business of the Provincial Court, 1649/50–1657, *Archives of Maryland*, 10:301–2; 1700: Inventory for Arthur Dickinson, September 7, 1702, York County, Virginia, Deeds, Orders, Wills, 1702–6, 29–32; 1750: Inventory for John Rochester, November 26, 1754, Westmoreland County, Virginia, Inventory Book 6, 52–52a; 1800: Inventory for John Rochester II, October 20, 1795, Westmoreland County,

Virginia, Inventory Book 8, 328–30. Drawings by Alan Adams; furnishings research by Betty Leviner.

CHAPTER 7

1. William Fitzhugh to Captain Henry Fitzhugh, January 30, 1686/87, in Richard Beale Davis, ed., *William Fitzhugh and His Chesapeake World, 1676–1701: The Fitzhugh Letters and Other Documents* (Chapel Hill: University of North Carolina Press for Virginia Historical Society, 1963), 193. See also Fitzhugh's order for silver, cited below. Cary Carson, "The Consumer Revolution in Colonial British America: Why Demand?" in *Of Consuming Interests: The Style of Life in the Eighteenth Century*, ed. Cary Carson and Ronald Hoffman (New York: Oxford University Press, 1990), 215–16.

2. Robert Beverley, *The History and Present State of Virginia* (London, 1705; reprint, Chapel Hill: University of North Carolina Press, 1947), 289–90.

3. Fraser Neiman, "Domestic Architecture at the Clifts Plantation: The Social Context of Early Virginia Building," *Northern Neck of Virginia Historical Magazine* 28 (December 1978): 3122–28.

4. Dell Upton, "Early Vernacular Architecture in Southeastern Virginia," 2 vols. (Ph.D. diss., Brown University, 1975), 1:218–20; see also J. Richard Revoire, *Homeplaces: Traditional Domestic Architecture of Charles County, Maryland* (La Plata, Md.: Charles County Community College, 1990).

5. Upton, "Early Vernacular Architecture in Southeastern Virginia," 1:220, 232; Cary Carson and Lorena Walsh, "The Material Life of the Early American Housewife," unpublished paper presented at the Conference on Women in Early America, Williamsburg, 1981.

6. Camille Wells, "Social and Economic Aspects of Eighteenth-Century Housing on the Northern Neck of Virginia" (Ph.D. diss., College of William and Mary, 1994), 113.

7. Thomas Jefferson to James Ogilvie, February 20, 1771, in Julian P. Boyd, ed., *The Papers of Thomas Jefferson*, 20 vols. (Princeton: Princeton University Press, 1950–82), 1:62–63.

8. George McDaniel, *Hearth and Home: Preserving a People's Culture* (Philadelphia: Temple University Press, 1982); Michael Ann Williams, "The Little 'Big House': The Use and Meaning of the Single-Pen Dwelling," in *Perspectives in Vernacular Architecture, II*, ed. Camille Wells (Columbia: University of Missouri Press, 1986), 130–36; Edward Williams, "Virginia: More Especially the South Part Thereof," in *Tracts and Other Papers Relating Principally to the Origin, Settlement, and Progress of the Colonies in North America, from the Discovery of the Country to the Year 1776*, 4 vols., ed. Peter Force (Washington, D.C.: P. Force, 1836–46), 3:30.

9. *Virginia Gazette*, July 18, 1766.

10. Willie Graham, Carter L. Hudgins, Carl R. Lounsbury, Fraser D. Neiman, and James P. Whittenburg, "Adaptation and Innovation: Archaeological and Architectural Perspectives on the Seventeenth-Century Chesapeake," *William and Mary Quarterly*, 3d ser., 54 (July 2007): 451–522.

11. Upton, "Early Vernacular Architecture in Southeastern Virginia," 1:294–96.

12. William Fitzhugh to Dr. Ralph Smith, April 22, 1686, in Davis, *William Fitzhugh and His Chesapeake World*, 175.

13. Ibid., William Fitzhugh to John Cooper and Nicholas Hayward, June 1, 1688, 244.

14. Ibid., 246.

15. William Byrd I to Perry and Lane, August 8, 1690, in Marion Tinling, ed., *Correspondence of Three William Byrds of Westover, Virginia, 1684–1776*, 3 vols. (Charlottesville: University Press of Virginia, 1977), 1:135.

16. Upton, "Early Vernacular Architecture in Southeastern Virginia," 1:103; Jan Gilliam and Betty C. Leviner, *"Upon Going to Housekeeping": Furnishing Williamsburg's Historic Buildings* (Williamsburg: Colonial Williamsburg Foundation, 1991), 11–22.

17. Minutes of the Vestry: Truro Parish, Virginia, 1732–1785 (Lorton, Va.: Pohick Church, 1974), 15, cited in Upton, "Early Vernacular Architecture in Southeastern Virginia," 1:265.

18. Upton, "Early Vernacular Architecture in Southeastern Virginia," 1:209–11; see Gunston Hall's Room Use Study, http://www.gunstonhall.org/mansion/room_use_study/domestic.html.

19. Upton, "Early Vernacular Architecture in Southeastern Virginia," 1:211. Arthur Allen's 1711 inventory is transcribed and published in Stephenson B. Andrews, *Bacon's Castle* (Richmond: Association for the Preservation of Virginia Antiquities, 1984), 84–86. The room over the chamber was clearly the best upper room. The chamber, on the other hand, was furnished with objects associated at the time with housewifery—in addition to two beds, a desk, two sugar boxes, and ironing equipment, the chamber was furnished with a large collection of stored linens and a still, together with a mortar and two pestles—probably for making medicines.

20. Terry K. Dunn, ed., *The Recollections of John Mason: George Mason's Son Remembers His Father and Life at Gunston Hall* (Marshall, Va.: EPM Publications, 2004), 64.

21. For Carter's inventory, see "Carter Papers," *Virginia Magazine of History and Biography* 6 (October 1898): 145–52; 6 (January 1899): 261–68; and 6 (April 1899): 365–70. It is clear from the seating listed in other rooms that the chairs had not been placed in Carter's chamber for purposes of storage.

22. Rodris Roth, "Tea-Drinking in Early America: Its Etiquette and Equipage," *Contributions to the Museum of History and Technology, United States National Museum, Bulletin 225* (Washington, D.C.: Smithsonian Institution, 1961), 63–77.

23. Robert Bolling's journal mentions an evening passed in his chamber in the company of several ladies, including Anne Miller, whom he was courting. Leo Lemay, ed., *Robert Bolling Woos Anne Miller, Love and Courtship in Colonial Virginia, 1760* (Charlottesville: University Press of Virginia, 1990), 55. At the house of Tappahannock merchant Archibald McCall, Robert Hunter recounted reading Junius aloud to female acquaintances in the upstairs chamber of McCall's daughter, Catherine. See Louis B. Wright, ed., *Quebec to Carolina in 1785–1786: Being the Travel Diary of Robert Hunter, Jr., a Young Merchant of London* (San Marino, Calif.: Huntington Library, 1943), 242.

24. Early evidence for waiting servants is copious. As a child, Eliza Custis recalled dancing in the dining room to entertain visiting guests, while, in her words, "the servants in the passage would join their mirth." Quoted in Daniel Blake Smith, *Inside the Great House* (Ithaca: Cornell University Press, 1986), 43. During a 1783 visit to Williamsburg, Scotsman Alexander McCaulay confided his resentment at being made to wait in Christiana Campbell's passage with her black servants. See the 1783 journal of Alexander Macaulay, reproduced in Jane Carson, ed., *We Were There: Descriptions of Williamsburg, 1699–1859* (Charlottesville: University Press of Virginia, 1965), 68–69. At Nomini Hall, in Westmoreland County, Virginia, one of Robert Carter's slaves—a male child loitering in the passage—was injured when the front door blew shut, cutting off his finger. See Rhys Isaac, *The Transformation of Virginia, 1740–1790* (Chapel Hill: University of North Carolina Press, 1982), 75. Hunter Dickinson Farish, ed., *The Journal and Letters of Philip Vickers Fithian, 1773–1774: A Plantation Tutor of the Old Dominion* (Williamsburg: Colonial Williamsburg, 1968), 51. In Philadelphia, the sight of slaves waiting about the front doorway of the house was a matter of concern to Thomas Jefferson, who asked that his rented accommodation have no seats outside "to collect lounging servants." Jefferson to William Temple Franklin, July 25, 1790, in Boyd, *Papers of Thomas Jefferson*, 17:268.

25. Shortly after his return from London to take up his inheritance, William Byrd compared life in Virginia to being "buried alive." Bernard Bailyn, *To Begin the World Anew: The Genius and Ambiguities of the American Founders* (New York: Knopf, 2003), 8.

26. Dell Upton, "Domestic Vernacular Architecture in Eighteenth-Century Virginia," *Winterthur Portfolio* 17 (Spring 1982): 98–103.

27. Ibid., 103–4.

28. Wright, *Quebec to Carolina in 1785–1786*, 229.

29. Carson, *We Were There*, 68–69.

30. Farish, *Journal and Letters of Philip Vickers Fithian*, 129.

31. Gregory A. Stiverson and Patrick H. Butler III, eds., "Virginia in 1732: The Travel Journal of William Hugh Grove," *Virginia Magazine of History and Biography* 85 (January 1977): 28.

32. Hugh Jones, *The Present State of Virginia*, ed. Richard L. Morton (London, 1724; reprint, Chapel Hill: University of North Carolina Press, 1956), 71; Stiverson and Butler, "Virginia in 1732: The Travel Journal of William Hugh Grove."

33. William Fairfax to Bryan Fairfax, July 14, 1735, in Papers on the Fairfax Estate 1703-85, Add. Ms. 30306, f. 144, British Museum, London, microfilm copy Rockefeller Library, Colonial Williamsburg Foundation. The author is indebted to Robert Teagle and Camille Wells for this reference.

34. John Custis to Bell & Dee, 1717, in Josephine Little Zuppan, ed., *The Letterbook of John Custis IV of Williamsburg, 1717–1742* (New York: Rowman and Littlefield, 2005), 35.

35. The framing problem was that of supporting the rear rafters when there were no joists in the stairwell to extend over the rear plate and receive them. To carry these rafters, Chesapeake carpenters eventually relied on out-lookers dovetailed into the upper edge of the rear plate. For construction dates of these houses, see Herman J. Heikkenen, "Construction Years for Eight Historical Structures in Colonial Williamsburg, Va., as Derived by Key-Year Technique," unpublished report, Architectural Research Department, Colonial Williamsburg Foundation, April 1984; see also "The Last Year of Tree Growth for Selected Members within the St. George Tucker House, Period I, as Derived by Key-Year Dendrochronology," unpublished report, Architectural Research Department, Colonial Williamsburg Foundation, March 1995.

36. Sarah Fouace Nourse, Diary, 1781–83, entries for July 1781, in Nourse and Morris Family Papers, Alderman Library, University of Virginia, Charlottesville, typescript, Colonial Williamsburg Foundation.

37. Farish, *Journal and Letters of Philip Vickers Fithian*, 130; William Lee to Landon Carter, May 19, 1775, Virginia Historical Society, Richmond, cited in William Rasmussen, "Sabine Hall: A Classical Villa in Virginia" (Ph.D. diss., University of Delaware, 1979), 132; Jack P. Greene, ed., *The Diary of Colonel Landon Carter of Sabine Hall, 1752–1778*, 2 vols. (Charlottesville: University Press of Virginia, 1965), 2:786.

38. Westmoreland County Will Book, 1756–67, 111–12, June 30, 1760.

39. York County Wills and Inventories, 1771–83, 107–12.

40. Mark R. Wenger, "The Dining Room in Early Virginia," in *Perspectives in Vernacular Architecture, III*, ed. Thomas Carter and Bernard L. Herman (Columbia: University of Missouri Press), 149–59.

41. Norfolk County Will and Deed Book, 1736–53, 198–204.

42. Richmond County Will Book, 1725–53, 635–38.

43. See, for example, the 1665 Norfolk County inventory of Thomas Keeling. Of sixty-nine Virginia inventories that mention dining rooms, sixty-seven date to 1727 or later.

44. H. R. McIlwaine, William Hall, and Benjamin Hillman, eds., *The Executive Journals of the Council of Colonial Virginia*, 6 vols. (Richmond: Virginia State Library, 1925–66), 4:135.

45. Upton, "Early Vernacular Architecture in Southeastern Virginia," 1:103.

46. Of twenty-one Virginia inventories that mention back rooms, seventeen date to the half century between 1725 and 1775.

47. Heikkenen, "Construction Years for Eight Historical Structures." Of ten Virginia inventories that mention "old halls," five date to the forty-year period between 1725 and 1765, after which the term disappears entirely from probate records.

48. "Architectural Investigations at Sotterley, St. Mary's City County, Maryland, 1999–2000," unpublished report, Colonial Williamsburg Foundation; D. W. Miles and M. J. Worthington, "Tree-Ring Dating of Sotterley Mansion, Hollywood, Maryland," unpublished interim report, Oxford Dendrochronology Laboratory, January 2006.

49. Evidence for an L-shaped passage is associated with the present stair, which appears to date from the early nineteenth century.

50. Earlier, less satisfactory attempts to achieve the same end can be seen in the Williamsburg houses of William Timson (1715–

16) and John Blair (1723), where the floor joists of the upper rooms extended well past the back wall, thus enlarging those rooms.

51. Upton, "Early Vernacular Architecture in Southeastern Virginia," 1:108–9.

52. Ibid., 1:232, 240.

53. Original in the manuscripts collection of the George Washington Foundation, Fredericksburg, Virginia.

54. For George Washington's rooms and their contents, see Worthington C. Ford, ed., *Inventory of the Contents of Mount Vernon, 1810* (Cambridge, Mass.: University Press, 1909).

55. Wells, "Social and Economic Aspects," 109, 126–27.

56. The writer is indebted to Camille Wells for this observation.

57. St. Mark's Parish Vestry Book, Culpeper County, Virginia, 1730–1843.

58. Thomas Lee Shippen to his parents, December 30, 1783, transcribed in *Westover Described in 1783* (Richmond: William Byrd Press, 1952).

59. Landon Carter inventory, Robert Carter Papers, Library of Congress, Washington, D.C., 1779, transcribed in Rasmussen, "Sabine Hall."

60. Gunston Hall Room Use Study, 2002, http://www.gunstonhall.org/mansion/room_use_study/methodology.html.

61. For the male associations of early dining rooms, see Mark R. Wenger, "Gender and the Meal in Early Virginia," in *A Taste of the Past: Early Foodways of the Albemarle Region, 1585–1830*, ed. James C. Jordan (Elizabeth City, N.C.: Museum of the Albemarle, 1991).

62. Diary entries, September 20, 1710, 232–33, and November 12, 1711, 436, in Louis B. Wright and Marion Tinling, eds., *The Secret Diary of William Byrd of Westover* (Richmond: Dietz Press, 1941).

63. For the design of this structure, see Carl Lounsbury, "An Elegant and Commodious Building: William Buckland and the Design of the Prince William County Courthouse," *Journal of the Society of Architectural Historians* 46 (September 1987): 228–40.

64. Dunn, *Recollections of John Mason*, 67.

65. The present house was completed by 1738, when John Carter wrote to his brother Charles that his steps at Shirley had been made "extravagantly dear by the drunkenness and laziness of old Taylor." Plummer-Carter Letterbook, Virginia Historical Society, Richmond. The present woodwork in this house is known to date from the 1770s, when Charles Carter advertised in the *Virginia Gazette* for three or four shop joiners "capable of executing the best wainscot work." *Virginia Gazette*, January 14, 1775. Recent examinations revealed the existence of whitewashed plaster behind some portions of the present wainscoting. Most of this had been removed in the 1770s remodeling. See Theodore Rinehart, *The Archaeology of Shirley Plantation* (Charlottesville: University Press of Virginia, 1984), 68.

66. The present "fireplace" is a nonfunctioning feature and has always been so. It appears to be original and was created purely for the sake of appearance—it broke up a large expanse of wall and provided a visual focus for the wall that people first saw as they entered. It also fulfilled expectations that a room of this size would be heated.

67. A chamber with similar attributes is to be seen at Wilton (1753), now moved to Richmond. One of a series of floor plans for Prospect Hill, Spotsylvania County, seat of the Holliday family, shows a ground-floor chamber with a private stair. Though beds appear in each of the chambers, those in the room at the top of the private stair are quite small, as if for servants or children. This plan, now in the Holliday Papers, Virginia Historical Society, Richmond, is illustrated in Camille Wells, "The Multi-Storied House: Twentieth-Century Encounters with the Domestic Architecture of Colonial Virginia," *Virginia Magazine of History and Biography* 106 (Autumn 1998): 417. A similar stair existed at Soldier's Joy, in Nelson County, Virginia, ascending from a lobby by the chamber.

68. Marcia Miller and Orlando Ridout V, eds., *Architecture in Annapolis: A Field Guide* (Crownsville: Vernacular Architecture Forum and Maryland Historical Trust, 1998), 42–44.

69. Ibid., 129–33.

70. Fielding Lewis inventory, 1781, transcription, Colonial Williamsburg Foundation.

71. Isaac, *Transformation of Virginia*, 312–20.

72. Timothy Breen, *Tobacco Culture: The Mentality of the Great Tidewater Planters on the Eve of the Revolution* (Princeton: Princeton University Press, 1985), 105–6, 122, 161–75.

73. Isaac, *Transformation of Virginia*, 302–5, 313–20.

74. Henry Glassie, *Folk Housing in Middle Virginia: A Structural Analysis of Historic Artifacts* (Knoxville: University of Tennessee Press, 1975), 120–22; Isaac, *Transformation of Virginia*, 302–5; Camille Wells, "Virginia by Design: The Making of Tuckahoe and the Remaking of Monticello," *Arris* 12 (2001): 64–67; Marlene Heck, "Palladian Architecture and Social Change in Post-Revolutionary Virginia" (Ph.D. diss., University of Pennsylvania, 1988), 315–37.

75. Smith, *Inside the Great House*, 284–99; Jan Lewis, *The Pursuit of Happiness: Family and Values in Jefferson's Virginia* (New York: Cambridge University Press, 1983); *Margaretta* M. Lovell, "Reading Eighteenth-Century American Family Portraits: Social Images and Self Images," in *Critical Issues in American Art: A Book of Readings*, ed. Mary Ann Calo (Boulder, Col.: Westview Press, 1998), 35–42.

76. Nurseries are rarely mentioned in early documents before 1750. Thereafter, their incidence in probate records and other documents increases markedly. An early example is the 1754 inventory of James Ball, Lancaster County Records, Wills, 1750–58, 195–96. In 1774, Philip Vickers Fithian described a ground-floor nursery at Nomini Hall and later a separate outbuilding given to lodging rooms and a nursery at Mount Airy. Farish, *Journal and Letters of Philip Vickers Fithian*, 95, 184–85. For the mention of Humberston Skipwith's room, see the 1805–6 inventory of Sir Peyton Skipwith of Prestwould, Skipwith Papers, box 23, folder 2, Special Collections, Swem Library, College of William and Mary, Williamsburg. For rooms denominated according to "Boys" and "Girls," see the 1820 inventory of Norfolk merchant Moses Meyers, Norfolk City Deed Book, 1820–22, 9–16.

77. Wright, *Quebec to Carolina in 1785–1786*, 243.

78. Dunn, *Recollections of John Mason*, 63–64.

79. Willie Graham and Mark R. Wenger, "Eppington," in *The Early Architecture of Tidewater Virginia* (Williamsburg: Colonial Williamsburg Foundation, 2002), 89–91.

80. Gaillard Hunt, ed., *The First Forty Years of Washington Society: Portrayed in the Family Letters of Margaret Bayard Smith* (New York: Charles Scribner, 1906), 234.

81. Laura Carter Holloway, *Ladies of the White House* (San Francisco: H. H. Bancroft, 1870), 388–92.

82. Heck, "Palladian Architecture and Social Change in Post-Revolutionary Virginia," 300–337; see also Willie Graham and Mark R. Wenger, "Battersea: A Historical and Architectural Study," unpublished research report, Friends of Battersea Committee and Historic Petersburg Foundation, 1988, chap. 3, 1–7; and *Early Architecture of Tidewater Virginia*, 98.

83. Wells, "Virginia by Design," 48–53.

84. Thomas Anburey, *Travels through the Interior Parts of North America in a Series of Letters*, 2 vols. (London: William Lane, 1789), 2:358–59.

85. Mark R. Wenger, "Jefferson's Designs for Remodeling the Governor's Palace," *Winterthur Portfolio* 32 (Winter 1997): 223–42.

86. For the public character of gentry life, see Margaret Bayard Smith's account of her 1809 visit to Montpelier, in Hunt, *First Forty Years*, 81–83.

87. Sidney George Fisher, *Mount Harmon Diaries of Sidney George Fisher, 1837–1850* (Wilmington: Historical Society of Delaware, 1976), 21.

88. Skipwith inventory, Skipwith Papers, Special Collections, Swem Library, College of William and Mary, Williamsburg.

89. Until recently, the Brockenbrough Room was installed in the Nelson-Atkins Museum, in Kansas City. It has recently been removed and sold at auction.

CHAPTER 8

1. Exceptions would include some seventeenth-century buildings financed by indentured labor before the principal shift to slavery in the 1690s, but the largest seventeenth-century planters and major building clients embraced slavery early. John C. Coombs, "The Phases of Conversion: A New Chronology for the Rise of Slavery in Early Virginia," *William and Mary Quarterly*, 3d ser., 68 (September 2011): 332–60; Lorena S. Walsh, *Motives of Honor, Pleasure, and Profit: Plantation Management in the Colonial Chesapeake, 1607–1763* (Chapel Hill: University of North Carolina Press, 2010).

2. W. L. G. Smith, *Life at the South: or "Uncle Tom's Cabin" as It Is, Being Narratives, Scenes, and Incidents in the Real "Life of the Lowly"* (Buffalo: George H. Derby, 1852). An earlier novel romanticizing the condition of Virginia slaves is John Pendleton Kennedy's *Swallow Barn; or a Sojourn in the Old Dominion* (1832; reprint, Baton Rouge: Louisiana State University Press, 1986).

3. For the enslaved population of Williamsburg, see Thad W. Tate, *The Negro in Eighteenth-Century Williamsburg* (Williamsburg: Colonial Williamsburg Foundation, 1965), 26–27; for An-

napolis, see General Assembly House of Delegates (Assessment Record), 1783, Annapolis Hundred, 1–5, MSA S1161-1, Maryland State Archives, Annapolis.

4. For discussion of the housing for Chesapeake slaves during the colonial period, see Philip D. Morgan, *Slave Counterpoint: Black Culture in the Eighteenth-Century Chesapeake and Lowcountry* (Chapel Hill: University of North Carolina Press, 1998), 104–24; Dell Upton, "Slave Housing in Eighteenth-Century Virginia," unpublished report, Department of Social and Cultural History, National Museum of American History, Smithsonian Institution, 1982; and Edward Chappell and Vanessa E. Patrick, "Architecture, Archaeology, and Slavery in the Early Chesapeake," paper presented at the Society for Historical Archaeology Conference, Richmond, January 10, 1991.

5. Christ Church Parish Vestry Book, 18.

6. Norfolk County Order Book, 1771–73, 162–63, March 19, 1773.

7. Dorchester County Orphans' Court Valuations, 1727–86, no. 10-0096, transcripts in Architectural Research Department, Colonial Williamsburg Foundation.

8. "Observations in Several Voyages and Travels in America," *William and Mary Quarterly*, 1st ser., 15 (January 1907): 148.

9. Richard Beale Davis, ed., *William Fitzhugh and His Chesapeake World, 1676–1701: The Fitzhugh Letters and Other Documents* (Chapel Hill: University of North Carolina Press for Virginia Historical Society, 1963), 175.

10. John Custis Letterbook, 1717–42, Library of Congress, Washington, D.C.

11. Fraser D. Neiman, "The Lost World of Monticello: An Evolutionary Perspective," *Journal of Anthropological Research* 64 (Summer 2008): 170.

12. Morgan, *Slave Counterpoint*, 110.

13. Ibid.

14. Second Book of Miscellanies, 1787–90, Robert Carter Papers, Library of Congress, Washington, D.C.

15. Matching workers in tithable lists to multiple properties owned by wealthy Virginians is commonly difficult, and it is possible that some of Bolling's fifteen workers occupied another "Quarter 24 by 20," worth £10.10, at a nearby tract named Cattails, but the latter was probably separate, tenanted property. Amelia County Court Order Book 1, 217; Amelia County Court Order Book 2, 247; Amelia Land Causes; Michael L. Nicholls, "Building the Virginia Southside: A Note on Architecture and Society in the Eighteenth Century," unpublished paper, Historical Research Department, Colonial Williamsburg Foundation, 1989.

16. Presumably the *Virginia Gazette* sample is skewed in favor of larger buildings. Camille Wells, "The Planter's Prospect: Houses, Outbuildings, and Rural Landscapes in Eighteenth-Century Virginia," *Winterthur Portfolio* 28 (Spring 1993): 1–31.

17. Dorchester County Orphans' Court Valuations, transcripts in Architectural Research Department, Colonial Williamsburg Foundation.

18. On the size of landowner housing in one Piedmont subregion, see Clifton Ellis, "Dissenting Faith and Domestic Landscape

in Eighteenth-Century Virginia," in *Exploring Everyday Landscapes: Perspectives in Vernacular Architecture, VII*, ed. Annmarie Adams and Sally McMurry (Knoxville: University of Tennessee Press, 1997), 24–26.

19. Allan Kulikoff, *Tobacco and Slaves: The Development of Southern Cultures in the Chesapeake, 1680–1800* (Chapel Hill: University of North Carolina Press, 1986); Morgan, *Slave Counterpoint*.

20. Walsh, *Motives of Honor, Pleasure, and Profit*, 380–82.

21. Russell R. Menard, "The Maryland Slave Population, 1658 to 1730: A Demographic Profile of Blacks in Four Counties," *William and Mary Quarterly*, 3d ser., 32 (January 1975): 53; Morgan, *Slave Counterpoint*, 61, 103.

22. See Walsh, *Motives of Honor, Pleasure, and Profit*, on separation of parents.

23. Fraser D. Neiman, "Sub-Floor Pits and Slavery in Eighteenth- and Early Nineteenth-Century Virginia," paper presented at Society for Historical Archaeology conference, Corpus Christi, 1997; Neiman, "Lost World of Monticello," 170, 175–80. See also Patricia M. Samford, *Subfloor Pits and the Archaeology of Slavery in Colonial Virginia* (Tuscaloosa: University of Alabama Press, 2007).

24. Garrett Randall Fesler, "From Houses to Homes: An Archaeological Case Study of Household Formation at the Utopia Slave Quarter, ca. 1675–1775" (Ph.D. diss., University of Virginia, 2004); Samford, *Subfloor Pits*, 42–50.

25. This site was probably called Debb's Quarter or Jacko's Quarter, the former suggesting it was female-headed. Lorena S. Walsh, *From Calabar to Carter's Grove: The History of a Virginia Slave Community* (Charlottesville: University Press of Virginia, 1997), 94.

26. Samford, *Subfloor Pits*, 50–59.

27. Garrett Fesler, "Excavating the Spaces and Interpreting the Places of Enslaved Africans and Their Descendants," in *Cabin, Quarter, Plantation: Architecture and Landscapes of North American Slavery*, ed. Clifton Ellis and Rebecca Ginsburg (New Haven: Yale University Press, 2010), 35–39.

28. Samford, *Subfloor Pits*, 60–66.

29. William M. Kelso, *Kingsmill Plantations, 1619–1800* (Orlando: Academic Press, 1984), 119–23; Samford, *Subfloor Pits*, 66–75.

30. Walsh, *From Calabar to Carter's Grove*, 217.

31. Fesler, "From Houses to Homes," 258–62, 333–50; Barbara Heath, "Space and Place within Plantation Quarters in Virginia, 1700–1825," in Ellis and Ginsburg, *Cabin, Quarter, Plantation*, 162–68.

32. Most if not all workers at Philip Ludwell's Rich Neck, also in James City County, lived from the 1740s to the 1770s in a house similar to Nathaniel Burwell's duplex. Maria Franklin, *An Archaeological Study of the Rich Neck Slave Quarter and Enslaved Domestic Life* (Williamsburg: Colonial Williamsburg Foundation, 2004).

33. Rhys Isaac, *The Transformation of Virginia, 1740–1790* (Chapel Hill: University of North Carolina Press, 1982), 339; Rhys Isaac, *Landon Carter's Uneasy Kingdom* (Oxford: Oxford University Press, 2004).

34. Joseph Ball Letterbook, 1743–80, Library of Congress, Washington, D.C., microfilm, M-21, Colonial Williamsburg Foundation, 9–10.

35. Ibid., 65, November 13, 1746.

36. Ibid., 133, February 5, 1754.

37. Jack P. Greene, ed., *The Diary of Colonel Landon Carter of Sabine Hall, 1752–1778*, 2 vols. (Charlottesville: University Press of Virginia, 1965), 1:291.

38. Joseph Ball Letterbook, 1743–80, 134.

39. Jameson's possessions were contained in an 80-gallon "harness" barrel, a small chest, and a box. Ibid., 135, April 23, 1754.

40. Ibid.

41. Ibid., 135–37.

42. Ibid., 16, February 18, 1744.

43. Ibid., 149, January 18, 1755. On owners' favorable comparisons of the living conditions of slaves in their own regions to European workers and enslaved workers in other lands, see Edward A. Chappell, "Accommodating Slavery in Bermuda," in Ellis and Ginsburg, *Cabin, Quarter, Plantation*, 77–78.

44. Joseph Ball Letterbook, 1743–80, August 31, 1754, to Ball, and August 31, 1754, to Jameson. James Grainger's advice to "Compel by threats, or win by soothing arts" is found in his 1764 poem "The Sugar-Cane." James Grainger et al., *On the Treatment and Management of the More Common West-India Diseases (1750–1802)*, ed. J. Edward Hutson (Mona, Jamaica: University of West Indies Press, 2005), 81. For Robert Carter rewarding an enslaved driver with private housing, see Walsh, *Motives of Honor, Pleasure, and Profit*, 262.

45. Hunter Dickinson Farish, ed., *The Journal and Letters of Philip Vickers Fithian, 1773–1774: A Plantation Tutor of the Old Dominion* (Williamsburg: Colonial Williamsburg, 1968), 107–9.

46. *Virginia Gazette*, October 8, 1767, February 5, 1767, and February 5, 1780.

47. A cellar kitchen was included at the William and Mary President's House, John Blair House, Mary Stith House, the Blue Bell and Campbell's taverns on Waller Street, and apparently below the first-floor chamber at Flournoy Tavern (c. 1710) and the hall of Shields Tavern on Duke of Gloucester Street.

48. Richard Henry Lee Memorandum Book, 1776–94, 34, January 16, 1780, and 40, April 7, 1780, Brock Collection, Huntington Library, San Marino, California.

49. Dorchester County Orphans' Court Valuations, Maryland, Land Records, Old Number 27, f. 425, May 20, 1774, transcripts in the Architectural Research Department, Colonial Williamsburg Foundation.

50. *Boston Evening Post*, May 5, 1741.

51. Greene, *Diary of Colonel Landon Carter of Sabine Hall*, 1:291.

52. There were two generations of kitchens north of the Wythe House, each with a sizable cookroom and heated secondary room served by a central chimney. Broadnax's presumed room was about 16 feet deep and of unclear length and was beside her cookroom in the earlier kitchen. The later lodging room was roughly 12 by 15 feet.

53. York County Wills and Inventories, 22, 337–46. An 1818 entry for Thomas G. Peachy Jr.'s estate provides the building's name. Williamsburg Land Books, 1782–1861, M-1-48, Colonial Williamsburg Foundation.

54. Unlike many contemporary English three-part ensembles, they seldom contained stables. The James Brice and Upton Scott Houses in Annapolis are exceptions, both incorporating stables in one flanking building.

55. Dennis Pogue, "The Domestic Architecture of Slavery at George Washington's Mount Vernon," *Winterthur Portfolio* 37 (2002): 3–22.

56. Precise dates of the earliest surviving flankers at Shirley are unknown, but they may predate John Carter's death in 1742. Son Charles Carter did not move to Shirley as an adult until 1771. It is conceivable that his mother, Elizabeth, and stepfather, Bowler Cock, built them.

57. Harrower called the one-room building where he lodged and taught "a neat little house … at 500 yds from the Main house." He conceived of the household at Belvidera as all the whites: "Our Family consists of the Coll. His lady & four Children a housekeeper and overseer and myself all white. But how many blacks young and old the Lord only knows for I believe there is about thirty that works every day in the field besides the servants about the house; such a Gardner, livery men and pages, Cooks, washer & dresser, sewster, and waiting girle." Housekeeper Gaines slept in the mansion. Edward Miles Riley, ed., *The Journal of John Harrower, an Indentured Servant in the Colony of Virginia, 1773–1776* (Williamsburg: Colonial Williamsburg Foundation, 1963), 41, 56, 68, 85, 112, 129, 131, 139–40, 142–44; Farish, *Journal and Letters of Philip Vickers Fithian*, 108.

58. Both flankers at Blandfield were built with large work fireplaces in the principal first-floor room. The south flanker was remodeled as refined domestic space, apparently for Beverley family use soon after 1800. At Mount Airy, one flanker was built as kitchen and plain lodgings and the other provided refined domestic space. Fithian described the wings at Mount Airy as "a kitchen, & the other, for a nursery & Lodging Rooms." Farish, *Journal and Letters of Philip Vickers Fithian*, 126. Menokin offers an exception. The relatively more modest arrangement there was that second-floor residents of the flankers walked through the larger first-floor room, including the cookroom and its inner room (identified as the laundry), suggesting that the upper lodging there was of lower status. For the design drawing attributed to William Buckland, see Camille Wells, "Dower Play/Power Play: Menokin and the Ordeal of Elite House Building in Colonial Virginia," in *Constructing Image, Identity, and Place: Perspectives in Vernacular Architecture, IX*, ed. Alison K. Hoagland and Kenneth A. Breisch (Knoxville: University of Tennessee Press, 2003), 10.

59. Fithian described in his diary how in 1774 the young slave Sukey was frightened by a human or spectral intruder in her bed in the nursery at Nomini Hall and that she ran to the bed of housekeeper Sally Stanhope. Harrower recorded that affluent Priscilla Dawson visiting from Williamsburg in 1775 died at Belvidera in the chamber where her daughter and an enslaved waiting maid slept.

Dawson was the widow of Thomas Dawson, president of the College of William and Mary. See Farish, *Journal and Letters of Philip Vickers Fithian*; and Riley, *Journal of John Harrower*, 87, 184n.

60. Greene, *Diary of Colonel Landon Carter of Sabine Hall*, 1:495.

61. Archaeological excavation adjoining the fireplace revealed faunal and artifact remains interpreted as evidence of small-scale cooking and domestic work like sewing, as well as evidence for a sub-floor pit. Kim Tinkham and Matthew Reeves, "Mansion Cellars Report: Excavations of the Cellar Spaces for the Main Block of the Mansion (2003–2005 Seasons)," unpublished report, Montpelier, Orange, Virginia, 2010.

62. Andrew Levy, *The First Emancipator* (New York: Random House, 2005).

63. Problems with water leaks in the esoteric treble roof led Carter or his successor to add upper rafters above the valleys. Riven clapboards were then jerry-rigged into the resulting openings to raise the partition and maintain separation of the two spaces. Microscopy reveals that the plaster has two coats of whitewash and the clapboards none.

64. Orlando Ridout V, "Re-editing the Architectural Past: A Comparison of Surviving Documentary and Physical Evidence on Maryland's Eastern Shore," paper presented at the Society of Architectural Historians Conference, New Haven, April 1982.

65. It was not until the 1780s, for example, that "Negro quarters" began to be listed among the facilities at properties offered for sale in Maryland newspapers. Early American Newspapers, infoweb.newbank.com.

66. Neiman, "Lost World of Monticello."

67. Annette Gordon-Reed, *The Hemingses of Monticello: An American Family* (New York: W. W. Norton, 2008), 28, 512–15; Lucia Stanton, *Slavery at Monticello* ([Charlottesville, Va.]: Thomas Jefferson Memorial Foundation, 1996); Lucia Stanton, *Free Some Day: The African-American Families of Monticello* (Charlottesville, Va.: Thomas Jefferson Foundation, 2000).

68. Neiman, "Lost World of Monticello."

69. John Hill, "Tract of Sir Peyton Skipwith's Land," February 1–15, 1798, Prestwould Foundation, Clarksville, Virginia.

70. St. Mary's County Orphans' Court Valuations, 1780–1807, f 193 and 236, transcripts in Maryland Historical Trust, Annapolis, 19–0073 and 19–0084.

71. Pogue, "Domestic Architecture of Slavery," 8–11.

72. Farish, *Journal and Letters of Philip Vickers Fithian*, 265.

73. Frasier D. Neiman, "Housing Slavery at Monticello and Beyond: Models, Expectations, Data," paper presented at Society for Historical Archaeology conference, Baltimore, 2012.

74. Nicholls, "Building the Virginia Southside."

75. Ridout, "Re-editing the Architectural Past."

76. St. Mary's County Orphans' Court Valuations, 1780–1807, transcripts in Maryland Historical Trust, Annapolis.

77. J. F. D. Smythe, *Travels through the Interior Parts of America*, 2 vols. (London, 1789), 2:381–82.

78. Johann David Schoepf, *Travels in the Confederation*, 2 vols. (1788; reprint, New York: Bergman, 1968), 2:32–33.

79. Mary Browne to Alexander D. Galt, September 13, 1823, Galt Papers, Swem Library, College of William and Mary, Williamsburg, quoted in Gerald Mullin, *Flight and Rebellion: Slave Resistance in Eighteenth-Century Virginia* (New York: Oxford University Press, 1972), 52.

80. James O. Breeden, ed., *Advice among Masters: The Ideal in Slave Management in the Old South* (Westport, Conn.: Greenwood Press, 1980), 106–10.

81. Dell Upton, "Lancasterian Schools, Republican Citizenship, and the Spatial Imagination in Early Nineteenth-Century America," *Journal of the Society of Architectural Historians* 55, no. 3 (September 1996): 238–53.

82. Bernard L. Herman, "Slave Quarters in Virginia: The Persona behind Historic Artifacts," in *The Scope of Historical Archaeology: Essays in Honor of John L. Cotter*, ed. David G. Orr and D. G. Crozier (Philadelphia: Temple University Press, 1984), 253–83.

83. Letter from Shepard, n.d., Josiah Collins Papers, PC417, North Carolina State Archives, Raleigh, cited in Carl Lounsbury, "The Building Process in Antebellum North Carolina," *North Carolina Historical Review* 60, no. 4 (October 1983): 437. Shepard died in 1852.

84. Douglas W. Sanford and Dennis J. Pogue, "Measuring the Social, Spatial, and Temporal Dimensions of Virginia Slave Housing," performance report for NEH Grant R2-50619–06, 2009.

85. The now-altered central building may have been an overseer's house, measuring about 26 feet by 18 feet and set forward of the other four, but it, too, had a dirt floor. Goochland County, Virginia, Land and Personal Property Lists, 1830 and 1850.

86. Breeden, *Advice among Masters*, 125.

87. Dendrochronological date from Sanford and Pogue, "Measuring the Social, Spatial, and Temporal Dimensions," appendix 2.

88. Larry McKee, "The Ideals and Realities behind the Design and Use of 19th-Century Virginia Slave Cabins," in *The Art and Mystery of Historical Archaeology: Essays in Honor of James Deetz*, ed. Anne Elizabeth Yentsch and Mary C. Beandry (Boca Raton: CRC Press, 1992), 201.

89. Edward A. Chappell, "Housing a Nation: The Transformation of Living Standards in Early America," in *Of Consuming Interests*, ed. Cary Carson, Ronald Hoffman, and Peter J. Albert (Charlottesville: University Press of Virginia, 1994), 221–22.

90. Ira Berlin, *Generations in Captivity: A History of African-American Slaves* (Cambridge, Mass.: Harvard University Press, 2003); Walsh, *Motives of Honor, Pleasure, and Profit*.

91. Carl Lounsbury and George McDaniel, "Recording Plantation Communities," unpublished report, North Carolina Department of Archives and History, Raleigh, 1980, 8.

92. Eppes Diaries, Sept. 3, Oct. 1, 1851; Apr. 30, Oct. 20, Nov. 4, 1852; Eppes Papers, Virginia Historical Society.

93. Cameron to Cameron, February 15, 1826, Cameron Family Papers, Southern Historical Collection, Wilson Library, University of North Carolina at Chapel Hill, cited in Lounsbury, "The Building Process," 437.

94. Frederick Law Olmsted, *The Journey through the Seaboard Slave States: The Upper South, 1852–1853*, in *The Papers of Frederick Law Olmsted*, ed. Charles E. Beveridge and Charles Capen McLaughlin (Baltimore: Johns Hopkins University Press, 1981), 2, 89.

CHAPTER 9

1. Edwin M. Betts, ed., *Thomas Jefferson's Farm Book* (Charlottesville: University Press of Virginia, 1976); Jack P. Greene, ed., *The Diary of Colonel Landon Carter of Sabine Hall, 1752–1778*, 2 vols. (Charlottesville: University Press of Virginia, 1965).

2. J. Hall Pleasants, ed., *Archives of Maryland, LIV: Proceedings of the County Courts of Kent (1658–1676), Talbot (1662–1674), and Somerset (1665–1668)* (Baltimore: Maryland Historical Society, 1937), 151.

3. Ibid., 151–52.

4. Arthur Pierce Middleton, *Tobacco Coast* (Newport News, Va.: Mariner's Museum, 1953); Aubrey C. Land, ed., *Bases of the Plantation Society* (New York: Harper and Row, 1969); Carville V. Earle, *The Evolution of a Tidewater Settlement System* (Chicago: University of Chicago Press, 1975); Rhys Isaac, *The Transformation of Virginia, 1740–1790* (Chapel Hill: University of North Carolina Press, 1982); Cary Carson et al., "Impermanent Architecture in the Southern American Colonies," *Winterthur Portfolio* 16 (Summer/Autumn 1981): 135–96.

5. Lois Green Carr and Russell R. Menard, "Immigration and Opportunity: The Freedman in Early Colonial Maryland," in *The Chesapeake in the Seventeenth Century*, ed. Thad W. Tate and David L. Ammerman (New York: W. W. Norton, 1979), 207; William Tatham, *An Historical and Practical Essay on the Culture of Tobacco* (London: Vernor and Hood, 1800), 195. Tatham cited Thomas Jefferson, *Notes on the State of Virginia* (London: John Stockdale, 1787), 276–78. Records from the 1640s and 1650s indicate that hogsheads weighed in the range of 300 to 333 pounds, but size and capacity grew to perhaps 500 pounds in the 1690s, and by the mid-eighteenth century had been enlarged to 1,000 pounds or more. For the conversion of crop production to tobacco houses, see "On the Cultivation of Tobacco," *American Farmer*, 1 (March 10, 1820): 395.

6. Paul G. Clemens, *The Atlantic Economy and Colonial Maryland's Eastern Shore: From Tobacco to Grain* (Ithaca: Cornell University Press, 1980); Elizabeth Gallow, "Observations from the 1798 Tax Record for Maryland," unpublished research report, Architectural Research Department, Colonial Williamsburg Foundation, 2005.

7. Hugh Jones, *The Present State of Virginia* (London, 1724; reprint, Chapel Hill: University of North Carolina Press, 1956), 77; Greene, *Diary of Colonel Landon Carter of Sabine Hall*; Tatham, *Historical and Practical Essay on the Culture of Tobacco*, 113–29; A. Lawrence Kocher and Howard Dearstyne, *Shadows in Silver: Virginia, 1850–1900* (New York: Charles Scribner's, 1954), 15–33; Christopher Martin, *Calvert County Tobacco Culture Survey, Phase II: Oral History and Folklife* (n.p.: Engineering-Science, 1991).

8. For "killing" tobacco, see Greene, *Diary of Colonel Landon Carter of Sabine Hall*, 2:735, 742.

9. *American Husbandry*, 2 vols. (London: J. Bew, 1775), 1:224–25, cited in Land, *Bases of the Plantation Society*, 77; Greene, *Diary of Colonel Landon Carter of Sabine Hall*, 2:780; Tatham, *Historical and Practical Essay on the Culture of Tobacco*, 33–37.

10. Tatham, *Historical and Practical Essay on the Culture of Tobacco*, 47–48, 128–29, 195; Jones, *Present State of Virginia*, 77.

11. Tatham, *Historical and Practical Essay on the Culture of Tobacco*, 69–84; Elizabeth Cometti, ed., *The American Journals of Lt. John Enys* (Syracuse: Syracuse University Press, 1976), 243; Frederic Emory, *History of Queen Anne's County, Maryland* (Baltimore: Maryland Historical Society, 1950), 21–22.

12. Elizabeth Merritt, ed., *Archives of Maryland, LXVII: Proceedings of the Provincial Court, 1677–1678* (Baltimore: Maryland Historical Society, 1956), 345; W. W. Abbot, Dorothy Twohig, and Philander D. Chase, eds., *The Papers of George Washington, Colonial Series*, 10 vols. (Charlottesville: University Press of Virginia, 1983–95), 5:447; Greene, *Diary of Colonel Landon Carter of Sabine Hall*, 1:487–88, 490.

13. Francis Jerdone Account Book, July 12, 1759, Manuscript 29.4, Colonial Williamsburg Foundation; Joseph Ball Letterbook, 1743–80, Library of Congress, Washington, D.C., microfilm, M-21, Colonial Williamsburg Foundation.

14. Richmond County Miscellaneous Record Book, 1718, 206–7; J. Richard Rivoire, *Home Places* (La Plata, Md.: Southern Maryland Studies Center, 1990), 166–67.

15. Joseph Ball Letterbook, 1743–80, February 18, 1744.

16. Lewis C. Gray, *History of Agriculture in the Southern United States to 1860*, 2 vols. (Washington, D.C., 1933; reprint, Clifton, N.J.: Augustus M. Kelley, 1973), 1:22; H. R. McIlwaine, ed., *Minutes of the Council and General Court of Virginia, 1622–1632, 1670–1676* (Richmond: Virginia State Library, 1924), 27; Susie M. Ames, *County Court Records of Accomack-Northampton, Virginia, 1640–1645* (Charlottesville: University Press of Virginia, 1973), 118–19, 354.

17. If the relatively small sample for St. Mary's County is accurate, it is likely that adoption of 4-foot rooms was occurring apace in the adjoining counties of southern Maryland, such as Charles and Calvert.

18. Gray, *History of Agriculture*, 1:36–37, 171–74; Peter Kalm, "Description of Maize, How It Is Planted and Cultivated in North America," trans. Esther L. Larsen, *Agricultural History* 9 (April 1935): 98–117; Edward Miles Riley, ed., *The Journal of John Harrower, an Indentured Servant in the Colony of Virginia, 1773–1776* (Williamsburg: Colonial Williamsburg Foundation, 1963), 52–53.

19. Gray, *History of Agriculture*, 1:171–74; W. W. Abbot, Dorothy Towhig, Philander D. Chase, Theodore J. Crackel, et al., *The Papers of George Washington, Presidential Series*, 16 vols. to date (Charlottesville: University of Virginia Press, 1987–), 1:221; Riley, *Journal of John Harrower*, 52–53.

20. Crop cycles can be followed through multiple years in the weekly work reports filed for each of the subsidiary farms that made up Mount Vernon for the period 1784–99. Comparable records appear in a less continuous and organized format by Landon Carter and John Harrower in the late colonial period.

"Mount Vernon Weekly Reports," Smith Library, Mount Vernon Ladies' Association, Mount Vernon, Alexandria, Virginia. For cross-plowing, spacing, and planting, see Riley, *Journal of John Harrower*, 52–53, 93; Greene, *Diary of Colonel Landon Carter of Sabine Hall*, 2:678, 930–31; and Richard Parkinson, *A Tour in America in 1798, 1799, and 1800*, 2 vols. (London: J. Harding and J. Murray, 1805), 1:413.

21. The practice of gathering fodder, blades, and tops is summarized by Gray, *History of Agriculture*, 1:174. For additional references to these practices, see "Mount Vernon Weekly Reports," Smith Library, Mount Vernon Ladies' Association, Mount Vernon, Alexandria, Virginia; Riley, *Journal of John Harrower*, 52–53, 64, 66, 69; and Greene, *Diary of Colonel Landon Carter of Sabine Hall*, 2:622, 641, 734, 895, 907.

22. In Queen Anne's County, 82 of 182 valuations (45 percent) for the period 1708–75 include at least one corn house; in Dorchester County the count is 66 of 130 (51 percent) for 1727–76; and in St. Mary's County the count is 47 of 85 (55 percent) for the somewhat later period of 1780–1807. By the first decade of the nineteenth century in Queen Anne's County, 80 percent of valuations included at least one corn house. Precise statements regarding materials are complicated by the tendency to describe the building as log or to omit materials entirely.

23. I am indebted to Camille Wells for transcriptions of property advertisements from the Virginia newspapers. Note that this schedule includes hewing the timbers and preparing the framing members for assembly. Francis Taylor, "Diaries, 1786–1799," entries for November 10–17, 1794, Library of Virginia, Richmond.

24. Queen Anne's County Deeds, RT No. H: 206, RT No. I: 374, and RT No. C: 228; Dorchester County Orphans' Court Transcripts 10-0101 and 10-0096; Queen Anne's County Guardian Bonds and Valuations, WHN #1:116 and WHN #3:152.

25. Of 182 valuations for the period 1708–75, tobacco houses were listed in 120 and corn houses in 82. For the tax data, see Gallow, "Observations from the 1798 Tax Record."

26. Queen Anne's County Guardian Bonds and Valuations, WHN #1:39; Gallow, "Observations from the 1798 Tax Record," charts for County Building Type Frequency (Anne Arundel yielded one and Somerset five). Virginia crib references drawn from Architectural Database, Colonial Williamsburg Foundation; and Elizabeth City Parish Vestry Book, January 1, 1767.

27. Queen Anne's County Guardian Bonds and Valuations, WHN #1:39, WHN #3:144, and WHN #4:1. A survey of the two-man teams of appraisers involved in the key period 1814–22 reveals that eighteen different individuals were involved, but that two men account for nine of the fourteen valuations that use the term "crib." Of eighty-one descriptions from the 1850s, thirty-two use the term "crib."

28. Gray, *History of Agriculture*, 1:161–71; Harold Gill, "Wheat Culture in Colonial Virginia," *Agricultural History* 52, no. 3 (July 1978): 380–93; Jefferson, *Notes on the State of Virginia*.

29. Gray, *History of Agriculture*; Gill, "Wheat Culture in Colonial Virginia"; Clemens, *Atlantic Economy*, 168–98.

30. Crop cycles are derived from diary entries by Landon

Carter, John Harrower, and George Washington and from "Mount Vernon Weekly Reports," 1785–99, Smith Library, Mount Vernon Ladies' Association, Mount Vernon, Alexandria, Virginia.

31. George Washington, "Notes & Observations," manuscript, 1785–86, Washington Papers, Library of Congress, Washington, D.C., 43–47; Donald Jackson and Dorothy Twohig, eds., *The Diaries of George Washington*, 6 vols. (Charlottesville: University Press of Virginia, 1976–79), 2:80–81, 2:171, 5:8–10; "Mount Vernon Weekly Reports," 1785–99, June 25–July 8, 1797, Smith Library, Mount Vernon Ladies' Association, Mount Vernon, Alexandria, Virginia; Riley, *Journal of John Harrower*, 50, 102; John C. Fitzpatrick, ed., *The Writings of George Washington from the Original Manuscript Sources, 1745–1799*, 39 vols. (Washington, D.C.: Government Printing Office, 1931–44), 32:470–73.

32. Greene, *Diary of Colonel Landon Carter of Sabine Hall*, July 10, 1775, 2:920.

33. Riley, *Journal of John Harrower*, 47–68.

34. Ibid., 104. George Washington noted 177 shocks of wheat "in the field" in 1786, each equal to about 1½ to 2 bushels. Jackson and Twohig, *Diaries of George Washington*, 5:11–14.

35. English agricultural reformer Arthur Young describes threshing by hand on temporary floors in the field, in Arthur Young, *Six Months Tour through the North of England*, 2 vols. (London: W. Strahan, 1771), 1:4. Quality issues related to treading were raised by William Strickland, *Observations on the Agriculture of the United States of America* (London: W. Bulmer, 1801), 47. For Landon Carter on hand flailing or "whipping out" wheat, including daily production per man, see Greene, *Diary of Colonel Landon Carter of Sabine Hall*, 2:600–601, 612–14. Harrower describes treading with horses in 1775, in Riley, *Journal of John Harrower*, 85, 107.

36. Greene, *Diary of Colonel Landon Carter of Sabine Hall*, 2:630, 781.

37. Queen Anne's County Deeds, RT No. D: 75. Of 87 valuations from this county for the period 1800–1809, 23 had separate granary structures (26 percent), another 9 had granaries within multipurpose buildings (10 percent), and 21 more had barns that may have included storage for grain (21 percent). The Dorchester County sample includes 130 pre-Revolutionary valuations (1727–76) and 3 from the following decade. The St. Mary's County sample consists of 85 valuations for the period 1780–1808; four granaries are described, all from the years 1802–7.

38. *Virginia Gazette*, October 11, 1751.

39. *Maryland Gazette*, February 2, 1769.

40. *Virginia Herald*, April 22, 1800.

41. Northampton County Deed and Will Book, 1655–68, 2.

42. Stratton Major Parish Vestry Book, 1729–83, 5.

43. Fairfax Parish Vestry Book, May 24, 1773.

44. *Maryland Gazette*, August 8, 1780.

45. Ibid., December 28, 1786.

46. Queen Anne's County Guardian Bonds and Valuations, November 3, 1795, SC:257.

47. Dorchester County Orphans' Court Valuations, 10-0046 and 10-0080.

48. Space allocations can be determined from three kinds of evidence—field documentation of a small number of extant stables, scale drawings that survive from the period, and documentary descriptions with sufficient detail to allow analytical conclusions.

49. "Journal of the Meetings of the President and Masters of [the College of] William and Mary, June 26, 1761," in *William and Mary Quarterly*, 1st ser., 3 (January 1895): 195.

50. Cumberland Parish Vestry Book, January 15, 1766.

51. *Virginia Gazette*, September 27, 1783.

52. *Maryland Gazette*, April 14, 1767; Riley, *Journal of John Harrower*, 141.

53. Whitehall Plantation Accounts, June 21, 1774, Manuscripts Collection, Winterthur Library, Winterthur, Delaware; York County Loss Claims for January 1, 1781, transcript, Rockefeller Library, Colonial Williamsburg Foundation; *Virginia Herald*, March 7, 1800; *Maryland Gazette*, October 25, 1764.

54. *Virginia Herald and Fredericksburg Advertiser*, January 22, 1789; *Alexandria Gazette*, August 27, 1795; *Maryland Gazette*, July 2, 1812.

55. Richmond Croom Beatty and William J. Mulloy, eds., *William Byrd, Natural History of Virginia* (Richmond: Dietz Press, 1940), 18.

56. Gray, *History of Agriculture*, 1:22, 28; G. E. Fussell, "Science and Practice in Eighteenth Century British Agriculture," *Agricultural History* 43 (October 1969): 10; *American Husbandry* (London: J. Bew, 1775), 266–67, 277.

57. Greene, *Diary of Colonel Landon Carter of Sabine Hall*, 2:777; "Mount Vernon Weekly Reports," 1785–95, Smith Library, Mount Vernon Ladies' Association, Mount Vernon, Alexandria, Virginia. Documentary evidence for eighteenth-century cow stall sizes in the Chesapeake is limited, but stall data can be derived from model farm layouts published in British pattern books, and these are consistent with advice from American sources such as John Beale Bordley, who recommended an area 3 by 6 feet for each cow. John Beale Bordley, *Sketches on Rotation of Crops* (Philadelphia: Charles Cist, 1797), 55.

58. Gray, *History of Agriculture*, 1:145. Fencing types can be derived from a diverse array of primary sources, but the Queen Anne's County valuations provide a particularly rich source for details.

59. Dorchester Orphans' Court Valuations, 10-0094, 10-0097, and 10-0044.

60. William Hand Browne, ed., *Archives of Maryland, IV: Judicial and Testamentary Business of the Provincial Court, 1637–1650* (Baltimore: Maryland Historical Society, 1887), 110, 455.

61. Greene, *Diary of Colonel Landon Carter of Sabine Hall*, 2:897.

62. Ibid.

63. Jackson and Twohig, *Diaries of George Washington*, 4:231; Washington, "Notes & Observations," 47.

64. W. Emerson Wilson, ed., *Mount Harmon Diaries of Sidney George Fisher, 1837–1850* (Wilmington: Historical Society of Delaware, 1976), 216–17; "A Memorandum of Passing Events by

William H. C. Roe, October 1856–June 1861," transcription by Orlando Ridout V, 1979, Maryland Historical Trust, Crownsville.

CHAPTER 10

1. Much of the seventeenth-century portion of this chapter is derived from my contribution to a published essay: Cary Carson, Joanne Bowen, Willie Graham, Martha McCartney, and Lorena Walsh, "New World, Real World: Improvising English Culture in Seventeenth-Century Virginia and Maryland," *Journal of Southern History* 74 (February 2008): 31–88. See also Willie Graham, Carter L. Hudgins, Carl R. Lounsbury, Fraser D. Neiman, and James P. Whittenburg, "Adaptation and Innovation: Archaeological and Architectural Perspectives on the Seventeenth-Century Chesapeake," *William and Mary Quarterly*, 3d ser., 54 (July 2007): 451–522. I am greatly indebted to Cary Carson for his help in shaping this chapter.

2. J. Eric Deetz, "Architecture of Early Virginia: An Analysis of the Origins of the Earth Fast Tradition" (master's thesis, University of Leicester, 2002); William Kelso and Beverly Straube, *Jamestown Rediscovery, 1994–2004* (Richmond: Association for the Preservation of Virginia Antiquities, 2004), 49–61.

3. Cary Carson, Norman F. Barka, William M. Kelso, Garry Wheeler Stone, and Dell Upton, "Impermanent Architecture in the Southern American Colonies," *Winterthur Portfolio* 16 (Summer–Autumn 1981): 136–38. These authors advanced the hypothesis that the oldest buildings known to archaeologists in the region in 1981—those discovered at Flowerdew Hundred dated to 1619—had been built too early to reflect the process of New World invention. The fort buildings at Jamestown push that date back to the first years of settlement.

4. J. G. Hurst, "A Review of Archaeological Research," in *Deserted Medieval Villages*, ed. Maurice Beresford and John G. Hurst (London: Lutterworth Press, 1971), 76–168.

5. Philip L. Barbour, ed., *The Complete Works of Captain John Smith*, 3 vols. (Chapel Hill: University of North Carolina Press, 1986), 1:233.

6. Documentary evidence for clay-walled buildings, a continuation of the practice of nogging walls with clay, and the haphazard alignment of posts inside clay walls suggest a robust regional practice throughout the first half of the seventeenth century. See, as an example, Willie Graham, "A Report on the Nature of the Kirbye House Frame and Wall System," unpublished report, Architectural Research Department, Colonial Williamsburg Foundation, 2004.

7. From "Anonymous Notes for the Guidance of Raleigh and Cavendish," entitled "For Master Rauleys Viage," quoted in *The Roanoke Voyages, 1584–1590: Documents to Illustrate the English Voyages to North America under the Patent Granted to Walter Raleigh in 1584*, 2 vols., ed. David Beers Quinn (London: Hakluyt Society, 1955; reprint, New York: Dover, 1991): 1:136. The tradition of expeditions relying upon these ancient construction methods continued throughout the seventeenth century, even as late as the Scottish expedition to Darien, Panama, in 1698. Although earthfast buildings were discovered during a preliminary excava-

tion, no report was written of the findings. It was featured in a 2004 BBC Scotland program, *Darien: Disaster in Paradise*, by the expedition leader, Mark Horton. See also Charles Hodges, "Forts of the Chieftains: A Study of Vernacular, Classical, and Renaissance Influence on Defensible, Town and Villa Plans in Seventeenth-Century Virginia" (master's thesis, College of William and Mary, 2003).

8. Carson et al., "Impermanent Architecture," 135–96.

9. Norman F. Barka, *The Archaeology of Flowerdew Hundred Plantation: The Stone House Foundation Site* (Williamsburg: Southside Historical Sites, 1976); Garry Wheeler Stone, "Society, Housing, and Architecture in Early Maryland: John Lewger's St. John's" (Ph.D. diss., University of Pennsylvania, 1982); Nicholas Luccketti, "The Road to James Fort," in William M. Kelso, Nicholas M. Luccketti, and Beverly A. Straube, *Jamestown Rediscovery, V* (Richmond: Association for the Preservation of Virginia Antiquities, 1999), 27–29. For mud-and-stud, which was common to the Lincolnshire fens, see Deetz, "Architecture of Early Virginia"; and Rodney Cousins, *Lincolnshire Buildings in the Mud and Stud Tradition* (Sleaford, England: Heritage Lincolnshire, 2000). See also Database of Early Chesapeake Architecture (DECA), www.deca.swem.wm.edu.

10. Al Luckenbach, *Providence 1649: The History and Archaeology of Anne Arundel County Maryland's First European Settlement* (Crownsville: Maryland State Archives and Maryland Historical Trust, 1995).

11. Letter from Thomas Cornwaleys to Lord Baltimore, April 16, 1638, in *The Calvert Papers, Number One* (Baltimore: Maryland Historical Society, Fund Publication No. 28, 1889), 174.

12. Richard Beale Davis, ed., *William Fitzhugh and His Chesapeake World, 1676–1701: The Fitzhugh Letters and Other Documents* (Chapel Hill: University of North Carolina Press for Virginia Historical Society, 1963), 202–3.

13. Edward Arber and A. G. Bradley, eds., *Travels and Works of Captain John Smith, President of Virginia, and Admiral of New England, 1580–1631* (Edinburgh: John Grant, 1910), 114, 121.

14. *Information and Direction to Such Persons as Are Inclined to America, More Especially Those Related to the Province of Pennsylvania* (1682), in *Pennsylvania Magazine of History and Biography* 4 (1880): 335. Although intended for settlers bound for Pennsylvania, this tract included instructions needed to build what was essentially a vernacular house in Virginia.

15. Eric Mercer, *English Vernacular Houses* (London: HMSO, 1975), 125–26; Richard Harris, *Discovering Timber-Framed Buildings* (Aylesbury: Shire Publications, 1978), 23–24; Dell T. Upton, "Early Vernacular Architecture in Southeastern Virginia," 2 vols. (Ph.D. diss., Brown University, 1979), 1:58–59.

16. Mercer, *English Vernacular Houses*, 125; Nina Jennings, *Clay Dabbins: Vernacular Buildings of the Solway Plain, Cumbria* (Kendal, Cumbria: Cumberland and Westmoreland Antiquarian and Archaeological Society, 2003), 61–66, 143–47.

17. See Carl Lounsbury, "The 1608 Church at Jamestown: A History and Precedents for Its Design and Reconstruction," unpublished research report, Architectural Research Depart-

ment, Colonial Williamsburg Foundation, 2010; Edward Maria Wingfield, *A Discourse of Virginia* (Boston: John Wilson, 1860), n52.

18. Willie Graham, "Preindustrial Framing Technology in the Chesapeake," in *Constructing Image, Identity, and Place: Perspectives in Vernacular Architecture, IX*, ed. Alison K. Hoagland and Kenneth A. Breisch (Knoxville: University of Tennessee Press, 2003), 180–96.

19. Cary Carson, "The Virginia House in Maryland," *Maryland Historical Magazine* 69, no. 2 (Summer 1974): 185–96.

20. Although other bay dimensions show up in the archaeological record, 10-foot bays were the most common into the early eighteenth century.

21. The rafters in the 1715 wing at Sotterley are an example, measuring less than 2 inches square in cross section.

22. For instance, justices in Essex County "agree[d] with a workman to build a house to hold court in, of *common clapboard work* thirty foot long and twenty foot wide." Essex County, Virginia, Court Order Book, 1726–29, 84; Dell Upton, "Board Roofing in Tidewater Virginia," *Association for Preservation Technology* 3, no. 4 (1976): 22–43.

23. Unpublished fieldwork by Cary Carson in southwest England reveals the use of a light wall plate to carry the feet of secondary rafters, which at times also supported the tops of wall studs. This framing timber may have been the inspiration for the false plate that developed in the Chesapeake.

24. Carson et al., "Impermanent Architecture in the Southern American Colonies," 166–71.

25. C. G. Chamberlain, ed., *Vestry Book and Register of St. Peter's Parish, New Kent, and James City Counties, Virginia, 1684–1786* (Richmond: Division of Purchase and Printing, 1937), 129.

26. Marcia M. Miller and Orlando Ridout V, eds., *Architecture in Annapolis: A Field Guide* (Crownsville: Maryland Historical Trust Press, 1998), 55–56, 118–20.

27. Dell Upton, *Holy Things and Profane: Anglican Parish Churches in Colonial Virginia* (Cambridge, Mass.: MIT Press, 1986), 35–40.

28. *Minutes of the Vestry, Truro Parish, Virginia, 1732–1785* (Lorton, Va.: Pohick Church, 1974), 15.

29. Graham, "Preindustrial Framing Technology in the Chesapeake," 179, 190–91.

30. For instance, tree-ring analysis of Bruton Parish Church by Herman J. Heikkenen revealed that timbers for the roof frame were felled as early as 1707, with some as late as 1714, this despite that plans for the new church were only approved in 1711.

31. John Steele Papers, #689, Southern Historical Collection, Wilson Library, University of North Carolina at Chapel Hill.

32. The reason these three buildings survive is that each, respectively, was eventually underpinned with brick, or the walls were encased in brick, or the walls were replaced altogether with brick—each sometime in the eighteenth century.

33. J. Hall Pleasants, ed., *Archives of Maryland, LIII: Charles County Court Proceedings, 1662–1666* (Baltimore: Maryland Historical Society, 1936), 357, May 12, 1663.

34. The emergence of log construction as a replacement for earthfast practices in the Chesapeake is discussed in Graham et al., "Adaptation and Innovation," 516–18; and in Carl R. Lounsbury, "Log Building in the Chesapeake," *Vernacular Architecture* 41 (2010): 77–82.

35. Graham et al., "Adaptation and Innovation," 517–18.

36. Matthew Reeves, "Examining a Pre-Georgian Plantation Landscape in Piedmont Virginia: The Original Madison Family Plantation, 1726–1770," paper delivered at the Society for Historical Archaeology Conference, Providence, R.I., 2003.

37. Estate of T. Baughan, account with Benjamin Harrison, 1837, original owned by Edward Ayres, copy on file at Architectural Research Department, Colonial Williamsburg Foundation.

38. William K. Boyd, ed., *William Byrd's History of the Dividing Line betwixt Virginia and North Carolina* (Raleigh: North Carolina Historical Commission, 1929; reprint, New York: Dover, 1967), 36.

39. For a summary of the 1798 direct tax record for selected Maryland counties, see Liz Gallow, "Observations from the 1798 Tax Record for Anne Arundel, Baltimore, Prince George, and Somerset Counties, Maryland," unpublished report, Architectural Research Department, Colonial Williamsburg Foundation, 2005.

40. Bates recorded 145 dwellings, 67 cabins, 1 smith shop, and 26 households with no associated buildings. James Bates, "A List of White Persons and Houses Taken in the County of Halifax, 1785," in "Lists, Inhabitants, and Buildings, 1782–1785," box 2, Virginia State Library, Richmond. See Michael L. Nicholls, "Building the Virginia Southside: A Note on Architecture and Society in the Eighteenth Century," unpublished paper, Architectural Research Department, Colonial Williamsburg Foundation, 1985.

41. Terry G. Jordan attempted to trace the European ancestry of log forms and their associated joints, in *American Log Buildings: An Old World Heritage* (Chapel Hill: University of North Carolina Press, 1985). What is clear from the documentary record and surviving buildings is that a range of forms were selected for use in the Chesapeake and Piedmont regions. By this time, their association with a particular people and place in Europe had long been lost. What became paramount for builders and clients was how each type of log form and its joinery would fit a particular need in the new context of Maryland and Virginia.

42. Baynham's house is better known today as the Bundy House, named for a free black family that was a later owner. Tax valuation for the house rose in 1840 and then remained constant until Baynham sold the property in 1859, suggesting that construction took place in 1839 or 1840. See Julie Richter to Edward Chappell, "The Bundy House, Essex County, Virginia," unpublished research report, Architectural Research Department, Colonial Williamsburg Foundation, February 4, 1993; Essex County Personal Property Tax Lists, 1850–60; and Essex County Deed Book 51, 367, October 15, 1859.

43. Bates, "A List of White Persons and Houses Taken in the County of Halifax, 1785."

44. Cedar Park (1702), the Thoroughgood House (c. 1720),

the Poe House (c. 1720), Pear Valley (1740), and the Benjamin Waller House (c. 1749) reflect the geographical diversity of clapboard use as a base for shingles, in both town and country, during the first half of the eighteenth century.

45. Abbott Cummings notes the prevalence of sheathed roofs on surviving seventeenth-century houses in Massachusetts. Abbott Lowell Cummings, *The Framed Houses of Massachusetts Bay, 1625–1725* (Cambridge, Mass.: Harvard University Press, 1979), 143; Henry A. Hazen, *History of Billerica, Massachusetts, with a Genealogical Register* (Boston: A. Williams, 1883), 275, quoted in Cummings, *Framed Houses*, 143.

46. Joseph Moxon, *Mechanick Exercises or the Doctrine of Handy-Works* (London, 1683; 3d ed., 1703).

47. Daniel W. H. Miles and Michael J. Worthington Miles, "The Tree-Ring Dating of Ware Church, Gloucester County, Virginia," unpublished report, Oxford Tree-Ring Laboratory, 2006.

48. One such exception is the single-pile, Dutch-roofed Travis House in Williamsburg, which was standing when recorded by a French cartographer for a map of Williamsburg in 1782.

49. Joseph Gwilt, *The Encyclopedia of Architecture: Historical, Theoretical, and Practical* (London: Longmans, Green, 1867; reprint, New York: Crown, 1982), 606–7; Carl R. Lounsbury, *An Illustrated Glossary of Early Southern Architecture and Landscape* (New York: Oxford University Press, 1994), 125.

50. Tree-ring analysis by Herman J. Heikkenen derived a date of 1681 for this last year of tree growth for timbers in the Sands House. However, despite the oddity of its roof frame, such an early date seems implausible, especially since a board false plate was used in its roof. Construction more likely took place in the 1720s or 1730s and possibly as late as 1739, when the site was subdivided into three parcels by its new owner, Dr. Charles Carroll.

51. Later, additional trenched purlins were added to take a conventional round-butt shingle roof. Miller and Ridout, *Architecture in Annapolis*, 142–44.

52. Edward R. Cook, William J. Callahan Jr., and Camille Wells, "Dendrochronological Analysis of Rural Plains, Mechanicsville, Hanover County, Virginia," unpublished report for the Richmond National Battlefield Park, 2007. One of the earliest documented southern Dutch roofs is mentioned in the *South Carolina Gazette* in 1734. Soon after, in 1738–39, Judge John Brice built a house in Annapolis with a gambrel roof; Pemberton Hall was erected two years later in Wicomico County; and in 1743–45 William Brown built Four Mile Tree in Surry County with a Dutch roof and clipped gables. These houses represent the beginnings of a Dutch roof tradition in the Chesapeake.

53. An early reference to what was likely a tilted false plate used for an agricultural building called for "plates 12 inches square, False plate 4 by 5 inches." Hubbard Papers, Southern Historical Collection, Wilson Library, University of North Carolina at Chapel Hill.

54. Peter Cottom, *The Richmond and Alexandria Builders' Price Book Containing the House Carpenters' and Joiner's Book of Prices* (Richmond: Peter Cottom, 1820), 43.

CHAPTER 11

1. Areas of easily collectible fieldstone did not exist east of the fall line in the Chesapeake. A few bands of fieldstone in Maryland made it possible for builders to construct an occasional foundation, cellar, or chimney. On the Eastern Shore of Maryland, there were sufficient veins of fieldstone in northern Dorchester, southern Talbot, and central Kent Counties for the construction of a few smokehouses, dairies, cellars, and parts of dwellings. Stone becomes much more common at the head of the bay near the Pennsylvania border. Except for parts of northern Maryland and certain areas between the Rappahannock River and the Potomac River in Virginia, the region also lacked quarryable building stone. One of the earliest quarries in operation was located at Aquia Creek in Stafford County, Virginia, where workers excavated buff-colored sandstone.

2. A good Chesapeake bricklayer charged nearly twice as much for his services per day as a provincial mason in England, one outside of London. For English labor costs, see James Ayres, *Building the Georgian City* (New Haven: Yale University Press, 1998), 114. See also Edward Miles Riley, ed., *The Journal of John Harrower, an Indentured Servant in the Colony of Virginia, 1773–1776* (Williamsburg: Colonial Williamsburg Foundation, 1963), 109.

3. I would like to thank historic brickwork consultant Gerard Lynch for his review of the following material on English brickwork. Gerard Lynch, *Brickwork: History, Technology, and Practice*, 2 vols. (London: Donhead, 1994), 1:6–11; R. W. Brunskill, *Brickmaking in Britain* (London: Victor Gollancz, 1990), 130–31. A statute in 1729 revised the standard size of bricks made within a 15-mile radius of London to $8\frac{3}{4}$ inches in length, $4\frac{1}{8}$ inches in width, and $2\frac{1}{2}$ inches in height. Batty Langley, *London Prices of Bricklayers' Materials and Works* (London: Richard Adams and John Wren, 1749), 2. A survey of seventeenth-century brick structures in southeastern England indicates that brick lengths ranged from $8\frac{1}{2}$ to $9\frac{1}{2}$ inches, headers from 4 to $4\frac{5}{8}$ inches, with most $4\frac{1}{4}$ inches, and heights as little as $1\frac{7}{8}$ inches to as much as $2\frac{3}{4}$ inches, with the average falling between 2 and $2\frac{1}{4}$ inches. Willie Graham and Carl Lounsbury, "Seventeenth-Century Precedents and Parallels in Brick Construction in England and Virginia," unpublished paper for Jamestown Rediscovery, Jamestown Island, Virginia, August 2001.

4. Dutch-style bricks were made in England and Sweden as well as in the Low Countries. They have been found in a number of early colonial sites associated with hearths, including Structure 139 in Jamestown, the Hallowes in Westmoreland County, Virginia, and at the mid-seventeenth-century Puritan settlement at Providence in Anne Arundel County, Maryland. The use of these bricks continued well into the eighteenth century. A planter purchased a shipload of Swedish yellow bricks for use at Notley Hall in St. Mary's County in the 1670s. Calder Loth, "Notes on the Evolution of Virginia Brickwork from the Seventeenth Century to the Late Nineteenth Century," *Bulletin of the Association for Preservation Technology* 6 (1974): 84; Al Luckenbach, "The Excavation of an Eighteenth-Century Dutch Yellow Brick Firebox and

Chimney Stack in Anne Arundel County, Maryland," *Maryland Archaeology* 30 (September 1994): 9–22.

Brick sizes remained constant for more than two centuries. The brick foundations of the church erected in Jamestown around 1618 measure 8½ to 9 inches in length, 4½ inches in width, and 2⅜ inches in height. Specifications for bricks burned for a project in Talbot County, Maryland, in 1687 called for them to be 9 inches long, 4 inches wide, and 2½ inches high. And eighty years later, the vestry of Truro Parish, in Fairfax County, Virginia, noted that a new church was "to be built of good bricks well burnt, of the ordinary size, that is nine Inches long, four and an half Inches broad, and three Inches thick." A 1792 law passed to regulate brickmaking in Kent County, Maryland, specified that place bricks were to be 9 inches by 4¼ inches by 2½ inches. The better-made stock bricks were to be the same length and width but an additional ⅛ inch in height. Talbot County, Maryland, Land Records, August 16, 1687; Truro Parish Vestry Book, Fairfax County, Virginia, February 4, 1766; *Archives of Maryland, 644: Session Laws, 1792* (Annapolis: Maryland State Archives, 2003), 19–20, December 22, 1792.

5. The comparison is based on fifty randomly sampled buildings in states north of the Delaware River dating between 1641 and 1800 and 145 random samples from the Chesapeake dating between 1617 and 1800.

6. For a description of traditional brickmaking as still practiced in the early twentieth century, see Warren Scott Boyce, *Economic and Social History of Chowan County, North Carolina, 1880–1915* (New York: Columbia University Press, 1917), 113–14.

7. *Scientific American*, October 1, 1853, 24.

8. On the immensity of oyster deposits in the Chesapeake, see "A Letter from Mr. John Clayton Rector of Crofton at Wakefield in Yorkshire, to the Royal Society, May 12, 1688," in *Tracts and Other Papers Relating Principally to the Origin, Settlement, and Progress of the Colonies in North America, from the Discovery of the Country to the Year 1776*, 4 vols., ed. Peter Force (Washington, D.C.: P. Force, 1836–46), 3:14.

9. James Crenshaw, of Froehling & Robertson, "Petrographic Report of Hardened Mortar, Ludwell Statehouses, Jamestown, Virginia," unpublished paper, Architectural Research Department, Colonial Williamsburg Foundation, March 2001, 2–4. For other examples that differentiated between the content of mortar intended for exterior locations and that intended for interior locations, see Robert A. Rutland, ed., *The Papers of George Mason, 1725–1792*, 3 vols. (Chapel Hill: University of North Carolina Press, 1970), 1:56; and Truro Parish Vestry Book, Fairfax County, Virginia, February 4, 1766.

10. Construction dates and owners' initials picked out in glazed headers appeared infrequently in eastern Virginia. Maryland seems to have more examples from the colonial period, perhaps due to the influence of Delaware Valley masons, who used the convention with great alacrity in southern New Jersey and southeastern Pennsylvania. On the decorative brickwork tradition in that region, see Paul Love, "Pattern Brickwork in Southern New Jersey," *Proceedings of the New Jersey Historical Society* 73

(July 1955): 182–208; and Michael Chiarappa, "The Social Context of Eighteenth-Century West New Jersey Brick Artisanry," in *Perspectives in Vernacular Architecture, IV*, ed. Thomas Carter and Bernard Herman (Columbia: University of Missouri Press, 1991), 31–43.

11. Paul Touart, *Along the Shore: The Architectural History of Worcester County, Maryland* (Snow Hill: Worcester County, 1994), 237–39; Paul Touart, *Somerset: An Architectural History* (Princess Anne: Somerset County Historical Trust, 1990), 42–43, 193–94. In a similar vein, the Mason House (1729) in nearby Accomack County, Virginia, has a series of glazed diamond patterns on its long walls, though now much obscured by later whitewash.

12. Frances Benjamin Johnson and Thomas T. Waterman, *The Early Architecture of North Carolina* (Chapel Hill: University of North Carolina Press, 1947), 31–32, 65.

13. John Summerson, *Architecture in Britain, 1530–1830*, 9th ed. (New Haven: Yale University Press, 1993), 142–56.

14. "Report of the Excavations Made at Jamestown in 1901 and 1902," in John L. Cotter, *Archaeological Excavations at Jamestown, Virginia*, 2nd ed. (Richmond: Archaeological Society of Virginia, 1994), 224.

15. In 1742, the Bruton Parish vestry ordered "the brick Ornaments of the Gavel ends to be taken down, and finished with wood, answering the rest." William A. R. Goodwin, ed., *The Records of Bruton Parish Church* (Richmond: Dietz Press, 1941), 139.

16. Bishop Roberts's view of Charleston painted in the late 1730s depicts a number of buildings with shaped gables on or near the Cooper River waterfront. In the countryside, shaped gables were used at Prince George, Winyah in Georgetown (1745–47), Pon Pon Chapel, St. Bartholomew's Parish (c. 1758), and St. Stephen's Parish Church (1767).

17. Gerard Lynch, *The History of Gauged Brickwork* (New York: Butterworth-Heinemann, 2007), 125–36.

18. Gerard Lynch, letter to the author, January 16, 2003.

19. There is conflicting physical and documentary evidence as to whether the windows on the first story on the front side also had stuccoed surrounds.

20. Westover in Charles City County, Virginia (1750–51), and the nearby Charles City County Courthouse (1757) are noteworthy late examples of the use of segmental arches on principal facades.

21. In London, at midcentury, the estimated cost of fabricating straight-headed arches and moldings was 1 shilling 4 pence per superficial foot, while the price of circular openings and moldings rose to 2 shillings per superficial foot. Langley, *London Prices of Bricklayers' Materials and Works*, 295.

22. The two-story addition built at right angles to Governor Berkeley's original house at Green Spring had a compass-headed opening in the upper level of the entrance porch. See Benjamin Henry Latrobe's drawing of 1797, Maryland Historical Society, Baltimore.

23. Timothy Easton, "The Disguise of Historic Brickwork Rediscovered," in *Material Culture in Medieval Europe*, ed. Guy De Boe and Frans Verhaeghe (Zellik, Belgium: Instituut voor het

Archeologisch Patrimonium, 1997), 485–95; Lynch, *Brickwork: History, Technology, and Practice*, 1:38–39.

24. Evidence for the early red coating at Bacon's Castle is still very visible on most of its walls. The primary pigment is red ochre with some burnt sienna. The binding media appears to be a limewash. Since there was no defined boundary between the paint and the mortar, the paint appears to have been applied before the mortar had completely cured. Susan Buck, "Cross-Section Microscopy Report: Bacon's Castle Painted Mortar Sample, Surry County, Virginia," unpublished report for the Architectural Research Department, Colonial Williamsburg Foundation, June 18, 2002, 2. The eastern unit of Structure 144 had traces of red staining in the surviving mortar joints above the water table. Mark Kutney to Carl Lounsbury, April 5, 2002. Red wash covered the brick joints at the Mount, the Taliaferro House in Caroline County, dating to the last decade of the seventeenth century. Susan Buck, "Cross-Section Microscopy Report: Brick, Mortar, and Limewash Coating Samples from the Mount, Carter's Grove, the Masonic Lodge and Store [Eastville, Northampton County, Va.], and the Debtors' Prison [Gloucester County, Va.]," unpublished report for the Architectural Research Department, Colonial Williamsburg Foundation, December 6, 2003.

25. For paint analysis of the cartouche, see Susan Buck, "Page House Painted Cartouche, Williamsburg, Virginia," unpublished report for the Architectural Research Department, Colonial Williamsburg Foundation, July 13, 2002, 3.

26. Susan Buck, "Montpelier Red Wash on Brick Investigation Continued," unpublished report for John Jeanes, director, Architectural Restoration, Montpelier, Orange, Virginia, June 22, 2006.

27. Other examples of red wash in the putty joints of frontispieces appear at Ware Church, Gloucester County (1719), and on the Nelson House, Yorktown (1729–30). A red wash was applied to the stringcourse during the construction of Wilton, a house originally built in Henrico County around 1753. Natasha Loeblich, "Wilton: Cross-Section Microscopy Paint Analysis," unpublished report for the Architectural Research Department, Colonial Williamsburg Foundation, February 2006. For a more detailed discussion of color washes, see Susan Buck, Carl Lounsbury, and Alfredo Maul, "Color Washes and Penciling on Bricks and Mortar Joints in the Chesapeake," October 2003, Colonial Williamsburg Research Division, http://www.history.org/research.

28. Susan Buck, "Matthew Jones House: Cross-Section Microscopy Report," unpublished report for the Architectural Research Department, Colonial Williamsburg Foundation, May 27, 2005.

29. See, for example, Catherine Matsen, "Cross-Section Microscopy Report: Esmont, Albemarle County, Virginia," unpublished report for the Architectural Research Department, Colonial Williamsburg Foundation, August 30, 2002; Buck, "Cross-Section Microscopy Report: Brick, Mortar, and Limewash Coating Samples from the Mount, Carter's Grove, the Masonic Lodge and Store [Eastville, Northampton County, Va.], and the Debtors' Prison [Gloucester County, Va.]"; Susan Buck, "Cross-Section Microscopy Report: Aiken-Rhett House [Charleston,

S.C.]," unpublished report for the Historic Charleston Foundation, July 2, 2003.

30. According to historic masonry specialist Raymond Cannetti, this was the most standard method used by bricklayers in the Tidewater. Another method was to swing arcs from the corners of the upper corners of the opening so that they bisected in the center of the opening. This usually created a 60-degree splay. Raymond Cannetti to author, January 15, 2010.

31. Only a handful of buildings in Virginia are known to have had all-header bonding. These included the Foushee Tebbs House (c. 1760, now destroyed) and the Old Hotel or Williams Ordinary (c. 1765), both in Dumfries, Prince William County, and Old Princess Anne County Jail (c. 1789) in Kempsville. Loth, "Notes on the Evolution of Virginia Brickwork," 96; Thomas Tileston Waterman, *The Mansions of Virginia, 1706–1776* (Chapel Hill: University of North Carolina Press, 1946), 230–36. On header bonding in Annapolis, see Marcia Miller and Orlando Ridout V, eds., *Architecture in Annapolis: A Field Guide* (Crownsville: Maryland Historical Trust, 1998), 129.

32. Widehall, a two-story, double-pile house built in Chestertown in Kent County, Maryland (1769), employs header bond on the two principal facades, while the side and back walls are laid in one-to-three bond. Otternbein Church in Baltimore (1785) has Flemish-bond entrance facades and one-to-three and one-to-five back walls. For other early examples, see Michael Bourne, *Historic Houses of Kent County: An Architectural History, 1642–1860* (Chestertown: Historical Society of Kent County, 1998).

33. Gadsby's Tavern in Alexandria (1782–85) has one-to-three bonding in the front foundations and the lower half of the rear wall. The upper portion of the rear wall is laid in one-to-five bond. This early use of common bond in Alexandria is another example of the influence of Maryland brickwork on the south side of the Potomac.

34. Pilastered facades were not uncommon in England in the late seventeenth century and the eighteenth century. However, many of these buildings had brick cornices and parapets, features rarely found on Chesapeake buildings in the colonial period. Brick cornices generally became fashionable in Virginia and Maryland in the early nineteenth century. Front-wall parapets were never in vogue.

35. Camille Wells, "The Planter's Prospect: Houses, Outbuildings, and Rural Landscapes in Eighteenth-Century Virginia," *Winterthur Portfolio* 28 (1993): 7–12.

36. Percy G. Adams, ed., *William Byrd's Histories of the Dividing Line betwixt Virginia and North Carolina* (New York: Dover, 1967), 96.

37. Gregory A. Stiverson and Patrick H. Butler III, eds., "Virginia in 1732: The Travel Journal of William Hugh Grove," *Virginia Magazine of History and Biography* 85 (1977): 30.

38. Donald Jackson and Dorothy Twohig, eds., *The Diaries of George Washington*, 6 vols. (Charlottesville: University Press of Virginia, 1976–79), 6:161.

39. Stiverson and Butler, "Virginia in 1732," 22.

40. Edward Kimber, "Observations in Several Voyages and Travels in America," *William and Mary Quarterly*, 1st ser., 15 (January 1907): 11. Within a decade of Kimber's visit to Snow Hill, the vestry of All Hallows Parish demolished the wooden church and erected a large brick one, measuring 45 by 65 feet, with sizable compass-headed openings.

41. Federal Direct Tax Census, 1798, Annapolis. Enumerators listed 211 dwellings in their survey, of which 133 were framed and 86 were brick. Of the 133 frame dwellings, 79 were one story and 34 were two stories. Of the 86 brick dwellings, 13 were three stories, 53 were two stories, and 20 were one story. There were 216 outbuildings listed in the schedule: 108 frame, 85 brick, 1 stone, 6 log, and 16 of unidentified building materials.

By way of comparison, Philadelphia some ten years later was overwhelmingly a brick city. A guide to Philadelphia in 1810 counted 13,241 buildings within the city limits. Of these, 8,640 were brick and 4,601 were frame structures. This two-to-one ratio of brick to wood rises to three-to-one when only dwellings are counted. Philadelphia had 6,351 brick houses, compared to 2,523 built of wood. However, in the Philadelphia suburbs, wooden buildings predominated. When the dwellings, commercial buildings, public buildings, stables, and workshops are combined for Philadelphia, the Northern Liberties, Penn Township, Kensington, Southwark, Moymamensing, and Passyunk, brick barely outnumbered wood. The metropolitan area contained 22,769 buildings. Of this number 11,978 were brick and 10,841 were frame. John Adems Paxton, *(The Stranger's Guide): An Alphabetical List of All the Wards, Streets, Roads, Lanes, Alleys, Avenues, Courts, Wharves, Ship Yards, Public Buildings, &c. in the City and Suburbs of Philadelphia* (Philadelphia: Edward Parker, 1810), 18–20.

42. Elizabeth Gallow, "Preliminary Analysis of the 1798 Tax Record in Maryland," unpublished research report for the Architectural Research Department, Colonial Williamsburg Foundation, 2005.

43. Willie Graham, Carter L. Hudgins, Carl R. Lounsbury, Fraser D. Neiman, and James P. Whittenburg, "Adaptation and Innovation: Archaeological and Architectural Perspectives on the Seventeenth-Century Chesapeake," *William and Mary Quarterly*, 3d ser., 64 (July 2007): 475–84.

44. Dell Upton, *Holy Things and Profane: Anglican Parish Churches in Colonial Virginia* (Cambridge, Mass.: MIT Press, 1986), 11–13.

45. Carl Lounsbury, "Anglican Church Design in the Chesapeake: English Inheritances and Regional Interpretations," in *Building, Image, and Identity: Perspectives in Vernacular Architecture, IX*, ed. Alison K. Hoagland and Kenneth A. Breisch (Knoxville: University of Tennessee Press, 2003), 27–28.

46. Carl Lounsbury, *The Courthouses of Early Virginia: An Architectural History* (Charlottesville: University of Virginia Press, 2005), 91–92, 239–41.

47. Thomas Henderson Letterbook, 1810–11, Duplin County, Thomas Henderson Papers, North Carolina Division of Archives and History, Raleigh.

CHAPTER 12

1. Mark Kostro, "Excavating Sites Unseen," in *Between Dirt and Discussion: Methods, Methodology, and Interpretation in Historical Archaeology*, ed. Steven N. Archer and Kevin M. Bartoy (New York: Springer, 2006), 183–99.

2. Louis B. Wright and Marion Tinling, eds., *The London Diary, 1717–1721, and Other Writing: William Byrd of Virginia* (New York: Oxford University Press, 1958), 566.

3. William Waller Hening, ed., *Statutes at Large; Being a Collection of All the Laws of Virginia*, 13 vols. (Richmond, 1809–23; reprint, Charlottesville: University Press of Virginia, 1969), 1:291; St. Mary's County Orphans' Court Valuations, 1780–1807, f 3 and 4, transcripts in Maryland Historical Trust, Annapolis.

4. P. P. Barbour Papers and Account Books, Virginia Historical Society, Richmond.

5. *The Builders' Price Book* (Alexandria: Cottom and Stewart, 1812), 16. The price book suggested that builders should charge less for floors that were "nailed in sight" than for floors that were secret nailed.

6. For names, sizes, and uses of nails, as well as a note on botching, see "Nails," in *The Builder's Dictionary* (London: A. Bettesworth, 1734), n.p.; and Batty Langley, *London Prices of Bricklayers' Materials and Works* (London: Richard Adams, 1749), 58–64.

7. Lee H. Nelson, "Nail Chronology as an Aid to Dating Old Buildings," *Technical Leaflet* 48 (Washington, D.C.: National Park Service, November 1968); Tom Wells, "Nail Chronology: The Use of Technologically Derived Features," *Historical Archaeology* 32 (1998): 78–99.

8. Richard Neve, *The City and Country Purchaser's and Builder's Dictionary* (London: B. Sprint, 1703), 166.

9. N. W. Alcock and Nancy Cox, *Living and Working in Seventeenth-Century England* (including manuscripts for Randle Holme, *The Academy of Armory (1688)* (London: British Library, CD-ROM, 2000), book 3, chap. 7, sect. 1b; emphasis added.

10. Stay hooks slightly raised the price of hook-and-eye hinges. William Salmon, *Country Builder's Estimator* (London: James Hodges, 1733–35), 77.

11. Frances Norton Mason, ed., *John Norton & Sons, Merchants of London and Virginia* (Richmond: Dietz Press, 1939), 120.

12. Thomas Pollock Letterbook, 21, North Carolina Division of Archives and History, Raleigh.

13. Neve, *City and Country Purchaser's and Builder's Dictionary*, 166; Ephraim Chambers, *Cyclopedia* (London: J. F. Rivington, 1786), 1; William Salmon, *Palladio Londinensis* (London: J. Hodges, 1748), 69; Salmon, *Country Builder's Estimator*, 75.

14. Joseph Moxon, *Mechanick Exercises or the Doctrine of Handy-Works* (London, 1703; reprint, Scarsdale, N.Y.: Early American Industries Association, 1979), 21.

15. Kirsten E. Travers, "Cross-Section Microscopy Report: Shirley Plantation Main House, Charles City County, Virginia: Selected Interior Finishes," unpublished report, Architectural Research Department, Colonial Williamsburg Foundation, 2010, 33; Susan Buck, "The Benjamin Waller House, Colonial Williamsburg, Virginia: Interior Woodwork Cross-Section Microscopy

Report," unpublished report, Architectural Research Department, Colonial Williamsburg Foundation, 1999.

16. Salmon, *Palladio Londinensis*, 69; Salmon, *Country Builder's Estimator*, 75–76.

17. Beverley to Athawes, Robert Beverley Letterbook, 1761–93, Library of Congress, Washington, D.C.

18. The 1727 inventory of Chowan County joiner Patrick Ogleby included one pair of butt hinges, presumably intended for furniture. Secretary of State, Wills, 1722–35, Chowan County, 109–12, North Carolina Division of Archives and History, Raleigh.

19. John C. Fitzpatrick, ed., *The Writings of George Washington from the Original Manuscript Sources, 1745–1799*, 39 vols. (Washington, D.C.: Government Printing Office, 1931–44), 29:216.

20. Prince William County Deedbook, 1787–91, April 1788, 101–3.

21. Box 6, folder 54a, Skipwith Papers, Special Collections, Swem Library, College of William and Mary, Williamsburg.

22. Salmon called them "Bastard-Banbury stock locks." Salmon, *Palladio Londinensis*, 71.

23. Drop handles could cost two or three times the price of knobs. See Peabody Essex catalog 739.4.S19.2, 10, book 22021, watermark 1804; compare items 1856–58 with 1880–83 and 2813–14. Phillips Library, Peabody Essex Museum, Salem, Massachusetts. New Bern, North Carolina, storekeeper John Coart offered rim locks named for their handles, "Ring and Knob Locks," in 1817. *Carolina Federal Republican*, October 25, 1817.

24. Robert Beverley ordered "22 Mortise Locks, 5 Inches long with Scutcheons" for the main floors at Blandfield in 1771. Robert Beverley Letterbook, 1761–93, Library of Congress, Washington, D.C. He felt that rim locks sufficed for doors in the wings and cellar.

25. As Henry Fielding illustrates in *Joseph Andrews*, such uncovered openings could provide unseemly peepholes into private spaces and personal matters.

26. Mason, *John Norton*, 169.

27. An 1820 Virginia price book set the price for installing mortise locks at $1.00; installing common locks cost 25¢ to 30¢. Peter Cottom, *The Richmond and Alexandria Builders' Price Book Containing the House Carpenters' and Joiner's Book of Prices* (Richmond: Peter Cottom, 1820), 17. Prices were similar in 1812, in *The Builders' Price Book*, 11.

28. George Washington reported in 1787 that he could "get them here [Philadelphia] of good quality from Seven Inches downwards." He had previously used brass rim locks on most first-floor doors. Fitzpatrick, *Writings of George Washington*, 29:254.

29. St. Mark's Parish Vestry Book, Culpeper County, Virginia, 408–9, Library of Virginia, Richmond.

30. Orlando Ridout V, *Building the Octagon* (Washington, D.C.: American Institute of Architects Press, 1989), 110.

31. Hunter Dickinson Farish, ed., *The Journal and Letters of Philip Vickers Fithian, 1773–1774: A Plantation Tutor of the Old Dominion* (Williamsburg: Colonial Williamsburg, 1968), 242, 245.

32. Neve, *City and Country Purchaser's and Builder's Dictionary*, 181; Salmon, *Palladio Londinensis*, 70.

33. Round bolts with knobs were favored for exterior shutters in the region by the 1760s and became a more common choice for doors by about 1810, much later than in Pennsylvania, New York, and England.

34. William Hogarth places an example, along with boards wedged against the door, in a poor and disreputable setting in his print "The Idle Prentice Returned from Sea & in a Garret with a Common Prostitute," in the "Industry and Idleness" series.

35. Some of the Jamestown padlocks and hasps were for securing chests, a common alternative to locking rooms when unrelated residents shared spaces. Personal communication from Beverly Straub, curator, Jamestown Rediscovery to author, November 20, 2011.

36. Louis B. Wright and Marion Tilling, eds., *The Secret Diary of William Byrd of Westover, 1709–1712* (Richmond: Dietz Press, 1941), 5.

37. George Wythe referred to the better sort as "wainscot pullies" in 1771. Mason, *John Norton*, 169. Walthoe's storehouse had the cheaper variety.

38. James A. Bear Jr. and Lucia C. Stanton, eds., *Jefferson's Memorandum Books: Accounts, with Legal Records and Miscellany, 1767–1826*, 2 vols. (Princeton: Princeton University Press, 1997), 1:403.

39. Builders charged extra for including "boxes for weights" in the window frames as well as for purchasing the pulleys and weights, which shifted increasingly from lead in the eighteenth century after 1790. *The Builders' Price Book*, 10; Cottom, *Richmond and Alexandria Builders' Price Book Containing the House Carpenters' and Joiner's Book of Prices*, 16.

40. The term "sash fasteners" is used for related latches in a hardware trade catalog from about 1789 (NK7899 B61e TC, no. 1763, Winterthur Library, Winterthur, Del.) and as "sash fastenings" in a catalog from about 1825 (TS573 B61f no. 1 TC, 251–52, ibid.). Close in appearance is Metropolitan Museum of Art brass hardware catalog 1985.1103, l with 1818 watermark, no. 3324, opposite 117, and 38.45 with 1812, 1814, and 1816 watermarks, 14, no. 1686, priced at 13 shillings. Metropolitan Museum of Art, New York.

41. Jack P. Greene, ed., *The Diary of Colonel Landon Carter of Sabine Hall, 1752–1778*, 2 vols. (Richmond: Virginia Historical Society, 1987), 2:787.

42. Bear and Stanton, *Jefferson's Memorandum Books*, 1:29.

43. The fine Richmond house Michael Hancock built in 1809 had pulls at the front door, dining room, and nursery above it, all of which rang bells in the cellar kitchen below the dining room.

44. In another version, Jean Skipwith order to James Maury, August 27, 1795, Skipwith Papers, Alderman Library, University of Virginia, Charlottesville.

45. Ridout, *Building the Octagon*, 116, 141; William Seale, *The President's House: A History*, 2 vols. (Washington, D.C.: White House Historical Association, 1986), 1:78, 84, 92.

46. The bells at Prestwould were mounted on the side of the house facing a detached kitchen.

47. See, for example, Albert H. Sonn, *Early American Wrought Iron*, 3 vols. (New York: Scribner's, 1928), 3:190–97.

48. Robert Beverley Letterbook, 1761–93, 1770, Library of Congress, Washington, D.C.

49. Tony Weston, "English Roasting Jacks, Part 2: Standard Weight-Driven Spit Jacks of the Eighteenth Century," *Journal of the Antique Metalware Society* 18 (June 2010): 32–47.

50. In Governor Francis Fauquier's inventory in 1768, the jack in the Governor's Palace kitchen was assessed at £3. Graham Hood, *The Governor's Palace in Williamsburg: A Cultural Study* (Williamsburg: Colonial Williamsburg Foundation, 1991), 297, 302.

CHAPTER 13

1. My sincere thanks to the many colleagues who gave advice, provided examples from their own research, and cajoled me into finishing this chapter, not the least of which are Carl Lounsbury, Edward Chappell, Jeffery Klee, Orlando Ridout V, and Mark R. Wenger. I owe special gratitude to Cary Carson, who helped me think through and craft much of what I have to say.

2. See the introduction to Carl R. Lounsbury, *An Illustrated Glossary of Early Southern Architecture and Landscape* (New York: Oxford University Press, 1994), ix–xiv.

3. Richard L. Bushman, *The Refinement of America: Persons, Houses, Cities* (New York: Knopf, 1992); Cary Carson, "The Consumer Revolution in Colonial British America: Why Demand," in *Of Consuming Interests: The Styles of Life in the Eighteenth Century*, ed. Cary Carson, Ronald Hoffman, and Peter J. Albert (Charlottesville: University Press of Virginia, 1994).

4. Quoted in Louis B. Wright, *A Voyage to Virginia in 1609* (Charlottesville: University Press of Virginia, 1964), 81.

5. Plaster is commonly found on the interior and exterior walls of early mud-walled buildings in Britain but is not universal. It is common for archaeological sites of mud-walled buildings in Maryland and Virginia to have plaster associated with them, but it is often unclear whether the plaster was applied to the interior or to the exterior of the walls.

6. A list of the known building sites in the Chesapeake that predate 1720 is compiled in the Database of Early Chesapeake Architecture (DECA) by the Colonial Williamsburg Foundation and the College of William and Mary. It can be viewed at www.deca.swem.wm.edu.

7. Cary Carson, "The Virginia House in Maryland," *Maryland Historical Magazine* 69 (Summer 1974): 185–96.

8. Some of the clapboarded Williamsburg buildings include the Brush-Everard House, which initially had an exposed clapboard roof, the John Blair House, which had both clapboard walls and roof, and the Benjamin Waller House, which at the least had a clapboard roof. Clapboards did a poor job of shedding water over a sustained period of time. The addition of shingles on these examples—in some cases demonstrably not long after construction—is suggestive that clapboards were often an expedient for drying in a building while waiting for a more permanent covering.

9. Carole Shammas, "The Housing Stock of the Early United States: Refinement Meets Migration," *William and Mary Quarterly*, 3d ser., 64 (July 2007): 549–90.

10. Augusta Parish Vestry Book, Virginia, November 25, 1760.

11. "Featheredge" is a common alternate term for weatherboards, so-called because of their tapered cross section. "Featheredge" is also occasionally used to mean any kind of board tapered in cross section, including clapboards and side-lapped shingles.

12. Edward A. Chappell, "Housing a Nation: The Transformation of Living Standards in Early America," in Carson, Hoffman, and Albert, *Of Consuming Interests*, 167–232.

13. The development of bent principal roofs as adopted in the Chesapeake early in the eighteenth century is likely, in part, the result of merging the earlier convention, which lacked a structural overhang, with the need for a classical cornice. Bent principals transfer the load of the roof directly to wall plates and allow the secondary joist extensions, which bear little weight except for short kick rafters, to frame a classical cornice. Bent principals were used in a slightly different context at Bruton Parish Church in Williamsburg. There they were limited to the two gable ends, presumably as a way to accommodate now lost gable parapets and ornaments.

14. In 1681, for instance, a building was "to be Lathed, filled, and white limed, or filled and sealed." Northumberland County, Virginia, Court Order Book, 1678–98, 89.

15. Thatch was a common medieval and postmedieval roof covering whose use was concentrated in the south of England. Buildings with a variety of wall material—stone, half-timbered, and clay—were frequently thatched. But clay-walled construction has a particular association with thatch, since the two materials are some of the most basal of vernacular technologies. See Pamela Egeland, *Cob and Thatch* (Tiverton, Devon: Devon Books, 1988); and Jo Cox and John R. L. Thorp, *Devon Thatch: An Illustrated History of Thatching and Thatched Buildings in Devon* (Tiverton, Devon: Devon Books, 2001). Even in the north of England, thatch and cob had a strong association, particularly in the seventeenth and eighteenth centuries. See Nina Jennings, *Clay Dabbins: Vernacular Buildings of the Solway Plain* (Kendal, Cumbria: Cumberland & Westmorland Antiquarian & Archaeological Society, 2003).

16. "A Brief Description of the Plantation of Virginia during the First Twelve Years, When Sir Thomas Smith Was Governor of the Company Down to This Present Time: By the Ancient Planters Now Remaining in Virginia, 1623," in *Jamestown Narratives: Eyewitness Accounts of the Virginia Colony, the First Decade, 1607–1617*, ed. Edmund Haile (Oxford: Roundhouse, 1998), 893–901; Jack P. Greene, ed., *The Diary of Colonel Landon Carter of Sabine Hall, 1752–1778*, 2 vols. (Charlottesville: University Press of Virginia, 1965), 1:608.

17. Seventeenth-century Virginians sometimes referred to the grassy, rushlike material they used for thatch as "sedge." A Charles County man in 1680 was "gone about a weeke to get seidge to cover ye tobacco houses." Charles County, Maryland, Court and Land Records, 1678–80, 259.

18. Although tiles were found on each of these sites, archaeolo-

gists have concerns—that tile evidence is so slight (in the case of Structures 116, 123, and 163) or tile locations are not sufficiently obvious to have originated from these buildings to argue convincingly that their roofs were tiled. Data was collected from Cary Carson, "Structures," in Cary Carson, Audrey J. Horning, Beverly A. Straube, and Ronald W. Fuchs II, "Jamestown Archaeological Assessment, 1992–1996: Evaluation of Previous Archaeology" (Williamsburg: Colonial Williamsburg Foundation and the College of William and Mary, 2006), 83–87; information on Structures 144 and 163, excavated by the Association for the Preservation of Virginia Antiquities, Richmond, in Cary Carson, Willie Graham, Carl Lounsbury, and Martha McCartney, "Description and Analysis of Structure 144 [Ludwell Statehouse Group],unpublished report to Association for the Preservation of Virginia Antiquities, Jamestown Rediscovery, Williamsburg, Virginia, August 20, 2002.

19. An anonymous propaganda tract, "A Perfect Description of Virginia," first published in London in 1649, discusses the lack of a tile-making trade in the region: "They have lime in abundance made for their houses, store of bricks made, and house and chimnies built of brick, and some wood high and fair, covered with shingle for tile, yet they have none that make them, wanting workmen; in that [tile-making] trade the brick makers have not the art to do it, it shrinketh." *Virginia Historical Register, and Literary Advertiser* 2 (April 1849): 67.

20. See letter from Henry Cary to Edmund Jenings, April 16, 1709, quoted in *Virginia Magazine of History and Biography* 16 (July 1908): 83–84.

21. Robert Beverley, *The History and Present State of Virginia* (London, 1705; reprint, Chapel Hill: University of North Carolina Press, 1947), 290.

22. Marion Tinling, ed., *The Correspondence of the Three William Byrds of Westover, Virginia, 1684–1776*, 3 vols. (Charlottesville: University Press of Virginia, 1977), 1:111; John Metz, Jennifer Jones, Dwayne Pickett, and David Muraca, *"Upon the Palisado" and Other Stories of Place from Bruton Heights* (Williamsburg: Colonial Williamsburg Foundation, 1998); Carson, "Structures," 83–87.

23. Note, for instance, that the Poe House in Annapolis had a shingle covering that lasted more than one hundred years, and portions of the shingle roof on Mount Vernon were more than ninety years old before they were covered by an addition.

24. "A Perfect Description of Virginia," 7.

25. William Hand Browne, ed., *Archives of Maryland, XIII: Proceedings and Acts of the General Assembly of Maryland, April 1684–June 1692* (Baltimore: Maryland Historical Society, 1894), 224. Ironically, it was the failure of the Maryland statehouse pantile roof that called for its replacement in shingle.

26. St. Peter's Parish Vestry Book, 1682–1758, 80, October 22, 1701.

27. The Eastern Shore of Virginia is well known for its pegged shingled roofs, with remnants still surviving at Pear Valley and evidence only recently destroyed at the Mason House. A shingle roof has also been discovered on the west side of the bay at Taliaferro's Mount in Caroline County, but this remains the only known example not on the Eastern Shore.

28. Of the 116 houses in the region studied with surviving evidence of shingles, fully 38 percent were coated with either tar or paint at some point in their use.

29. In Fredericksburg, Virginia, on May 13, 1774, English visitor John Harrower described the houses in the city as "generally at a little distance one from another, some of them being built of wood made and some of them of brick, and all covered with wood in the form of slates about four Inches broad, which when painted blew you wou'd not know it from a house sclated with Isedell sclate." Edward Miles Riley, ed., *The Journal of John Harrower, an Indentured Servant in the Colony of Virginia, 1773–1776* (Williamsburg: Colonial Williamsburg Foundation, 1963), 38.

30. Observations about the use of side-lap shingles in these places is based on the fieldwork of Thomas Reinhart, Maryland Historical Trust, Crownsville. Personal communication, July 16, 2010.

31. Gary Stanton, "'Alarmed by the Cry of Fire': How Fire Changed Fredericksburg, Virginia," in *Shaping Communities: Perspectives in Vernacular Architecture, VI*, ed. Carter L. Hudgins and Elizabeth Collins Cromley (Knoxville: University of Tennessee Press, 1997), 122–24. The early replacement of the lead roof with slate on the capitol in Richmond was unsuccessful. Only a small amount of slate that was ordered to be completed in October 1796 had been installed by December 1797. It was removed, and the roof was covered with traditional wooden shingles instead. See S. Allen Chambers Jr., "'Of the Best Quality': Buckingham Slate," *Virginia Cavalcade* 38 (Spring 1989): 159–61.

32. George P. Merrill and Edward B. Mathews, *The Building and Decorative Stones of Maryland* (Baltimore: Johns Hopkins University Press, 1898), 214–21.

33. Note that the Mutual Assurance Society covered rural areas only until 1820, and most policies even in this brief period were written for town buildings.

34. A home industry did arise in Charleston, South Carolina, where pantiles found more success. One local manufacturer boasted that, unlike most of those made by American companies, his were superior to those of Holland and England, noting that "they are all of a *true line*, calculated to *lie close into each other*, and they do not require to be *pointed* [with mortar] on their outside, which is a considerable saving of labour and expense, and adds much to the clean and handsome appearance of a roof. Another advantage they possess is, that from their lightness, they are peculiarly well adapted to the covering of *wooden* buildings, and have been employed for that purpose with great satisfaction." *Charleston Times*, October 7, 1800.

35. William L. Beiswanger, "Jefferson and the Art of Roofing," *Chronicle of the Early American Industries Association* 58 (March 2005): 18–25.

36. Peter Cottom, *The Richmond and Alexandria Builders' Price Book Containing the House Carpenters' and Joiner's Book of Prices* (Richmond: Peter Cottom, 1820), 43.

37. Mortar applied as a sealant between roof and chimney was used at Salubria in 1757 and can be found as late as the middle of the nineteenth century on the Tatum House in Petersburg.

38. For example, the Ridout House, built in 1764–65 during Annapolis's second building boom, used flashing in the valleys instead of fanned shingles and had lead-lined gutters masked by the exterior cornice.

39. See Database of Early Chesapeake Architecture (DECA), www.deca.swem.wm.edu.

40. Dorchester County, Maryland, Land Record Book, 1669–83, quoted in Carl R. Lounsbury, *The Courthouses of Early Virginia: An Architectural History* (Charlottesville: University of Virginia Press, 2005), 124.

41. H. R. McIlwaine, ed., *Journals of the House of Burgesses of Virginia*, 13 vols. (Richmond: Virginia State Library, 1905–15), 3:272–73. See Lounsbury, *Courthouses of Early Virginia*, 124–25.

42. *Wilmington Gazette*, April 28, 1807.

43. Mark R. Wenger, "The Central Passage in Virginia: Evolution of an Eighteenth-Century Living Space," in *Perspectives in Vernacular Architecture, II*, ed. Camille Wells (Columbia: University of Missouri Press, 1986), 137–49.

44. The porch is depicted on a Mutual Assurance Society policy for the house, which dates to 1797, indicating that it was present by this time. Mutual Assurance Society Policies, microfilm, reel 1, vol. 4, 186, Library of Virginia, Richmond.

45. Jon Prown, "A Cultural Analysis of Furniture-Making in Petersburg, Virginia, 1760–1820," *Journal of Early Southern Decorative Arts* 18, no. 1 (May 1992): 1–113.

46. William Martin, *Journal of William D. Martin: A Journey from South Carolina to Connecticut in the Year 1809* (Charlotte, N.C.: Heritage House, 1950).

47. William Salmon, *Palladio Londinensis: Or the London Art of Building* (London: Ward and Wicksteed, 1734), plates XXV and XXVI. Mark R. Wenger observes that the frontispieces were likely added by Byrd after his return to Westover from Philadelphia in the 1760s.

48. Susan D. Hanna, Barry Knight, and Geoff Egan, "Marked Window Leads from North America and Europe," unpublished report, Historic St. Mary's City, Maryland, 1992.

49. Arthur Pierce Middleton and Henry M. Miller, "'Mr. Secretary': John Lewgar, St. John's Freehold, and Early Maryland," *Maryland Historical Magazine* 103 (2008): 132–65, especially the illustration on p. 141.

50. Turned window lead marked "Iohn: Byshopp of Exceter Gonnar: 1625" was recovered from the Harwood plantation site (Site A) at Martin's Hundred. Ivor Noel Hume and Audrey Noel Hume, *The Archaeology of Martin's Hundred*, 2 vols. (Philadelphia: University of Pennsylvania Museum of Archaeology and Anthropology, 2001), 1:127.

51. Personal communication with Beverly Straube, Jamestown Rediscovery, Jamestown Island, Virginia, February 11, 2011.

52. Personal communication with Al Luckenbach, Lost Towns Project, Anne Arundel County, Maryland, July 7, 2007. Of the roughly twenty seventeenth-century sites tested by Luckenbach,

only three did not reveal the presence of cames: Chockely, the site of a poor farmer; Broadneck, one of the first houses at Providence (perhaps indicating that lead and glass simply were not available there until the place was more settled); and the Lord Mayor's Tenement at London Town. Al Luckenbach and James G. Gibb, "Dated Window Leads from Colonial Sites in Anne Arundel County, Maryland," *Maryland Archaeology* 30 (September 1994): 23–28.

53. See Nicholas M. Luccketti, "Archaeology at Bennett Farm: The Life Style of a Seventeenth-Century Middling Planter in York County, Virginia" (master's thesis, College of William and Mary, 1990).

54. John Hammond, *Leah and Rachel, or the Two Fruitfull Sisters Virginia and Mary-land: Their Present Condition, Impartially Stated and Related* (London: T. Mabb, 1656), in *Tracts and Other Papers Relating Principally to the Origin, Settlement, and Progress of the Colonies in North America, from the Discovery of the Country to the Year 1776*, 4 vols. (Washington, D.C.: P. Force, 1836–46), 3: Tract 14.

55. For a discussion of glass manufacture, the varying types available in England and America in the seventeenth and eighteenth centuries, and their relationship to the evolution of casement and sash windows, see Hentie J. Louw, "Window-Glass Making in Britain c. 1660–c. 1680 and Its Architectural Impact," in *Construction History* 7 (1991): 47–68; and Isabel Davies, "Window Glass in Eighteenth-Century Williamsburg," in *Five Artifact Studies* (Williamsburg: Colonial Williamsburg Foundation, 1973).

56. *Virginia Gazette*, May 4, 1769.

57. Based on fieldwork by Orlando Ridout V.

58. Hentie J. Louw, "The Origin of the Sash-Window," *Architectural History: Journal of the Society of Architectural Historians of Great Britain* 26 (1983): 49–72.

59. Letter from Thomas Bannister, Boston, to Thomas Bettsoe, London, April 29, 1701, quoted in Charles F. Montgomery, "Thomas Bannister on the New Sash Windows, Boston, 1701," *Journal of the Society of Architectural Historians* 24 (May 1965): 170.

60. The Reverend James Blair recruited Thomas Hadley from England to serve as the surveyor of the building. Foreign expertise was required to erect such a large building in the new refined taste and incorporate sash windows. Marcus Whiffen, *The Public Buildings of Williamsburg* (Williamsburg: Colonial Williamsburg, Incorporated, 1958), 21.

61. James D. Kornwolf, *"So Good a Design": The Colonial Campus of the College of William and Mary, Its History, Background, and Legacy* (Williamsburg: College of William and Mary, 1989), 37.

62. Ibid., 42; St. Peter's Parish Vestry Book, 1682–1758, 60–62, October 22, 1701.

63. Carl R. Lounsbury, "An Architectural Summary of the Timson House," unpublished report, Architectural Research Department, Colonial Williamsburg Foundation, 2003, 5.

64. Louis B. Wright and Marion Tinling, eds., *The Secret*

Diary of William Byrd of Westover, 1709–1712 (Richmond: Dietz Press, 1941), 5, February 5, 1709.

65. Charles E. Peterson, ed., *The Carpenters' Company of the City and County of Philadelphia 1786 Rule Book* (New York: Bell, 1971).

66. To accomplish this feat, a single sash weight with a pulley at the top was used on each side of the opening. The rope was threaded through the tops of both weights and attached to the sides of both sash. Weights of this type were imported to Barbados early in the nineteenth century, and their widespread use in the colonies suggests an English origin.

67. "Mr. Reed's Store," drawn by Fedor Vasil'evich Karzhavin during his first visit to Williamsburg, between May 1777 and January 1780. F. V. Karzhavina, bez no. 1.1, National Library of Russia, St. Petersburg, Russia.

68. Louis Simond, *An American in Regency England: The Journal of a Tour in 1810–1811*, ed. Christopher Hibbert (London: Robert Maxwell, 1968).

CHAPTER 14

1. The contrivance of eighteenth-century gentry landscapes and associated buildings created as part of planters' self-presentation was orchestrated to regulate movement through them. The stage serves as a useful metaphor for understanding how these buildings and spaces were made into an artificial setting used by the families and visitors, who became the actors and audience in the social and work interactions that unfolded there, and by the slaves, who made the play work as if by invisible stagehands. See Dell Upton, "White and Black Landscapes in Eighteenth Century Virginia," in *Material Life in America, 1600–1860*, ed. Robert Blair St. George (Boston: Northeastern University Press, 1988), 357–70.

2. Thomas Lee Shippen to William Shippen Jr., December 30, 1783, Shippen Family Papers, Library of Congress, Washington, D.C.

3. Talbot Hamlin, *Benjamin Henry Latrobe* (New York: Oxford University Press, 1955), 75.

4. Hugh Jones, *Present State of Virginia* (London: J. Clarke, 1724), 32.

5. Edward Chappell, "Looking at Buildings," *Fresh Advices*, supplement to *Colonial Williamsburg Interpreter* 5, no. 6 (1984): i–vi.

6. Cary Carson, Audrey J. Horning, and Bly Straube, "Evaluation of Previous Archaeology," in *Jamestown Archaeological Assessment, 1992–1996*, ed. Cary Carson (Williamsburg: National Park Service, 2006), 52–57, 138–43.

7. Marsha Miller and Orlando Ridout V, *Architecture and Change in the Chesapeake: A Field Tour on the Eastern and Western Shores* (Crownsville: Vernacular Architecture Forum and Maryland Historical Trust Press, 1998), 36–39.

8. Northampton County Miscellaneous Records, 1818, North Carolina State Archives, Raleigh.

9. Peter Cottom, *The Richmond and Alexandria Builders' Price Book Containing the House Carpenters' and Joiner's Book of Prices* (Richmond: Peter Cottom, 1820), 25–26, 46.

10. Julia A. King, Scott M. Strickland, and Kevin Norris, "The Search for the Court House at Moore's Lodge: Charles County's First County Seat," unpublished manuscript, Citizens of Charles County, 2008; J. Hall Pleasants, ed., *Archives of Maryland, LX: Proceedings of the County Court of Charles County, 1666–1674* (Baltimore: Maryland Historical Society, 1943), 615–18.

11. The finest of these is a court cupboard in the collection of the Museum of Early Southern Decorative Arts, Winston-Salem, North Carolina, which was made about 1680 in, it is thought, York County. The cupboard has wainscot ends with typical shallow-cut moldings planed onto the edges of the stiles and rails that embrace a floating flat panel. Another survival is a chest that was provided by Richard Perrott Jr. to the lower chapel of Christ Church Parish, Middlesex County, in 1677.

12. The evolution of wainscoting in England is discussed in Linda Hall, *Period House Fixtures and Fittings, 1300–1900* (Newbury, England: Countryside Books, 2005), 133–53.

13. The suggestion of the use of the Corinthian order comes from observations of Lucy Page Saunders. The pedestal to a stool owned by the Virginia Historical Society, Richmond, is made in part of mahogany Ionic capitals and is thought to have been taken from the hall at Rosewell. See Betty Crowe Leviner, "Rosewell Revisited," *Journal of Early Southern Decorative Arts* 19 (November 1993): 19.

14. Mark R. Wenger and Willie Graham, "Architectural Analysis of the Nelson House, Yorktown, Virginia," unpublished report for the National Park Service, 2003.

15. Thomas Jefferson, *Notes on the State of Virginia*, ed. William Peden (Chapel Hill: University of North Carolina Press, 1995), 152.

16. Mrs. Riddell to John Donaldson, December 12, 1811, Riddell Papers, Maryland Historical Society, Baltimore.

17. For a detailed discussion of "fancy" as a decorative style, see Sumpter Priddy, *American Fancy: Exuberance in the Arts, 1790–1840* (Milwaukee: Chipstone Foundation, 2004).

18. Marcia Miller and Orlando Ridout V, eds., *Architecture in Annapolis: A Field Guide* (Crownsville: Vernacular Architecture Forum and Maryland Historical Trust, 1998), 22–25.

19. Matthew Webster, "Plaster Composition," unpublished report, George Washington Foundation, Fredericksburg, Virginia, July 2003; Emily Brackbill, "Location of Nails in Overmantel," unpublished report, George Washington Foundation, Fredericksburg, Virginia, November 2005.

20. Thomas Jefferson to John Hemings, August 7, 1825, quoted in S. Allen Chambers Jr., *Poplar Forest & Thomas Jefferson* (Forest, Va.: Corporation for Jefferson's Poplar Forest, 1993), 159.

21. Cottom, *Richmond and Alexandria Builders' Price Book Containing the House Carpenters' and Joiner's Book of Prices*, 23–24.

22. Doweled flooring shows up regionally at least by 1739, when it was installed in the Judge John Brice House in Annapolis, and its use dies out soon after the end of the Revolution.

23. A secondary way to gauge a floorboard was to scribe its sides an inch below the top face and then drawknife a bevel below that

line. Undercutting was then achieved in the same way, as with rabbeted edges.

24. Miller and Ridout, *Architecture in Annapolis*, 42–44.

25. The earliest recovered Delft fragments come from a site in Virginia Beach, dating sometime between the mid-1630s and the mid-1650s, and from the homestead of Governor William Harwood at Wolstenholme Town, where tiles were probably discarded about 1640. See Floyd Painter, "The Chesopean Site," *Quarterly Bulletin of the Archeological Society of Virginia* 13, no. 3 (1959): 24–36; Ivor Noel Hume and Audrey Noel Hume, *The Archaeology of Martin's Hundred, Part I: Interpretive Studies* (Williamsburg: Colonial Williamsburg Foundation, 2001), 127.

26. Indenture, March 16, 1680, Talbot County, Maryland, Court Judgments, 1675–82, 194–95.

27. Queen Anne's County, Maryland, Deed Book D, 1751.

28. *Federal Gazette and Baltimore Daily Advertiser*, May 31, 1797.

29. See Mark Reinberger, *Utility and Beauty: Robert Wellford and Composition Ornament in America* (Newark: University of Delaware Press, 2003).

30. Indenture, March 16, 1680, Talbot County, Maryland, Court Judgments, 1675–82, 194–95.

31. Will of John Custis II, Northampton County Orders and Wills, 1689–98, 355–60. For a discussion of room use, see Edward A. Chappell, "Arlington," unpublished report, Architectural Research Department, Colonial Williamsburg Foundation, 2008, 27–29.

32. Hall, *Period House Fixtures and Fittings*, 105–7.

33. Jeffrey E. Klee, "Thomas Everard House Architectural Research Report," unpublished report, Architectural Research Department, Colonial Williamsburg Foundation, March 2010.

34. For a discussion of the role that the passage played in the development of private spaces, see Dell Upton, "Vernacular Domestic Architecture in Eighteenth-Century Virginia," *Winterthur Portfolio* 17, nos. 2/3 (Summer/Autumn 1982): 103–4. Mark R. Wenger discusses the changing role of the center passage and its ornamentation in "The Center Passage in Virginia: Evolution of an Eighteenth-Century Living Space," in *Perspectives in Vernacular Architecture, II*, ed. Camille Wells (Columbia: University of Missouri Press, 1986), 137–49.

35. Edward A. Papenfuse, *In Pursuit of Profit: The Annapolis Merchants in the Era of the American Revolution, 1763–1805* (Baltimore: Johns Hopkins University Press, 1975), 16–32.

36. Marcia Miller, "The Chase-Lloyd House" (master's thesis, George Washington University, 1993).

37. A surviving slave house built at Wales in Dinwiddie County, for instance, has an enclosed stair in each of its two units.

38. Asher Benjamin, *American Builder's Assistant* (Greenfield, Mass.: Thomas Dickman, 1797). Quotation from Asher Benjamin, *American Builder's Companion* (Boston: R. P. & C. Williams, 1816), 20.

39. Cottom, *Richmond and Alexandria Builders' Price Book Containing the House Carpenters' and Joiner's Book of Prices*, 20; Accounts, Mrs. Riddell to John Donaldson, December 12, 1811, Riddell Papers, Maryland Historical Society, Baltimore.

CHAPTER 15

1. Letter from Walter M. Macomber to Susan H. Nash, August 29, 1930, Archives, Colonial Williamsburg Foundation.

2. Alfred J. Morrison, ed., *Travels in the Confederation, 1783–1784, from the German of Johann David Schoepf* (Philadelphia, 1911; reprint, New York: Bergman, 1968), 73.

3. Letter from Susan H. Nash to Walter M. Macomber, September 4, 1930, Archives, Colonial Williamsburg Foundation. See Willie Graham, "Architectural Paint Research at American Museums: An Appeal for Standards," in *Architectural Finishes in the Built Environment*, ed. Mary A. Jablonski and Catherine R. Matsen (London: Archetype Publications, 2009), 3–18; and Edward A. Chappell, "The Colors of Williamsburg: New Analysis and the Chesapeake Town," in ibid., 30–44.

4. The term "showplace" to describe the polite house comes from Cary Carson, "Culture Transfer, Culture Shock: How the English Farmhouse Was Redesigned for British North America," unpublished paper, Architectural Research Department, Colonial Williamsburg Foundation, 2006.

5. John Smith, *The Art of Painting in Oyl* (London: Samuel Crouch, 1687). Smith's work is significant for discussing architectural finishes, which he calls "vulgar work." More sophisticated finishes, such as oriental lacquer made with materials readily available in England, including shellac, are presented in John Stalker and George Parker, *A Treatise of Japaning and Varnishing* (Oxford: Richard Wood, 1688).

6. Ian Bristow cites 1664 as the earliest discovered reference to pitchmaking. This was the work of John Winthrop the younger, governor of Connecticut. Ian Bristow, *Architectural Colours in British Interiors, 1615–1840* (New Haven: Yale University Press, 1996), 71.

7. Petsworth Parish Vestry Book, 1677–1793, 1690. The parish allocated 80 pounds of tobacco for Samuel Iremonger to bring tar to the church and 3,000 pounds of tobacco to Thomas Powell to plaster the church.

8. See Abbott Lowell Cummings and Richard M. Candee, "Colonial and Federal America: Accounts of Early Painting Practices," in *Paint in America: The Colors of Historic Buildings*, ed. Roger M. Moss (Washington, D.C.: Preservation Press, 1994), 13–16. Investigation of seventeenth-century New England houses suggests that limewashes were standard interior coatings. In the Chesapeake, however, the recorded use of tar far outweighs the number of documents that referred to limewashing until well into the nineteenth century.

9. Morgan W. Phillips, "A Survey of Paint Technology: The Composition and Properties of Paints," in Moss, *Paint in America*, 233–35.

10. Bristow, *Architectural Colours in British Interiors*, 111.

11. St. Peter's Parish Vestry Book, New Kent, Virginia, 1682–1758, 62, November 22, 1701.

12. H. R. McIlwaine, ed., *Journals of the House of Burgesses of Virginia*, 13 vols. (Richmond: Virginia State Library, 1905–15), 2:282.

13. Color analysis was undertaken by Mark Kutney in 2002.

Mark Kutney email communication to Willie Graham, March 8, 2002.

14. John Hammond, *Leah and Rachel, or the Two Fruitfull Sisters Virginia and Mary-Land: Their Present Condition, Impartially Stated and Related* (London: T. Tobb, 1656), in *Tracts and Other Papers Relating Principally to the Origin, Settlement, and Progress of the Colonies in North America, from the Discovery of the Country to the Year 1776*, 4 vols., ed. Peter Force (Washington, D.C.: P. Force, 1836–46), 3:18.

15. The few buildings of the seventeenth century that do survive are arguably the best of their time, and even their woodwork is largely devoid of paint. Third Haven Meetinghouse, in Talbot County—a finely built and finished English frame structure—has had few of its interior surfaces whitewashed and none have been painted. Much of its interior is later, and yet still unpainted. It might be argued that its Quaker association was the cause for its simplicity, but not so at Bacon's Castle, whose elaborately molded summer beams and joists clearly date to the seventeenth century and were not painted, nor were they whitewashed during the hundred years they were left exposed. Beyond the use of pine tar and whitewash, painted public and private buildings alike are glaringly absent from the documentary and physical record until the end of the seventeenth century. Not limited to the Chesapeake, this scarcity also appeared in New England as well where paint was sparingly used before the last quarter of the seventeenth century. Meetinghouses were infrequently painted or even stained before 1700. Peter Benes, *Meetinghouses of Early New England* (Amherst: University of Massachusetts Press, 2012), 191.

16. See Cary Carson, "The Consumer Revolution in Colonial British America: Why Demand?" in *Of Consuming Interest: The Style of Life in the Eighteenth Century*, ed. Cary Carson, Ronald Huffman, and Peter J. Albert (Charlottesville: University Press of Virginia, 1994), 483–697; and Richard L. Bushman, *The Refinement of America: Persons, Houses, Cities* (New York: Alfred A. Knopf, 1992).

17. Lancaster County Order Book, 1696–1702, December 14, 1699.

18. McIlwaine, *Journals of the House of Burgesses of Virginia*, 4:117–18, May 10, 1705.

19. James Carroll Boyd, *Ocean Hall: Discovery of an American Classic* (n.p., 2011), 48–50.

20. Carole Shammas, "The Housing Stock of the Early United States: Refinement Meets Migration," *William and Mary Quarterly*, 3d ser., 64 (July 2007): 549–90; Edward A. Chappell, "Housing a Nation: The Transformation of Living Standards in Early America," in Carson, Huffman, and Albert, *Of Consuming Interest*, 167–232; Dell Upton, "White and Black Landscapes in Eighteenth Century Virginia," in *Material Life in America, 1600–1860*, ed. Robert Blair St. George (Boston: Northeastern University Press, 1988), 357–69.

21. For instance, shingles on the statehouse in Williamsburg were ordered to be tarred in 1705. Likewise, those on the back slope of the Ringgold House in Chestertown, Maryland, built about 1743, are now protected by the roof of a 1771 extension and still retain traces of tar on them. Clapboards on an eighteenth-century addition to the rear of Linden Farm in Richmond County were tarred, along with those of the earlier wall, although yellow ochre paint was used to highlight the window jambs. McIlwaine, *Journals of the House of Burgesses of Virginia*, 4:117, May 10, 1705.

22. Natasha Loeblich to Willie Graham, "Cross-Section Microscopy Analysis of Finishes on Exterior Cornice Modillion Fragment from Yeocomico Church, Westmoreland County, Virginia," unpublished report, Architectural Research Department, Colonial Williamsburg Foundation, May 12, 2008.

23. For instance, analysis of tar on a shingle from Wetherburn's Tavern and another from a gutter at the Robert Carter House revealed very similar compositions, with iron oxide red and carbon black particles suspended in an oil-resin (perhaps pine resin) binder. Analysis was conducted by Susan L. Buck using cross-section paint analysis, polarized light microscopy, and Fourier Transform Infrared Spectroscopy (FTIR) microspectroscopy analysis techniques. The FTIR analysis was conducted at the Winterthur Museum Analytical Lab under the supervision of senior scientist Janice H. Carlson.

24. Note that tar, as a viscous material, was most malleable and paintlike when warm and was therefore often applied during the warm seasons. The May 10, 1705, entry in the *Journals of the House of Burgesses of Virginia* indicates this seasonality: "Resolved that the Roofs of the Capitol and prison be Tarred again this Summer as often as ye Overseer of the Building shall think fit." McIlwaine, *Journals of the House of Burgesses of Virginia*, 4:117.

25. St. George's Parish Vestry Book, Spotsylvania County, Virginia, April 10, 1732.

26. Edward M. Riley, ed., *The Journal of John Harrower, an Indentured Servant in the Colony of Virginia, 1773–1776* (Williamsburg: Colonial Williamsburg Foundation, 1963), 38.

27. The common use of red-brown for painting shingle roofs in the Chesapeake was likely an attempt, along with their shape, to simulate clay pantiles. Whereas the orange cast of the shingles on the Sands House in Annapolis and those used on the Mason House in Accomack County, Virginia, matched the color most often associated with clay tiles, this orange color was more typically tempered with Spanish brown. Black- and gray-painted roofs are occasionally seen in Virginia and North Carolina, such as at Prestwould in Mecklenburg County, Virginia, and Battersea in Petersburg. George Washington had the roofs of some dependencies at Mount Vernon painted gray, perhaps in the 1770s, but was advised by his nephew and estate manager to switch to red, at least for the green house, in 1792: "Spanish brown will I think answer very well for painting the Roof of the Green House and the wings to it for white lead which is the principal paint in forming a slate color is very expensive[.] I think there is in the store half as much spanish brown as will be wanting for the purpose mentioned and the further quantity that may be required may perhaps be obtained on as good terms in Alexandria as in Philadelphia and Oil also of which a good deel will be wanting." George Augustine Washington to George Washington, April 15–16, 1792, in Philander D. Chase, ed., *The Papers of George Washington: Presiden-*

tial Series, 16 vols. (Charlottesville: University of Virginia Press, 1987–2011), 10:270.

28. Memorandum of agreement between St. George Tucker and Jeremiah Satterwhite, August 30, 1798, Tucker-Coleman Collection, Swem Library, College of William and Mary, Williamsburg.

29. McIlwaine, *Journals of the House of Burgesses of Virginia*, 4:117–18, May 10, 1705.

30. Smith, *Art of Painting in Oyl*, 44.

31. Original paint schemes used on Robertson's Tenement and those applied during Peyton and Betty Randolph's ownership are reviewed in Mark Kutney, "Painting Peyton Randolph's House," *Colonial Williamsburg Interpreter* 20 (1999): 25–30.

32. Memorandum of agreement between St. George Tucker and Jeremiah Satterwhite; Susan Buck, "Colonial Williamsburg Foundation Walthoe Storehouse Paint Analysis Report," unpublished report, Architectural Research Department, Colonial Williamsburg Foundation, 1997; Matthew J. Mosca, "Historic Paint Finishes Report, Paint Analysis of Selected Samples for the Preservation Plan, Sotterley Plantation, St. Mary's County, Maryland," unpublished report, Architectural Research Department, Colonial Williamsburg Foundation, 1999; *Carolina Comments* 59 (January 2011): 15–16.

33. Willie Graham and Mark R. Wenger, "A House Befitting Mr. Attorney," *Colonial Williamsburg Interpreter* 20 (1999): 19–24; Ronald Hurst, "Refurbishing the Randolph House . . . Again?" *Colonial Williamsburg Interpreter* 20 (1999): 37–42.

34. Susan L. Buck, "Paint Cross-Section Microscopy Report: Peyton Randolph House Phase II Paint Analysis, Colonial Williamsburg," unpublished report, Architectural Research Department, Colonial Williamsburg Foundation, 1998; Kutney, "Painting Peyton Randolph's House"; Frank Welsh, "Peyton Randolph House—Four Exterior Paint Samples," unpublished report, Architectural Research Department, Colonial Williamsburg Foundation, 1998.

35. Natasha Loeblich, "Cross-Section Microscopy Analysis of Interior and Exterior Paint: Bruton Parish Church," unpublished report, Architectural Research Department, Colonial Williamsburg Foundation, 2008.

36. John Keefe was one such artisan who advertised his services as a painter in the *Virginia Gazette*: "The Subscriber, lately arrived from London, performs all sorts of Landskape, Herald, and House Painting, in the best and exactest Manner, at reasonable Rates." *Virginia Gazette*, April 18, 1751.

37. William Beverley letter, July 24, 1739, Manuscript Division, New York Public Library.

38. Bristow, *Architectural Colours in British Interiors*, 20.

39. John Harris, *The Palladian Revival: Lord Burlington, His Villa and Garden at Chiswick* (New Haven: Yale University Press, 1994), 129; Helen Hughes, "'With the Feather Edge of a Goose-Quill': Experimental Archaeology at the Little Castle Bolsover," in Jablonski and Matsen, *Architectural Finishes in the Built Environment*, 123–36.

40. Prussian blue was found in the bright blue paint on the columns of a 1715 Hadley, Massachusetts, court cupboard, which appears to be the first solidly dated use of Prussian blue for decorative paints in the colonies. See Philip Zea and Suzanne L. Flynt, *Hadley Chests* (Deerfield, Mass.: Pocumtuck Memorial Hall Association, 1992). The presence of Prussian blue on the paint brush was identified by Susan L. Buck by polarized light microscopy and confirmed by Winterthur Museum senior scientist Janice H. Carlson using FTIR microspectroscopy.

41. William Farington, letter to Isabella and Mary, Surry Street Strand, February 18, 1756, as cited in appendix A of Desmond Fitz-Gerald, *The Norfolk House Music Room* (London: Victoria and Albert Museum, 1973), 48.

42. Marcia Miller and Orlando Ridout V, *Architecture and Change in the Chesapeake: A Field Tour on the Eastern and Western Shores* (Crownsville: Vernacular Architecture Forum and Maryland Historical Trust Press, 1998), 129.

43. Susan L. Buck, "Preliminary Results from the Marmion Room Cross-Section Microscopy Paint Analysis," unpublished memo for the Metropolitan Museum of Art, April 29, 2008; Natasha Loeblich, "Cross-Section Microscopy Analysis of Interior and Exterior Paint: Marmion," unpublished report, Architectural Research Department, Colonial Williamsburg Foundation, 2008.

44. Susan L. Buck, "Cross-Section Paint Microscopy Report: Interior and Exterior Paint Investigation, Four Mile Tree," unpublished report, Architectural Research Department, Colonial Williamsburg Foundation, 2009.

45. Margaret Pritchard and Willie Graham, "Rethinking Two Houses at Colonial Williamsburg," *Magazine Antiques* 149 (January 1996): 166–73.

46. John Ferdinand Dalziel Smythe, *A Tour of the United States of America: Containing an Account of the Present Situation of that Country*, 2 vols. (London: G. Robinson, 1784), 1:12.

47. Frank S. Welsh, "Microscopical Analysis to Determine and Evaluate the Nature and Colors of the Original Surface Coatings: Gloucester County Courthouse, Hanover County Courthouse, King William County Courthouse, Charles City Courthouse, Fork Church, Hanover County, Abingdon Church, Gloucester County, Aquia Church, Stafford County," unpublished report, Architectural Research Department, Colonial Williamsburg Foundation, 1989.

48. Lead white in linseed oil produced a warm, creamy white that is characteristic of eighteenth-century paint and contrasts with the more brilliant cool whites produced by modern titanium-based paints.

49. McIlwaine, *Journals of the House of Burgesses of Virginia*, 12:83, June 20, 1770.

50. William Allason to Gerard Hooe, August 27, 1775, Allason Letterbooks, Virginia State Library, Richmond.

51. Norton Papers, Architectural Research Department, Colonial Williamsburg Foundation. The complete order included 100 pounds of white lead, 20 pounds of yellow ochre, a barrel of oil, 20 pounds of Venetian red, 2 gallons of spirits of turpentine, 5 pounds of red lead, 3 pounds of lampblack, and 2 pounds of white copperas.

52. Graham and Wenger, "A House Befitting Mr. Attorney";

Kutney, "Painting Peyton Randolph's House"; Susan L. Buck, "Paint Cross-Section Microscopy Report: Peyton Randolph House Phase II Paint Analysis, Colonial Williamsburg," unpublished report, Architectural Research Department, Colonial Williamsburg Foundation, 1998.

53. The first of these books was Hezekiah Reynolds, *Directions for House and Ship Painting*, which was published in 1812 (facsimile reprint, Worcester, Ma.: American Antiquarian Society, 1978).

54. Willie Graham and Orlando Ridout V, "Architectural Analysis of Tudor Place: An Interim Report," unpublished report, Tudor Place Foundation, Washington, D.C., 2002.

55. Paint contract, Mutual Assurance Society Records, Miscellaneous Records, 1794–1869, Virginia State Archives, Richmond.

56. Two early examples of oak graining in principal spaces are the repainting of Prestwould in 1831 and Philip St. George Cocke's remodeling of Four Mile Tree in 1835. Early architectural finishes at Prestwould were examined by Frank Welsh in 1994 to assist in interior restoration of the house. Susan L. Buck, "Cross-Section Paint Microscopy Report: Interior and Exterior Paint Investigation, Four Mile Tree," unpublished report, Architectural Research Department, Colonial Williamsburg Foundation, 2009.

CHAPTER 16

1. Textile hangings can also be documented on the walls of New England houses. See Florence Montgomery, *Textiles in America, 1650–1870* (New York: W. W. Norton, 1984), 214–15.

2. York Country Records, Deeds, Orders, Wills, 1691–94, 161.

3. Richmond County Will Book, 1725–53, 547–53.

4. For tapestry hangings in New England, see *Boston Newsletter*, August 3, 1755; and Walter Kendall Watkins, "The Early Use and Manufacture of Paperhangings in Boston," in *Old Time New England* 12, no. 3 (January 1922): 109.

5. Mary Newton Stanard, *Colonial Virginia, Its People and Customs* (Philadelphia: J. B. Lippincott, 1917), 73; Richard Beale Davis, ed., *William Fitzhugh and His Chesapeake World, 1676–1701: The Fitzhugh Letters and Other Documents* (Chapel Hill: University of North Carolina Press for Virginia Historical Society, 1963), 142, 175.

6. "Rosewell," *Southern Literary Messenger* 10 (January 1844): 41.

7. "Abstracts of Land Patents," *Virginia Magazine of History and Biography* 1 (1894): 439; *Virginia Magazine of History and Biography* 32 (1924): 3n.

8. Schedule of Losses Sustained by the Earl of Dunmore, His Majesty's Late Governor of the Colony of Virginia, February 25, 1784, quoted in Graham Hood, *The Governor's Palace in Williamsburg: A Cultural Study* (Williamsburg: Colonial Williamsburg Foundation, 1991), appendix 3.

9. Ibid., appendix 4, 298. Probably during Governor Fauquier's residence at the Governor's Palace, from 1758 to 1768, some fifty years after the leather may have been installed, the Upper Middle Room was redecorated with back stools upholstered in crimson damask and "2 long looking Glasses with red gilded frames." The windows were newly hung with crimson damask curtains to match the chairs. The current fashion would have favored hanging the walls with crimson damask to match the chairs and windows.

10. Hood, *Governor's Palace in Williamsburg*, appendix 5, 300.

11. E. A. Entwisle, "The Blew Paper Warehouse in Aldermanbury, London," *Connoisseur* (May 1950): 95.

12. Abbott Lowell Cummings, "The Use and Manufacture of Wallpaper in New England," in Richard C. Nylander et al., *Wallpaper in New England* (Boston: Society for the Preservation of New England Antiquities, 1986), 3.

13. "Ledger of Imports and Exports, Christmas 1699– Christmas 1700," Customs 3/4, Public Record Office, Kew, microfilm reel 452, Rockefeller Library, Colonial Williamsburg Foundation.

14. Cited in Charles Saumarez Smith, *Eighteenth-Century Decoration: Design and the Domestic Interior in England* (New York: Harry N. Abrams, 1993), 128.

15. Robert Beverley Letterbook, 1761–75, April 15, 1771, Library of Congress, Washington, D.C., and microfilm reel M-3, Rockefeller Library, Colonial Williamsburg Foundation.

16. *Virginia Gazette*, April 6, 1739, and November 28, 1745.

17. *Virginia Gazette*, December 28, 1769.

18. The identification of the lining paper would seem to associate the fabric and lining paper with Carter's 1762 installation. Physical evidence for such furring was also installed at Mount Pleasant, Surry County, Virginia, in 1803.

19. Cartridge paper was a heavyweight plain paper, usually white.

20. Botetourt's accounts with Joseph Kidd, "The Governor's Palace Historical Notes," 214–15, Department of Research and Record, Colonial Williamsburg Foundation.

21. Though no fragments of the original paper survive on the wooden sheathing at Rock Castle, the scoring lines made by the paperhanger are still evident in 21¾-inch intervals throughout the room.

22. A keyword search of the America's Historical Newspapers database identified the newspaper fragments. They were from the *Baltimore Federal Gazette* and date between November 20 and 30, 1797. http://www.newsbank.com/Readex/index.cfm?content=96

23. *Pennsylvania Packet*, August 19, 1786, cited in Alfred Coxe Prime, *The Arts and Crafts in Philadelphia, Maryland, and South Carolina, 1786–1800*, Series Two (Topsfield, Mass.: Walpole Society, 1932), 276.

24. Investigations by painting historians Frank Welsh at Kenmore and Susan Buck at Montpelier revealed that paper was applied directly to the brown coat of plaster.

25. Christopher Gilbert, *The Life and Work of Thomas Chippendale*, 2 vols. (New York: Macmillan, 1978), 1:200.

26. Botetourt's accounts with William Fenton record that he spent £18, 15 shillings, for 500 feet of papier-mâché, as opposed to Lascelles, who spent £110, 5 shillings, 0 pence, for 420 feet of gilt wooden border. Botetourt's accounts also document that he purchased "50 lb of the best Verdeter," "24 lb of prusian blue," and "2 Ream of fine large Elephant paper." Botetourt Account Book, Badminton House Archives, England.

27. Botetourt inventory, in Hood, *Governor's Palace in Williamsburg*, appendix 1, 290–91.

28. Robert Beverley Letterbook, 1761–93, Library of Congress, Washington, D.C.

29. John C. Fitzpatrick, ed., *The Writings of George Washington from the Original Manuscript Sources, 1745–1799*, 39 vols. (Washington, D.C.: Government Printing Office, 1931–44), 27:305.

30. James A. Bear Jr. and Lucia C. Stanton, eds., *Jefferson's Memorandum Books: Accounts, with Legal Records and Miscellany, 1767–1826*, 2 vols. (Princeton: Princeton University Press, 1997), 1:27. Investigations of the paint and paper layers by paint historian Susan Buck did not reveal this blue paper layer.

31. See Cummings, "Use and Manufacture of Wallpaper in New England, 1700–1820," 5.

32. J. Thomas Savage and Robert A. Leath, "Buying British: Merchants, Taste, and Charleston Consumerism," in *In Pursuit of Refinement: Charlestonians Abroad, 1740–1860*, ed. Maurie D. McInnis (Columbia: University of South Carolina Press, 1999), 59.

33. Excerpted from "Carlyle House Furnishings Plan," original in Gunston Hall Library and Archives, Lorton, Virginia.

34. Rosamond Randall Beirne and John Henry Scarff, *William Buckland, 1734–1774: Architect of Virginia and Maryland* (Baltimore: Maryland Historical Society, 1958), 150.

35. "Invoice of Sundry Goods Shipd by Richd Washington on bord the Peggy and Elizabeth," November 1757, *George Washington Papers at the Library of Congress, 1741–1799*, Series 5, Financial Papers, image 241, http://lcweb2.10c.gov.

36. *Maryland Gazette*, March 5, 1761.

37. *Virginia Gazette*, October 5, 1769.

38. Fitzpatrick, *Writings of George Washington*, 2:23.

39. R. Campbell, *The London Tradesman* (London, 1747; reprint, Newton Abbot, Devon: David and Charles, 1969), 170.

40. Robert Carter to Thomas Blandon, London, February 16, 1762, Robert Carter Letterbook, 1761–64, microfilm reel M-114, Rockefeller Library, Colonial Williamsburg Foundation.

41. London, April 27, 1762, Carter-Keith Papers, reel 3, Virginia Historical Society, microfilm, Rockefeller Library, Colonial Williamsburg Foundation.

42. *Virginia Gazette*, May 9, 1771.

43. Quoted in Cummings, "Use and Manufacture of Wallpaper in New England, 1700–1820," 12.

44. Robert Beverley Letterbook, 1761–93, February 10, 1772, Library of Congress, Washington, D.C.

45. Ibid.

46. Ibid. Later, in the same invoice, Beverley ordered another set of chairs, upholstered in black horsehair, "for a dining Room."

47. Architectural examinations of the original window moldings in this room also revealed evidence of cloak pins, used to tie off curtains drawn up in drapery, of the type described by Beverley.

48. Robert Carter to Thomas Blandon, February 16, 1762, Robert Carter Letterbook, 1761–64.

49. Invoice of goods shipped to Nathaniel Lyttleton Savage, 1769. See Beatrix Rumford, "Wallpaper in Williamsburg," unpublished report, Colonial Williamsburg Foundation.

50. In 1756, William Farington described the Norfolk House to his sisters, noting that "the Hall is very Plain." Desmond Fitz-Gerald, *The Norfolk House Music Room* (London: Victoria and Albert Museum, 1973), appendix A, 48.

51. Trade card illustrated in Treve Rosoman, *London Wallpapers, Their Manufacture and Use, 1690–1840* (London: English Heritage, 1992), 6.

52. Occasionally, combinations of light and dark woods were used for visual effect. See, for example, Celia Fiennes's description of Chippenham, in Cambridgeshire, in Mark R. Wenger, *The English Travels of Sir John Percival and William Byrd II: The Percival Diary of 1701* (Columbia: University of Missouri Press, 1989), 67n127.

53. *Massachusetts Centennial*, February 4, 1789, quoted in Cummings, "Use and Manufacture of Wallpaper in New England, 1700–1820," 14.

54. Robert Beverley Letterbook, 1761–93, Library of Congress, Washington, D.C. The term "stucco" was used to represent both printed imitations of plasterwork and molded papier-mâché, as well as the color. In addition to the stucco-colored pillar and arch paper that Beverley ordered, he also included "No. 9 Stucco Color" and "No. 11 Large yellow Pattern mixed with stucco Colour."

55. Orders to Robert Stark, March 1763, Gunston Hall Archives, Lorton, Virginia.

56. Papers of this same type were also purchased by Philip Van Schuyler in 1761 (now destroyed) and by Stephen Van Rensselaer between 1765 and 1769 (now in the Metropolitan Museum of Art) and were requested by New Jersey governor William Franklin, although no actual order survives.

57. *Daily National Intelligencer* (Washington, D.C.), October 20, 1825, quoted in Catherine Lynn, *Wallpaper in America: From the Seventeenth Century to World War I* (New York: W. W. Norton, 1980), 229. Business records for the Zuber manufactory still survive at the Musée du Papier Peint in Rixheim, France, and they document the shipment of scenic wallpapers to numerous cities in the United States, including Norfolk and Richmond.

58. John Cornforth, *Early Georgian Interiors* (New Haven: Yale University Press, 2004), 95.

59. Quoted in John Cornforth and John Fowler, *English Decoration in the Eighteenth Century* (Princeton: Pyne Press, 1974), 202.

60. Robert Carter Letterbook, II, 74–75, manuscript, Duke University Library, Durham.

61. Thomas Jefferson to William Short, New York, April 6, 1790, in Julian P. Boyd, ed., *The Papers of Thomas Jefferson*, 20 vols. (Princeton: Princeton University Press, 1950–82), 16:322.

62. Susan R. Stein, *The Worlds of Thomas Jefferson at Monticello* (New York: Harry N. Abrams, 1993), 71.

63. Ibid., 71–79, 281, 304, 311–12, 425. James Madison's drawing room at Montpelier also contained furnishings similar to those recorded in Jefferson's parlor, and the room was certainly used in a similar manner. Tiny fragments of a crimson flocked paper have recently been discovered there, confirming the continuity of the

fashion for hanging the most formal entertaining spaces with this color.

64. "Decoration of paper machee for a ceiling 14f. 4 I. sq. Divided into 6 + 2 compartments and resembling as much as may be Gibbs' rules for drawg. Pl.58. upper figure, & Palladio B. 4. Pl. 26. fig. C.D.F." Bear and Stanton, *Jefferson's Memorandum Books*, 1:27.

65. Jefferson subsequently installed jasperware plaques in the chimneypiece, probably in the 1796–1809 renovation. Stein, *Worlds of Thomas Jefferson*, 86.

66. John Evelyn, trans., *A Parallel of Architecture Both Ancient and Moderne by Roland Freart St. De Chambray* (London: Tho. Reycroft, 1664), 10.

67. Richard Neve, *The City and Country Purchaser's and Builder's Dictionary* (London: B. Sprint, 1736), 2–3.

68. Louis B. Wright and Marion Tinling, eds., *The Secret Diary of William Byrd of Westover, 1709–1712* (Richmond: Dietz Press, 1941), October 21, 1710, 246.

69. "Invoice of Sundry Goods Shipd by Richd Washington on bord the Peggy and Elizabeth." Two years later, Washington ordered bed furniture, upholstered chairs, and window curtains to coordinate with the paper.

70. Quoted in Cummings, "Use and Manufacture of Wallpaper in New England, 1700–1820," 12.

71. Thomas Jefferson to William Short, New York, April 6, 1790, in Boyd, *Papers of Thomas Jefferson*, 16:322.

72. The *Oxford English Dictionary* describes "furbelow" as "anything having a flounce." The practice of hanging fabrics drawn up in flounces as wall decoration originated with Daniel Marot's designs created for William III in Holland and England. See plate 99, in Peter Thornton, *Authentic Decor: The Domestic Interior, 1620–1920* (New York: Crescent Books, 1984), 81.

73. Quoted in Gilbert, *Life and Work of Thomas Chippendale*, 1:50.

74. "Invoice of Sundry Goods Shipd by Richd Washington on bord the Peggy and Elizabeth."

75. Fitzpatrick, *Writings of George Washington*, 2:23, April 1757.

76. "Invoice of Sundry Goods Shipd by Richd Washington on bord the Peggy and Elizabeth."

77. Other Chesapeake references support the use of large quantities of varying patterns of paper within a single dwelling. See Robert Beverley's order with Samuel Athawes for Blandfield in 1771, in Robert Beverley Letterbook, 1761–93, September 1771, Library of Congress, Washington, D.C. Other Virginia invoices document a similar aesthetic: Robert Carter of Williamsburg, Colonel George William Fairfax of Belvoir, Thomas Jefferson, and Sir Peyton Skipwith of Prestwould.

78. *Maryland Gazette*, April 14, 1767.

79. Rawleigh Downman in London to Joseph Chinn at Morattico, Lancaster County, Virginia, November 12, 1764, Rawleigh Downman Letterbook, microfilm, Rockefeller Library, Colonial Williamsburg Foundation.

80. *Virginia Gazette*, August 6, 1777.

81. Fitzpatrick, *Writings of George Washington*, 2:138.

82. W. W. Abbot, Dorothy Twohig, and Philander D. Chase, eds., *The Papers of George Washington, Colonial Series*, 10 vols. (Charlottesville: University Press of Virginia, 1983–95), 4:377; Fitzpatrick, *Writings of George Washington*, 2:320.

83. Robert Beverley Letterbook, 1761–93, February 10, 1772, Library of Congress, Washington, D.C.

CHAPTER 17

1. Colonial building accounts are generally fragmentary and rare. One relatively complete set of records exists for the construction of Carter's Grove, a two-story brick dwelling erected near Williamsburg in the early 1750s. These accounts demonstrate the high cost of labor in the traditional building process. Carter Burwell spent nearly £1,300 over a four-year period, between 1751 and 1755. Burwell paid more than three-quarters of that amount to his many workmen—only about a quarter of it was spent on materials. Carter Burwell Account Book, 1738–55, Colonial Williamsburg Foundation.

2. Gregg Kimball, *American City, Southern Place: A Cultural History of Antebellum Richmond* (Athens: University of Georgia Press, 2003), 19; *Twenty-sixth Annual Report of the Railroad Commissioner of the State of Virginia* (Richmond: J. H. O'Bannon, 1902), ix.

3. William Mahone laid out the Norfolk and Petersburg branch line in the mid-1850s. Following the Civil War, the railway was linked to towns such as Lynchburg and the coalfields in the western part of the state. It was consolidated as the Atlantic, Mississippi, and Ohio Railroad in 1870, and its name was changed again, to the Norfolk and Western, in 1881. *Seventeenth Annual Report of the Railroad Commissioner of the State of Virginia* (Richmond: J. H. O'Bannon, 1893), lxxiv.

4. Fernand Braudel, *Capitalism and Material Life, 1400–1800* (New York: Harper and Row, 1973), 193.

5. Fred Kniffen, "Folk Housing: Key to Diffusion," *Annals of the Association of American Geographers* 55 (December 1965): 553.

6. For a detailed study of the industrialization of the building process, see Catherine Bishir, Charlotte Brown, Carl Lounsbury, and Ernest Wood, *Architects and Builders in North Carolina: A History of the Practice of Building* (Chapel Hill: University of North Carolina Press, 1990), 193–239.

7. In the 1880s, a number of firms shipped several million feet of timber from the depot at Ivor to Norfolk, Petersburg, Boston, New York, and Philadelphia. There were sawmills, planing mills, and sash and blind factories up and down the line. *The Virginias, a Mining, Industrial, and Scientific Journal Devoted to the Development of Virginia and West Virginia* 3 (June 1882): 91; *Reference Book of the Norfolk & Western Railroad Co., 1885* (n.p., 1885), 12, 64.

8. Horace Greeley et al., eds., *The Great Industries of the United States* (Hartford: J. B. Burr and Hyde, 1872), 40–41.

9. *Manufacturer and Builder* 2 (February 1870): 57.

10. *Manufacturer and Builder* 17 (March 1885): 52.

11. *Manufacturer and Builder* 5 (April 1873): 78.

12. *American Agriculturist* 46 (May 1887): 214.

13. *Milton Chronicle*, March 10, 1859.

14. *Eighth Census of the United States, 1860*, vol. 3, *Manufactures* (Washington, D.C.: Government Printing Office, 1865).

15. J. Thomas Sharf, *History of Baltimore City and County* (Philadelphia: Louis H. Everts, 1881), 436.

16. George Howard, *The Monumental City* (Baltimore: J. D. Ehlers, 1873), 191.

17. Ibid., 248; William Bullock Clark and Edward B. Mathews, eds., *Maryland Mineral Industries, 1896–1907* (Baltimore: Johns Hopkins University Press, 1908), 112.

18. Pamela Simpson, *Cheap, Quick, and Easy: Imitative Architectural Materials, 1870–1930* (Knoxville: University of Tennessee Press, 1999).

Contributors

SUSAN BUCK completed her Ph.D. in Art Conservation Research from the University of Delaware in 2003, where her research focused on establishing a standard architectural paint analysis methodology and the use of paint archaeology to help understand the evolution of an 1818 Charleston, South Carolina, house and its outbuildings. She has a B.A. from Williams College, an M.B.A. from Boston University, and an M.S. from the Winterthur/University of Delaware Program in Art Conservation, and she co-teaches a course in that program in cross-section microscopy analysis. She works privately on paint analysis and conservation treatment projects for many historic sites.

CARY CARSON is a historian, student of material culture, and museum educator. Employed by Colonial Williamsburg beginning in 1976, he served as vice president for the Research Division, retiring after thirty years. During that time, he worked alongside most of the contributors to this book. He conducts his own field research in New England, Maryland, Virginia, and Great Britain. He writes about the social history of early America, the transformation of English architectural traditions brought to the colonies, the history of Americans' love affair with consumer goods, and the role that history museums play—or should play—in public education.

EDWARD A. CHAPPELL is the Shirley H. and Richard D. Roberts Director of Architectural and Archaeological Research at Colonial Williamsburg, where he began as head of Architectural Research in 1980. Chappell has responsibility for historic preservation, as well as archaeological excavation and the research and design that have distinguished the Colonial Williamsburg Foundation's restoration and reconstruction projects for three decades, and he has made wide-ranging fieldwork an essential part of scholarship at Colonial Williamsburg reconstruction projects. He studied history at the College of William and Mary and architectural history at the University of Virginia.

WILLIE GRAHAM has, since 1981, overseen investigations, restorations, and reconstructions of buildings for the Colonial Williamsburg Foundation, where he serves as the Curator of Architecture. He has promoted the use of advanced technologies to probe buildings as a way to better understand how and when they were built and used, including working on national and international standards for the application of dendrochronology and scientific paint analysis. His research focuses on traditional building design and construction technology.

CARL R. LOUNSBURY is Senior Architectural Historian at the Colonial Williamsburg Foundation and teaches in the history department at the College of William and Mary. His research interests have concentrated on English and American churches and meetinghouses, public buildings, and theaters. His books include *Essays in Early American Architectural History* (2011), *The Courthouses of Early Virginia* (2005), and *An Illustrated Glossary of Early Southern Architecture and Landscape* (1994).

MARGARET BECK PRITCHARD is the Curator of Prints, Maps, and Wallpaper for the Colonial Williamsburg Foundation. She is responsible for selecting appropriate prints, maps, and wallpaper to hang on the walls of buildings in the historic district and has lectured and published on numerous subjects relating to the collection for which she is responsible. Her most recent publication was a comprehensive catalog of the map collection at Colonial Williamsburg, *Degrees of Latitude: Mapping Colonial America*. She has also authored books and articles on English natural history artists, the graphics in the collections at the Museum of Early Southern Decorative Arts, and Pennsylvania cartographers and naturalists, as well as several articles on eighteenth-century wallpaper.

ORLANDO RIDOUT V is Chief of the Office of Research, Survey, and Registration at the Maryland Historical Trust (the state historic preservation office), where he has worked since completing his B.A. in architectural history at the University of Virginia. He teaches courses at George Washington University. For over thirty years, Ridout has conducted extensive research on the early architecture of the Chesapeake region. He has served as a consultant for Colonial Williamsburg, Mount Vernon, Historic Charleston Foundation, Tudor Place Foundation, and the Montpelier Foundation. His books include *Building the Octagon* and *Architecture and Change in the Chesapeake*.

LORENA S. WALSH retired after twenty-seven years as a historian at the Colonial Williamsburg Foundation, where she worked on Chesapeake social and economic history, consumer behavior, agricultural history, urban food systems, African American history, and the trans-Atlantic slave trade. She is the author (with Lois Green Carr and Russell R. Menard) of *Robert Cole's World: Agriculture and Society in Early Maryland* (1991); *From Calabar to Carter's Grove: The History of a Virginia Slave Community* (1997); and *Motives of Honor, Pleasure, and Profit: Plantation Management in the Chesapeake, 1607–1763* (2010).

MARK R. WENGER was, from 1980 to 2003, an architectural historian with the Colonial Williamsburg Foundation, where he studied and worked on many major buildings in the Historic Area, including the reconstruction of Charlton's Coffeehouse. Since 2003, he has been employed with Mesick Cohen Wilson Baker, Architects, where he has participated in a number of significant projects, including the restoration of Montpelier and the drafting of a preservation plan for the University of Virginia.

Image Credits

1.0. Cameron Davidson
1.1. Studio Ammons
1.2. Maryland Historical Society
1.3. Library of Congress
1.4. Maryland Historical Society
1.5. Metropolitan Museum of Art
1.6. Maryland Historical Society
1.7. Maryland State Archives
2.0. David Doody, CWF
2.1A-C. CWF; 2.1D. Massachusetts
    Historical Society
2.2. Frank Nivison, CWF
2.3. Thomas Williams, CWF
2.4. Condé Nast
2.5. Stephen Toth, CWF
2.6. David Doody, CWF
2.7. Billie Graham and Jeffrey Klee,
    CWF
2.8. Studio Ammons after Mark Schara,
    Edward Chappell, and Jeffrey
    Bostetter, CWF
2.9. Studio Ammons after Cary Carson,
    CWF
2.10. Studio Ammons after Cary Carson,
    David Bergstone, Carl Lounsbury,
    Willie Graham, CWF
2.11. Jeffrey Klee after Cary Carson, CWF
2.12. David Doody, CWF
2.13. Tom Green, CWF
2.14. Mark Tucker, CWF
3.0. Willie Graham, David Doody, CWF
3.1. Singleton P. Moorehead, CWF
3.2. HABS
3.3. Edward Chappell, CWF
3.4. Willie Graham, CWF
3.5. Edward Chappell, CWF
3.6. Studio Ammons after Edward
    Chappell, CWF
3.7. Edward Chappell, CWF
3.8. Clyde Holmes, CWF
3.9. Albert Koch, CWF
3.10. Kirsten Travers, CWF

3.11. Studio Ammons after HABS
3.12. Jonathan Owen, CWF after
    James Gibbs
3.13. Willie Graham, CWF
3.14. Willie Graham, CWF
3.15. Studio Ammons, Jeffrey Klee, CWF,
    after Billie Graham, Edward Chappell,
    Jeff Bostetter, CWF
3.16. Willie Graham, CWF
3.17. Carl Lounsbury, CWF
3.18A. Studio Ammons after Doug
    Taylor, CWF; 3.18B. Jeffrey Klee after
    HABS, Edward Chappell, CWF;
    3.18C. Studio Ammons after Travis
    McDonald, Edward Chappell, CWF
3.19. Jeffrey Klee, CWF
3.20. Craig McDougal, CWF
4.0. Barbara Temple Lombardi, CWF
4.1. Keith Rocco, National Park Service
4.2. Timothy Riordan, Historic St.
    Mary's City
4.3. CWF.
4.4. Studio Ammons
4.5. Princeton University Library
4.6. CWF.
5.0. David Doody, CWF.
5.1 Library of Congress
5.2. Library of Congress
5.3. Library of Virginia
5.4. Royal Institute of British Architects
5.5. Loring J. Turner, CWF.
5.6. Barbara Temple Lombardi, CWF
5.7. Barbara Temple Lombardi, CWF
5.8. Adam Wright and Jeffrey Klee, CWF,
    Peter Wyld
5.9. Willie Graham, CWF
5.10. Jeffrey Klee, CWF.
5.11A. Jeffrey Klee; 5.11B. Billie Graham,
    CWF
5.12. Jeffrey Klee, CWF
5.13. Clerk's Office, Northampton
    County, Virginia
5.14. Yale University Art Gallery
5.15. Mount Vernon Ladies Association;
    inset: CWF
5.16. Carl Lounsbury, CWF
5.17. Barbara Temple Lombardi, CWF
6.0. CWF

6.1. Studio Ammons after Jamie May,
    David Given, Charles Hodges, Taft
    Kiser, and Cary Carson, CWF
6.2. Studio Ammons after Jamie May
    and Cary Carson, CWF
6.3. Studio Ammons after Mark J.
    Wenger, Garrett Fesler, Patricia
    Samford, and Cary Carson, CWF
6.4. Studio Ammons after Cary Carson,
    CWF
6.5. Studio Ammons after Ivor Noël
    Hume and Cary Carson, CWF
6.6. Studio Ammons after Norman Barka
    and Cary Carson, CWF
6.7. Jeffrey Klee after Garry Wheeler
    Stone and Cary Carson, CWF
6.8. Studio Ammons, Jeffrey Klee, Tricia
    Miller after Ivor Noël Hume, Edward
    Chappell, and Cary Carson, CWF
6.9. Jeffrey Klee after David Muraca,
    Andrew Edwards, and Cary Carson,
    CWF
6.10. Studio Ammons after William
    Buchanan Jr., Edward Heite, and
    Cary Carson, CWF
6.11. Studio Ammons after Fraser Neiman
    and Cary Carson, CWF
6.12. Jeffrey Klee after Silas Hurry, Henry
    Miller, Timothy Riordan, and Cary
    Carson, CWF
6.13. Studio Ammons after Ivor Noël
    Hume and Cary Carson, CWF
6.14. Studio Ammons after William
    Kelso, Garrett Fesler, and Cary
    Carson, CWF
6.15. Studio Ammons after Cary Carson,
    CWF
6.16. Billie Graham, CWF
6.17. Billie Graham and Jeffrey Klee,
    CWF
6.18. Studio Ammons after Edward
    Chappell and Cary Carson, CWF
6.19. CWF
6.20. Roger Guernsey after Cary Carson,
    CWF; inset: William Salt Library
6.21. Jeffrey Klee after Richard Anderson,
    Willie Graham, and Cary Carson,
    CWF

6.22. Jeffrey Klee after John Metz, Jennifer Jones, Dwayne Pickett, David Muraca, and Cary Carson, CWF

6.23. David Doody, CWF

6.24. Studio Ammons after Dennis Blanton, Nicholas Luccketti, Willie Graham, Edward Chappell, and Cary Carson, CWF

6.25. Studio Ammons, Tricia Miller after Cary Carson, CWF

7.0. David Doody, CWF

7.1. Rendersphere after HABS

7.2. Rendersphere after Willie Graham, CWF

7.3. Willie Graham, CWF

7.4. Rendersphere after Cary Carson, HABS

7.5. Valentine Richmond History Center

7.6. Rendersphere, Allan Adams after Willie Graham, CWF

7.7. Rendersphere after Laura J. Wilson, CWF

7.8. Mrs. Nony Ollerenshaw

7.9. Billie Graham, Willie Graham, CWF

7.10A. Billie Graham, CWF; 7.10B. Jeffrey Klee after Mark R. Wenger, Willie Graham, CWF; 7.10C Billie Graham after Mark R. Wenger

7.11A. Studio Ammons after Mark R. Wenger, CWF; 7.11B. Rendersphere after Mark R. Wenger

7.12. Carl Lounsbury, CWF

7.13A. Rendersphere after HABS; 7.13B. Rendersphere after Mark R. Wenger, CWF

7.14. Huntington Library

7.15A. Willie Graham, CWF; 7.15B. Jennifer Glass

7.16. Jennifer Glass

7.17. Willie Graham, CWF

7.18. Jeffrey Klee, CWF

7.19A. Rendersphere after Mark R. Wenger, CWF; 7.19B Rendersphere after HABS; 7.19C. Rendersphere after Billie Graham, CWF

7.20. Jeffrey Klee, CWF

7.21A. Jeffrey Klee, Billie Graham, CWF; 7.21B. Rendersphere after Mark R. Wenger

7.22. Studio Ammons after Arthur A. Shurcliff and Jeffrey Bostetter, CWF

7.23. Rendersphere after Orlando Ridout V and Nancy Kurtz

7.24. HABS

7.25. HABS

7.26. HABS

7.27A. Rendersphere after Carl Lounsbury, CWF; 7.27B. Rendersphere after Willie Graham, Mark R. Wenger, CWF

7.28. Jeffrey Klee after Mark R. Wenger, CWF

7.29. Willie Graham, CWF; inset: Barbara Temple Lombardi, CWF

7.30. Studio Ammons, Jeffrey Klee after Mark R. Wenger, CWF

7.31. Willie Graham, CWF

7.32A. Jeffrey Klee after HABS; 7.33B. Studio Ammons after Mount Vernon Ladies Association

7.33. Jeffrey Klee and Jennifer Glass after Gardiner Hallock, Montpelier Foundation

7.34. Billie Graham, CWF

7.35. Rendersphere after HABS, Mark R. Wenger, CWF

7.36. Jeffrey Klee after Carl Lounsbury, CWF

8.0. David Doody, CWF

8.1. Rendersphere after Edward Chappell, CWF

8.2. Edward Chappell, CWF

8.3. Rendersphere after Edward Chappell, CWF

8.4. Carl Lounsbury, CWF

8.5. Thomas Williams, CWF

8.6. HABS

8.7. Jeffrey Klee, CWF

8.8. Rendersphere after Willie Graham, CWF

8.9. Jeffrey Klee, CWF

8.10. Studio Ammons, Jeffrey Klee after Edward Chappell, CWF

8.11. Jeffrey Klee after Edward Chappell, CWF

8.12. Studio Ammons after Edward Chappell, CWF

8.13. Studio Ammons after Mark Schara, CWF

8.14. Edward Chappell, CWF

8.15. Willie Graham, CWF

8.16. Frances Benjamin Johnston, Library of Congress

8.17A. Jeffrey Klee after Doug Taylor and Edward Chappell, CWF; 8.17B. Jeffrey Klee

9.0. David Doody, CWF

9.1. Rendersphere after Cary Carson, CWF

9.2. E. H. Pickering, HABS

9.3. Special Collections, University of Virginia Library

9.4. Jack Boucher, HABS

9.5. Jeffrey Klee after Orlando Ridout V

9.6. Jack Boucher, HABS

9.7. Orlando Ridout V

9.8. Jack Boucher, HABS

9.9. Jack Boucher, HABS

9.10. Studio Ammons, Allan Adams after Willie Macintire, CWF

9.11. Studio Ammons, Allan Adams after Doug Taylor, CWF

9.12. Orlando Ridout V

9.13. Orlando Ridout V

9.14. Studio Ammons, Allan Adams after John Bernard, CWF

9.15. Willie Graham, CWF

9.16. Orlando Ridout V

9.17. William Bodenstein, Maryland Historical Trust

9.18. Studio Ammons, Allan Adams after John Bernard, CWF

9.19. Willie Graham, CWF

9.20. Willie Graham, CWF

9.21. HABS

9.22. Rendersphere after Robert Ray, CWF

9.23. HABS

9.24. E. H. Pickering, HABS

10.0. Lael White, CWF

10.1. Studio Ammons, Allan Adams after Willie Graham, CWF

10.2. Willie Graham, CWF

10.3. Studio Ammons after Cary Carson, CWF

10.4. Rendersphere after Willie Graham, CWF

10.5. Rendersphere after Nicholas Luccketti, Willie Graham, CWF

10.6. Studio Ammons, Allan Adams after Willie Graham, CWF

10.7. Loring Turner, CWF

10.8. Rendersphere after Willie Graham, CWF

10.9. Studio Ammons, Allan Adams after Willie Graham, CWF

10.10. Rendersphere after Willie Graham, CWF

10.11. Studio Ammons after Willie Graham, CWF

10.12. Studio Ammons after Willie Graham, CWF

10.13. Willie Graham, CWF

10.14. CWF

10.15. Rendersphere, Studio Ammons, Allan Adams after Willie Graham, CWF

10.16. Willie Graham, CWF

10.17. Jeffrey Klee, CWF

10.18. Willie Graham, CWF

10.19. Willie Graham, CWF

10.20. Rendersphere after Willie Graham, CWF

10.21. Rendersphere, Jeffrey Klee after Willie Graham, CWF

10.22. Studio Ammons after Cary Carson, CWF

10.23. Studio Ammons after Cary Carson and Chinh Hoang

10.24. Rendersphere after Singleton P. Moorehead, CWF

10.25. Willie Graham, CWF

10.26. Rendersphere after Willie Graham, CWF

10.27A. Rendersphere after Willie Graham, CWF; 10.27B. Studio Ammons, Rendersphere after Willie Graham, CWF

10.28. Carl Lounsbury, CWF

10.29. Willie Graham, CWF

10.30. Studio Ammons after Willie Graham, CWF

11.0. Tom Green, CWF

11.1. Willie Graham, CWF

11.2. CWF

11.3. David Doody, CWF

11.4. Tom Green, CWF

11.5. Carl Lounsbury, CWF

11.6. Tricia Miller after Edward Chappell, CWF

11.7. Carl Lounsbury, CWF

11.8. Carl Lounsbury, CWF

11.9. Barbara Temple Lombardi, CWF

11.10. Carl Lounsbury, CWF

11.11. Tricia Miller after Carl Lounsbury, CWF

11.12. Edward Chappell, CWF

11.13. Carl Lounsbury, CWF

11.14A. Jeffrey Klee, CWF; 11.14B-C. Carl Lounsbury, CWF

11.15. Carl Lounsbury, CWF

11.16. Jeffrey Klee, CWF

11.17. Carl Lounsbury, CWF

11.18. Carl Lounsbury, CWF

11.19. Willie Graham, CWF

12.0. David Doody, CWF

12.1. Tricia Miller after Edward Chappell, CWF

12.2. Orlando Ridout V

12.3. Edward Chappell, CWF

12.4. Edward Chappell, CWF

12.5. Willie Graham, CWF

12.6. Edward Chappell, CWF

12.7. Tricia Miller after Robert Teagle, Edward Chappell, CWF

12.8. Jeffrey Klee, CWF

12.9. Tricia Miller after Carl Lounsbury, Edward Chappell, CWF

12.10. Tricia Miller after Edward Chappell, CWF

12.11. Willie Graham, CWF

12.12. Willie Graham, CWF

12.13. Orlando Ridout V

12.14. Willie Graham, CWF

12.15. Willie Graham, CWF

12.16. Rick Guthrie, CWF

12.17. Craig McDougal, CWF

12.18. Rendersphere and Jeffrey Klee, CWF after Billie Graham and Edward Chappell, CWF

12.19. Tricia Miller after Willie Graham, William Macintire, and Edward Chappell, CWF

12.20. Willie Graham, CWF

12.21. Tricia Miller after Edward Chappell, CWF

12.22. Tricia Miller after Edward Chappell, CWF

12.23. Willie Graham, CWF

12.24. Willie Graham, CWF

13.0. Tom Green, CWF

13.1. Frances Benjamin Johnston, Library of Congress

13.2. Willie Graham, CWF

13.3. Willie Graham, CWF

13.4. Willie Graham, CWF

13.5. Willie Graham, CWF

13.6. Willie Graham, CWF

13.7. Willie Graham, CWF

13.8. Willie Graham, CWF

13.9. Willie Graham, CWF

13.10. Willie Graham, CWF

13.11. Library of Congress

13.12. Willie Graham, CWF

13.13. Studio Ammons after Willie Graham, CWF

13.14. Virginia Historical Society

13.15. Brooke Clagett

13.16. Willie Graham, CWF

13.17. Willie Graham, CWF

13.18. Willie Graham, CWF

13.19. Willie Graham, CWF

13.20A. Rendersphere after Willie Graham, CWF; 13.20B. Studio Ammons after Willie Graham, CWF

13.21. Willie Graham, CWF

13.22. Tricia Miller, Rendersphere after Willie Graham, CWF

13.23. Rendersphere after Willie Graham, CWF

13.24. Willie Graham, CWF

13.25. Willie Graham, CWF

13.26. National Library of Russia

13.27. Digital History Center, CWF

14.0. David Doody, CWF

14.1. Willie Graham, CWF

14.2. Rendersphere after Jeffrey Bostetter, CWF

14.3. Rendersphere after Cary Carson, CWF

14.4. Studio Ammons after Willie Graham, CWF

14.5. Willie Graham, CWF

14.6. Willie Graham, CWF

14.7. Allan Adams after Willie Graham, CWF

14.8. Willie Graham, CWF

14.9. Willie Graham, CWF

14.10. Willie Graham, CWF

14.11. Willie Graham, CWF

14.12. Jeffrey Klee, CWF

14.13. Jeffrey Klee, CWF

14.14. Willie Graham, CWF

14.15. Willie Graham, CWF

14.16. Willie Graham, CWF

14.17. Rendersphere after Willie Graham, CWF

14.18. Rendersphere and Jeffrey Klee after Orlando Ridout V, Willie Graham, CWF

14.19. Studio Ammons after Willie Graham, CWF

14.20. Willie Graham, CWF

14.21. Willie Graham after Cary Carson, CWF

14.22. Willie Graham, CWF

14.23. Willie Graham, CWF

14.24. Willie Graham, CWF

14.25. Jeffrey Klee, CWF

14.26. Willie Graham, CWF

14.27. Willie Graham, CWF

14.28. Willie Graham, CWF

Index

Page numbers in *italics* refer to illustrations.

New England, 1, 2, 61, 71, 80, 217, 226, 228, 231, 241, 276, 281, 283, 304, 306, 316, 343, 348, 378, 381–82, 437 (n. 8), 438 (n. 15), 440 (n. 1)

New England Palladium, 382

New Kent County, Va., 32, *33*, 47, 70, 78, 248, 278, 295, 308, 358, 405; courthouse, 32. *See also* St. Peter's Church; Springdale

Newport News, Va., 95, *95*, 101, *101*, 125, *125*, *211*, 219, 251, 267, *269*, 273, 315, 326, 405

Newport Parish Church (Isle of Wight Co., Va.), 73, 245, 247–50, *247*, *350*, 404

New World, 48, *49*, 50–51, 68, 79, 86–87, 94, 206–7, 220, 426 (n. 3)

New York, 348, 377, 399

New York City, 60, 398, 442 (n. 7)

Niche, 248, 340, 383

Nicholls, Michael, 172

Nicholson, Mary, 172

Nicholson Shop (Williamsburg), 380, *389*

Nigeria, 55

Nomini Hall (Westmoreland Co., Va.), 80, 126, 163, 168, 170, 257, 387, 406, 418 (n. 24), 419 (n. 76), 422 (n. 59)

Norfolk, 2, *3*, 57, 60–61, 64–66, *65*, 70, 85, 157, 171, 203, 272, 296, 298, 313, 320, 341, 398, 405, 419 (n. 76), 441 (n. 57), 442 (n. 7). *See also* Myers House

Norfolk, England, *91*

Norfolk and Western Railroad, *394*, 395, 398, 442 (n. 3)

Norfolk County, Va., 128, 325; courthouse, 70

Norfolk House (London), 367, 441 (n. 50)

Northampton County, Va., 69, 112–14, *112–13*, *122*, 196, 218, *218*, 250, 257, 315, *315*, 336, 385–86, *385*, 405, 427 (n. 44), 434 (n. 27), 437 (n. 31); courthouse, 247, *247*

North Carolina, 45, 121, 132, 174, 178, 217, 222, 241, 246, 256–58, 260, 267–68, 289, 302, *306*, 316, 364, *380*, 432 (n. 23), 436 (n. 11), 438 (n. 17)

Northern Neck, 60, 80, 96, 105, 109, 160, 163, 387

Northwest Territories, 397

Norton, John, 267, 275

Notching. *See* Log construction

Nourse, Sarah, 127

Nursery, 101, 132, 145, 276, 308, *327*, 328, 419 (n. 76), 422 (nn. 58, 59), 432 (n. 43)

Oak, 23, 40, 68, 161, *180*, 184, 191–92, 196–97, 212, 223, 273, 279, *279*, 318, 325, 363, 375, 384

Ocean Hall (St. Mary's Co., Md.), 229, *230*, 359, *359*, 361, 366, 403

Octagon (Washington, D.C.), 275–76, 281, 403

Office, 21, 31, 74, 83, 99, 119, 123, 141, *141*, 143, *152*, 176, 179, 253, 325, 375, 404, 412 (n. 62)

Ogee. *See* Moldings: cyma

Ohio, 55, 61

Old World, 8, 12, 25, 48–49, *49*, 50, 53, 67, 86, 98, 215, 220. *See also* Britain; England

Olmsted, Frederick Law, 178

Onancock, Va., 171, 282

Orange County, Va., 146, 150, *152*, 164, 169, 222, 251, 263, 279, *279*, 302, 310, *310*, 380, 405, 441 (n. 63)

Orchard, 56, 102

Orrell, John, house (Williamsburg), 40, 406

O'Sheal, John, 128

Overdoor, *316*, 328–29

Overmantel, 41–43, *67*, 82, 319, 322, 325, 332–33, *333*, 335, 358, 366. *See also* Chimneypiece; Mantel/mantelpiece

Overseer, 100, 126, 157–58, 160, *161*, 162–63, 168–69, 171–73, 175–76, 187, 196, 308, 422 (n. 57), 423 (n. 85)

Overzee, Simon, 101

Ovolo. *See* Moldings: ovolo

Oxford, England, 79

Oxford, Md., 2, 57

Oxford Dendrochronology Laboratory, 9, 37

Oxfordshire, *91*, 274

Oyster shells, 239, 243, *367*

Page, John, 111, 164, 257, 295; house (Middle Plantation), *111*, 248, 336, 404

Page, John, Jr., 257, 372

Pain, William, 82

Paint, 9, 37–43, 45–46, 64, 73, 109, 128, 214–15, 251, 259, 267, 270–71, 274, 289, 296, 330, 356–75, 377, 379, 381, 384, 386, 390–91, 401, 434 (n. 28), 438 (n. 15); coat(s), 24, 64, 289, 357, 361–62, 364, 372–73, 375; distemper, 357–59, *358*, 379, 391; faux/graining/ imitation/marbleized, 317, 322, 357, 359, *359*, 361–62, 367–69, *379*, *371*, 373–75, *374*, 385, 387, 401, 440 (n. 56); gilded/gilding, 113, 312, 363–64, 366, 377, *377*, 380–81, *381*, 386–87, 389, 392, 440 (n. 9); oil, 39, 42–43, 251, 357–64, 366, 370, 372, 375, 439 (n. 48); photo micrographs, *37*, *370*; primer, 38, 42, 361, 370; shellac, *357*, 361, 437 (n. 5); unpainted, 40, 168, 173, 268, 296, 362–64, 372, 438 (n. 15); varnish, 356, 370, 375. *See also* Color wash; Limewash; Paint analysis; Paint colors/pigments; Painters

Paint analysis, 37, 42, 308, 356, 361, 365–66, 371–72, 375

Paint brush, *251*, 367, *367*, 372, 375, 439 (n. 40)

Paint colors/pigments, 24, *41*, 42, 45, *46*, 251, *251*, 270, 296, 348, 356, 362–73, 384, 391, 430 (n. 24), 434 (n. 29), 438 (nn. 21, 27), 439 (n. 40); black, 24, 296, 312, 391, 438 (n. 27); blue, 32, *41*, 42–43, 358, 362, 367, 370, 378, *379*, 381–82, 387–91, *390*, 434 (n. 29), 439 (n. 40), 441 (n. 30); blue-green, *41*, 42; brown, 40, 42; chocolate, 363; cream, 370; crimson, 382, 387–88, 391–92, 440 (n. 9), 441 (n. 63); gray, 24, 296, 362–64, 370, 372, 438 (n. 27); green, 40, *41*, 42, 137, *368*, 370, *370*, 373, 375, 377, 381, 384, 387–88, 391–92; lampblack, 357, 439 (n. 51); lead, 363; oak, *359*, 363; olive, 366; orange, 296, 358, 362, 364, 438 (n. 27); pink, 42, 358–59; Prussian blue, 24, 366–67, 379, 439 (n. 40), 440 (n. 26); red-brown, 24, *357*, *360*, 361–64, *365*, 367, 370, 372, 374, 391, 438 (n. 27); red lead, 251, 296, 357–58, *360*, 362–64, *363*, *366*, 367, 372, *373*, 439 (n. 51); red ocher, 112, 251, 357–58, 430 (n. 24); sienna, 357, 430 (n. 24); sky blue, 367; slate, 438 (n. 27); Spanish brown, *360*, 362–64, 366, 438 (n. 27); Spanish white, 358; stone, 24, 363; stucco, 362, 383–85, 441 (n. 54); umber, 357; Venetian red, 372, 439 (n. 51); verdigris, 366, *368*, 370, *370*, 373; verditer, 358, 379; walnut, 370; white, 40, 270, 363, 391; white lead, *251*, 356, *360*, 362, 366–67, 370, 372–74, 438 (n. 27); 439 (nn. 48, 51);